Vol. II

THE AUTOPOIESIS OF ARCHITECTURE

To Zaha Hadid

Vol. II

Patrik Schumacher

THE AUTOPOIESIS OF ARCHITECTURE

A New Agenda for Architecture

A John Wiley & Sons, Ltd., Publication

This edition first published 2012

Registered Office
John Wiley & Sons Ltd, The Atrium, Southern Gate, Chichester, West Sussex, PO19 8SQ, United Kingdom

For details of our global editorial offices, for customer services and for information about how to apply for permission to reuse the copyright material in this book please see our website at www.wiley.com.

Executive Commissioning Editor: Helen Castle
Project Editor: Miriam Swift
Assistant Editor: Calver Lezama

ISBN 978-0-470-66615-9 (hardback)
ISBN 978-0-470-66616-6 (paperback)
ISBN 978-1-119-94046-3 (ebk)
ISBN 978-1-119-94047-0 (ebk)
ISBN 978-1-119-94048-7 (ebk)
Design and cover design by Kate Ward
Typeset in 9.5/12.5pt TradeGothic by Aptara Inc., New Delhi, India
Printed and bound in Great Britain by CPI Antony Rowe, Chippenham, Wiltshire

Contents

Introduction to Volume 2 1

6. The Task of Architecture **5**

6.1 Functions 7
6.1.1 Functions versus Capacities 11
6.1.2 Substantial versus Subsidiary Functions 17
6.1.3 Tectonics 19
6.1.4 The Categorization of Function-types 22
6.1.5 Problem-types (Function-types) vs Solution-types (Archetypes) 24
6.1.6 Patterns of Decomposition/Composition 30
6.1.7 Functional Reasoning via Action-artefact Networks 32
6.1.8 Limitations of Functional Expertise 39
6.2 Order via Organization and Articulation 42
6.2.1 Organization and Articulation: Historical and Systematic 47
6.2.2 Architectural Order 52
6.2.3 A Definition of Organization for Contemporary Architecture 57
6.2.4 Complicated, Complex, Organized, Ordered 61
6.3 Organization 70
6.3.1 Relating Spatial to Social Organization 72
6.3.2 Territorialization and Integration 77
6.3.3 Systems, Configurations, Organizations 80
6.4 Supplementing Architecture with a Science of Configuration 88
6.4.1 Set Theory 88
6.4.2 Harnessing Network Theory 93
6.4.3 Excursion: Network Theory 99
6.4.4 A City is not a Tree 106
6.4.5 Space Syntax: Concepts and Tools of Analysis 112
6.4.6 Space Syntax: Theoretical Claims 125
6.4.7 From Organization to Articulation: Taking Account of Cognition 131
6.5 Articulation 134
6.5.1 Articulation vs Organization 134
6.5.2 The Problem of Orientation and the Problematic of Legibility 137
6.5.3 Articulate vs Inarticulate Organization 138
6.5.4 Articulation as the Core Competency of Architecture 139
6.5.5 Generalizing the Concept of Function 140
6.6 The Phenomenological vs the Semiological Dimension of Architecture 142

6.7 The Phenomenological Dimension of Architectural Articulation 145
6.7.1 The Perceptual Constitution of Objects and Spaces 147
6.7.2 Cognitive Principles of Gestalt-Perception 153
6.7.3 Parametric Figuration 165
6.8 The Semiological Dimension of Architectural Articulation 167
6.8.1 The Built Works of Architecture as Framing Communications 171
6.8.2 Analogy: Language and Built Environment as Media of Communication 176
6.8.3 Signs as Communications 181
6.8.4 Territory as Fundamental Semiological Unit 183
6.8.5 Saussure's Insight: Language as System of Correlated Differences 189
6.8.6 Extra-Semiological Demands on Architecture's Medial Substrate 193
6.8.7 Syntagmatic vs Paradigmatic Relations 196
6.9 Prolegomenon to Architecture's Semiological Project 200
6.9.1 The Scope of Architecture's Signified 201
6.9.2 The Composite Character of the Architectural Sign 206
6.9.3 Absolute and Relative Arbitrariness 210
6.9.4 Natural and Artificial Semiosis 215
6.9.5 Designing Architecture's Semiological Project 222
6.9.6 Cognitive and Attentional Conditions of Architectural Communication 229
6.9.7 Speculation: Expanding the Expressive Power of Architectural Sign Systems 232
6.10 The Semiological Project and the General Project of Architectural Order 238
6.10.1 The Semiological Project in Relation to the Organizational and the Phenomenological Project 239
6.10.2 Relationship between Architectural Languages and Architectural Styles 244
6.10.3 The Requisite Variety of Architectural Articulation 246

7. The Design Process 251
7.1 Contemporary Context and Aim of Design Process Theory 254
7.2 Towards a Contemporary Design Process Reflection and Design Methodology 257
7.2.1 Method vs Process 258
7.3 The Design Process as Problem-solving Process 263
7.3.1 The Design Process as Information-processing Process 264
7.3.2 The Structure of Information-processing Systems 269

7.3.3 Programmes 272
7.3.4 The Task Environment and its Representation as Problem Space 277
7.3.5 Problem Solving as Search in a State Space 284
7.3.6 Planning Spaces 295
7.3.7 Heuristic versus Exhaustive Problem-solving Methods 298
7.4 Differentiating Classical, Modern and Contemporary Processes 311
7.5 Problem Definition and Problem Structure 318
7.5.1 Wicked Problems 319
7.5.2 The Structure of Ill-structured Problems 323
7.5.3 An Information-processing Model for Information-rich Design Processes 332
7.6 Rationality: Retrospective and Prospective 337
7.6.1 Rational in Retrospect: Observing Innovative Design Practice 341
7.6.2 Prospective Rationality 355
7.6.3 Processing the Three Task Dimensions of Architecture 358
7.7 Modelling Spaces 361

8. Architecture and Society **379**
8.1 World Architecture within World Society 382
8.2 Autonomy vs Authority 385
8.3 Architecture's Conception of Society 390
8.3.1 The Crisis of Modernism's Conception of Society 394
8.3.2 Social Systems Theory and the Theory of Architectural Autopoiesis 396
8.4 Architecture in Relation to other Societal Subsystems 398
8.4.1 Architecture In Relation to the Economic System 401
8.4.2 The Economy and the Design-Principle of Economy of Means 402
8.4.3 Economic Conditions of Architectural Discourse 406
8.4.4 Architecture and Education 407
8.5 Architecture as Profession and Professional Career 410
8.5.1 Authorship, Reputation, Oeuvre 411
8.5.2 Centre-periphery Differentiation within Architecture 414
8.5.3 The Absorption of Uncertainty 418
8.5.4 The Architectural Design Studio as Organization 420
8.6 The Built Environment as Primordial Condition of Society 422
8.6.1 The Built Environment As Indispensable Substrate of Social Evolution 423
8.6.2 From Spatial Order to Conceptual Order 426
8.6.3 Beauty and the Evolution of Concepts of Order 434

9. Architecture and Politics **439**
9.1 Is Political Architecture Possible? 440
9.1.1 Political Vacuum 441
9.1.2 Normal vs Revolutionary Politics 445
9.2 Theorizing the Relationship between Architecture and Politics 448
9.2.1 The Incommensurability of Architecture and Politics 448
9.2.2 Architecture Responds to Political Agendas – Three Scenarios 450
9.2.3 Service Provisions Between Architecture and Politics 453
9.3 Architecture Adapts to Political Development 459
9.3.1 Modern Architecture Calls on Politics 461
9.3.2 The ABC Group: Political Agitation Within Architecture 462
9.3.3 The Vicissitudes of Political Polarization 466
9.4 The Limitations of Critical Practice in Architecture 470
9.4.1 General Political Critique and Macro-political Ambitions 470
9.4.2 Architecture's 'Micro-Political' Agency: Manipulating Non-political Power 472
9.4.3 Who Controls the Power-distributing Capacity of Design? 474
9.4.4 Public Competitions As Structural Coupling between Architecture and Politics 477

10. The Self-descriptions of Architecture **484**
10.1 Theoretical Underpinnings 485
10.1.1 Reference as Self-reference 489
10.1.2 Levels of Self-reference 490
10.2 The Necessity of Reflection: Architectural Theory as Reflection Theory 496
10.2.1 Continuity vs Consistency 501
10.2.2 Categorical vs Variable Structures of Communication 504
10.3 Classic Treatises 509
10.3.1 Alberti's *De re aedificatoria* 511
10.3.2 Durand's *Précis des leçons d'architecture* 543
10.3.3 Le Corbusier's *Vers une architecture* 568
10.3.4 *The Autopoiesis of Architecture* 592
10.4 Architectural Historiography 606
10.4.1 History of Architecture's Autonomization and Internal Structuration 608

10.4.2 History of Architectural Styles as Responses to Epochal Shifts in the Societal Environment 610
10.5 Architectural Criticism 615

11. Parametricism – The Parametric Paradigm and the Formation of a New Style 617
11.1 Parametricism as Epochal Style 622
11.1.1 Historiographical Sketch: The Epochal Alignment of Styles 627
11.1.2 A Unified Style for the 21st Century 642
11.1.3 The Maturity of Parametricism 646
11.1.4 Polarized Confrontation: Parametricism versus Minimalism 648
11.1.5 Styles as Design Research Programmes 651
11.2 The Parametricist Research Programme 654
11.2.1 Conceptual Definition of Parametricism 654
11.2.2 Operational Definition of Parametricism: The Defining Heuristics of Parametricism 656
11.2.3 Genealogy of the Parametricist Heuristics 660
11.2.4 Analogies: Emulating Natural Systems 663
11.2.5 Agendas Advancing Parametricism 669
11.2.6 The Agenda of Ecological Sustainability 676
11.3 Parametricist vs Modernist Urbanism 680
11.3.1 Simple Order, Disorder, Complex Order 681
11.3.2 Implementing Parametricist Urbanism 686
11.4 Elegance 700

12. Epilogue – The Design of a Theory 710
12.1 Theoretical Foundation: Communication Theory vs Historical Materialism? 714
12.2 The Theory of Architectural Autopoiesis as Unified Theory of Architecture 719
12.3 Notes on the Architecture of the Theory 722
12.4 The Theory as the Result of Contingent Theory Design Decisions 726

Concluding Remarks 735

Appendix 3: *The Autopoiesis of Architecture in the Context of Three Classic Texts* 737

Appendix 4: Theses 25–60 742

References 748

Index 759

The author and the publisher gratefully acknowledge the people who gave their permission to reproduce material in this book. While every effort has been made to contact copyright holders for their permission to reprint material, the publishers would be grateful to hear from any copyright holder who is not acknowledged here and will undertake to rectify any errors or omissions in future editions.

p 59 (t) © Hochhausstadt, east-west street, project for a high-rise city, 1924. Ludwig Karl Hilberseimer. Ludwig Karl Hilberseimer Papers, Ryerson and Burnham Archives, The Art Institute of Chicago. Digital File #070383.HochhOst. © The Art Institute of Chicago; pp 59 (b), 621, 647 (b), 649, 650, 655 (b), 656, 675, 676, 679 (t & b), 687, 688 (t, c & b), 689 (t & b), 690 (t & b), 691 (t & b), 692, 693, 701 (b), 702, 706, © Zaha Hadid Architects; p 60 (t) © Hans Strand/Corbis; p 60 (b) © Susumu Nishinaga/Science Photo Library; pp 76, 90 (t & b), 95, 97 (t & b), 159 (t & b), 160 (t & b), 161 (b), 307, 308, 309 (t & b), 310, 701 (t) © Patrik Schumacher; p 108 (t) © Mrs Kenzo Tange, Paul NoritakaTange and Tange Associates, Tokyo; pp 108 (b), 110 Image redrawn by Patrik Schumacher, according to the original © Christopher Alexander; p 111 Image redrawn by Patrik Schumacher, according to the original © Simon Nicholson; pp 115, 120, 123, 214, 126, 129 © Bill Hillier; p 117 © From Bill Hiller and Julia Hanson, The Social Logic of Space, 1984, figures on p 150. © Cambridge University Press, reproduced with permission of the author and publisher; p 118 © From Bill Hiller and Julia Hanson, The Social Logic of Space, 1984, figures on p 151. © Cambridge University Press, reproduced with permission of the author and publisher; p 151 © From Gyorgi Kepes, Language of Vision, Dover Publications Inc., New York 1995, originally published by Paul Theobald, Chicago 1944, p.102; p 152 courtesy of gta Archives, ETH Zurich: legacy of Bernhard Hoesli; p 161 (t & c) © From Max Wertheimer, Laws of Organization in Perceptual Forms, First published in 1923 as Untersuchungen zur Lehre von der Gestalt II, in Psycologische Forschung, 4, 301-350. Translation published in Ellis, W. (1938). A source book of Gestalt psychology (pp. 71-88). London: Routledge & Kegan Paul; p 162 © From Hermann Rorschach, Psychodiagnostik: Methodik und Ergebnisse eines wahrnehmungsdiagnostischen Experiments (Deutenlassen von Zufallsformen) / Mit den zugehörigen Tests bestehend aus zehn Teils mehrfarbigen Tafeln. Bern; Berlin : H. Huber, 1932 2nd Edition: Dr. W. Morgenthaler; p 164 © Patrik Schumacher, redrawn by the author with permission from Fondation Le Corbusier; p 165 © Zaha Hadid and Patrik Schumacher; p 425 © From Bill Hiller and Julia Hanson, The Social Logic of Space, 1984, figures on p.63. © Cambridge University Press, reproduced with permission of the author and publisher; p 426 © From The Winnebago Tribe by Paul Radin, published by the University of Nebraska Press; p 620 (t) courtesy OMA © Rem and Madelon Koolhaas-Vriessendorp; p 620 (b) © Udo Hess; pp 622, 682 © Frei Otto; p 629 © The Bridgeman Art Library; p 629 © The Walters Art Museum, Baltimore; p 638 (b) © Austrian Archives/Corbis; p 647 (t) © Daniel Köhler and Rasa Navasaityte (www.lab-eds.org); p 655 (t) © Francis DK Ching; p 670 © Werner Forman/Corbis p 671 © Maren Klasing, Martin Krcha, Manuel Froeschl and Konrad Hofmann; University of Applied Arts, Vienna, 2007, Project Simultaneity and Latency; p 672 © Konrad Hofmann, Maren Klasing, Martn Krcha and Manuel Froeschl; University of Applied Arts, Vienna, 2006, Project Compressed Complexity; p 673 (t & b), 674 © Mario Gasser and Philip Weisz; p 684 (t & b) © Institut für Leichtbau Entwerfen und Konstruieren, Universität Stuttgart, Germany; pp 694, 695, 698, 699 (t & b) © Ludovico Lombardi (on behalf of Craft_id); p 701 (c) © ILEK Universität Stuttgart, Germany p 705 (t & b) © Gerry Cruz, Spyridon Kaprinis, Natalie Popik and Maria Tsironi.

Introduction to Volume 2

This is the second volume of *The Autopoiesis of Architecture*. The two volumes together present a complete outline of the theory of architectural autopoiesis, a systematic treatise on architecture. This treatise proceeds via a comprehensive discourse analysis of the discipline, and on this basis tries to steer the discipline's self-conception and development.

Volume 1 introduces a new theoretical framework within which architecture may analyze and confront itself in terms of its most fundamental concepts, methods and values. Volume 2 continues to analyze architecture's discourse *and* proposes a new agenda for contemporary architecture in response to the challenges and opportunities posed by current societal and technological developments. The Volume ends with a manifesto for the new style of Parametricism, promoted as candidate to become the unified, epochal style for the 21st century. To be credible, a unified style must be backed up and guided by a unified theoretical edifice that is able to integrate many partial theories: a theory of architecture's societal function, a theory of the discipline's self-demarcation, a theory of the avant-garde, aesthetic theory, media theory, process theory etc. The theory of architectural autopoiesis presents such an integrated theoretical edifice. It is nothing other than the rational reconstruction and systematization of the discursively evolving discipline, made explicit as unified theory and opened up to criticism and constructive elaboration. Selective rational reconstruction and systematization are necessary to give *coherent* guidance to a comprehensive architectural practice that covers the totality of the built environment and its contemporary adaptive challenges.[1]

Architecture is one of the great function systems of modern, functionally differentiated society. The theory of architectural autopoiesis is a ***reflection theory*** or ***self-description*** of architecture formulated from within architecture. As such its purpose is to contribute to the necessary self-steering of the autopoiesis of architecture. Like all reflection theories – for example, economic theories, jurisprudence, the

1 The coherence of a unified theory helps to avoid self-contradiction in addressing the different theoretical and practical questions a multi-faceted discipline like architecture poses. A unified theory gives one's various statements and practical engagements consistency. Without such guidance one is prone to get in one's own way, blocking yesterday's achievements with today's efforts. A unified theory is necessary to give leadership to the discipline. It is of practical urgency with respect to giving consistent leadership to a large firm like ZHA operating globally across all programmes and scales.

epistemologies formulated within science, political theories etc – the theory of architectural autopoiesis oscillates between ***descriptive*** and ***normative*** modes of theorizing. Of necessity, as ***committed inside communication***, it is simultaneously a descriptive and a normative theory. By describing, conceptually systematizing and reconstructing the ***rationality*** of architecture's history and current state, the theory gathers the necessary internal connectivity to make normative claims and projections plausible. The tension between descriptive and normative moments permeates the totality of *The Autopoiesis of Architecture.* However, the balance between the two moments is struck differently in the two volumes. From Volume 1 to Volume 2, as we move from *framework* to *agenda*, the balance shifts towards the normative pole, and indeed includes more projective, speculative moments.[2]

The elaboration of architecture's agenda in Volume 2 proceeds in six parts, parts 6–11:

Part 6 *The Task of Architecture* sets out the general task of architecture in the terms of architecture's lead-distinction: *to give form to function.* An adequate concept of how to understand and address functions within contemporary architecture is proposed. Architecture's task is then elaborated along two dimensions: organization and articulation. To meet contemporary challenges architecture must enhance its capacity in both dimensions. Theoretical resources that contribute to this enhancement are brought to bear: network theory, Gestalt theory and semiology. In particular, an axiomatic framework for reinvigorating the semiological project within architecture is provided. The elaboration of spatial complexes as systems-of-signification is promoted as a core competency of architecture.

Part 7 *The Design Process* elaborates the second item on the agenda: the enhancement of architecture's design process reflection. Here the achievements of the design methods movement are recuperated. Design rationality is challenged by the expectation of continuous innovation as well as by the increasing complexity of architecture's task domain. Many design tasks are new and complex. This double burden demands a new theoretical reflection concerning the methodological credentials of design processes as rational decision processes. The theory of architectural autopoiesis offers a conceptual apparatus for the description and analysis of design processes, promotes innovative design process heuristics and

2 The fact that every ambitious self-description enters an ideological battleground concerning the discursive culture and direction of the discipline/profession is more palpable in Volume 2. However, aggressive polemics have been deliberately avoided in order to allow the elaboration of a coherent theoretical system to take precedence. The hope is that the analyses, theses and projections deliver a package that convinces without polemical battles.

attempts to formulate adequate contemporary criteria of design rationality.[3]

Part 8 *Architecture and Society* addresses the necessity for the autopoiesis of architecture to update and upgrade its internal representation of society in line with society's development. Luhmann's conception of a polycontextual, functionally differentiated world society is – once more – offered as adequate conceptual horizon for architecture's orientation. The dialectical relationship – coevolution – between the autopoiesis of architecture and its societal environment is addressed in Luhmann's terms. Then the reflection goes deeper and touches on the fundamental dependence of society's emergence and ongoing development on the built environment as the indispensable substratum of socio-cultural evolution. Finally, the investigation turns to the manifold societal conditions and institutions on which the autopoiesis of architecture depends.

Part 9 *Architecture and Politics* addresses architecture's relationship with one of the subsystems within its societal environment: the political system. Architecture's relationship with the political system is singled out for in-depth analysis not because of the inherent importance of this relationship but because of the widespread, disorienting illusions that abound concerning this relationship. The theoretical clarification of architecture's systemic position relative to the political system becomes the premise for the attempt to define an adequate, productive role for avant-garde architecture in relation to contemporary politics.

Part 10 *The Self-descriptions of Architecture* presents key treatises that have been seminal in the historical evolution of architecture's autopoiesis. This agenda item – architecture's self-descriptions – reveals the general requirement that architecture, like all function systems of society, must reflect its own constitution with respect to its societal function in order effectively to steer itself in the absence of authoritative directives from outside. Comprehensive theoretical treatises are the most adequate form this necessary reflection can take. Three key texts have been selected and subjected to a detailed, parallel analysis: Alberti's treatise of 1485,[4] Durand's treatise of 1802–5, and Le Corbusier's treatise of 1923. These treatises are confident, comprehensive accounts of the discipline, each reflecting architecture's societal function and arguing for principles, methods and repertoires that should guide the

3 Adequacy here means that the criteria allow us to critique and enhance design proposals without imposing sterile and unrealistic ideals.

4 Alberti's *De re aedificatoria* was written in 1450. It first circulated as a hand-copied manuscript and was then published in 1485 as the first printed book on architecture.

discipline in discharging its function. Each of these texts had been seminal in inaugurating or representing one of the epochal styles of architecture: the Renaissance, Neo-Classicism and Modernism respectively. The analysis of these three texts has been structured by the conceptual grid that underlies and organizes *The Autopoiesis of Architecture* itself, thus directly confronting the theory of architectural autopoiesis with these prior attempts at providing architecture with a comprehensive self-description. Here thus arises another occasion of autological self-inclusion for the theory of architectural autopoiesis: an occasion for the theory to analyze and historicize itself as an attempt, once more, to provide architecture with a viable self-description, this time expounding the emerging epochal style of Parametricism.

Part 11 *Parametricism – The Parametric Paradigm and the Formation of a New Style* moves beyond the general theory of architectural autopoiesis[5] and utilizes the theory's conceptual apparatus and theses to distil, analyze and evaluate a powerful new tendency within contemporary architecture. The author is himself a contributor to this tendency, as designer, teacher and author.[6] Parametricism is expounded as candidate to become the new epochal style with global reach and universal scope.

Patrik Schumacher, London, February 2012

5 The theory of architectural autopoiesis does not stand or fall with the success of Parametricism. Its scope and validity are broader. As a general theoretical framework it might be embraced by theorists and architects who do not agree with the author's evaluation of certain contemporary architectural tendencies.

6 The author first coined the label 'Parametricism' in 2008 during the Venice Architecture Biennale, and then further expounded the style in a series of articles and lectures.

6. The Task of Architecture

The theory of architectural autopoiesis identifies architecture's societal function[1] as the innovative framing of social *interaction*. Interaction is defined as communication between participants who are physically present, as distinct from remote communication via writing, telephone, Internet etc. All communications, and thus all interactions, are embedded within social systems understood as systems of communications. All social interactions take place in designed spaces filled with designed artefacts. Architectural artefacts – as well as other designed artefacts such as furniture, appliances and clothing – thus participate in the reproduction of social systems of communications. Architectural artefacts frame virtually all social communication systems, with the exception of those systems that exclusively reproduce outside the interaction between physically present participants. The designed environment matters: it frames all interactions. Only on the basis of the designed environment as complex system of frames can society be reproduced on the level of complexity it has attained.[2]

All architectural communications, as well as all communications of all the design disciplines, are communications in the medium of space.[3] Architecture frames social interaction. This very general formula characterizes architecture's societal role, responsibility and *raison d'être*. At this level of abstraction the formula can say nothing about *how* architecture might be able to discharge its responsibility, ie, *how* it might be able to order and frame the manifold social interactions that reproduce society.

1 See Volume 1, part 5 *The Societal Function of Architecture*, in particular, Chapter 5.1.3 *Framing as Societal Function of Architecture*.

2 To understand the power of architecture's societal function – namely to frame, order and orient social interaction – one might consider the following thought experiment. Imagine that the complex built environment of a city like London is replaced by a flat, undifferentiated surface. Now try to imagine how the 10 million inhabitants of the city stranded on this surface might try to recreate and order social interaction on the level of complexity that is currently sustained by the built environment.

3 All architectural communications are spatial communications. This also applies to drawings and models, including digital models. The drawing/model is architecture's specialized medium developed with the advent of architecture as self-referentially enclosed function system. See Volume 1, part 4 *The Medium of Architecture*.

Architecture's *raison d'être* – its general societal function or responsibility – must be translated into more concrete terms that allow for the formulation of tangible tasks for architecture. The autopoiesis of architecture itself has always – since its very inception – provided for this translation, namely in the terms of its lead-distinction: form (= frame) vs function (= interaction). Architecture's general societal role is thus continuously reassured, elaborated and made concrete via the continuous application of its lead-distinction on successive scales and levels of abstraction/concretization. The 'functions' architects address refer to clusters of social interactions understood as social systems. For instance the function-type 'residence' frames families or households, the function-type 'school' frames the respective social system. Many such functions can be distinguished, named and listed, at different levels of abstraction/concretization, and then confronted with various spatial forms that might also be distinguished, named and listed.

The historical coevolution of the built environment's pre-architectural repertoire and society's pre-Modern manifold of interactions led to the sedimentation of a catalogue of social institutions that correlates with a catalogue of spatio-formal types, ie, the traditional catalogue of building-type solutions. But these traditional 'solutions' are not yet conceptualized as solutions to problems. Rather they are naturalized as unquestioned essences. The traditional concepts like villa, church, palace, town hall, town house etc represent the as yet undifferentiated unity of sedimented form-function complexes. The emergence of architecture as autopoietic system – armed with its lead-distinction – implied the possibility to break down these fixed, taken-for-granted form-function unities. The old canon becomes available for dissection and recombination, in both the formal and the functional dimension. Now function and form can be distinguished as aspects of an artefact. The unification of these aspects becomes problematic. The distinction of form and function poses the question of their effective correlation. The presumed essences are dissolved. Traditional forms can now be criticized with respect to their ability to satisfy functional demands. Functions are now posed as problems. Forms are probed, selected and elaborated as solutions to problems. The distinction of form vs function marks the inauguration of architecture as rational-reflective discipline. It is the precondition of innovation.[4] Only the distinction of form vs function allows the framing of social interaction – a necessary dimension of all social evolution – to become a subject of critique and innovation.

4 Innovation is the *raison d'être* of the discipline's reflective rationality.

The task of architecture can thus be cast in terms of architecture's lead-distinction: ***to give form to function***. This general task formula confronts an increasingly rich world of social institutions with an expanding panoply of forms. Within this abstract conceptual horizon the designer can tackle every concrete design task as the concrete confrontation of a given functional problem with a specific set of forms. As will be elaborated below, this uniform task formulation can be further unfolded by a second, crucial distinction: the distinction between ***organization*** and ***articulation***. This distinction is as general and universally applicable as the distinction of form and function. The distinction is equally defining for architecture, and indeed equally venerable in terms of its pedigree in the history of architectural theory.[5] Architectural forms function via organization and articulation. Articulation can be further analyzed into phenomenological articulation and semiological articulation.

Organization and articulation are the constituent dimensions of architecture's task. However, before elaborating these dimensions, it seems useful to further clarify the general architectural concept of function and to reflect upon how the understanding of functions in architecture might be further developed and upgraded in the light of the current/emergent challenges the autopoiesis of architecture must cope with.

6.1 Functions

THESIS 25

While functional typology remains indispensable as initial orienting framework, functional reasoning in architecture has to upgrade towards a conceptualization of function in terms of action-artefact networks.

The distinction of form and function is architecture's lead-distinction and as such a permanent communication structure of architecture's autopoiesis. The concern with function is an inescapable feature of all architectural communications. It concerns all architectural artefacts, from the overall building, to each space, each architectural element, and tectonic detail.

The *concept* of function is a primary concept within architecture right from its ancient inception and then again from its rebirth in the Renaissance. The classical Vitruvian trinity of *firmitas*, *utilitas* and

5 See Chapter 6.2.1 *Organization and Articulation: Historical and Systematic*.

venustas attests to this.[6] The *term* 'function' entered the autopoiesis of architecture only in the 19th century, perhaps most prominently in the writings of Viollet-le-Duc. The term seems to have been borrowed from the biology of Georges Cuvier. Cuvier insisted that the understanding of the structure of organisms had to be grounded in relating structures to their functions. He emphasized the principle of functional organization that allocates specific functions to the various parts of the organism in correlation to all its other parts and its overall conditions of existence.[7] The influence of Cuvier's idea of functional analysis and his principle of the correlation of parts is evident in Viollet-le-Duc's writings. 'In every specimen of mason-work each piece taken separately in the case of dressed stone, or each section in concrete works, should clearly indicate its function. We ought to be able to analyze a building, as we take a puzzle to pieces, so that the place and function of each of the parts cannot be mistaken.'[8]

In the case of Viollet-le-Duc's notion quoted above, the concept of function refers to the contributions that the different parts of a structure make to the overall performance of a structure. Here these contributions are primarily technical. The different parts have no independent social function. The case is different if we consider the different rooms of a villa. Here each room has an individual social function and as such contributes to the overall functioning of the villa as ordering frame for the family's life. This second way of applying the concept of function can also be found in Viollet-le-Duc: 'There is in every building, I may say, one

6 Alberti's corresponding terms are *commoda, firmitatem* and *gratiam*.

7 Cuvier argued that an animal should be understood as a functional unit, whose structure is determined by its relationship to its specific environment. Each animal part or organ has its specific function: for example, the lung's function is respiration etc. All of the organism's organs relate functionally to one another and operate together. Cuvier believed that no part could alter its form or function without adversely affecting the entire organism. Cuvier emphasized this principle of biological integration – the correlation of parts – as one of the most fundamental laws of comparative anatomy. Cuvier explained his principle with the following example: if an animal's teeth are such as they must be, in order for it to nourish itself with flesh, we can be sure without further examination that the whole system of its digestive organs is appropriate for that kind of food, and that its whole skeleton and locomotive organs, and even its sense organs, are arranged in such a way as to make it skilful at pursuing and catching its prey. For these relations are the necessary conditions of existence of the animal; if things were not so, it would not be able to subsist. The principle of the correlation of parts – underpinned by the idea of conditions of existence – led Cuvier to the claim that one can infer the structure of the whole animal from any one of its parts. See: Georges Cuvier, *The Animal Kingdom – Arranged in Conformity with its Organization*, G & C & H Carvill (New York), 1832.

8 EE Viollet-le-Duc, *Lectures on Architecture*, 2 vols (1863, 1872), trans B Bucknall (1877, 1881), Dover Publications (New York), 1987; Vol 2, p 33, quoted in: Adrian Forty, *Words and Buildings*, Thames & Hudson (London), 2000, p 176.

principal organ – one dominant part – and certain secondary orders or members, and the necessary appliances for supplying all these parts, by a system of circulation. Each of these organs has its own function; but it ought to be connected with the whole body in proportion to its requirements.'[9] Although the term function was imported into architectural discourse only in the 19th century, and was given a new impetus by the advancing science of biology of the time, both the concept and its underpinning analogy with the animal organism were already fully operative in Alberti's foundational treatise. Alberti writes: 'Just as with animals, members relate to members, so too in buildings part ought to relate to part. . . . Each member should therefore be in the correct zone and position; it should be no larger than utility requires, no smaller than dignity demands.'[10] Alberti parallels functional integration with aesthetic harmony: 'The parts ought to be so composed that their overall harmony contributes to the honour and grace of the whole work.'[11] However, the primacy of the functional determination and correlation of the parts is clearly stated: 'Each part should be appropriate and suit its purpose. For every aspect of building, if you think of it rightly, is born of necessity, nourished by convenience, dignified by use, and only in the end is pleasure provided for.'[12] Alberti's implied notion of function (utility, purpose, convenience, necessity) is of equal generality as Viollet-le-Duc's notion.

More detailed and comprehensive accounts of the emergence and development of the concept of function within architecture can be found in works by Adrian Forty, Christoph Feldtkeller and Philip Steadman, among others. Here the main point is to establish the universal presence of the concept of function since architecture's inception as well as its generality that encompasses both the architectural artefact's functioning with respect to social demands and the functioning of the artefact's parts with respect to their contribution to the artefact's overall function. Thus the concept of function refers to both the architectural artefact's ends and its means. Since this generality might lead to confusion, a distinction is called for: the distinction between substantial and subsidiary functions. This distinction will be elaborated below. Before introducing this distinction and elaborating how the substantial functions of architecture are ordered by means of a system of fundamental function-types, another important distinction must be introduced: the

9 Ibid, p 90.

10 Leon Battista Alberti, *On the Art of Building in Ten Books*, translated by Joseph Rykwert, Neil Leach & Robert Tavernor, MIT Press (Cambridge, MA), 1988, p 23.

11 Ibid.

12 Ibid, p 24.

distinction between functions and capacities. This distinction will be introduced in the following chapter.

An important aspect of the concept of function as indicated by the historical references quoted above seems to be the idea of the functional integration of parts. The function of an architectural artefact is always defined relative to an encompassing functioning unit to which it is considered to contribute. Therefore, for any particular application of the notion of 'function' it is necessary to specify a system-reference, ie, the functioning whole with reference to which the functional element is supposed to contribute by fulfilling its allocated function. An architectural artefact is built up as a cascade of functions serving functions. This cascade is usually ordered hierarchically: encompassing functions are fulfilled via a series of subsidiary functions. One can also find webs of functions that cannot be neatly decomposed into distinct levels. However, the cascade or web of functions always culminates in categorical social functions that are given to architecture as its external reference, its *world-reference*.

That functions constitute architecture's world-reference, and that functions are always embedded within cascades and networks of functions, does not tell us what kind of entities the functions of architecture and design are. The fundamental starting point of the theory of architectural autopoiesis is that everything within its domain is communication. This is a consequence of the theory's self-embedding within Luhmann's social systems theory. Everything social is communication. Therefore everything architectural is communication. The theory operates within an ontologically homogeneous domain: everything is communication.

Architecture's lead-distinction is the distinction of form vs function. According to the theory of architectural autopoiesis, both forms and functions are communications. ***Forms are framing communications, functions are framed communications.*** This is the fundamental, necessary axiom of all further theorizing about form and function within the theory of architectural autopoiesis. The built forms of architecture are the final communications of architecture that are released into society to serve as framing communications within the respectively accommodated social systems. The functions of architecture are those communications, communicative interactions and communicative event scenarios that are framed by architecture's forms. All design is ultimately communication design.

We might demonstrate the pertinence of this axiom by considering some examples. What is, for instance, the function of a bread knife? To cut bread. Or to be more precise: the function of a designed bread knife is the ***action*** or ***action type*** of cutting bread. What is the function of a phone? The action (or action type) of having a phone conversation. The function of a designed car is the action type of driving a car, including (perhaps most importantly) when the user of the car is picking up his girlfriend. The function of a dinner table is the action type of sharing a dinner. The function of a lecture theatre is the social event type that we call lecture. What is important to note here is that all these functions are in fact communications. To cut bread at the dinner table is a communication. All actions, as distinct from mere bodily movements, are communications. By cutting the bread at the table the user of the knife might communicate that he wants to guide the event, as a good host, that he wants to express concern, hospitality etc. The knife itself frames this communication. It is itself a framing communication. The design features of the knife participate and give connotation and nuance to the communicative action of cutting the bread. Its weight and size modulate the gesture. Its appearance – modern versus traditional – gives identity to the user etc. It is these communicative aspects of the action that are the concern of the contemporary product designer. The technical feasibility of the knife's cutting operation is the concern of the product engineer. (The functions engineers are concerned with are physical processes.) In a similar fashion a lecture theatre can be analyzed as a framing communication whose function is the communicative interaction scenario that is the lecture or lecture event. The lecture is a communication that is framed and modulated by the specific design of the lecture theatre. It matters whether the theatre is long or broad, flat or steep, open or closed, with a lot of space between the seats or tightly packed etc. These differences are framing communications that regulate the participants' expectations and put them in a particular mood and provide a sense of anticipation.

All design is ultimately communication design. The design of social networking software, the design of tableware, the design of an evening dress, as well as the design of a living room, embedded within the design of the encompassing apartment, which is in turn embedded within the design of an apartment building. The functions of architecture and design are communications, communicative interactions, communicative event scenarios and communication systems, all operating within cascades of subordination/superordination, as well as in more loosely structured networks.

6.1.1 FUNCTIONS VERSUS CAPACITIES

The distinction of functions versus capacities is a relatively recent acquisition within the autopoiesis of architecture. This conceptual augmentation of architectural discourse responds to the increasing fluidity of architecture's task environment.

Rapidly shifting and differentiating life/communication processes with rather fluid requirements imply that thinking in stereotypical functions is no longer always appropriate. At the same time new design techniques deliver new formal repertoires with as yet unclear utilization potentials.

While a ***function*** of a building, space or architectural element is an actual, regular utilization effect of the respective building, space or element, a ***capacity*** of a building, space or architectural element is an occasional or only potential utilization effect. (The concept of utilization effect is coextensive with the concept of social communication (action, interaction). All utilization effects of architectural artefacts are social communications.) Functions might be manifest or latent. A function is ***manifest*** if it is explicitly acknowledged as the purpose of the building, space or element. Most buildings, spaces or elements have one single manifest function that is referred to in the space/element's name. For instance, the manifest function of an office building is to be utilized for office work, the manifest function of a lecture theatre is to accommodate lectures, the manifest function of a bedroom is its regular night-time utilization as sleeping place, and the manifest function of an entrance door is to be utilized as point of entry etc. (All these activities can be understood as communicative action: working, sleeping, lecturing, listening to a lecture, entering a building.) In addition to its manifest function, a building, space or architectural element might routinely be utilized in ways that are not explicitly acknowledged. However, these unacknowledged utilizations might still occur regularly, offering advantages that continue to motivate the reproduction of the respective forms of the buildings, spaces or elements in question. For instance, generous entrance steps into a public building might have the implicit or ***latent*** function of serving as informal lingering space that gives the respective institution a sense of welcoming animation. Reception desks in lobbies have the latent function of controlling access.[13] Their typical placement within lobbies indicates that this latent function is an aspect of their reproduction. (This distinction of manifest versus latent functions has been borrowed from sociology.)

The ***routine utilization*** of a certain form of building, space or architectural element is decisive for defining its functions, both manifest and latent. Further, the ascription of a function requires that this routine utilization feeds back to and ***motivates*** the ***regular reproduction*** of the

13 Controlling glances are deterrent communications. Even the mere occupation of a strategic entry position is a communication.

specific form of building, space or element. Capacities are effects where this aspect of a routine utilization that motivates regular reproduction is absent. Functions are declared or hidden ***purposes***. Capacities are ***potentials*** rather than purposes. They are affordances that have neither been asked for by the client, nor are they expected by user groups. Capacities might occasionally be utilized, however, without becoming a factor in the reproduction of the forms that have these capacities. With respect to capacities one might distinguish ***actual*** from ***virtual*** capacities. Actual capacities are current affordances that are occasionally utilized within the life/communication processes of the accommodated social system. For instance, all the rooms of a residential apartment have the capacity to become students' studios if the apartment is taken up by a student commune. Virtual capacities are as yet undiscovered, potential affordances that might be actualized only within a transformed life-process. Virtual capacities are involved when architectural design research has its most speculative moments. Virtual capacities are to be transformed into actual capacities. To the extent that these actual capacities become recognized, regularly utilized and then expected, they become functions. If they acquire a name that is used to designate buildings, spaces or elements they become manifest functions.

The distinction of functions versus capacities might be illuminated by reference to a similar distinction that is being made in relation to biology. Biological functions can be defined as selected effects.[14] An effect of a certain organic structure or trait of an organism can only be described as a function of the respective organic structure or trait if this effect presents an advantage for the organism and has contributed to the differential survival of the organism's ancestors utilizing the effect. The respective structures/traits have been *selected* in the sense that the population with the structure/trait exhibits a higher rate of reproduction than a comparable population without the structure/trait. The concept also requires that these selected effects are still contributing to the ongoing survival and reproduction success of the population in question. Functions are relative to a given life-process within a given environment. The underlying capacity might lose its function – becoming a mere rudiment – if the life-process changes within a transformed environment. At the same time, capacities that were dormant might become active and relevant for survival/reproduction within the new life-process. At any time,

14 Concerning the selected effects theory of function see: Karen Neander, 'Functions as Selected Effects: The Conceptual Analyst's Defense', in: *Philosophy of Science*, Vol 58, No 2 (June 1991), pp 168–84. The paper defends an etiological theory of biological functions according to which the proper function of a trait is the effect for which it was selected by natural selection.

any organism has an inexhaustible excess of virtual capacities. These capacities include the sum total of all traits that emerged as yet unutilized side effects of structures that evolved under certain selection pressures: differences that make no difference yet. The limit for the identification of capacities is located in the observer – biologist, architect, user-group – and his/her/its resources of discrimination. Any feature that can be described at all becomes a virtual capacity if a potentially relevant effect can be imagined that would put the feature to work within an (imagined) future environment or life-process. With a change in selective pressure – induced either by an environmental change or by a change of survival strategy on the part of the organism – these capacities might become relevant contributors to the further survival and proliferation of the organism in question. Side effects become selected effects, capacities transform into functions. This process whereby hitherto redundant features become vital functions is called ***exaptation***[15] in contrast to ***adaptation*** where a given functional feature is gradually optimized relative to a stable selection criterion. Exaptation includes both the first utilization of fallow features and the re-functionalization or 'détournement' of functional features, ie, their enlistment for new functions. In retrospect both the redundant features and the functional traits reveal their capacities by becoming evident as so-called ***pre-adaptive advances***. Both biological and cultural evolution proceed as much via exaptation as via adaptation. Exaptations are usually followed by further adaptations.

As indicated above, exaptation does not only involve the utilization of hitherto unutilized features but also (and perhaps predominantly so) the re-utilization of features or structures in new capacities that eventually stabilize into functions. The human hand evolved from extremities that were originally (like the feet) organs of locomotion. The evolution of the human speech organs (tongue, voice) involved the détournement of structures that originally evolved as organs with the functions of eating, breathing, and perhaps signalling via screaming. The significant fact with respect to highly evolved, complex organisms is that their body's organization and its structures are much more fixed and stable than their life-processes. The utilization (functionalization) of these structures and their capacities is much more malleable than these structures themselves. When a new pattern of utilization has been established, optimizing adaptation is set onto a new course and slowly reshapes and refines the structures in question according to the exigencies of the new

15 Stephen J Gould & Elisabeth S Vrba, 'Exaptation: A Missing Term in the Science of Form', in: *Paleobiology* 8 (1), 1982, pp 4–15.

life-process and its selection pressures. In the domain of architecture it can also be observed that evolution largely proceeds via the re-utilization of already evolved spatial types for new purposes rather than starting from scratch with each new requirement. In the world of architectural and artefactual evolution, a similar dialectic between exaptation and adaptation can be observed. Revolutionary, creative advances happen when new capacities are discovered and transformed into reproducible functions. Further cumulative advances are possible by means of adaptive refinement in view of the new function and its criteria. A new capacity for both the engine and the carriage was discovered in their combination within the first motor car. Since then a cumulative advancement of this new 'life form' has been witnessed, and it is still ongoing on the basis of a fundamental body plan that is now over 100 years old.

Contemporary avant-garde architecture has discovered the category of capacities, and the attendant concept of an always excessive virtuality, as a vehicle for evolutionary acceleration. The proliferation of as yet uninterpreted forms is not only tolerated but promoted as the production of as yet uncharted capacities.[16] The conversion of abstract forms into speculative proto-capacities is proceeding in design processes that employ a form-to-programme heuristics. Sometimes this creative work of functional interpretation is left to audiences that encounter and inhabit experimental projects after their construction. In any case, the architect has no control over which of his/her discovered and promoted capacities are finally selected, recognized and reproduced as designated functions. Architects control form (internal reference), they do not control function (external reference).[17]

If architectural functions are selected effects then the question does indeed arise of how this selection process takes place. The ascription of functions is safe, trivial and even inevitable only in the case of stable, stereotypical social institutions. The standard set of rooms in a modern, residential apartment is an example here: living room, dining room, kitchen, bathrooms and bedrooms have designated functions that the designer can rely on and work with in his design thinking.[18] The final

16 See, for example: John Rajchman (guest editor), 'The Virtual House', *Any* magazine, September 1997.

17 The lead-distinction of form vs function effects the re-entry of the distinction between system and environment into the system. Form is architecture's internal reference (self-reference). Function is architecture's external reference (world-reference). See: Volume 1, chapter 3.4.2 *Form vs Function as the Lead-distinction within the Design Disciplines*.

18 Strictly speaking even these stereotypical functions are up for détournement. All rooms in an apartment that is taken up by a commune of students are re-utilized as studios, including the living room and the dining room. The détournement sometimes goes even further: the first

arbiter of the advancement of social functionality, of the transformation of capacities into functions, is indeed the appropriation of the designed territories by the accommodated life-processes of the users. The more fluid and uncertain those life-processes become, the more must the discourse of architecture shift its attention from the anticipation of ascribed/designated functions to speculation about capacities. The plausibility of such speculations can be enhanced via an upgraded medium of architecture that is able to build up and visualize various social scenarios that tease out the virtual capacities of a designed spatial configuration and morphology.

Although the notion of a territory's capacities is certain to gain more prominence within architectural discourse, the concept of function cannot be replaced or eliminated by the promotion of the concept of capacity. The latter concept requires the former in its definition: a capacity is defined as a potential function. It is a ***proto-function*** in the sense that it has yet to acquire a determinate and desired effect by being selected according to the purposes and pursuits of the social communication processes framed by the territory in question. What must be refuted decisively here is the idea that all stable functions, and by implication all stable social institutions and expectations, are about to dissolve into a maelstrom of ever-changing forms of spontaneous communicative interaction. There can be no complex, productive social process that is just built upon fluid spontaneity. Complex social processes are ordered social processes. The very societal *raison d'être* of architecture is to stabilize and order patterns of social communication. That's the meaning of framing.[19] Without the stabilizing force of architecture no social complexity can be built up. Neither can social complexity be maintained without architectural stabilization on the high level of artificiality and thus improbability that has been achieved within contemporary society. What we must focus on is the innovation of frames and their functions, not their dissolution. Capacities must ossify into functions, within ever accelerating cycles of innovation. There can be no social life without expectations, without institutions, without (manifest and latent) functions. The functional designation of territories might become loose, multiple and transient, but it will not disappear. Functions will mutate from fixed stereotypes into more variable event scenarios. The functional distinctions will evolve from rigid dichotomies into richer

London studio the author occupied as independent apartment was originally designed as a kitchen.

19 *Framing* has been identified as architecture's societal function. See Volume 1, chapter 5.1.3 *Framing as Societal Function of Architecture*.

manifolds that might be susceptible to architectural ordering via gradients, allowing for smooth transitions and interpenetrations. All this is welcome and necessary, a higher, more complex and variegated order, requiring a more sophisticated repertoire of architectural framing. As will be explored below, the challenge of framing more complex patterns of social communication requires the upgrading of architecture's framing power along three dimensions that collaborate in the establishment of architectural order: the organizational, phenomenological and semiological dimensions of architectural order. The speculation about new capacities of new architectural forms will play an important part in architecture's attempt to address the evolving challenges of contemporary life. Their condensation into new function-types must remain the aim of such speculations.

6.1.2 SUBSTANTIAL VERSUS SUBSIDIARY FUNCTIONS

To elaborate a general concept of function, it is crucial to distinguish *direct* vs *indirect* contributions to social purposes (social interactions). The functioning of an architectural artefact that contributes to a social use or purpose only indirectly, via its encompassing unit, needs to be distinguished from such architectural artefacts that by themselves directly address a social use or concern.[20] Architectural theory needs to conceptualize the difference between, for example, the function of the posts that make up the balustrade and the social function of the balustrade itself, for example, its latent provision of a comfortable place to lean against, linger and look about. To express this difference, the theory of architectural autopoiesis distinguishes ***subsidiary*** functions from ***substantial*** functions. The substantial functions of architecture are always self-sufficient communicative actions, interactions, situations, events, scenarios or systems. At this point it is important to identify the architectural units that are capable of carrying substantial functions. The question arises whether architectural elements or components below the level of a room or territory are capable of sustaining a social function. The answer is no. All design disciplines produce artefacts that frame social interaction. Within the domain of architecture – as distinct from product and fashion design – the artefacts that frame social communication are ***territories*** that establish a difference between inside and outside.[21] Thus only territories have substantial functions. Therefore, the example of the balustrade is pertinent only to the extent to which the balustrade has

20 Social uses are always communicative actions or interactions: working, conferencing, learning, shopping, dining, hanging out etc.

21 See Volume 1, Chapter 2.5.5 *The Specificity of Architecture within the Design Disciplines*.

been designed to define a place, and does indeed define a self-sufficient territorial unit that can routinely frame social interactions. This might usually not be the case with balustrades, except perhaps if the balustrade describes a semi-circle to produce a niche and is perhaps further augmented with a wide handrail to lean upon etc. Such a niche or balcony overlooking a lobby is indeed a territorial unit that can sustain a substantial function, ie, the activity of overlooking the events unfolding in the lobby space. The niche communicates an invitation to reside there in this way. If the niche is occupied, people passing by will understand and respect this. (In this sense the niche communicates a single occupancy rule.) The niche might also invite two or three friends to gather there for a chat. The niche thus has two substantial functions sustaining two distinct types of social interaction: solitary lingering and chatting. Both are latent rather than manifest functions. (A flat, nondescript balustrade might have the capacity to host such events. Since, in this case, such events are not expected or considered in the brief and design of the balustrade they are mere capacities and not functions.) Strictly speaking the balustrade itself does not have its own substantial function. It is subordinate to the niche as frame. It contributes to the framing effect of the niche by means of various subsidiary functions: the function of supporting the weight of the communicating bodies, the space-delimiting function and the provision of an inviting aesthetic or atmospheric identity. Thus we can distinguish three types of subsidiary function: technical, organizational (space-delimiting) and articulatory functions. Each subsidiary effect or function contributes, in its own way, to the creation of the niche and its framing action. The strictly technical aspects, as external constraints, can be taken up by the engineering disciplines. However, even if the responsibility for the technical feasibility of these aspects is renounced, the architect must be able to discuss and integrate the technical requirements.

The distinction introduced here allows explicit differentiation between the merely subsidiary functioning of a staircase as device to reconnect a space that has been severed into levels, and a situation where the staircase is expected to address its own substantial function as a communicative space that has its own social significance. In the first instance the staircase has only a subsidiary function. In the latter instance the staircase has a substantial function. We might also envision a situation where a staircase serves both a subsidiary function, for example, reconnecting a severed programmatic unit, as well as a (latent) substantial function, for example, giving space and occasion to desired communicative encounters. The example of the staircase thus implies that an architectural artefact might, at the same time, but with respect to different social purposes (situations, audiences), fulfil both subsidiary and substantial functions.

Subsidiary functions always serve substantial functions, either immediately or via a cascade of intermediate subsidiary functions. Substantial functions always address social purposes directly. However, since human purposes are themselves ordered into cascades, hierarchies and networks, so must be the substantial functions that are the external reference and *raison d'être* of any architectural design. Relations of subordination (or superordination) do not only hold between substantial and subsidiary functions, they also hold among substantial functions as well as among subsidiary functions. The substantial function of the staircase as catalyst and hub for informal communication might be feeding into the encompassing (superordinate) substantial function of a communicative entrance lobby which in turn contributes to the overall function of the corporate headquarters building within which it is located: the overall spatial framing of the social system that is the corporate business organization. The various territorial units within the corporate building have their own (manifest and latent) substantial functions. These functions are meant to collaborate to produce the superordinate, encompassing function of the building. The function of each individual territory is thus conceptually subordinated to the encompassing function. The functions of the parts are meant to be coordinated to add up to an integrated, global function: the designated function of the building as (productive) corporate headquarters for a given business organization. The dimensions of organization and articulation come into play here as follows. The overall constitution and thus ordering/framing communication of the building depends upon the organization (distribution, clustering, nesting) of the elemental territorial units. Also, the internal organization of the territorial units is relevant here. The same integrated concern for both global and local aspects applies to the dimension of articulation. The overall range of atmospheres, their spatial distribution and the contrasts between atmospheres of different units etc, are as important as the individual atmospheres and their connotations and affects. In both dimensions part-to-whole relations (system-subsystem relations) have to be reckoned with and must be orchestrated. Further, dependencies between the three dimensions – technical, organizational and articulatory – need to be considered.

6.1.3 TECTONICS

The relationship between the technical and the articulatory dimensions leads to the concept of tectonics. There are plenty of examples in the history of architecture where architectural elements and features with technical, subsidiary functions become the object of articulatory endeavours. This is the domain of tectonics. For many architectural theorists, tectonics is the very essence of architecture. However, for these theorists the point of tectonics is the didactic, visual clarification of the building's material and technical constitution. The theory of architectural autopoiesis rejects this understanding of tectonics as a distraction from architecture's societal *raison d'être*. In what follows, tectonics is given its appropriate station within the discipline's rationality.

How can a designer articulate the substantial function of an architectural space or element? What becomes the material substrate of his/her effort of articulation? As introduced above, subsidiary functions might be classified into three categories: technical, organizational and articulatory functions. This classification of functional dimensions is important to order the designer's search for functional equivalents. One and the same architectural element – for example, a particular wall – might operate in all three dimensions: it has many technical functions (load-bearing, thermal insulation), organizational functions (separation of domains), as well as articulatory functions (giving a characteristic atmosphere). In each dimension the designer can search for different possibilities for the wall's functional substitution. These might or might not coincide again in a single alternative artefact. The load-bearing capacity of the wall might be taken up by columns, the separation of domains might be handled by a light partition wall, and the atmospheric characterization of the space might be achieved by the ceiling etc. The design process might proceed in the following sequencing of concerns: organization, technical materialization, articulation.

The materialized organization, materialized according to the concerns of technical efficiency, produces a certain morphology with a certain appearance. Before adding an additional material layer for the purposes of articulation, it thus makes sense to investigate whether this technically given phenomenological material is suited to serve the wall's required articulatory function.

A technically selected morphology thus assumes articulatory functions. This initially unconscious, evolutionary, historical process becomes a conscious design strategy under the banner of tectonics, albeit often with the tendency to hypostatize the tectonic expression as an end in itself rather than as a means to articulate the substantial (social) function of the artefact/space in question. Structural expressionism as primary design agenda is an example of this hypostatization of tectonic expression. However, this kind of hypostatization of a valid design strategy does not invalidate the design strategy as such. If we define tectonics as the strategic détournement of an element's technically induced morphology in order to address substantial functions in the articulatory dimension, then tectonics can be redeemed and integrated within contemporary notions of handling form-function relations. We might call this strategy of opportunizing on technical details ***tectonic articulation***. The engineering logic of adapting member sizes in proportion to stresses can be taken up within an architectural strategy of articulation. For instance, the skeleton of a tower might be expressed on the outside as exo-skeleton. It might be differentiated along the vertical axis describing a gradient transformation from massive to filigree. This structural logic might be correlated with an occupational logic and the structure's articulation might in turn come to signify the occupational distribution.

Historically, the transformation of a technically motivated form into an articulating motif has tended to conventionalize and fix the form. The articulatory function comes to dominate. It often unfolds its own developmental dynamic. Eventually the technical realization of a motif might change, ie, a certain motif loses its original technical *raison d'être*. (At this point, contemporary sensibility would suggest the abandonment of the motif.) This happened to the details of the Classical orders as they moved from wood construction to stone construction. In this case the motif's articulatory function remains in operation. It is not 'mere decoration' without function. However, it no longer constitutes tectonic articulation in the sense defined here. It has become *ornamental* articulation.

The theory of architectural autopoiesis recognizes the rationality of tectonic articulation as opportunizing strategy serving articulation. It is no self-serving pursuit and must remain subordinated to the concern of articulating a substantial function. The advantage of tectonic articulation is that what is required anyway, for technical reasons, is utilized as convenient means of articulation. The drawback here is that the articulatory repertoire is thereby constrained, so that this strategy might not succeed if the task of articulation is very complex. For instance, the exposure of the primary structure can be very effective in giving an identifiable character and atmosphere to certain spaces. The internal ordering of large spaces might be facilitated by the lawful differentiation of the structural system: the different (longitudinal versus transversal) directions of the space are indicated by the direction of the primary beams. The centre of a large space is indicated by the greatest depth of the beams etc. These features might serve as orienting clues within a large, otherwise visually partitioned space like a large market space. However, if a rich network of different and differently related spaces needs to be articulated then the enlistment of the (technically homogeneous) structure might not be feasible because it is not versatile enough. On the other hand, to force the structure into articulatory differences might become too forced and costwise prohibitive. Therefore tectonic articulation cannot be made an absolute priority. Articulation[22] as such, by any means necessary, has precedence.

The articulatory integration of the morphological consequences of technical requirements is always more elegant and satisfying than the attempt to fight and deny them by hiding or obfuscating them. In order for architects to attempt this they need to guide and orchestrate the engineering investigations and then select the engineering options that most suit their primary task to fulfil the posed substantial functions. The adaptive differentiation of structures as well as the adaptive differentiation of volumes and envelopes according to the building's environmental performance (with respect to its exposure to internal heat loads, as well as sun, wind, rain etc) afford many opportunities for differential tectonic articulation. Although there can be no doubt that architecture remains a discourse that is distinct from engineering, a close collaboration with these disciplines as well as the acquisition of reliable intuitions about their respective logics are increasingly important conditions for the design of contemporary high performance architecture.

6.1.4 THE CATEGORIZATION OF FUNCTION-TYPES

The basis for the overall order of substantial functions in architecture is the functional differentiation of society itself. The panoply of architecture's substantial functions is the full range of social interaction types, filtered and worked through within the autopoiesis of architecture. This longstanding and ongoing filtration process has produced a relatively stable, categorical system of programmatic distinctions or ***function-types*** (programme types) that gives a primary order to the substantial functions of architecture. Function-types are architecture's registration of types of social interaction.

There is no functionality in the abstract. There's only functionality with respect to a specified programmatic type or function-type. Therefore, all functional reasoning in architecture starts within the framework of an assumed programme-typology as a given set of distinct social uses (programmatic types, or function-types). However, this does not imply that typological distinctions – like residential vs commercial – are absolute or immutable. Programme types might develop, transitional variants might be derived etc. But the dimension of programme typology cannot be suspended. It remains the starting point for architecture, the inescapable logic of its external reference. The functions that are handled

22 The concept of articulation will be elaborated in detail in section 6.5 *Articulation*.

within architecture are always conceptually subsumed under a certain overarching function-type. This is the structure of architecture's world-reference. It reflects a key structural property of architecture's societal environment and is not an arbitrary invention that can be undone by a radical innovation produced within architecture.[23]

A speculative sociology might go beyond any received institutional typology and speculate radically about possible social formations or societies and thus unravel any given programme types, in order to reconstitute a new way of differentiating the social system, proposing a new set of programmatic types. A certain degree of such sociological imagination, on the level of nuance rather than on the level of revolution, might be admissible and even called for as ingredient of avant-garde architectural work. Otherwise, however, architecture has to accept the given categorical differences between different types of programmes as starting point.

For modern society the distinction between industrial, administrative, residential and recreational functions has been categorical. Further, modernity crystallized a series of stable, specialized, institutional building types like schools, hospitals and museums etc. Even if the attempt is made to subvert those categories, for example, by introducing hybrid typologies like live-work, those categories remain the starting point of this (only partial) subversion. This categorical differentiation of social uses implies that there is, from the start, a multiplicity of substantial functions to be fulfilled rather than a single unified function such as 'urban life'. A design effort taking on urban life would have to start by breaking this unity into components. This basic principle of functional differentiation is particularly intransigent within modern, functionally differentiated society.

The Middle Ages too knew different building types. The church was not a house. The town hall was distinguished from the houses surrounding it. In principle, however, the mass of the medieval city was segmented rather than differentiated, ie, segmented into multifunctional household units. The house of the burghers carried the whole life of the family and its extended household. It was dwelling, place of work and place of exchange. Within the house the rooms were not specifically differentiated. Segmentation and stratification were the primary modes of differentiation in traditional societies. Functional differentiation is the

23 The slogan of a supposed transition 'from typology to topology' that has been put forward in recent avant-garde discourse must be bracketed by this insight. The distinction of fundamental function-types cannot be eradicated from within architecture. It belongs to architecture's external reference. However, the slogan makes sense in relation to solution-types or archetypes.

primary mode of differentiation in modern society. This is a fundamental external condition for the autopoiesis of architecture, and this condition is recognized by the fact that the identification of the function-type is the fundamental starting point and headline for any architectural project.[24]

6.1.5 PROBLEM-TYPES (FUNCTION-TYPES) VS SOLUTION-TYPES (ARCHETYPES)

The programmatic typology that categorizes substantial functions has been a crucial factor at the root of most of what has been called 'typology' within architecture. However, as stable social functions created a stable environment for the development of stable substantial functions for architecture, equally stable spatio-structural solutions emerged to address and fulfil these substantial functions. Those spatio-structural solutions – for example, the hut, the courtyard building, the basilica, the hall, the mall etc – have their own inertia and their own capacity to fulfil new functions. They persist in the history of architecture across a certain diversity of substantial functions, and a concept could therefore be formed that abstracts from the aspect of a specific function. In fact the same respective spatio-structural solutions have been developed over and over again for different social functions at different historical times in different cultures. These abstract, general solutions became the basis of another concept of 'typology' in architecture. Bill Hillier talks about 'solution typologies', defined as 'fields of strategic possibility defined by past practice'.[25]

We might take this cue from Hillier and distinguish problem typologies from solution typologies.[26] Problem types lead to function-types and solution-types lead to what we might call 'archetypes'. Archetypes, or more general solution-types, belong to the discourse on form. Aldo Rossi explicitly emphasized this abstraction from specific function, referring to such types as *archetypes*, and tried to argue for the virtues of such enduring forms and their potentially open-ended capacities.[27] The

24 A project that avoids this identification is a proto-architectural study rather than an architectural project. Proto-architectures in this sense are viable vehicles of design research. The AADRL is currently pursuing a three-year design research agenda under the title *Proto-design*.

25 Bill Hillier, *Space is the Machine – A Configurational Theory of Architecture*, Cambridge University Press (Cambridge), 1996, p 429.

26 This double meaning of the notion of typology that is here unfolded reflects the fundamental double-orientation of architecture: the orientation towards function (problems) and forms (solutions).

27 Function-types – as problem types – remain relatively stable across styles, while the conceptualization of archetypes, conceptualized in the context of solution typologies, shifts as the discipline moves from one style to the next.

traditional city was seen as a reservoir of such archetypes with multivalent capacities with respect to (new) functions.

Although there are insights to be captured here, it has to be said that such collections of 'archetypes' can never be expected to form a stable system of categories that could give long-term order to the discipline of architecture. Such archetypes stabilized primarily on the basis of longstanding technical limitations of the craft of construction in unison with the long-term stability of social institutions. The enumeration of historical archetypes – courtyard house, basilica etc – produces a rather haphazard collection of items that can hardly form the basis of a systematic theory. Instead solution typologies might be constructed on the basis of an abstract principle that delivers a systematically constituted, exhaustive solution space. One might formulate solution typologies based on abstract classificatory principles, for example, a typology of basic building shapes based upon the relative expansiveness of their respective spatial dimensions. On this basis we might thus distinguish six basic solution-types for buildings (or for components of larger building complexes):

- point-shape (pavilion)
- horizontal line-shape (bar)
- vertical line-shape (tower)
- horizontal plane-shape (shed)
- vertical plane-shape (slab)
- and cubic-shape (block)

With respect to the basic aspect of the building's outward dimensional ratios, this is an exhaustive universe: pavilions, bars, towers, sheds, slabs and blocks. The six building forms represent all there is, in terms of the basic modules of our cities. There are typical combinations like vertical line-shapes on top of horizontal plane-shapes (tower over podium), or vertical plane-shapes over horizontal plane-shapes (slab over podium). Complexes, with volume shapes that do not immediately fit into this system, can nevertheless be analyzed: for instance, dumb-bell shopping malls can be analyzed as two parallel bars running between two sheds or two blocks.

These basic, generic types are in principle open with respect to their substantial function. This typology of basic building forms might then enter into a typology of urban morphologies, distinguishing ways of multiplying, arraying and combining these types of volume-shape into types of urban massing. We might also proceed inwards and distinguish different patterns of internal voiding and patterns of internal partitioning. On all three levels – on the level of the internal subdivision, on the level of the basic building shape and on the urban level – such solution typologies might be related to problem typologies.

At Zaha Hadid Architects we analyzed all our prior oeuvre with respect to this categorization. We did this in connection with a theoretical design project that was presented under the general headline of 'Form Informing Urbanism',[28] conceived within the paradigm of 'Parametric Urbanism'.[29] In this project we took this basic building-shape typology – after enhancing each basic type with a scale-dependent void – as a starting point for a systematic field-differentiation whereby we subjected the six types to a multi-dimensional morphing process. The results are still analyzable in terms of the six categories, albeit on a more sophisticated level: each building is now indexed with respect to a series of percentiles that indicate the morphing mix of the building in question. This was a purely formal exercise (resulting in interesting formal field qualities as the morphing mix and scale were correlated with river-proximity and topography).

However, the purpose of setting up such a typology is not only to have a systematic, exhaustive register of building forms for the sake of setting up formal operations. Indeed, with respect to formal proliferation this catalogue is rather too reductive. The primary purpose of such a categorization is to have a starting point for thinking through systematic form-function relations. The 'colloquial' type-names like tower, slab, block, shed etc indicate that this basic form-categorization might systematically correlate with certain functional capacities that tend to attract preferred substantial function-types.

Alejandro Zaera-Polo is probing precisely this intuition with his ambitious 'unitary theory of the building envelope'.[30] His typology takes nearly the same approach of distinguishing according to volumetric proportions. He distinguishes four types and starts to characterize them in terms of their functional capacity and probable social (and 'political') import:

- $X = Y > Z$ Flat-horizontal envelopes: loose fit
  This category comprises functions such as train stations, airports, trade fairs, markets, stadiums etc. According to Zaera-Polo: 'Their ability to host crowds, enclose public space, and control flow in an artificially controlled environment, as well as their conflictual relationship with the

28 'Form Informing Urbanism – Parametric Urbanism', is a display and animated film created by Zaha Hadid & Patrik Schumacher for the *Global Cities* exhibition at Tate Modern, June 2007.

29 See part 11. *Parametricism – The Parametric Paradigm and the Formation of a New Style.*

30 Alejandro Zaera-Polo, 'The Politics of the Envelope – A Political Critique of Materialism', in: *Volume*, Archis, 2008, #17, pp 77–105.

local, qualifies flat-horizontal envelopes as highly politically charged. . . . The material and geometrical configuration of the edge is crucial to the articulation of inside and outside: insets of the footprint or corrugation of the vertical surface and the use of permeable materials may contribute to enhancing osmosis between the contained programme and its surroundings. The problem of inserting a large shed into an urban fabric is . . . large scale obstacles to urban flows, sterilizing their surroundings . . . resulting in a struggle between . . . developers who want to swallow as much space as possible within their complexes, and urban planners who want to keep as much permeability as possible.'[31]

- X = Y = Z Spherical envelopes: relaxed fit
'The specificity of this type is precisely the relative independence that the skin acquires in relation to its programmatic determinations as function is not usually determined by proximity to the outside. . . . The spherical type often contains gradients of publicness within. Spherical envelopes often correspond to public buildings, buildings that gather a multiplicity of spaces rather than a repetitive type of space. . . . Political expression and identity are particularly important. . . . The spherical envelope features the lowest level of environmental constraints and the highest levels of representational demands.'[32] The way Zaera-Polo characterizes this envelope type identifies it with the manifesto-style programme Rem Koolhaas has put forward with his notion of 'Bigness'.[33]
- X = Z > Y Flat-vertical envelopes: tight fit
'Flat-vertical envelopes are generated by the horizontal displacement of a section of space, which in order to support a specific function, optimizes density, daylight, ventilation, structural constraints and the building's relationship with public space and infrastructure. Land uses and orientation are also important drivers for this type of envelope. We can probably include within this category most mid-rise residential and many office buildings as they respond to the need to host a large volume of homogeneous programme. . . . Modern fabrics tend to be predominantly matrices of Flat-vertical envelopes.'[34]
- Z > X = Y Vertical envelope: slim fit
'The collusion between extreme technical performance and high visual impact produces a maximum tension between efficiency and expression. . . . As the envelope increases in visibility and iconographic

31 Ibid, p 82.
32 Ibid, p 87.
33 See chapter 2.39 *Retroactive Manifestos*.
34 Zaera-Polo, 'The Politics of the Envelope', p 92.

potential, so do the environmental and structural demands.... As a result of this intensification of the environmental parameters the vertical envelope is becoming increasingly complex and anisotropic. It is reacting very specifically to the surrounding urban context with specific inflexions that provide views, solar exposure, natural ventilation and profile.... The current urban core densification is reviving the drive for monumental high-rise construction. Tall buildings are paradigmatic of the representation of power in the city.... The manipulation of the envelope's crowning, where the technical determinations are weaker, is the technique to distinguish buildings otherwise designed as mere extrusions of an optimized footprint.... Tall buildings are no longer an expensive extravagance but a crucial development vehicle engaging the middle classes. In this process of democratization the high-rise has exceeded its natural milieu as workspace and pervaded all aspects of urban life.... Because of its engagement with domestic protocols and specific climatic conditions, the vertical envelope is now producing culturally-specific, vernacular varieties.'

These excerpts might not do justice to the intentions of Zaera-Polo's attempt to reconstruct the 'politics of the envelope'. Here they should act as an example of the kinds of generalizing statements about form-function relations we find in contemporary architecture. The excerpts also serve as an initial pointer towards a type of research that would aim to establish systematic correlations between forms (solutions) and functions (problems). This is the core business of substantive architectural theory. Both *solution typologies* and *problem typologies* – whether based on inductive retrieval or deductive construction – are an essential first step in the attempt to develop a substantive architectural theory. The next step is to try to map solution typologies onto problem typologies, on the basis of both empirical observation and rational reconstruction, in order to establish theoretical premises for a creative expansion of new, viable form-function complexes. Zaera-Polo's solution typology, and his (so far rather unsystematic) attempt to gather and reconstruct evidence concerning the functional capacities and performative effects of these types, is a first step that deserves to be noted.

Obviously the outer shape (ratios of primary dimensions) is only one among many dimensions of formal classification. Although we can presume that articulated building complexes might be analyzed as composites of those types, we should not over-emphasize this thinking in terms of convex containers. We cannot afford to forget the significance of the switch from edifice to space. Also, types like the flat-horizontal envelope sometimes extend to dimensions where the external shape opens up so many possibilities of internal organization that the identification of the type leaves everything yet to be determined. The notion of an 'interior urbanism'[35] has been coined for this condition (airports, malls etc). Working with the (inevitably reductive) method of solution *types* always runs counter to the radical openness that was gained by the switch from edifice to space. However, an analytic architectural theory has to find ways of ordering this universe of possibility, and the indicated shape-types have the advantage of possessing close empirical correlates. Thus they are a good starting point even if the intention is to move 'from typology to topology'.

The 'parametric' approach to design, which is sometimes supposed to supersede typology, might rather be theorized as a refinement within the typological discourse. While parametric design indeed dissolves formal types understood as rigid archetypal forms, it cannot replace functional typology as a necessary framework for the elaboration of the functional/performative dimension of architecture. Meaningful parameters can only be defined within a classification that allows for the specification of performance criteria relative to corresponding types of activities. Ideas of gradual transition or hybridization obviously depend upon prior categories to be hybridized or morphed. Even assuming a totally smooth series of continuous transformation, gradual quantitative change will lead to qualitative differences that must be conceptualized by some form of classification: typology.

Traditional schemes of classification are thus augmented by the possibility of hybridization, and the ordering of a spectrum of smooth transitions[36] between types via ordinate or quantitative (parametricized) concepts. Function-types are thus placed within a continuous order and redefined as variable, parametricized constructs. The result is more complex than a traditional typology. This increased complexity does not only result from the addition of the in-between variants, but is also due to the much stronger sense of integration achieved within such a ***topo-typological system.***

35 *Interior Urbanism* was one of the key slogans that guided the generative design research at the AADRL, Design Research Lab founded in 1996 as Master of Architecture Programme at the Architectural Association School of Architecture.

36 Obviously, such ideas of typological hybridization and smooth transitions require corresponding tendencies within the societal environment, for example, the tendency of knowledge based self-employment and home-work leading to the new hybrid typology of live-work, which in fact has already been institutionalized within the planning guidelines, for instance in London.

6.1.6 PATTERNS OF DECOMPOSITION/COMPOSITION

The notion of function refers to the role a territorial unit or architectural subsystem plays with respect to the ordering/framing operation of an encompassing territory. The function of the part/subsystem is its contribution to the function of the superordinate system which in turn is itself a part or subsystem of a yet larger territorial system. The function of the staircase for instance is the integration of the stack of floors into a functional unit, a certain (wing of a) building. This building might in turn be a component that makes a specific functional contribution to the functioning of an encompassing building complex. In this way a nested chain of system-subsystem relations might be constructed. Certain spatial items or artefacts might be parts of several systems. This multiple system-reference should be distinguished from multifunctionality which implies that a unit might have several functions within a single system. In each case, functionality is defined with respect to the most immediate level of system integration, within an overall (hierarchical) order of system levels.

According to which organizational pattern should a network of territorial/architectural system-subsystem relations be constructed? The answer must depend upon the structure of the life-process of the accommodated social system. How should a given institutional totality, for example, the life of a family or household that is to be framed by a residential architecture, be decomposed into interaction/activity subsystems? The point here is to note that there are many possible patterns of decomposition/composition that might be proposed to resolve a global function, like the function of a residence, into its contributing parts. A residential unit might be decomposed into the standard room-types like living room, and dining room, kitchen, bedroom, bathroom, ie, the unit breaks into five parts. Or one might proceed more abstractly via several levels of decomposition and first distinguish those areas to which visitors have access versus those areas to which there is no such access by visitors. Then one might take each of these subsystems, the public versus the private subsystem, and decompose further, either by trying to maintain a general principle of differentiation that applies to successive levels of subsystem formation, for instance the differentiation of (more) public versus (more) private activities/spaces, or alternatively by introducing a new principle like distinguishing servicing vs served activities/spaces, or finally proceeding independently in each branch of the initial bifurcation, distinguishing, for example, the public subsystem into lounging versus dining, while distinguishing the private part into sleeping, dressing and bathing. The decision or preference might depend upon the criterion of parsimony. In this case the single principle approach should be chosen. A further abstract-formal a priori would be to proceed by dichotomous bifurcation only. If this seems too forced or artificial, and instead close adherence to common sense is the criterion, then one might utilize familiar concepts and change the principle of differentiation on each level, without regulating the span of differentiation. The different ways of architectural ordering considered here are at the same time different ways of ordering the social life-processes that are expected to unfold within the designed architecture. The architectural order is assumed to coincide with and sustain the social order. The main point to establish here is that whatever pattern of decomposition or systems-integration is assumed, the notion of function can only be specified in such a context of decomposition or integration.

The decomposition is supposed to produce functional subsystems. These subsystems are integrated via a unifying function that is performed for the encompassing system. These subsystems might be decomposed further into elements that ideally all cooperate via relations that are internal to the subsystem, ie, without getting entangled in interdependencies that stretch across the subsystem boundaries. For instance, a bathroom is an autonomous functional unit that requires no contribution from facilities that are located outside the bathroom. The towel should be ready to hand and not be placed in the dressing room. On the next level of system integration, the bathroom and the dressing room function together as private backstage unit that allows the inhabitants to prepare themselves to face the public. Together they form an autonomous subsystem separated off from the rest of the residential unit. This avoidance of boundary-crossing dependencies – full (or near) decomposability – has the advantage of allowing for a controlled build up of complexity. However, this principle limits the ability to articulate the increased levels of connection intensity that marks many contemporary social institutions. Therefore the principle of full (or near) decomposability cannot be set up as a universal rule or preference. This principle gives up on the potential efficiencies of overlapping utilization. Another way to proceed might be via the opposition of several systems of differentiation that each operate across the overall domain, intersecting like a matrix rather than building up a hierarchy of nesting distinctions. Public versus private might be intersected by servicing versus served. Christopher Alexander proposed this possibility with respect to urban differentiation in his seminal text 'A City is not a Tree'.[37]

37 Christopher Alexander, 'A City is not a Tree', in: Jonathan Crary (Ed), *Zone 1/2, The Contemporary City*, Urzone Inc (New York), 1987.

The arrangement of a network of criss-crossing functional contributions of territorial units or architectural subsystems is conceivable, whereby each unit/subsystem might contribute to multiple further units/subsystems in a way that does not allow for the analysis into a hierarchical tree-like decomposition of functions. To track such complex patterns of functional collaboration the use of 'network analysis' or 'graph theory'[38] can be recommended.

6.1.7 FUNCTIONAL REASONING VIA ACTION-ARTEFACT NETWORKS

Within a societal environment where social communication processes become increasingly diverse, multifaceted and nuanced, architecture must think of upgrading its understanding and handling of functions. The disposition over a mere handful of standard function-types that trigger routine design responses can no longer satisfy sophisticated clients. A more detailed and nuanced understanding of architecture's audiences and user groups – in terms of their actual and potential patterns of communicative interaction – seems to be called for.

Does this imply that architects should try to design the life-processes that are to unfold within the spaces of their buildings? Such a pretension is evidently preposterous. (Architects have indeed been accused of such pretensions.) How should architectural theory conceive the relation of the designed architectural artefacts to its users within its design projects?

The user or, to be more precise, the user's communicative activities[39] that utilize architectural spaces, are located in architecture's most immediate and most relevant societal environment. The user's communications and communicative interactions are not architectural communications. They belong to the social systems of communications that are serviced/framed by architecture. The communications unfolding within a lecture theatre during a lecture belong to the temporary system of communications that we can identify with the lecture as autopoietic system of communications.[40] At the same time the lecture is embedded

38 See section 6.4 *Supplementing Architecture with a Science of Configuration*.

39 There is a general theoretical predisposition to be observed here. This predisposition resides in one of Luhmann's fundamental theoretical decisions: the decision to locate human beings (as psychic and living/organic systems) within the environment of society. Society, according to Luhmann, consists of nothing but communications connecting to communications. To follow this theoretical decision here implies that not the users but their communications and communicative interactions constitute the immediate and most relevant societal environment of architecture.

40 A lecture is an autopoietic system of communications because during its course it develops a unique mood, understanding and rapport among the participants, ie, it self-referentially closes and builds up temporary communication structures. A latecomer will find it difficult to catch up with what is going on.

within a lecture series, which in turn is embedded in the larger communication system that is the university department within which the lecture has an allocated role to play. It is within these social systems that the communications unfolding within the lecture theatre belong. The same applies to the designed lecture theatre itself as framing communication. The main lecture theatre of the university department is a communication within the social system of this department. Its location, size and atmosphere communicate about the department, on behalf of the department. This communication is attributed to the department as much as the lecture series unfolding within it is attributed to it. Both belong to the same system of communications. Both are located in the environment of architecture. However, the designed lecture theatre might also be circulating as communication within the autopoiesis of architecture. Perhaps it is recognized as avant-garde contribution to a certain emerging style and as such might be attracting appraisals within the architectural discourse. Architectural students might come to visit and debate its design features. In this way all built works of architecture lead a communicative double life, as framing communications within the social systems they accommodate, and as communications within the autopoietic system of architecture. (The framing role of specific architectural works within their framed social systems might become the topic of communication within architectural discourse. This, however, would not overcome the sharp distinction that exists between these two domains of communication.)

To reiterate: the users and their patterns of utilization and communication cannot be made an immediate object of design within an architectural project. They constitute architecture's external reference, outside the architect's control. Architects control the construction of forms, architecture's internal reference. However, both the final built architectural forms and the functions they sustain are communications that together reside in architecture's environment. It is this environment that is modelled within architecture's design medium. Traditionally, the architectural drawing only depicts the forms that are under architecture's control. Functions are not depicted beyond simple designations that appear as room labels within the drawing. Sometimes furniture configurations are drawn to indicate the utilization of a particular spatial layout. The thesis here is that the autopoiesis of architecture should aim to go beyond this and deepen its engagement with the potential utilization of its designs. Occupation and communication patterns should become the key reference point of architectural design speculation and discussion. In order for this to happen, these patterns of communicative interaction (that are to be ordered, framed and thereby sustained by the architectural design effort) must be represented within architecture's design medium. Each ambitious design project that is confronted with the task of designing for advanced contemporary social institutions (like universities or sophisticated corporations) must find ways to explore and discuss in detail the framing role specific architectural forms should take up within the social systems they engage with. The architectural design process and discourse must develop the tools and intelligence to anticipate and evaluate the framing efficacy of their design proposals. It is a key thesis of the theory of architectural autopoiesis that complex, sophisticated communication systems like advanced corporations can no longer be adequately framed via a given standard set of stereotypical solutions.

The development of more versatile and nuanced solutions requires not only the expansion of the formal repertoire on the basis of a new formal design heuristics, but equally a new functional heuristics, ie, a new way of understanding and handling functions that is able analytically to break up stereotypical monolithic functions to get into their underlying constitution from multiple, communicative interaction scenarios. What is required here is, first of all, the interpretation of functions as communicative interaction scenarios and, secondly, a close reading and speculation about how the various aspects of a framing architectural setting intervene in such scenarios, ie, how architectural spaces and their furnishings become 'actors' or 'agents' within the unfolding event scenarios. The task is to understand and simulate how architectural agents might gather, order, prompt, cajole and inspire desired patterns of social communication. The phrase or formula that the theory of architectural autopoiesis proposes for this reads: architecture must conceive of its function in terms of ***action-artefact networks***.[41] The architectural design process should be able credibly to speculate about probable social scenarios. This implies that the design medium represents and animates such scenarios. This requires that artefacts (forms) and communicative actions (functions) are modelled together. The artefacts/forms are the independent variable under the manipulative control of the designer. The actions/functions are the dependent variable that serves as feedback and selection criterion for the manipulation of forms.

The substantial functions of architecture have to be addressed in terms of action-artefact networks. The inclusion of communicating actors

41 The concept is loosely inspired by *actor-network theory*. Although the context and purpose of the concept of actor-networks are rather different, the perspective shares the aspect of theorizing communicative complexes that involves actors and material objects (as well as the routines that bind them). See Bruno Latour, *Reassembling the Social: An Introduction to Actor-Network-Theory*, Oxford University Press (Oxford), 2005.

within action-artefact networks is the only viable way forward with respect to a contemporary, upgraded functional reasoning that would be able to cope with the level of sophistication and innovation demanded by contemporary society. For instance, with respect to the design of a high performance private residence, we might consider the example of hosting a dinner party, understood as a complex and ambitious communicative institution. The success of the party hinges upon its ability to engender stimulating conversations, its ability to facilitate individual efforts in making new acquaintances etc. One crucial parameter of the design might be the density and arrangement of props capable of creating situations that facilitate the deepening of networks of friendship and allow a measured increase in the level of intimacy with selected guests. Such a dinner party is in effect a complex and layered configuration of communication and community building. Ideally an extended scenario might be orchestrated, unfolding in choreographed stages. The party begins as people are moving in, gathering in the entrance hall and taking a stand-up cocktail. A cluster of stand-up tables, in conjunction with a window affording a stimulating view of the city, facilitates the necessary physical proximity of human bodies and the shared attentional focus that is required to stimulate communication. Here opportunities for informal acquaintance are afforded. At the next stage, the host starts to call everybody to the big, unified dining table. Everybody has extended time to converse with their respective neighbours at the table. After dinner this stable configuration is transformed into the fluid play of small groups gathering and dispersing at the various lounging points. Shifting conversational clusters can be formed. Diverse spatial settings with various types of furnishings might be called for to catalyze and orchestrate this scenario. The subsystems and elements of this social institution of the dinner party are the communicative actions of the users. However, those communicative actions, all along, involve architectural settings and artefacts as integral parts of the communicative events. We might refer to those artefacts as *architectural agents*. Armchairs are shifted and turned, cushions are adjusted, legs crossed over, wine glasses are refilled, light levels are adjusted. The intimate conversation at the small side-table is a subsystem contributing to the overall event of the party by remaining in view and by contributing to the background noise. This way of functional reasoning and analysis leads to the shift of attention from the form and spatial arrangement of the artefacts to the description of action patterns with emphasis on the contribution of the respective architectural agents within these social situations.

Each level of the architectural analysis involves action-artefact complexes, never the mere artefacts. Obviously, this conception of architectural design discourse is rather ambitious. A kind of scenario thinking, on the level of anecdote, has long since been woven into the design considerations of sensitive architects. The point here is to raise the stakes by radicalizing this aspect towards a vigorous demarcation of architecture. Lack of concern for architecture's communicative engagement either by focusing on simple physical functions like shelter, durable construction etc or by focusing solely on the form of the artefact, spells the ejection from the discourse of architecture. These escapes from the central concern of architecture lead to the domain of engineering in the first case and to the domain of art in the second case. The threshold of the presupposed intelligence and sophistication with respect to the participation within the discourse of architecture is significantly raised by this move towards the explicit emphasis upon communicative interaction patterns. An ability to talk about and model such patterns (in relation to architectural form) becomes an entrance threshold for competent participation within the autopoiesis of architecture.

This upgraded design speculation is only possible on the back of an upgraded medium of design. Current animation software affords the tools to elaborate 4D scenarios involving the modelling of agent-systems and character animation to speculate about use-patterns in varying settings. The completed design would then no longer rest with a full set of drawings plus photorealistic renderings. A new layer of representation would have to be added: a series of animated scenarios that demonstrate the anticipated action-artefact networks that have been guiding the design process. This move from mere spatial figures to space-time figures would accompany the design process all the way from the initial animated diagrams to the final life-like simulations in the form of movie-clips.[42]

The conventional mode of design speculates only about spatial form as a response to fixed, presupposed use-patterns. This limits innovation to formal variations. In this way a dining chair remains forever a dining chair (gathering participants facing each other around a dining table), in all sorts of formal variations that leave intact the basic social diagram and the expectations it encodes. The institution of the dinner is always fixed and presupposed and remains outside the domain of architectural speculation. The same goes for higher levels of system-integration: domestic life at home, corporate life at the office, educational life on the university campus. Radical innovation only broke ground in the late

42 At the AADRL, the Design Research Laboratory at the Architectural Association School of Architecture, this type of elaborate scenario modelling was a key component of each thesis design during a three-year research agenda 'Responsive Environments' in 2001–4.

1960s, pushed on by the social revolutions of the time. While modern furniture design was typologically rigid all the way to the mid 1960s, radical mutations and an expansion of the given furniture typology have been achieved since the late 1960s. Superstudio's 'Superwave' might act as example here. Similar mutations happened in other institutions and their respective building types. For instance, schools, universities, museums and many workplaces changed both their patterns of communication and their spatial physiognomy. The example of the radical transformations that were achieved in the late 1960s indicates that architectural innovations require a conducive societal environment. In fact the societal environment pushes without knowing where it wants to go architecturally. This question can only be answered within the autopoiesis of architecture. The underlying premise of this chapter is thus that societal mutations are currently under way in various domains of social life that create an environment conducive to the promoted concept of action-artefact networks. Functional reasoning in terms of action-artefact networks increases architecture's capacity to analyze, dissolve, vary and reconstitute its elements in relation to a more versatile and nuanced understanding of its substantial functions. It is in the context of modelling and discussing action-artefact networks that the concept of capacity will flourish.

The attempt to transcend functional reasoning in stereotype solutions and to leave the familar solutions behind dramatically increases the inherent risk that is bound up with all design activity projecting into an unknown future. Communication on this enhanced level of uncertainty would be highly improbable and indeed impossible without a dramatic increase in the power of architecture's medium. The key is the incorporation of credible ways of representing the occupation and interaction scenarios that are to guide and test the formal manipulations during the design process. On the organizational level of general layouts and plan configurations, user groups and their patterns of occupation can be simulated via agent modelling. The computational representation of human actors as rule-governed automatons does not contradict the emphasis on communication. Patterns of pedestrian movement, crowd behaviour, queues etc are communication scenarios. Pacing down the pavement is as much a communicative action ('out of my way!') as is the relaxed, hand-in-hand strolling (window shopping).

Patterns of observed crowd behaviour can be simulated via scripted agents. For instance, the spontaneous ordering of pedestrian flows into a right and left stream moving in opposite directions within a busy corridor or underground passage can be recreated with agents. The introduction of a narrow point (door-frame) within such a computational model spontaneously produces a new pattern of ordering the flows. In this case, time rather than space is used and the flow breaks into an oscillating pattern where one direction flows for a while until pressure builds up at the other side and the flow direction is reversed. A junction of four inflowing lines of movement spontaneously produces a circular flow pattern. Such patterns can be reproduced with very simple agent profiles. The probable impact of manipulating spatial forms can be observed in real time. However, the possibility of modelling occupational patterns with agents is not restricted to such basic phenomena. Lingering in the foyer, stopping at a notice board, sitting down on the staircase outside the entrance etc are communicative actions that can still be simulated with a high degree of veracity by automatons. More sophisticated agents can be programmed. For example, in the context of a corporate space-planning project, University College London's Space Syntax Lab conducted a study of space occupation and communication patterns via camera recordings of patterns of movement, resting, gathering etc within the existing spaces of the corporation. An extensive analysis tried to abstract the rules that governed these observed patterns in their dependence on the architectural environment. Where were the attractors that made short gatherings more likely? What are the properties of settings that correlate with longer gatherings? How many agents were likely to gather where and for how long? How about the differential speed of moving relative to the spatial conditions? These were the kinds of questions that were asked and answered. The rules that answered these questions were embodied in the agent definitions. The success of this exercise could be demonstrated by the verisimilitude of the reproduction of the observed patterns. On this basis the spatial configuration of the environment (independent variable) could be manipulated and tested with respect to its effect in terms of probable communication patterns (dependent variable).

The next step in the design, beyond the abstract plan configuration, can still be supported by a further expansion of architecture's design medium. A fully modelled 3D scene might be turned into a 4D animated scene including character animation and scenario development in the form of small movies depicting patterns of communication within the designed environments. The intuitive plausibility of such animations would be the guiding evaluation criterion here. The important fact is that the designer has a medium within which slowly to work on and elaborate both forms and their probable functions together, with a nearly infinite level of detail resolution in both respects. A thus enhanced medium can – to a certain extent – overcome the inherent improbability of successful communications about strange environments and their claim to be innovative facilitators of desired communication patterns. The exact content of the hosted communications can obviously not be steered in this way. However, the density and distribution of encounters and the general social or atmospheric character of the various gatherings and interactions can be influenced. On the basis of these discursive and medial enhancements of working in terms of action-artefact networks, the risk of venturing into unfamilar territory can be contained and managed. A narrative scenario with animated visualizations might convince not only the designers themselves but also their clients and user groups that unfamiliar spaces could sustain and encourage desired interaction patterns that are more productive (albeit equally plausible) than what is to be expected within current form-function stereotypes.

6.1.8 LIMITATIONS OF FUNCTIONAL EXPERTISE

The architectural discourse on (substantial) function constitutes architecture's world-reference. The upgrading of the discipline's environmental adaptivity involves the upgrading of its analytic-predictive resources. This raises the question: how far must the discipline of architecture penetrate the various societal domains in order to fulfil the promise of an upgraded action-artefact reasoning?

At this stage in the argument the question of the demarcation and autonomy of the discipline of architecture is once more posed. Obviously, architectural design cannot dissolve into the education system and incorporate the theory of pedagogy when it comes to the design of a school. In the case of workplace design, architecture does not dissolve into corporate management or management consulting, even if it has to engage in a close collaboration with these domains.

There seems to be an occasion for an interdisciplinary project (and discourse) here that equally engages architects and management consultants in a single concerted effort. We can observe the beginnings of a new type of service for corporations whereby corporate space-planning and interior design are integrated and offered in conjunction with management consultancy and organization design. One of the world's leading corporate space-planning firms – London-based DEGW – was bought and integrated within management consultancy firm Twynstra Gudde. DEGW has been developing space-planning expertise for corporations that goes far beyond the usual architectural service of arranging spaces according to a given schedule of accommodation. Instead DEGW is offering to develop the client's brief on the basis of a detailed analysis of how the client's current pattern of space occupation correlates with its current profile of activities. Social science research tools like interviews and questionnaires are deployed to relate the ongoing communication patterns to both organizational and spatial relations. The Space Syntax Lab[43] is a direct competitor of DEGW that works in much the same way, but in addition deploys agent-based simulations of space occupancy in terms of circulation and informal communication patterns. The initial empirical research involves the placement of inconspicuous cameras in lobbies and corridors of the client's current premises. The recordings are then analyzed in terms of movement patterns with particular attention to the way people might initiate short communications upon the occasion of random encounters. Attention is paid to the relationship between spatial conditions and the probability and duration of the communicative encounters. The results of this analysis are then used to programme a population of agents in such a way that they spontaneously approximate the observed patterns at the respective locations within the model of the corporate space. On the basis of the successful replication of the observed patterns, the agent's behaviour within a modified spatial configuration can be regarded as a simulation of the communication patterns that might be expected within the newly configured space. The simulation is effectively a parametric model of an action-artefact network and can be operated as a predictive design tool.

These examples do *not* imply that all ambitious architects must now aspire to become social scientist and agent programmers. Such an integration of expert knowledge and specialized skills is highly unlikely to become generalized. What is more likely is that the professional design team – led by the architect – is augmented by new specialized contributors. This in turn also implies the expansion of the architect's typical horizon of expertise and knowledge together with the overall retooling of the discourse of the discipline that is required to adequately address the new societal challenges and technological opportunities. New forms of knowledge need to be integrated into the discourse and new techniques need to be integrated into the design process – together leading to an invigorated architectural autopoiesis. This indirect utilization of scientific expert knowledge and specialized skills is based upon a partial assimilation of key concepts that inspire the adaptation of architecture's own communicative structures. A full integration of social science into architecture is unrealistic.

43 The Space Syntax Lab is a research lab at UCL (University College London) that also operates as a professional consultancy.

The case is comparable to the challenge placed upon architecture by the general ascendance of ecological concerns and demands for sustainability. Here too we witness both the enlisting of new experts into the architecture-led design team and the partial assimilation of key concepts and general principles into the discursive constitution and system of values of the discipline. Architects start to talk about ecological principles and integrate such talk into the formation of their design concepts, but they are not becoming sustainability experts, nor do, by this token, scientific principles dominate the design process and its attendant communications. Architects call upon external experts to upgrade their game but keep their own design prerogatives under the spell of utility, beauty and originality.

The cases of DEGW and the Space Syntax Lab are also instructive on this question of the maintenance of the disciplinary boundaries. Although the background of the partners and key staff, in both cases, is architecture, we can observe two developmental paths that seem open here to architectural firms. DEGW – although temporarily acquired by a management consultancy group – stayed within the domain of architecture. They soon separated from Twynstra Gudde and continued as architects (space planners and interior designers), albeit with a special client base and with an especially innovative, augmented design intelligence and process. How influential their innovations prove to be within the larger field has yet to be seen. The Space Syntax Lab started out from an architectural academic base about 20 years ago, setting out to augment the architectural and urban discourse with new concepts, methods and techniques, especially focusing on rigorous configurational analysis. Both as an academic research project and as a professional practice, the success of the Space Syntax Lab has been very impressive. However, its theoretical and practical achievements have not penetrated the heart of the discipline. Their concepts, techniques and specific mode of reasoning have not made an impact within the wider architectural discourse. Their call for scientific rigour in the design discourse and for a design process informed by scientifically rigorous analysis has not been heeded. Instead of impacting the core of the discipline through its discourse, the Space Syntax Lab has been successfully operating like a specialist consultancy service advising and supporting architects, albeit – despite its success – without yet finding any followers. Only on the basis of an expanding utilization as specialist consultancy, so it seems, can the insights of space syntax research be expected to exert a certain influence and indirectly augment the discourse of architecture and urbanism. Although it might be hoped for, a full-blown inclusion of space syntax thinking into general architectural thinking should perhaps not be expected. Despite these caveats, below the attempt is made to assimilate key insights of space syntax theory within a broader theory of architectural order.

Space syntax operates as an engineering discipline or applied science. Its discourse is regulated by the code of truth and by the code of utility but does not concern itself with either beauty or design originality. The theory of architectural autopoiesis can thus explain the failure of space syntax to impact architectural discourse, despite its otherwise compelling theoretical and practical achievements. The discursive structure of architecture is too different to incorporate segments of science-based engineering wholesale. Architecture can be perturbed and stirred by science/engineering, but how, and to what extent, scientific knowledge is filtered and absorbed into architecture, and perhaps transmuted and codified into design principles or routine processes, is a matter of its own evolving autopoiesis. Scientists will never rule architecture and design.

This obstinacy of architecture should not in itself be a cause for concern. In fact, the author is rather optimistic that many of the preoccupations, concepts and insights of space syntax research will filter into the avant-garde discourse and finally into the generalized design intelligence of architecture – albeit in a mutated form that allows these insights to be fitted into the distinct communication structures of architecture. Hillier's *Space is the Machine*[44] is not only promoted here; it is widely read within architectural academia. Key terms like configuration and integration and a general sense that what Hillier calls configurational properties matter for functionality and orientation with respect to complex buildings or urban fields are spreading. However, the detailed, analytical science that can concretely operationalize these insights will always require a specialist expert service.

6.2 Order via Organization and Articulation

THESIS 26

Architectural order is symbiotic with social order and its effective realization requires organization and articulation as crucial registers of the design effort.

The distinction of form and function poses the question of their effective correlation. The question is how functional requirements can be addressed by architectural forms. This is the ultimate question of architectural theory and the most general formulation of the task posed to

44 Bill Hillier, *Space is the Machine*.

architecture. The autopoiesis of architecture, ie, architecture as a discipline and discourse, is dedicated to innovating the resources and processes that can be brought to bear on this task.

The theory of architectural autopoiesis analyzes the task of giving form to functions via a crucial distinction: the distinction between ***organization*** and ***articulation***. Organization and articulation are the two irreducible, constituent components of architecture's task. Organization is concerned with the physical distancing, separation and connection of domains and is thus *framing*[45] communication physically, by physically channelling movement and interaction. Articulation is concerned with orientation and is *framing* communication cognitively. Articulation is guiding movement and interaction via atmospheres, and perceptual as well as semiotic clues. Organization recognizes and operates via social communication's dependence on human beings as mobile bodies in space, while articulation recognizes and operates via social communication's dependence on human beings as perceiving/comprehending systems.

Organization and articulation are worked out in architecture's design medium of the drawing/model. The built results – the organized and articulated buildings and spaces – operate in the medium of *space*. All framing communications are spatial communications. In Volume 1, architecture's design medium was theorized as symbolically generalized medium of communication that is able to make otherwise improbable communications probable. The medium was compared to *money* as the medium of the economic system and to *power* as the medium of the political system. The theory of architectural autopoiesis now poses *space* as the medium of architecture.[46] The idea of a symbolically generalized medium for architectural communications might thus be applied once more, namely to the completed buildings and spaces that are architecture's final communications. We thus need to distinguish between architecture's *design medium* – the medium of the drawing/model – and architecture's *success medium*, ie, space as the medium within which architecture delivers its service to society: the buildings and spaces that are architecture's final communications that function as spatial frames and premises for all further communicative

45 The concept of framing is central within the theory of architectural autopoiesis. It pinpoints architecture's unique societal function. See Volume 1, chapter 5.1.5 *Framing Double Contingency*.

46 The switch from edifice to space and the further switch from space to field should not be seen to contradict this statement. The theoretical concept of space as medium proposed here should be distinguished from the concept of space as historically specific regulating idea used by Modernist architects to characterize the scope of their work.

interactions. Space has thus been appropriated to be the success medium of the autopoietic function system of architecture.[47]

To give form to functions in architecture translates into the task of (spatially) organizing and (morphologically) articulating the substantial functions that represent the demands of the social life-process within architecture. Although at first sight it may seem as if organization is concerned with function, judged according to its utility, and as if articulation is concerned with form, judged according to its beauty, the theory of architectural autopoiesis resists this latent alignment, and insists instead that the distinction organization vs articulation cuts orthogonally across architecture's lead-distinction of form vs function. Both the organization and the articulation of a space/building involve both form and function, and thus call forth both sides of the double code of beauty and utility. During the design process or when judging completed buildings, the parti or organization of a scheme might not just be judged in terms of its utility – functional or dysfunctional – it might also be judged to be either formally resolved (beautiful) or formally unresolved (ugly). The same goes for the aspect of articulation. Here it seems as if formal judgement is more pertinent: the atmosphere pleases or displeases. However, articulation can, is, and should be judged according to utility as well. A certain scheme of articulation might ease orientation and wayfinding or not. It might define the various required/expected atmospheres and moods of the destination spaces appropriately or inappropriately, and thus either serve to enhance the ease of communicative interaction, or irritate, confuse and distract.

Organization involves the functional allocation of spaces, ie, the distinction, designation and spatial distribution of uses. Articulation is concerned with making the distinction and designation of uses, as well as their spatial relations, conspicuous and legible. To illustrate this conceptual pair one might point to the architectural order of the typical Renaissance Palazzo as inaugurated by Alberti's Palazzo Rucellai completed in 1451 in Florence, and perhaps more vigorously expressed in Michelozzo di Bartolomeo's Palazzo Medici-Riccardi completed in 1459. The organizational and articulatory schema of the Renaissance Palazzo became a ubiquitous trope of architecture for the following

47 However, the space referred to here is not the space that results as a haphazard, uncontrolled side product of human intervention, but only the carefully designed, organized and articulated space. As we shall see below, this architectural, framing space is always a phenomenologically and semiologically charged space. Only selected aspects of what we might otherwise include in the general idea of space become available as medium of a framing communication. These aspects are mostly limited to those that can be controlled via architecture's design medium. Design medium and success medium must thus be closely related.

450 years. A stratified, tripartite organization of uses is articulated by the different architectural treatment of each of the three levels.[48] On the ground floor are allocated the storage, production and business quarters, expressed as a solid, rusticated base with small windows. The second level – the 'piano nobile' – is allocated to public receptions. Here the walls are usually smoother and the windows much larger. The third floor contains the private living quarters and bedrooms of the noble family. Here the height might be somewhat reduced and the windows are once more smaller and the wall is smoother still. The servants' bedrooms on top are made virtually invisible by the large cornice that terminates the facade. While the differentiation of the three strata is overall more conspicuous in the Palazzo Medici-Riccardi, Alberti's Palazzo Rucellai offers a further, more subtle, semiological rather than phenomenological differentiation: the differentiation by means of pilasters expressing the three Classical column orders.

The typical schema of the Renaissance Palazzo illustrates the dialectic of organization and articulation. It shows how the functional designation motivates certain morphological adaptations, for example, in terms of differential heights, wall thicknesses and window sizes, that follow both functional requirements of use as well as a structural rationality. The spatial distribution of the designated uses follows the logic of the social life and communication process. The example also makes clear that architecture involves the expressive heightening of the functional distinctions and the attempt to characterize them via tectonic or ornamental features.[49] The rustication of the base expresses its protective solidity. The Doric order, as the expressly sturdiest order, further symbolizes this aspect. Neither rustication nor pilasters serve any necessary physical function. They are clearly articulatory devices that communicate. The progression of successive smoothening and ornamental refinement is expressive of a definite, deliberate order. It communicates order. The same is true for the Classical sequence Doric, Ionic, Corinthian. A definite order is applied resulting in an overall architectural order that is understood to be meaningful.

48 Other typical examples are: Palazzo Pitti by Brunelleschi, Florence 1464; Palazzo Strozzi by Benedetto da Maiano, Florence 1489; Palazzo Vidoni-Caffarelli by Raffaello Sanzio, Rome 1515; Palazzo Farnese by Antonio da Sangallo il Giovane and Michelangelo Buonarroti, Rome 1536. The same tripartite organization/articulation is also evident, in an even more expressive fashion, in Michelangelo's Palazzo Senatorio in Rome, designed in 1536 as part of the Piazza del Campidoglio, as well as in Palladio's Villa Foscari designed in 1549.

49 These ornamental features are usually of tectonic origin, ie, they originate in features that are due to technical function and material fabrication.

The two key concepts that act here to define the task of architecture – organization and articulation – are well established within current architectural discourse. However, these concepts are here promoted to a new level of significance: as a conceptual pair they are designated to encompass the totality of architecture's task. These concepts, and the agendas they sponsor, are elaborated here to an extent that goes beyond a mere analysis of current practice and discourse. The attempt is made to contribute to the *retooling* of the discipline by giving indications about how the organizational and articulatory capacity of contemporary architecture can be enhanced. This enhancement proceeds along the two primary dimensions of architecture's task: the dimension of organization and the dimension of articulation. As will be elaborated below, the dimension of articulation includes two distinct sub-tasks: phenomenological articulation and semiological articulation. Thus we can distinguish three agendas – the ***organizational***, the ***phenomenological*** and the ***semiological*** agenda – for the retooling of architecture's expertise. Each of these agendas is given a separate treatment. The semiological dimension receives the most extensive treatment here, not only because it is currently the least developed and the least prominent of the three dimensions, but also because the theory of architectural autopoiesis argues that it is this dimension which should represent the core competency of the discipline. The theory speculates that it is in this dimension that contemporary avant-garde architecture can and must demonstrate its superiority. However, all three dimensions are indispensable aspects of architecture's task. Accordingly, each ambitious contemporary avant-garde design project should contain and synthesize an organizational, a phenomenological and a semiological project. The three dimensions together procure what we call here architectural order. Thus we can summarize the conceptual set up of this section as follows:

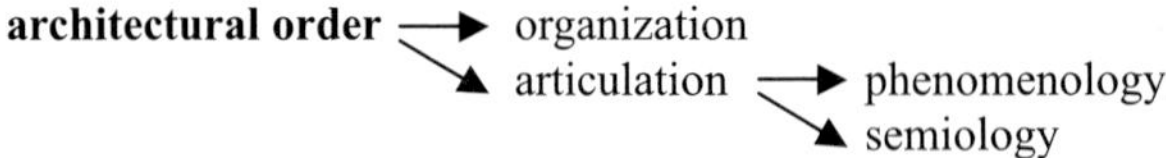

This diagram relates the key terms of this section. At the same time it gives a summary map of what the theory of architectural autopoiesis suspects are the most promising avenues for architecture's theory-led self-enhancement. First ventures in this direction are offered in what follows. However, only when these dimensions are placed on architecture's collective design research agenda, and only when these aspects begin to be mastered, should we be satisfied that the autopoiesis of architecture is on the way to fulfil its societal function on the new level of sophistication that would be conducive to the advances made in the other great function systems of contemporary world society.

6.2.1 ORGANIZATION AND ARTICULATION: HISTORICAL AND SYSTEMATIC

Architecture facilitates interaction by providing spatio-morphological frames that firstly structure patterns of encounter, and secondly help to define the encounters to be expected. The first aspect – the aspect of organization – operates primarily via spatial separation and connection. The second aspect – the aspect of articulation – operates primarily via the priming of the participant's perceptions, inducing pertinent expectations, and thus preparing the appropriate mood and readiness to interact.

Both key concepts – the concept of organization and the concept of articulation – have noteworthy precursors in the history of architectural theory. To recognize this is important. The distinction of organization vs articulation – denoting two fundamental dimensions of architecture's task – is a permanent communication structure of architecture. As such it must have had a conceptual registration within the history of architectural theory. This is indeed the case.

The first precursor of the concept of organization was Alberti's concept of ***partitio*** (compartition). Compartition is one of six topics that together structure the whole subject matter of architectural design. The six topics are sequenced in accordance with the design process: locality, area, compartition, wall, roof, openings. The compartition of the building, essentially the internal division into rooms, is determined by means of the floorplan, after the site and the footprint of the building have been determined, and before the walls, roof and openings are raised in elevation over the plan. Alberti defines: 'Compartition (*partitio*) is the process of dividing up the site (footprint of the building) into yet smaller units, so that the building may be considered as being made up of close-fitting smaller buildings, joined together like members of the whole body.'[50] This analogy of the organization of the building with the organization of the body, and with organisms and organic systems in general, has been inspiring architecture from its beginning (with Alberti) all the way to the most current agenda of avant-garde architecture (Parametricism). The importance of compartition is duly emphasized by Alberti: 'All the power of invention, all the skill and experience of the art of building are called upon in compartition; compartition alone divides up

50 Alberti, *On the Art of Building in Ten Books*, trans Rykwert, Leach & Tavernor, p 8.

the whole building into the parts by which it is articulated, and integrates its every part by composing all the lines and angles into a single, harmonious work that respects utility, dignity, and delight. . . . Just as with animals, members relate to members, so too in buildings part ought to relate to part. . . . Each member should therefore be in the correct zone and position.'[51] It is important to note here that according to Alberti, organization – and not just decoration – is subject to both codes, the code of utility and the code of beauty (dignity and delight). This relationship between compartition and beauty is further emphasized: 'If the compartition satisfies these conditions completely, the cheerfulness and elegance of the ornament will find the appropriate place and will shine out; but if not, the work will undoubtedly fail to retain any dignity. The entire composition of the members, therefore, must be so well considered, conform so perfectly with the requirements of necessity and convenience, that this or that part should not give as much pleasure separately as their appropriate placing, here or there, in a particular order, situation, conjunction, arrangement, and configuration.'[52] This final proliferation of terms – order, situation, conjunction, arrangement, configuration – does indeed testify to the importance of the thus denoted concern: the concern of organization.

Although much of subsequent architectural theory focused on the Classical orders and their proportions, the much more fundamental notion of organization continued to be registered under various titles, most notably under the title of ***distribution***. Distribution was considered within an overall tripartite division of architecture's teachings: distribution, construction and decoration. This tripartite division of architectural knowledge was established in French architectural theory by Augustin-Charles d'Aviler in his *Cours d'architecture* (1691). This work was a standard reference during the whole of the 18th century. The triad of distribution, construction and decoration is also found in Jacques-François Blondel's celebrated *Cours d'architecture* (1771–7). Karl Friedrich Schinkel (1802) refers to this tripartite division in his (unfinished) architectural treatise. According to Schinkel 'the purposefulness of any building can be considered from three principal perspectives: purposefulness of spatial distribution (Raumverteilung) or of the plan, purposefulness of construction or the joining of materials appropriate to the plan, purposefulness of ornament or decoration.'[53]

51 Ibid, p 23.

52 Ibid, p 163.

53 Karl Friedrich Schinkel, *Das Architektonische Lehrbuch*, Deutscher Kunstverlag (Munich/Berlin), 2001, p 22, the text from 1805 remained an unpublished fragment during Schinkel's time.

Schinkel goes on to elaborate as follows: 'The purposefulness of spatial distribution or of the plan contains the following three principal attributes: greatest economy of space, greatest order in the distribution, greatest comfort in the space.'[54] Sir John Soane's second series of six Royal Academy Lectures in 1815 was also structured by this tripartite division: 'The great points or objects now to be considered might be classed and separately treated of, under the heads of Distribution, Construction, and Decoration.'[55] Soane defines distribution as follows: 'Distribution comprehends the divisions and arrangements of the various parts of buildings of every kind as to solidity, convenience, elegance and beauty. Distribution must therefore be viewed as one of those essential and important objects of architectural study that must claim the most serious consideration of the architect, and require the fullest exertion of his talents and genius.'[56] The emphasis on the importance of distribution is reminiscent of Alberti's emphasis of the importance of *partitio*. The core of the definition – *division* and *arrangement* – also matches Alberti's core definition that compartition *divides* and *integrates*.

We should also note that in the quote above, Soane – again in line with Alberti's theory – assumes that distribution is contributing to *both* the functionality (convenience, solidity) *and* the beauty (elegance) of the building. However, Soane remains ambiguous in this respect. Later in the same lecture he maps the tripartite division of the discipline into distribution, construction and decoration onto the Vitruvian triad of solidity, convenience and beauty: 'In buildings of every description... three things are indispensably necessary, viz., solidity in construction, convenience in distribution, and beauty in its characteristic decoration.'[57]

Although this alignment seems to be compelling, the theory of architectural autopoiesis proposes a different arrangement of concepts. First of all we recognize that the concern of construction and solidity has drifted out of the central domain of architecture into the domain of engineering. (This also suits our preference for conceptual pairs over conceptual triads.) We are thus left with two conceptual pairs or distinctions: *organization vs articulation* on the one hand, and *utility vs beauty* on the other hand, respectively indicating the ***task*** of architecture and the ***code*** of architecture. The conceptual scheme proposed here sets these two distinctions orthogonal rather than parallel to each other. Both

54 Ibid.
55 John Soane, *The Royal Academy Lectures*, Cambridge University Press (Cambridge), 2000, p 157.
56 Ibid, p 158.
57 Ibid, p 165.

tasks have to respond to both codes. Organization has to answer both the demand of functionality and the demand of formal resolution, and articulation equally has to answer both the demand of functionality and the demand of formal resolution. If we define architectural order as the result of the conjoined effort of organization and articulation, we can summarize the essential concern of architecture as the elaboration of a functional and formally resolved architectural order.

		task	
		organization	**articulation**
code	**utility**	functional organization vs dysfunctional organization	functional articulation vs dysfunctional articulation
	beauty	formally resolved organization vs formally unresolved organization	formally resolved articulation vs formally unresolved articulation

The formal judgement of organizational patterns seems odd at first sight. Also, the utility/function of articulation has not always been recognized. The rationality and advantages of this arrangement will transpire in the following chapters where this conceptual schema is going to be further explicated and put to work. At the current juncture of the argument it suffices to point out that the proposed arrangement can make claims to count as a reconstruction and clarification of the theoretical heritage rather than an arbitrary conceptual invention or imposition. As documented above, the aesthetic import of organization has been stated by both Alberti and Soane, among others. This point will be further reinforced if we recognize that much of what we encompass under the heading of organization has traditionally been treated under the heading of *composition*. Thus we can note that the traditional notions of compartition, distribution and composition are now to be absorbed within the concept of organization, although the traditional treatment of composition also covers aspects of what we now encompass under the concept of articulation.

Aspects of what we today understand (and shall further elaborate here) under the heading of articulation had been alluded to within the history of architectural theory under the titles of *character* and *expression*. The notion of character has indeed been related to the building's function, as its expression, and as such it fulfils a function, ie, the function of communicating the purpose of the building. The ideas of 'character' and 'expression', taken from the theatre, were together first introduced into architectural theory by Germain Boffrand, a student of Mansart, and an important French architect of the early 18th century. He introduced the discussion of character in his *Livre d'architecture* of 1745: 'Architecture ... its component parts are so to speak brought to life by the different characters that it conveys to us. Through its composition a building expresses, as if in the theatre, that the scene is pastoral or tragic; that this is a temple or a palace, a public building destined for a particular purpose or a private house. By their planning, their structure and their decoration, all such buildings must proclaim their purpose to the beholder. If they fail to do so, they offend against expression and are not what they ought to be.'[58] It is noteworthy here that all three terms of the Classical tripartite division – planning (distribution), structure (construction), decoration – are together involved in expressing the character of the building. The positive function of character expression is to proclaim the purpose of the building to the beholder. The notions of expression and character imply a particular way in which this proclamation is effected: 'If you are setting out to build a music room, or a salon in which to receive company, it must be cheerful in its planning, in its lighting, and in its manner of decoration. If you want a mausoleum, the building must be suited to its use, and the architecture and decoration must be serious and sad; for Nature makes us susceptible to all these impressions, and a unified impulse never fails to touch our feelings.'[59] The unified impulse that touches our feelings might best be translated into our contemporary language in terms of the *atmosphere* of a space we might be immersed within. Jacques-François Blondel referred to 'imperceptible nuances' in connection with the concepts of character and expression: 'It is by the assistance of these imperceptible nuances that we are able to make a real distinction in the design of two buildings of the same genre but which nevertheless should announce themselves differently: preferring in one a style sublime, noble and elevated; in the other a character naïve, simple and true. Distinct particular expressions ... that need to be felt ... contribute more than one ordinarily imagines in assigning to each building the character that is proper to it.'[60] This type of architectural effectiveness, via atmospheric values that

58 Germain Boffrand, *Book of Architecture Containing the General Principles of the Art*, Ashgate Publishing (Aldershot), 2003, pp 21–2, French original *Livre d'architecture*, 1745, excerpt in: Harry Francis Mallgrave (Ed), *Architectural Theory*, Blackwell Publishing (Oxford), 2006, p 193.

59 Ibid.

60 Jacques-François Blondel, *Course of Architecture*, 1771, excerpt in: Harry Francis Mallgrave (Ed), *Architectural Theory*, p 198. Blondel goes on to utilize the distinction of male versus female as an analogical character distinction applicable to buildings. The male character

are taken in semi-consciously, is to be considered when we theorize the task of articulation. Articulation operates largely via the modulation of morphological features that are perceived in passing, in a mode of *distraction*,[61] rather than focused attention. The information processing, which is relevant for the quick, intuitive orientation of users and for their behavioural priming appropriate for the respective social setting, is largely unconscious. This intuitive, even 'feeling'-based processing of articulated spaces must find recognition within a design research programme of articulation that suggests the calculated build up of phenomenological and semiotic effects.

6.2.2 ARCHITECTURAL ORDER

How can functional requirements be effectively addressed by architectural forms? To narrow the scope of this very general question it is pertinent to concentrate on the most fundamental, primary part of the question, ie, the question of how a given ***social order*** can be facilitated by a corresponding ***architectural order***. The term *social order* should denote the overall system of *substantial*[62] functional requirements posed by the specific social institution or life-process to be accommodated. We are speaking of a social or institutional *order* to the extent to which we assume that the communications and interactions that constitute the social practice or institution in question are subject to non-arbitrary relationships and interdependencies.

We might assume that an important architectural pendant of this notion of social order is the ***parti*** of the project. The parti addresses functional requirements on the level of global *organization*. At this level – mostly in the initial stages of the design process – we are more concerned with the basic distinctions and organizing principles employed. The overall organizational diagram serves as premise for further design decisions.[63]

entails massiveness, firmness, grandeur, should be sparse in the detail of its ornament, show simplicity in the general composition and feature projecting bodies that throw large shadows.

61 Walter Benjamin, *The Work of Art in the Age of Mechanical Reproduction*, in: Walter Benjamin, *Illuminations: Essays and Reflections*, Schocken Books (New York), 1968.

62 See section 6.1 *Functions*, in particular chapter 6.1.2 *Substantial vs Subsidiary Functions*.

63 For instance, in the case of designing a residence, the parti is concerned with the location of the private quarters in relation to the public reception spaces, rather than being concerned about the natural light in the corridor or addressing the pros and cons of different kitchen layouts. A specific architectural order is always about the facilitation and manifestation of a particular life-process implying a particular social order with its respective substantial functions that need to be addressed. For instance, the pertinence of a sharp separation of the private domain from the reception areas in a family where the different family members maintain quite separate social circles might suggest a bipolar parti with both front and back garden rather

With respect to architectural organization, the globally defined parti is only one possible starting point. It is equally possible to proceed in a bottom-up process of agglomerating local micro organizations, for example, via local rules in the fashion of cellular automata, or via agent-based models. The resultant *emergent* global pattern is no less organized than an organization that is elaborated in a top-down process starting with the overall parti. The main difference is that the parti starts with a global concept while the organization emerging from a bottom-up generative process starts with constitutive local relationships and ends up with an emergent organization that requires an additional effort to be described with respect to its global outcome. However, neither globally imposed parti, nor emergent global patterns, are automatically recognized as ***architectural order***. The theory of architectural autopoiesis reserves the concept of order for organizations that become apparent – visible and legible – via the effort of articulation.

The ***concept of order*** proposed here thus denotes the result of the combined effort of organization and articulation. Architectural order – symbiotic with social order – requires *both* spatial organization *and* spatio-morphological articulation. Spatial organization and morphological articulation together produce architectural order. With respect to the question of how to design an architectural order we might thus pose two related sub-questions:

1. How can a workable organization (parti or emergent pattern) be found and ascertained?
2. How can this organization (parti or emergent pattern) be made intelligible and effectively brought to life with respect to the perceiving/conceiving/navigating social actors?

The first task is ***the task of organization***. The second, dependent task is ***the task of articulation***. These two tasks deserve to be distinguished. Each demands its own distinct design effort.

The reference to intelligibility/navigability is necessary to tie the concept of order to performance. This, however, complicates matters. It transforms the concept of order from a category that merely describes and compares an objective property of an architectural

than the unified diagram of the courtyard villa. Subsidiary concerns like the handling of natural light within the house or the kitchen typology should in the final analysis also be guided by their contribution to the architectural order that facilitates and manifests the social order, ie, the order of the life-process that is supposed to unfold within the house. Order understood as the integration of all substantial functions is thus the alpha and omega of the design effort. Obviously this abstract statement gives no hint as to how such effective order can be achieved or ascertained.

artefact/configuration to a category that describes and compares a relation that holds between an architectural artefact and a (socialized) user/audience that perceives and (hopefully) comprehends this artefact/configuration. The concept of order proposed thus has an objective as well as subjective aspect. The objective aspect is the (degree of) ***organization*** within a configuration. The subjective aspect is the (degree of) ***articulation*** within an organized configuration, ie, the extent to which the organization is retrievable by a navigating/perceiving subject.

Organization is based upon the constitution and distribution of positions for elements and their pattern of linkages. Articulation is based upon the constitution and the distribution of *morphological identities, similitudes and differences* across the elements to be organized. Organization is instituted via the physical means of distancing, barring, as well as connecting via vistas and/or circulatory channelling. These mechanisms can operate independently of all nuanced perception and comprehension, and can thus in principle succeed without the efforts of articulation. However, the restriction to a mere organization without articulation, and thus without facilitating the participants' active navigation, would severely constrain the level of complexity that would be possible in the social communication thus framed. Articulation, the distinction and distribution of morphological characteristics, presupposes cognition. It enlists the participant's perception and comprehension and thus facilitates the participant's active orientation. The two registers relate as follows. Articulation builds upon and reveals organization. Articulation makes the organization of functions apparent. In doing so it elevates organization into order. Articulation might also, to a certain extent, compensate for organizational patterns that deviate from the intended relations. For instance, if a given physical configuration separates what belongs together or pushes together what should be separated (for example, because of tight packing constraints), articulation can counteract these shortcomings by morphologically assimilating what is spatially distant and by morphologically distinguishing what is spatially continuous.

The concept of organization is updating and systematizing the concerns traditionally addressed in the concepts of compartition, distribution and composition. The concept of articulation is updating and systematizing the concerns traditionally addressed in the concepts of decoration (ornamentation), character and expression. The notions of character and expression hinted at the *goal* of articulation, and the notion of ornament was seen as the primary *means* of articulation. Contemporary architecture operates with a vastly expanded formal repertoire if compared with Classical architecture – with respect to both its organizational and articulatory registers. Morphological articulation is a much more fundamental register than traditional ornamentation – it encompasses the global shape, tectonic constitution and surface treatment of the architectural elements in question.

The crucial conceptual difference between those traditional notions and the contemporary concepts of organization and articulation is that the latter are ultimately seen as instrumental with respect to the social life-process and its functional requirements, while composition and ornamentation were often considered to be serving beauty as a value in its own right.

However, the ultimate functional instrumentalization of organization and articulation does not imply that the theoretical elaboration of those concepts must be directly tied to the discussion of functional concerns. Just like composition and ornamentation were discussed and taught in their own right, the theory of organization and the theory of articulation must be able to develop their respective concepts, criteria and repertoires with a degree of abstract generality and versatility that prevents instant performative evaluation, even if its effective instrumentalization remains its destiny. Instead of operating with fixed form-function unities like (Gothic) 'church', (Renaissance) 'villa', (Baroque) 'palace' etc, contemporary architecture must develop three initially independent conceptual registers, each with a rich apparatus of distinctions. There must be an organizational register, an articulatory register and a functional-programmatic register.[64] These registers must first be unfolded independently. Only on this basis can the architect inquire into how these three registers might best be brought together to establish viable designs. On the basis of a rich, threefold repertoire, and threefold intelligence, the architect can experiment with pertinent correlations and inquire which functions select which organizations, and which organizations select which articulatory morphologies. The clear differentiation and independent elaboration of these three registers are a precondition for finding ever more effective possibilities (solutions) for their effective collaboration. This enhancement of architecture's ability to analyze and recombine its concepts is a precondition of architectural innovation.

The concepts of order, organization and articulation all make sense for both domains that are to be correlated – for the domain of the social process *and* for the domain of architectural space. Thus we can speak of

64 The first two registers together prepare the formal side in the build up of form-function correlations.

both social and architectural order, of both social and spatial organization, and also of both social and spatio-morphological articulation. However, there can be no direct translation from a social, language-based articulation to the required architectural articulation. The path of translation is routed via organization. Social organization translates into spatial organization by way of translating the patterns of social distinction, social grouping and social communication into spatial partitions, enclosures and connections. The sequence of design then moves from organization to articulation.

Articulation cannot be dispensed with. This is due to the fact that cities, urban spaces and buildings function only via their utilization by perceiving and comprehending subjects who need to recognize and understand the built environment in order to navigate and utilize it effectively. The effective social order requires an articulated spatial organization: architectural order. Even without articulation as consciously guided design effort, the inevitable spatio-morphological ('compositional' and 'decorative') features of the resultant design will be (more or less successfully) utilized as orienting clues within the social life-process accommodated within the designed territory. Every designing architect articulates intuitively. Both phenomenological and semiological aspects are taken into account even without an explicitly theorized expertise.[65] This is also the case with vernacular building. The city confronts society with its image. This was perhaps clearer in the old days when most social relations were literally enclosed within the bounds of the city wall. Anthropologists are able to detect the structure of primitive societies in their settlement structures. This is certainly more difficult with respect to modern urban environments. An ordered built environment remains, however, an indispensable aspect in the ordering of social interaction. The sociologist Dirk Baecker sees urban space as a 'symbiotic mechanism of society that makes the complex relations of life . . . phenomenologically palpable'.[66] The important point here is that this spatial representation of society and its various social systems does itself become a productive (and indeed indispensable) factor in the functioning of society. The more complex the social order becomes, the more it pays to upgrade architecture's ability to construct visual order and legibility in the face of this increasing social complexity.

65 The theory of architectural autopoiesis proposes that it is time to move beyond this intuitive handling of the environment's legibility. The task of articulation must become the explicit subject of a principled and self-critical intelligence.

66 Dirk Baecker, *Die nächste Stadt: Ein Pflichtenheft*, unpublished manuscript, 2009/2010, www.dirkbaecker.com.

6.2.3 A DEFINITION OF ORGANIZATION FOR CONTEMPORARY ARCHITECTURE

In very general terms organization (and therefore by extension order) is understood as the opposite of arbitrary randomness. This very basic definition must be our uncontested point of departure. The task of spatial organization is working against utter randomness or chaos by establishing a pattern, a spatial organization. The encompassing concept that comprises both spatial organizations and spatial chaos is the concept of ***configuration***: comprising both organized and arbitrary (unorganized) configurations.

While traditional notions of organization and order sought to constrain arbitrariness via the adherence of a configuration to a preconceived, ideal pattern or scheme, for instance via grids, preconceived proportional schemes and symmetries, contemporary notions of organization are much more open with respect to the mechanisms that might restrict randomness. Contemporary mechanisms might hinge on the establishment of local interdependencies between elements rather than on the dependency of elements on prior, global schemata.

Both Classical and Modernist architecture display compositions that arrange a handful of preconceived, identifiable parts – geometric figures like rectangles/cubes, circles/cylinders/semi-spheres and triangles/prisms/pyramids – according to simple relations/operations as follows: Classical architecture uses repetition, symmetry and proportion. Modernism uses fewer constraints, allowing for asymmetry as well as for stretched proportions without proportional coordination. Modernism allows for an increased heterogeneity within large architectural configurations like institutional buildings or ensembles. However, usually orthogonality is presupposed throughout in both the global configuration and its parts and details. Modernist design operates by means of separating parts and allowing each part to develop an independent morphology according to functional requirements. Within each separated part of the composition repetition is used extensively. To give a certain sense of global unity to these compositions, Modernism uses the loose concept of dynamic equilibrium.

Modernist compositions are more open/incomplete than Classical compositions, and are overall less constrained. In this sense we can say that Modernist compositions are less organized in comparison to Classical compositions. This trajectory of decreasing organization by removing constraints continues with Postmodernism and Deconstructivism. Deconstructivism removes the presupposition of orthogonality, and it allows new moves – like the overlap of geometric figures and the interpenetration of different grids – that both expand the repertoire and decrease the degree of organization and thus predictability of the design. By predictability we mean here two related things: first, the ***predictability*** of a particular design move/decision within the design process (*design progress predictability*) and, second, the ability to make predictions or successful guesses – while moving through the building – about how the building continues (*configuration predictability*), ie, local to local inferences as well as local to global inferences that facilitate successful navigation. We can thus observe a historical trajectory in the development of 20th-century architecture that paid for successive repertoire expansions (that in turn afforded increases in architecture's response versatility) with a successive decrease in organization and thus navigability.

The question thus arises here whether this trade off is inevitable or whether it is possible to combine further, necessary increases in architecture's response versatility with a simultaneous increase in organization. The thesis proposed here is that the contemporary style of *Parametricism*[67] is – in principle – geared up to accomplish this combined advance of versatility and organization. The style is further set up to augment complex organizations via pertinent techniques of articulation that make the elaborated organization legible, thus potentially establishing an architectural order capable of addressing the complexities of contemporary society. The demonstration of the thesis demands first of all a more precise concept of organization that allows at least the comparison (if not measurement) of *degrees of organization.* As a priori criterion for such a definition of degrees of organization we stipulate that higher degrees of a thus defined organization must, if appropriately articulated, lead to a higher intelligibility and navigability.

The theory of architectural autopoiesis values organization and order in the sense defined here. Organization implies organized complexity as distinct from both *configurations that lack determination* (organization) and *configurations that lack complexity* (diversity). Both types of spatial configurations are equally disorienting and incapable of effectively ordering/framing the processes of contemporary society. From the perspective of the spatial needs of contemporary network society, the Modernist regime of serial repetition lacks complexity. The Modernist urban and architectural repertoire – well-adapted to the era of Fordist mass society – can no longer accommodate the complexity of Post-Fordist network society. However, the unregulated expression of diversity that has followed in the wake of the crisis and abandonment of Modernism is equally disorienting: it lacks organization.

67 See section 11: *Parametricism – The Parametric Paradigm and the Formation of a New Style*.

Figure 1 Fordist urbanism: determination without diversity, Ludwig Hilberseimer, *Groszstadtarchitektur*, 1927

Figure 2 Moscow City, 21st century: diversity without determination

The relentless seriality of Modernism made way for the Postmodern principle of collage where no regulation constrains the agglomeration of difference. In urban agglomerations like the one depicted in Figure 2, all elements and their properties are chosen without regard to each other. There are no relations or interdependencies set up between buildings. Everything is equally possible and equally unexpected. Neither the repetition of the same nor the collage of the different is appropriate for

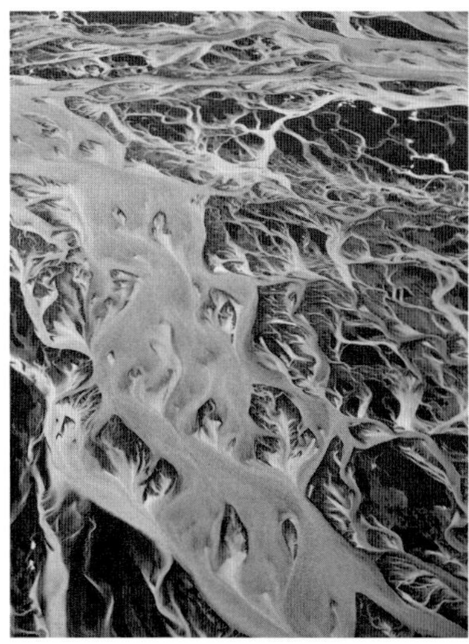

Figure 3 Organized complexity: inorganic natural system, river delta

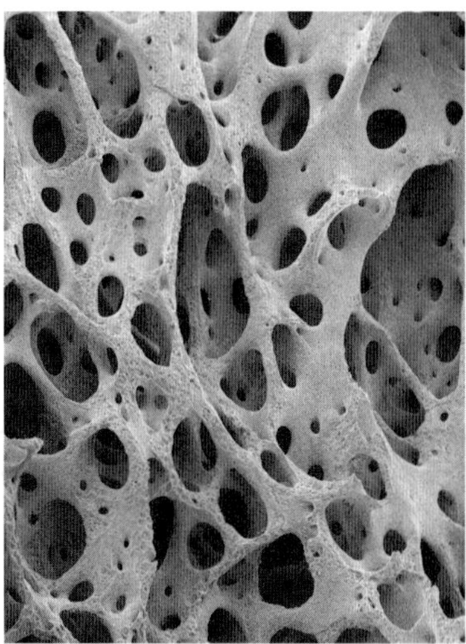

Figure 4 Organized complexity: organic natural system, bone structure

the spatial organization and architectural articulation of contemporary society. The key to a much more appropriate urban and architectural response might be found in the kind of organized complexity one can observe in natural systems. Here lies the profound motivation for the recent interest in natural systems.

Natural systems display the coincidence of rich differentiation *and* rigorous determination that we recognize as the key characteristics of *organized complexity*.[68] Complexity theory – with the aid of digital computation – has been able to analyze and simulate the rule-based formation of this kind of organized complexity. These systems have been referred to as 'self-organizing systems' because the build up of the organization has been revealed to proceed bottom-up, often via the build up of hierarchical levels, but always without the need to presume that an a priori mould or telos is being imposed from outside.

6.2.4 COMPLICATED, COMPLEX, ORGANIZED, ORDERED

Architectural order facilitates social order[69] and its effective realization requires organization and articulation as crucial registers of the design effort. The first task is the task of spatial organization.[70] The second, dependent task is the task of spatio-morphological articulation.[71] The combined effort results in architectural order.

The theory of architectural autopoiesis distinguishes organizations from mere configurations. To be more precise: the class of all configurations encompasses organizations as a special subclass. Organizations are then to be understood as configurations that satisfy some additional criterion, namely the criterion to be organized. In what follows here this tautology will be unpacked, and an operational definition of relative degrees of organization will be offered.

An *organized* spatial configuration is defined in opposition to an *arbitrary* or *random* configuration. A configuration is *random* when *no* position/property of *any* element within the configuration in any way constrains the positioning or property of any other element within the configuration. No rules exist that regulate the configuration, no correlations are prescribed. The result is a zero degree of organization. A random configuration is the outer limit of a spectrum that stretches

68 The concept of complexity will be elaborated and formalized below.

69 For social order we might stipulate the same aspects of organization and articulation. Social organization is more effective if it is articulated, ie, perceived and comprehended by the participants of social interactions. A police officer is more effective if his/her position and status is readily recognizable. In general language, the availability of single terms for social positions is a primary mechanism for articulating social organization. However, design and architecture participate as well in this articulatory effort.

70 The concept of organization is updating and systematizing the concerns traditionally addressed in the concepts of compartition, distribution and composition.

71 The concept of articulation is updating and systematizing the concerns traditionally addressed in the concepts of ornamentation, character and expression.The notion of character hinted at the goal of articulation (expression) and ornament was seen as the primary means of articulation.

between mere configurations and highly organized spatial systems. Random configurations in this sense define a limit case that we should not expect to exist in the built environment. The apparently 'random' patterns one finds in unplanned settlements do not constitute pure randomness. Bill Hillier has demonstrated that such irregular developments follow patterns that emerge from the observation of locally applied rules.[72] Those rules might best be characterized as constraints on an otherwise random agglomeration. What might appear as chaotic or arbitrary might reveal a hidden organization through an upgraded analysis that has a more advanced, richer repertoire of organizational notions at its disposal. It therefore makes sense to open the concept of spatial organization as much as possible and let the boundary of the concept be marked by the utterly arbitrary and formless, ie, configurations that resist any attempt to be predicted, summarized and reproduced.

From this definition of the limit case of a totally random configuration several ways open up to build up degrees of organization by working away from this radical arbitrariness. If we describe the configuration by describing its constitution via its sequential build up we can distinguish various ways of working away from randomness.

The first approach is the idea that a spatial organization is a configuration the description of which can be condensed into a formula.[73] This implies that a spatial organization can be constructed or reconstructed via some production rule. Such rules might give exact determinations that leave nothing to chance. The result will be totally organized, a *total organization* – the other limit case in the spectrum from configuration to system. Again, we should not expect a total organization in the reality of the built environment. Unique contextual conditions and other unexpected circumstances are likely to produce singularities that intervene with the unfolding of the deterministic rule.

The first way to build up an organized spatial organization is to define a formula, ie, a recursive rule that successively produces the overall pattern. The process starts with a single element and uses its position and properties as starting input for the stepwise proliferation of similar elements according to a recursively applied function. The resultant configuration is fully determined with respect to the positions and

72 Hillier analyzed and simulated the typical settlement patterns of the villages of the South of France. The typical pattern is the 'beady ring' pattern. Hillier's simulation involves rules that operate via specific local restrictions of an otherwise random process. Bill Hillier & Julienne Hanson, *The Social Logic of Space*, Cambridge University Press (Cambridge), 1984.

73 The string length of such a formula in a given formalized language can be taken as a measure of the organization's descriptive complexity, also referred to as Kolmogorov complexity. This measure is obviously relative to the language used.

properties of all its elements. Branching L-systems are a classic example of systems that are defined via such recursive rules. Grids can also be constructed by means of such recursive rules. The same goes for radial city systems with radials and concentric rings. These three types of systems are obvious and easy to recognize. However, the definition of the concept of organization does not imply that its systematic constitution is readily apparent. The retrieval of the generative rule is a matter of analytical reconstruction. The recognition of organization/systematicity is a matter of Gestalt perception. Neither can be taken for granted. It is the design task of articulation to enhance the chance of an organization's successful recognition.

The three typical urban systems mentioned above display *regularity*.[74] Regular organizations have a greater chance of being detected and understood. A *regular* spatial organization is not only determined with respect to the positions and properties of all its elements, it is also self-similar throughout its expanse. Not all recursive rules produce regularity. There are further constraints to be observed to achieve regularity. For instance, there must be a provision against the spatial interpenetration of elements. Also, the element parameters must be constrained within a certain range in order to preserve sufficient self-similarity.

Instead of working with fully deterministic rules, one might also script rules that integrate partial randomization. Such rules define conditions that allow for arbitrary choices, constrained within certain parametric boundaries.[75] If we compare two similar configurations based on two similar branching algorithms – one fully deterministic, the other partially deterministic – the fully deterministic configuration is stipulated to be more systematic, more organized. However, determination is not the ultimate endgame of the pursuit of high levels of organization. There is another key dimension of organization: complexity.[76]

Since there is an unlimited number of generative or recursive rules that can fully determine a spatial system, the degree of determination does not serve us well in distinguishing degrees of organization. There must be at least one other dimension that deserves to be taken into account. If we compare two branching systems – one where the branch length and the angle of branching stay constant from generation to

74 Regularity is a broader concept with weaker requirements than the concept of repetitiveness. Both repetition and iteration are compatible with the requirement of regularity.

75 These boundaries must either vary systematically across the expanse of the territory or vary according to local conditions that emerge and therefore lead to a self-induced concatenation of constraints.

76 The concept of complexity will be elaborated and formalized below.

generation versus another one where the branch length shortens (or elongates) and where the angle progressively opens (or closes) with each generation – which of the two systems should we consider to be more organized? The decision should not be too difficult: intuitively the latter system would be considered to be of a higher degree of organization (irrespective of the fact that without such a progressive rule the system would soon terminate due to self-intersection). The latter system displays a higher degree of complexity – it contains more variation – without losing its determinateness or systematicity. A system that only varies branch length but keeps the angle of branching constant would be less organized, displaying a lesser degree or lower level of organization. A spatial configuration that subjects the length and/or angle of branching to a more elaborate rule (rather than a mere linear progression) would be of higher organization. In general we stipulate that the degree of organization increases with the complexity of the rule system. The increase of complexity must be *determined* complexity. The degree of determined complexity is reflected in the complexity (length, elaborateness) of the formula or script that generates/determines the system. Thus we arrive at a second dimension of organization: the degree of determined complexity.[77] On this count the Manhattan grid is of (slightly) higher organization than a fully isotropic grid. The degree of organization – due to the build up of determined complexity – shows up as determined differentiation of the system. Taking up the example of the variously defined branching systems above, we can observe that the more organized branching systems that vary branch-lengths and angles according to a rule produce a spatial field that is lawfully differentiated. This lawful, rule-based differentiation affords an important property: it allows us to infer additional information from the given parameters.

The comparison between the two most typical urban systems – simple grid system and simple radial system – allows an assessment of their relative degree of organization. The radial system is more organized than

77 Determined complexity is thus the descriptive complexity of the condensed production formula that generates the determined complexity. Mirco Becker gives the following example: a set of 100 points with random distribution has to be determined by XYZ coordinates thus leading to 300 entries in a table in order to be fully described. 100 points with equal distance along an axis of a Cartesian coordinate system can be expressed in a compact formula stating the XYZ coordinates of the first point, the modulus – equal distance, and the total number, thus only requiring five entries in a table. (Becker talks about algorithmic rather than determined complexity and uses the term 'structure in a data-set' rather than organization in a configuration.) The random distribution has complexity of 300 but no organization, the equidistant set along an axis has a fully determined complexity 5 but a relatively low level of organization because of its low level of complexity. See: Mirco Becker, 'The Generative and the Synthetic', in: *Modulor*, February 2010.

the grid system because it is more complex and differentiated. The grid is undifferentiated and affords no local to local or local to global inferences. There is no local spatial difference between the interior (geometric centre) of the overall grid and its peripheral regions. In contrast, the radial system has a marked singularity – its centre – and the system is continuously differentiated: moving outwards the concentric rings increase in radius and the ring segments between the radials increase in length. The system establishes a ***correlation*** between a road's radius and its distance from the centre. This systematic, correlated variation in turn affords local information about the position within the overall system. The convex side of the road points towards the centre and the concave side points outward. The proximity to the centre can be read off the radius of the ring. This particular information is redundantly underlined by the length of the ring segments. These local properties are inherent in the geometry of the system. They are available – as potential orienting information – even without articulatory intent or effort. They become actualized to the extent to which the global system is understood and thus available as guiding mental map, and to the extent to which the local properties become perceptually available. (The aspect of perceptual availability might require further articulatory efforts.) However, the embedded information is relatively weak due to the large degree of symmetry within the system, ie, there are many positions with the same local parameters. Further systematic differentiation (symmetry-breaking) would lead to further potential orienting information.[78] In this sense a radial system built upon ellipses rather than circles would be of higher organization.

The first way to build up organization – in contradistinction to random configurations – is to determine the build up of the configuration from scratch, step by step, via a (partially) deterministic, generative formula or recursive rule. A second way can be described as follows: to build up organization one might start with a random disposition of more or less self-similar elements as a base configuration. Then – with respect to this initially arbitrary configuration – rules might be defined that place additional layers of elements according to parameters read off the initial random layer. The initial configuration might be generated by a random process. Often the given site and its context, or rather a specific analytical reading of a given site/context, might serve as a quasi-random starting point. Functions might then be defined that constrain all further moves on the basis of the initial layer. The parametric disposition of the

78 Potential orienting information becomes actual orienting information when the objective correlations within the system are further articulated to trigger subjective associations within the users of the system.

additional layers is then driven by the parameter distribution of the initial, random configuration. Systematic correlations are thus formed, and the degree of organization increases with each new layer. With each new rigorously scripted layer determined complexity, and thus the degree of organization, increases. Complexity increases with each new layer in relation to the number and variability of the new elements placed and with respect to the elaborateness of the rule that is applied. The increase of complexity without rule-based determination/correlation does not increase organization. We might say that this indeterminate increase of complexity results in *extensive complexity*. Consequently we might use the term *intensive complexity* for the result of the determined increase of complexity.

This elaborated concept of complexity is the key to give the concept of organization an ordinal-comparative meaning and measure. (However, the degree of complexity of a configuration is not the same as its degree or level of organization.) With respect to the relative measure of complexity[79] within a configuration we might distinguish two dimensions of comparison: ***extensive complexity*** and ***intensive complexity***, each comprising two sub-dimensions. These dimensions allow us to speak of a relative increase or decrease of organization within a given design process, ie, whether a certain design move increases or decreases organization, or which of two design moves engenders a larger increase in organization.[80] An increase in intensive complexity always increases the degree of organization. An increase in extensive complexity might reduce the degree of organization unless it is accompanied and captured by a simultaneous increase in intensive complexity. Complexity is thus Janus-faced.[81] It only increases organization to the extent to which its introduction is determined by rules of correlation. An increase of merely extensive complexity lowers the overall level of organization within a configuration.

extensive complexity:	this measure depends both on the number of distinguishable items and on the diversity of those items within the configuration

79 There are various attempts to measure complexity within different contexts. The one proposed here is not based on any specific source.

80 However, this definition neither allows us to measure across disparate, unrelated designs, nor do its dimensional values ever add up to deliver a single value that could rank different versions of a design that differ in several dimensions at the same time. The application of the concept is thus subject to severe *ceteris paribus* restrictions, ie, comparisons can only be made one dimension at a time, while assuming everything else to be equal.

81 Warren Weaver distinguished two forms of complexity: disorganized complexity and organized complexity. Warren Weaver, 'Science and Complexity', in: *American Scientist*, 36: 536 (1948).

intensive complexity: this measure depends both on the density of interdependencies between the distinguishable items and on the diversity of those interdependencies within the configuration

Extensive complexity provides only the necessary basis upon which *intensive complexity* can be built up via the establishment of interdependencies. To the extent to which the number/diversity of items (extensive complexity) in the configuration is *not* becoming the basis of establishing interdependencies (producing intensive complexity), it is producing mere ***complication.*** The degree of complication – measured by those items that remain unrelated/independent and by those types of items (diversity) that do not make a difference in terms of the establishment of interdependencies – detracts from the relative degree of organization, and thus finally from the degree of order the respective configuration achieves.

Intensive complexity builds upon extensive complexity by grouping items into sets and then defining (scripting) correlations (functions, mappings) between those sets. Extensive and intensive complexity relate differently to organization. While intensive complexity increases organization, merely extensive complexity reduces organization. But the relationship is not one of simple reversal. The increase of extensive complexity – while initially reducing organization – increases the opportunity/potential for intensive complexity and thus for an enhanced degree of organization, if further interdependencies are established.

The process of organization is a process of establishing interdependencies. As the design progresses, the density of these interdependencies should increase. This means that organized complexity is built up rather than mere complication. Any parameter (property or relation) of any item might be associated with any parameter (property or relation) of any other item (or sets of items). The perfect technique/vehicle for this is scripted functions.

The two dimensions of complexity are incommensurable. Degrees of complexity cannot be measured on a unitary scale. It is a multi-dimensional 'measure' that cannot be reduced to a single scale. This does not invalidate the concept. The concept defined here is conceived to allow comparisons within an ongoing design process. The concept/measure is operational as long as it allows the designer to assess whether a certain proposed design move increases or decreases the organization of the design. With sufficiently small (or sufficiently decomposed) design steps there should be no problem in applying the criteria proposed here. The introduction of additional elements or layers within a configuration increases complexity. However, they increase rather than decrease *organization* only if their introduction is rule-based so that the positions and properties of the new elements are not only internally correlated but correlated with (and thus at least partially determined by) what had been built up already. Any random interference, deletion or distortion of what has already been determined/correlated decreases the level of organization. For instance, the injection of a random scatter of buildings into an urban grid or onto a radial urban system decreases the degree of organization. Even the imposition of a further internally systematic layer increases the overall level of organization only if there is a systematic correlation with what was there already. Bernard Tschumi's design strategy for his Parc de la Villette serves as an example. The project builds up complexity by layering multiple urban geometries: point grid system, system of primary geometric zones (circle, triangle, square), system of winding paths. Each configuration is internally systematic, but they are wholly indifferent (uncorrelated) with respect to each other. According to our stipulation there is a decrease of organization with each new superimposed layer. The project becomes ever more chaotic. However, this build up of extensive complexity prepares the ground for the build up of intensive complexity via correlations. Huge increases in organization would be possible if these layers were now to adapt to each other via rules of inflection and modulation.

A highly organized configuration is marked by a rich, systematic differentiation. For the design process this recommends the following two-step strategy. If the system lacks initial differentiation (grid, simple radial system) then first increase complexity by an initially random injection of elements or layers. The resultant differentiation could then be overdetermined by systematic rules of adaptation that take up and correlate at least some of the new material with what else is there. The first step establishes a complicated configuration via extensive complexity. The second step transforms this extensive complexity into intensive complexity, and thus increases the organization of the configuration.[82]

An example of this is the utilization of 'forces' to distort/differentiate a grid. The imposition of attractors is random, but their dynamic correlation leads to a coherently differentiated field and thus to an increase in the overall degree of organization. Once a sufficiently complex differentiation (with sufficient asymmetries and gradients) has been achieved, further injections of complexity might be determined by scripts without any

82 Due to the random component in the generation of the configuration it can never reach the total organisation or full determination of a pure system.

further injection of randomness. The determination via scripts ensures organization. The process increases both complexity and organization resulting in ***organized complexity***.

Within the prevailing trend of contemporary avant-garde architecture, organized complexity rather than total organization is the primary aim.[83] Guided by the ambition to increase organized complexity, the design creativity moves from individual manipulations of elements to the conception of collective manipulations that handle many instances simultaneously, each individually formed according to the intersection of global rules with local parameters. The build up of organized complexity according to the Parametricist rule-imposing heuristic is cumulative and implies that an initially arbitrary beginning leads to a more and more self-constraining organization where each additional element or design intervention must be ever more carefully elaborated to satisfy and continue the complex web of rules and interdependencies already established. The overall organization remains open – it never achieves completion or perfection like, for example, a Palladian villa – but the probability that a design move disrupts rather than enhances the design increases with every further move. The further elaboration of the design becomes increasingly difficult the more the design advances. (A sense of necessity is therefore the subjective corollary of this situation from the designer's perspective.) Successful Parametricist designs share this feature with highly evolved organisms. Modernist, Postmodernist and Deconstructivist designs do not experience this increasing tightening of the remaining space of possibilities and the attendant increase in the difficulty of elaborating satisfying solutions for further design requirements or details. For Modernist, Postmodernist and Deconstructivist designs, a late design move is nearly as easy and unconstrained as an early move. Nearly anything goes. These compositions are far less organized.

The Parametricist build up of organized complexity often proceeds hierarchically, whereby correlated/interdependent sets of items (systems) are set into correlations (functions, mappings) with other such integrated sets of items or systems. Such systems are often functional units or subsystems. One might think of the subsystems of a tower, such as envelope, structural skeleton, system of spatial divisions, circulation system etc. Each of these systems is itself comprised of interrelated parts. According to the design research programme of Parametricism, one would expect each of these systems to be internally differentiated rather than repetitive (as one could assume in Modernism), ie, the skeleton's

83 Parametricism aims for organized complexity while Minimalism aims for total organization.

elements and their pattern of connections should be differentiated along the vertical axis of the tower in accordance with load and moment/stability parameters. The skeleton's particular pattern of differentiation can now become the input data-set for driving (aspects of) the facade's internal differentiation while other aspects/properties might be differentiated in accordance with environmental parameters.The structural system might in turn adapt to this envelope differentiation by producing a secondary differentiation, albeit without undermining its primary differentiation.

To the extent to which such differentiations are articulated and become legible, their organization contributes to the establishment of ***architectural order***. For instance, the visible differentiation of the skeleton offers clues (facilitating positional local to global inferences) as to whether one is relatively high or low within the building, or the visible differentiation of the facade's shading devices along the tower's circumference might offer clues (facilitating positional local to global inferences) as to one's orientation. Again, to the extent to which the correlation between these two subsystems of the tower is legible, ie, to the extent to which the skeleton's differentiation shines through the facade or is even further accentuated and revealed by the facade, organization is elevated to become order. In this case the subsystems involved in the scripted correlations become indeed ***representations***[84] of each other.

Above we emphasized that a Parametricist design transforms an arbitrary beginning into a highly elaborate, complex order that assumes the semblance of necessity for the designer. To the extent to which this ever more tightened network of organizing correlations is articulated (made visible/legible), an awe-inspiring elegance[85] results.

6.3 Organization

THESIS 27

Proficiency in establishing compelling new form-function relationships requires a system of abstract mediating concepts that can guide the correlation of spatial with social patterns.

Although the importance of organization (compartition, distribution, composition) has often been emphasized, traditional architectural theory

84 The German word for mathematical function 'Abbildung' literally translates as 'representation'.

85 See Patrik Schumacher, 'Arguing for Elegance', in: *Elegance*, AD (Architectural Design), vol 77, no 1, January/February 2007, general editor: Helen Castle, guest-edited by Ali Rahim & Hina Jamelle.

gives more space to the discussion of construction and decoration. The relative sparsity of detailed thoughts on distribution might be due to the relatively simple layouts of most historical buildings. Recommendations are concerned with the orientation of various rooms – bedchambers to the east, dining rooms to the west etc – with the appropriate shape and proportions of the various rooms, and with symmetry in the overall arrangement. The absence of an elaborated theory of distribution continued throughout the 19th century and throughout most of the 20th century. Only since the 1960s have theoretical resources been developed that are able to facilitate the principled build up and tractability of much higher levels of organizational complexity. However, those resources have remained marginal within the autopoiesis of architecture. It is one of the ambitions of the theory of architectural autopoiesis to shift these resources further into the centre of attention, at least (initially) within the avant-garde segment of architecture. Since these theoretical resources are capable of being handled computationally (parametrically) there is a justified hope that the current intensification of Parametricist design research will take note of this demand and opportunity.

The task of architectural design, project by project, is the elaboration of an architectural order that catalyzes, facilitates and maintains the specific social order to be accommodated. The first component of this task pertains to organization, ie, the translation of social organization into spatial organization. One might call this first subtask the ***projection of social structure into space***. The accomplishment of this task can then form the basis for the task of articulation. Organization and articulation together establish a legible architectural order as the precondition to speculate about and simulate effective action-artefact networks understood as architecturally framed scenarios of social interaction.

It is the *global spatial organization* of the design that constitutes the first problem that any architectural design has to solve. The global spatial organization might be conceived in top-down fashion or might result from a bottom-up process. In the first case we might speak of a ***parti***. In the second case we are dealing with an ***emergent pattern***. The initial parti or pattern has to be further manipulated and adapted if the project is to accommodate a complex social institution or life-process beyond the threshold of the trivial. How can this parti or pattern be found and ascertained? The problem is how to guide the search of promising correlations between social institutions and spatial arrangements. The ability to address this task hinges on the repertoire of possible organizational patterns as well as on the methods of evaluating the options available within the given repertoire.

Architectural design is first of all concerned with organization. Few architects would disagree with this. But when faced with the request to elaborate this general dictum by describing specific patterns of organization most architects remain mute, or are at best able to hint at vague distinctions like hierarchical versus non-hierarchical organization. The truth is that the discipline does not have any sophisticated descriptive terminology at its regular disposal. It seems high time that architecture overcomes this muteness and acquires a much richer and more precise conceptual apparatus to cope with contemporary demands to organize increasingly complex institutions.

The continued autopoiesis of architecture must allow for the replenishment of the universe of possibilities that is the source domain or solution space within which the organizational forms are searched for in this crucial initial design stage. How can this universe of possibilities be systematically expanded? And where can we find the appropriate search heuristics and evaluation criteria that must complement the expanded repertoire?

The aim of this section on organization is to give initial indications towards the elaboration of a detailed and systematic 'art of organization' that builds its principles upon a rich descriptive terminology and systematic apparatus of concepts, measures and theorems. Only on this basis can the discipline develop an effective organizational design intelligence that is adequate to the task of framing the increasing complexity of contemporary communication patterns.

6.3.1 RELATING SPATIAL TO SOCIAL ORGANIZATION

The original, most general question, 'How can functional requirements be effectively addressed by architectural forms?', has been broken down to arrive at the formulation of a first crucial subtask: architectural design is first of all the translation of social organizations into spatial organizations. What has been gained by this re-formulation?

What has been gained or acquired here is the concept of organization as central mediating concept between social function and spatial form. The concept of organization is a crucial lever to retool the discipline. If contemporary designers locate their efforts on the level of abstraction that is afforded by the concept of organization – the central concept that is shared between the domains of social organization and spatial organization – then they can adequately address the task of correlating complex social processes with complex architectural arrangements – provided that architectural theory can sufficiently unfold this concept of organization. This implies the systematic distinction of different types of organizational patterns – the construction of an organizational taxonomy – and the definition of pertinent qualities and measures of organization that apply to both the social and the spatial dimension. Such a system of organizational concepts provides a viable set of mediating terms, ie, terms that can mediate the domain of social functions with the domain of spatial forms and thus facilitate the effective correlation of social and spatial organization.[86]

The correlation between social and spatial patterns of organization is well prepared by the fact that the language for the conceptualization of the social world has been derived primarily from the language of space. Spatial relations form the primary source domain for metaphors and concepts of social order. Fundamental spatial concepts like position, distance, domain, boundary and symmetry have all been borrowed to describe social order. The very concept of order itself has its roots in spatial order and architecture.

Architectural organization is the spatial organization of a given social organization. Spatial organization primarily proceeds by means of boundaries. Boundaries both enclose and divide space. Originally this was very much an act of claiming and defining a bounded domain or territory against an undifferentiated, virgin background. However, such virgin ground has long since disappeared and architectural organization takes the form of a re-division or further subdivision of a given system of boundaries/territories. The initial task of architectural design might indeed be concisely defined as the distribution of (permeable) boundaries that both separate and selectively connect social domains and activities.[87]

Enclosure produces unities that might be further divided. Further enclosures might be established within enclosures thus producing a system of nesting enclosures within enclosures. Thus a hierarchical (but not necessarily stratified) organization is established. ***Division*** produces parallel spatial segments (segments next to segments) that might represent a segmented, stratified or functionally differentiated social organization.[88]

86 The theoretical paradigm of 'space syntax' is an interesting example where the formal elaboration of computational measures of spatial organisation has spurned an interdisciplinary discourse – with enlisting contributors from the social sciences – around the diverse application of the basic concepts and computational tools of space syntax. See Bill Hillier, *Space is the Machine*.

87 Compare: Christoph Feldtkeller, *Der architektonische Raum: eine Fiktion. Annäherung an eine funktionale Betrachtung*, Bauwelt Fundamente 83, Vieweg (Braunschweig/Wiesbaden), 1989.

88 A hierarchy of access might then be used to support a stratified social organization, for example, with the deepest, most remote space being of the highest social importance. A parallel access via corridor might support a segmented or functionally differentiated organization without ranking.

The theory of architectural autopoiesis adopts/adapts Deleuze and Guattari's concept of ***territorialization*** as a general concept of organization by means of boundaries whereby a spatial continuum is broken down into discrete spatial units: ***territorial units***. Territorialization thus encompasses both enclosure and division. This primary operation of territorialization – the drawing of a line (or outline) representing a boundary – produces the distinction of inside vs outside. The operations of enclosure and/or division might be repeated on the inside of the domain thus established. This way a complex system of nested inside/outside relations might be built up. This distinction of inside and outside – although relative to an assumed position – is (nearly) always applicable as the primary means of orientation within architectural organizations. Key terms in architecture that refer to organizational patterns like 'plan', 'diagram', 'layout' or 'parti' are mostly concerned with the pattern of spatial territorialization.

All the more significant is the radical break and expansion of organizational possibilities that architecture enacted when it set itself the aim of undermining the clear distinction between inside and outside, introducing concepts like overlap and phased transitions. These concepts, which in their Modernist guise still rely on the underlying operation of spatial division and the setting of boundaries, were further radicalized during the 1980s and 1990s, to the point where a whole new organizational paradigm beyond boundary formation becomes possible: the notion of space as a ***continuously differentiated field*** or medium in which gradients, vectors of transformation, directionalities and the distribution of densities etc replace the system of domains next to/within domains. Deleuze and Guattari distinguished smooth space from striated space.[89] This distinction became influential within the architectural avant-garde discourse of the 1990s. The theory of architectural autopoiesis reaffirms and incorporates this distinction as denoting an important and powerful innovation in the theory and practice of contemporary architectural organization. In the terminological apparatus forged here, both smooth and striated regimes of spatial organization are territorializing regimes that produce 'territorial units'. Even fuzzy sets are sets, and transitional zones operate like expanded boundaries. Territories might be defined by intensive field qualities rather than extensive enclosures. The theory of architectural autopoiesis requires a general, abstract category for the elemental units of spatial organization that can

89 Gilles Deleuze & Felix Guattari, *A Thousand Plateaus*, University of Minnesota Press (Minneapolis), 1987, French original: *Mille Plateaux*, Les Editions de Minuit (Paris), 1980.

be applied across all regimes or modes of organization. The concept of ***territory*** fulfils this requirement.

Although the discovery and promotion of smooth organization marks an extremely important innovation, the bulk of architectural production – both mainstream *and* avant-garde – and most of social life continue to operate under the regime of striation by means of boundaries.[90] The result of striation, a territorialized space, might be obtained by two rather different design operations: the operation of enclosure/division on the one hand, and the operation of aggregating cells on the other hand. The successive (hierarchical) enclosure/division might be substituted by a (functionally equivalent) operation of successive (hierarchical) aggregation of territorial units into larger, encompassing territorial units. The result is the same: a striated world made up of discrete units of space. The organizational regime of striation thus encompasses the operations of enclosure, division as well as aggregation. The overarching concept of territorialization encompasses all processes of striation as well as the processes of smooth and intensive differentiation.

Territorialization must be complemented by defining connections between the delineated territories. The established boundaries must be opened up by means of apertures as points of access or visual connection. This way the established domains are linked and related. The concatenation and three-dimensional integration of these linkages might be abstracted and investigated as integrated path-systems each with their own respective configuration. The pattern of these path-systems is as important as the pattern of territorialization. Together they produce the effective system of spatial relations which can be considered as a spatial mapping or projection of social relations, reinforcing the relevant social distinctions, positions, linkages etc, and organizing the required social activities.

A spatial organization is thus only fully specified and established once a given pattern of territorialization is complemented by a pattern of ***connection***. However, a comprehensive theory of architectural organization has to take account of both striated spaces and smooth fields.[91] A smooth field pattern needs to be complemented by a pattern

90 Even most avant-garde work still operates via patterns of enclosure and division – although these patterns are more intricate than traditional and modern patterns. Contemporary patterns involve broken boundaries and interpenetrating domains.

91 In order to remain terminologically consistent, the theory of architectural autopoiesis must transmute Deleuze & Guattari's concept of smooth space into the concept of smooth field. This is in line with the proposal to reserve the concept of space (as much as possible) for the Modernist conception of architecture as space. Against this concept of space the contemporary

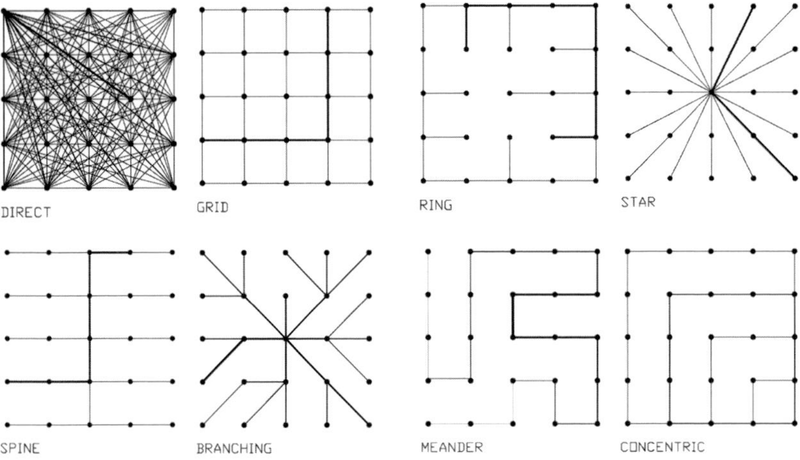

Figure 5 Typology of connection patterns

of ***penetration***. The penetration of fields does not necessarily involve fixed lines of movement. The actual patterns of movement observed might describe path networks. However, the field itself produces only a differentiated movement potential. The field might thus be described in terms of differential permeability maps, with different (gradually transforming) biases or resistances in various directions. If we utilize the general term ***territorialization*** to comprise the differentiating operations of both striation and smooth distribution, and take the general term ***integration*** to denote both the operations of connection and penetration, we can formulate as follows: there are two general dimensions of spatial organization that have to be addressed in every spatial organization – territorialization and integration.

The patterns depicted in Figure 5 might equally apply to the connection of striated space and the penetration of smooth fields. Each diagram connects the same 25 territories. The direct-lines pattern serves here as theoretical limit case against which all other types can be understood and measured. Each organizational type selects from the all-lines diagram according to a rule. The types can be evaluated via the double measure of total network length on the one hand, and average point-to-point path length (or imposed detour factor) on the other hand.

avant-garde – here theorized under the title of Parametricism – has been pushing the field concept. See Volume 1, chapter 5.4.4. *From Space to Field.*

These are important efficiency measures[92] that urban planners/designers should take into account. These measures might also factor in the network formation of unplanned urban development processes. Besides these quantitative concerns, urban planners/designers should be cognizant of the fact that the different organizational types make a difference in terms of the systems of positions they establish. These respectively established spatial positions might take account of social significance, and thus the choice of spatial organization can be presumed to impact (if not impose) the social order of the accommodated population. The grid produces an array of (nearly) equivalent positions. In contrast, the star type creates a very strong centre that 'controls' all movements, or is able to take advantage of all movements. The branching system also establishes a centre but in addition sets up a series of subcentres. Both star and branching system establish a hierarchy of positions that will irresistibly produce a social or functional hierarchy. These organizational patterns operate like sorting machines. They are bound to structure the organization of the social communication processes that are unfolding in the respective territories. We might speak here about the demiurge-like power of architecture.

6.3.2 TERRITORIALIZATION AND INTEGRATION

The distinction of territorialization and integration[93] is the most general and universally applicable distinction that might be placed at the starting point of a theory of spatial organization. Territorialization comprises striation (enclosure, division, cell aggregation) as well as smooth differentiation. It differentiates otherwise continuous, undifferentiated space[94] into more or less distinct (fuzzy) *territorial units* (domains,

92 The smaller the overall path network and the smaller the average detour factor, the more efficient is the network. However, the simultaneous application of both criteria pulls the network in different directions.

93 The distinction of territorialization and integration generalizes Frei Otto's distinction of occupying and connecting. Frei Otto introduced this conceptual pair to identify the two complementary, constituent operations of all urban settlement processes. The conceptual pair of territorialization and integration generalizes this notion across all scales to include architecture and its interior divisions and connections. The notion of territorialization is substituted for Frei Otto's notion of occupying in order to keep the conceptual pair strictly within the realm of spatial operations. Frei Otto's notion of occupying conflates spatial and social operations. The conceptual apparatus developed here initially separates spatial and social organization to problematize their relationship. Compare: Frei Otto, *Occupying and Connecting – Thoughts on Territories and Spheres of Influence with Particular Reference to Human Settlement*, Edition Axel Menges (Stuttgart/London), 2009.

94 Obviously the natural landscape is always differentiated to a certain extent. Natural features and discontinuities are therefore often utilized and incorporated into the architectural pattern of territorialization.

regions, zones, sites, parcels, spaces, rooms). Spatial territorialization recurs on many scales. The process of territorializing differentiation thus becomes a continuous chain of sub-differentiations within differentiations. Urban design divides the urban territory into districts, urban blocks and individual parcels/sites. Architecture continues the process of division by segmenting the site or building complex into separate buildings, tracts or wings, floors and spaces/rooms. Territorializing differentiation might be effected by many means, ie, by means of boundaries (walls, fences etc) and sharp thresholds (curbs etc) or by means of continuous field differentiation (density gradients, light modulations etc) and morphological differentiation (morphing) as means of smooth field differentiations.

Integration integrates the differentiated territories. It connects the distinct domains within the subdivided space and penetrates the smoothly differentiated field. Integration might proceed by means of openings within boundaries and by delineating path-networks, or by means of distributing differential degrees of porosity that bias and thus pattern field penetration. Integration comprises both circulatory and visual integration.

The connection lines that channel the necessary movements between the domains either run along and between the boundary lines that set up the domains at each scale, or they run across the boundaries to cut across the various spatial domains and subdomains. Thus the connection lines are either parallel or orthogonal to the dividing lines. Beijing's Forbidden City is an extensive urban complex where orthogonal circulation dominates, both within the urban spaces and within the buildings. Modern society has all but eliminated the orthogonal variant of the relation between connection and division. In former times – before the advent of modern society – roads were often interrupted by barriers at the boundary of domains, for example, by customs barriers and by the city gates. Within most pre-Modern buildings circulation went right through the middle of the spaces, from adjoining space to adjoining space, en suite (enfilade). The invention of corridors has all but terminated this condition.[95]

Typically, territorialization is subject to the organizing principle of nesting, ie, domains are embedded within encompassing larger domains which are in turn embedded within even larger domains etc. This works as much with fuzzy, gradient domains as it does with strictly delimited zones. Although the principle of hierarchical nesting has been prevalent

95 See Robin Evans, 'Figures, Doors and Passages', in: *Translations from Drawing to Building and other Essays*, AA Documents 2, AA Publications (London), 1997.

throughout the history of human civilization, striations (enclosures, divisions) can cut across each other, so that domains might overlap or intersect. The organizing principle of intersection also operates with both crisp and fuzzy domains. Just like fuzzy set calculus builds upon ordinary set calculus, so we might look upon smooth field organization as an enhanced form of striated space organization.

The principle of nesting has its complement in the dimension of integration: paths typically branch off larger and longer paths, which in turn branch off even larger/longer paths etc. Thus the principle of nesting enclosures is mirrored in the *principle of successive connective branches and sub-branches*.

Territorialization and integration complement each other and are tightly correlated. Neither of the two dimensions can claim any logical priority over the other. The same is true with respect to the design sequence in which these dimensions are addressed: the design of either dimension can (temporarily) take the lead. The same applies to (unplanned) developmental processes. Pathways through the open landscape set up lines along which subdivisions can proceed to segment the adjoining land, or the lines dividing the (for example, agricultural) domains acquire the function of circulation lines. Both with respect to design and with respect to developmental processes, the build up of an effective spatial organization involves the oscillation between territorialization and integration.

The contemporary built environment is fully territorialized and integrated. Spatial subdivision is directly linked with social appropriation across all scales: administrative domains, property in land and buildings, socially appropriated/dedicated spaces within buildings. Modern circulatory irrigation of space reaches nearly every domain independently. Every territorial unit is linked up with every other territorial unit. (There are no longer any 'caught' territories.) We can therefore equate circulatory connection with the public domain while spatial enclosure and subdivision can be – with very few exceptions – equated with the private domain. This rigorous distinction between the category of the private vs the public domain is a characteristic hallmark of modern society. Spatially this is reflected in the combination of total connection and total territorialization, ie, the spatial organization of modern society uniquely combines total territorialization (spatializing the private domain as inviolate social category, mostly via relentless striation) with total connection (spatializing the public as inviolate social category). It might seem that this condition represents a deep structural feature of modern society and that we should expect the attendant fundamental feature of the organization of space to remain dominant for a long time to come.

However, the new concept and repertoire of smooth field organization dissolves the strict dichotomy of public circulation versus private destination spaces and thus between public and private zones. The avant-garde interest in smooth and interpenetrating differentiations is not an unfounded enthusiasm. It is based on the identification of societal tendencies that at least point in the direction of more complex and dynamic forms of social organization that would find a better, more conducive registration and support in the regime of smooth differentiation that allows for conditions of smooth interpenetration and transitioning rather than relying on strict and determinate zoning. In any event, the distinction of the regime of striated space versus the regime of smooth fields is no either/or dichotomy. The two regimes can coexist. While the partition of space into private parcels within separate buildings dominates the building scale, on the urban scale the boundless urban sprawl and the continuous modulation of the urban fabric tend to produce smooth field conditions. Also, within large private parcels, for example, within malls or within large corporate headquarters, an interior urbanism becomes possible that is based on the smooth differentiation of field qualities rather than relying on enclosure and subdivision with their attendant strict distinction of circulation and destination spaces.

6.3.3 SYSTEMS, CONFIGURATIONS, ORGANIZATIONS

A configuration is defined as a set of spatial elements that can be considered as a unit of interaction. Such a set of spatial elements might be either ontologically *homogeneous* or *heterogeneous*. If the spatial elements within the configuration are of the same type we speak of an ontologically ***homogeneous*** configuration, for example, nothing but lines of circulation (channels), or nothing but territorial cells (with or without overlap), or nothing but a scatter of destination points etc. An analysis that would be able to describe an architectural or urban artefact by simultaneously referencing different types of spatial elements, for example, channels, cells, destination points, would be analyzing the architectural or urban artefact as an ontologically ***heterogeneous*** configuration.[96]

While all but the most simple design projects must inevitably become heterogeneous, during the design process the designer might be temporarily concerned with a particular subsystem of the project. Such a subsystem, if studied at a sufficiently high level of abstraction, might be considered and handled as a homogeneous configuration. The same

96 Space syntax seems to restrict its scope to the analysis of homogeneous configurations – a rather severe and artificial restriction.

might occur for the purposes of the theoretical analysis of a given built project, for example, the high level analysis of a project's structural system (skeleton) as a homogeneous configuration of linear structural members, or the high level analysis of a project's circulation system as a homogeneous configuration of linear paths. Notions like 'structural system' and 'circulation system' are commonplace. Not much thought is given to their designation as *systems*. The theory of architectural autopoiesis proposes to sharpen and regulate the use of this term: it is a fact that all members of a structure or all the paths of a path-network hang and act together and thus form a functional unit that warrants their qualification as system. Another example is a building's outer envelope. It is a system because it is a continuous, functional unit. A breach at any point compromises the performance of the whole envelope. Thus we can define: architectural and urban ***systems***[97] are ***collaborative unities.*** The minimum requirement here is that their parts (elements or subsystems) are ***functionally interdependent.*** This relation of functional dependence must be reciprocal or mutual, ie, each part impacts all other parts and is impacted by all other parts, directly or indirectly.

This definition alters some of the common uses of the term. For instance, a building envelope is a single, unitary system even if it is a collage or patchwork of disparate facade types, or a city's circulation system is a single system even if it comprises zones with grids, zones with radial organization, 'irregular' areas, as well as zones where these three types of configuration interpenetrate. Usually one might distinguish the gridded from the radial part as two different systems. In contrast the system concept proposed here does not require adherence to a unitary scheme. Indeed, no regularity is implied at all. The same applies to structural systems. Usually one might distinguish a post-beam system, from a portal-frame system, from a vaulting system etc. This usage of the term system – its indication of a certain internal coherence, generative principle, or rule – is taken up by the notion of organization. Instead of talking about different structural systems or different circulation systems in this way the theory of architectural autopoiesis proposes to talk about different principles of structural organization or different principles of circulatory organization etc.

On the other hand, certain classes of elements in the city are usually talked about as systems even if there is little or no evidence of them being functionally collaborative. That all the parks or green areas in a city form a system – the city's system of parks – cannot be taken for granted. Rather it is an empirical question that depends upon the citizens'

97 This definition encompasses subsystems. Subsystems are systems in this sense.

patterns of usage, ie, it depends, for instance, on whether and to what extent most citizens consider the different items within the named class – 'parks' – as functional substitutes for each other, so that, for example, a local park expansion is an effective expansion of the overall provision. Even the question of whether a city's street network in its totality does indeed form a system is not absolutely settled. Some of its parts might be so isolated and cut off from the actual flows moving through the city that their modification would have virtually no impact on the overall network. Such an isolated zone would therefore not belong to the city's circulation system, even if it were vitally to depend upon the rest of the city's network. According to our definition dependency has to be mutual. One-sided chains of dependency do not constitute systems.

The old way of thinking in distinct systems understood as different types – grid, spine or ring etc – is typical of the Modernist paradigm, and leads to questions such as: 'Which system should we employ here?' Contemporary sensibility – as well as contemporary reality – suggests a different approach. The different structural or circulatory typologies are hybridized or morphed into each other. What matters is that there emerges a collaborative unity. This collaborative unity might be internally differentiated in terms of different patterns of configuration. Different principles of organization might be distributed across the system. For instance, the different types of organization shown in Figure 5 might coexist in an overall patchwork configuration. Or they might coexist in the sense of an interpenetration, for example, an urban zone might be a spine in terms of vehicular circulation and a grid in terms of pedestrian circulation.

The system concept defined here admits both homogeneous and heterogeneous configurations. All that matters is that the components act together or at least mutually depend upon each other with respect to their respective performance. The term configuration is more general. Any co-present collection of spatial items can be taken and investigated as configuration. Christopher Alexander employed nearly the same concept of system defined here: 'When the elements of a set belong together because they co-operate or work together somehow, we call the set of elements a system.'[98] Alexander gives an example of a system that is interesting because of its extremely heterogeneous make up: 'For example, in Berkeley at the corner of Hearst and Euclid, there is a drugstore, and outside the drugstore a traffic light. In the entrance to the

98 Christopher Alexander, 'A City is not a Tree', in: Jonathan Crary (Ed), *Zone 1/2, The Contemporary City*, published by Urzone (New York), 1987, p 130, first published in: *Architectural Forum*, Vol 122, Nos 1 & 2, 1965.

drugstore there is a newsrack where the day's papers are displayed. When the light is red, people who are waiting to cross the street stand idly by the light; and since they have nothing to do, they look at the papers displayed on the newsrack which they can see from where they stand. Some of them just read the headlines, others actually buy a paper while they wait. This effect makes the newsrack and the traffic light interactive; the newsrack, the newspapers on it, the money going from people's pockets to the dime slot, the people who stop at the light and read papers, the traffic light, the electric impulses which make the lights change, and the sidewalk which the people stand on form a system – they all work together.'[99] Alexander's notion of a collaboratively functioning system anticipates the concept of an integrated action-artefact network[100] as the basis for analyzing and distilling the functional requirements that are to be fulfilled by the architectural system in question: 'From the designer's point of view, the physically unchanging part of this system is of special interest. The newsrack, the traffic light and the sidewalk between them, related as they are, form the fixed part of the system. It is the unchanging receptacle in which the changing parts of the system – people, newspapers, money and electrical impulses – can work together. I define this fixed part as a unit of the city. It derives its coherence as a unit both from the forces which hold its own elements together and from the dynamic coherence of the larger living system which includes it as a fixed invariant part.'[101] The only difference in the conceptualization proposed within the theory of architectural autopoiesis is the attempt to interpret the operations of both actors and artefacts as communications. A designed pavement communicates an invitation to pedestrians to stroll here. The actions of its pedestrian users communicate, in their manner of walking and overall demeanour, that they have understood and accepted the framing communication of the pavement.

The question whether a specifically defined or identified configuration is a system is a question that involves the concept of function. A system must function as a system. In contrast, the concept of configuration, as well as the concept of organization, is located in the domain of form. The forms, features and measures of configurations and organizations are initially analyzed without functional prejudice or reference to functional capacities. Only in a second step are the identified and described forms, features and measures of configurations and organizations investigated in

99 Ibid.

100 See chapter 6.1.7 *Functional Reasoning via Action-artefact Networks*.

101 Christopher Alexander, 'A City is not a Tree', in: Jonathan Crary (Ed), *Zone 1/2, The Contemporary City*, published by Urzone (New York), 1987, p 130, first published in: *Architectural Forum*, Vol 122, Nos 1 & 2, 1965.

terms of their functional capacities and possible functional application. The question whether a given configuration or organization works as a system, how it functions and whether it functions well, are questions that are best approached on the basis of a prior configurational/organizational analysis. Both the forms (configurations, organizations), understood as repertoire of potential solutions, and functions (activity networks), understood as problems, need to be theoretically prepared in order to be intelligently related to each other in the search for new, viable (high-performance) form-function complexes.[102]

A city's road-network hangs together. Any local blockage might have effects that ripple through the network and impact many distant (if not all) points. Therefore we must speak of a unified *system* of circulation, even if there are no systematic principles or general features that pervade the circulation network in all its parts. A system is given whenever many parts operate together, independent of the degree of organization and coherence of the system. There might be only one, several, or no principles of organization at work. In the latter case the circulation system is a mere configuration.

To mark the difference between a chaotic, random, unprincipled configuration and a configuration that is based on rules that pervasively structure the configuration, we employ the concept of organization defined above. Thus in terms of, for example, urban circulation networks, the notion of *circulation organization* should be reserved for the latter case where the whole circulation network is indeed patterned according to a certain systematically applied principle and therefore possesses a coherent global organization as well as general properties that pervade the respective system all the way through. Otherwise, in the absence of a systematically applied principle, we should restrict ourselves to speak of a given *circulation configuration*. Circulation configurations are therefore either *organized* or *unorganized*. However, the mere positing of this distinction does not imply that it is easy to operationalize and apply this distinction.

Above, organization was defined as the opposite of randomness. However, at this preliminary stage of setting out the basic concepts of a theory of organization, there is no strict a priori operational criterion of organization available that would allow us to dismiss an apparently

102 This theoretical project of enhancing the conceptual repertoire of formal (configurational, organizational) description and design is tentatively sketched out and started in section 6.4 *Supplementing Architecture with a Science of Configuration*. Mathematical network theory provides a purely formal repertoire while space syntax offers both formal measures and functional hypotheses.

random configuration as unorganized only because we can neither reproduce its rule nor recognize its organization. Rather, the theory of architectural autopoiesis is reckoning with an ever expanding repertoire of organizational processes/patterns. This does not mean that the unorganized is merely a receding limit case. No. Given the fragmented and haphazard way in which large urban agglomerations have been built up over long periods of time according to shifting and inconsistent influences, we should assume the absence of organization until we have decoded the underlying principles that have constrained randomness and thus imposed a certain degree of organization. The idea that organization in the case of urban settlement patterns should not only be thought of in terms of deterministic rules but rather in terms of certain rule-based constraints upon an otherwise random growth process is a fruitful starting point. Often these rules are rather local and take on only a few key parameters as factors that constrain the next move. The more aspects of an already given configuration are taken into account to constrain (if not determine) the next move, the more organized does the resultant configuration become.

Traditional notions of organization sought to avoid arbitrariness via adherence to a preconceived, ideal pattern or scheme. Contemporary notions of organization are much more open with respect to the mechanisms that might restrict randomness. Contemporary mechanisms hinge on the establishment of internal interdependencies between elements rather than on the dependency of elements on prior global schemata. (Accordingly, a notion of relative degrees of organization was defined on the basis of the relative density and diversity of interdependencies between the elements within a configuration.) However, here in the context of setting out the basic concepts for a comprehensive theory of architectural organization, simple schemata like grids or concentric-radial patterns cannot be excluded from the concept of organization versus mere configuration.

All circulation systems have a certain configuration. Circulation organizations are a subset of circulation configurations. The extent to which any given configuration can be specified by means of an explicit ordering principle might be referred to as circulation organization. Typical examples are the rigorous American street grids, or radial city plans with converging radials and concentric ring-roads. Karlsruhe and Moscow might serve as examples here. London might act as a typical example of a configuration without any evident, pervasive organizing principle. Different local patches might adhere to different local organizing principles. There are, however, certain general structural features that seem to be nearly ubiquitous throughout London. A good heuristic criterion for this is the fact that Londoners can navigate areas with which they have no familiarity. There seems to be a certain intuitive predictability at play here. Most probably this predictability relies not only on the organization of the street system itself, but could instead involve correlations with the lawful distribution of the built fabric. This indicates that an initially random or nearly random pattern can climb the gradient of relative organization by adding further elements according to mapping rules that create interdependencies and thus predictability (and, in our terms, more organization) without relying on prior schemata.

The same distinction and relationship between the concept of organization and the more general, encompassing concept of configuration can be defined with respect to the dimension of territorialization. Enclosure-and-division organizations are then set against mere enclosure-and-division configurations. We might also apply this distinction to conjunctions of differentiation- and integration-configurations. Some are organized – to a certain relative degree – and some seem unorganized.

Organizations are to be preferred over mere configurations. However, it should be clear by now that the distinction between organizations and mere configurations is not a simple, absolute and objective distinction. The distinction is relative to what is understood and accepted as an explicit principle of organization. There are degrees of organization that can be assessed only comparatively, when comparing configurations that are somehow versions of each other. The distinction of organizations in relation to mere configurations thus depends upon what can be analyzed with a given theoretical apparatus.

What might appear as unorganized or arbitrary might reveal a hidden organization through an upgraded analysis that has a more advanced, richer repertoire of organizational notions at its disposal. Recently the available canon of organizational principles has been expanded to include formation processes that allow for a certain degree of unpredictability, freedom or randomization while still affording the ascertainment of certain global statistical properties. Modernists like Le Corbusier were operating with a rather restrictive notion of organization. He admired the urban regularity of Roman cities and rejected the irregularity of medieval cities as 'the pack-donkey's way'.[103] Le Corbusier's limitation is not his insistence upon regularity but his limited concept of regularity in terms of

103 Le Corbusier, *The City of Tomorrow and its Planning*, Dover Publications (New York), 1987, translated from French original *Urbanisme*, Crès & Cie (Paris), 1925, p 8.

Classical geometry. Complexity theory (chaos theory) in general, and the research of Frei Otto in particular, have since taught us to recognize, measure and simulate the complex patterns of organization that emerge from processes of self-organization. Phenomena like the 'donkey's path' of least resistance and the urban patterns resulting from unplanned settlement processes can now be analyzed and appreciated in terms of their hidden organizational principles, and thus (at least approximate or stochastic) predictability.

The question whether an agglomeration of multiple organizations can be construed as an organization is also open to debate. This relative vagueness and openness of the distinction is rather an advantage at this stage of building a theory of architectural organization. It leaves scope for evolving the concepts together with the development of the theory.[104] The more configurations are recognized and understood as spatial organizations, the more advanced is the state of the discipline's organizational intelligence.[105] At this stage of the theory it makes sense to open up the concept of spatial organization as much as possible and let the boundary of the concept be marked by the utterly arbitrary and formless, ie, configurations that resist any attempts to be predicted, summarized and reproduced.

In contrast, the concept of order imposes a rather strict selection criterion with respect to pertinent organizations. Order requires that articulation is able to make the underlying organization perceptually palpable and legible. The theory of architectural autopoiesis insists that any claim concerning the accomplishment of urban or architectural *order* must simultaneously reflect the conditions that impact the cognition of the proposed organization. We can only claim that a complex order has been achieved, if the constructed/conceived organization has a reasonable chance to be perceived/understood, not by organizational scientists but by the (well-socialized) users of architecture.

104 Are Voronoi patterns systems of spatial organization? All or only some? How about L-systems? This depends upon how these patterns are explicitly set up, analyzed, understood and handled. There is an open-ended number of networking algorithms that might be defined and applied to any given point cloud. As scripting becomes ever more widespread as design technique we might raise the question: should we classify any configuration that results from recursive, rule-based pattern-formation as spatial organisation? The theory of architectural autopoiesis answers this question in the affirmative.

105 The theory of architectural autopoiesis concurs with Bill Hillier's assessment that the difficulty of talking about spatial configuration in architecture is a central problem of architectural theory. Bill Hillier, *Space is the Machine*, p 38.

6.4 Supplementing Architecture with a Science of Configuration

THESIS 28

The task of organization today requires a more explicit and more elaborate repertoire of organizational patterns and more explicit, precise criteria for their evaluation than what can be reasonably expected from the tacit knowledge and accumulated wisdom of an experienced architect.

To give traction to the distinction of organized versus unorganized configurations requires a repertoire of concepts and principles of organization. What follows is an attempt to contribute to the build up of such a repertoire.

So far we have only established some basic definitions in preparation for a theory of architectural organization.

Above, the need for a systematic 'art of organization' was stipulated, ie, a theory and technique of organization that build their heuristic principles upon a rich descriptive terminology and a systematic apparatus of concepts, measures and theorems. How can such an 'art of organization' be developed? Are there intellectual resources to draw on? Is there a science that can be consulted and exploited for the task of architectural organization?

There are indeed well-elaborated resources that architecture can draw upon to enhance its organizational intelligence: the resources of discrete mathematics (or finite mathematics), most generally ***set theory***, and more specifically combinatorics with its subdisciplines of ***network theory*** (graph theory) and order theory.

6.4.1 SET THEORY

The concepts of set theory have become the most fundamental and ubiquitous concepts of all logic and mathematics. Two of the most basic concepts within set theory – the concept of membership and the concept of containment – can be perfectly well illustrated by the fundamental architectural relation of enclosure. That this fundamental concept of logic should find its most illustrative exemplification in architecture should encourage architects to explore this domain further.

Set theory commences with a very simple ontology. There are two primitive entities: *elements* and *sets*, and the basic relation of membership – *being an element of* – relating elements with sets. A set is an unordered collection of elements. A given element either does or does not belong to a given set. The are some basic relationships that can hold between a given number of sets:

1. *containment*, whereby one set is fully contained within another. A contains B implies that B is a *subset* of A, ie, all of B's elements are also elements of the containing set A.
2. *intersection*, whereby two (or more) sets intersect and share some elements common to both (all).
3. *disjointedness*, whereby sets are disjoint, ie, they do not have any elements in common.
4. *complementarity*, whereby two sets are disjoint and together fully dissect the domain within which they are defined.

There are some basic operations performed on sets: *set union*, *set intersection, set subtraction* and *set complement*. These are operations that produce a new set from any one, two, or more given sets. The *union* of two sets A and B is the set C which features all of the elements that are in A or B or in both. The resultant set C contains both A and B. The *intersection* of two sets A and B is the set C which features only those elements which are in both A and B. The *complement* of set A is the set B that features all of the objects in the universal set except those in A.

To visualize relationships between elements and sets, as well as relationships between different sets, a graphic notation called ***Venn diagrams*** might be used. Venn diagrams represent sets by convex bounding lines that encircle all the elements the set contains. The 'paper space' represents 'the universe'. The complement set is thus the area that surrounds a closed outline. The containment or subset relation is depicted by means of one outline fully encircling another, and the relation of intersection is depicted by the overlapping or interpenetration of the respective bounded areas. The area of overlap then represents the set generated by the intersection of the intersecting sets and might be denoted in its own right.

The representational device of the Venn diagrams allows us to ascertain some key logical relations by visual inspection. For instance, the transitivity of the containment relation can be immediately read from the graphic representation as relation of spatial inclusion: the nesting of bounded domains. This law of the transitivity of the containment relation is in fact the fundamental figure of logical inference since Aristotle. His first ***syllogism*** reads: if all A are B and all B are C then all A are C. The graphic representation of its set-theoretic equivalent is the simple diagram of three concentric circles, with A in the centre and C on the

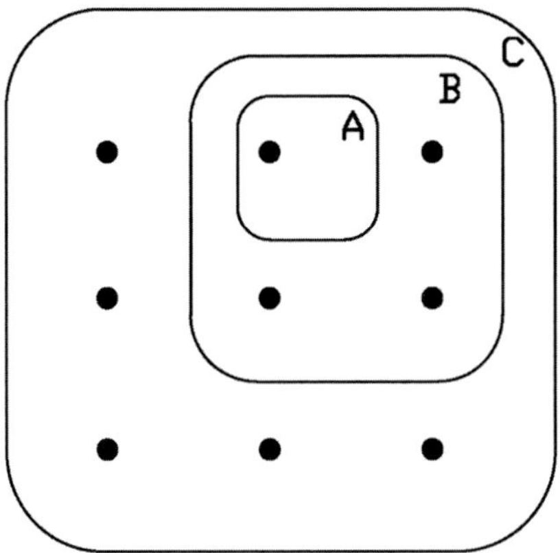

Figure 6 Syllogism Barbara as Venn diagram

outside. Set B is in the middle, representing the so-called middle or mediating term in Aristotle's first syllogism.[106]

We might interpret bubble diagrams, the architect's primary tool for setting out the primary spatial organization or parti of his/her design, as a variant of Venn diagrams that operates with relations of spatial containment. The difference is that bubble diagrams are usually processing further information like the adjacencies of the domains to be organized, and perhaps the rough relative sizes of the domains. While bubble diagrams give meaning to the relative position of the bubbles that are collected within an enclosing bubble, Venn diagrams do not interpret this (graphically unavoidable) feature of relative spatial position. It is noteworthy that until relatively recently bubble intersection in bubble diagrams was taboo. Relations of disjointedness and relations of containment were the only relations considered.

In Venn diagrams spatialization is only utilized to represent the abstract relations of containment, intersection and disjointedness while the relative sizes and adjacency positions are irrelevant and might be chosen arbitrarily, or according to the exigencies of illustrative clarity. The Venn diagram proper, if applied to architecture, would spatialize neither more nor less than the logical relations of subsumption that are usually presented in the schedule of accommodation with its chapter and subchapter titles, each heading a list of spaces to be accommodated under the various chapters.

106 The philosophical significance of this parallelism between primary logical relations and tropes of spatial organization will be reflected below, in the chapter 8.6.2 *From Spatial Order to Conceptual Order*.

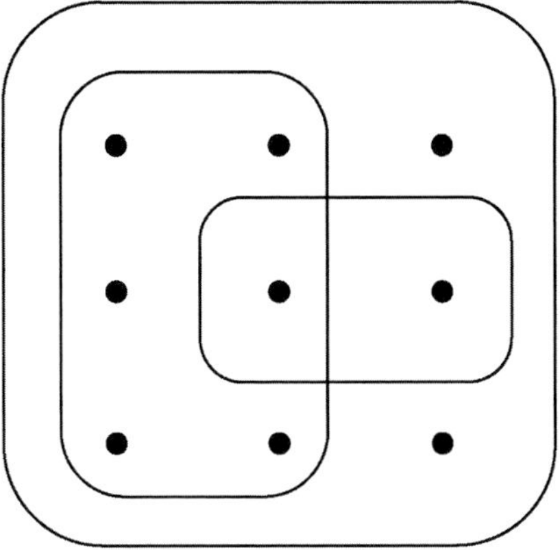

Figure 7 Venn diagram with intersecting sets

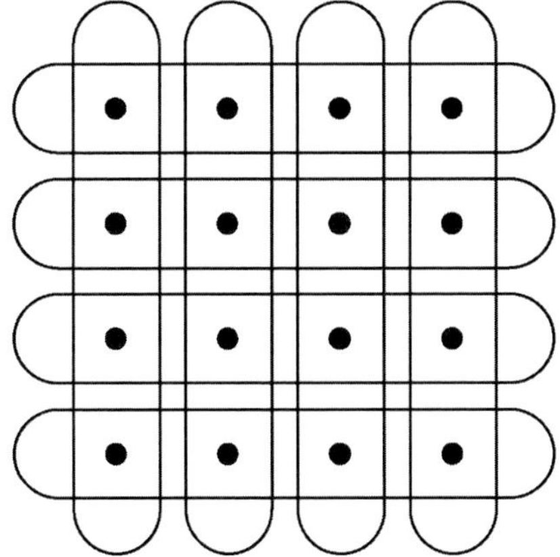

Figure 8 Matrix of 4 x 4 sets

If we thus juxtapose the conceptual apparatus of set theory with the usual structure of architectural briefs given in the form of schedules of accommodation, one blindspot is again salient: the total absence of intersection or overlap within the normal form of the architectural brief. Intersection, one of the key relations of interest within set theory, seems to be excluded from architectural organization from the very start. Only relations of full containment and relations of full disjointedness are recognized. As already mentioned, until relatively recently the overlap of domains was not only absent from architectural briefs but was also absent from the design repertoire of architecture and urbanism. The interpenetration of domains – a key pursuit of Deconstructivist and

Parametricist architecture – was not considered as a meaningful spatial operation.

This rejection of overlap had for a long time also been a hallmark of modern social organizations such as government bureaucracies and business corporations. The overruling idea of organization theory during the first half of the 20th century was clarity of the lines of command. Departmental affiliation should be unambiguous, ie, the domains of competency were supposed to be clearly and singularly allocated. Overlap implied confusion. However, this has since changed drastically, and the idea of overlapping domains of competency has become a part of standard organizational strategies establishing so-called matrix organizations where functional and divisional segmentations cross.

In terms of a mathematics of organization inspired by set theory, one might point here to the exponential increase in differentiation and complexity that can be achieved if one works with intersecting sets rather than being restricted to disjointedness and containment. Both in the case of the juxtaposition of disjointed sets and with respect to the concentric nesting of sets within sets, the further placement of each set increases the complexity of the overall organization by one additional position only. With the admission of intersection the complexity of the overall organization increases by multiplication rather than addition. With each single new set that intersects the given cluster of sets, the overall number of positions increases by the number of sets intersected by the new set. Each set that is intersected by the new set allows for the establishment of a new position in the respective area of overlap generated. The result is a rapid increase in organizational complexity that has the advantage of being reducible to a very small number of key determinants.

The absence of architectural and urban overlap was famously criticized by Christopher Alexander in relation to modern urban planning. Commencing with Alexander's influential polemic 'A City is not a Tree' published in 1965 and with Colin Rowe's and Robert Slutzky's nearly simultaneous landmark article 'Transparency: Literal and Phenomenal', first published in 1963, the idea of spatial intersection and 'super-position' gathered pace during the 1970s, in the work of Michael Graves, Peter Eisenman, and others, to become one of the key preoccupations of the architectural avant-garde during the 1980s, perhaps best exemplified by Bernard Tschumi's 1985 winning entry for the grand competition for Paris' Parc de la Villette. The idea of spatial super-position was followed by further concepts that instantiate the logic of intersecting sets within architecture: cross-programming, hybridity and multiple affiliation.

6.4.2 HARNESSING NETWORK THEORY

That the resources offered within discrete mathematics might be pertinent with respect to the task of spatial organization in architecture and urbanism is most immediately obvious with respect to ***network theory*** (graph theory). The mathematics of networks seems to be most pertinent to the field of urbanism. However, both the logic and the graphic representations that illustrate the basic concepts of network theory are also instantiated in the familiar connection diagrams that often accompany the schedule of accommodation in design briefs, whereby each required connection between programme components is indicated by a line linking the labelled boxes representing the respective programme components. The architect's first task is to translate this abstract connection diagram into a spatial configuration that takes the relative sizes of the required spaces into account and interprets connection as adjacency.[107]

The most basic entities (primitives) that constitute networks or graphs – the elements and the relations between those elements – are referred to as nodes (or vertices) and links (or edges). In its most simple, default mode the links are binary, symmetric and irreflexive relations.[108] However this basic ontology might be expanded to include directional links (*directed* vs *undirected* graphs), and a further expansion allows for links to be *weighted* or *signed* (plus vs minus). Street networks might be presented by undirected, but weighted networks, whereby the capacities, or the metric distances between junctions might be translated into weights.

The network theoretical representation of, for example, a circulation configuration (street pattern) – given or to be designed – allows for a series of rigorous definitions and computational solutions, for instance for the shortest path between any two nodes measured by the number of intervening nodes, or various measures for node positions like the relative centrality of a node within a given network, definable in a variety of ways. Graph theory provides the solution for various problems that are relevant in certain architectural or urban problem-contexts. For instance, the famous Königsberg Bridges problem: is it possible to cross the seven bridges of Königsberg (connecting two islands in the river with each other and with the opposite riverbanks) in a continuous walk without recrossing

107 In complex briefs the desired connections mostly overreach the possibility of being solved via immediate adjacency relations.

108 The characterization of the basic relation as binary, symmetric and irreflexive relation implies that each relation links only two elements, and if vertex *a* is linked to vertex *b*, then *b* is *eo ipso* linked to *a*. Links are only defined between different vertices, ie, a vertex cannot be linked to itself.

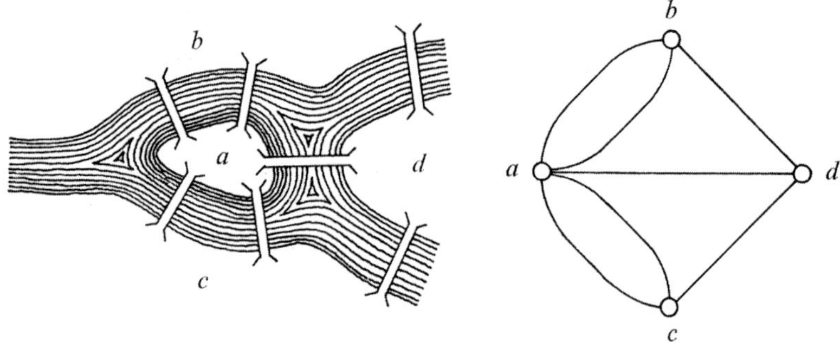

Figure 9 Euler's solution to the famous problem of the seven bridges of Königsberg. From March & Steadman, *The Geometry of Environment*, 1971

them? Graph theory can prove that the multi-graph representing the situation has no trail containing all links. The graph-theoretic formalism facilitates the implementation of various graph algorithms such as the depth-first-search, shortest path search, single-source shortest path problem, the route inspection problem (also called the 'Chinese Postman Problem') and optimal routing problems such as the famous travelling salesman problem.[109]

There are numerous problems that can be formalized with graphs, especially problems that have to do with flows in networks. A *network flow* is an assignment of flow to the edges of a directed graph (called a *flow network* in this case) where each edge has a *capacity*, such that the amount of flow along an edge does not exceed its capacity. In addition you have the restriction that the amount of flow into a node equals the amount of flow out of it (unless it is a *source*, which only has outgoing flow, or *sink*, which has only incoming flow). A flow network can be used to simulate fluids in pipes, currents in an electrical circuit, or anything where something travels through a network, including, for example, the traffic that might flow within a given road system.

Networks/graphs are represented graphically by plotting a dot for every node (vertex), and by drawing a line between two nodes if they are connected by a link (edge), and by drawing arrows in the case of directed graphs. A network/graph drawing should not be confused with the network/graph itself (the abstract organizational structure). There are always multiple ways to draw the network/graph. All that matters is the

109 A salesman starts at a certain point and has to reach all of a given set of points. If the distances between every pair of points are known, what is the shortest route which visits all points and returns to the point of origin?

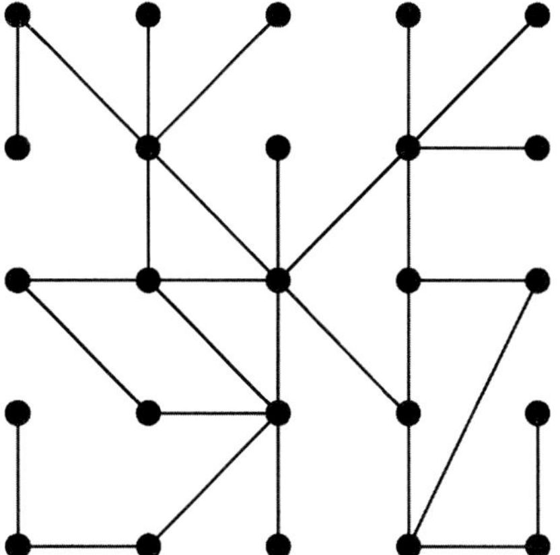

Figure 10 Network diagram

logic of the connection pattern, not the spatial layout. In practice it is often difficult to decide whether two drawings represent the same network/graph. Depending on the problem domain, some layouts may be better suited and easier to understand than others. In fact this multitude of possible drawings (spatializations) of the abstract organizational pattern is the first part of the problem of architectural design understood as projection of abstract (social) organization into space.

We can therefore introduce the following distinction for our specific architectural purposes: the distinction between ***logical configuration*** and ***spatial configuration*** and the related distinction between *spatio-configurational* equivalence and *logico-configurational* equivalence. This distinction makes sense with respect to the graphic (spatial) representation and architectural/urban instantiation of networks, and goes beyond network theory proper. We define two spatial network patterns to be *logico-configurationally* equivalent if they represent the same network/graph as defined by network/graph theory. We define two spatial network patterns to be *spatio-configurationally* equivalent if they are *logico-configurationally* equivalent and also conserve the same adjacency relations – left of, right of, above, below, or: north of, south of, west of, east of – between the plotted node positions. Two spatial networks that are *spatio-configurationally* equivalent will exhibit the same pattern of link-intersection, while *logico-configurationally* equivalence is consistent with rather different patterns of link-intersection. While link-intersections in plotted network/graphs carry no meaning in network/graph theory, they might be significant with respect to certain architectural/urban applications. A specific task might for instance suggest that a given logical configuration should be spatialized with a minimum (or conversely with a maximum) of link intersections.

We surmise here that the abstract structure of a homogeneous spatial configuration – be it a differentiation (parcellation) pattern or an integration (circulation) pattern – can be fully described and analyzed within the formalization offered by set theory and/or network theory. So far we have introduced two formalisms with their attendant graphic languages: a set-calculus spatialized in Venn diagrams and a network-calculus spatialized in node-link diagrams. Venn diagrams seem to be able to abstract (or construct) the logic of parcellation or zoning configurations in as much as relations of spatial disjointedness (segmentation), containment (nesting) and intersection (interpenetration) between domains are involved or intended. Node-link diagrams seem predestined to represent, explore and measure the configurational characteristics of circulation configurations on both urban and architectural scales. However, node-link diagrams are also well suited to represent, explore and measure any given parcellation configuration by representing parcels as nodes and shared boundaries as links. The node-link diagram can even be used to represent the set-theoretical relation of containment. In this case, since containment is asymmetrical, we need to employ directed graphs. The directed link from A to B can thus represent that A contains/encloses B. (Figures 11 & 12 encode the containment relation – A contains B – as a downward link from A to B.) The concentric nesting sequence becomes a monodirectional chain of directed links. The typical nesting pattern, whereby each set in the order of subsumption contains multiple subsets, can be represented by a branching pattern of directed links. This pattern is referred to as a *tree*. In the tree pattern each node receives one incoming link from the node representing the containing set (or enclosing parcel) and generates multiple outgoing links representing the various contained subsets (or fully enclosed parcels).[110] Those subsets are disjoint and the node from which they spring is their union. This graphic notation can also represent set-configurations with intersecting sets. In this case the directed graph is no longer a tree, but instead allows nodes to have multiple incoming links implying that the respective element or set (parcel) is the intersection set of the various sets represented by the incoming links. This possibility of establishing an isomorphism between network diagrams and Venn diagrams is a rather interesting opportunity for organizational analysis and synthesis in architecture.

110 Trees have the interesting property that any two nodes are connected by *exactly one* path.

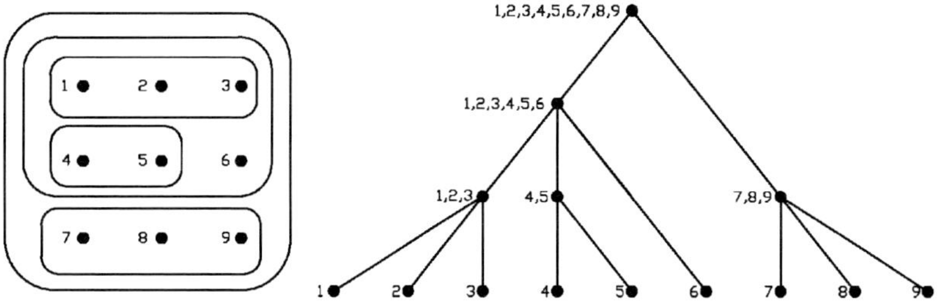

Figure 11 Nested sets: Venn diagram vs network diagram (tree); links are directed downwards encoding the containment relation

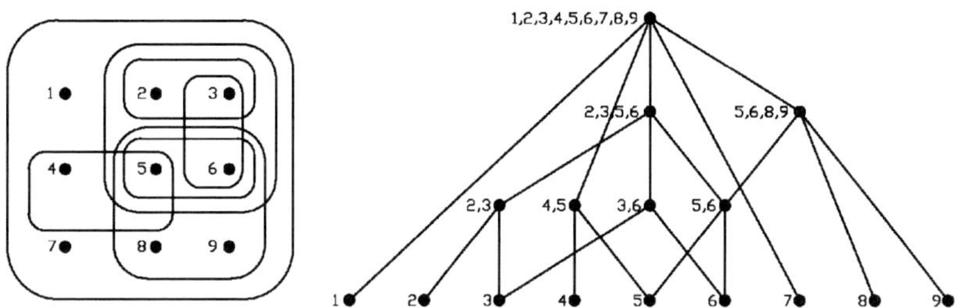

Figure 12 Intersecting sets: Venn diagram vs network diagram (semi-lattice); links are directed downwards encoding the containment relation

Venn diagrams and network diagrams might also be combined in a single graphic notation. So-called *hypergraphs* constitute such a combination. Hypergraphs might be used to depict partitioned networks. Partitioned networks are networks that are partitioned into zones by enclosing bounding lines that segment off and collect a certain number of nodes. Within an architectural design process one might use and interpret a hypergraph as follows: the nodes might represent programme components (activities). Links between nodes might represent adjacencies, perhaps categorized or even weighted to represent the quality or degree of direct accessibility (wall with opening vs wall with door vs low partition wall etc). The enclosing lines can operate very much like the encircling lines in Venn diagrams, expressing the basic relationships of inclusion, exclusion and intersection between sets. The nodes within the enclosures are now the elements within the sets or parcels. The operation of encirclement or segmentation within a partitioned network implies that some of the links within the network are now crossing a partition boundary with one node of the binary link being inside the bounded domain while the other node is outside. This new expanded ontology comprising nodes and links plus enclosures is still fully encompassed within network/graph theory. In fact the enclosing lines might be considered to be so-called hyperlinks. Hyperlinks are a variation of the network-theoretical link whereby one basic constraint of the link is lifted: the hyperlink is no longer constrained to represent a binary relation, but can instead link up an arbitrary number of nodes. Networks or graphs that use hyperlinks are called hyper-networks or hyper-graphs. A possible graphical representation for hyper-graphs is an enclosing outline capturing all and only those nodes to be linked by the hyperlink. The captured nodes can be interpreted as sets of related activities/programmes that are to be enclosed within a domain. In the absence of any rule that a node can only be captured by one hyperlink, the formalism allows for overlap or intersecting sets/domains.

With the hyper-network formalism both spatial differentiation and integration patterns can be built up and analyzed within a single representation: layout diagrams showing the partitioning of space together with the accessibility network of connections. Thus we have identified some pertinent diagramming formalisms for constructing and analyzing complex spatial organizations. There are various mathematical measures/calculations that tie in with these formalisms and thus allow for the utilization of mathematical techniques that might help architecture to cope with the increasing complexity of its task. These formalisms provide a basic conceptual, computational and notational set up on the basis of which concepts, measures and organizational principles can now be developed.

The mathematics of network theory does indeed hold the promise of an enhanced descriptive, analytical and constructive power for the organizational intelligence of architecture. Obviously, the primitives, various compound definitions, and especially the mathematical questions and theorems have not been crafted in response to the particular problems of architectural organization. Thus we will encounter a lot of material that is not readily applicable or useful. Pure mathematics is in permanent exchange with a wide range of applications. It also has its own immanent dynamic. The overabundance of conceptual material compensates for its lack of specific focus. In fact, it is the very promiscuity of mathematics – coupled with its radical abstractness – that makes mathematics so fertile as an exchange hub and transmission system for conceptual structures.[111]

111 This function as conceptual exchange hub makes mathematics comparable to philosophy. Both mathematics and philosophy fulfil parallel functions and are equally abstract. The difference is in the kind of conceptual structures that are being traded and the type of user manuals that are

The application domains of network theory (graph theory) include the basic fields of physics (force vectors), chemistry (analysis of molecular structures) and biology (metabolic networks). A lot of the recent work in network theory evolved in exchanges with computer science and related domains of application like chip design, neural networks, analysis of Internet link-structures, search engines etc. But network theory is also heavily utilized with respect to many spatial problem domains that more or less directly interface with urban and architectural questions, like geographic mapping and traffic analysis/simulation. Network theory has also been productive in linguistics, and most importantly in the social sciences under the name of *social network analysis*.

Of course, nothing stops architecture from constructing its own specifically crafted mathematics of spatial configuration, and this might indeed happen. There is in fact a rather successful example of a specifically crafted utilization of the basic concepts and techniques of network theory in the context of architecture and urbanism: Bill Hillier's theory and practice of 'space syntax'. Hillier also demonstrates how the mathematical reconstruction of a question paves the way for its computer-aided solution.

Before taking a closer look at Hillier's achievements we will briefly scan through some mathematical raw material, roughly filtered according to what seems to hold a potential for architectural application. The purpose here can only be to inspire curiosity and motivation for future work.

6.4.3 EXCURSION: NETWORK THEORY

This excursion offers a short exposition of network theory, presented via the successive build up of definitions, at times augmented by brief notes indicating typical applications in various fields. This short exposition avoids all mathematical notation. Hunches concerning the potential for fruitful applicability within architecture will emanate between the lines. What will become evident is a general sense of the productivity of a systematic build up of well-defined, complex concepts resulting in an overall system of concepts that combines expressive and heuristic power with precision.

Basic definitions:

Graph: An (undirected) graph (or network) is a finite set – the so-called vertex set with each element being referred to as ***vertex*** (or node) – together with an irreflexive, symmetric relation that defines ordered

provided. While philosophy trades in the most fundamental categories (paradigms) and provides epistemologically self-reflective user guides, mathematics provides technically precise formalisms and fully operational, technical user manuals.

pairs of vertices called ***edges*** (or links), together forming the edge-set that completely determines the respective relation. The *order* of a graph is the number of vertices within the graph. The *size* of the graph is the number of edges within the graph.

Adjacency: Two vertices (nodes) are *adjacent* if and only if they are joined by an edge (link).

There are a number of cross-cutting qualifications that define various modifications of the basic definition of a graph:

Directed graph: A directed graph (or *digraph*) is a graph whereby the defining relation is non-symmetric, for example, as might be used to indicate the direction of traffic in a traffic analysis graph.

Mixed graph: A mixed graph may contain both directional and non-directional (symmetric) links.

Signed graph: A signed graph is a graph whereby each edge receives either a plus sign or a minus sign. (Often used in social network analysis where a relationship might be positive or negative.)

Weighted graph: A weighted graph is a graph where the links are numerically weighted.

Multi-graph: A multi-graph is a graph where the restriction that the defining relation should be binary is lifted, ie, there might be more than one direct link between two nodes.

Further definitions:

Degree: The *degree* of a node is the number of nodes it is adjacent to; or, equivalently, it is the number of edges that are incident upon it. A node with degree 0 is an *isolate*, with degree 1 a *pendant*. In a *directed graph*, we can distinguish *indegrees* and *outdegrees*. A node with a positive outdegree but no indegree is called a *source*. A node with a positive indegree but no outdegree is called a *sink*.

Subgraph: A *subgraph* of a graph G is a graph whose vertices and edges are also in G. If we select a set of nodes from a graph, and then select *all* the edges that connect those nodes within this graph, the resulting subgraph is called an *induced subgraph*.

Walk: A *walk* is a sequence of adjacent vertices (nodes) together with the edges (links) that connect them. A walk might traverse nodes/links more than once, ie, a walk is a path in which segments may be repeated.

Path: A path is a walk in which no node is visited more than once. A path is a subgraph that is a linear sequence of connected vertices through a given graph. A path is itself a connected graph with degree 2 at every vertex.

Cycle: A cycle or *circuit* is a closed path without self-intersections. It is a connected graph with degree 2 at every vertex.

Disjointedness: A set of walks that share no vertices is called *vertex-disjoint*. A set of walks that share no edges is called *edge-disjoint*. Obviously, vertex-disjoint paths are also edge-disjoint. If a pair of nodes are connected by three vertex-disjoint paths, this means that there are three completely independent ways of getting from one point to the other.

Geodesics: A *geodesic* path is a shortest path between two nodes. There can be more than one geodesic path joining a given pair of nodes. The *graph-theoretic distance* or *geodesic distance* between two nodes is the length of the shortest path between them.

Complete graph: In a *complete graph* each pair of vertices is joined by an edge, ie, the graph contains all possible edges.

Bipartite graph: In a *bipartite graph* the vertices can be divided into two sets, so that every edge has one vertex in each of the two sets.

Complete bipartite graph: In a *complete bipartite graph* the vertex set is the union of two disjoint subsets, so that every vertex in one is adjacent to every vertex in the other but there are no edges within either.

Planar graph: A planar graph can be drawn in a plane with no crossing edges. The graph is *'embedded'* in a plane.

Fáry's theorem: The theorem states that any simple planar graph can be drawn without crossings so that its edges are straight line segments. That is, the ability to draw graph edges as curves instead of as straight line segments does not allow a larger class of graphs to be drawn.

Clique: A clique within an undirected graph is a subgraph or set of vertices such that for every two vertices in the subgraph there exists an edge connecting the two, ie, every vertex in the clique is joined with every other vertex in the clique. This is equivalent to saying that the subgraph is a complete graph. The *clique number* of a graph is the order (number of vertices) of the largest clique within this graph.

Connected graphs: A graph is *connected* if there exists a path from every node to every other node. A digraph that satisfies the connectedness definition is called *strongly connected*, ie, for any pair of nodes *a* and *b*, there exists both a path from *a* to *b* and from *b* to *a*. A digraph is *unilaterally connected* if between every unordered pair of nodes there is at least one path that connects them. A digraph whose underlying graph is connected is called *weakly connected*.

Maximal subgraph: A *maximal subgraph* is a subgraph that satisfies some specified property (such as being connected) and to which no node can be added without violating the property.

Component: A maximal connected subgraph is called a *component*.

Cutpoint: A cutpoint is a node whose removal would disconnect the graph. Alternatively, we could define a cutpoint as a node whose removal would increase the number of components of the graph. For instance, a social network that contains a cutpoint will break apart if the person who occupies the cutpoint leaves.

Bridge: A *bridge* is a link or edge whose removal disconnects the graph.

Block: A *block* is a subgraph which contains no cutpoints.

Cutset: A cutset is a set of points whose removal would disconnect a graph. A *minimal cutset* is a cutset that contains the minimum possible number of nodes that disconnect the graph. An *edge cutset* is a set of lines whose removal disconnects the graph.

Vertex connectivity: The size of a minimal cutset is called the *vertex connectivity* of the graph. The smaller the value, the greater the vulnerability of the network to disconnection. We can also define a pairwise version of vertex connectivity, which gives the minimum number of (intermediary) nodes that must be removed in order to disconnect two nodes.

Menger's theorem: Menger's theorem states that the minimum number of nodes that must be removed to disconnect two nodes is equal to the maximum number of vertex-disjoint paths that join *those* two nodes. This also works for lines.

Edge-connectivity: The edge-connectivity between two edges is equal to the maximum number of edge-disjoint paths that join the two edges.

Tree: A tree is a graph in which any two nodes are connected by *exactly one* path. A tree is a connected graph with no cycles, ie, trees are *acyclical*. A tree is called a *rooted tree* if one vertex has been designated the *root*, in which case the edges have a natural orientation, *towards* or *away* from the root. Rooted trees are well suited to analyze social hierarchies, for example, in business organizations where every member of the organization has one and only one superior. The single path translates into the single line of command and reporting. All parts of the hierarchy which are not vertically linked to one another can nevertheless be linked by travelling up the hierarchy to find a common direct or indirect superior, and then down again. Every finite tree structure has a single member that has no superior. This member is the root or root node. A node without outgoing link is called *end-node* or *leaf*. In a tree a directed edge refers to the link from the superior node (*parent*) to the inferior node (*child*).

Depth: The depth of a node n is the length of the path from the root to the node. The set of all nodes at a given depth is called a *level* of the tree (like a level within a hierarchy).

Height: The height of a tree is the length of the path from the root node to its furthest leaf.

Ancestors/descendants: If a path exists from node p to node q, then p is an ancestor of q and q is a descendant of p.

Size: In a tree the size of a node is the number of descendants it has including itself.

Binary tree: A rooted binary tree is a rooted tree in which every node has at most two children.

Full binary tree: A full binary tree, or proper binary tree, is a tree in which every node has zero or two children.

Perfect binary tree: A perfect binary tree (sometimes complete binary tree) is a *full binary tree* in which all *leaves* are at the same *depth*.

Spanning tree: A spanning tree of a graph is a selection of edges from this graph that form a tree *spanning* every vertex. That is, every vertex is connected to the tree, but no cycles (or loops) are formed.

Forest: A forest is a graph in which any two vertices are connected by *at most one* path. An equivalent definition is that a forest is a union of disjoint trees.

Network measures and node measures:

Centrality: There are different centrality measures for nodes within networks, describing the relative position or importance of the nodes and links in a network. The *degree* is the simplest measure distinguishing relative importance. More pertinent is the measure of centrality that considers both direct and indirect links and measures centrality by shortest number of total steps by which all other nodes within the network can be reached from the node in question.

Chromatic number: The chromatic number is the least number of colours needed to colour the graph whereby no joint vertices can have the same colour. For instance, six colours suit a complete graph with six vertices, but fewer colours would result in adjacent vertices of the same colour.

Perfect graph: A perfect graph is a graph in which the chromatic number of every induced subgraph equals the clique number of that subgraph. In any graph, the clique number provides a lower bound for the chromatic number, as all vertices in a clique must be assigned distinct colours. The perfect graphs are those for which this lower bound is tight, not just in the graph itself but in all of its induced subgraphs. For more general graphs, the chromatic number and clique number can differ; for example, a cycle of length five requires three colours in any proper colouring but its largest clique has size two.

Related theorem: The complement of a bipartite graph is perfect.

Arboricity: The arboricity of a graph is the minimum number of spanning trees needed to cover all the edges of the graph.

Thickness: The thickness of a graph is the minimum number of planar subgraphs into which its edges can be partitioned. As any planar graph has arboricity three, the thickness of any graph is at least equal to a third of the arboricity, and at most equal to the arboricity.

There are a number of standard operations that operate on graphs to produce new graphs:

Line graph: The operation line graph converts nodes into links and vice versa.

Dual graph: A dual graph of a given planar graph *G* has a vertex for each plane region of *G*, and an edge for each edge joining two neighbouring regions. This property is symmetric, ie, these graphs come in pairs.

Complement graph: The complement or inverse of a graph *G* is a graph *H* on the same vertices such that two vertices of *H* are adjacent if and only if they are not adjacent in *G*.

Concerning complex networks:

***Complex network*:** The term *complex network* refers to a network/graph that has certain non-trivial topological features that do not occur in simple networks. Such non-trivial features include: a *heavy-tail* in the degree distribution, a high *clustering coefficient*, *assortativity* or *disassortativity* among vertices; *community structure* at many scales; and evidence of a *hierarchical* structure. In contrast, simple networks have none of these properties and are typically represented by graphs such as a lattice or a random graph, which exhibit a high similarity no matter what part is examined.

Heavy-tailed: A heavy-tailed probability distribution is one that assigns relatively high probabilities to regions far from the mean or median.

Clustering coefficient: The clustering coefficient for a vertex is the proportion of links between the vertices within its neighbourhood divided by the number of links that could possibly exist between them. This measures 1 if every neighbour connected to the vertex is also connected to every other vertex within the neighbourhood, and 0 if none of vertices that are connected to the vertex in question connects to any of the other vertices connected to the vertex in question. The clustering coefficient is a graph measure that can be used to determine whether or not a graph is a small-world network.

Assortativity: Assortativity refers to a preference for a network's nodes to attach to others that are similar or different in some way. Though the specific measure of similarity may vary, network theorists often examine assortativity in terms of a node's degrees. Correlations between nodes of similar degree are found in many social networks: highly connected nodes tend to be connected with other high degree nodes.

***Dissortativity**:* Conversely *dissortativity* implies that high degree nodes tend to attach to low degree nodes.

***Community structures**:* A community structure within a network is a group of nodes which are more densely interconnected with each other than with the rest of the network. A network might contain multiple communities. This inhomogeneity suggests that the network has certain natural divisions within it. Communities might overlap. Social networks often include community groups based on common location, interests, occupation, etc. Metabolic networks have communities based on functional groupings. Citation networks form communities by research topic.

Small-world networks: A small-world network is a graph in which the average number of edges between any two vertices is very small (mathematically, it should grow as the logarithm of the size of the network), while the clustering coefficient stays large. A network is called a small-world network by analogy with the small-world phenomenon known as *six degrees of separation*: the small world hypothesis is the idea that two arbitrary people are connected by only six intermediaries. With the addition of only a small number of long-range links, a regular graph, in which the *diameter* is proportional to the size of the network, can be transformed into a 'small world'. A wide variety of abstract graphs exhibits the small-world property, for example, scale-free networks and random graphs.

***Scale-free networks**:* Scale-free networks are *complex networks*. A network is named scale-free if its degree distribution, ie, the probability that a node selected uniformly at random has a certain number of links (degrees), follows a particular mathematical function called a *power law*. The power law implies that the degree distribution of these networks has no characteristic scale. In contrast, a network with a single, well-defined scale is somewhat similar to a lattice in that every node has (roughly) the same degree. In a network with a scale-free degree distribution, some vertices have a degree that is orders of magnitude larger than the average – these vertices are often called 'hubs'. (There is no inherent threshold above which a node can be viewed as a hub. If there were, then it wouldn't be a scale-free distribution!) Power-law degree distribution is found in many real world networks such as the World Wide Web, the network of Internet routers, email networks etc, but also, for example, in protein interaction networks. Networks with a power-law degree distribution can be highly resistant to the random deletion of vertices, ie, the vast majority of vertices remain connected in a *giant component*.

Giant component: A giant component is a connected subgraph that contains a majority of the entire graph's nodes. Such networks can also be quite sensitive to targeted attacks.

Random graphs:The theory of random graphs studies typical properties of random graphs, those that hold with high probability for graphs drawn from a particular distribution. For example, that it has a path between any two nodes. Ramsey theory states that any sufficiently large random configuration will contain some sort of order. This theorem gives an interesting subtext to my earlier assertion that the difference between a system implying an explicit order and a mere configuration depends upon the repertoire of notions of order that is available in the analysis of the respective configuration.

6.4.4 A CITY IS NOT A TREE

'A City is not a Tree'[112] is the title of Christopher Alexander's 1965 seminal contribution to the theory of architectural and urban design, where he effectively deployed (a very small number of) concepts from set theory and graph theory to expose the organizational narrow-mindedness within the urban planning and design thinking of his day. The 'tree' in the title of Alexander's paper is the abstract structure as defined within graph theory: a directed graph constrained by the rule that every node has only one incoming link but may have multiple outgoing links, ie, the graph ramifies outwards from a root-node without ever reconnecting the branches.

In 'A City is not a Tree', Alexander contrasts this tree organization with patterns that do admit nodes with more that one incoming link and therefore allow multiple paths between nodes. He calls such a less constrained pattern a 'semi-lattice' and interprets both as patterns of decomposition for urban and architectural systems, ie, as patterns of how a system might be decomposed into various subsystems. The link of the directed graph thus stands for the inverse relation of being a subsystem or a subset. 'Both the tree and the semi-lattice are ways of thinking about how a large collection of many small systems goes to make up a large and complex system. More generally, they are both names for structures of

112 Originally published in: *Architectural Forum*, Vol 122, No 1, April 1965, Part I, Vol 122, No 2, May 1965, Part II.

sets.'[113] This interpretation of the nodes of the graph as sets together with the interpretation of the links as relation of set-containment – as discussed above – affords the conversion of any given Venn diagram of disjoint and nesting circles into a corresponding tree diagram and vice versa.[114] If the tree is drawn from top (root-node) to bottom (end-nodes), nodes that are laterally positioned imply disjoint sets that fall into the encompassing domain corresponding to the node at which their respective upward path/branches meet. The defining restriction of the tree translates into the exclusion of overlap or intersection between the domains. In the semi-lattice pattern two incoming links would imply that the respective set belongs to two containing sets as their intersection set. Alexander therefore gives the following definition: 'The tree axiom states: *A collection of sets forms a tree if and only if, for any two sets that belong to the collection either one is wholly contained in the other, or else they are wholly disjoint.*'[115] And he cites the axiom of the semi-lattice thus: '*A collection of sets forms a semilattice if and only if, when two overlapping sets belong to the collection, the set of elements common to both also belongs to the collection.*'[116]

Alexander distinguishes artificial city plans that are designed as trees from natural cities that are usually semi-lattices, and emphasizes their difference in complexity: 'We are concerned with the difference between structures in which no overlap occurs, and those structures in which overlap does occur. It is not merely the overlap which makes the distinction between the two important. Still more important is the fact that the semilattice is potentially a much more complex and subtle structure than a tree. We may see just how much more complex a semilattice can be than a tree in the following fact: a tree based on 20 elements can contain at most 19 further subsets of the 20, while a semilattice based on the same 20 elements can contain more than 1,000,000 different subsets. This enormously greater variety is an index of the great structural complexity a semilattice can have when compared with the structural simplicity of a tree. It is this lack of structural

113 Christopher Alexander, 'A City is not a Tree', in: *Architectural Forum*, Vol 122, No 1, April 1965, part I, p 58.

114 This means: all tree diagrams can be converted into Venn diagrams, but with respect to semi-lattice configurations this translation into Venn diagrams is practical only for rather simple configurations.

115 Alexander, 'A City is not a Tree', Part I, p 60.

116 Ibid.

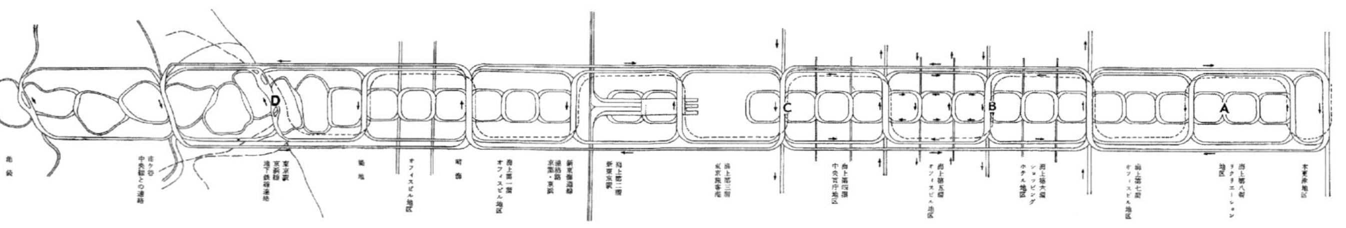

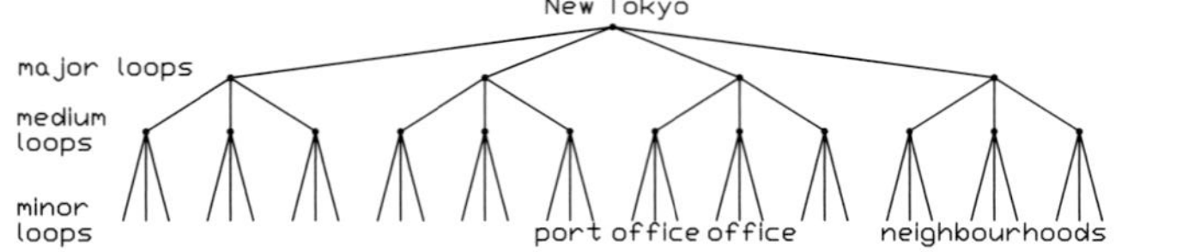

Figure 13 Analysis: Kenzo Tange's Tokyo Bay Project. From 'A City is not a Tree' by Christopher Alexander, 1987

complexity, characteristic of trees, which is crippling our conceptions of the city.'[117]

As Alexander analyzes a series of planned, 'artificial' cities it becomes clear that the set-structure implied in the plans can be read off the map in terms of the depicted parcellation and circulation patterns, ie, in terms of the zoning and road configurations. Alexander gives a series of examples, including Chandigarh which is based on a nested zoning diagram, and Brasilia which is based on an obvious tree-shaped circulation system. The most perfect example is Kenzo Tange's famous plan for Tokyo Bay, because here there is a direct coincidence between the pattern of roads and the pattern of the major parcels. The plan consists of a series of loops stretched across Tokyo Bay. There are four major loops, each of which contains three medium loops. Each medium loop contains three minor loops which are the residential neighbourhoods. Alexander comments: 'Each of these structures, then, is a tree. Each unit in each tree that I have described, moreover, is the fixed, unchanging residue of some system in the living city.... However, in every city there are thousands, even millions, of times as many more systems at work whose physical residue does not appear as a unit in these tree structures. In the worst cases, the units which do appear fail to correspond to any living reality; and the real systems, whose existence actually makes the city live, have been provided with no physical receptacle.'[118] Alexander continues to explicate: 'The units of which an artificial city is made up are always organized to form a tree.... Whenever we have a tree structure, it means that within this structure no piece of any unit is ever connected to other units, except through the medium of that unit as a whole. The enormity of this restriction is difficult to grasp. It is a little as though the members of a family were not free to make friends outside the family, except when the family as a whole made a friendship.... When we describe the city in terms of neighbourhoods, we implicitly assume that the smaller elements within any one of these neighbourhoods belong together so tightly that they only interact with elements in other neighbourhoods through the medium of the neighbourhoods to which they themselves belong.'[119]

This comparison of city patterns with the pattern of social connections implied by the tree model is of particular pertinence: while traditional society might indeed have been organized in the form of disjunct and

117 Alexander, 'A City is not a Tree', Part 1, p 60.
118 Ibid, Part 1, p 61.
119 Ibid.

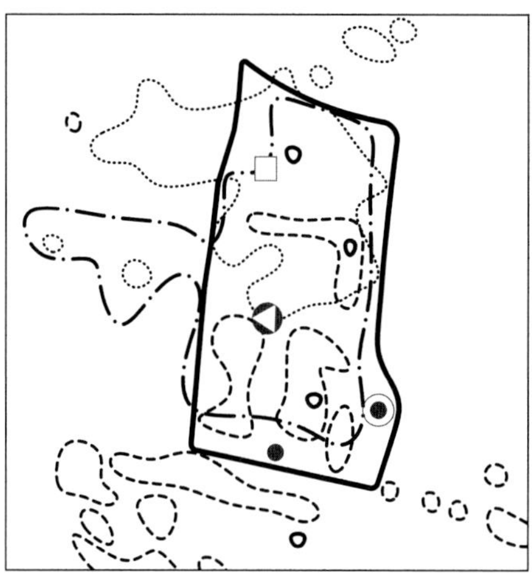

Figure 14 Middlesbrough: mapping of overlapping social systems. From 'A City is not a Tree' by Christopher Alexander

nesting groups, the patterns of social communication in modern society have exploded these restrictions.

After having analyzed a series of 'artificial' city plans, Alexander proceeds to use Ruth Glass' discourse about her redevelopment plan for Middlesbrough to demonstrate how the actual patterns of using space in a given modern city exceed the restrictive logic of the tree organization. Ruth Glass was trying to establish neighbourhoods but her efforts to establish a single pattern of decomposition were (bound to be) frustrated. The various real social systems she tried to capture each focused on a specific spatial node, like, for example, the primary schools, secondary schools, youth clubs, grocery shops etc. However, the catchment-areas of these nodes did not coincide, nor did they allow for arrangements of concentric nesting domains. The diagram that plotted these effective social groups – each defined by the node they utilized – was in fact a diagram of overlapping domains, whereby domains were neither disjunct, nor fully contained one within the other. Alexander summarized: 'There is nothing in the nature of the various centres which says that their catchment-areas should be the same. Their natures are different. Therefore the units they define are different.'[120] Conversely, however, the plotted catchment-areas find no architectural expression in the city fabric of Middlesbrough other than the node itself. The organizing capacity of

120 Alexander, 'A City is not a Tree', Part 1, p 62.

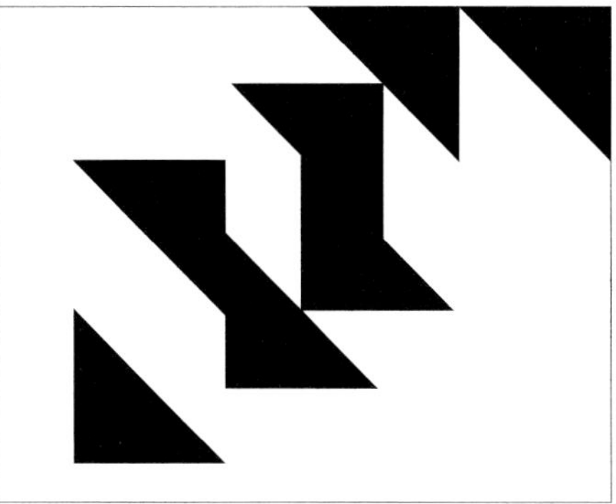

Figure 15 Diagram of painting with multiple readings/decompositions (after Simon Nicholson). From 'A City is not a Tree' by Christopher Alexander

this node is not supported by any particular urban spatial pattern. This lack provides an interesting urban design task.

Alexander cannot show us a design for a city plan that could provide a paradigm for urban semi-lattice organization. Instead he presents a remarkable painting by Simon Nicholson. The fascination of this painting lies in the fact that, although constructed of rather few simple triangular elements, these elements unite in many different ways to form the large units of the painting – in such a way that, if we make a complete inventory of the perceived units in the painting, we find that each triangle enters into four or five completely different units or figures, none contained in any of the others, yet all overlapping in that triangle. The proposal to use such an image as an analogy for the spatial organization of a city coincides with Colin Rowe and Robert Slutzky's notion of *phenomenal transparency* as expounded in 'Transparency: Literal and Phenomenal'[121] published one year in advance of Christopher Alexander's article. Alexander's proposal might be taken as the urban application of the concept of phenomenal transparency, with emphasis on organization rather than perception. Both Christopher Alexander's indication and Colin Rowe's treatise established an early, powerful anticipation of the ambitions that were to follow and occupy a whole generation of avant-garde architects, and still remains on the agenda of the avant-garde today.[122]

121 Colin Rowe & Robert Slutzky, 'Transparency: Literal and Phenomenal', in: *Perspecta 8*, Yale Architectural Journal, 1963.

122 This ambition to construct configurations within which multiple readings overlap lives on within the contemporary style of *Parametricism* under the heading of *parametric figuration*. See below, part 11 *Parametricism – The Parametric Paradigm and the Formation of a New Style*.

However, before turning to the organizational innovations that are fermenting within the current architectural avant-garde, it makes sense to introduce another strand of architectural research that was inspired by Christopher Alexander's introduction of new mathematics into the field of architecture and that remained closely tied to the instrumentalization of mathematical reasoning in relation to the problems of architectural and urban design. This research, which was pushed forward by Lionel March and Philip Steadman during the 1970s,[123] found its current point of culmination in the work of Bill Hillier and his Space Syntax Lab, based at London University. This mathematical research into the problematic of urban and architectural configuration was one of the first loci for the deployment of computational processes within the design disciplines.

6.4.5 SPACE SYNTAX: CONCEPTS AND TOOLS OF ANALYSIS

The work gathered under the heading of *space syntax* is perhaps the most impressive effort to date towards the enhancement of architectural intelligence in the problem-area of spatial configuration. Space syntax has been pioneered by Bill Hillier[124] as an organizationally focused approach to problems of architectural and urban design. This approach comprises a powerful set of techniques for the analysis of the spatial configurations of buildings, urban quarters and cities. In 1995 Bill Hillier established the Space Syntax Laboratory at The Bartlett Faculty of the Built Environment at University College London. The Space Syntax Laboratory operates both as academic institute and as consultancy firm.

Space syntax succeeded in elaborating a specific conceptual apparatus for architecture and urbanism, on the basis of the general conceptual tools of network theory, and it utilized this apparatus to build up an extensive body of analytical case studies, to formulate a series of noteworthy theoretical claims about the social functioning of the built environment, and finally to apply the tools and theorems of space syntax

123 See Lionel March & Philip Steadman, *The Geometry of Environment – An Introduction to Spatial Organization in Design*, RIBA Publications (London), 1971.

124 In his first book, *The Social Logic of Space* (1984), Hillier introduced the key configurational concepts and a first decade of research involving computational tools to analyze spatial configurations. Twelve years later, in his second book and magnum opus *Space is the Machine* (1996), Hillier presented the results of a further decade of research guided by the research programme outlined in *The Social Logic of Space*. Together the two works constitute one of the most original and profound contributions to architectural theory, a contribution which has as yet to be fully recognized and integrated into the ongoing autopoiesis of architecture. See Bill Hillier & Julienne Hanson, *The Social Logic of Space*, Cambridge University Press (Cambridge), 1984, and: Bill Hillier, *Space is the Machine*, Cambridge University Press (Cambridge), 1996.

within an ongoing design support service for architects and urbanists. The foundational concept of space syntax theory and practice is the concept of *configuration*. The concept aims at the whole of a complex to denote a set of relationships among things that are all interdependent. A relation between two elements is *configurational* 'insofar as it is affected by the simultaneous co-presence of at least a third element, and possibly all other elements, in a complex'.[125] A configuration is then defined as follows: 'Configuration is a set of interdependent relations in which each is determined by its relation to all the others.'[126] Thus Hillier's concept of configuration differs from the (weaker) concept of configuration defined within the theory of architectural autopoiesis. However, the difference is slight. The only additional criterion that Hillier's concept assumes is the criterion of continuity of access. All of Hillier's investigations ultimately focus on relations of access. When he investigates relations of visual connection they come in as supplementary to relations of access. The theory of architectural autopoiesis, as comprehensive theory of architecture, did not find it expedient to restrict the scope of relation-types that might be relevant for a general concept of configuration. The interdependency that enters into Hillier's definition is only relative to certain network measures, for example, the relative centrality or 'integration' of nodes or links within the network. Interdependency here means just that if you change the network locally, ie, by cutting a connection, the values of certain node measures that measure the node's direct and indirect connection with all other nodes change for every node. This formal interdependency might or might not impact on a corresponding functional interdependency. (This is a further question of substantial theory which Hillier tends to answer positively.) Hillier's concept of 'interdependent' spatial elements is, at least at its outset or definition, not to be confused with Alexander's concept of spatial system which demands the effective functional interdependence of spatial elements within action-artefact networks. Above, the theory of architectural autopoiesis placed the term configuration as the overarching term encompassing organizations as non-arbitrary, rule-constrained configurations. This implies that there are *mere* configurations that exhibit a zero degree of organization. Hillier is not working with this distinction arbitrary/random versus rule-based/organized, nor does he thus employ the concept of degrees of organization. Typology, ie, the distinction of (rule-based) types of configuration/organization (tree vs

125 Hillier, *Space is the Machine*, p 96.
126 Ibid, p 35.

semi-lattice, or grid vs ring vs star etc), is also missing from Hillier's discourse. These 'omissions' are not in any way criticized here, they are part of a very productive theoretical economy.

Space syntax is concerned with spatial configurations. However, Hillier's concern is not with the shape of the spaces, but only with their relative accessibility. All spaces must be accessible, but it matters how these relations of accessibility between spaces are patterned. Space syntax focuses exclusively on the density and distribution of the connections between spatial elements. The space syntax techniques measure connectivity. This base notion of spatial connection can be applied with respect to variously defined spatial elements: to rooms within a building, zones within larger spaces, or streets within street networks.[127] Two elements in a configuration are either directly connected or not. This relation is symmetrical. Those elements that are not directly connected are indirectly connected.

The most fundamental relational measure between any two elements within a configuration is their ***depth*** with respect to each other. The depth – or configurational distance – between two spatial elements is defined as the minimum number of intervening elements plus one, ie, the minimum number of boundary crossings or street corners that need to be passed on the way from one of the elements to the other. From this binary relation Hillier moves on to an element's *total depth* as the sum of all binary depth measures of this element, ie, measuring the accessibility of this element from all the other elements in the configuration. The element with the lowest total depth is the most accessible or most ***integrated*** element within the configuration. From these measures a series of global measures that serve to characterize the overall configuration can be derived: the configuration's *total depth* or *universal distance* sums all the individual elements' total depth values and thus gives the total number of links that must be traversed to move from each element to every other elemental space within the configuration. The average integration value of the configuration's elements allows us to distinguish deep from shallow configurations. The standard deviation (the average deviation from the average), and the ratio of the number of different integration values relative to the number of elements, both give a measure of the degree of the configuration's differentiation. The more symmetry a configuration

127 While rooms as closed cells are easy to identify, with respect to zones and streets space syntax requires operational definitions that unambiguously decompose a spatial configuration into elements, thus establishing where one element stops and another starts. With respect to given urban street patterns, space syntax analysis often chooses to consider straight street segments as elements. Thus a long street with multiple changes of direction breaks into as many elements as there are bends or changes of direction.

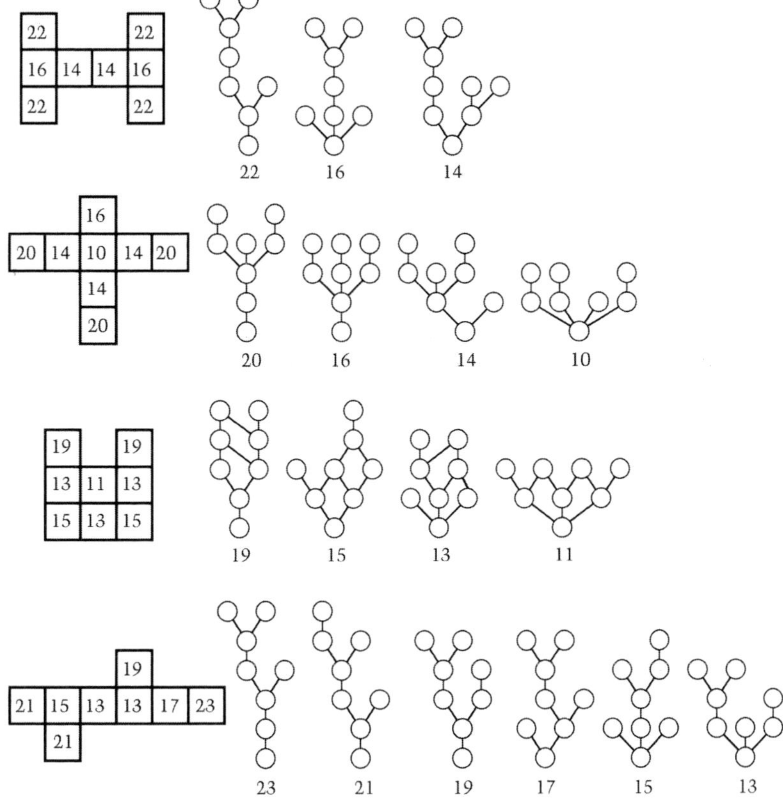

Figure 16 Space syntax – plan diagrams and their different justified adjacency/permeability graphs.The graphs read all full face adjacencies between spatial elements (cells) as connections. The numbers represent the total depth values (universal distances) of the cells. From Hillier, *Space is the Machine*, 1996

exhibits, the more equivalent parts does it contain and thus the smaller will be the ratio of different integration values. Within a perfect ring of cells, all cells have the same integration value. In a totally asymmetric configuration all cells might have different integration values. A high differentiation of integration values – high ratio of differently integrated elements and high standard deviation – means that the configuration offers a high variety of positions. What we might call the element's position within a configuration is not fully described by a mere numerical value. The position of an element within a configuration – in terms of the configurational key aspect of relative accessibility – can best be brought out by the utilization of certain graphic representations.

It is the combination of quantitative and graphic analysis that is the hallmark of Hillier's method. The so-called justified graph (short: j-graph) presents the permeability map or network of accessibility of a configuration from the point of view of a chosen spatial element. The j-graph of an element lays out all the other elements of the configuration in the order of their accessibility from the chosen element. The element chosen to be analyzed is placed at the *root* of the graph. From the root upwards the graph first plots all the elements that are immediately accessible, ie, that are accessible with one step from the root element. Then the second layer is plotted above with all the elements at depth two, then all those elements that can be reached with three steps, and so forth until all elements in the configuration are reached. The j-graph thus depicts all the elements of the configuration ordered by way of their depth from the chosen root element. The j-graph also shows all the links that exist between all the elements within the configuration.

Each element has its own j-graph. However, the *global* properties of the configuration that can be read off the different j-graphs must obviously remain invariant across the different graphs, for example, whether the configuration is a tree or a semi-lattice, and in the case of the latter, its degree of ringiness, ie, the number of rings within the configuration etc.[128] Despite the invariance of these global properties, different elements within the configuration might have rather differently patterned j-graphs with a different number of layers and different total depth. J-graphs thus characterize the different positions within a spatial configuration. There might also be elements with equivalent j-graphs. This depends on the degree of internal symmetry within the configuration.

The four plan diagrams depicted above show different arrangements of eight cells each. Each configuration has a different number of different j-graphs. The more symmetrical the figure is, the smaller is the number of different j-graphs and thus the less positional difference is available. J-graph isomorphism indicates equivalence of positional information and offers a more pertinent definition of symmetry than the usual definition as 'invariance under motion'. Along these lines more nuanced definitions of symmetry are also possible. For instance, one might distinguish *local symmetry* from *global symmetry*, ie, considering local rather than global j-graph isomorphism by taking only the first few layers of the graph into account. *Weak symmetry* might be defined by specifying various types of similarities (rather than identity) with respect to the positional information of the respective spatial elements. Hillier also suggests that

128 In the j-graphs depicted above only the j-graphs of the second shape contain rings: here each j-graph contains two rings. The j-graphs of the other two shapes are trees.

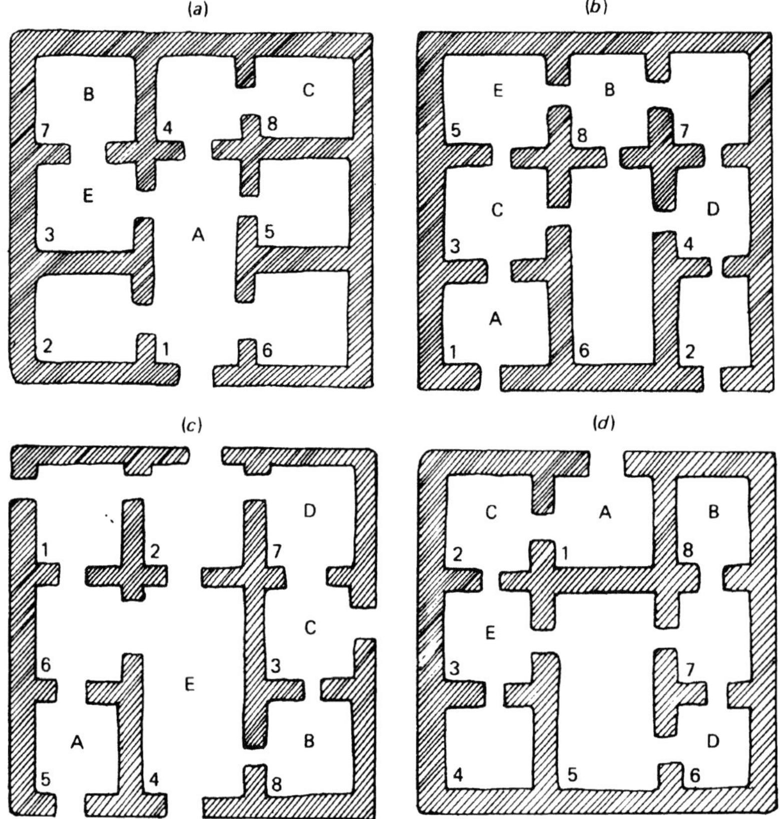

Figure 17 Four layouts with identical geometry and adjacencies. From Hillier & Hanson, *The Social Logic of Space*, 1984

he can give a formalization of balanced asymmetry where the total depth in each of the two sides is equal but the pattern of connectivity is different. The fourth plan diagram in Figure 16 displays balanced asymmetry in this sense.[129]

J-graphs give a *topological* rather than geometric image of a spatial layout. Above, the assumption was made that cells connect at all full face adjacencies. If we interpret the cells as rooms within a building we would not expect doors at all points of adjacency. The graphs above therefore present connection potential rather than implemented connections.

129 Hillier did not depict all the different j-graphs. For instance, with respect to the third shape, the two cells which both have a total depth value of 13 have *different* j-graphs. Hillier only depicts one of them. Between the two elements holds the relationship of balanced asymmetry.

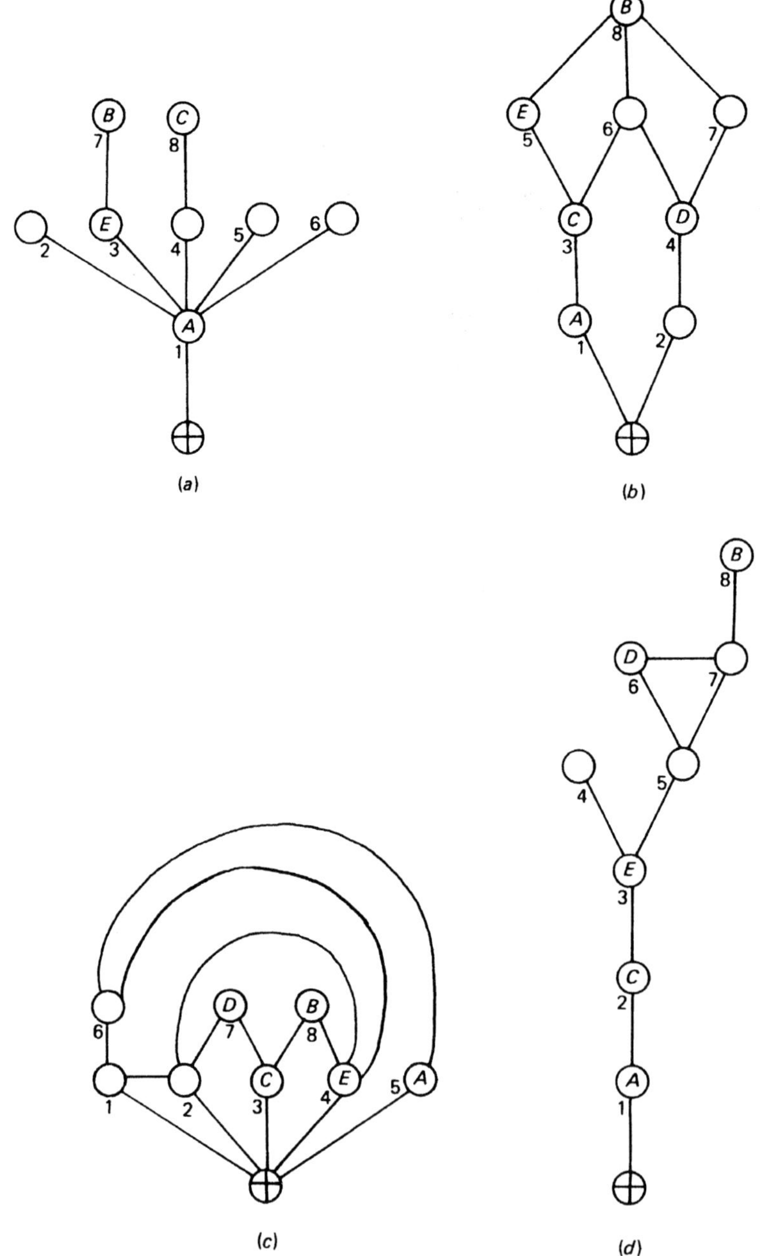

Figure 18 Four different justified permeability maps. From Hillier & Hanson, *The Social Logic of Space*, 1984

The four plan diagrams below (Figure 17) all show the same spatial arrangement of nine rooms, however, in each case with a different arrangement of doors. The depicted j-graphs are taking the surrounding exterior space as root to look at the syntax of each variant. Despite the geometric identity of the four plans they are syntactically distinct: their respective j-graphs are strikingly different.

It should be clear that the j-graph is a more pertinent map of the respective plan's spatial logic – and of the social logic of its occupation – than the geometric plan itself. The visual order of the respective plan's bird's-eye view is rather deceiving. Only from the syntactic point of view is it possible to identify what Hillier calls *genotypes*, ie, recurrent spatial configurations that sustain and stabilize recurrent patterns of social life. As example of such a genotype, Hillier has been analyzing French farm houses, discovering a stable syntactic pattern that distinguishes two similarly sized spaces: the *salle commune* and the *grande salle*. Hillier uses the example of French farm houses to explain the significance of genotypes: 'We can ask how the different functions in the house are "spatialized", that is how they are embedded in the overall spatial configuration. . . . We find that it is very common that different functions are spatialized in different ways, and that this can often be expressed clearly through "integration" analysis. . . . To the extent that there are commonalities in the sequence of inequalities, then we can say that there is a common pattern to the way in which different functions are spatialized in the house. We call such common patterns "inequality genotypes".'[130]

The French farm houses analyzed by Hillier displayed the reverse condition from the four layouts shown above in Figure 17: their topological/syntactic patterns are more similar than their geometric shape. The figure below represents the genotype as an abstracted plan diagram. The two following diagrams utilize a graphic technique that allows combination of the spatial shape information with syntactic information. Here the total depth-values (integration values) are used to drive a colour coding that reveals how the key property of integration is distributed across the plan. Hillier works with two variants of this technique. The first takes each convex space – the rooms as well as the corridor – as a single spatial element. The second variant tessellates the plan and then takes each square module as a separate spatial element. Walls feature here as interruptions in the grid of cells. The second variant

130 Hillier, *Space is the Machine*, p 36.

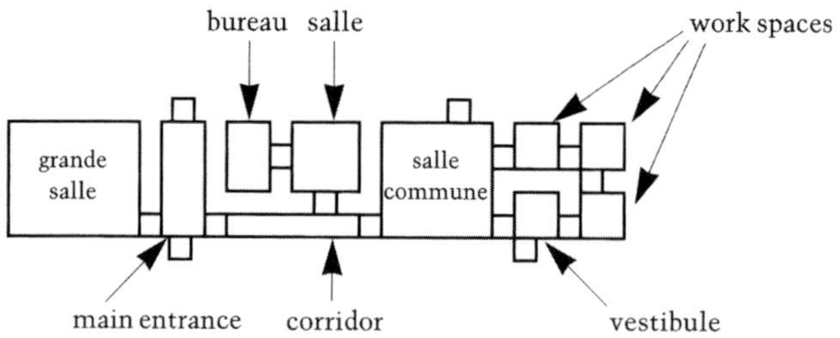

Figure 19 Space syntax: abstracted plan diagram of typical French farm house. From Hillier, *Space is the Machine*, 1996

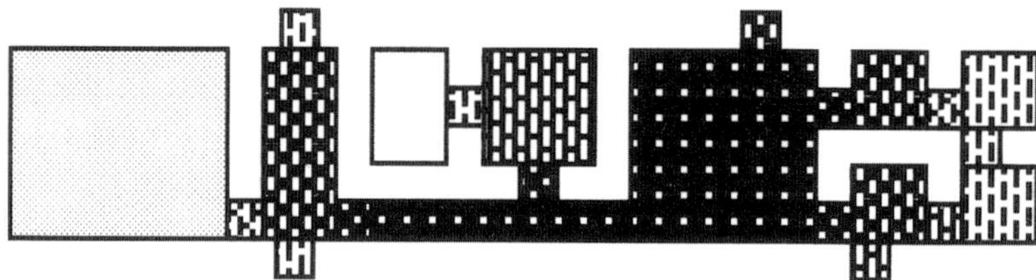

Figure 20 Space syntax: graphic integration analysis decomposing the plan into convex spaces. From Hillier, *Space is the Machine*, 1996

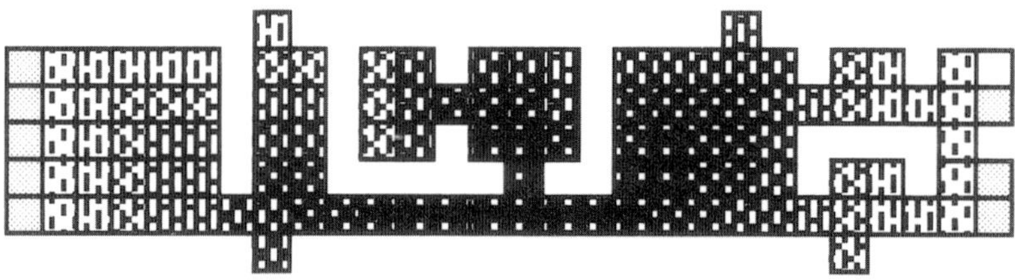

Figure 21 Space syntax: graphic integration analysis decomposing the plan into a tessellation of same sized cells. From Hillier, *Space is the Machine*, 1996

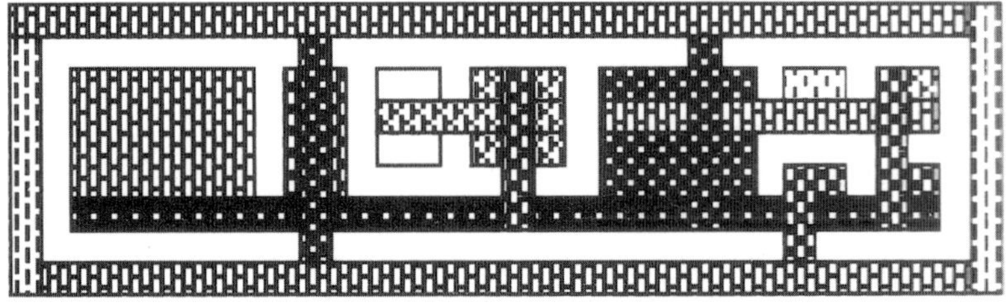

Figure 22 Space syntax: graphic integration analysis superimposing convex space analysis with strips of visual connection. From Hillier, *Space is the Machine*, 1996

captures two factors over and above the pure logic of space-to-space accessibility: the metric distances and the size of the spaces. The first factor is relevant in terms of the physiological effort required to move through the plan. The second factor recognizes that larger rooms are more important and can be expected to attract more people independent of relative position. While the first variant ignores these factors, the second variant allows them to influence the distribution of integration within the plan. In the specific case of the genotype of the French farm house, both analyses show both the *salle commune* and the corridor as the spaces with the highest level of integration. Hillier suggests that these two ways of decomposing a plan as a basis for integration analysis can be operated simultaneously by superimposing the calculations. He is also suggesting a third form of decomposition in terms of axial strips representing visual connectivity. All three variants of analysis might be superimposed within a single multi-layered analysis, or might be placed next to each other, each displaying its specific emphasis.

The possibility of superimposing the calculations of multiple decompositions suggests that integration analysis can be applied to decompositions that within themselves recognize overlapping or interpenetrating spaces. This is important because the most interesting architectural designs since the advent of Modernism no longer work with cellular rooms. Instead space is often conceived as open and continuous, and in recent years spatial overlap and the interpenetration of domains have been pushed onto the design agenda. Areas of overlap are areas of intensity that will also be highlighted by the attendant integration analysis.

Within Hillier's space syntax, conditions of spatial overlap are primarily found in the analysis of urban space. Within urban environments, space is rarely unambiguously contained. Instead space flows continuously. With the exception of American cities that display relentlessly regular grid layouts, most urban layouts present the urban space structure Hillier calls *deformed grid*. Here the street pattern deviates from strict orthogonality. Most cities in Europe fall into this category. In these deformed grids lines of sight do not continue all the way through but streets keep changing direction and lines of sight keep striking the facades of buildings. As we move through the city, the shape of our field of vision continuously changes.

A typical urban space defined by urban blocks might be decomposed into spatial elements in a number of ways. One plausible way to define spatial segments within the continuity of urban space is to use the faces of the blocks as references. Each face or facade sponsors a determinate field of visibility: the union of the isovists of all points on the respective

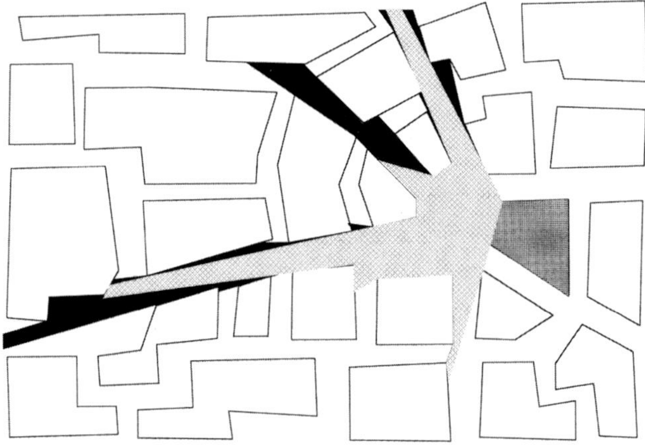

Figure 23 Facade isovist within typical urban space with urban blocks. Light grey shows the full-facade isovist. Black: part-facade isovist. From Hillier, *Space is the Machine*, 1996

facade defines a spatial zone that can be seen from the facade. This zone collects all points from where the facade can be seen. Such a field of visibility can be constructed for each face of each urban block. These fields of vision overlap. The zones of overlap can themselves be taken as spatial elements. There are zones of overlap that are convex. In such zones all points are mutually visible to each other. Such zones are of special interest in so far as they might serve as unified event spaces or spaces of congregation. The high visibility spaces where many fields of vision overlap are also central to the orientation within an urban field. The convex overlap areas might be taken as spatial elements of an integration analysis. This is one way space syntax analysis can be applied to the continuous and ambiguous shape of urban space.

Another, more straightforward way to analyze urban patterns is in terms of straight lines striking through the urban space. These lines depict the street spaces in terms of the relevant aspect of straight lines of sight directing movement. These lines extend further through the deformed grid and thus generate higher values of total integration. The space syntax toolbox distinguishes 'all line maps' and 'axial line maps'. The latter just take the street axes of the deformed urban grid as long as they are straight. Any bend in the street generates a new segment for the axial analysis. The urban space is thus decomposed into a network of connected straight line segments. The most salient property space syntax focuses on is once more the depth of those street segments from each

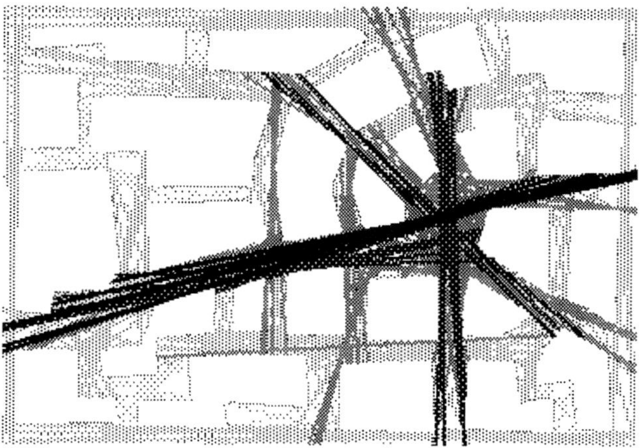

Figure 24 Space syntax: all line map, integration analysis. From Hillier, *Space is the Machine*, 1996

other. On this basis the total depth (or degree of integration)[131] of each segment and the total depth/integration of the whole configuration are measured. There are two rules of thumb: segments in the centre tend to have a higher degree of integration than segments on the periphery, and the longer the segment the higher is its potential level of integration. However, this rule can be subverted by the way the elements are networked. The attendant graphic technique reveals each element's relative integration by colour-coding the elements according to their integration ranking. The colour-coded axial maps are thus depicting the differentiation and distribution of integration across the configuration. The integration value of an element qualifies the element in its relation to the global configuration. Space syntax analysis also works with more local measures, for example, different measures of *local integration* can be defined by measuring how many elements can be reached by one or two steps. In large global systems, a three-step analysis might also serve as a measure of local integration. The axial map analysis is the most widely used tool in the practical applications of space syntax analysis.

The configurational properties of streets, as visualized in the axial map below (Figure 25), and the configurational properties of rooms, as visualized in Figure 22, are invisible, hidden ('non-discursive') properties.

131 While total depth values are simple summations of individual depth counts, so that larger configurations generate larger total depths, the inverse measure of integration is corrected for the overall size of the configuration. Therefore integration values can be compared across configurations of different size.

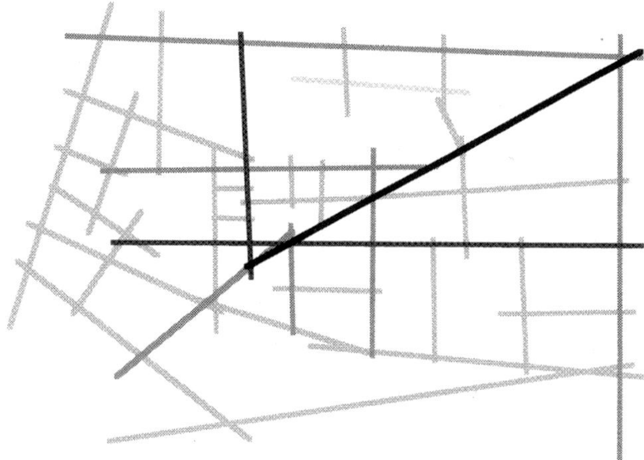

Figure 25 Space syntax: axial map, integration analysis. From Hillier, *Space is the Machine*, 1996

These properties are, supposedly, operationally effective. They certainly have the capacity or potential for operational effectiveness. The correlations that Hillier detects between these invisible configurational properties and social patterns of utilization imply that these properties, or rather the advantages these properties entail, have *somehow* been detected by social actors, even if only in a collective process of trial and error, symmetry-breaking and self-amplification. Small, initial, visible, functional concentrations along invisibly advantageous lines lead to further concentrations along the same lines etc. Can this haphazard process of discovering these functional potentials (hidden in the configurational maze) be facilitated by architectural design? The possibility of tracking and revealing important configurational properties creates the possibility of making them visible, not only in an analytical diagram but within the medium of built architecture via dedicated means of articulation. It seems Hillier never considered this possibility but his tools open up the possibility to turn the objective configurational properties into subjectively available information by making the space syntax of buildings and urban fields transparent to its users, for instance by using variable intensity of ornamentation to track degrees of integration. This idea leads us to the more general recognition that articulation in architecture does not have to be restricted to the articulation of local functional features. It includes the local morphological registration of positional properties, and indeed of relational properties in general, that exceed the immediate contiguous present. The information that might be encoded might allow local to local as well as local to global inferences of all kinds. Articulations that should transport these kinds of non-present information can only function through systematically coded systems-of-signification. They belong to architecture's semiological rather than organizational dimension.[132]

6.4.6 SPACE SYNTAX: THEORETICAL CLAIMS

The central idea of space syntax is that the crucial aspect of the built environment that needs to be analyzed in order to understand how buildings function within society is the *spatial configuration* that exists within and between them. Hillier denounces the preoccupation of a lot of architectural theory with style and visual appearance as missing the essential point about the social efficacy of architecture. Space syntax also implies that buildings respond to functional requirements not primarily by giving shape to individual spaces but by the patterns of connections it affords. The neutral, rectilinear shape of most spaces attests to this. This relative shape neutrality makes buildings inherently multifunctional. Although the fact that buildings are usually erected for (more or less) specific purposes cannot be denied, it seems pertinent to focus theoretical attention on more generic patterns of social organization in terms of access, encounter and avoidance that are shared across many different function-types.

The built environment and the buildings within it provide a spatial patterning of activities and relationships. The simple act of creating a spatial boundary separates an inside from an outside and thus creates (or reflects) a socially significant distinction or relation. Hillier's theoretical interest focuses on relations and on the more complex relational schemes he calls *configurations*.[133]

He insists that architectural space should be analyzed in terms of configuration because 'it is as configuration that it has its most powerful and independent effects on the way buildings and built environments are formed and how they function for their purposes'.[134] This is so because 'individual spaces place little limit on human activity, except for those of size and perhaps shape. . . . The relation between space and social existence lies in the relations between configurations of people and configurations of space.'[135] The emphasis on *systems* of spatial relations

132 This dimension, and the potential for upgrading architecture's capacity within it, will be explored below, in sections 6.8 to 6.10.

133 Hillier prefers the term configuration over the term pattern because he feels that the word pattern suggests an expectation of a recognizable regularity.

134 Hillier, *Space is the Machine*, p 27.

135 Ibid, p 31.

(configurations) in architecture is an important pendant to the importance of *systems* of relations in the societal environment that architecture is to serve. It is not isolated individual users who are important but the organization of social relations. Hiller clearly realizes this: 'Encountering, congregating, avoiding, interacting, dwelling, conferring are not attributes of individuals, but patterns, or configurations formed by groups or collections of people. They depend on an engineered pattern of co-presence, and indeed co-absence.'[136] Systems of relations are crucial. This creates an inherent difficulty for architects, because it is much more difficult to grasp relations and systems of relations than to grasp objects and their properties. 'Related spaces, almost by definition, cannot be seen all at once, but require movement from one to other to experience the whole. This is to say that relationality in space is rarely accessible to us as a single experience.'[137] According to Hillier the difficulty of thinking about relations has led architectural theory astray. Systems of relations – like languages, symbolic systems and also the complex spatial systems that architecture should be concerned with – are 'much easier to use and to take for granted than to talk about analytically'.[138] As a result, Hillier suggests that 'the discourse about architecture that is a necessary concomitant of the practice of architecture is afflicted with a kind of permanent disability'.[139] It is this disability that space syntax as an analytically rigorous theory of spatial configuration sets out to address and overcome. This task is crucial for architectural theory, Hillier claims, because it is only on the basis of syntactic analysis – focusing on space-to-space permeability – that the social logic of space can be detected.

More specifically, space syntax theory claims that the space syntax techniques of analysis are able to predict the likely occupation effects of architectural and urban designs on the basis of a purely configurational analysis that can proceed on the basis of maps or geometric surveys without requiring additional information about traffic or the distribution of functions. In fact, the claim is that traffic patterns and functional distributions can be inferred from the results of a space syntax analysis of the spatial configuration. The most effective and thus most likely occurrence of certain urban functions – like shops and restaurants – that feed on movement and high visibility can also be read off the space

136 Ibid, p 29.
137 Ibid, p 267.
138 Hillier & Hanson, *The Social Logic of Space*, p 2.
139 Ibid.

syntax map of the urban geometry. These claims have been corroborated in extensive empirical studies involving functional mappings, measurements of traffic flows as well as pedestrian movement densities.

However, Hillier's space syntax paradigm is not only confined to quantitative analyses and measurements. Hillier argues that his techniques can serve to explain, formalize and thus demystify otherwise elusive qualitative concepts like urbanity and intelligibility.

According to Hillier, the noticeable lack of urbanity of many new cities in comparison with old cities, and the respective lack of urbanity of the modern parts in comparison with the historical parts of cities, has more to do with spatial syntax than with the aesthetic feel of the respective places. Modern cities and parts of cities are often characterized by both an overall shortfall of integration and by a lack of differentiation of integration values across the configuration of streets. This is especially the case with the much maligned modern housing estates. The estate type of development is characterized both by its segregation from the rest of the city – giving it an overall low integration score – and by an evenness in the distribution of integration values across the estate. The integration analysis of three London housing estates confirms this general pattern: 'The estate is substantially more segregated than the rest of the urban surface and, what is more problematic, segregated as a lump. Good urban space has segregated lines, but they are close to integrated lines, so that there is a good mix of integrated and segregated lines locally.'[140] Urbanity – a vibrant street life – thrives on the local concentration of movement that is generated both locally and globally.

Hillier makes another pertinent point about modern housing estates that is revealed when global integration analysis is related to a three step local integration analysis. The analyzed housing estates evidence a 'poor relation between local and global integration'[141] and thus an 'unclear relation between local and global structure'.[142] This implies a disalignment of localized and less localized movement and thus between inhabitant and stranger. This observed lack of coincidence between local and global integration has another, more general significance. According to Hillier this mismatch between local and global integration implies a lack of 'intelligibility'.

140 Hillier, *Space is the Machine*, p 175.
141 Ibid.
142 Ibid.

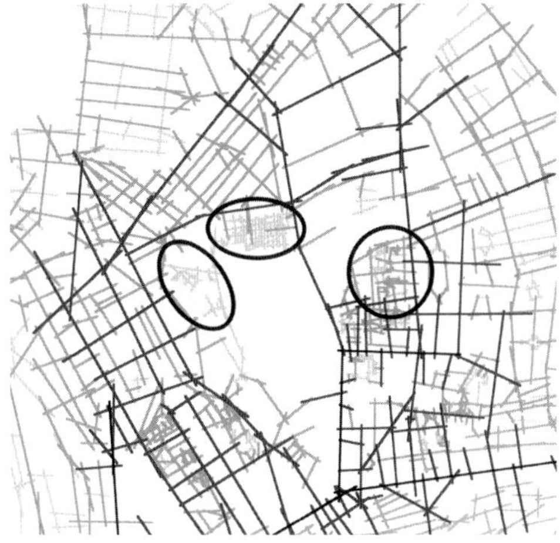

Figure 26 Integration analysis focusing on three housing estates, King's Cross area, London. From Hillier, *Space is the Machine*, 1996

This notion of 'intelligibility'[143] is rather interesting because it expands the type of performance criteria that a spatial configuration might be subjected to. So far Hillier has considered concepts/criteria that describe/measure characteristics that pertain to the configuration itself. A configuration has a certain degree of symmetry, a certain degree of ringiness or a certain degree of overall depth/integration etc. It seems that the import of the criterion of 'intelligibility' cannot be understood merely by reference to the objective characteristics of the configuration itself. The concept makes claims about the relationship between certain measurable properties of the configuration itself and a human occupant's capacity to successfully navigate the system. The pair of diagrams in Figure 27 are presented by Hillier to give the reader an intuitively accessible illustration of intelligibility: the first configuration seems to be a proper urban space while the second looks rather labyrinthian. It seems like a reasonable intuition to presume that those moving through these spaces find the first configuration more 'intelligible' and thus easier to orient within than the second configuration.

143 The term intelligibility is placed in quotation marks throughout the discussion of Hillier's account of the concept. This should not imply any disrespect for Hillier's original, insightful contribution around this concept. However, the theory of architectural autopoiesis prefers to withdraw this term – with its connotations implying reference to the cognition of users/observers – from the concept Hillier operationalizes with space syntax theory. What Hillier defines is not degrees of intelligibility but degrees of internal correlation, specifically the correlation of local with global integration.

Figure 27 Space syntax: two urban configurations, urban vs labyrinthian configuration. From Hillier, *Space is the Machine*, 1996

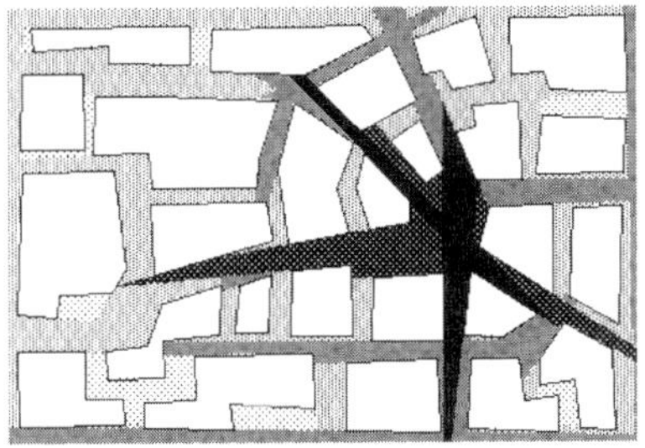

Figure 28 Space syntax: two configurations, orderly vs disorderly distribution of integration values. From Hillier, *Space is the Machine*, 1996

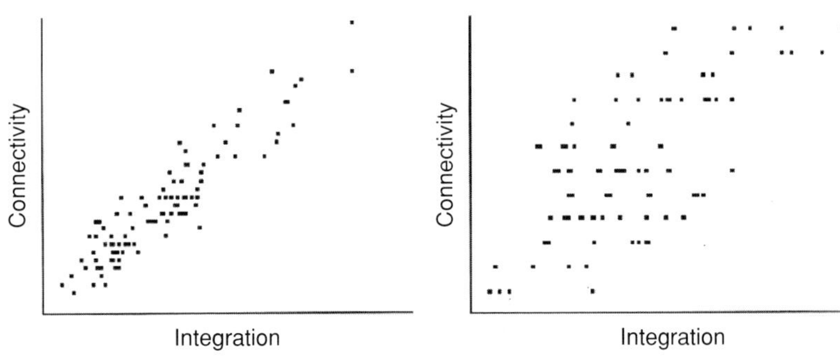

Figure 29 Space syntax: two urban configurations, high intelligibility vs low intelligibility. From Hillier, *Space is the Machine*, 1996

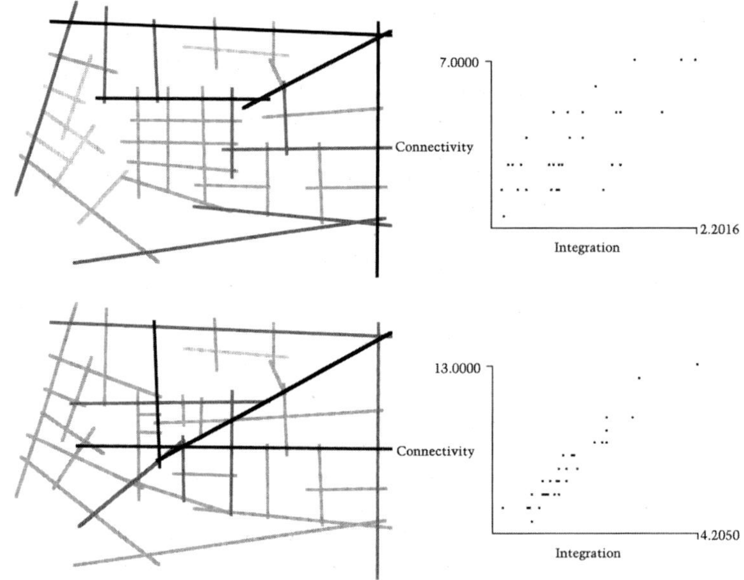

Figure 30 Space syntax: designing with instant feedback on integration and intelligibility. From Hillier, *Space is the Machine*, 1996

Hillier claims that this intuitively available quality of 'intelligibility' has an underlying syntactic cause. His initial heuristic definition of 'intelligibility' is noteworthy: 'The property of "intelligibility" in a deformed grid means the degree to which what we can see . . . is a good guide to what we cannot see.' Hillier then moves on to operationalize this definition by means of relating two measures: the visible measure of immediate *connection* (local integration) and the invisible measure of global *integration*. Hillier's thesis then reads: 'An intelligible system is one in which well-connected spaces also tend to be well-integrated spaces. An unintelligible system is one where well-connected spaces are not well integrated, so that what we can see of their connections misleads us about the status of that space in the system as a whole.'[144] The two scattergrams plot all convex spatial elements with respect to the two coordinates of visible connectivity and invisible integration. The superior degree of 'intelligibility' of the first configuration is indicated by its relative tightness of correlation between connectivity and integration in comparison with the loose, uncorrelated scatter of the second configuration.

144 Hillier, *Space is the Machine*, p 127.

The analytical techniques of space syntax can also be integrated in the creative design process, especially as the invisible numerical properties of the configuration can be handled graphically. It is the computational implementation and graphical representation of the various organizational measures that allow designers to utilize space syntax analysis within the design process. As the urban designer builds up his/her urban configuration he/she receives instant feedback about the distribution and redistribution of integration within the evolving configuration. In parallel, the 'intelligibility' of the configuration can be monitored, and thus pursued as a strategic goal, as the design progresses.

6.4.7 FROM ORGANIZATION TO ARTICULATION: TAKING ACCOUNT OF COGNITION

Above, the term intelligibility is placed in quotation marks in the discussion of Hillier's account of the concept. This should not imply any disrespect for the insights that Hillier gathers around this term. However, the theory of architectural autopoiesis prefers to withdraw this term – with its connotations implying reference to the cognition of users/observers – from the concept Hillier operationalizes within space syntax theory. What Hillier defines is not degrees of intelligibility but degrees of *internal correlation* within *a* configuration, specifically the correlation of local with global integration.

Above it was suggested that the import of the criterion of 'intelligibility' cannot be understood merely by reference to the objective characteristics of the configuration itself. Indeed, it seems that the intuitive concept makes a claim about the relationship between certain measurable properties of the configuration itself and a human occupant's capacity to perceive and comprehend, and thus successfully navigate the configuration. However, Hillier's operationalization of the concept does not capture the intuitive intent of the concept: Hillier's operational definition of 'intelligibility' does *not* include any reference to specific cognitive capacities. Hillier's notion of 'intelligibility' remains fully within the realm of objective configurational properties irrespective of what one presumes about the cognitive capacities of users/observers. All that Hillier's concept asserts is that the configuration is structured in a way that *allows* for an inference from local properties to global positional properties. This is in itself an important notion. One might talk about *local-to-global coherence* or *local-to-global correlation* as an objective precondition for anybody's local-to-global orientation. This kind of objective local-to-global correlation – here specifically of local and global integration values – can indeed be considered to be a precondition of local-to-global intelligibility, but cannot in itself already constitute or guarantee intelligibility.[145] The dispute revolves around the appropriate use of a term, but it is motivated by the attempt to build a theory with a further enhanced level of analytical resolution.

What the theory of architectural autopoiesis can take up and preserve from Hillier's discussion of 'intelligibility' is the fundamental notion of *correlation* in general, and of correlations that allow for ***local to global inferences*** in particular. These are important notions that lead the theory to move from the realm of *organization* to the concern with *articulation*.

Hillier's insight is that the correlation of local and global integration is a desirable property of urban configurations, a property that might – under certain further conditions – serve to facilitate orientation. These further conditions must be as much a concern for a comprehensive theory as the configurational precondition that Hillier has aptly identified. To the extent that local connectivity can indeed be *perceived* and if such a correlation is being assumed or *expected*, this correlation can indeed become a powerful orienting mechanism for urban navigation.[146] Architecture's ability to facilitate orientation via perception and pattern recognition will be elaborated and theorized under the auspices of a general concept of articulation.

It is important to note that the notion of local-to-global correlation can be generalized beyond the rather narrow focus on the correlation of local with global integration. There can be many more potentially significant forms of local-to-global correlation as so many objective preconditions of so many orienting local-to-global inferences. The concept of ***correlation*** can and must be generalized further, beyond local-to-global correlations, to local-to-local correlations, and indeed to correlations in general. For instance, given the fact that the inside and outside of a building can rarely be simultaneously perceived, the correlation between the properties of the outside of a building and the inside of the building should be an

145 In a sense, implicit in Hillier's choice of terminology is the rather strong theoretical claim that objective 'intelligibility' as detected and measured in real urban environments produces or facilitates real, subjective intelligibility with the effect that environments that have this property function better. The claim has the status of a prima facie worthwhile hypothesis but its validation would require empirical or experimental corroboration. It should perhaps not be written into the very terminology of the theory.

146 It seems as if Hillier takes both assumptions for granted: first, that connectivity can be easily perceived, and further that users habitually expect local hubs to lead to global hubs. Perhaps this is not an unreasonable assumption with respect to habitual life in traditional city layouts, and perhaps this justifies Hillier's deployment of the term 'intelligibility'. That might very well be so, but this cannot deter the theory of architectural autopoiesis from proposing a different terminology in the attempt to construct a richer and more comprehensive theory that takes less for granted and focuses more on future design potentials than on the explanation of well established urban patterns.

important type of correlation as precondition for vital ***outside-to-inside inferences***. Finally, in general, and most importantly, there is the correlation of forms with functions, on all scales, creating the objective preconditions for ***form-to-function inferences***. (The construction of form-to-function correlations, like the construction of any correlation, cannot be achieved via isolated instances, but only by mapping one range of differences (the dependent variable) onto another range of differences (the independent variable). An *ordered range* of different forms might be correlated with a corresponding *ordered range* of different functions.)

With these formulations we are indeed arriving at the point where a definition of the concept of ***articulation*** can be refined. The facilitation of form-to-function inferences is the task and agenda of articulation, with specific attention to the cognitive conditions of the design's prospective users. Because the form-to-function inferences must operate intuitively, in a state of 'distraction' rather than via an effortful step by step analysis, it is more appropriate to talk about *associations* than about inferences. We can thus formulate the following general thesis: articulation presupposes correlation. From systematic ***correlation*** as an objective condition we must progress to ***association*** as its (potential) subjective consequence. Articulation is then that design effort that facilitates the transformation of objective correlations into subjective associations.

For the sake of 'intelligibility', ie, in order to establish the objective, organizational preconditions for intelligibility, a spatial configuration – urban or architectural – should be designed in such a way that it is saturated with such correlations. The resultant configuration might be called ***information rich***. We might also talk about a high *degree of organization*. Above we defined architectural *order* as an articulated organization. A high degree of organization is the organizational basis for a high level of architectural order. To realize this order an additional design effort is necessary, an effort that takes the cognitive capacities/constraints of the users/observers into account. This design effort is what the theory of architectural autopoiesis emphasizes under the title of ***articulation***. Architectural order is the result of organization *and* articulation, whereby objective correlations are transformed into subjective associations. It is this more elaborate concept of architectural/urban order that is the theoretically appropriate place where the concept of *intelligibility* might be applied. A mere spatial organization cannot be qualified in terms of its degree of intelligibility. Intelligibility is a property of architectural or urban orders. It signifies the perceptual/cognitive transparency or lucidness of the order in question, and constitutes one of the most important qualities that architectural and urban design, and indeed design in general, aspire to. The intelligibility of a particular architectural or urban order depends upon two factors: its organization and its articulation. Accordingly, the degree of intelligibility of the respective order must be assessed along two dimensions: the *degree of organization* on the one hand, and its *degree of articulateness* on the other hand. The latter dimension is elaborated below.

6.5 Articulation

THESIS 29

The degree to which the effective functioning of architecture must (and can) rely upon articulation rather than mere physical organization is a barometer of societal progress.

Articulation reckons with the fact that buildings function only via the user's active 'reading' of the building's spatial and functional organization. At a certain level of social complexity a building's *order*, designed to structure an intended life-process, can only realize its intended role if it reckons with and enlists the user's capacity actively to 'read' and comprehend the order of the building.[147] Only on the basis of ***articulate*** organizations will users be enabled to navigate, appropriate and collectively utilize the built environment to its fullest potential. The ability thus to enlist the perceiving/comprehending users depends upon a design effort that systematically reflects the legibility of a spatial arrangement. As organizational complexity is being built up during the design process, 'aesthetic' control is required to prevent visual chaos and to preserve legibility. Legibility has a phenomenological and a semiological dimension. The phenomenological aspect requires reflection upon the conditions of effective perception, and the semiological aspect requires reflection upon the conditions that allow the interplay of spatial, morphological and material differentiations to produce a semiological code that can inform and direct the socialized users. The task of imbuing the organized environment with a heightened legibility is the architectural design task of ***articulation***.

6.5.1 ARTICULATION VS ORGANIZATION

The distinction of articulation versus organization cannot be aligned with the distinction of form versus function. The two distinctions intersect

147 According to the definitions of the theory of architectural autopoeisis only those spatial/functional organizations that are designed so as to enlist the user's capacity actively to 'read' and comprehend them are elevated to the title of *orders*.

each other. Both organization and articulation have functional as well as formal aspects. Both organizational diagrams *and* strategies of articulation are subject to the formal a priori, and *both* need to be selected on the basis of their social functionality.

The task of architecture as a functional subsystem of modern society is to *organize and* ***articulate*** new social functions by means of new spatial forms. Articulation is not adornment, but the continuation of the organizing effort by other means. Articulation augments the effectiveness of organization. Adornment can become a means of articulation if it is employed as a phenomenologically effective accentuation, or if it is integrated into a semiologically effective code, or both at the same time.

Beyond organization by means of establishing appropriate adjacencies, distances, barriers and connections etc emerges the task of ordering by means of *articulation*.[148] Thus we may distinguish ***physical organization*** from ***articulated organization***. The abstract organizational diagrams discussed in the previous section are open with respect to whether they will be concretized as merely physical organizations ***channelling bodies*** or as articulated organizations ***guiding subjects***.

In ambitious architectural designs, physical organization is usually augmented by means of articulation, resulting in an articulated organization. Articulated organizations presuppose physical organization as their basis. However, we cannot assume that articulation merely emphasizes an organization that is already functioning as such. There are many social organizations that can only function if their spatial organization is articulated, because their efficient functioning relies upon the quick comprehension of the users, and this cannot be achieved by focusing on physical operations (distancing, physical separation, physical connection) only. One of the main arguments developed here is that advanced social institutions and life-processes can no longer be ordered by physical means only, but increasingly rely on spatial organizations that are highly articulated. Articulation is always selective. It involves both the accentuation and the suppression of features, revealing and concealing, making conspicuous as well as inconspicuous. It is often necessary to conceal, avoiding the conspicuity of certain features that might otherwise impress themselves and distract/disorient the users.[149]

The distinction between organization and articulation recognizes the difference between the organizing operations of the building that work via

148 'Articulation' comprises both phenomenological articulation and semiological articulation (signification).

149 A lot of ingenuity and effort are invested in Minimalist detailing which essentially consists in the suppression of construction details.

physical imposition and those ordering effects that work via the user's perception, conception and comprehension of their environment. The effective structuring of the social process via channelling, separating and aggregating human bodies serves as the criterion of successful physical organization. Objective measures like the absolute/relative size, proximity/distance and the relative position of spaces, as well as the capacity/speed of circulation possible between these spaces are relevant here.[150] In contrast articulation is 'measured' subjectively, on the basis of the degree of ***navigation***, ***orientation*** and ***immersion*** or ***atmospheric priming*** it affords the respective users. These three aspects constitute the three main functions of all articulatory efforts within architecture. Navigation refers to wayfinding within a territorial matrix. Orientation refers to the grasping of the social situation and the anticipation of the social interaction-scenarios that might be expected within a particular environment. Immersion or atmospheric priming instills mental and emotional disposition that initiates and sustains successful social interaction. All three functions of articulation contribute to architecture's capacity to address its societal function: the framing of social communication.

The three aspects of legibility thus furnish the criteria for what is to be considered well articulated. In order to anticipate and predict these subject-dependent affordances we need to work with quasi-objective 'phenomenological qualities' and the presumed 'semiological charge' of a projected spatial configuration and architectural morphology.[151]

Articulation over-determines organization. Articulation can even substitute for organization where demarcation no longer equals physical separation and instead relies on the 'reading' of space. Orientation within a sufficiently complex social space indeed requires ***active conceptualization*** rather than mere passive perception. As stated above, any simple concept of a built organization that is construed as functioning by means of the physical channelling of bodies only, and that receives articulation only as a secondary add-on that is merely improving this prior functionality by making it transparent, is insufficient. Today we witness many complex spheres of social life – for example, the open

150 Bill Hillier's measure of 'integration' of a spatial unit within a network of such units belongs in this category of objective measures the geometric (physical) organization of space. Hillier goes on to suggest that a further objective measure – the degree of coincidence between global and local integration – can be used as an indication of the *intelligibility* of the system. However, Hillier's concept does not reflect the user's cognition and thus remains in the realm of organisation rather than articulation.

151 The design process relies on the designer's own continuous, critical assessment of the legibility of the design – trying to see the design through the eyes of its future audience and users.

office landscapes of contemporary corporations – where physical separation is far too crude and restrictive a measure to order and frame the process. The environment is obviously always physical, but the contemporary means of ordering – lightweight screens, soffits, steps, morphological distinctions, light levels etc – are too nuanced and subtle to function via their (far reduced) physical presence. Physically the thresholds would simply be overrun, if they were not perceived, conceived and understood as communications. The meaning of these articulations is not always explicit, and may be navigated subliminally. They order the ongoing communication as framing context. Although primarily operating via subliminal cognition, the implicit meaning of spatial settings can – at any time – be made the subject of a clarifying, explicit communication.

6.5.2 THE PROBLEM OF ORIENTATION AND THE PROBLEMATIC OF LEGIBILITY

The reference problem for the task of articulation is ***orientation***.[152] Articulation should facilitate orientation by making the spatial organization and the social order within it legible. Orientation includes wayfinding within a spatial configuration, but it encompasses much more than that. Orientation includes the steering of expectations about the social scenarios that might unfold within a space and about the conduct that is appropriate within the space. The built environment is always *more or less* legible, whether there was an articulatory effort at work or not. ***Articulation*** therefore does not establish legibility as such. Rather articulation is the competent, purposeful effort to *increase* the legibility of a proposed spatial/functional organization.[153]

Again: the built environment is always *more or less* legible. Organizations that are designed by paying attention to their physical effect only, nevertheless end up with an outward form that can be taken as an orienting clue (or so-called 'index'). Users can indeed always learn to read their physical environments, extracting clues from the observation of regularities. In theory this is always possible, just as we can learn to read and navigate a landscape on the basis of observed regularities. The problem is that the contemporary diversity and complexity of social institutions *and* the contemporary proliferation of construction technologies/materials give far too much scope for random variety. The

152 For the sake of brevity the term orientation is used as *pars pro toto*, referring to the three functions of navigation, orientation and priming/immersion.

153 This may not only be a form of graphic post-production – like a post-fitted signage system – but also a concern that is folded into the very conception of the design.

same materials/forms are used for diverse social institutions and the same social institutions might be constructed with very diverse forms/materials. This condition requires a strategic approach to the selection of spatial forms and materials, with the view to visual clarification and systematic codification. The aim should be to establish systematic correlations that map the social differentiation onto spatial, morphological and material differentiations. The more complex the social system, the more resourceful must be the articulatory repertoire of any architectural style to cope with the sharpened problematic of legibility.[154]

6.5.3 ARTICULATE VS INARTICULATE ORGANIZATION

We have distinguished physical organization from articulated organization. Then we had to admit that merely physically ordered organizations can nevertheless be (more or less) legible. We defined articulation as the conscious design effort towards increasing legibility. As conscious effort directed towards a (more or less) generic audience, the articulatory effort constitutes a *communication*, to the extent to which it is recognized, understood and attributed[155] as communication. The fact that the articulated organization is being recognized as deliberate communication is itself a factor enhancing its potential effectiveness. The audience's attention level and perspective can be expected to shift favourably once an intention to communicate is detected in the built environment.[156] However, even under this favourable disposition, there is no guarantee that the articulatory effort succeeds in increasing legibility. The opposite might hold and confusion might be introduced into a complex that might otherwise have been reasonably legible. Therefore we need to distinguish ***articulate*** organizations from (potentially badly) articulated organizations. The achievement of a truly articulate organization is the name of the game in architecture. The opposite term ***inarticulate*** organization thus comprises everything that is in one way or another deficient with respect to articulation: the merely physically ordered organization – legible or illegible – as well as the articulated organization that remains or turns out to be illegible to all or most users. It is important to note that the concept of articulate organization includes the designer's deliberate effort as a necessary moment of its definition. What the concept requires is not only successful legibility but a

154 It has to be noted here that the solution cannot be the mere simplification of the visual field. This would imply the obliteration rather than the articulation of complexity.

155 Communications via built architectural works are attributed to the client, host, occupying organization rather than to the architect.

156 We are referring here only to the relevant audience that is trying to read and navigate the space and is thus motivated to look for clues.

successful legibility that has been achieved through a conscious design effort deploying deliberate strategies of articulation. Articulate organization is posited here as the prized endgame of architecture as conscious design discourse, in contradistinction to the vernacular tradition.

The section on architectural style stated that styles differ with respect to the way they handle form-function relations. We can further state that they represent specific ways of translating social into spatial order. We can observe that the requirements of articulation historically advance in prominence over and above the requirements of mere physical ordering. Now we can further specify that styles may differ in their ability to cater for this increasing demand of the advancing social order. The Baroque style, for instance, seems more articulate than the Renaissance. In general, we might surmise that the progression of styles, that is the history of architecture, might be written from the vantage point of a hypothesized increase in the capacity to cope with the advancing social demand to generate articulate spatial organizations. The degree of articulateness is then a primary criterion for the competitive evaluation of styles.

6.5.4 ARTICULATION AS THE CORE COMPETENCY OF ARCHITECTURE

Contemporary efforts at architectural articulation address the need for an increasingly rapid orientation in an increasingly complex built environment/social arena. This quest for orientation demands legibility in the face of mounting complexity.

The problematic of legibility provides the decisive *differentia specifica* that distinguishes architecture from engineering. While engineering is concerned with the provision of physical support systems (stability, climatic control etc), architecture is concerned with the spatial framing of social processes. This is a task that needs to go beyond physical organization to include articulate organization, addressed to perceptive, comprehending subjects. Thus the overall architectural design task, the spatialization of social processes, has two aspects: physical organization and articulation. Both aspects are currently handled by the discipline of architecture.

However, a potential future differentiation of the discipline into independent subsystems (rather than dependent subdivisions within a single system) can be detected here. Should the evolution proceed in this direction, the time-honoured title of architecture could only be given to one of the two social systems. Given the social cachet that comes with this title, the representative of the other of the two contending subdisciplines is likely to be demoted to become either a 'mere engineer' or a 'mere decorator' respectively. It is my thesis here that, should this differentiation occur, it will be the task of articulation that most probably can seize the prized title of 'architecture'.

The recent emphasis on 'operativity' and 'performance' fails to take account of this crucial moment of articulation that distinguishes architecture from engineering. The opposition of performance versus representation that has dominated the polemic against both Postmodernism and Deconstructivism is a false opposition. This one-sided emphasis on operativity and the related ambition to 'determine' rather than intuitively 'invent' form[157] induces avant-garde design research to gravitate towards those problems that tend to be operation focused, such as transport interchanges where physical organization seems to be primary, involving objective processes only. Attention to such physical operations is always involved in solving architectural problems, but the more *specific* task of architecture involves the articulation of space with reference to perceiving and comprehending subjects and their communicative interactions. This, in turn, involves the question of phenomenology, ie, *how are pertinent percepts solicited?*, as well as the question of semiology, ie, *how are pertinent systems of significations constructed and activated?* Answers to the semiological question do not necessarily imply the utilization of well-established references. 'Signification' might involve the negation, decoding or subversion of known references and, within sufficiently large structures, new semiological systems can be forged (as will be elaborated below). That the semiological dimension of architecture has been denigrated in recent avant-garde discourses is due to the dialectical overreaction against the undue over-emphasis of issues of meaning during the previous periods of Postmodernism and Deconstructivism. The suppression of semiotic concerns is therefore a reactive rather than inherent trait of the recent avant-garde. It is a key contention of the theory of architectural autopoiesis that it is necessary to reintegrate both phenomenology and semiology into the design research programme of the current avant-garde.

6.5.5 GENERALIZING THE CONCEPT OF FUNCTION

All the above implies that phenomenology and semiology in architecture should not be opposed to function. Rather, phenomenological and semiological concerns should be subsumed within an updated, more general and more demanding notion of function, in line with the reconceptualization of functionality in terms of action-artefact networks.

157 For instance in Winy Maas' programme of architecture as datascape.

Both the phenomenological and the semiological dimension of architecture, together, have to be theorized as catering for the articulatory demands placed upon architecture, over and above the basic demand for hard, physical organization. We might accordingly distinguish ***hard functioning*** and ***soft functioning***. A physical distance functions as an undeniable, physical imposition. A solid wall constitutes a hard territorial boundary by physical force. In contrast, a step, balustrade or ceiling design might articulate a territorial distinction without barring movement and communication from territory to territory. These devices function softly, via suggestion rather than via imposition. The territorial boundary no longer imposes a physical barrier. This coincidence of territorial distinction and uninterrupted communication across territorial boundaries lies beyond the capacity of mere physical organisation. But it is this coincidence that affords much enhanced efficiencies in the spatial ordering of complex social systems. Even where physical organization is operating already, an articulatory overlay further enhances the social functionality of the space. The *soft* function of the wall is to create a perceptually palpable identity and atmosphere over and above the hard physical separation. The articulation of the space might also be involved in semiological coding operations that indicate the space's relative position in the overall spatial organization as well as its particular, designated function within an overall system of distinguished functions.

The utility of a spatial organization might be considerably enhanced by means of an effective articulation that makes the underlying physical organization and the functional distribution of the territory legible to its users. The more complex and intricate the accommodated social institution, the more important, and indeed indispensable, becomes the articulatory enhancement of the spatial organization. Full functionality can no longer be sustained without a well-articulated design that satisfies both phenomenological and semiological criteria. This implies that the effective spatial ordering of the accommodated social institution can only be achieved by the coincidence of both physical organization *and* articulation. The solid wall operates as overpowering physical device separating domains in terms of access and visual/acoustic isolation. Thus it produces an organizational effect by means of physical power. In contrast to this *physical organization* the *phenomenological/semiological ordering* uses the necessary physical substrate in its articulatory (rather than in its physical) capacity. Obviously both operations rely on a physical substrate that can be specified in a set of construction documents. However, the conditions of effective phenomenological/semiological ordering stretch far beyond what can be delineated and specified within a traditional architectural drawing. Virtuoso articulation cannot be designed via abstract diagrams or 2D line-drawings. Thus the task of articulation, especially under the condition of complexity and radical innovation, calls for a significant expansion of the design media of the discipline. The designer needs the enhanced visual simulation capacities of 3D rendering and animation to calibrate the perceptual efficacy of the design.

The visual appearance of buildings and spaces matters enormously within architecture. Both architects and clients demonstate their investment in appearances and aesthetic matters. The theory of architectural autopoiesis shows why this investment is not a fetish or indulgence. The rationality of this investment lies in the fact that architecture functions as much via its appearance as it functions via its physical sorting of bodies. This has always been the case. However, architectural theory has tended to set appearance against function. In contrast, the theory of architectural autopoiesis incorporates the concern for the visual appearance of architectural works within an expanded or generalized concept of architectural functioning. This generalized concept of function in turn demands that appearances are consciously functionalized within the design process. What is new in recent times is that the physical sorting of bodies recedes in relative importance. What is also new is that societal development has accelerated and social complexity has increased to a point where the conscious functionalization of appearances within a strategic, theory-led design effort becomes more and more urgent. This fact is recognized by positing articulation as fundamental dimension of architecture's task.

6.6 The Phenomenological vs the Semiological Dimension of Architecture

THESIS 30

Phenomenology and semiology address different dimensions of the task of architectural articulation that are equally indispensable for the built environment's functionality: the perception of spatial order and the comprehension of social order.

Both the phenomenological and the semiological dimension of architecture are dimensions of architecture's functionality.

Thus far we have coupled the phenomenological and semiological dimensions, to distinguish them, as subject-dependent dimensions, from the objective organizational dimension. Now it is necessary to distinguish phenomenology from semiology leading to the following tripartite distinction:

- The ***organizational dimension*** of architecture is the part of the architectural discourse/design-effort that is concerned with the physical conditions of the built environment's social functionality. The organizational dimension is based on the fact that the effective use of the built environment depends upon the physical ordering of the user's activities and relative movements.[158]
- The ***phenomenological dimension*** of architecture is the part of the architectural discourse/design-effort that is concerned with the perceptual conditions of the built environment's social functionality. The phenomenological dimension is based on the fact that the effective use of the built environment depends upon the user's fast and comprehensive perception of its spatial organization.
- The ***semiological (semantic) dimension*** of architecture is the part of the architectural discourse/design-effort that is concerned with the semantic conditions of the built environment's social functionality. The semiological dimension is based on the fact that the effective use of the built environment depends upon the user's fast and comprehensive understanding of the built environment as system of signification that reveals its social meaning, ie, the types of social interactions that are to be expected within the encountered environment.

Between these three dimensions obtains a relation of successive presupposition such that the successful activation of the semantic dimension presupposes a prior accomplishment within the phenomenological dimension which in turn presupposes at least a certain minimum of physical organization. The final result of these staggered achievements is the accomplishment of a designated and articulated spatial organization, ie, an architectural order that frames and thus facilitates the participating actor's orderly communication processes.

Architecture functions only if it is understood by its users. This understanding presupposes the recognition of figures and configurations as well as the observation of regular correlations of spatial forms with social functions within the built environment. These regular correlations might be a side effect of physical organization or the result of a conscious articulatory effort of the designer. Independently of their origin as side effects or intended effects, in each instance, regular correlations consolidate to more or less fixed ***signs***. In the first case, where the sign emerges on the basis of unintended regularities, the observed

158 The physical dimension of architecture is the dimension where functionality is established by means which do not depend upon specifically sharpened perceptual and semantic capacities of the occupants to achieve its organizational objectives.

spatio-physical feature operates as a so-called ***indexical sign***. In the second case, where the relationship is consciously crafted it operates as a so-called ***symbolic sign.*** Irrespectively, the emerging sign system belongs to the semiological dimension of architecture. This semiological dimension of architecture thus emerges partly by default semiosis and partly on the basis of intended signification.

It is important to note that effective meanings cannot be established by fiat. Deliberate strategies of signification are no more than suggestive steering efforts that rely on the user's acceptance and routine utilization to become effective. This user-dependency limits the degree of novelty/strangeness that can be introduced at any one time. For radical novelty to succeed, a certain critical mass of construction – as a critical quantum of material for semiosis – is required. Within mainstream architecture, deliberate strategies of signification are often just imitating the results of unconscious vernacular building, following on from the indexical signs as conventional condensation of the originally unintended correlations. For instance, there might be the deliberate intention to make sure that a villa looks like a villa, a hotel looks like a hotel etc. Thus emerges a ***conventional symbolic canon*** of (all too) familiar architectural signs. It is one of the primary agendas of the theory of architectural autopoiesis to contribute to the development of a semiological expertise that can be confident enough to break through this barrier of conventionality.

The ***phenomenological dimension*** refers to pre-semantic cognitive processes where less familiar figurations and configurations are perceived and percepts are constructed rather than simply retrieved via indexical, iconic or symbolic triggers. The construction of percepts might be both bottom-up – as in the famous Gestalt-grouping principles (proximity, similarity, continuity, symmetry, closure) – as well as top-down on the basis of prior schemata and mental maps. These schemata, like axes, grids, concentric organizations etc, are abstract and thus open to novel interpretation. Here, in the pre-semantic domain, articulation facilitates perception by means of visual clarification in terms of general criteria of perceptibility and conspicuity, as have been elaborated by the Gestalt psychologists in the early 20th century. It is important to recognize the phenomenological dimension as independent, pre-semantic domain of articulation that operates in advance of any iconography or conventional symbolic canon. Over-reliance on the semiological dimension of architecture tends towards iconography, which is often rather inimical to radical innovation. It is possible to articulate abstract configurations that can be navigated without yet being coded with fixed social meanings, thus giving scope to creative appropriation.

Avant-garde architects should be fully aware of the complex semiological codings that always operate within the social utilization of the built environment. But this understanding of the prevailing semiological codes should enable the architect to break up and subvert the prevailing meanings rather than only use and perpetuate them. This practice of 'making strange' is indeed a hallmark of all avant-garde design practice – although this is not always reflected and instrumentalized in relation to a programme of articulation.[159] In order to facilitate the build up of a new legible order, eventually engendering a new semiosis, the architect must reflect upon the cognitive capacities of its users, and perhaps tap into the relevant psychological research. In fact, there has been an interesting historical lineage whereby the insights of Gestalt psychology have been channelled into the discourse of architecture. Le Corbusier, László Moholy-Nagy, Sigfried Giedion, György Kepes, Colin Rowe, Christian Norberg-Schulz, Michael Graves and Peter Eisenman are among those who concerned themselves with questions of perception and took note of Gestalt psychology.

The study of the psychological science of perception might be helpful, but is no *conditio sine qua non*. The architect can work quite intuitively and use his own perceptual capacity as ongoing control mechanism. However, reliance on the average architect's intuitions is insufficient to address society's increasingly rich and complex life-processes. The task of articulation requires the explicit recognition of architecture's phenomenological dimension as a field of design research. It is one of the agendas of the theory of architectural autopoiesis to instigate a collective, investigative discourse as well as theoretically informed design experiments in this dimension.

6.7 The Phenomenological Dimension of Architectural Articulation

THESIS 31

Within the avant-garde stage of a style, articulation strategies must emphasize the phenomenological dimension as independent, pre-semantic arena of articulation that gives scope to creative appropriation beyond fixed meanings.

While architecture shares the semiological dimension with other design disciplines like product and fashion design, the phenomenological dimension, although perhaps not exclusive to architecture, is of unique

159 This practice of 'making strange' was first formulated in the art system (Surrealism) and within the context of modern theatre (Brecht).

importance to architecture and urban design. The perception of architectural and urban territories presents some unique cognitive challenges in comparison with the perception of objects of the kind product designers deal with. The perceptual identification and isolation of objects like mobile phones, handbags, chairs and bicycles is unproblematic because they move against their background. The integrity and demarcation of architectural entities is, in comparison, always more problematic. The distinction of buildings within a contiguous urban fabric is often difficult. Strictly speaking, the built environment is a single, continuous entity. Its decomposition into units lacks the hard criterion of independent mobility. The perceptual identification of architectural unities is further made difficult by the fact that most relevant architectural unities (buildings, territories) elude the scope of individual vistas. While the totality of a mobile phone is in view all the time (or can be brought to view and easily grasped by swivelling it in one's hand), the totality of a building always eludes the scope of what can be seen at any one time. Cognition has actively to synthesize architectural unities from perceptual fragments. Thus phenomenological articulation is required to support the perceptual decomposition of a global scene into relevant units, both via the perceptual severing of an otherwise continuous contiguity, and via the synthesis of asynchronous parts into unities.

Thus in the case of architecture, the synthesis of parts into relevant unities is burdened by the fact that movement and time are required to synthesize the perceptual totality of the building. The front and back of the building can never be experienced at the same time. The same separation in time exists with respect to inside and outside. They can never be experienced simultaneously.[160] The same applies to interior spaces. Human vision is not 360 degree vision. The perception of an enveloping space requires time and synthesis, even in the case of simple convex spaces. Also, the different, collaborating parts of the building's interior – although intended to form a functional unity – can never be apprehended together. Instead a mental map needs to be constructed to make orientation possible. But in order to construct such a map the spatial organization of those parts relative to each other has to be grasped. The subject/user has to understand what belongs together and where a different zone or territory begins. What is required here is that the phenomenological articulation furnishes conspicuous visual contrasts

160 The distinction of inside versus outside is the *differentia specifica* that demarcates architecture from the other design disciplines. See Volume 1, chapter 2.5.5 *The Specificity of Architecture within the Design Disciplines*.

and continuities that support the individuation of different territories. These visual differentiations should be ordered into a system of visual similitudes and contrasts that corresponds to the system of social distinctions. Thus, especially in view of articulating larger complexes, the establishment of these contrasts and continuities should be rule based. What is further required is the grasp of the spatial relations and access opportunities between the distinguished units.

The subject's mastery of all these perceptual challenges can be facilitated by the design effort of phenomenological articulation. Phenomenology thus facilitates orientation and navigation. It should do so, as much as possible, on the basis of the subject's cognitive background processing rather than requiring the subject's concentrated observation.

6.7.1 THE PERCEPTUAL CONSTITUTION OF OBJECTS AND SPACES

Fast orientation in complex scenes is based on the capacity to perceive configurations as whole figures.[161] This instant (re)cognition of the whole figure without prior (re)cognition of the parts might be referred to as the psychological primacy of wholes. The recognition of individual parts is not implied, and requires a further, separate focus and cognitive effort. The recognition of wholes, ie, simple or complex objects that form a functional unit or unit of interaction, is a vital capacity of all higher organisms that have to identify prey and avoid predators. Perception, involving object- and pattern-recognition, is not a matter of passive reception. The identification of stable objects within the ongoing stream of impressions is an act of cognitive synthesis. Perception is proactively involved in the very construction or constitution of objects and patterns. The achievement of synthesizing the multitude of impressions from the tactile, auditory and visual sense, each delivering ever-changing sensory inputs (sense-data), relies on a capacity that is species-dependent and to a certain extent subject to cultural overdetermination. The acquisition of such an interpretative capacity is an evolutionary achievement of the species and a developmental achievement within each individual. According to the pioneer of developmental psychology, Jean Piaget, the full achievement of this competency – which Piaget terms the achievement of *object permanence* (OP) – is realized at the age of two and marks a definite stage in the cognitive development of the child.

161 The German word for figure is 'Gestalt'. Accordingly, Gestalt psychology is the psychology of figure recognition. (*Gestalt-psychologie* is the name Max Werheimer and his followers gave their original, groundbreaking research into and theory of the psychology of perception.)

The evolved human mind constructs or calculates the world of stable objects from the ever-changing stream of sensory inputs. The input for this calculation comprises the coincidence and concatenation of ever-changing, fragmented, tactile encounters and visual sensations. The visual sensations are subject to perspective distortions as well as to continuously shifting conditions of visual overlap and reflections due to modulated conditions of light/shadow. The perspective distortions are regularly concatenated and correlated with the sense of bodily movements. Reflections and overlap are also correlated with the sense of bodily movement indicating the subject's shifting spatial position. The fluidity and subjectivity of sensory impressions have led philosophers to ruminate upon the reality of the 'external world'.

The empiricist philosopher Bertrand Russell considers physical objects to be nothing but 'logical constructions from sense-data' whereby the criterion that distinguishes stable objects from hallucinations is the regular, predictable concatenation of the sequence of sense-data. Bertrand Russell defined sense-data as follows: 'Let us give the name of "sense-data" to the things that are immediately known in sensation: such things as colours, sounds, smells, hardnesses, roughnesses, and so on.'[162] Russell's analysis of the perception of a simple everyday object is instructive:

> ... let us concentrate attention on the table. To the eye it is oblong, brown and shiny, to the touch it is smooth and cool and hard; when I tap it, it gives out a wooden sound.... Although I believe that the table is 'really' of the same colour all over, the parts that reflect the light look much brighter than the other parts, and some parts look white because of reflected light. I know that, if I move, the parts that reflect the light will be different, so that the apparent distribution of colours on the table will change.... This colour is not something which is inherent in the table, but something depending upon the table and the spectator and the way the light falls on the table.... The *shape* of the table is no better. We are all in the habit of judging as to the 'real' shapes of things, and we do this so unreflectingly that we come to think we actually see the real shapes. But, in fact, as we all have to learn if we try to draw, a given thing looks different in shape from every different point of view. If our table is 'really' rectangular, it will look, from almost all points of view, as if it had two acute angles and two obtuse angles. If opposite sides are parallel, they will look as if they converged to a point away from the spectator; if they are of equal length, they will look as if the nearer side were longer. All these things are not commonly noticed in looking at a table, because experience has taught us to construct the 'real'

162 Bertrand Russell, *The Problems of Philosophy*, Home University Library, 1912, Oxford University Press (Oxford/New York), paperback, 1959, chapter I.

> shape from the apparent shape, and the 'real' shape is what interests us as practical men. But the 'real' shape is not what we see; it is something inferred from what we see. And what we see is constantly changing in shape as we move about the room . . .[163]

The underlying philosophical quest of Russell to explicate the ontological status of physical objects of experience and to give a critical foundation to science is of no concern to us here. (Russell's philosophical efforts in these respects have long since been superseded.) What is of interest here is the illustration of the difference between immediate appearances and the 'inferred' reality. In everyday life our experience of this 'inferred' reality is immediate, although we have the ability to reflect upon the underlying appearances. Painters need to be able to concentrate on appearances to simulate the visual impression of reality. The theory of architectural autopoiesis argues that architects too should pay close attention to how spatial reality is 'inferred' or 'constructed' from appearances. This process of construction or inference is a cognitive process that happens preconsciously. In a cognitive science of perception something like sense-data (retinal images) are taken as the primary input to perceptual processes. Within consciousness the complete object is the primary given. The process of constructing stable mental images is an automatic process that renders that which is immediately given to our senses virtually invisible. It takes a rather artificial mode of attention to abstract from the automatic recognition of objects and to focus instead on what is given to the senses. This artificial mode of concentrated attention and reflection is at the root of the philosophical methodology of phenomenology, the so-called phenomenological reduction. A similar, artificial focus on unprocessed sense-data is required for the task of realistic painting. When a child tries to depict a familiar object it lacks realism. It seems as if the child goes by what it knows rather than what it really sees. This shows that the realism we expect from a skilful rendition – supposedly depicting the thing or scene just as we see it – is a rather effortful, artificial achievement that in no way comes naturally. Seeing cannot easily be separated from knowing and recognizing. But that is what is required in order to produce the kind of realistic simulation of visual reality that we admire in virtuoso painting. This kind of simulation requires us to invert our natural perceptual attitude. It requires

163 Ibid. See also: Bertrand Russell, *Our Knowledge of the External World*, Routledge Classics (London/New York), 2009, first published by Open Court Publishing Company (Chicago), 1914; and Bertrand Russell, 'The Philosophy of Logical Atomism', first published in: *The Monist* 1918/1919, also in: Bertrand Russell, *Logic and Knowledge – Essays 1901–1950*, Capricorn Books (New York), 1951.

us to realize what is projected onto our retina when we experience objects within an environment. It took thousands of years of development before the art of drawing/painting was able effectively to simulate the visual sense-data that our senses receive and upon which the acts of perceptual synthesis are performed to deliver our experience of the tangible world. The simulation of perspective distortion was a first major step – understood and promoted by Alberti. Perspective did not only advance painting, it also inaugurated architecture's skilful engagement with the phenomenological dimension of the built environment by establishing its capacity to simulate the visual impressions that a building or space would make. Leonardo da Vinci's simulation of air-perspective indicating far distances was another step. The advanced simulation of light and shadow effects followed, most notably by Caravaggio and Rembrandt. The architecture of the Baroque reflects this new sensibility towards light and shadow effects with its emphasis of deep relief and plasticity.

The history of painting can thus be written as a long march back to the sensory base of perception. The last stage and final moment of arrival – Impressionism – both delivers compelling simulations and, at this very moment of delivery, shows its own artifice and thereby finally reveals the creative act of perceptual synthesis. The Impressionist canvas, if viewed from a distance, displays a convincing simulation of a real-life scene. Upon close inspection the image dissolves into an amorphous flux of elementary colour patches.

Impressionist painting might very well be interpreted as either an anticipation or an illustration of the radically empiricist philosophy of sense-data that emerged at about the same time.[164] The next step was Cubism. Like Impressionism, Cubism was concerned with the investigation of perception. Both Impressionism and Cubism were working with quasi-scientific series. Analytical Cubism goes further and, as it were, moves from the Impressionist's real-life experiments in perception to abstract 'laboratory' experiments that allow for the systematic manipulation of critical variables in order to home in on some profound and compelling effects.[165] The key dichotomy of all perception and all prior representation – the distinction of figure and ground – was probed. The figures are broken into fragments and assimilated to the

164 Although Russell's text dates from 1912, similar ideas had been discussed earlier, most notably Ernst Mach's *The Analysis of Sensations and the Relation of the Physical to the Psychical*, Open Court Publishing Company (Chicago/London), 1914. The German original – *Die Analyse der Empfindungen und das Verhältnis des Physischen zum Psychischen*, Verlag Gustav Fischer (Jena), 1886.

165 This interpretation of Cubism does not make any claims with respect to Picasso and Braque's self-conscious intentions.

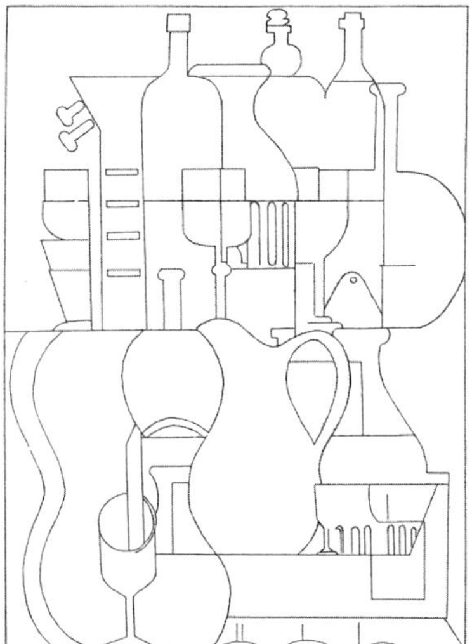

Figure 31 György Kepes, diagram of painting of Ozenfant. From Kepes, *Language of Vision*, 1947

background in the attempt to find the threshold where a figure crystallizes from the amorphous background and dissolves back into it. The paintings try to capture this tipping point. If one looks successively at a whole series of such works, one can realize that this threshold or tipping point depends on what one has been looking at before. Thus the sequencing of images – or vistas in a spatial sequence – can determine how each individual image or vista is perceived. Within the psychology of perception this effect is called 'priming'. The Gestalt psychologist Kurt Koffka, following Edgar Rubin, talks about 'figural after-effects'.[166]

The early Cubist paintings worked with the fragmentation of the human figure. The Cubists also worked with still lifes: simple scenes of everyday life with the most mundane and taken-for-granted objects like bottles or vases on a table. Their pictorial problematization of these most simple and clear objects mirrors the philosophers' preferred examples – chairs, tables and the book on the table in front of them – as vehicles for the problematization of reality and knowledge.

Le Corbusier experimented with the ambiguity and volatility of perceptual object synthesis in his paintings from the 1920s. His *Still Life* from 1920, at first glance, seems to depict a guitar as the most prominent, central figure in the painting. Further exposure to the painting

166 Kurt Koffka, 'Perception: An Introduction to the Gestalt-Theorie', in: *Psychological Bulletin* *19*, 531–85, 1922.

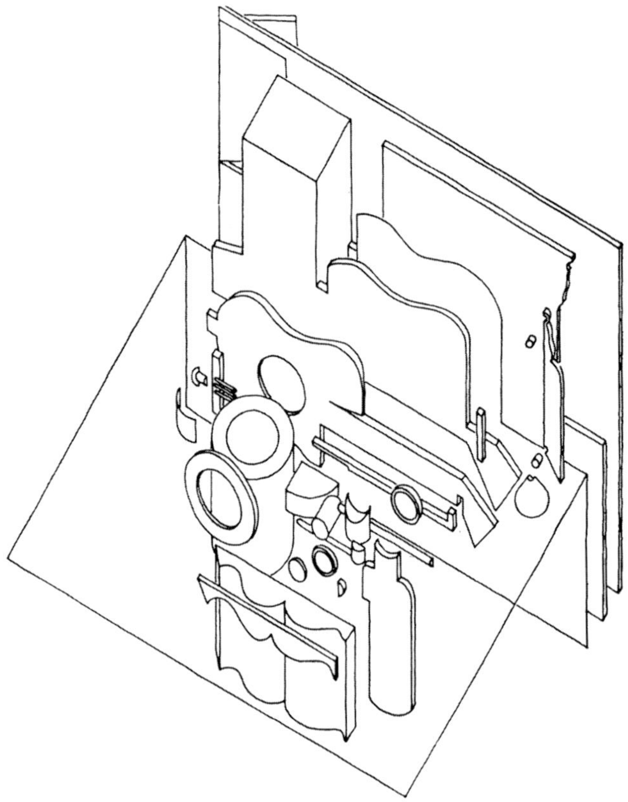

Figure 32 Phenomenal transparency, diagram of 1920 *Still Life* by Le Corbusier. From Rowe & Slutzky, *Transparency: Literal and Phenomenal*, 1997

slowly reveals other objects. However, these other objects cannot coexist with the guitar. They dissolve the guitar by reinterpreting its supposed parts within other object formations. The circle in the centre of the body of the guitar (supposedly depicting the guitar's rosette) becomes the top plate of a pile of plates. What seemed to be the tuning keys of the guitar turn out to be the mouths of various bottles, glasses and pipes placed upon the table. Even the body of the guitar disappears and re-appears as the back of a chair that is pushed against the table. The painting thus calibrates a multiplicity of equally plausible decompositions. What is a whole and what is a part, and to which wholes the parts assemble remains unresolved.

The synthesis of a multitude of impressions into a set of stable objects is the fundamental task of perception. Ephemeral appearances have to be distinguished from recurrent properties. Another, related task – or perhaps another way to pose the same problem – is the task of decomposing a complex scene or perceptual totality into relevant units of interaction. Effective units of interaction, like people, animals, flocks of animals, plants etc, have to be distinguished from each other, from their background, and from coincidental clusters of features that do not form an integrated, functioning whole. The surest criterion for what should be considered an effective unit of interaction is what moves together: the various body parts of an animal, the flock of birds, the stone that rolls down the hill. Within the built environment, architecture's domain of intervention, this ultimate criterion of object individuation is not available. In architecture, object identities are always problematic. What should be considered as an integral whole, as effective unit of interaction, must remain a precarious inference. There is no ultimate test of wholeness. Yet, within the built environment it remains as vital as it is within nature to understand what belongs together to form an effective unit of interaction. What works together should be perceived as integral entity. The perceived visual decomposition of a scene should match the functional decomposition of the territory.

Where does a space, a territory, or a building begin and where does it end? What works together? What functions as a unit? Which sequence or cluster of spaces belongs together as spatial system sustaining a social system and its integral life-process? Functional units must be recognized as such in order to function. Therefore spatial elements must be allocated and understood as parts of larger, effective wholes. The potential for ambiguity is enormous here. But this ambiguity is not only a problem. This ambiguity entails an exciting potential that can be exploited in respectively astute design strategies. Architectural and urban design are creative fields where the reflection upon the principles that govern perceptual synthesis and decomposition is most pertinent.

6.7.2 COGNITIVE PRINCIPLES OF GESTALT-PERCEPTION

At the exact same time when Picasso and Braque developed Cubism, and Russell analyzed the constitution of objects in terms of sense-data, Max Wertheimer (1880–1943) – together with his collaborators Kurt Koffka (1886–1941) and Wolfgang Köhler (1887–1967) – started to develop a new approach to the psychology of perception that was soon termed *Gestalt psychology*. The key concept of *Gestalt* – the German word for figure or pattern – indicates the keen interest in the fact that perception involves the organization of integral figures or patterns. The problematic of the previous chapter – the perceptual constitution of objects and the related decomposition of a complex scene – is the key problematic of Gestalt psychology.

The key tenet of Gestalt psychology is the insistence on the experiential primacy of wholes and the rejection of the notion of atomistically conceived sensations, insisting that 'percepts have characteristics which cannot be derived from the characteristics of their ultimate components, the so-called sensations'.[167] The Gestalt psychologists discovered and documented through extensive experiments that the identity and properties of the various elements within a perceptual field are relational rather than autonomous. The properties of parts are determined by the wholes they are perceived to be a part of. And, as Koffka insists, 'these properties need not be like those of traditional psychology, "dead" attributes, possessing a "so-being" only, but that many of them are alive and active, possessing a "so-functioning".'[168] Experiments can be constructed in which the elements that constitute an experience change their perceived character and properties when shifted into a new constellation despite the fact that the underlying elemental stimulus remains the same. Conversely, a perceived whole, for example, a chord, melody or characteristic spatial shape/configuration, is perceived as being the same even if all its elemental stimuli are being changed, for instance, when a melody is transposed into a different key or a shape is perspectively distorted. These experiments suggested that it is to the *Gestalt*, the relational organization or figural whole, rather than to individual sensory elements, that the organism responds. Especially when a scene or figure is exposed only for a very short moment, essential Gestalt qualities are grasped and recognized without any ability to recall or identify components. Before Gestalt psychology, the psychology of perception was focusing on elemental sensations and the habitual association between such sensations. According to Wolfgang Köhler, psychology has been 'ignoring all processes, all functional interrelations, which may have operated before there is a perceptual scene and which thus influence the characteristics of this scene'.[169] The recognition of a Gestalt is a 'whole undivided experience'. But, as Koffka points out, 'undivided does not mean uniform, for an undivided experience may be articulated and it may involve an immense richness of detail, yet this detail does not make of it

167 Wolfgang Köhler, 'Gestalt Psychology Today', in: *American Psychologist*, *14*, 1959, pp 727–34.
168 Koffka, 'Perception: An Introduction to the Gestalt-Theorie', pp 531–85.
169 Köhler, 'Gestalt Psychology Today', pp 727–34.

a sum of many experiences'.[170] Koffka writes: 'What we find is an undivided, articulated whole. Let us call these wholes "structures", and we can then assert that an unprejudiced description finds such structures in the cases underlying all psycho-physical experiments, but never any separate sensations.'[171] The importance of structures is that they determine the qualities of all subsidiary parts. 'Structures, then, are very elementary reactions, which phenomenally are not composed of constituent elements, their members being what they are by virtue of their "member-character", their place in the whole; their essential nature being derived from the whole whose members they are.'[172] Max Wertheimer summarized the essential insight of his approach as follows: 'The fundamental "formula" of Gestalt theory might be expressed in this way: There are wholes, the behaviour of which is not determined by that of their individual elements, but where the part-processes are themselves determined by the intrinsic nature of the whole.'[173]

According to the Gestalt psychologists there are certain universal principles that order human visual perception, most importantly the separation of 'figure' and 'ground' as precondition for further discriminations within the figure or for comparisons from figure to figure. Confronted by a rich visual scene, we need to separate a dominant shape (a 'figure' with a definite contour) from what our current concerns then relegate to the 'background' (or 'ground'). An illustration of figure-ground separation as perceptual act is the famous ambiguous figure devised by the Danish psychologist Edgar Rubin which appears alternately as vase or as two human profiles facing each other. Kurt Koffka considers the 'figure-ground structure' to be 'one of the most primitive of all structures'. He describes the essential features of this structure as follows: 'As a rule the figure is the outstanding kernel of the whole experience. Whenever I give attention to a particular part of a field, this part appears in the figure-character. . . . Whatever I am looking at, watching, acting upon, stands forth, grows fixed, becomes an object, while the rest recedes, grows empty, and becomes the ground. . . . The ground is always less "formed", less outlined, than the figure. . . . Phenomenally, the figure is always a stronger and more resistant structure than the ground, and in extreme cases the ground may be almost formless, a mere background.'

170 Koffka, 'Perception: An Introduction to the Gestalt-Theorie', pp 531–85.

171 Ibid.

172 Ibid.

173 Max Wertheimer, *Gestalt Theory*, German original: *Über Gestalttheorie* (an address before the Kant Society, Berlin, 7 December 1924), Erlangen, 1925, translation by Willis D Ellis published in: *Source Book of Gestalt Psychology*, Harcourt, Brace & Co (New York), 1938.

Figure 33 Figure-ground ambiguity, Edgar Rubin 1915

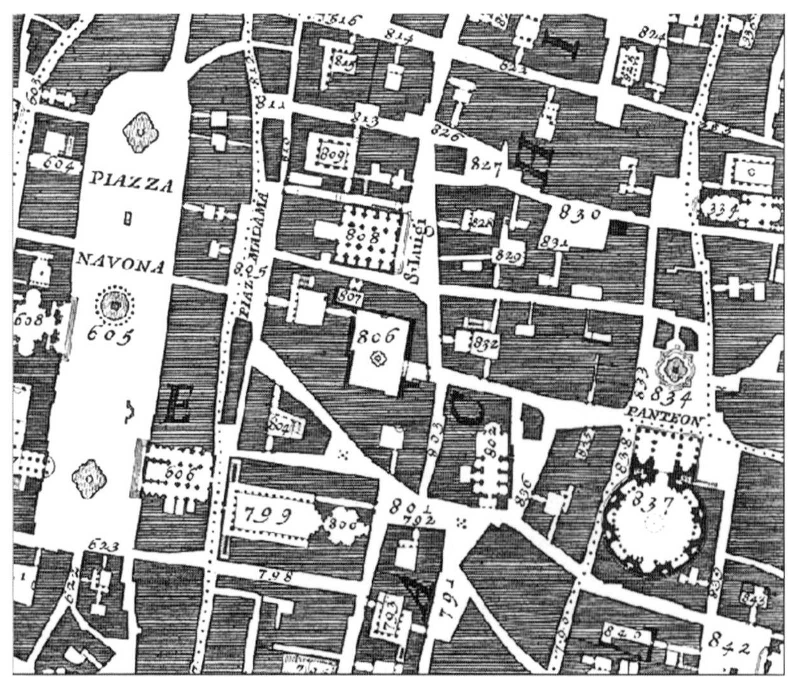

Figure 34 Giambattista Nolli, Plan of Rome, 1748, small segment

Koffka is once more emphasizing the act of perceptual synthesis: 'Phenomenal figures have boundary lines even when the corresponding objective figures have none. A good figure is always a "closed" figure, which the boundary line has the function of closing.'

The classic architectural application of the figure-ground structure is manifest in the so-called figure-ground plan that distinguishes urban mass from urban void. Giambattista Nolli's famous 1748 Plan of Rome depicts the non-public urban mass as black solids while letting the urban voids and important public interiors show up in white. Here it is the voids rather than the built forms that are perceived as figures against the background of a nearly amorphous fabric. What inclines us to focus on the voids here? It is the sense of convex closure of the white areas – although this feature is objectively always interrupted by the incoming and outgoing streets. Furthermore it is the greater regularity and symmetry of the white areas. (These factors will be thematized below under the heading of 'Gestalt-grouping principles'.) With respect to urban scenes there is always this double-sidedness, this twofold possibility of reading the structure as a structure of voids or as a structure of solids. Colin Rowe has noted that traditional and modern city stand opposed, with the latter focusing on solids with a continuous void as background and the former focusing on voids with a continuous background of solids: 'the traditional city . . . is so much the inverse of the city of modern architecture that the two of them together might, sometimes, almost present themselves as the alternative reading of some Gestalt diagram illustrating the fluctuations of the figure-ground phenomenon.'[174] However, even if one reading is privileged, either as solid or as void, depending upon the type of urban formation, there remains an inherent ambiguity. The potential for a Gestalt-switch remains. An urban design strategy might involve strategic shifts between the two tendencies and set up conditions that induce subjective figure-ground reversals. One might set up zones that clearly privilege the reading of solid figures and then move on to zones that privilege the reading of the figural voids. There might be a zone of transition where the matter becomes ambiguous and thus prone to the experience of Gestalt-switches. While Rubin's abstract ambiguous figure-ground structure leads to an unpredictable oscillation between two possible perceptions, in a concrete ecological condition one of the two readings might be contextually primed. The reading of the transition zone might depend on the direction from which an observer enters the transitional scene. It is in such a situation that figural after-effects come into play. Koffka elaborated on this phenomenon as follows:

174 Colin Rowe & Fred Koetter, *Collage City*, MIT Press (Cambridge, MA), 1978, p 62.

> The figure-ground distinction cannot be identified with a mere difference of the attention-level. . . . The organism's structural reaction to a pair of stimuli depends upon its attitude. . . . Before the subject is confronted with the stimulus, the structure that eventually will ensue must be prepared for by a mental attitude, and this attitude consists mainly in a readiness to carry out a certain structural process. 'Attitude' has now become a well-defined term as distinguished from 'attention'. It means that in entering a given situation the organism has in readiness certain modes of response, these modes being themselves what we have called 'structures'. . . . If a structural process is thus adequately prepared for, it may come to its full effect under conditions which of themselves would have provoked a different structural process.[175]

However, before or rather alongside all after-effects and attitudinal preparedness there might be hard-wired structuring processes that are part of an invariant make up of our perceptual/cognitive apparatus. The question must be raised which aspects of an objective spatial configuration become decisive factors for the emergence of patterns and figures within human perception/apprehension. Gestalt psychology talks about ***Gestalt-grouping principles*** which regulate how one (rather than another) whole figure is perceived in the face of a certain arrangement of 'stuff'. (We say 'stuff' because to speak of parts, elements or even fragments already implies a certain whole as reference.) Although habituation plays an important role in perception, Wertheimer insists and demonstrates that the operation of the Gestalt-grouping principles cannot be explained on the basis of a subject's prior experience, as a mere tendency to recognize the familiar.[176]

The major Gestalt-grouping principles are: the law of proximity, the law of similarity, the law of continuation, the law of closure and the law of symmetry.

These principles designate conditions that promote the perceptual synthesis of the 'given' visual 'stuff' into the wholes which imprint themselves so irresistibly in our minds. For instance, within a scatter of dots we tend to perceive groups/figures where dots are more proximate to each other. With respect to interpreting lines as outlines that define an object or figure, a smooth/curvilinear/convex line dominates over concave lines, or lines which are broken by kinks. Symmetry also inclines

175 Koffka, 'Perception: An Introduction to the Gestalt-Theorie', pp 531–85.

176 Max Wertheimer, *Laws of Organization in Perceptual Forms*, first published in 1923 as 'Untersuchungen zur Lehre von der Gestalt II', in *Psychologische Forschung*, 4, 301–50. Translation published in W Ellis, *A Source Book of Gestalt Psychology*, Routledge & Kegan Paul (London), 1938, pp 71–88.

perception to draw complementing elements into a whole. The Gestalt-grouping principles thus compose/decompose the visual scene into a particular configuration. Usually this entails the so-called *figure-ground segregations* as basic result.

1. The law of proximity:
   Grouping proceeds on the basis of contiguity, or in the absence of contiguity, grouping is guided by the closest proximity. The left image suggests vertical lines while the right image suggests horizontal lines. However, it should be observed that an inverse reading is still possible.

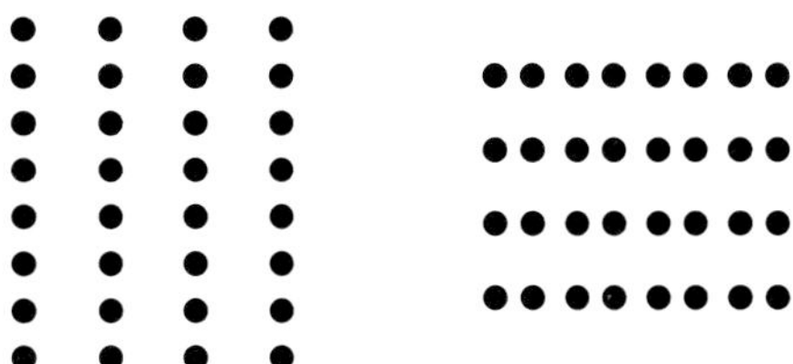

Figure 35 Gestalt grouping principle: the law of proximity

2. The law of similarity:
   Grouping proceeds on the basis of similarity. Despite the fact that the proximity principle would privilege the perception of vertical lines, the principle of similarity suggests horizontal lines. This example thus shows that the different principles might be in conflict with each other. Here similarity dominates.

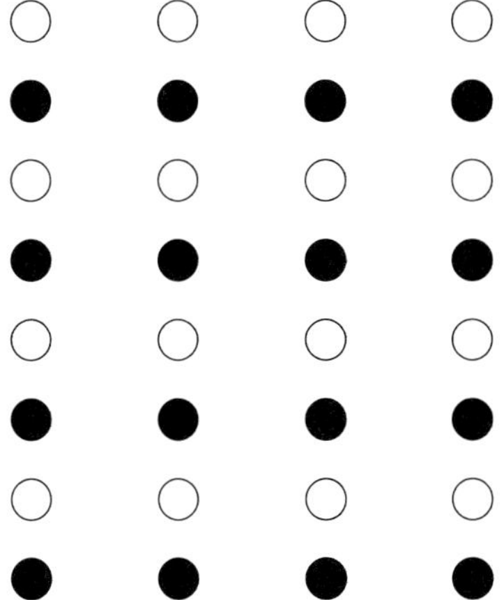

Figure 36 Gestalt-grouping principle: the law of similarity

3. The law of continuation:
   Grouping proceeds on the basis of smooth continuation. The first option of decomposition is most likely, it is privileged by the law of continuation. Again, the other two ways of decomposing the scene remain latent possibilities. Such latent possibility might be triggered by the introduction of minute geometric manipulations, for example, the introduction of a small gap at the junction, or by prior lead in experiences.

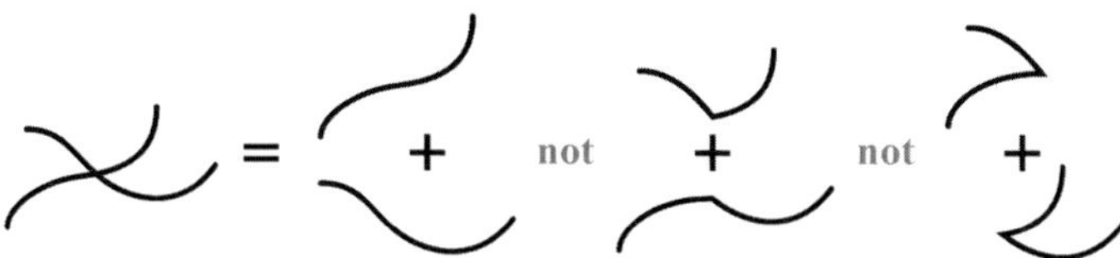

Figure 37 Gestalt-grouping principle: the law of continuity

4. The law of closure:
   The synthesis of the given elements (here line segments) – or rather the decomposition of the scene into figures – privileges closed forms. The first decomposition of the scene into a closed, convex figure that is framed by two lines is the most natural one. This effect holds despite the fact that the other two possibilities of synthesis/ decomposition reveal the latent presence of equally familiar figures, namely the letters K, W and M. Closure as a primary Gestalt-grouping principle trumps familiarity.

Figure 38 Gestalt-grouping principle: the law of closure

This can be confirmed with the image Wertheimer himself uses. Here the familiar figure of the square is avoided. The first part of Figure 39 does not privilege the decomposition into the letters W and M but rather suggests a (strange) shape squeezed between two lines.

Wertheimer uses the configuration in Figure 40 to show a conflict between closure and continuation. Here the continuation of the curve dominates over the option to see three separate closed figures.

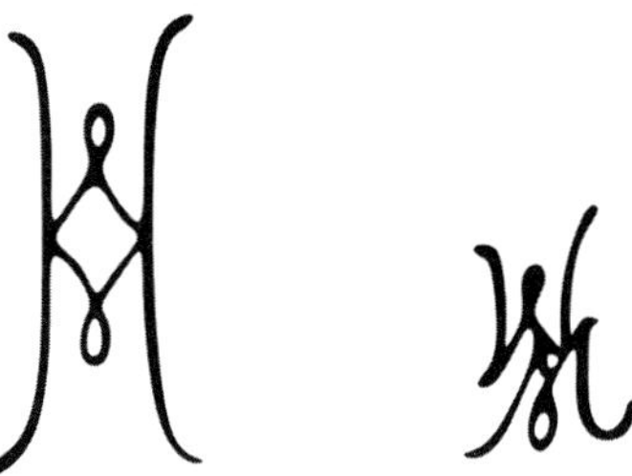

Figure 39 Closure dominates familiarity

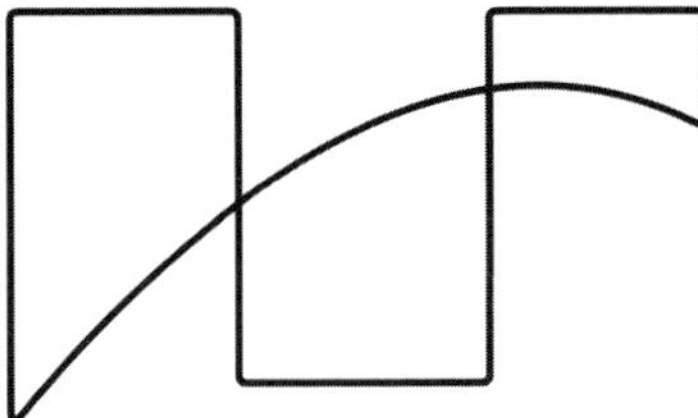

Figure 40 Continuity dominates closure

5. The law of symmetry:
   Figure identification privileges symmetrical figures. This explains why we tend to focus on the white in the top row and on the black in the bottom row. However, the effect seems rather unstable here.

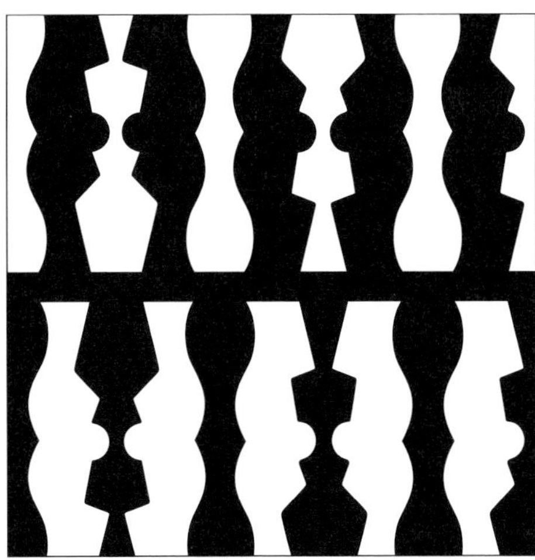

Figure 41 Gestalt-grouping principle: the law of symmetry

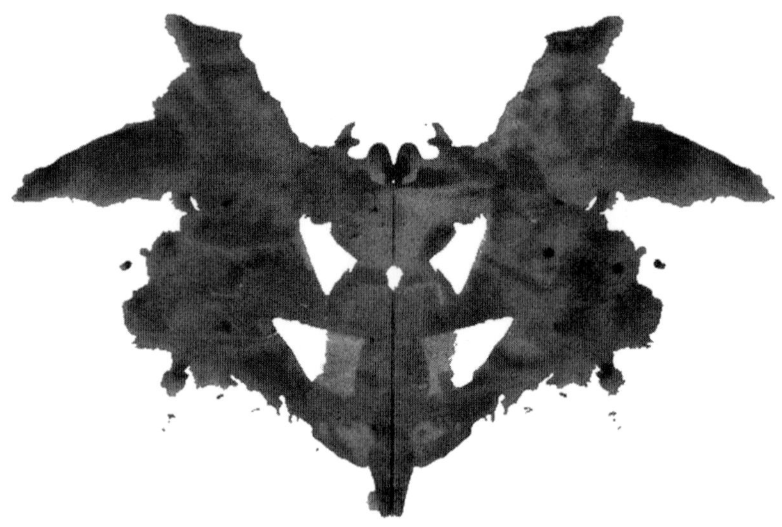

Figure 42 Inkblot #1, from Hermann Rorschach, *Psychodiagnostik*, 1921

The power of symmetry with respect to catching our attention can also be demonstrated with the images utilized in the so-called Rorschach test.[177] These images emerge from random ink splashes that are then folded into symmetrical figures that trigger the test participant's imaginative figure reading. Our predisposition towards reading such shapes as creatures implies that we seek out credible units of interaction in whatever visual material we are confronted with.

One can observe here that the attention-grabbing impact of the symmetry increases with the degree of complex irregularity/asymmetry of the half-image that is then mirrored to produce the final image. The figure is so strongly integrated because its parts lack independent figural qualities. Thus there is little chance that this whole falls apart into autonomous segments. The hidden rationality of this effect lies in the improbability that such a complex configuration could be accidental. It therefore makes sense that such a configuration commands attention. In fact, this dialectic whereby incompleteness, asymmetry and complexity in the parts is sublated into an all the more powerful impression of unity in

177 The Rorschach inkblot test is a psychological assessment to examine and evaluate the personality characteristics, in particular with respect to the detection of psychotic thinking. The test was created by Hermann Rorschach in 1921. There are 10 official inkblots. Five inkblots are black ink on white paper. Two are black and red ink on white paper. Three are multicoloured. The image depicted above is the first of the official black inkblots. Rorschach's test was first published in his 1921 publication *Psychodiagnostik* (Berlin/Leipzig),1921.

the whole was effectively utilized by the Baroque. Here lies the primary advance of the Baroque over the Renaissance: the Baroque's far superior capacity to forge large, complex unities.

Architectural composition can utilize these principles to aggregate building components into strong and coherent, highly legible objects and configurations of objects. But it is equally possible, and this has been the ambition of Colin Rowe's concept of ***phenomenal transparency***,[178] to take the cue from the ambiguous figures and multivalent patterns[179] that serve as research material in the psychology of perception, and allow the various Gestalt-grouping principles to compete against each other, setting up arrangements that oscillate between several latent 'readings'.[180] Phenomenal transparency implies the formal multi-tasking of the parts of a formal arrangement. Even what is a nameable part (or distinct sub-whole) is a function of the overall reading of the arrangement as figure. Two-dimensional ambiguous figures are the perfect example. But we can also observe this phenomenon in three-dimensional space. This strategy allows for the simultaneous articulation of different social orders, catering for different events or audiences sharing a complex social space. For each audience, with its particular expectations, a latent reading is presented. In this way visual ambiguity or multiple readings give phenomenological support to multifunctionality within a single territory that is simultaneously utilized according to two different event patterns. However, in the history of architectural thinking the idea of phenomenal transparency was, so far, only a concept concerned with formal/experiential effects.

Le Corbusier's 1920 still life described above can serve as a paradigmatic example of phenomenal transparency. Colin Rowe used Le Corbusier's 1927 competition design for the League of Nations as one of several examples of how the phenomenal transparency effect can operate

178 Colin Rowe & Robert Slutzky, 'Transparency: Literal and Phenomenal', *Perspecta* 8 (Yale Architectural Journal), Yale University, 1963. Jeff Kipnis proposed an interesting expansion of Rowe's concept, ie, he proposed the term 'phenomenal transparency' to describe conditions where an indeterminate number of latent readings seems to be embedded within a rich pattern.

179 A fascinating, in-depth exploration of ambiguous figures and multivalent patterns can be found in George Stiny's brilliant *Shape*. According to Stiny, shape ambiguity and the continous re-reading of figures/shapes is an essential aspect of the design process. See George Stiny, *Shape: Talking about Seeing and Doing*, MIT Press (Cambridge, MA), 2006.

180 In architectural design (as distinct from product design), this notion of latency is of particular relevance, because in architecture part to whole relationships are always somewhat precarious. In architecture everything is immobile. There are no objects in architecture if one assumes that the paradigm of the integral object is the mobile object that moves with all its parts and thus severs itself unambiguously from its background. In architecture this final, absolute criterion of distinct objecthood – its independent, integral mobility – is lacking. Therefore in architecture objecthood remains precarious. There are – *stricto sensu* – no architectural objects.

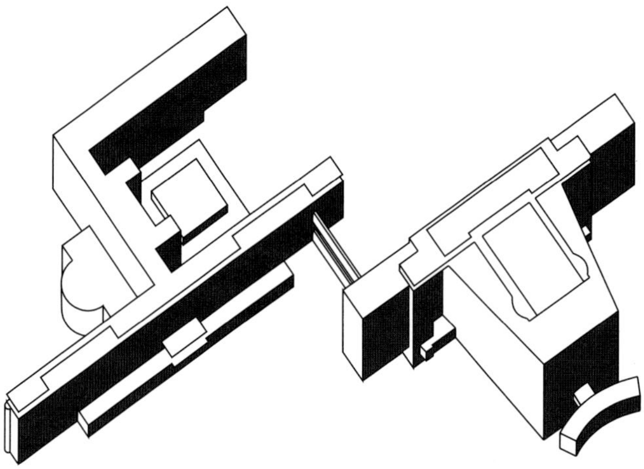

Figure 43 **Le Corbusier, Competition Design for the League of Nations, 1927. From Rowe & Slutzky, 'Transparency: Literal and Phenomenal', 1963**

in space. The different readings of the overall spatial composition are triggered by a shifting subject position when the subject moves through the complex and thus gains and loses aspects of the composition. The two main readings between which Le Corbusier's design oscillates are its reading as monumental, symmetrical composition (perceived when approached on axis), and its reading as asymmetrical, dynamic composition of planes sliding against each other.

One of the author's own attempts to utilize the phenomenal transparency effect within a spatial composition was realized in the context of an exhibition design, the design for 'Wishmachine – World Invention' curated by Brigitte Felderer and Herbert Lachmayer. The two primary readings (decompositions) of the spatial composition were functionalized in terms of two ways of ordering the exhibits into storylines. The first decomposition of the scene presented four different walls that traversed the space: a zigzag wall, an S-curved wall, a boomerang-shaped wall and a wall in the shape of a giant ramp. Each wall traversed the given bounding box, intersecting with all (or some of) the other walls. Each wall carried a chronological, monothematic sequence of objects. The intersection of the walls produced a series of enclosures between them and the bounding box. This series of enclosed territories presented the second decomposition of the scene. Here clusters of the objects, from different themes, came together in particular, synoptic, multi-theme time-slices. Thus the concept of phenomenal transparency is

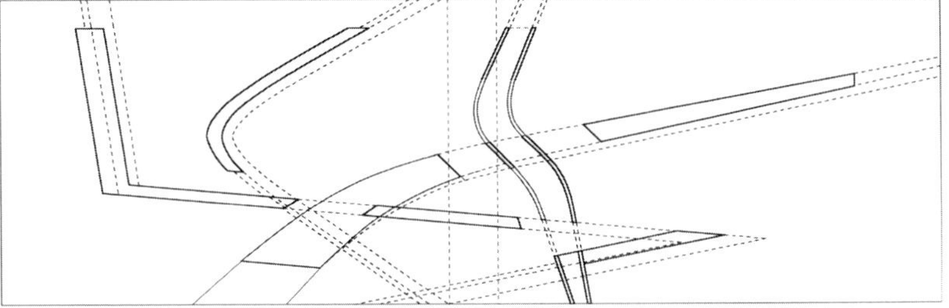

Figure 44 Zaha Hadid & Patrik Schumacher, exhibition design for 'Wishmachine – World Invention', Vienna, 1996

utilized to support the perceptual presence of two different spatial ordering principles, allowing for the double association of exhibits, and thus installing a richer field of content relations than would have been possible with a traditional, unitary ordering principle.

6.7.3 PARAMETRIC FIGURATION

As the example of the design for 'Wishmachine – World Invention' demonstrates, the inherent volatility of the perceptual interpretation of complex scenes offers the opportunity to be functionalized for the programmatic coexistence of multiple social agendas in a single territory. The articulatory ambition here is to give all simultaneously operating life-processes a strong phenomenological registration. The different life-processes might also utilize the territory at different times, for example, weekend life versus weekday life. The switch between the two (or more) possible phenomenological interpretations does not have to be left to chance. It is possible to trigger latent readings by means of parametric levers that overturn a reading by a small, strategic intervention.

The author has seized upon this possibility within a design research project that has been conducted at various undergraduate and postgraduate design studios.[181] The projects were conducted under various titles – *Parametric Urbanism and the Perception of Complexity, Simultaneity & Latency, Figure-field Symbiosis & Parametric Figuration* – but they shared the same original ambition that is perhaps best referred to as ***parametric figuration***. The underlying thesis suggests that multi-stable urban/architectural configurations can be devised that are

181 Institute of Experimental Architecture, Innsbruck University; Design Research Laboratory, Architectural Association School of Architecture, London; University of Applied Arts, Vienna; Yale University, New Haven.

pregnant with a multiplicity of variously conspicuous readings. This latency can be set up as a parametric model whereby the variables are extremely ***Gestalt-sensitive***, ie, the quantitative modification of these parameters triggers qualitative shifts – ***Gestalt-catastrophes*** – in the perceived order of the urban/architectural configuration. The key parameters of the model are chosen with respect to the Gestalt-potentials that are embedded in the configuration. This parametricization is initially a design tool. However, it then can also be treated literally as a mechanism to trigger Gestalt-switches in the real building. For the parametric set up we distinguish ***object parameters*** (geometry, material textures), ***ambient parameters*** (lighting conditions, contexts) and ***observer parameters*** (camera position, movement, priming) as registers for the parametric calibration of the latent figuration.

The build up of such multivalent arrangements is a fragile balancing act, and very context sensitive. The aim of the set up is to achieve a maximal perceptual reconfiguration of a scene with a minimal intervention. Potential interventions (triggers) include the shifting of observer position and perspective (observer parameter), the change of lighting conditions (ambient parameter) and the manipulation of kinetic elements (object parameter). An object parameter, for instance, could be the opening or closing of a gap that creates or breaks a spatial figure, or creates/breaks visual connections.

The figural reading of a scene and its parts is subject to various context effects. All perception and pattern recognition is context dependent – both with respect to the spatial context, as well as with respect to the context of time (before and after). In both respects – time contexts and space contexts – we have to distinguish so-called low level context effects (like light/dark contrast, or colour contrast, relative direction, relative size etc) from high level context effects which work on the basis of the context implicating our prior knowledge, concepts, schemata and expectations. The final achievement of a reading/percept involves both bottom-up processes like the Gestalt-grouping principles, and top-down processes of recognition on the basis of memory, expectations and higher level concepts. High level context effects (top-down perceptual processes) are strongly influenced by the prevailing semiological conventions, but – as perceptual processes – belong to the phenomenological dimension and must be distinguished from semiology proper. Top-down processing implies that figures and patterns are recognized as looking like something familiar, nameable, thus terminating the game of discovery and interpretation.

Architecture's societal function is the innovation of the spatial means that can be deployed to order social processes. Beyond the basic physical organization articulation is required. Articulation operates through the related registers of phenomenology and semiology. These three staggered dimensions of spatial organization – the organizational, the phenomenological and the semiological dimension – can be effected either by separate sets of building elements, or by superimposing the physical, phenomenological and semiological effect within one set of architectural elements. For instance, a step that cuts across a space and imposes a certain (but not impenetrable) physical barrier, can *in addition* assume phenomenological prominence, for example, via symmetry, *and* finally a semantic significance, for example, via a semiological system that distinguishes socially significant levels within the space. Each successive register/dimension reinforces the function of the step as ordering device, enhancing its capacity to facilitate social order and orientation.

The given/evolving built environment is a more or less integrated universe of organizational, phenomenological and semiological orderings. It is a product of the coevolution of specific social communication processes in specifically shaped architectural environments. Not all of this is consciously and strategically available to the designing architect, because a lot of the nuances are not explicitly reflected within the architectural expert discourse. The designer's active intervention within this universe goes on irrespectively. Design decisions need to be made. It is the academic branch of the discipline that we must look to if we wish to gain more explicit, intelligent control over the intuitive efforts of designers to produce sophisticated architectural orders that operate along all three dimensions of architecture's task.

6.8 The Semiological Dimension of Architectural Articulation

THESIS 32

The semiological dimension makes a significant contribution to the architecturally inspired process of social structuration that occurs all the time, at all scales.

The premise and challenge of this section can be conveyed in the following words by Roland Barthes: 'The city is a discourse, and this discourse is actually a language: the city speaks to its inhabitants, we speak to our city, the city where we are, simply by inhabiting it, by traversing it, by looking at it. Yet, the problem is to extract an expression like "the language of the city" from the purely metaphorical stage. . . . We must confront this problem: how to shift from metaphor to analysis when we speak of the language of the city?'[182] This problem has been posed many times. A convincing solution to this question is bound to empower architecture. However, the analytical task is only the first stepping stone: the required semiological intelligence has to sponsor an effective semiological design project.

To meet the posed challenge, the theory of architectural autopoiesis filters, assimilates and reconstructs the field of ***semiology*** or ***semiotics***. The two competing names in the field are due to its two independent, modern originators[183]: the linguist Ferdinand de Saussure (sémiologie) and the philosopher and logician Charles S Peirce (semiotics). The double origin of the field led to two traditions and two broad conceptual lineages. The two traditions differ already with respect to their conceptual analyses of the base concept of the ***sign***. Saussure defines the sign as the unity of a signifier (sign-vehicle) with a signified (meaning). Peirce analyzes the sign into three components: the sign itself (equivalent to Saussure's signifier), the interpretant (equivalent to Saussure's signified), and the object. The subsequent cross-fertilization of the two lineages only complicated matters. While linguistics became a highly evolved, technical discipline, the rest of the field of semiology/semiotics remained as rugged and confusing on the side of theory as it is broad and unwieldy on the side of empirical content. Like many human sciences it lacks a singular and clear paradigmatic framework. Therefore, each effort in the field needs to sort, select and restructure the basic categories and axioms of the field before moving on to specific studies. That's why, on the one hand, the all too familiar terms of the field – code, sign, signifier, signified, referent, icon, index, symbol, syntagmatic, paradigmatic, metaphor, metonym, denotation, connotation, semiosis etc – are defined and networked differently in each account or study, while on the other hand, equivalent or very similar conceptual distinctions are often given different terms.

The field came to general intellectual prominence during the 1960s. This also led to its reception and influence within the autopoiesis of

182 Roland Barthes, *The Semiotic Challenge*, Basil Blackwell (Oxford), 1988, French original: *L'aventure sémiologique*, Éditions du Seuil (Paris), 1985, p 195.

183 There have been many precursors to the modern general theory of signs, starting with Ancient Greek philosophy. Umberto Eco names Plato's *Cratylus* and *Sophist*, Aristotle's *Poetics* and *Rhetoric*, as well as the medieval philosopher William of Ockham, the *Port-Royal Grammar*, Kircher's *Semiologia*, then Locke, Vico, and Lambert's *Semiotik*, as well as Bolzano and Husserl. See: Umberto Eco, 'The Influence of Roman Jakobson on the Development of Semiotics', in: Martin Krampen et al (Eds), *Classics of Semiotics*, Plenum Press (New York), 1987, p 109.

architecture and became a factor in the crisis of Modernism and in the attempts to work through this crisis. One of the first milestone publications that recognized and enhanced the reflection of the semiological dimension within architecture was the anthology *Meaning in Architecture*, edited by Charles Jencks and George Baird, in 1970.[184] The book comprises 15 articles by leading architectural theorists (and theoretically minded architects) of the time including, besides the editors, contributions from Geoffrey Broadbent, Reyner Banham, Kenneth Frampton, Aldo van Eyck, Christian Norberg-Schulz and Alan Colquhoun, among others. Charles Jencks' own lead-in article was entitled 'Semiology & Architecture'. The various attempts to make the concepts and insights of semiology/semiotics fruitful within architecture each tapped into different sources. Although, in general, the influence of the semiological lineage dominates over the semiotic one, concepts have been mixed and matched as seemed appropriate. Even where roughly the same sources come into play, their respective application within the domain of architecture has been rather varied. The appropriation of semiology/semiotics within architecture roughly spans two decades, the 1970s and the 1980s. The first decade mostly relied on the theoretical resources of Structuralism, going back to Saussure. Besides Saussure, the main source was Claude Lévi-Strauss, with occasional references also to Roland Barthes, Roman Jakobson and Umberto Eco. In the 1980s architectural discourse was shifting by catching up with Post-Structuralism. The main author referred to now was Jacques Derrida, with references as well to Michel Foucault, Julia Kristeva, Jean Baudrillard, Jean-François Lyotard etc. The discourse became more sophisticated but also more critical rather than constructive and systematizing. In any case, within architecture the discourse had never reached a stage of cumulative design research on the basis of a shared theoretical paradigm. Furthermore, the discourse on signification in architecture has been more or less dormant for 20 years now.[185]

This situation leaves us no other choice than, once more, to try to filter, assimilate and reconstruct insights, concepts and terminology in a new way, fit for our specific purposes. Moreover, this creative

184 Charles Jencks & George Baird (Eds), *Meaning in Architecture*, George Braziller (New York), 1970.

185 In the early 1990s the concern with 'representation' had been repudiated in favour of a concern with 'performance' within the discourse of the architectural avant-garde. The problem with this confrontation is that architecture, to a large extent, performs through representation.

reconstruction is, in any case, unavoidable because we approach the field of semiology/semiotics (as well as its tentative prior applications to the domain of architecture) with a fully formed, coherent, overarching conceptual framework, namely the adopted framework of Luhmann's social systems theory – adopted, adapted and extensively elaborated within the two volumes of *The Autopoiesis of Architecture*. Whatever we appropriate from the field of semiology/semiotics must be fitted into the evolving edifice of the theory of architectural autopoiesis.

From which sources should the theory of architectural autopoiesis start its assimilation of the required semiological intelligence? Given the impressive development of linguistics in comparison with the relatively primitive and inconclusive status of the field of semiology/semiotics as a whole, it seems to make sense to look primarily to linguistics for inspiration and guidance. But is the medium and function of verbal languages not too different from the medium and function of what might be called (initially only metaphorically) architectural languages? The risk here is that the analogy that is to be elaborated is too forced to become productive. However, to take this risk is worthwhile, especially as the task here is not merely an analytical one. The ambition is also the creative advancement of the discipline's design capacity. To this end a mere analytical penetration of how the built environment currently operates as a system-of-signification does not suffice. Ideas on how these operations might be systematized and intensified need to be generated. Linguistics might become a source of inspiration in this sense. However, with the project of an architectural semiology being effectively still in its infancy, it would make little sense to confront it with the latest, most advanced and technically detailed researches.[186] The decision has thus been taken to start once more with the founding document of modern structural linguistics, Ferdinand de Saussure's *Cours de linguistique générale*, first published posthumously in 1916, and to use Saussure's original insights, concepts and suggestions, that proved to be so seminal for the inauguration of linguistics and semiology, as the primary guide to explore the basic categories upon which to construct a theoretical framework for a prospective architectural semiology that must ultimately be design oriented and generative rather than merely analytical in ambition. Before returning to Saussure, with this ambition in mind, it is necessary to prepare the conceptual ground of this engagement within the already elaborate conceptual framework of the theory of architectural autopoiesis.

186 In any case, the acquisition of expertise in advanced linguistics lies beyond the capacity of the author, as well as beyond the capacity of architectural discourse in general.

6.8.1 THE BUILT WORKS OF ARCHITECTURE AS FRAMING COMMUNICATIONS

The theoretical decision to include spaces and buildings among the communications that constitute the ongoing autopoiesis of architecture predisposes the theory of architectural autopoiesis towards a semiological understanding of architectural works. Perhaps the most sustained and convincing analytical attempt to apply semiology/semiotics to the built environment can be found in the writings of the art historian Donald Preziosi. In 1979 Preziosi published two substantial works in the subdiscipline of architectural semiotics: *the Semiotics of the Built Environment*,[187] and *Architecture, Language, and Meaning*.[188] Preziosi's works display a number of insights and conceptual stipulations that coincide with the theoretical premises and decisions promoted within the theory of architectural autopoiesis. The first shared premise is entailed in the following excerpt: 'Like verbal language . . . the architectonic code is a panhuman phenomenon. No human society exists without artificially reordering its environment – without employing environmental formations (whether made or appropriated) as sign-tokens in a system of visual communication. . . . Every human society communicates architectonically . . . in media addressed to visual perception.'[189] The second shared premise is that the pertinent theoretical scope here encompasses the totality of the built environment *and* the world of artefacts (as well as appropriated natural spaces/objects). The theoretical task of the semiotics of the built environment is to explain: 'how it is that we come to scaffold our individual and collaborative lives through the appropriation of and interaction with this omnipresent world of objects'.[190] The third shared premise is that any 'architectonic code' can only function within a matrix of multiple, simultaneously operating systems-of-signification: 'As a system of signs, a built environment does not exist in a vacuum but is co-occurrent with ensembles of other sign systems in different media. . . . The architectonic code is one of several fundamental panhuman sign systems which in concert provide individuals and groups with a multi-modal and multi-stereoscopic template for the creation of humanly-meaningful realities.'[191]

187 Donald Preziosi, *The Semiotics of the Built Environment – An Introduction to Architectonic Analysis*, Indiana University Press (Bloomington), 1979, p 1.

188 Donald Preziosi, *Architecture, Language, and Meaning – The Origins of the Built World and its Semiotic Organization*, Mouton Publishers (The Hague/Paris/New York), 1979.

189 Preziosi, *The Semiotics of the Built Environment*, p 1.

190 Ibid.

191 Ibid, p 3.

In the conceptual framework adopted by the theory of architectural autopoiesis, the multiplicity of simultaneously operating sign systems is thought to be orchestrated by the unity of a social system – conceptualized as ***autopoietic system of communications*** – that underlies all human communication processes. This most fundamental concept of the theory of architectural autopoiesis was not available to Preziosi. Preziosi's work, however, shares the functional outlook of the theory of architectural autopoiesis and looks out for functional equivalences: 'Each sign system offers certain advantages over others. . . . A built environment does certain things which verbal language does not do, or only does by weak approximation and circumlocution – and vice versa. Sign systems often provide partially redundant ways of doing functionally equivalent things. I can maintain my privacy, for example, by building a wall around myself, putting up a "no trespassing" sign, wearing a loincloth, or gesturing dramatically whenever a stranger comes within six meters of my person.'[192] Another coincidence between Preziosi's work and the attempt made here to develop a theoretical framework for the effective handling of architecture's semiological dimension lies in the important theoretical problem of identifying the specific, pertinent, elemental units within the built environment that are capable of carrying social meaning in the specific mode of architecture. According to Preziosi, the organizing units of any architectonic code are what he calls 'space-cells' characterized by the 'topological property of boundedness'.[193] Being built up from this type of elemental unit is seen as architecturally universal, as the common denominator of all 'architectonic systems' and human built environments. The theory of architectural autopoiesis, as will be elaborated below, on its own account, has come to the same conclusion. Whether understood as empirical generalization or theoretical stipulation, what Preziosi calls 'space-cell', and what the theory of architectural autopoiesis prefers to call ***frame*** or ***territory***, is the fundamental unit of all communications that are operating via built architectural works. This proposition is fully consistent with the identification of architecture's societal function as ***framing***.

As stated above at the outset of this chapter, the basic premise to include built works among the communications of architecture's autopoiesis predisposes the theory towards a semiological approach. We have now reached a point in the build up of the theory where this initial decision compels us to corroborate, through a more detailed theoretical elaboration, that buildings and the spaces within them do indeed

192 Ibid, p 3.
193 Ibid, p 15.

communicate. The theory of architectural autopoiesis postulates that architectural spaces are *framing* communications that communicate through predefining and ordering the social situations and attendant expectations that structure all communicative interactions.[194] In this sense all built works of architecture have a semiological dimension, ie, all architectural works operate as signs and can be analyzed as such, independently of whether the architect/designer has paid explicit expert attention to this fact or not.[195]

According to Luhmann's theoretical premises – which have been adopted here – communications are events that acquire and process meaning via their recursive concatenation within autopoietic systems of communication.[196] The insistence that communications are events produces a prima facie difficulty for the inclusion of architectural/design artefacts. Luhmann often emphasizes the ephemerality of communication events. They perish quickly as they succeed each other in often rapid succession. But this does not hold for all communications Luhmann recognizes. A written inscription is a communication that persists through time. The same is the case with buildings and designed artefacts. Their physical permanence implies that their respective message is broadcast ceaselessly. Luhmann has never explicitly counted, nor has he ever explicitly excluded, buildings, spaces or any other designed artefacts among the communications his theory is concerned with. Luhmann's theory is claiming comprehensiveness, and he was wise enough never to attempt a comprehensive list of types of communication. Concerning the supposed event character and ephemerality of communications, this cannot be construed as a necessary, definitive condition of communications within Luhmann's theoretical system. As hinted above, a powerful example that stands against such an interpretation is the example of written communications, including books, which Luhmann (like Derrida and Marshall McLuhan) recognizes as a crucial form of communication. Our civilization is, in a very profound sense, a literary

194 See Volume 1, chapter 5.1.3 *Framing as Societal Function of Architecture*.

195 It can safely be assumed that architects, as socialized members of society, are intuitively paying tribute to the dimension of social meaning in their design work. And should they lack the respective sensibility, or violate such concerns due to an avant-gardist radicality, their clients will surely steer them in ways that recognize the potential social meanings that the designed works are likely to acquire.

196 The circularity of this statement is inevitable and does not interfere with the statement's function as criterion. Circularity is an inevitable mark of the definition of base concepts. What can be provided here is a criterion of coherency of concept deployment, but not an indisputable foundation.

and print based civilization, it is 'Gutenberg's galaxy'.[197] Books can thus serve as example to argue that architectural- and design-artefacts cannot be excluded from the realm of communications just on account of their persistence and their lacking event character.

The notion that architectural spaces and buildings are communications implies that they participate within recursive networks of communications. To secure our starting premise – architectural works communicate – we merely have to establish that spaces and buildings can function within networks of communications, not that they, between themselves alone, form a complete system of communications. In fact, in the strict sense of the concept *system of communications* employed here, this possibility must be excluded. An 'architectural system of communications' can only exist in a looser, more general sense of 'system', in the sense that, for instance, structuralist linguists refer to language as a system, namely as a system of signification. This employment of the term system refers to an abstractum rather than a social reality that can be observed. To avoid the proliferation of the term system, the theory of architectural autopoiesis thus proposes to restrict its use – as much as possible – to the designation of autopoietic systems. Instead of 'architectural system of communications', phrases like 'architectural system-of-signification', or better still 'architectural language' should be used here. In Luhmann's theoretical edifice (presupposed here), general societal languages like English, French etc are categorized as a medium of communication, a medium using articulated speech. The more specific languages of autopoietic subsystems with their more narrowly defined systems-of-signification fall under the general category of communication structures. This terminology will also be adopted here in order to avoid ambiguity with respect to the term 'system'. In this sense the terminological apparatus of the theory of architectural autopoiesis will refer to building in general as medium of communication. It categorizes specific architectural languages or systems-of-signification as specific communication structures. These specific languages or communication structures, in terms of their formal formation, are tied to specific architectural styles, oeuvres or individual projects, depending on the specificity of the rules of signification implied. However, in terms of their meanings, these specific structures/languages are tied to the specific social systems that communicate through and within these structures. The built works of architecture function as

197 Below, in section 8.6 on *The Built Environment as Primordial Condition of Society*, the theory of architectural autopoiesis will explicate how our civilization is in an even deeper sense also an architectural civilization.

framing communications within the social system that utilizes these works. Therefore the architectural language employed is a medium or communication structure within the framed social system. The designing architecture can only provide the forms but never control the meanings of the respective architectural language.

Another defining criterion of communications is their tripartite constitution allowing for the distinction of *information*, *impartation*[198] and *understanding*. Some kind of information must be conveyed. Luhmann's favourite shorthand definition of information is Gregory Bateson's dictum: *a difference that makes a difference*. One can safely grant that (some if not all) design differences do make a difference with respect to the ongoing communicative interaction within a space. The second point requires that it must be possible to distinguish the impartation, conveyance or broadcasting of this information from the information or differential import. To grant this might be considered more problematic. It implies that architectural spaces are recognized *as* communications within social systems. In this sense, the third moment of understanding entails the distinction of information and impartation. Understanding does not only involve the reception of the information but also the recognition that this information was imparted within a particular, situated communication 'event'. This usually involves the attribution of the communication to a sender. This point of attribution, however, does not have to be a person. It might be a certain social organization (legal person) or the state, as in a statute. In the case of an architectural space such an attribution is indeed possible and even likely. The user of a building who recognizes a certain, specific arrangement of the spaces within the building, a certain style in the articulation of its interior, a certain atmosphere, is not only likely to be impacted by taking in the information about the social situations to be expected, he/she is also likely to attribute this message to the intentions of those who provided those arrangements and atmospheric steerings. The point of attribution is usually not the architect or designer, who will most probably be unknown to the user. It is much more likely and appropriate for the user to attribute the communication to the occupying institution or hosting owner of the building who is receiving the users and who originally acted as the architect's client. Thus we can establish that architectural spaces are usually *understood* as impartations that convey information. Architectural buildings and spaces can thus be construed to

198 Luhmann uses the German word *Mitteilung*, mostly translated as *utterance*. I believe the rendering as impartation captures Luhmann's concept much better. Another term that captures the meaning of impartation is *conveyance*.

fulfil Luhmann's defining criteria for the concept of communication. Therefore, our fundamental theoretical premise holds (so far), namely that built architectural works can (and must) be counted among the communications that constitute society.

The theory of architectural autopoiesis proposes that built architectural works constitute the 'final' communications of architecture.[199] Whether these final communications of the discipline form their own subsystem-of-signification, and whether this subsystem-of-signification exhibits systematicity, or whether it can be enhanced to become more systematic and language-like, is the (compound) question that will concern us within this section.

6.8.2 ANALOGY: LANGUAGE AND BUILT ENVIRONMENT AS MEDIA OF COMMUNICATION

In principle, the totality of the built environment, its spaces, furnishings, appliances, vehicles, as well as our outfits, is under the purview of architecture and the design disciplines. The totality of the man-made, phenomenological world is shaped by design. Everything has to go through the controlling gate or needle's eye of the design discourse.[200]

The premise here is that the built environment, together with the world of artefacts that populate it, is involved in processes of social communication. Spaces and artefacts are not only objects of communication but they function as specific means, media or modes of communication within all (multi-modal) systems of communication that together constitute society. This presumption implies that architecture and the design disciplines should be keenly interested to understand this involvement. Architecture and design – whether this is always consciously reflected or not – intervene in an ongoing semiosis that continuously evolves the semiological aspect of the built environment and the world of artefacts. This semiosis has been going on since the dawn of culture, long before architectural design was differentiated as a specialized discipline. This ongoing process of semiosis cannot be fully controlled by design, not even by a design discipline that is becoming more and more self-conscious about its role within this process. However, this process can be investigated and theorized in order to guide the strategic design engagement with it.

199 See Volume 1, *Introduction*. This system comprises built architectural works as well as drawings, models, talks, books, exhibitions etc. Built architectural works feature in two ways as points of discursive reference and as spatial frames, namely the territories in which architects work, talk and exhibit etc.

200 This design discourse is the topic and site of intervention of this book. Theory plays a crucial role in shaping this gate.

Where might the theoretical resources be drawn from to undertake such an investigation? The discipline of *semiotics* or *semiology* had been postulated 100 years ago, by Peirce and Saussure respectively, as a general science of systems-of-signification (media). Linguistics remains by far the most advanced subdiscipline, and thus remains the crucial source domain for conceptual and analogical transferences into an analysis of the built environment as semiotic or semiological system-of-signification that operates, like a language, within and across various social systems (autopoietic systems of communication).

Although there are obvious, significant differences between spoken languages and the presumed 'language' that operates via the built environment – the one unfolds in time, the other unfolds in space; one communicates via ephemeral utterances, the other via persistent and often massive constructions – there is no viable alternative to the language analogy and linguistics as source of theoretical guidance. Language is the most potent medium of communication. No other medium has received an equivalent level of detailed and sustained attention. Linguistics is a highly evolved science that offers a panoply of conceptual schemes that might be put to the test with respect to the domain of architectural theory.

It has been established here that the built environment can be used as a medium of communication. This implies that – to the extent that aspects of the built environment indeed operate as communications – it should be possible to analyze such built environments as systems-of-signification that encode social meanings. But to what extent are such systems-of-signification language-like?

The idea that architecture constitutes a 'language' has been formulated many times. For instance, Gottfried Semper starts the introduction of his *Style in the Technical and Tectonic Arts* with this idea: 'Art has a special language of its own, consisting of formal types and symbols that have changed in a great variety of ways over the course of cultural history. They offer as many ways of making oneself understood as language itself.'[201] Semper's interest focused on emulating the efforts of historical linguistics with respect to tracing the most basic forms and symbols of architecture just as historical linguistics have been able to trace the various languages and words to their common primeval forms. However, without really being able to substantiate and elaborate the language analogy, Semper claims: 'If an architect recognizes the primeval

201 Gottfried Semper, *Style in the Technical and Tectonic Arts: or, Practical Aesthetics*, Getty Publications (Los Angeles), 2004, original German: *Der Stil in den Technischen und Tektonischen Künsten; oder Praktische Aesthetik. Ein Handbuch für Techniker, Künstler und Kunstfreunde*, Verlag für Kunst & Wissenschaft (Frankfurt am Main), 1860, vol 1, p 103.

value of the oldest symbols of *his* language and takes account of the way in which they, along with art itself, have changed their form and meaning historically, then he will have the same advantage as a modern orator who studies comparative linguistics and the most ancient relationships among languages.'[202] Semper moves on to offer the following outlook on future research opportunities: 'It will not be long before research into linguistics will start to interact with research into art-forms; such a link is bound to lead to the most remarkable revelations in both fields.'[203] This seems like a rather prescient anticipation, except that it took a rather long time before efforts in this direction took off, and excepting that we are still in the infancy of exploiting this link.

Then there is John Summerson's *The Classical Language of Architecture*.[204] Summerson refers to Classical architecture as 'the Latin of architecture',[205] and the chapter headings read, among others, 'The Grammar of Antiquity', 'Sixteenth-Century Linguistics' and 'The Rhetoric of Baroque'. But again, the analogy remains on the level of simple metaphors rather than being instrumentalized for systematic analogical transferences. The same goes for Bruno Zevi's *The Modern Language of Architecture*.[206] Here the analogy is evoked in the introduction entitled 'Speaking Architecture', but it is not followed through in any detail. Zevi is introducing his book as a sequel to Summerson's book and suggests that: 'in the course of centuries only one architectural language has been codified, that of classicism. None other has been processed and put into the systematic form required of an acknowledged language.'[207] To do this for modern architecture is presented as the most urgent task facing architectural history and criticism. Zevi purports to 'formulate the modern idiom' and is referring to 'the vocabulary, the grammar, and the syntax of the contemporary language'.[208] But once more, these terms remain instant metaphors without any further elaboration. The same goes for Charles Jencks' *The Language of Post-Modern Architecture*.

In a reverse move linguists have sometimes used architectural analogies to explicate their concepts and insights. Saussure, for instance, uses the analogy of the Classical architectural orders to explicate the

202 Ibid, p 106.
203 Ibid.
204 John Summerson, *The Classical Language of Architecture*, MIT Press (Cambridge, MA), 1963.
205 Ibid, p 7.
206 Bruno Zevi, *The Modern Language of Architecture*, University of Washington Press (Seattle), 1978, Italian original: *Il linguaggio moderno dell'architettura*, Einaudi (Turin), 1973.
207 Ibid, p 3.
208 Ibid, p 4.

crucial distinction of the two basic types of relationship between linguistic elements that must be mastered by any speaker to achieve linguistic competence: *syntagmatic* and *paradigmatic* relations. Syntagmatic relations involve the coordination – *in praesentia* – of elements into syntagms or sequences, and paradigmatic relations – Saussure calls them *associative* – involve the association of present elements with absent ones that might have been chosen as alternative options instead of the chosen elements. Saussure constructs his analogy as follows:

> Neither order of relations is reducible to the other: both are operative. If we compare them to the parts of a building: columns will stand in a certain relation to a frieze they support. These two components are related in a way which is comparable to the syntagmatic relation. It is an arrangement of two co-present units. If I see a Doric column, I might link it by association with a series of objects that are not present, associative relations (Ionic column, Corinthian column). The sum total of word relations that the mind associates with any word that is present gives a virtual series, a series formed by the memory (a mnemonic series), as opposed to a chain, a syntagma formed by two units present together. This is an actual series, as opposed to a virtual series, and gives rise to other relations.[209]

This analogy is as instructive for architecture as it is for linguistics. Here seems to be a point of departure to make the analogy between language and architecture work with some detail, perhaps allowing us to appropriate an important theoretical distinction for architecture.

The language analogy and the comparison of architectural semiosis with linguistic semiosis might indeed afford clues and inspiration for the potential expansion of the semiotic power of architecture. That is the motivation for rehearsing the basic concepts and insights of linguistics. The most appropriate place to start should indeed be Ferdinand de Saussure's *Course in General Linguistics*, the foundational text of modern linguistics and semiology. It seems, before engaging with any particular linguistic approach, the fundamental plausibility of the language analogy has to be assessed. However, the real test of productivity of the analogy can only be the success of its detailed elaboration.

Before diving into this elaboration, two critical questions might be raised in advance, as probing devices. The first question was already raised above: does the built environment display sufficient systematicity or correlative regularity in relation to the social life and communication processes taking place within it? The second question is whether there is

209 Ferdinand de Saussure, *Course in General Linguistics*, 4th edition, Duckworth (London), 1995, original French: *Cours de linguistique générale*, Payot (Paris), 1916.

an architectural analogue of linguistic well-formedness? A linguistic utterance is either *well-formed* or not, grammatically correct or incorrect. With respect to the built environment, or within the practice and discourse of architecture, the question is whether we can find or construct an equivalent for this fundamental distinction? This distinction between correctly vs incorrectly formed expressions arises due to the fact that a language is not just a set of simple signs – each doing its job independently. Language builds up its meaningful signs as composites from elements according to rules. Is there something like architectural well-formedness vs architectural disfigurement? And does the signifying power of architecture depend upon this ability to construct well-formed, compound signs? Thus we have posed two fundamental preconditions for the plausibility of the language analogy within architecture.

These questions cannot be answered ad hoc, in advance of a more elaborate analysis. However, they might be addressed here with some initial considerations. The first question – the question of architecture's systematicity and consistency of correlation with social processes – seems to afford a clearly positive answer only with respect to pre-Modern societies. For instance, Claude Lévi-Strauss' structural analysis of South American villages suggests rather strict and tight correlations between the structure of the village and the observed social structure and communication patterns. In the village of the Bororo, the position of an individual's abode correlated strictly with the individual's moiety, clan, economic activity, role in religious ceremony and possible choice of mate. The same seems to apply to archaic Greek cities, and still to the early medieval towns of Europe. Later, in particular with the onset of modernity, this tight correlation of settlement structure and social communication processes seems to loosen. Or is this impression merely a matter of complication resulting in the difficulty of analytical penetration? And further, assuming that systematicity has indeed been eroded, is it possible to reverse this process, at least locally, by a conscious design effort? And further still, might we ask if it could be possible to steer the global autopoiesis of architecture into a mode of operation that can start to reverse this process of hyposignification[210] on a global level, to enhance the overall semiotic prowess of architecture and urbanism?

Concerning the second question about the applicability of the distinction well-formed vs disfigured: the case is not as straightforward as it is in the case of language. Architectural designs are composed of

210 Françoise Choay, 'Urbanism and Semiology', in: *Meaning in Architecture*, Charles Jencks & George Baird (Ed), George Braziller (New York), 1970, pp 27–39. According to Françoise Choay, the urban system, as system-of-signification, is threatened in its very existence.

elements. The distinction between well-formedness and disfigurement depends upon rules of composition. With respect to Classical architecture the presence of such rules is rather evident. Well-formedness according to rules can be asserted most rigorously within a style, less so across styles. But whether the compositional rules of an architectural style are – like a grammar – being mobilized for signification is less clear. However, again, the agenda here is not merely descriptive or analytical. Even if the grammars of architectural styles have so far been rather rudimentary, or are currently going through a process of disintegration, it might be worthwhile to explore the language analogy within the context of a theory that has placed its agenda of analysis and reflection within an agenda of adaptive enhancement. Perhaps the two agendas must be combined: shared criteria of well-formedness of multi-component architectural constructs might be a means to enhance the degree of systematicity in architecture's semiological operations and on this basis enhance architecture's chance to maintain/upgrade its semiotic prowess in a world of increasing social complexity.

6.8.3 SIGNS AS COMMUNICATIONS

The concept of the sign is the central, undisputed founding concept of semiology (semiotics). In order to engage with and appropriate the insights of semiology/semiotics within the theory of architectural autopoiesis it is necessary to clarify and redefine the sign concept in relation to Luhmann's concept of communication. The proposal here is to define signs as communications. The two concepts are taken here as coextensive, ie, they are taken to denote the same class of entities in the world. Every sign is a communication and every communication is a sign. This means, first of all, that signs are not abstracta that exist in Platonic heaven. They exist as communicative events in space and time, within a specific social system or societal context. Isolated words, slumbering in dictionaries, are therefore not signs in the sense defined here. Also, individual words within speech cannot be abstracted from their context and considered as self-sufficient signs in their own right. The minimal unit of language that can be considered a sign is the individual *speech act*.[211] Speech acts usually take the form of sentences, as minimal units conveying a determinate meaning. Occasionally, a single word might constitute a complete, self-sufficient speech act. In such cases, words

211 Communication is not only conveying information. Communication is social action. Speech act theory also emphasizes this fact. See John L Austin, *How to Do Things with Words*, Clarendon Press (Oxford), 1962; also: John Searle, *Speech Acts*, Cambridge University Press (Cambridge), 1969.

serve as compressed or abbreviated sentences, ie, it is always possible to unfold them to proper sentences, and thus explicate their meaning. For example, the appellation 'Come!' can be explicated as: 'You should come here!'

This identification of signs with communications does not contradict the standard definition of the sign found in expositions of semiology, namely its definition as the unity (coincidence, bond, relation) of a signifier and a signified. The signifier is initially introduced as the material aspect or physical body of the sign with all its empirically observable properties. This seems, prima facie, clear enough to work with. (However, if one probes deeper into how the signifier's identity is constituted and reproduced, one realizes that it is a pattern or class of phenomenal entities the identification of which depends dialectically on its use or correlation with the signified.) The other conceptual component of the sign concept – the signified – seems more problematic (obscure, mysterious) right from the start. The term refers to the 'meaning' of the sign, or better, to that which the sign signifies. Saussure, who first introduced this triad of sign (*signe*), signifier (*signifiant*) and signified (*signifié*), presumed the signified to be a mental entity. Here the philosophical quicksand abounds all around. As Umberto Eco alludes, 'the entire history of philosophy could be re-read in a semiotic perspective'.[212] That is why Luhmann understands meaning as network connectivity rather than mental entity.

The signifier is formed in a medium. In the case of verbal language the primary medium is the medium of articulated oral sounds, and its (by now at least equally important) secondary medium (or set of media) of writing/typing/printing with graphic alphabets. The medium of architectural design is the medium (set of media) of drawing and digital modelling. The relevant communication medium for built architectures is the medium of spatial construction utilizing the full panoply of materials as well as fabrication and construction processes offered by the construction industry. (This large and ever-extending palette, however liberating it might seem, also constitutes a problem, at least for the vital, spontaneous semiosis of the built environment.) This identification of the various media of various systems-of-signification is consistent with Luhmann's general concept of medium as a universe of loosely coupled elements that serves as reservoir for the formation of forms understood as strict couplings of elements selected from within the medium.

212 Umberto Eco, 'The Influence of Roman Jakobson on the Development of Semiotics', in: Martin Krampen et al (Eds), *Classics of Semiotics*, Plenum Press (New York), 1987, p 109.

6.8.4 TERRITORY AS FUNDAMENTAL SEMIOLOGICAL UNIT

The elaboration of the language analogy within architecture must start with the identification of the basic units within built architectures that function as communications. Any semiological interpretation and analysis of built architectures must answer this question: which minimal, self-sufficient units within the built environment function as full communications or communicating signs? What, in the domain of communication via built architectures, generates a self-sufficient social meaning? Or, in other words, what is the equivalent of the speech act or sentence in the language of architecture? The answer proposed here is that ***territories*** are the fundamental, minimal units of communication within built environments. This proposition stipulating the territory as the fundamental unit that underlies all processes of signification is a fundamental axiom of the architectural semiology sketched out here. Territories are communications. As such they constitute a form of social action. The establishment and provision of a territory is indeed a social act and communication, a territorializing act and communication.

Every territory – just like every speech act – is embedded within a context. It is to be expected that the meaning of the territory depends upon its context. There are two types of context that need to be distinguished. The *spatial context*, ie, the other surrounding territories on the one hand, and the *social context*, ie, the social events that are or have been unfolding within the territory.[213]

The concept of territory proposed here comprises all kinds of places, spaces, zones etc, interior, or urban. Anything that produces a sense of enclosure, separation, demarcation or distinction, in any way whatsoever, and that can be somehow recognized as *frame* for social interaction. The concept of territory, together with its derivatives of territorialization and territorial unit, has already been introduced above, in the context of discussing the organizational dimension of architecture.[214] Thus the fundamental unit of all spatial organization is at the same time the fundamental unit of all processes of semiosis within the built environment.

A territory functions – permanently, at certain times, or momentarily – as *designated* locus for specific forms of interaction. (Even if they are used for solitary activities by individuals, the very fact of their occupation for a certain legitimate purpose implies a social act, and thus a communication.) The type and the probable features of the designated

213 This distinction is analogous to the distinction of co-text vs context in linguistics (pragmatics).

214 See chapter 6.3.1 *Relating Spatial to Social Organization* and chapter 6.3.2 *Territorialization and Integration*.

social interaction can be anticipated on account of the territory's relative location and visible morphological features. The character of the expected social encounter can be sensed and intuited on account of the atmospheric ambience of the territory. The territory thus prepares or *primes* the participants.

The theory of architectural autopoiesis has identified the applicability of the distinction of inside vs outside as the defining *differentia specifica* that distinguishes architecture, including urban, interior and (to a certain extent) furniture design, from all the other design disciplines that (together with architecture) form the autopoietic function system of architecture/design.[215] This distinction of inside vs outside can now be employed as the crux in the formal definition of the concept of territory: a territory is an entity that distinguishes and thus establishes an inside (its inside) as distinct from an outside (its outside). That suffices.

Every communication is dialogical. Every communication offers itself, or is exposed to, the binary choice of being accepted or rejected. A verbal communication, for example, in the form of a declarative sentence or assertion, is either accepted as *true* or rejected as *false*. It makes no sense to accept or reject single words unless they represent a compressed sentence. A command is either *obeyed* or *resisted* etc. The acceptance of a communication allows it to become a premise and point of reference for further connecting communications. In the same way a territory or spatial frame can be rejected or accepted as premise for further communications: the territory can be entered – which implies an acceptance and engagement with the signified and anticipated type of social interaction to be expected within the entered territory – or the territory can be exited, or altogether avoided. This spells rejection, and implies the refusal to participate in the signified social interaction. The acceptance of a communication allows for the connection of further communications that build upon each other. To enter a designated territory implies the acceptance of the territory as meaningful frame, ie, the acceptance of its communication as grounding premise for further communications. Those who enter become participants agreeing to engage in the social interactions unfolding within this frame and thus allowing further communications to build upon the grounding premise and upon each other.

215 The centrality of the inside-outside distinction, the centrality of enclosure and territory, is expressed in Le Corbusier's dictum that 'the exterior is always an interior'. There is never an absolute outside. On the exterior of a building there is another composed interior. 'The elements of the site rise up like walls, . . . like the walls of a room.' Le Corbusier, *Towards a New Architecture*, Dover Publications (New York), 1986, unaltered republication of English translation of 13th French edition, published by John Rodker (London), 1931, pp 191–2.

Thus it should be evident that the territorial unit functions as a communication that can be accepted or rejected. Any smaller architectural unit, below the level of the territorial unit, for example, a column, is not subject to such a binary choice of acceptance vs rejection. The column's muteness in this respect implies that it is not to be counted as communication.[216] By itself the column means little, unless it is establishing its own (tenuous) place or territory, perhaps for an intimate rendezvous. In all other (usual) cases it has only a subsidiary meaning as it contributes somehow to the characterization of a territory. This territory might be established with or without the column as part of a demarcating boundary. This difference does not affect the column's status as dependent, subsidiary signifying component. As long as the column exists within the territory it is a potential contributor to the signification. The definition and analysis of the general semiological base category of the sign are thus instituted by the architectural territory as follows: the framing territory is the sign as the unity of its bounding and characterizing physical devices, which together constitute the signifier, with the framed (expected) type of social interaction constituting the signified. The signifier operates in the domain of architectural form, while the signified encompasses the domain of architecture's substantial functions. Thus the conceptual pair *signifier vs signified* is aligned with the conceptual pair *form vs function* and thus with the distinction of architecture's self-reference (internal reference) vs architecture's world-reference (external reference). However, the signifier is only a part of architecture's form, and the signified captures only a part of architecture's function.[217] The basic conceptual arrangement that underlies the analysis of architectural sign systems can thus be summarized and displayed as follows:

the sign	= designed and designated territory	< architecture	= communication
the signifier	= ensemble of territory-defining devices	< form	= self-reference
the signified	= type of social interaction to be framed	< function	= world-reference

This conceptual set up excludes much of what has traditionally been called 'architectural symbolism', for instance, in the sense that the Eiffel Tower might be construed to 'symbolize' the technological prowess of the

216 Every communication presents itself and its meaning as a proposal and invitation that is to be either accepted or rejected. This bifurcation unfolds the moment of understanding, one of the three necessary moments that constitute any communication.

217 Only substantial but not subsidiary functions belong to architecture's signified. Also, not all of architecture's formal operations are enlisted within the plane of the signifier. Thus the unequal (<) rather the equal sign (=) is used to indicate the alignment of the conceptual pair form/function with the conceptual pair signifier/signified.

French nation. The theory of architectural autopoiesis rejects this kind of symbolism as not belonging to the domain of architecture. Indeed, this kind of symbolism was fully expunged from the autopoiesis of architecture with its refoundation as Modern architecture. If there is meaningful 'symbolism' within architecture then it can only be 'self-referential symbolism'.[218]

To illustrate the conceptual set up we might use a very simple example: the bedroom in my London apartment is a sign/communication, that signifies/communicates the social act/interaction of going to bed. The signifier comprises the bounding surfaces, the apertures, as well as the furnishings of the room. The broadcast of the sign is contextualized within the ensemble of the apartment unit, which in turn is contextualized within the apartment block, estate, neighbourhood etc. The basic semiological operation involves the simple mapping of a typology of territories onto a typology of social interactions. Onto this primary constitution of a base meaning further, more nuanced meanings might be superimposed, for example, a sense of non-romantic, no frills, matter-of-factness, or perhaps a sense of romance and sensuousness, depending on the specific textures and colours of the surfaces as well as on the selection and arrangement of the furnishings. These additional characterizations of the territory are considered semiologically active, ie, communicative, to the extent to which they give further information as well as cognitive-emotive preparation about the social interactions that one might expect here. The semiological distinction of *connotation vs denotation* might serve here to label this kind of additional elaboration of the basic (denotative) meaning. The various architectural elements – below the level of the room or territorial unit – receive their always subsidiary meaning, like the words within a sentence, from their position within and contribution to the space-making and sense-making ensemble of the total sign that is always a territorial unit in relation to which one is either inside (with the choice of leaving) or outside (with the potential option to enter).

Above, the medium of architecture's built communications was characterized as the totality of the materials, fabrication processes and construction methods that the global construction industry makes available. One could also define the medium more theoretically, as Preziosi does: 'The physical medium of the built environment, then, is potentially coterminus with the entire range of material resources of the planetary biosphere which can be employed to construct significative

218 Term used by Stanislaus von Moos to characterize work by OMA in an article published in OMA issue of *L'Architecture d'aujourd'hui*, 238, April 1985.

formations addressed to the visual channel.'[219] If one conceptually opens the medium to this extent – beyond the domain of what is now industry-wise available to the contemporary professional architect – one has to introduce the conceptual restriction to material constructs that can be deployed in a territorializing capacity. This is indeed what Preziosi does: 'The medium of the built environment is in fact anything and everything visually palpable which can be employed to serve place-making functions.'[220]

The reference to perception is pertinent here (although the restriction to the visual channel is unnecessary). Architecture is always very much concerned with appearances (although not only appearances). It certainly never concerns itself with what remains invisible, ie, foundations, hidden ducts, hidden machines, hidden cables etc. To this extent we must admit that some of the products of the construction industry are excluded from the medium of architecture, even if the cool air and the electric light as effects of these invisible systems do belong to built architecture's medium of communication. They belong to the medium to the extent to which they can be deployed in a territorializing and/or atmospheric capacity.

The medium of building comprises virtually everything that can be used for perceptually palpable territorializing operations. If this defines the medium of all built architectures, of architecture's final communications delivered into society at large, what is its relationship with architecture's internal medium of communication, with architecture's own discursive design medium of the drawing? The crucial category of territory is recognized within the design medium of drawing by the prominence of lines and outlines in their capacity as delineating boundary operations. The importance of establishing, distinguishing and relating territorial units is also recognized in the crucial drawing type for diagramming and sketching that establishes the essential organization and parti of any design at the early design stages: the bubble diagram. The bubbles of bubble diagrams imply nothing but the unitary, topological primitive we are positing as the categorical substrate of all sense-making processes within architecture: the territorial unit.

If territorial units, as elemental semiological units and correlates of determinate social situations, are the alpha and omega of all processes of architectural semiosis, where does this leave the field-concept or, more precisely, the concept of the *continuously differentiated field* that seems

219 Preziosi, *The Semiotics of the Built Environment*, p 5.
220 Ibid, p 4.

to suspend the very concept of boundedness?[221] There is no doubt that this innovative concept needs to be integrated into any worthwhile contemporary theory of architectural semiosis. Can this be done if the precondition of ascribing meaning to built architectural works is that they are built up from (or can be decomposed into) territorial units? The insistence that this has to be possible was the reason why Preziosi's concept of 'space-cell' had to be replaced with the concept of territory. Territories might be variously bounded. A *blurred* boundary is still a boundary, even if its threshold operation is stretched and softened into a gradient zone of transition. Such a boundary is a more sophisticated territorializing device than a crisp outline. Fuzzy sets are still sets, albeit sponsoring a more sophisticated logic. But the concept of territory can be stretched even further to encompass territories defined by intrinsic field qualities rather than any sort of boundary. These field qualities might be structured by smooth gradients so that the concept of boundary is suspended altogether. The fundamental choice of staying, accepting and participating on the one hand, or avoiding, moving on and leaving, on the other hand, remains. Moving up or down the gradient makes a communicative difference. The subject is either (deliberately) approaching and moving closer to an anticipated type of social encounter, or is moving away to avoid the communication scenario expected in a certain direction. Both moves can be understood as communications responding to the framing communication of the field.

Territories, as the fundamental units of spatial organization and functional designation, are the fundamental units for the ascription of meaning within architecture and the built environment. In this sense they are analogous to sentences within verbal languages. We have also established that the meaning signified by a territory is the social interaction to be expected within its ambit. This does not yet tell us anything about how territories acquire and convey this meaning.

The basic denotative meaning of a territory is nothing but its functional designation, the basic type of social interaction to be expected. This much might be legible via the territory's spatial position within an array of territories, its position within a network of circulation, together with the bare volumetric proportions of the territory. Further connotations rely on the further architectural elaboration (nuanced characterization) of the territory. Various registers of architectural articulation are coming into play here: geometry, tectonic detail, materiality, texture, colour, light etc. These are the registers that are

221 See Volume 1, chapter 5.4.4 *From Space to Field*.

available on the level of the signifier. The totality of these registers might be referred to as ***architectural morphology***. The main question to be raised here is a question that is central to all semiological inquiries: what does it take to elevate such a panoply of articulatory registers to become a system-of-signification, ie, an operating medium of communication, a language that is able to coordinate the elements and features of an articulated spatial ensemble into a comprehensible, information-rich message? That the socio-cultural evolution has achieved this feat over and over again is clear. The point here is to unravel its mechanisms and structural devices in order to assess to what extent and how this feat can be made the (likely) result of a design effort.

6.8.5 SAUSSURE'S INSIGHT: LANGUAGE AS SYSTEM OF CORRELATED DIFFERENCES

As mentioned above, the two independent founding fathers of semiology/semiotics are Ferdinand de Saussure (1857–1913) and Charles Sanders Peirce (1839–1914). Saussure's work establishes linguistics as a science of human language understood as a synchronic system. He conceived of linguistics to be encompassed by an anticipated general science concerned with the totality of human sign systems. Saussure proposed to call this science *semiology* (sémiologie): 'A language system is a system of signs . . . comparable to writing, the deaf-and-dumb alphabet, symbolic rites, forms of politeness, military signals, and so on. . . . It is therefore possible to conceive of a science *which studies the role of signs as part of social life*. We shall call it semiology (from Greek semeion, "sign"). . . . The linguist's task is to define what makes languages a special type of system within the totality of semiological facts.'[222] Saussure's definition of the basic concept 'linguistic sign' can be (and has been) generalized to the concept of signs in general. 'In our terminology a *sign* is the combination of a concept and a sound pattern. . . . We propose to keep the term *sign* to designate the whole, but to replace *concept* and *sound pattern* by *signified* and *signifier*. The latter terms have the advantage of indicating the distinction which separates each from the other and both from the whole of which they are a part.'[223] This simple triad of terms should not deceive us. It does not imply that language is simply an arsenal of such signs, each by itself established as the correlation of a concept with a sound pattern.

222 Saussure, *Course in General Linguistics*, p 16.
223 Ibid, p 67.

Saussure warns against 'the superficial view taken by the general public, which sees a language merely as a nomenclature'.[224] He elaborates: 'For some people a language, reduced to its essentials, is a nomenclature: a list of terms corresponding to a list of things. . . . This conception . . . assumes that ideas already exist independently of words.'[225] Instead Saussure argued that concepts are a product of linguistic operations, ie, achievements of a social system of interaction beyond anybody's reach.[226] An individual speech act can only be meaningful as an instance that follows and reproduces the rules of a shared language system.[227] Each individual word within this system has meaning only due to its participation and specifically allocated role or position within the system. This allocated position or role Saussure terms (synchronic or linguistic) *value*. The identity and meaning of a word depend upon its value in the linguistic structure or system. Saussure illustrates his concept of value by analogy with what defines each of the pieces of the game of chess, namely the overall set of pieces, differentiated by the rules or 'grammar' of the game, and the relative role of the individual piece within the thus constituted system.[228] Saussure's notion of value implies that the individual sign cannot be isolated from the system to which it belongs, and that it would be 'a great mistake to consider a sign as nothing more than the combination of a certain sound and a certain concept, . . . to suppose that a start could be made with individual signs, and a system constructed by putting them together. On the contrary, the system as a united whole is the starting point, from which it becomes possible, by a process of analysis, to identify its constituent elements.'[229] Saussure's central groundbreaking insight,

224 Saussure, *Course in General Linguistics*, p 67.

225 Ibid, p 65.

226 This insight would have shaken up Western philosophy if Saussure's work had entered philosophical discourse at the time Saussure gave his lectures on general linguistics between 1906 and 1911. Instead philosophy had to develop this insight on its own. Ludwig Wittgenstein was one of the key protagonists of the later so-called *linguistic turn* in philosophy. His starting point – many years after Saussure's lecture courses – was also the rejection of the naive conception of language as the trivial operation of labelling pre-existing ideas. See Ludwig Wittgenstein, *Philosophical Investigations* (Philosophische Untersuchungen), Blackwell Publishing (Oxford), 1953.

227 It is impossible to give meaning to one's utterances by fiat, by intention, or force of one's will. To grasp this see Wittgenstein's arguments against the possibility of a private language in his *Philosophical Investigations*. Meaning is only conveyed via a language system or structure. That's why Saussure insists on the importance of the distinction of *language* (langue) and *speech* (parole).

228 The chess game was also one of Wittgenstein's leading analogies.

229 Saussure, *Course in General Linguistics*, p 112.

initially as counterintuitive as it is ultimately compelling, is stated in the first sentence of Chapter IV on 'Linguistic Value': 'Language itself can be nothing other than a system of pure values.'[230] And further: 'Values remain entirely a matter of internal relations.'[231] Saussure elaborates: 'What we find, instead of *ideas* given in advance, are values emanating from a linguistic system. If we say that these values correspond to certain concepts, it must be understood that the concepts in question are purely differential. That is to say they are concepts defined not positively, in terms of their content, but negatively by contrast with other items in the same system. What characterizes each most exactly is being whatever the others are not.'[232] And: 'The content of a word is determined in the final analysis not by what it contains but by what exists outside it.'[233] This leads Saussure to the following summary formulation: 'The language is, so to speak, an algebra which has only complex terms. . . . Nothing is simple. Always and everywhere one finds the same complex equilibrium of terms holding one another in mutual juxtaposition.'[234]

Concepts are co-produced together by somehow correlating experiences, perceptions, actions etc with an otherwise abstract, formal calculus of differentiated sound patterns. 'Just as the conceptual part of linguistic value is determined solely by relations and differences with other signs in the language, so the same is true for its material part. The sound of a word is not in itself important, but the phonetic contrasts which allow us to distinguish that word from another.'[235] But how to identify and individualize one sound pattern versus another? How to pick out the relevant from the irrelevant contrasts? There are many different idiosyncratic ways of pronouncing a certain word. What are the criteria for discriminating two individual utterances or alternatively identifying them as versions of the same sound pattern? This question cannot be solved in the domain of perception alone. Anybody trying to learn a foreign language realizes that the first and most persistent problem is simple listening comprehension. An utterly alien language appears like an undifferentiated blur of sound. We are confronted with the apparent

230 Ibid, p 110.
231 Ibid, p 111.
232 Ibid, p 115.
233 Ibid, p 114. This fundamental insight that apparent essences emanate from a patterned system of pure differences, without original positive terms, is the cornerstone insight of all post-metaphysical philosophies. It also underlies Luhmann's theory of social systems. Luhmann explicitly characterizes his theoretical system as based on difference rather than identity as foundational category.
234 Saussure, *Course in General Linguistics*, p 120.
235 Ibid, p 116.

paradox that the two levels that are both inherently indeterminate – the level of the signified and the level of the signifier – are able to act as each other's scaffold of determination, resulting in a determinate structure. Saussure poses the paradox as follows: 'No ideas are established in advance, and nothing is distinct before the introduction of linguistic structure. But do sounds, which lie outside of this nebulous world of thought, in themselves constitute entities established in advance? No more than ideas do. The substance of sound is no more fixed and rigid than that of thought. It does not offer a readymade mould, with shapes that thought must inevitably conform to. It is a malleable material which can be fashioned into separate parts in order to supply the signals which thought has need of.'[236] The description of how this happens, gradually, within a long process of historical evolution whereby language use coevolves within socio-cultural evolution as one of its primary tools and engines, lies outside the scope of Saussure's synchronic science of linguistics. To get a tangible sense of how a language gradually acquires meaning and builds up complexity within pragmatic circumstances of cooperation one might read Ludwig Wittgenstein's attempt to model such a process by describing very simple *language games* operating in very simple *forms of life*.[237] Saussure just offers the striking vista of the paradoxical, final achievement, the creation of order from chaos: 'So we can envisage the linguistic phenomenon in its entirety – the language that is – as a series of adjoining subdivisions simultaneously imprinted both on the plane of vague, amorphous thought (A), and on the equally featureless plane of sound (B). This can be represented very approximately in the following sketch. . . . The combination of both a necessary and mutually complementary delimitation of units. Thought, chaotic by nature, is made precise by this process of segmentation. . . . What takes place, is a somewhat mysterious process by which "thought-sound" evolves divisions, and a language takes shape with its linguistic units in between these two amorphous masses.'[238]

This co-production of structure out of the two levels implies that it is impossible to change the plane of the signifieds without at the same time changing the plane of the signifiers. Every sign is co-determined by all the other signs within the system. In large systems, the effects are more localized within the vicinity of a given sign constituted by its competing and collaborating signs. If a signifier drops out of use, the use of the neighbouring signs is inevitably affected. Similarly, if a signified drops

236 Ibid, p 110.

237 Ludwig Wittgenstein, *Philosophical Investigations*, Blackwell Publishing (Oxford), 1953.

238 Saussure, *Course in General Linguistics*, p 110.

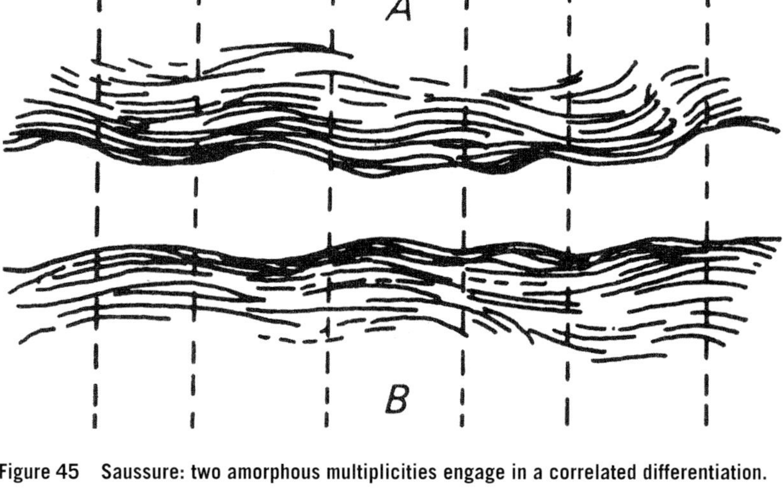

Figure 45 Saussure: two amorphous multiplicities engage in a correlated differentiation. From Saussure, *Course in General Linguistics*, 1995

away, other collaborating or contrasting signifieds will be affected. If a concept loses or changes its primary contrast it has become a different concept. If a new signifier pushes into a semantic field it squeezes and re-arranges positions of many if not all competitors. The two planes are inseparable as the two sides of a sheet of paper. The scissors always cut through both sides.[239]

6.8.6 EXTRA-SEMIOLOGICAL DEMANDS ON ARCHITECTURE'S MEDIAL SUBSTRATE

Above, Saussure is giving a dramatic image of a seemingly paradoxical process: two unstructured, amorphous planes use each other as scaffold in the build up of determinate structures. The cognitive processes that are coming into play here have been alluded to in the chapters on the psychology of perception.[240] However, what should be noted here is that the evolution of a language is not proceeding in the wilderness. Language coevolved with the built environment together with other media of conspicuous differentiation like body adornments etc. The settlement structures with their delimitation of spaces and the spatial sorting of

239 Historical linguistics offers a reservoir of evidence to corroborate these theses. Saussure notes that 'when one word gives birth to two alternative pronunciations . . . the phonetic difference which has emerged will tend to acquire significance, although perhaps not immediately.' Saussure, *Course in General Linguistics*, p 110.

240 See chapter 6.7.1 *The Perceptual Constitution of Objects and Spaces* and chapter 6.7.2 *Cognitive Principles of Gestalt-perception*.

people, objects and activities must have been an important scaffold for early language and concept formation. In turn, the evolution and structuring of the built environment must have been supported by the evolving language and its categorizations. This collaboration and coevolution of language and built environment as complementary systems-of-signification continues. Thus a comprehensive theory must reckon with a ***multi-modal*** social system of communications. This implies that additional layers must be added to Saussure's picture. These layers are somehow mapped onto each other, but never in simple one-to-one, item-to-item mappings. And certainly they do not all refer back to a single objective signified. Both verbal sign system and the sign system of the built environment have their own double articulation into the signifying and the signified layer. But they somehow function together in structuring the social life-process, as complementary media, each with its own specific affordances and limitations.

The central thesis of Saussure, namely that a language operates always on the basis of differences, as a complex system 'in which all the elements fit together, and in which the value of any one element depends on the simultaneous coexistence of all the others', should still hold, at least to some extent, for any 'architectural language' worthy of the name.[241]

However, there is a fundamental difference between verbal and architectural languages. Verbal languages are indeed pure communication media, purely concerned with information processing and the coordination aspect of social life. Accordingly, verbal languages possess an incredible material lightness. This sense of a nearly dematerialized physical existence has also been carried forth into the derivative medial forms of writing, printing and language-based telecommunication. This dematerialized purity also predestines verbal language to be the universal medium that can, in principle, communicate about anything and everything that could ever be communicated about. Its level of the signified is unlimited, unconstrained in comparison with other media like the built environment, the design media of drawing/modelling, body-language, body-adornment or fashion etc. These latter media are all characterized by a limitation of their domain of the signified.

241 Perhaps Saussure's thesis is even overstated for the case of verbal languages where semi-autonomous regions might exist where influences are bound to close neighbourhoods. But then, we might speak of different languages or, like Wittgenstein, of different language games. So what is at stake here is not the fundamental thesis or principle Saussure has discovered, but the theoretical decision about the criteria of individuation one should use with respect to the concept of a unified language. Perhaps English should not be considered as one language but a series of overlapping languages?

The built environment is not purely a medium of communication. The built environment does more: it shelters from (counteracts) the cold, hot, dark, bright, wet, dry, noisy and polluted environment. These physical operations are part of the medial substrate of the medium of built architecture. To the extent that these operations are deemed necessary for the bodily functioning of the accommodated social institutions, they impose limitations on the free disposition over the built matter in the service of functioning as medium of communication. Also, these physical aspects are no longer under the full control of the autopoiesis of architecture. They are engineering matters.

Thus the medium of built architecture is burdened with these non-architectural requirements that are imposed upon its medial substrate. There are also architectural aspects that cannot be construed as mere communications. These are the organizational requirements of the functioning of social institutions. These organizational aspects/requirements involve the distancing and separating of people who could be disturbing or dangerous to each other. The organization via distancing and solid/secure enclosures operates in ways that cannot be construed as mere communication (although such separations are always unavoidably communications). Organization involves the organization of connections and proximities via channels of movement. These connections also do not (primarily) function as communications. They involve the physical channelling of bodies. These organizational aspects – space planning layouts, accessibility networks etc – are (still) controlled within the domain of architecture.[242] However, they impose functional criteria on the medial substrate of built architecture that are not the same as the functional criteria of signification/communication. Every medium, even the medium of verbal language, is subject to physical-material constraints (as well as to the general constraints of human cognitive capacity). In the case of verbal languages these are the constraints of the articulatory organs, acoustic transmission properties of air etc. In the case of built architecture, the constraints involve the laws of physics (building physics, structural laws), as well as constraints inherent in the historically available fabrication and construction techniques. In principle, these material constraints *cannot* be summarily compared or weighted across such fundamentally different kinds of sign systems with so radically different material substrates. However, an important

242 It would in principle be possible for these aspects to be outsourced to another engineering discipline. However, the limitations on the medial substrate of any architectural sign system would be all the more severe if architecture were to lose control of the organization of the built environment.

difference between the two types of sign systems that *can* be asserted is the fact that the built environment serves more than just communicative functions. It cannot be monofunctionally driven to become a pure and 'perfect' instrument of communication. This is also the reason why the language of the built environment is not, as is verbal language, characterized by absolute and inherent arbitrariness. The different building forms of world history, even if they have evolved independently of each other, seem rather similar to each other. It seems comparatively easy to guess and grasp the meaning of buildings the world over, certainly in comparison with the utter hopelessness of understanding a foreign language. We will return to the discussion of arbitrariness below.

6.8.7 SYNTAGMATIC VS PARADIGMATIC RELATIONS

When Saussure introduces the concept of system or structure, what he has in mind initially is primarily the idea of a matrix or set of terms that co-depend on each other for defining and demarcating each other as different and opposed to each other in a 'complex equilibrium of terms holding one another in mutual juxtaposition'.[243] He is not, as yet, concerned how these different terms form a rational structure, or how they collaborate and function together. The concept of value – initially denoting the position of a term within the system of differences – is then augmented by considering the relations and connections such a term is able to engage in. Saussure is distinguishing two types of relations that terms might engage in that together elaborate the concept of value. 'The relations and differences between linguistic items fall into two quite distinct kinds, each giving rise to a separate order of values.'[244] Saussure distinguishes *syntagmatic* from *associative* relations. (The latter term has later generally been replaced by the term *paradigmatic*. Thus we get the mnemotechnically motivated pair syntagmatic vs paradigmatic.) Syntagmatic relations are the relations within strings, for example, within multi-syllable words, phrases, sentences and sequences of sentences. They are based on the linear, sequential character of language. Associative relations are relations of belonging to a certain associative group. An association might be based on semantic associations or on sound similarities, ie, associative relationships can operate on the level of the signifier, the signified or both. Saussure's concept of associative relations is a rather open-ended notion: 'Any given term acts as the centre of a constellation, from which connected terms radiate *ad*

243 Saussure, *Course in General Linguistics*, p 120.

244 Ibid, p 121.

infinitum.'[245] Later authors have not only supplanted the term 'associative relation' with the term 'paradigmatic relation' but have mostly tried to rein in the scope and openness of this notion to give it more precision. Usually, a set of terms is considered paradigmatically related, forming a paradigm, if they can somehow substitute for each other as contrasting and therefore significant alternatives of expression. 'Signs are in paradigmatic relation when the choice of one excludes the choice of another.'[246] Or, put another way: 'Paradigmatic relations are those which belong to the same set by virtue of a function they share. . . . A sign enters into paradigmatic relations with all the signs which can also occur in the same context but not at the same time.'[247]

Saussure contrasts the two types of relations as follows: 'Syntagmatic relations hold *in praesentia*. They hold between two or more terms co-present in a sequence. Associative relations, on the contrary, hold *in absentia*. They hold between terms constituting a mnemonic group.'[248] It has been noted that the concepts of syntagmatic and paradigmatic relations have general semiological application, also with respect to architecture. It is indeed a commonplace to rehearse this distinction within semiological accounts of architecture.[249] The syntagmatic relation, which in verbal language is a relation in time, is transposed into a relation in space. (In neither case must the concept be restricted to relations of immediate adjacency, succession or antecedence.) This transposition of the conceptual pair into architecture was made easy by the fact that Saussure chose to illustrate the distinction of the two types of relations with reference to architecture: 'Considered from these two points of view, a linguistic unit may be compared to a single part of a building, for example, a column. A column is related in a certain way to the architrave it supports. This disposition, involving two units co-present in space, is comparable to a syntagmatic relation. On the other hand, if a column is Doric, it will evoke mental comparison with the other architectural orders (Ionic, Corinthian etc), which are not in this instance spatially co-present. This relation is associative.'[250]

245 Ibid, p 124.
246 David Silverman & Brian Torode, *The Material Word: Some Theories of Language and its Limits*, Routledge & Kegan Paul (London), 1980, p 255.
247 Varda Langholz Leymore, *Hidden Myth: Structure and Symbolism in Advertising*, Basic Books (New York), 1975, p 8.
248 Saussure, *Course in General Linguistics*, p 124.
249 For instance see Geoffrey Broadbent, 'Meaning into Architecture', in: Charles Jencks & George Baird (Eds), *Meaning in Architecture*, George Braziller (New York), 1970, pp 51–2.
250 Saussure, *Course in General Linguistics*, p 122.

The point of introducing the two types of relations that can be identified in any communicative impartation (utterance, building) is to understand how they are involved in the functioning of communication. To say that one set of relations is 'present' and the other 'absent' is a poignant contrast but also a simplification that might lead to a misunderstanding. The meaning of any particular sequence or arrangement of terms/items presented depends not only on the different alternative items that might otherwise be chosen in place of each placed item, it also depends on the 'absent' rules of the language or system-of-signification that make a particular sequence/arrangement either expected, or surprising, or even incomprehensible. What has to be taken into account is the fact that syntagms are usually constructed on regular patterns and that a system of rules, a grammar, is involved that determines not only the well-formedness of a construct but also the particular meaning of the composite impartation. The question of the systematicity of the language thus arises, in particular with respect to any supposed architectural language. Not all built environments display the same degree of regularity. Superficial regularity is by itself not a sufficient criterion for language systematicity. Spatial and formal similarities and differences must be systematically correlated with differences in uses, types of social interaction and social structure. Mario Gandelsonas compares the systematicity of the Classical architectural canon that dominated architecture since the Renaissance with Modernism: 'In both circumstances the aim was to produce a systematic organization of the codes of architectural practice, to define an apparently finite and stable number of forms and their correlated meaning within a closed system. . . . But whereas in classicism a fully constituted language in this sense can be observed in the way in which the elements of antiquity, deployed in an entirely new way, sustained a grammatical framework, in modernism the linguistic organization was essentially illusory. . . . It proposed new words but no rules for their combination, no grammatical framework for their use.'[251] Whether Gandelsonas' assessment of Modernism is correct or doubtful, there can be no doubt that the radical expansion of architecture's repertoire and the abandonment of the strictures of symmetry and proportion initially implied a certain loss of overall redundancy and thus structure or systematicity. However, if one reads Henry-Russell Hitchcock and Philip Johnson's *International Style*, presenting the canonization of the first 10 years of the Modern

251 Mario Gandelsonas, 'From Structure to Subject: The Formation of an Architectural Language', in: *Oppositions* 17, Summer 1979, p 201.

Movement, a strong sense of systematization, at least on the side of the signifier, comes across.

Leaving this question of the language-likeness of the style of Modernism aside, the more important question concerns the built environment in general. The built environment is the outcome of the intersection of architectural efforts (that are programmed according to the heuristics of the dominant style) and the contingencies of the societal environment outside architecture's control. It is in this societal environment that processes of semiosis occur. Indeed, prima facie it seems that the built environments of traditional, closed societies developed much stricter rules and exhibited more regular syntagmatic patterns in their settlements than can be detected in the seemingly amorphous, randomly sprawling urban agglomerations of modern societies. The semiological systematicity of the global built environment seems to have further degenerated since the onset of globalization, Post-Fordism and the resultant crisis of architectural Modernism. The emergence of Postmodernism, Deconstructivism and Minimalism did exacerbate this situation rather than leading to more semiological systematicity. Although this historical tendency of semiological degeneration seems to be undeniable – despite the efforts of Postmodern architecture – this does not mean that the attempt to develop architectural grammars for new projects must be considered hopeless from the start.

If the natural semiosis of the built environment, left to its own devices within contemporary conditions, is failing, is there a chance to induce a new semiosis artificially? Is it possible to create, and to a certain extent steer, an artifical language for the built environment analogous to the artificial languages that were developed within early 20th-century philosophy? Proposing and launching more rigorously conceived and structured compositions is always possible. But can the semiosis that will engulf them be even vaguely anticipated, let alone predicted or controlled? As Charles Jencks put it 40 years ago: 'the minute a new form is invented it will acquire, inevitably, a meaning. This semantization is inevitable'.[252] There is some evident truth here, but what Charles Jencks includes in the concept of meaning in architecture is much more vague and wide-ranging than what the theory of architectural autopoiesis considers. Jencks thinks about symbolic allusions and all sorts of connotations that might cross the mind of a disengaged connoisseur, rather than the operative meanings that frame and orient the interaction

252 Charles Jencks, 'Semiology and Architecture', in: Charles Jencks & George Baird (Eds), *Meaning in Architecture*, George Braziller (New York), 1970, p 11.

processes of the immediate users. The latter, more constrained and precise definition of the concept of meaning in architecture is the definition proposed here, and further elaborated below. With respect to this notion, the envisioned semiological project has more plausibility, notwithstanding the fact that the only real and relevant meanings are produced within the social systems that communicate within the designed projects, with no regard to the intentions of the designer.

6.9 Prolegomenon to Architecture's Semiological Project

THESIS 33

Contemporary architecture must push the expressive power of its architectural language far beyond the simple correlations between forms and designations that have usually been considered under the heading of 'meaning in architecture'.

The theory of architectural autopoiesis states that the autopoiesis of architecture operates globally, as a single, worldwide system of communications. In this sense contemporary architecture is world architecture. Does this imply that the 'language of architecture' must be a single world architectural language? Not necessarily. We can speak about world society without necessarily assuming the existence of a single world language (although English might be a plausible candidate to become this world language). However, it does imply that a single world architectural language is possible in principle. As will be explored below, this idea of a world architectural language, not understood metaphorically as another term for a global architectural style but as a new level of semiosis involving a grammar that allows for the construction of composite architectural signs, cannot emerge spontaneously. This possibility, which until now existed only in theoretical speculation, can only be advanced by strategically selected design research projects, ie, via individual design projects of sufficient scale, and with briefs that imply a high level of social complexity and communication density to warrant the design of a new, autonomous, project-specific system of signification. Before outlining the conditions and criteria that such projects should meet, some further insights, concepts and premises must be assembled. For instance, before further investigating the general question of a language's systematicity or grammaticality, it is opportune to determine more precisely the particular types of meaning built architectural works might acquire. The theoretical task here is to define the domain of architecture's signified.

6.9.1 THE SCOPE OF ARCHITECTURE'S SIGNIFIED

Above it was asserted that the basic architectural sign is the designated territory. Its basic denotative signified is the social interaction type accommodated within it.[253] This demarcation of architecture's signified concurs with Ludwig Wittgenstein's general insight that the meaning of a sign is its use. The identification of architecture's signified with its function, understood as accommodated activity or social action, has often (although not always) been the basic premise for theorizing architecture as sign system. For instance, Mario Gandelsonas, one of the main protagonists of such theorizing in the 1970s, states that, for both Classical and Modern architecture, meaning coincides with function. Although he does not restrict the architectural sign to territories, he posits that the domain of architecture's content coincides with 'the system of social actions'.[254] The most condensed formula for this axiom reads: ***form signifies function.*** Or alternatively it might be put like this: architecture's signified must take the categorical form of a ***function-type.***[255]

An architectural sign – a territory – always points to itself, to its inside. That's the meaning of Stanislaus von Moos' phrase *self-referential symbolism*. All other forms of symbolism have or should have been expelled from the domain of architecture. The question now arises of the overall scope of possible contents of architectural communication. In which ways, to which of its aspects, does an architectural work – a building, space or field – refer?

In analyzing this question *in abstracto*, ie, without analyzing a concrete building, we will be guided primarily by the words/concepts that have sedimented within our (ordinary) verbal language (English). Architectural and verbal language have evolved together. Verbal conceptualization is omnipresent and thus prestructures and guides the decomposition of the world of experience, also the world of architectural experience. (In turn, verbal language is prestructured by the partitioning of space within the built environment.)

What are the types of information one might expect to be denotated or connotated by a built architecture?[256] The base information is the type of

253 Ontologically, the primary signified, the 'meaning' of the sign/territory, is neither a physical nor a mental thing. Neither is it an ideal (Platonic) entity. It is a socially attributed, dispositional property of a territory: its expected capacity to host specific activities and types of interaction.

254 Mario Gandelsonas, 'From Structure to Subject: The Formation of an Architectural Language', in: *Oppositions* 17, Summer 1979, reprinted in: K Michael Hays, *Oppositions Reader*, Princeton Architectural Press (New York), 1998, p 203.

255 The concept of function-type was formally introduced in chapter 6.1.4 *The Categorization of Function-types*.

256 To overcome the total abstraction of the following analysis, the reader might picture and keep in mind the Bauhaus in Dessau as illustration.

social interaction, ie, the function-type the territory instantiates. This function-type can be classified with various degrees of resolution or specificity, ie, the conveyed information might be more or less specific. The building or space might denote 'institution', or more specifically 'educational institution', or more specifically 'university', or more specifically still 'school of architecture'. Thus it seems as if the denotated signified is structured in layers or nested categories that conform to a system of classification within which function-types can be defined with a variable degree of resolution. The first point to be noted here is that in each layer the signified information is based on a system of implicit distinctions in the paradigmatic dimension. 'Institutional' is part of the paradigmatic set 'institutional vs commercial vs residential'. It is thus defined negatively as 'neither commercial nor residential'. 'Educational' is understood only in opposition to 'political', 'legal', 'medical', 'military' etc. 'University' is defined as distinct from both 'secondary education' and 'adult education', constituting the selection/substitution set: 'university vs secondary school vs adult education'. The second point to be noted here is that this kind of functional classification seems to have a natural point of termination. Perhaps 'university' (or 'university institute') suffices to inform about the patterns of interaction to be expected within the thus designated territory. The further qualification as 'school of architecture', or even more so as 'Modernist school of architecture', or nearly absurd, as 'German Modernist school of architecture and urbanism' seems to add rapidly diminishing returns in terms of offering orientation with regards to anticipated patterns of social intercourse and communication. To investigate another example, one might imagine, for instance, approaching one of the Bauhaus masters' houses in Dessau. Here there might be no series involved at all. The denotation might simply be 'family house'. Or there might be the short series: 'residential' (vs 'commercial' vs 'institutional'), and then more specifically 'single family house' (vs 'multi-parti territory'). Again, any further qualification, for instance in terms of architectural (rather than functional) typology – 'detached house, vs semi-detached, vs terrace house' – only delivers much diminished informational returns. Or consider the series 'commercial' (vs 'institutional' vs 'residential' vs 'offices'), or more specifically 'retail' (vs 'entertainment' vs 'catering'), or more specifically 'fashion store' (vs 'food store' vs 'book store' vs 'electronics store'). Here the last qualification also adds little of relevance. Here 'retail store' seems to be the terminal, most pertinent level for identifying the function-type that should be architecture's denotative signified here. The structure of the signified is thus a nesting structure or order of subsumption with a relative determinate, privileged, terminal level of classification. The function-types thus classified correspond to determinate, stable social institutions or types of interaction. This much can be asserted about the structure of architecture's signified on the fundamental level of denotation.

However, there is more relevant information about territories that could be communicated within an architectural language. For instance, information about which social strata or classes are to be encountered, to which social group the territory belongs. During the epoch when stratification was still the dominant mode of societal and social differentiation, this aspect of social status or stratum was indeed the dominant dimension of architecture's signified. In the era of Modern (and Postmodern) *functionally differentiated society*, functional classifications of the kind explored above provide the dominant and most pertinent categories structuring architecture's signified. It is the terminal level of the function-type that establishes the denotative signified of the architectural territory in question. The function-type dominates the determination of the expected social encounter/interaction almost irrespective of the class position (status in a general societal stratification) of those involved in the encounter/interaction. This strongly contrasts with the previous historical era. During the feudal order – when the stratification of society was of primary relevance in all circumstances – the pertinent, primary, denotative signified of all architecture (as well as of all fashion and product design) was the position and role of the territory in the system of status distinctions, almost irrespective of the function of the encounter/interaction. With the transformation of the predominantly stratified social order into an order based on functional differentiation, the respective roles of function-type and status-type have been reversed. Now the function-type is a matter of architecture's denotation and the status-type, to the extent to which it still exists in various new guises, is relegated to the domain of connotations. Not that connotations are irrelevant or to be neglected. But there is a definite hierarchy of determination to be observed here: first the pertinent denotation is to be settled, and within this primary frame, connotations, ie, secondary qualifications and nuances, can be played out.

The transition from a stratified to a functionally differentiated society coincides with the emergence of architecture as autopoietic system of communications as distinct from tradition-bound building. Thus, in theory at least, architecture's primary signified should have been functionally oriented since its inception. If one only consults architecture's theoretical self-descriptions – starting with Leon Battista Alberti's *De re aedificatoria* – this is indeed the impression one receives. Although references to social status are still relevant and explicit in Alberti's discourse, they seem to be subordinated to a fundamentally functional discourse. The real historical semiosis on the ground might still have been a different matter until about 1800.

Although the concept of status-type with its connotations of hierarchy and stratification still exists today, its general social relevance and acceptance are no longer guaranteed.[257] The concept of status-type should therefore be generalized to the concept of ***social-type***, comprising all qualifications on the basis of any possible social classification: ethnic group, race, age, gender, educational level, sub-cultural type, or lifestyle group in general. The expected or desired social-type is one of the primary connotative signifieds of architecture. Architecture can, does and should communicate social typologies of the kind indicated above, but only in the mode of connotation. Architecture shares this communicative task with the fashion system. However, what is the denotational signified of the fashion system is a mere connotational signified within architectural systems-of-signification. For example, a restaurant might be characterized as *formal* vs *informal*, or *cheap* vs *expensive* etc. A workplace is *corporate* vs *creative* etc. The rules of engagement are more or less the same – the social situations are of the same type – but there are nuances to be observed. This is what the theory of architectural autopoiesis proposes to capture via its assimilation of the linguistic distinction ***denotation*** vs ***connotation***. The connotative dimension of the social-type seems more open-ended and freewheeling than the denotative function-type. Function-types are based on social communicative institutions that are relatively stable in the time dimension and geographically nearly universal across global society. While status-types used to have this level of stability during the epoch of stratification, the social-types of today are much more unstable, and geographically more localized. That is another reason why social-types cannot be the primary signified for the medium of architecture, or even urbanism.

There is a third category of information that might be revealed or communicated via an architectural language or system-of-signification, namely information about the location or spatial position of the territory (zone, building, field, space, room) within a larger configurational matrix. Information about the otherwise hidden configurational measures of Hillier's space syntax, for example, the integration value of a territorial unit, might be coded and communicated.[258] This mode of

257 Anybody of supposedly high status will realize this when he/she enters a public place like a post office, or train station etc, and finds him/herself compelled to either join the queue or leave.

258 Concerning the suggestion of articulating space syntax information consult the end of chapter 6.4.5 *Space Syntax: Concepts and Tools of Analysis*.

communication is also concerned with indicating (leading to) adjacent or near territories that are somehow connected and relevant to the territory in question. This dimension of the signified might be called the dimension of navigation. The signified itself might be called ***location-type*** (as distinct from function-type and social-type). Its role is to assist wayfinding. The design strategy of contextual affiliation might be brought to bear here as a formal operation on the level of the signifier to signify/convey this kind of information. Within this dimension a navigation function (rather than denotative or connotative function) of the architectural sign also entails the task of making comprehensible the internal spatial organization of a complex territory into smaller territorial units. The location-type, comprising organizational (positional) information, looking spatially outwards from the territory as well as looking inwards into the internal organization of the territory, is a type of information that is necessitated by the fact that architectural works/territories, unlike other designed artefacts, mostly exceed what can be perceived in a single instance. It is not possible to simultaneously perceive both the inside and the outside of a building. (Even within a convex space it is impossible to perceive the totality of the territory in a simultaneous image.)

With regard to revealing the (outward and inward) organizational structure of a territory, semiological articulation is directly isofunctional (but not identical) with phenomenological articulation. The task is the same but the means are different. Semiological and phenomenological efforts might complement or substitute each other in this respect. They are functional equivalents here. Here the organization of the territory becomes the signified of the architectural language. The structure of the signified in this dimension is either the structure of spatial nesting – territories within territories – or a network structure like sequences, rings, branching systems etc. These structural logics would have to be taken into account by any language structure with the ambition to articulate the organization of the territory.

On the premise that the architectural sign always takes the form of a territory, the dimensions of architecture's signified, ie, the pertinent dimensions that any architectural sign might address as its information or content, can now be summarized as follows:

sign-function:	denotation	connotation	navigation
dimensions of the signified:	function-type	social-type	location-type

Communications comprise the moments impartation, information and understanding. Above, three types of information were distinguished in the domain of architecture's signified: the function-type, the social-type and the location-type. An information-rich built environment or architectural work should cover all three types of information. However, any graded notion of (the degree of) information-richness or ***information-density***, as a comparative term, depends upon the richness or ***expressive power*** of the architectural language. The expressive power of an architectural language, for example, in the domain of the function-type, depends upon the correlated conceptual and formal manifold that is co-created by the language as it builds up a structure between the planes of the signifier and the signified. It depends on the number of distinct alternative signs that is available in the domain of the function-type. The larger this number of possible alternatives to any chosen sign, the higher the amount of information conveyed with this single sign.

6.9.2 THE COMPOSITE CHARACTER OF THE ARCHITECTURAL SIGN

Above, the central category of semiology – the *sign*-concept – was imported into the theory of architectural autopoiesis as co-extensive equivalent to its central concept of *communication*. The more specific concept of *architectural sign*, synonymous with *built architectural communication*, was concretized by being identified with the concept of (designed and designated) *territory* as the minimal self-sufficient communicative unit within the domain of architecture, equivalent to the unit of the sentence as the minimal self-sufficient communicative unit of speech acts utilizing a verbal language.[259] However, it must be recognized (and terminologically accommodated) that architectural signs, as much as the sentences of a language, are composite entities. This composite character is not only to be observed in the case of larger territories like buildings or urban ensembles that can be analyzed as aggregation of elemental territorial units but, most importantly, concerns the constitution of the elemental territorial sign-units from components that by themselves do not constitute autonomous communications. These components are not complete signs. They might be referred to as ***sign-radicals***. The term alludes to the concept of (free) radicals in chemistry. Sign-radicals (in analogy to their chemical namesakes) have a certain connective force, and combinatory potential. They require each other to complete a sign. However, as in a chemical reaction, depending on the cojoining elements, the radical actualizes one of a set of meaning potentials. These potentials might be rather different. The re-use of

259 This usage/definition of the concept of the sign deviates from Saussure's usage. In Saussure's terminology, individual words count as signs. Words are even Saussure's paradigm case of signs.

sign-radicals in rather different contexts might lead to different overall meanings. The notion thus allows the combination of sign-radicals to be similar to chemical reactions where the components might lose their original identity in emergent results (signs) that would have been difficult to predict. There can be no inexorable logic or rationality that allows for the unfailing deduction of composite meanings from their components. However, although the concept thus allows for emergence and surprise, the theory does not privilege unpredictable outcomes. The normal case must be the predictable extrapolation of the uses of sign-radicals. It should be possible to guess the meaning of a sign even if the exact combination of sign-radicals was put together for the first time. Familiarity with the prior uses of sign-radicals should enable the anticipation (understanding) of new combinations. This must be the normal case in a well functioning language.

It is necessary to distinguish the ordinary use of language in familiar circumstances from the extension of language use to new situations. As Noam Chomsky has stressed, a competent language user should be able to understand a sentence even if he/she has never heard the exact same sentence before. This means that even with respect to ordinary language uses there can be 'new' sentences in the sense that they have not been uttered before. If the meaning of such sentences is unproblematic it is because the operation of the language's rules is predictable for the socialized language users. This case of ordinary, trivial newness must be distinguished from the process of language extension where new situations are encountered that exceed what can be covered by the ordinary usages of the given language. In such situations the meanings of words (sign-radicals) have to be stretched. Their usage has to be extrapolated. This usually happens via metaphor or metonomy. Or, if new words are coined (by resuscitating old language roots from Latin or Greek), they are usually domesticated by means of certain endings that bring them into alignment with known words of similar meaning. In all these cases of language extension, the situation is inherently open, and ultimately unpredictable. However, the extension of word uses can never be utterly arbitrary. That would be bizarre and unacceptable, and mnemotechnically irrational. It should be possible to guess the meaning of the new language use, even if the expression could not have been predicted. It must be motivated somehow, although there are no strict rules here.

Although the distinction between ordinary and extraordinary newness seems clear enough, it has to be noted that there is no strict dividing line here. Where does ordinary usage become extraordinary usage? Where does the ordinary creativity of language Chomsky talks about become an extraordinary creativity that creates a new language possibility rather than a new sentence within a given language? These questions escape general answers. (Here it can only be a matter of being aware of them.) However, even in the absence of a strict definition and dividing line, the distinction between ordinary and extraordinary extrapolations makes sense. Ordinary usage cannot be reduced to mere repetition. Otherwise the whole rationale and advantage of a systematic grammar over and above the individual conditioning of fixed phrases in fixed contexts would be inexplicable.

Actual language use is indeed acquired by training with individual examples, without explicit rules. To make the rules explicit is the task of grammarians. The difficulty of this task is attested to by several hundred years of painstaking attempts that never reached a satisfactory result. As Wittgenstein has pointed out, the formulation of explicit rules that fix everything in advance works only as long as it works, ie, until a situation emerges that exposes the rule's ultimate indeterminateness. Even with the supposedly ordinary usages there is no logical guarantee of the rule's functioning, only its pragmatic success. Grammar works, although there is no inexorable force of logic.

Although there is no inexorable force of logic in any language (not even in formal logic itself), there are and should be at least strong, shared biases within a community of socialized users of a language/built environment that make certain associations and understandings of given ensembles more likely than others, so that signification/communication does not only function with standing phrases and stereotypical set pieces. For this to be possible a language, whether verbal or spatial, must have a grammar. A grammar is a set of rules (super-strong biases) that regulates not only how (well-formed) composite signs can be constructed from sign-radicals but also how composite meanings can be retrieved on the basis of the meaning-potentials of the sign-radicals. For this to work, grammars have to severely restrict the ways in which sign-radicals can come together. These restrictions reflect the structure-potential of the domain of the signified. In most natural languages, grammatical rules defining the syntactic well-formedness of expressions are insufficient to prevent well-formed expressions that nevertheless produce nothing but incomprehensible nonsense. In certain artificial languages, the attempt was made to constrain the domain of the syntactically legitimate to the domain of the semantically meaningful. The syntax of such a language might be called logical syntax.[260] This is only possible if the semantic

260 Rudolf Carnap, *The Logical Syntax of Language*, Kegan Paul, Trench Trubner & Co Ltd (London), 1937. Programming languages might serve as examples here.

domain is circumscribed in advance. This cannot be the case with natural languages that should be able to take up anything whatsoever, including any future unknowns. In contrast, architectural languages, and especially project specific languages, have sufficiently pre-constrained signifieds to admit the attempt to construct a logical syntax, ie, a grammar that excludes nonsensical expressions.

Grammars allow for semiosis to progress beyond simple one-to-one mappings of atomic signifiers to atomic signifieds in the manner of behaviourist conditionings. For very simple societies or smaller social systems with a short list of rigidly defined institutions this kind of one-to-one correlation, every single one being fixed separately by repetition leading to convention, might be sufficient. But such a system of rigid spatial signs could not frame the social life-processes of contemporary society.

The concept of ***grammar***[261] allows for the identification of well-formed (grammatically correct) compositions. However, the concept of grammar cannot be reduced to the purely syntactical level. A grammar operates also in the semantic dimension. The grammar of a language determines how the meaning of a sign/communication is constituted or derived from the meaning-potentials or associative valencies of the involved sign-radicals. Although any grammar *as a whole* is inherently arbitrary – as the diversity of grammars and their continuous evolution demonstrates – each particular grammar introduces limitations to utter arbitrariness within the language in question. The logic of a language (as well as the language of logic) can take many structural forms or grammars, as long as it provides more than the one-to-one mapping of rigid institutions onto fixed territorial settings. (This mapping would imply that it would make no sense to analyze signs into constituent parts.) A separate convention would be required for each correlation which treats the correlated signs as atoms. 'One requirement that a grammar must certainly meet . . . the grammar cannot simply be a list of all morpheme (or word) sequences.'[262] Grammar presupposes that signs/communications are composed and that the composition is somehow structured, ie, limited. As a minimal requirement grammars must provide 'grammatical restrictions that limit the choice of the next word at this point in the

261 The concept of grammar presupposed here involves more than the everyday notion that mostly only implies grammaticality in the sense of well-formedness without regard to the constitution of meaningful communications. The notion implied here is aligned to Ludwig Wittgenstein's use of the term.

262 Noam Chomsky, *Syntactic Structures*, Mouton de Gruyter (Berlin/New York), 2002, 1st edition published in 1957, p 18. Chomsky and Carnap can both be enlisted here even if their concept of grammar (in the works quoted) is restricted to syntax.

utterance'.[263] These limitations concern both the syntactic as well as the semantic dimension. However, the limitation of the arbitrariness of the elements and their combinations that is (practically but not inexorably) given by any language's structure or logic, once a language is given or chosen, must be understood in the context of the inherent arbitrariness of its overall structure or logic (as well as of its particular material instantiation in comparison with other isomorphic material instantiations) that always could have been otherwise. As the logician Rudolf Carnap pronounced in connection with his famous 'Principle of Tolerance' with regard to the construction of systems of logic: 'We have in every respect complete liberty with regard to the forms of language; ... both the forms of construction for sentences and the rules of transformation (the latter are usually designated as "postulates" and "rules of inference") may be chosen quite arbitrarily.'[264] In Saussure, this tension between arbitrariness and its limitation by an 'arbitrarily chosen' systematicity is expressed in his distinction of absolute versus relative arbitrariness.

6.9.3 ABSOLUTE AND RELATIVE ARBITRARINESS

The notion that the connection between a sign's signified and its signifier is *arbitrary*, based on mere convention, is one of the most well-rehearsed commonplaces that trickled down from the discipline of semiology into the stock of insights of academic architects. The point seems obvious, and it could hardly have been overlooked. After all, in Saussure's *Course in General Linguistics*, the statement that 'the link between signifier and signified is arbitrary'[265] is posited as the first principle of linguistics: 'First principle: the sign is arbitrary.'[266] However, in this raw state as a singular truth the insight has perhaps done more harm than good for the development of architectural intelligence. Sure enough, in the further progress of Saussure's *Course*, the principle is relativized and receives a nuanced treatment that starts to do justice to the complexities involved. Saussure links his insistence on the centrality of the concept of *value* that reveals the dependency of any individual meaning on the total network of meanings to the central thesis of language's arbitrariness. Referring back to his diagram of the two planes of the signifier and the signified, Saussure states: 'Not only are the two areas which are linguistically linked vague and amorphous in themselves but the process which selects one

263 Ibid.

264 Carnap, *The Logical Syntax of Language*, p xv.

265 Saussure, *Course in General Linguistics*, p 67.

266 Ibid.

particular sound-sequence to correspond to one particular idea is entirely arbitrary. If this were not so, the notion of value would lose something. For it would involve a certain element of imposition from the outside world. But in fact values remain entirely a matter of internal relations, and that is why the link between idea and sound is intrinsically arbitrary.'[267]

The point of outward impositions is of interest here. The medial constraints inherent in any medium have been alluded to already above. They cannot undermine the ultimate arbitrariness of the particulars of any language. In verbal languages, the only case where individual words seem natural is the case of so-called onomatopoeia: for example, the word tick-tock referring to the sound of the clock via imitation. But as Saussure suggests, onomatopoeia is only ever an approximate, conventionalized imitation. In architecture the case is rather different: here the signifier stands in a much more direct relation to its signified. Also, the medial substrate of architectural signification is often directly involved in establishing the physical conditions of the signified, ie, the type of social interaction to be expected.

However, there is another important sense in which the arbitrariness of signification has to be relativized, and this applies even more to verbal languages than to any existing or projected architectural language. The requirement for ***systematicity*** constrains the utter arbitrariness of the signified-signifier correlations. This requirement is a general, internal rather than external, imposition that must be met by all systems-of-signification. Ultimately, this requirement refers back to the cognitive capacities of the participants who have to acquire the respective language competency. The systematicity of language, expressed in its grammar, does not only concern how words are composed into sentences but also the formation of words (sign-radicals), for example, the endings of regular verbs indicate tense etc. Irregular verbs violate this requirement of systematicity. If too much is irregular the language falls apart. For instance, languages tend to assimilate the terms of conceptual pairs to each other, or tend to use certain endings to characterize the general role a word plays in the discourse, for example, the ending 'ism' marks terms naming an ideological doctrine or attitude etc. Grammaticality implies that a complete sign or unit of meaning, ie, in our terms a particular, self-sufficient communication, like a sentence in the case of verbal languages and a territory in the case of architectural languages, must be composed of parts put together according to rules. Systematicity on the level of sign-radical formation is achieved by clustering sign-radicals into

267 Ibid, p 111.

groups or families so that some form of 'similitude', in whatever respect, in the domain of the signifiers finds a correspondence in a clustering based on another 'similitude', constituted in whatever respect, in the domain of the signified. The inherent, inevitable vagueness of the (ultimately undefinable) base concept of similitude, as well as the recurrent phrase 'in whatever respect', indicate that the signifier-signified relations remain ultimately arbitrary, or to put it in more functional terms: the options for making connections and stitching up correlations between the two planes remain flexible and open ended. Or to put it in even more positive terms: the inventiveness and resourcefulness of semiosis are inexhaustible. But the mnemotechnic necessity to build up some form of systematicity after all, implies that initial choices constrain further choices, and that the arbitrariness that might have been nearly absolute becomes a relative and constrained arbitrariness. As complexity is accrued within a language, many paths remain open for further elaboration. But not all paths can count as further elaboration.

Saussure recognizes that the sign, although in the last analysis ultimately arbitrary, in the sense that the form it takes can never be deduced or predicted with certainty, might to a certain extent be *motivated*. Motivation works against absolute arbitrariness and produces relative arbitrariness. Saussure introduces this concern with systematicity as follows: 'So far we have looked upon units as values, as elements of a system, and considered principally the oppositions between them. But now we are taking stock of their interdependencies, both associative and syntagmatic, which combine to set a limit on arbitrariness.'[268] The importance of understanding systematicity in sign systems is acknowledged by Saussure: 'Everything having to do with languages as systems needs to be approached . . . with the view to examining the limitations of arbitrariness.'[269] The principle of arbitrariness remains the first principle: 'For the entire linguistic system is founded upon the irrational principle that the linguistic sign is arbitrary. Applied without restriction, this principle would lead to utter chaos. But the mind succeeds in introducing a principle of order and regularity into certain areas of the mass of signs. That is the role of relative motivation.'[270] This relative motivation of the signs, and the regularities they participate within, follow a functional rationality. However, this rationality 'provides

268 Saussure, *Course in General Linguistics*, p 131; Saussure gives a simple example: the French word *vingt* (20) is wholly arbitrary, or unmotivated, whereas *dix-neuf* (19) is to a certain extent motivated.

269 Ibid.

270 Ibid.

only a partial correction to a system which is chaotic by nature'.[271] Not all languages exhibit the same degree of systematicity. Saussure distinguishes *lexico-logical languages* in which the absence of motivation reaches a maximum from *grammatical languages* in which it falls to a minimum. Chinese is offered as an example of the former and Sanskrit as an example of the latter extreme. 'There exists no language in which nothing is motivated. Even to conceive of such a language is an impossibility by definition. Between the two extremes – minimum of organization and minimum of arbitrariness – all possible varieties are found. Languages always exhibit features of both kinds – intrinsically arbitrary and relatively motivated.'[272]

Language evolution is not necessarily an evolution towards more systematicity. French, for instance, is much more arbitrary than Latin. Saussure discusses the mechanisms that are involved on the plane of the signifiers. There is a tendency for languages to degenerate by sound changes that obscure the network rationality of words and phrases. 'Sound change is a linguistic disturbance loosening the grammatical connections which link words together. It increases the sum total of linguistic forms to no purpose.'[273] Although elsewhere Saussure recognizes that all initially arbitrary sound changes and arbitrary sound differentiations eventually lead to meaning changes and meaning differentiations, and thus operate creatively like mutations, here he focuses on the aspect that they initially create mere irregularity: 'The linguistic mechanism becomes obscure and complicated.'[274] Another spontaneous process, *agglutination*, also reduces the rationality of a language. It is an involuntary process whereby the components of motivated composite words fuse into an unanalyzable single word or standing phrase. Originally the components came together to construct an overall meaning that could be traced back to the meaning of the component parts. The process thus involves a loss of structure. There are also structure elaborating processes. The primary process here is ***analogy***. 'Analogy works in favour of regularity and tends to unify formational and flexional processes.'[275] Saussure celebrates analogy, its ability 'to replace old, irregular and ailing formations by new ones of greater regularity, composed of living elements'.[276] If new words are introduced by analogy

271 Ibid.
272 Ibid.
273 Ibid, p 160.
274 Ibid.
275 Ibid, p 161.
276 Ibid, p 169.

with existing forms, the speaker tries to detect and extend the rationality of the language he is trying to augment. Although somehow prepared by the existing systematicity of the language, the analogical innovation is an intelligent, creative act that convinces and finds imitators. Here is Saussure's definition of analogy: 'Analogy presupposes a model, and regular imitation of a model. *An analogical form is a form made in the image of one or more other forms according to a fixed rule.*'[277] We should not be deceived here by the phrase 'fixed rule'. The rule might be fixed, or seem clear, only as long as it is followed. But as Wittgenstein revealed in his famous discussion on rule following, there is nothing in a rule that predetermines or forces its extension to new, unforeseen cases. And what is new rather than the same can also not be fixed in advance. Saussure seems to have grasped this inherent precariousness and potential instability of the rule concept: 'it is impossible to say in advance how far imitation of a model will extend'.[278] Rules make things orderly and predictable only until someone finds another, prehaps more convincing way to follow the rule. What is logical or illogical is a question of practice evolving on the basis of pragmatic criteria. Nothing predetermines which analogies are drawn in which way and how far. The inherent arbitrariness of all semiological constructions remains the first principle to be remembered even in the discussion of how to achieve a relative move away from total arbitrariness to relative arbitrariness. This is good and encouraging news for avant-garde designers who are keen to try their luck in the creative construction of semiological potential.

However, this creative construction effort can indeed only create a ***semiological virtuality***. For this to become an actual language, the accommodated social system has to be enlisted and relied upon. The actualization of the architecture's semiological offerings is altogether outside the architect's control, and in fact outside anybody's control. Semiosis is an evolutionary process that unfolds within and contributes to the evolution of a social system. In the case of natural, verbal languages that evolve with a whole society or, like English, with world society, the uncontrollable dynamic of language is part of the autopoietic self-organization of a society that has long since lost its control centre. The size and complexity of natural languages, and the fact that they are unrestrictedly available across the totality of a given society, being used by everybody every day, imply that they are 'immune from arbitrary

277 Ibid, p 160.
278 Ibid, p 161.

alteration'.[279] This aspect of the inherent inertia and tenacity of natural languages comes across strongly in Saussure: 'No individual is able . . . to modify in any way a choice already established in the language. Nor can the linguistic community exercise its authority to change even a single word. . . . The rules the community accepts are imposed upon it and not freely agreed. . . . Any given linguistic state is always the product of historical factors. . . . Historical transmission is the overriding factor, to the point of excluding the possibility of any general or sudden linguistic change.'[280] These features of gradualism and resistance to control are the general features of any distributed evolutionary process that has reached a high level of organized complexity. The balance of variation and redundancy is heavily tilted in the direction of redundancy. This relative slowness distinguishes natural languages from other social institutions and communication structures that rely upon it (and its stability) as a medium for their own accelerated evolution. 'If stability is a characteristic of languages, it is not only because languages are anchored in the community. They are also anchored in time. The two facts are inseparable. Continuity with the past constantly restricts freedom of choice.'[281] Historical continuity is preserved despite the lightness of its medial substrate and the ephemerality of individual speech acts. Inertia and historical depth are also features of the built environment and its system-of-signification. However, here it might be more anchored in the heavy physicality and thus permanence/inertia of its material substrate than in the highly evolved and organized complexity of its code. The question of the systematicity and complexity of the language of the built environment, and to what extent it is language-like at all, will be, once more, considered in the following chapters. Saussure closes his chapter on language's invariability with a reflection on the dialectic between the inertia of tradition and arbitrariness: 'It is because the linguistic sign is arbitrary that it knows no other law than that of tradition, and because it is founded upon tradition that it can be arbitrary.'[282]

6.9.4 NATURAL AND ARTIFICIAL SEMIOSIS

It is necessary to recuperate some further basic concepts and insights from semiology/semiotics that can serve to inform our ambition to

279 Ibid, p 72.
280 Ibid.
281 Ibid, p 74.
282 Ibid.

enhance architectural intelligence with respect to the task of articulation. The triadic distinction ***iconic*** vs ***indexical*** vs ***symbolic*** signs stems from Charles Sanders Peirce and is a commonplace in semiology/semiotics. Not unlike Saussure, Peirce conceived of the sign as the unity of the 'sign itself' and the 'interpretant'.[283] These terms might be translated into the terms signifier versus signified taken up from Saussure. Peirce then distinguished three principal types of signs – iconic signs, or icons, indexical signs, or indexes, and symbolic signs, or symbols – based upon the distinction of three different modes by which the relationship between the signifier and the signified is established and maintained. Peirce's typology of signs can be integrated into the framework synthesized here. The three types of signs might be characterized as follows:

- The ***iconic sign*** or ***icon*** is a sign whereby the relationship between the signifier and the signified is established on the basis of a direct resemblance between the signifier and the signified, via imitation. Examples are the Olympic graphic icons that signify the different types of sport, cartoons, 'realistic' sounds in a radio drama, or imitative gestures. It might be noted here that drawings and models are also to be classified among the iconic signs. Buildings that are designed to act as iconic signs are rare. Venturi gave examples like the hamburger stand that is designed to look like a gigantic hamburger. To a certain extent Saarinen's TWA terminal at JFK has been designed as iconic sign representing flight by shaping the roof to look like wings.

283 Peirce's system also distinguishes a third term, the thing or object being referred to as distinct from the interpretant understood as the (supposedly mental) concept of the thing/object. This ontological doubling of the level of the signified seems, at first sight, to enrich and complete the discussion in comparison with Saussure's neglect of the referent (extension) as distinct from the concept. However, the philosophical quicksands are closing in all around any such attempt. Peirce's own life-long struggle with clarifying this distinction attests to this. With Luhmann's theory of communication this ontological schism can be closed as follows: instead of posing the two ontological domains everything is reduced to observable communications. The distinction between the signifier ('object') and the signified ('concept') comes down to the distinction of impartation, information and understanding as observable moments of communication. The moment of impartation/signifier is observed on the simplest level of observing a direct presence. The signified, both in terms of information and understanding, is observable (and analyzable, reconstructable on the basis of many more simple observations) in terms of the networkedness and connectivity of the communication events. The moment of information can be analyzed in terms of paradigmatic relations, both actual and virtual. The moment of understanding can be observed by focusing on responses in terms of syntagmatic relations, ie, in terms of the retrospective and prospective connectivity of the communications within an ongoing process. Everything remains in a single, socially observable domain, the domain of communications hooking up to, referring back to and triggering further communications. The semiological discourse itself becomes observable as communication about communications.

- The ***indexical sign*** or ***index*** is a sign whereby the relationship between the signifier and the signified is established because the signifier is directly (causally) *connected* in some way to the signified. This link can be observed or inferred, for example, 'natural signs' (smoke, thunder, footprints), medical symptoms (pain, a rash, pulse rate), measuring instruments (thermometer), 'signals' (a knock on a door, a phone ringing), or unintended 'trademarks' like accents or idiosyncratic cultural habits.[284] The built environment is full of indexical signs. For instance, facades usually indicate the type of institution accommodated behind, ie, an experienced city dweller can usually read the type of function a building accommodates from its facade. Umbrellas mounted along a pavement index/signify 'street café' or at least more generally 'street business'. There is no need here to impute the intention to communicate. Indexicality is based on an act of judgement or inference (whereas iconicity is closer to direct perception).
- The ***symbolic sign*** or ***symbol*** is a sign whereby the relationship between the signifier and the signified is *arbitrary* or purely conventional – so that the relationship must be learnt, for example, alphabetical letters, words and language in general, Morse code, traffic lights, national flags etc. There is neither any resemblance, nor any natural connection between the signifier and the signified. In architecture a pertinent example would be the deliberate use of a Classical Doric portico to signify that the respective building accommodates a law court, or the use of Gothic motifs in the design of churches and city halls in the 19th century. The 19th century was the great era of symbolic signs in architecture. The symbolic sign *does* presuppose an intention to communicate.

The three types of signs differ with respect to their degree of ***conventionality***. Symbolic signs are highly conventional; iconic signs always involve some degree of conventionality; while indexical signs are initially not based on any conventionality, but instead 'direct the attention to their objects by blind compulsion', as Peirce observed. The three types of signs differ with respect to the degree of constraint that operates between the signifier and the signified and/or vice versa, ie, icon, index and symbol differ in the degree to which the signifier is constrained by the signified and, inversely, with respect to the degree to which the signified is constrained by the signifier as an element in a system of interrelated signifiers. *Indexical* and *iconic* signifiers can be

284 Sometimes pointers (a pointing 'index' finger, a directional signpost) are listed alongside the examples given above. However, this makes the concept ambiguous as these signs are ultimately conventional in nature, even if they seem somehow natural or motivated.

seen as more constrained by their referential *signifieds*. Saussure would talk about 'motivation' here. The more a signifier is constrained by the signified, the more 'motivated' the sign is: iconic signs are highly motivated; symbolic signs are unmotivated. This traditional teaching of the unmotivated character of the symbolic sign can, in relation to verbal languages, only refer to words only, or in our terms, to sign-radicals only. Once we enter the realm of composite signs based on the syntactic and semantic rules of a grammar, motivation enters without requiring either iconicity or indexicality. We might therefore distinguish *internal motivation* from *external motivation*. Then we can say that symbolic signs are internally motivated but externally unmotivated.

The less motivated the sign (sign-radical), the more learning of an arbitrary convention is required. To a certain extent, even iconic signs (like the drawings and models of architecture's medium) are built on conventions which must be learned to be 'read'. Such evolving conventions are the essence of semiosis. In the case of *symbolic* signs, the reverse determination holds: the *signified* can be seen as being defined to a greater extent by the *signifier*. This is due to the fact that meanings, as discussed above, are a function of how the language system dissects and conceptually orders the world. Meanings are constituted by language, ie, they are constituted by the interplay of the planes of the signifiers and the signified. This dependency on the plane of signifiers – in terms of its substrate as well as in terms of its evolving formal structure – imposes a strong constraint upon what can be distinguished and referred to as a signified. However, also in the case of iconic signs, the individual signs sometimes constitute their meaning within a system of signifiers that to a certain extent mutually define each other rather than operating in isolation. However, the possibility of isolated operation is not absolutely excluded in the case of icons.

One important peculiarity about semiosis within the domain of architecture has to be noted at this point. While semiology/semiotics describes the symbolic sign as arbitrary and assumes determination here to run only from the signifier to the signified, in architecture there is sometimes a certain constraining force that runs in the opposite direction, from the signified to the signifier. This is due to the fact that in the case of the architectural articulation the always necessary physical embodiment of the signifier is mostly *not* constructed in such a relatively light-footed, dematerialized domain such as, for example, the spoken words in the domain of acoustic waves, or the printed word in the domain of nearly immaterial ink-marks or in the domain of the states of an electronic computer screen. In architecture, signifiers are often the tectonic forms of the heavy and physically burdened structures themselves, which in turn are determined by the signified, in as much as the signified, in the case of architecture, is precisely the social life-process that the architectural components (like walls, roofs, windows, doors) are supposed to serve. The signifying aspects of the sign-radicals that constitute the territory as sign are also burdened to physically organize, support and accommodate the denoted life-processes. Of course, there are also some lighter registers of articulation like colour, texture and ornament etc. But even the available colour spectrum might be constrained by the fact that the signified life-process might be disturbed by the coloured light that might otherwise be available to signify this life-process.

All three types of signs – indexical, iconic and symbolic – feature within architecture. However, the symbolic signs – which are the most evolved/advanced type of sign that dominates in all verbal languages – are least prominent within architecture. Within architecture most signs are either iconic signs or indexical signs or, if they progressed to operate as symbols, they nevertheless still betray their origin as either icon or index. This betrays the fact that 'the language of architecture' (architectural semiosis) is in a very primitive and crude state when compared with spoken/written language proper.

The language analogy might therefore afford clues and inspiration for the potential expansion of the semiological power of architecture. That is the motivation for rehearsing the basic concepts and insights of linguistics within architecture. The semiological project within architecture (as distinct from vernacular building/decorating) must replace intuitive sensitivity with theoretically grounded expertise. The theoretical conclusion to insist on and elaborate here is that the primarily indexical functioning of the current architectural and vernacular built environment must be challenged and overcome by a primarily symbolic-conventional articulation based on a systematic, grammar-based architectural language.

Strictly speaking, the principle of indexicality does not really belong to the proper domain of semiology, at least not in its pure state, unmediated by conventionalizing selections. Indexes can function in isolation. Pure indexes should not even be classified as signs. They are not communications. The moment of impartation is lacking. They cannot be attributed and understood *as* communications. They are analogous to behaviours as distinct from actions. Pure indexes do not operate as parts of systems-of-signification. Reading the built environment as a collection of indexes is very much like reading natural environments. Everything is full of clues on the basis of regular correlations. Indexicality functions to the extent to which built environments exhibit quasi-natural regularities.

Indeed, in nature such regularities or correlations exist so that nearly everything is a 'sign' of many other things. Certain flora indicate soil-quality, or allow for the anticipation of certain fauna. The movement of the topography indicates the direction where a river might be found etc. Within nature such regularities are very deeply and rigorously determined. This is the natural precondition on which the natural sciences succeed. However, in nature these spontaneous regularities never become the material for a selective, amplifying systematization, ie, there is no semiosis in nature, at least not in inorganic nature and flora that determines our natural landscapes. Within built environments indexicality operates too but far less rigorously and consistently. There is no full equivalent to nature's determinism. The attempt to develop a science to uncover the laws of formation of built environments, modelled on the methodologies of the natural sciences, for example, via computational simulations, can only succeed on a very abstract, urban, organizational level, if at all, and only historically localized. Most facts and nuances uncovered by a morphological close reading of the human habitat must remain outside the scope of such an analysis. Here, indexicality still operates somehow, but not with rigorous correlations that would allow for predictability. Historically, the more modernization has progressed, the more fabrication and construction processes have proliferated, the less legible has the built environment become. Its indexical functioning is weakened when compared with earlier periods with much more constrained and thus uniformly applied construction materials and processes. This progressive degeneration of the environment's indexical legibility, it seems, is being compensated for by the spontaneous process of semiosis that, to a certain extent, selects and orders the materiality of the built environment according to communicative intentions. Indexes are transformed into symbols. Contrasts are amplified, alignments tightened etc. This has been happening all along, and perhaps more during the pre-architectural, vernacular eras (dominated by traditional user-led building) than during the past 500 years of architecture.

At least since the advent of architecture as autopoietic expert discourse and profession, the sign system of the built environment, to the extent that it operates as such, exhibits the peculiarity that the architectural impartations ('utterances') are not directly produced within the accommodated social system itself. Instead they are delivered from outside, by the hired expert architect, as shells to be appropriated. Of course, a certain more ephemeral level of furnishings, or at least the artefactual paraphernalia of everyday life that accompany most appropriations, are still operating as utterances of the users, albeit as selections rather than as creations. On this level of the occupant's personal fitting out the vernacular still exists. Thus a close, nuanced evolutionary adaptation of these environments with respect to the specific communicative interactions that they accommodate and frame can be expected to lead to some kind of spontaneous semiosis that might develop some of the characteristics that can be observed in natural languages. This process works even, and perhaps all the more, under the premise of a world of artefacts/products that are largely provided by a professional design discipline together with a worldwide industrial production and distribution system. On this basis at least the conditions for globally operating codes or 'languages' are in place. The interior fit-out of the architect's shells is thus more closely looped with the interaction processes than the architectural shells themselves. Recently, the fit-out of more and more interiors has come under the auspices of professionals (and their discourses): enriched provisions in places of work in depersonalized work environments, restaurants, hotels, shops and cafés that are taken over by chains are designed by professionals. Semiological nuance is getting lost when articulation is decoupled from the adaptive loops that keep it close to communicative interaction.

Does this decoupling of the production of the signifier (impartation) altogether compromise the status of designed architectural works as communications that operate within the accommodated social systems? No, this question was answered at the very outset, and is not undermined by the closer look provided here: the framing environment is understood as communication and locally attributed to the client, owner, host etc, no matter whether the host – individual, family, organization, or institution – has built and decorated the provided place of interaction, or whether he/she/it has provided for it by selecting, hiring and instructing a professional architect. The following scenario can illustrate this: the suitor who takes his date to a certain restaurant of his choice – with its particular location, style, ambience – as scene for a romantic evening becomes the point of attribution for the architectural communication that frames the ensuing communicative interaction of the date itself. Architectural signs/communications, although conceived within the autopoiesis of architecture, come alive as framing communications only within the social systems they are delivered to.[285]

285 Architectural signs, the built architectural communications – architecture's service to society – are delivered to all social systems that rely on them. They are the final, boundary-crossing communications of architecture. They circulate as communications both within architecture and within the social systems they have been delivered to.

The following six theses/pointers are to serve as summary of the results of this chapter – with some references back to preceding chapters – and as premises for the final chapters to come:

- The legibility of the built environment relies heavily on indexes or conventionalized indexical signs.
- Pure indexes do not belong in the domain of semiology. They are not communications and do not integrate into *systems-of-signification*.
- The indexical functioning of the contemporary built environment is degenerating. Spontaneous semiological selection/correlation is too weak and fragmented to compensate for this. Overall legibility of the environment decreases resulting in a sense of urban chaos.
- The diversity of materials, construction/fabrication techniques and styles leads to a richness of architectural morphologies that is insufficiently correlated with the increasing diversity of types of social interactions. Spontaneous semiosis is in crisis.
- The language-likeness of the built environment as system-of-signification, to the extent that it operates as such, hinges on the systematicity or ordering of its signs, as well as on the build up of composite signs from sign-radicals on the basis of a *grammar*.
- The lack of an effective grammar is the key limitation of the built environment and spells out the key task for the development of an architectural language.

6.9.5 DESIGNING ARCHITECTURE'S SEMIOLOGICAL PROJECT

The idea of an architectural semiology poses two related theoretical challenges. It poses an analytical challenge, ie, the attempt to describe, analyze and critique how the built environment is already functioning as system-of-signification, and it poses the challenge of developing a semiological model that allows architects to design projects that might be able to function as new, artificial systems-of-signification.[286] Above, insights from general semiology and linguistics have been gathered, a conceptual apparatus for the application of semiological concepts within architecture has been elaborated, and a series of first theses and pointers has been assembled. On this basis architecture's semiological project should be further outlined and directed.

At the peak of the Postmodern, semiological wave in architecture, Mario Gandelsonas contrasted 'two entirely opposed . . . extensions of the

286 With respect to the progress of linguistics these two strands of theoretical work can also be identified. An extensive body of descriptive linguistic research on the one hand and the synthetic-constructive work on artificial languages on the other hand were combined into the analytic/generative model of Chomsky's transformational grammar.

traditional modes of generating meaning in architecture'[287] as represented by the work of Robert Venturi and Peter Eisenman respectively, both positioned as reaction against Modern Functionalism. 'The first... Robert Venturi... advocates the reinstatement of a multivalent and eclectic language.... This position... understands in a critical way the nature of conventional meanings, and relishes the complexity of a plurality of meanings. The second... Peter Eisenman... tries to address the more basic questions of language, the grammatical questions.'[288] Eisenman reacts against the 'open condition in which there exists no syntactic criteria for the language and no definitions of its formal structure'.[289] Instead he focuses on the constitution of a formal, purely syntactical system, that considers only architecture's formal aspect, 'structured according to finite and specific rules, prescribing particular lines of action'.[290] Eisenman's approach and design process, as experimented with in his series of houses, are inspired by the idea of rewriting rules taken from Chomsky's generative, *transformational* grammars. He starts with a general, abstract geometrical primitive, mostly a cube, and then proceeds to rewrite or redraw this primitive according to rules – regulating operations like subtraction, division, rotation etc – that successively substitute parts with more articulated parts. The process, if rigorously defined, is a rather powerful one. The power of such a formalized or regulated process – as distinct from just regulating the final result – had already been established by Jean-Nicolas-Louis Durand's system of composition.[291] As in the case of Durand, Eisenman's developmental sequence thus moves from the simple to the complex. Often, the same operations are applied recursively. Eisenman progresses beyond Durand by going from a single rule set offered as *the* rational method to solve the tasks of architecture, to a series of experiments in rule-set construction as exemplified in the series of houses from *house I* to *house X*. Supposedly, 'at every stage there are rules that permit the selection of what can be called correct configurations'.[292] Eisenman's work in the domain of architectural syntax must be recognized as an important, original contribution here. However,

287 Mario Gandelsonas, 'From Structure to Subject: The Formation of an Architectural Language', in: *Oppositions* 17, Summer 1979, reprinted in: K Michael Hays, *Oppositions Reader*, Princeton Architectural Press (New York), 1998, p 202.

288 Ibid.

289 Ibid.

290 Ibid, p 203.

291 See below, chapter 10.3.2 Durand's *Précis des leçons d'architecture*.

292 Mario Gandelsonas, 'From Structure to Subject: The Formation of an Architectural Language', p 206.

there are two fundamental problems with Eisenman's work. First, it is doubtful that Eisenman's processes were really rule-based in a strict sense. The rules that governed a particular house were never explicitly stated. Even if they were somehow stated, in the verbal terms of a natural language like English the rules would have lacked precision and completeness. Only the operationalization via computationally realized algorithms can guarantee the operation of an invariant rule set. The only other way in which rules can be established and maintained is via a collective process of intersubjective socialization and control. Eisenman's informal, solitary process lacks either condition and thus implies that the 'logically correct' next step was whatever seemed to be somehow 'logically correct' to Peter Eisenman at the moment when the next step was to be taken.[293] The second problem is that the lack of explicitness of the rule set prevents the possibility of an iterative process of rule-modification on the basis of a feedback loop with the results of the rule application. These problems of rule-based design have been solved by current computational techniques. The much more serious limitation of Eisenman's approach is the fact that his process lacks explicit criteria that could guide the selection and improvement of the (supposed) rule set employed. These criteria must, in the last analysis, refer to the social functioning of the architectural language that is to be constructed. Because Eisenman's work lacks engagement with social meanings, his approach can only reach the status of a preliminary exercise.

The idea of constructing a language for architecture on a purely syntactical basis without concern for and correlation with the semantic and pragmatic levels is not a meaningful endeavour. It effectively reduces the idea of language, even the idea of syntax, to a mere metaphor. Eisenman is indeed explicitly rejecting social function as the domain that gives meaning to architectural form. He presumes that architecture should aspire to a supposedly generalizable 'new cultural attitude' or 'Modernist sensibility' evident in the abstract art, atonal music and non-narrative film of protagonists like Mondrian, Schoenberg and Richter.[294] The exclusive focus on syntax is certainly not how Noam Chomsky understood the task of linguistics. Work on syntax can never be regarded as an autonomous project that could on its own fulfil the aims of linguistics or semiology/semiotics. This can be said independently of the

293 On this point the reader might refer to Wittgenstein's discussion on rule following and on the impossibility of a private language. See: Ludwig Wittgenstein, *Philosophical Investigations* (Philosophische Untersuchungen), Blackwell Publishing (Oxford), 1953.

294 Peter Eisenman, 'Post-Functionalism', in: *Oppositions* 6, Fall 1976, reprinted in: K Michael Hays, *Oppositions Reader*, Princeton Architectural Press (New York), 1998, pp 9–12.

validity of the thesis of the autonomy of syntax, ie, whether syntactical mechanisms are in themselves sufficient to establish the 'grammatical' correctness of speech acts.[295] When it comes to the creative endeavour of conceiving, constructing and developing a new language-model for architectural design that should have a chance to be actualized in the social life-process of the end users, a purely syntax-based approach is out of the question. The potential for semantic interpretation and pragmatic contextualization provides the required selection criterion for proposed syntactic structures in an iterative process of developing a spatial language. The specificities of architecture's signified must be considered. Syntactic and semantic principles have to be developed together. It is this richer concept of a semantically interpreted syntax that is implied with the concept of ***grammar*** proposed here as key ambition of architecture's semiological project.

The final elaboration of an architectural language must proceed as architectural design research project in architecture's medium of drawing/modelling/scripting. What can be done here are pointers about what might be heuristically promising parameters and criteria for such a project. Despite the criticisms launched above, the kind of project recommended here is certainly more in the tradition of Eisenman's rather than Venturi's work. Considering the totality of aspects discussed so far, perhaps the best way to proceed in advancing the semiological project within architecture is via individual design projects that are of sufficient size and complexity to plausibly warrant the establishment of an ***autonomous, project specific language*** without regard to conventional semantic associations otherwise circulating in the environment at large.[296] Starting with an autonomous sign-system for a single (large-scale) project implies a decoupling from the general, spontaneous semiosis of the built environment.[297]

295 This question has stimulated much debate in philosophy. Willard van Orman Quine's position, for instance, is that grammatical concepts must be defined on the basis of semantic notions, that the concept of phoneme must be defined in terms of synonymy. This implies, crudely speaking, for example, that *r* and *l* are different phonemes because *ramp* and *lamp* do not have the same meaning. See: Noam Chomsky, *On Language*, New Press (New York), 2007, p 138.

296 Below will be discussed how this relatively circumscribed ambition might be extended by proposing a general semiological heuristics that might serve to systematize a whole architectural style in view of enhancing its capacity to contribute to a unified architectural system-of-signification that is able to operate beyond single projects.

297 The author has indeed started to experiment with semiological design projects in two of his teaching arenas: *The Semiological Project* was a year-long design project for the academic year 2010/2011 at the Zaha Hadid Masterclass, University of Applied Arts in Vienna. At the AADRL in London, the author introduced *Parametric Semiology* as design research project for 2011. In both cases the complex programme of a university campus is being utilized as basis for

Engagement with the given network of meanings is too constraining for an avant-garde design research project that wants to push the capacity of the discipline beyond its current status. The development of a new, separate architectural language could be compared to the specialist languages that have been developed in various branches of science. Any new language must cut the contaminating associations with ordinary discourse. The more radical the cut and thus the strangeness of the new, artificial language, the greater is the likelihood that new associations, internal to the project, can form. For this to happen, scale and internal coherence are important factors. Then the design can take the risk of making a radically new start, creating something analogous to the artificial languages that have been created in the domain of mathematical logic: 'to cast the ship of logic off from the *terra firma* of the classical forms'.[298]

The initial disengagement from existing meaning contexts allows a language to be designed as an original, internally coherent system where the meaning of every term depends solely on the structure of the system of formal differences and their correlation with different types of social interaction within the project. The language can be learned by the users detecting the differences that make a difference, without any presupposed prior knowledge.

The overall size of the project, as well as the richness and complexity of the brief, are critical parameters, if the ambition is to make architectural semiosis more language-like in the sense of building up a grammar rather than a mere lexicon of features. Indeed, only project briefs that imply a very high complexity in terms of the diversity, dynamism and communicative density of the expected/required patterns of social interaction are able to make use of complex proto-grammars. (Individual family residences certainly do not require the kind of semiological upgrade aspired to here.) Perhaps the most pertinent task domain, where a semiological design experiment would find a sufficiently complex (as well as sufficiently analyzed and documented) life-process, is the domain of the large-scale, highly integrated and

the elaboration of a design brief. The complex institutional organization of a university, its rich/diverse schedule of events, the different status groups to be distinguished, and the spatial expanse of its premises together make the university the perfect project category for the exploration of the semiological project in architecture.

298 Rudolf Carnap, *The Logical Syntax of Language*, p xv. The radical reconstruction of logic as abstract calculus, arbitrary, but internally coherent, and backed up by an artificial language that allows logical processes to be mechanized, was the pioneering effort of Frege, Russell, Carnap and others during the early 20th century. This work must be recognized as one of the fundamental contributions that enable the creation of our computer-based civilization.

communication-intensive business organizations of today's knowledge economy. It is with respect to the organization and articulation of these highly ambitious and complex social systems that the semiological upgrade of architecture's capacity would make pragmatic sense. The design briefs of large corporations contain complex challenges in all three dimensions of architecture's signified: function-type, social-type and location-type. The legibility of the environment with respect to all three types of information is very useful, if not vital, to the establishment and overall productivity of the complex network of coordinated communications that is supposed to evolve and operate within the space (or field) of the corporate territory.

The corporate life-process is the object of intense attention and study within the corporation itself, mediated by professional management consultants armed with the reflection theories provided by management theory as well as organizational sociology and psychology. Empirical studies of current communication patterns accompany the continuous efforts in space planning as part of the overall, ongoing organizational reform processes. These facts are mentioned here to indicate that such projects offer a rich informational resource upon which to construct sufficiently rich criteria of semantic adequacy that could motivate an equally rich architectural syntax.

The fact that the corporate business organization as social system, and thus the communication processes within it, is at least to a certain extent subject to organizational design, rather than being based wholly on spontaneous processes of self-organization, adds to the viability of the idea of starting the project of architecture's semiological upgrade via the construction of artificial proto-languages within this particular task domain.

Design research concerning the 'spatialization of the complexities of contemporary business'[299] was conducted over a period of three years utilizing London-based corporations as quasi-clients within the context of the Design Research Lab at the Architectural Association in London. The design research effort focused on the architectural response to emergent forms of corporate organization. This general agenda was specified in seven project briefs which became manifest in 24 experimental design

299 Patrik Schumacher, 'Research Agenda: Spatializing the Complexities of Contemporary Business', in: Brett Steele (Ed), *Corporate Fields – New Office Environments by the AADRL*, AA Publications (London), 2005, pp 74–82. See also: Patrik Schumacher, 'Business – Research – Architecture', in: *Daidalos* 69/70, December 1998/January 1999; Patrik Schumacher, 'Arbeit, Spiel und Anarchie', in: Herbert Lachmayer & Eleonora Luis (Eds), *Work & Culture – Büro.Inszenierung von Arbeit*, Ritterverlag (Klagenfurt), 1998; Patrik Schumacher, 'Produktive Ordnungen', in: *ARCH+* 136, *Your Office Is Where You Are*, April 1997, Berlin.

projects elaborated by 56 architects working in teams of two to five. Each project team was collaborating with one of the following corporate quasi-clients: BDP, DEGW, M&C Saatchi, Ove Arup, Microsoft UK, Razorfish. The results of this research were published under the title *Corporate Fields*.[300]

In retrospect, these projects can be classified as following the style of Parametricism. Starting with the corporation's official organigrams, the projects developed abstract spatial systems that were trying to register and accommodate the actual patterns of communication of the investigated corporate organizations. Both issues of spatial organization and issues of visual articulation were prevalent. The problem of articulation was approached more in terms of phenomenology than of semiology, at least not in terms of an advanced semiological ambition involving the construction of a grammar. Thus the results cannot be taken as examples or illustrations for design research in the domain of architectural semiology or as experiments in the construction of an artificial architectural language. However, these projects revealed enough to recommend this task domain as the most prominent within which to launch semiologically focused design research projects.

The rich design briefs that can be developed for such firms cover the dimensions of both function-type and social-type. The task of articulating the location-type can only be posed later, on the basis of the spatial organization developed within the design. The dimension of the function-type contains the various activity types and types of social interaction that one can distinguish within the life-process of a corporation: individual, concentrated work; concentrated work taking place in parallel, in close proximity; one-to-one formal talks; one-to-one informal chats; small formal meetings; small informal gatherings; anonymous, quasi-public encounters; large conferences etc. All these function-types occur with various departmental affiliations which qualify or mark each of these situations. The dimension of the social-type is equally rich and differentiated: first of all there are the different specialisms or professional qualifications that need to be considered; second, there are all the general levels and positions within the corporate hierarchy that call for consideration; further, there are relations of immediate subordination; finally, there are various social-types that come from outside the firm to join social interactions within the designed space of the firm, including clients, consultants, job applicants etc. All these types that exist within the domain of the signified are prestructured by

300 Brett Steele (Ed), *Corporate Fields – New Office Environments by the AADRL*, AA Publications (London), 2005.

our shared language and by the official operational categories of the business firm. Many more nuanced, connotational distinctions might be relevant once insider knowledge and careful observation are enlisted to further enrich the brief. Each (official or unofficial) function-type or social-type that is architecturally articulated is thereby made prominent and thus reinforced. Thus, to a certain extent, Saussure's image of two amorphous planes engaging in the co-creation of a definite structure does also apply here. The designed spatial organization – together with its phenomenological and semiological articulation within a designed architectural language – reinforces and further structures the latent, prestructured function-types and social-types, by making them public, explicit and relatively permanent.

6.9.6 COGNITIVE AND ATTENTIONAL CONDITIONS OF ARCHITECTURAL COMMUNICATION

Before considering how the domain of the signifier might be structured and related to the domain of the signified to achieve this (mutual) reinforcement, the pragmatic and cognitive conditions under which an architectural sign system has to operate must be considered because there are some important differences here, in comparison with the pragmatic and cognitive conditions of verbal (spoken or written) languages. These differences affect the further elaboration of the language analogy within architecture.

The comprehension and information retrieval via a complex verbal language – both in its spoken/heard as well as in its written/read form – requires focused, concentrated attention. The same level of attention cannot always be expected from the users and supposed 'readers' of architectural information. Thus any conception of an architectural language that presupposes this level of attention is doomed to fail. Most (although certainly not all) of the information embedded within built environments, designed or not, is retrieved subliminally. The level of attention given to the environment is not always the same. When entering a new environment our level of attention is heightened, in particular if we are trying to orient ourselves or if we are looking for something specific. Thus two modes of engaging the frames of architecture must be distinguished according to the level of attention subjects give to the specific characteristics of the architecture that surrounds them. The two ***modes of engagement*** relative to architecture are ***attention*** vs ***distraction***. The mode of distraction prevails when subjects are absorbed in specific activities or social interactions, or in an environment where subjects feel familiar, safe and thus are willing to daydream. The mode of attention prevails in new environments, when subjects are trying to find their way, or when they first enter a territory and try to orient themselves and read the situation. Later, when the territory is revisited for repeat interactions, the mode of attention subsides. Now what was previously carefully read and (intuitively) analyzed is condensed into a quickly recognized, wholistic Gestalt. Such routinization also happens with respect to verbal messages. They condense into phrases that no longer need to be analyzed but are taken in as a whole, integral Gestalt. A certain level of verbal information retrieval is also possible in the mode of distraction. For instance, subjects understand sentences even if they are caught out by being addressed unawares without anticipation. However, the distinction of attentional levels in the mode of engagement is of particular importance in the domain of architectural communication.

There is a lot of specific research on attention in the field of cognitive psychology that might be consulted. The distinction *mode of distraction* vs *mode of attention* proposed here is roughly equivalent to concepts like *pre-attention* vs *attention*, or *parallel attention* vs *focal attention* one can find in the relevant literature: 'A first important distinction in the processing of information in visual search tasks is its separation in two stages. The first, early "preattentive" stage operates in parallel across the entire visual field extracting single "primitive features" without integrating them. The second "attentive" stage corresponds to the specialized integration of information from a limited part of the field at any one time, ie, serially. . . . There are two experimentally observed modes of visual attention, namely: the serial focal attention and the parallel spread of attention over space.'[301] The critical aspect that affects the ambition to construct a grammar that regulates the construction and comprehension of composite architectural signs is the distinction between the wholistic comprehension of a sign as a Gestalt, or integral figure that doesn't rely on being somehow deciphered or analyzed on the one hand, and, on the other hand, architectural signs that presuppose such an analysis, however quick and intuitive, as a capacity in the 'reading' subjects. Such analysis would be required if the composite architectural sign, ie, a given territory that has its relevant information encoded via the rule-based assembly of recognizable sign-radicals, is encountered for the first time. Here information retrieval would require a concentrated, close reading of the territory. Can such a 'reading' of an architectural ensemble ever be presumed or presupposed? That this presumption is not implausible is indeed an important premise of the

301 Gustavo Deco, Olga Pollatos & Josef Zihl, 'The Time Course of Selective Visual Attention: Theory and Experiments', *Vision Research* 42 (2002), 2925–45.

semiological project promoted here. Of course the reading of the territory is not presumed to take the form of explicit forensic analysis, nor should it take the form of effortful deciphering as when a child first learns to read. The extensiveness of the required 'analysis', operating intuitively rather than explicitly as conscious mental effort, depends on the complexity of the language, in terms of both signifier and signified.[302]

Above, three types of architectural information were distinguished, ie, function-type, social-type and location-type. It is also important, independently, to distinguish the functions that these types of architectural information are utilized for. One might distinguish the facilitation of ***navigation***, ***orientation*** and (successful) ***immersion*** as the three functions of architectural information. *Navigation* is concerned with wayfinding, ie, with finding desired sites of social interaction. The retrieval of the spatial type of information (location-type) is relevant for the facilitation of navigation. Navigation might oscillate or switch between the two modes of engagement. For example, close attention is required in new territories, at junctions where decisions about the further path have to be made. *Orientation* is concerned with understanding and anticipating the communicative situation upon entering a designated territory. Here, especially if the territory is entered for the first time, the mode of attention can be presumed to dominate, and indeed would be required to prepare the next step, the immersion in the social interaction. With respect to *immersion*, which implies the mode of distraction in relation to the surrounding environment, it is the atmospheric ambience of the territory, its operation as an undifferentiated Gestalt, that supports this function.

Architectural signs (territories) that operate as undifferentiated atmospheres might be referred to either as ***atomic signs***, if they are inherently undifferentiated, or ***condensed signs***, if they operate as atomic signs if encountered in the mode of distraction, while operating as ***composite signs*** if engaged in the mode of attention. This theoretical set up implies that the same architectural ensemble should be able to operate as both composite and condensed sign, first facilitating orientation in the mode of attention, and then sustaining immersion in the mode of distraction. Thus the same ensemble lives a double life, one regulated by a relatively elaborate grammar that allows for the rule-governed construction of signs from sign-radicals, and another one,

302 Since we are entering a kind of virgin ground here, speculation can only be advanced in parallel with design experiments. The questions raised here can only be answered via empirical evidence generated on the basis of theoretically controlled design experiments.

regulated by a rudimentary grammar that operates only with a simple series of contrastive opposites that correlate with a simple series of distinguished interaction types.

The conceptual set up can be summarized in the following matrix:

informational function:	**navigation**	**orientation**	**immersion**
information type	location-type (relative position)	function-type (interaction-type) social-type (status, affiliation)	function-type (interaction-type) social-type (status, affiliation)
mode of engagement	oscillating between modes of attention / distraction	mode of attention	mode of distraction
sign type	composite sign condensed sign	composite sign	atomic sign condensed sign
grammar	elaborate grammar	elaborate grammar rules composing sign-radical	rudimentary grammar contrastive oppositions

The foregoing reflections upon the modes of cognitive engagement that any architectural language must reckon with have not compromised the plausibility of conceiving an architectural language that is able to communicate information via the rule-based composition of composite signs. The following chapter will push speculation about the possibility of such an architectural language further than has hitherto been attempted.

6.9.7 SPECULATION: EXPANDING THE EXPRESSIVE POWER OF ARCHITECTURAL SIGN SYSTEMS

The amount of information conveyed in a single impartation (speech-act or built piece of architecture) depends on the expressive power of the language's signs, the number of signs used and the degree of redundancy in the imparted ensemble of signs. (Redundancy makes messages robust, but reduces the potential amount of information that can be packaged into a certain number of sign units.) The expressive power of a language depends not only on its lexicon, the number of fixed, standing terms available. It depends on its capacity to combine its simple terms in many different ways. It also depends on the kinds of terms it has available, ie, the categorical character of these terms. For instance, it makes a difference if a language has only simple predicates or also allows for the expression of relations, ie, predicates that accept two or more terms as their arguments, rather than only a single term.

The architectural sign, the essential unit of any architectural system-of-signification, is the territory. The notion of territory comprises both *elemental* and internally *differentiated* territories. Both elemental and differentiated territories are located within *encompassing* territories. Differentiated territories encompass at least one or more *encompassed* territories (sub-territories). To the extent that the participation in multiple events or interactions is plausible, interpenetrating or superimposed territories are also to be considered. All the organizational tropes of contemporary architecture must be accommodated. However, it has to be remembered that the concept of territory is conceived as the synthesis of signifier and signified and thus its identification or individuation as *this* versus *another* territory always includes the aspect of the expected or unfolding social interaction. In the standard case, at least, the assumption is that a territorial unit denotes a unitary social interaction type. Considering differentiated territories, an architectural code can be expected to include the spatial disposition (relative position) of the sub-territories within the encompassing territory, as well as in relation to each other, to have signicative import. The dimension of spatial organization will thus, on the one hand, be a syntactic register that can modulate/contextualize the meanings of signs (sub-territories), while, on the other hand, it is a dimension of the signified, ie, the location-type. Thus a feedback loop must be established between the organizational and the semiological project.

The more detailed discussion of *how* an encountered territory can be ***coded*** and then recognized *as* a territory with a certain designation should commence with the case of the elemental territory. The task – initially thought to be limited to a single, sufficiently large/complex design project – is thus to define a correlation or ***mapping*** from the universe of the signified (function-type, social-type, location-type) to the universe of the signifier. One early design decision that might recommend itself here is to allocate to each information type a distinct formal register within the domain of the signifier. Which registers can be distinguished and made available here? (It must be remembered here that we are considering only fully fitted and furnished territories. Urbanism, architecture, interior design, as well as furniture design, are assumed to operate together here.) Above we have broadly distinguished between the registers of spatial organization (territorial configuration) and morphological articulation (comprising tectonic form as well as materiality, texture and colour). This distinction must now be developed and refined in conjunction with the proposed alignment with the dimensions of the signified:

- The ***configurational geometry*** is the register that might be aligned with the function- or interaction-type. In the case of the elemental territory it comprises the ***bounding geometry*** of the territory in question as well as anything that serves to configure ***the spatial diagram of the social interaction***, ie, the relative position and geometric orientation of the communicating users (bodies) relative to each other.
- The ***morphological geometry*** is the register that might be aligned with the social-type. It comprises geometric articulations below the scale/scope of territory formation, and includes everything that one can include under the traditional concepts of ***ornament*** (mouldings) and ***tectonics*** (joints, articulation into components).
- The placement, geometry and morphological articulation of ***openings and perforations*** might be utilized as register for the coding of location information. In the case of elemental territories, this information concerns the location of the territorial unit within a larger territorialized context.
- The further registers of ***materiality, colour, texture, lighting*** etc might be utilized for various further connotational qualifications and nuances of both function-type and social-type.

These alignments are here no more than illustrative suggestions. They are certainly not meant as general theoretical postulates. These ***registers of semiological coding*** that together constitute the plane of architecture's signifiers are, in principle, functionally equivalent. They can substitute for each other with respect to the task of coding. However, they are, evidently, not freely disposable purely for the purposes of signification. They are not only burdened by the conditions and constraints imposed by the engineering disciplines, they are also burdened by functional concerns that are internal to architecture, namely the concerns of organization and phenomenological articulation. Here resides potential for conflict but also opportunities for partially motivating signs.

The different registers operate as sign-radicals that together compose the composite sign. These registers, as layers or aspects of the overall design of the territory, can be classified as sign-radicals because each has a (semi-autonomous) semantic alignment, potential, or bias that contributes to the constitution of the final meaning that is attributed to the territory. The distinctions within each separate register combine to contextualize and fulfil each other's semantic potential. However, these distinct registers are not the only way to establish sign-radicals. An architectural language or code might operate with a lexicon of discrete geometric components as sign-radicals that can come together in various significant ways, for example, to delineate the boundary of the territory. One might think here of the walls, columns, balustrades etc or various types of opening. Just like the riders on the library cards in the library catalogue constitute a sentence-like proposition, namely the book is loaned out and thus absent from the shelf, so might the ensembles of architectural sign-radicals produce propositional statements. The rider on the library card, and indeed the card itself, are sign-radicals constituting the composite sign which is the card contextualized within the catalogue, with or without rider. The example shows that within a system-of-signification absences can be made to speak as much as presences. The capacity of a system of signification to signify via absences depends upon the existence of a grammar.

Above, the territory was compared to the sentence as a minimal unit of determinate signification. Both territory and sentence are constituted from sign-radicals. This implies a grammar that regulates the systematic re-use of sign-radicals according to semantic rules. However, the deployment of these sign-radicals is also subject to the rules of syntax that determine – certainly in the case of language use – what is usually referred to as the grammatically[303] correct use of words. The basic syntax of a sentence, for instance, demands the presence of a *subject* and a *predicate*, and sometimes an *object*, usually in this order (SPO). Chomsky prefers to speak of a *noun phrase* and a *verb phrase*. These are necessary types of components (sign-radicals) that constitute the sentence. In the same way a new, systematic architectural language might involve a syntax that distinguishes and posits types of components that are necessary for the constitution of a meaningfully organized and articulated territory. For instance, it seems pertinent to pose ***territorial demarcation*** and ***occupiable surface*** as two necessary types of sign-radicals that must be present to correctly constitute a meaningful territory.

Rather than starting with the invention of a formal syntax here, it is important to consider in more detail what kinds of information and which proposition-types might be communicated via architecture. The general form of architectural signs is propositional. For instance, consider: *this is an individual office* (function-type) *for a director/board member* (social-type), *in this direction leading to the boardroom, in that direction*

303 The theory of architectural autopoiesis does not restrict the term grammar to syntax. A more comprehensive concept of grammar includes syntactic, semantic and pragmatic rules.

leading to a conference room (location-type). In this case the quest for the language's systematicity would demand that the signifier expressing the location-type by indicating the adjacency or direction to the boardroom shares, according to a rule, certain signifying characteristics with the generic signifier denoting the function-type 'boardroom'.

Considering that the coded information that is communicated within an architectural language takes the logical form of the proposition, leads to the idea that an architectural language might be designed that allows for the utilization of the logical operations of the so-called ***propositional calculus***, ie, ***negation***, as well as connectives like ***conjunction***, ***disjunction***, ***implication*** etc. (These more abstract, propositionally composed modes of architectural communication might indeed be accessible to users engaging within the mode of attention, eager to close-read the environment's rich information.) One might consider negation in comparison to disjunction as follows: rather than only working with positive statements like *this is public,* ***or*** *communal,* ***or*** *individual*, a negative qualification might sometimes hit the mark quicker without needing to be overdeterministic: this is ***not*** restricted. One might also consider extending the expressive power of the designed architectural proto-language by allowing for the incorporation of modal operators and probabilities. The classic ***modal qualifications*** of propositions are ***necessity***, ***possibility*** and ***contingency***. Rather than mere declarative propositions like *this is a meeting room for managers*, the language might be able to express modal propositions like *this* ***might*** *be a meeting room for managers* (possibility), or *this is* ***currently*** *a meeting room* (contingency), versus *this* ***must*** *remain a meeting room* (necessity). A possibility statement might be combined with an implication or conditional statement: *this* ***could*** *be used as a meeting room,* ***if so then*** *social restrictions do* ***not*** *apply*. How could ***modality*** be expressed on the plane of the signifier? The possibilities are infinite. For instance, one might use colour, or just colour saturation, or just brightness, exclusively and rigorously throughout the project to indicate modality. The spectrum from necessary (fully determined) to contingent (indeterminate) might be mapped onto the brightness spectrum from very dark to very light, across all function-types. In this case the modality of territories would be a prominent layer of information that could even be navigated and immersed in while engaging the environment in the mode of distraction. How about ***quantifiers*** like ***all, some, one, none?*** That might be yet another useful expansion of the expressive power of the envisioned architectural language. For instance, a long row of (differently sized) office cells might be marked with the all-quantifier: ***all*** *meeting units here are restricted to* *managers*. This kind of information saves the potential user checking availability individually. Another possibility is the utilization of the variable components of the environment, like doors being open or closed, curtains being drawn or open, light being switched on or dimmed etc to dynamize an architectural language (like the rider on the library card). This variable layer of the built environment already functions in terms of indexicality, sometimes even via an individual user's communications, for example, when a manager keeps the door open to indicate that his subordinates are free to enter his office without prior appointment. One might conceive of the total environment as comprising various layers of transience, from the structure, via flexible partitions to all the mobile and kinetic elements.[304] The most variable and responsive layer could be electronically augmented and systematized under the auspices of a rigorous code. Within a corporate environment with facility management and intelligent building systems, such a code could be implemented according to a designed language incorporating dynamic sign-radicals.

The various, suggested lines along which the possible content of an architectural language could be enhanced – negation, the logical connectives of propositional calculus, modal operators, degrees of determinacy, quantifiers, variables – would push the expressive power of an architectural language far beyond the simple correlations between forms and designations that have usually been considered under the heading of 'meaning in architecture'. How plausible are these extensions, and how can they be implemented? This is perhaps the point where this book reaches its most speculative moment. The author can cite no precedents or successful design experiments that could back up the intuitions and proposals put forward here. This is where avant-garde design must take over and lead further research. Theory must hand over to design research until further problems are posed by progressing design work.

304 After completing the three-year research agenda of *Corporate Fields* (1998–2001), the AA Design Research Lab conducted a three-year design research on *Responsive Environments* (2001–4), concerned with the design of architectural systems that are capable of interaction by means of real-time reconfiguration in response to users via embedded electronic intelligence. The agenda was focused on social organization via action-artefact networks with carefully designed interaction patterns. (However, no emphasis was placed on the semiological dimension.) See: Patrik Schumacher, 'Responsive Environments – From Drawing to Scripting', in: *01 AKAD – Experimental Research in Architecture and Design – Beginnings*, Katja Grillner, Per Glembrandt, Sven-Olov Wallenstein (Ed), Royal Institute of Technology (Stockholm), 2005.

6.10 The Semiological Project and the General Project of Architectural Order

THESIS 34

The semiological dimension of architecture engages most directly with architecture's unique societal function. It is the leading dimension of architecture's task. It is the expertise in this dimension that is most required to succeed in the provision of effective communicative spatial frames.

This section theorizes the relationship of semiology to phenomenology and organization. All three aspects contribute to the achievement of architectural order. The thesis that transpires in this section is that the semiological dimension is the leading dimension of architecture's three tasks: organization, phenomenological articulation and semiological articulation. However, the semiological dimension must lead from behind. Also, its leadership has mostly been obscure, hidden by stealth. To enable it to assert itself more fully and openly, as a precondition of its further advancement, is the task that the theory of architectural autopoiesis posits here.

The semiological project depends and builds on both the organizational and the phenomenological project. There seems to be a logical sequence of project development that starts with the organizational project, then moves to the phenomenological project and finally to the semiological project.[305] Leadership from behind means that an experienced designer reflects on and employs the conditions for a successful semiological project as selection criteria within the build up of organization and phenomenological articulation. The phenomenological project tries to enhance the perceptual palpability of the spatial organization. The semiological project in turn relies on the perceptual presence of forms that are to acquire meaning within the semiological system. The inherent ambiguity of the perceptual decomposition of a scene directly affects the expected semiosis. In fact, a sophisticated semiological project should be able to take advantage of the possibility of phenomenological double readings to further enrich the expressive power of the respective architectural language. The semiological structuration of the perceptual material will in turn feed back into stabilizing some rather than other perceptual possibilities via so-called top-down processing. The exploration of these relations of mutual dependence, embeddedness and feedback merits further detailed research. In this final section on

305 Concerning the sequencing of the three projects see below, chapter 7.6.3 *Processing the Three Task Dimensions of Architecture*.

architecture's semiological dimension, some further reflections and conceptual preparations are offered that can help to frame this research.

6.10.1 THE SEMIOLOGICAL PROJECT IN RELATION TO THE ORGANIZATIONAL AND THE PHENOMENOLOGICAL PROJECT

The theory of architectural autopoiesis is bringing the phenomenological and the semiological dimension of architecture under the shared heading of articulation, as distinct from organization. The latter distinction is based on the difference between handling ***passive bodies*** versus enlisting active, ***cognitive agents***. The former distinction is based on the difference between the enlistment of behavioural responses from cognitive agents and the communicative engagement of ***socialized actors***. The phenomenological project enlists the users as cognitive agents perceiving and decomposing their environment along the lines of the cognitive principles of pattern-recognition or Gestalt-perception. The phenomenological project is all about making organizational arrangements perceptually legible by making important points conspicuous, avoiding the visual overcrowding of the scene etc. To do this well requires either a special intuitive talent or an expertise in the psychology of perception. This project of increasing the perceptual palpability of the main structural features of the environment does not yet constitute a communication in the strict sense of Luhmann's concept adopted here. A more loose, everyday meaning of the word communication seems to be satisfied here. But for the concept adopted in the theory of architectural autopoiesis this does not suffice. The three moments that need to be distinguished and satisfied here are impartation, information and understanding. The third moment is not satisfied in the case of the phenomenological project. The moments of impartation and information are not distinguished, they fuse in the case of perception. Also, the moment of understanding is not reached. Understanding not only presupposes the distinction of impartation and information, it also involves the attribution of the communication, as communication, to some person, organization or general social institution. (It is this attribution that requires the distinction of impartation and information.) Understanding thus implies a communicative engagement, or social interaction, even if it only consists in an action of avoidance, for example, the refusal to enter. Here an important distinction comes into play, the distinction on which the discipline of sociology was originally founded: the distinction between mere behaviour and social action. Social action only exists in the domain of social meaning. This distinction also relates to the central distinction between the modes of knowledge in the social sciences versus natural sciences: explanation vs understanding. Behaviour can be explained, action has to be understood.[306] The apparent ontological gulf between the two categories has since been closed by social systems theory. A behaviour becomes an action only if an intention and a social meaning are attributed to it in the context of a social action system. Luhmann generalized the sociological concept of action to the concept of communication and insisted upon its systemic rather than individual constitution. His arguments run a similar course to Saussure's: the system constitutes its elements rather than vice versa. Communications can thus be observed and explained with reference to the specific medium or system-of-signification that is being used and reproduced within the respective autopoietic system of communications. The scientific analysis and explanation of communications are thus in principle possible. This, however, does not vitiate the theoretical (and practical, real-life) distinction of action vs behaviour. The understanding of an action on the basis of shared meanings remains distinct from the observation and explanation of behaviour.

A behaviour becomes a communication if it solicits connections that draw it into a structured network of behaviours-become-communications. In the context of built architectural offerings this happens all the time, but to become a virtuoso in making this happen as a designer one needs either an intuitive sensitivity with respect to socially circulating meaning structures or to develop a theoretical expertise with respect to the functioning of systems-of-signification within autopoietic social systems. The intuitive talent in this respect might be due more to the general social sensitivity of the respective architect than to his/her training and experience as a designer, due more to general rather than specifically architectural socialization. In any case, whether strategically designed on the basis of theoretical grasp and expertise or intuitively on the basis of a more general social sensitivity, only such aspects of the design that engage its users as communicative agents, via the nuanced deployment of the medium as a system-of-signification, are communications. Thus only these aspects operate, *stricto sensu*, as communicative *frame* as defined in the context of theorizing architecture's societal function. However, the assessment of which aspects and features of a building operate semiologically, rather than merely phenomenologically, or merely organizationally, is not a trivial matter. It certainly cannot simply be read

306 See Max Weber's *Economy and Society* as locus classicus for this distinction as founding distinction of sociology. Max Weber, *Economy and Society*, The Free Press (New York), 1947, German original: *Wirtschaft und Gesellschaft*, Mohr (Tübingen), 1922. Also: Georg Henrik von Wright, *Explanation and Understanding*, Cornell University Press (Ithaca, NY/London), 1971.

off the material construct itself. Neither does the reference to the designer's intentions help. This assessment can also not merely rely on the social expertise of the architectural analyst as a socialized participant with respect to the social institution accommodated. Although such familiarity helps, and might indeed be the precondition for any successful assessment, it must be complemented by the theoretically guided self-reflection of the analyst's intuitive perceptions, associations and responses, as well as by a close, theory-led observation of the social communication processes unfolding within the building.

In accordance with the three dimensions of architecture's task – as it is posed by architecture's societal function – we can distinguish three levels of framing: physical, perceptual and communicative framing. Although we might say that both the organization of space, and its perceptually palpable presentation 'frame' processes of social interaction, it is only through processes of semiosis that gather the topology and the figural features of the material construct into a system-of-signification that the conditions are prepared for the functioning of the respective building or space as *frame* in the sense required by architecture's societal function, namely to address the exigency of communication's inherent double contingency by helping to define and stabilize the always required definition of the communicative situation.[307]

To summarize, we can thus distinguish the contributions the three fundamental dimensions of architecture make (via their respective design projects) to architecture's essential societal function:

task dimension	**framing contribution**	**engagement of users**	**solicited response**
organizational project	as physical frame	as physical bodies	passive movement
phenomenological project	as perceptual frame	as cognitive beings	active behaviour
semiological project	as communicative frame	as socialized actors	communicative action

Strictly speaking, it is only the semiological project that addresses the core societal function of architecture. The other two dimensions either provide services that might eventually be outsourced – following the fate of the engineering project that has already been outsourced – or their contributions are subsidiary to the semiological project in the sense that they must be redeemed by being incorporated within a successful

307 See Volume 1, chapter 5.1.4 *The Definition of the Situation as Precondition of Social Interaction.*

semiological project as its building blocks. The configurational arrangements worked up within the organizational project do indeed become relevant within the semiological project. Both the relative spatial positions of territorial units as well as their circulatory linkages become important factors in the construction of the communicative frame. An architectural system-of-signification that has configurational relations at its disposal is much empowered in comparison to a language that can only work within the morphological register. There might exist many coincidences where organizational criteria and concerns harmonize with and support semiological concerns, for example, if the alignment of two entrances on two opposing ends of an axis both establishes the most efficient connection between two institutions that produce frequent circulatory movement between them, and at the same time works in terms of signifying an important social distinction between symmetrically opposed institutions of equal rank. Although such coincidences might exist and should be looked for, there is plenty of scope for conflict because the two dimensions of the architectural project follow different functional prerogatives. They need to be balanced. To put it another way, the organizational project becomes a medial constraint for the medium of architecture which is handled and advanced within the semiological project. The same dialectic of potential support vs potential distraction exists between the organizational and phenomenological project, as well as between the phenomenological and semiological project. The three projects might be aligned as in the example of the symmetrically opposed entrances. Here the phenomenological project would consist in making both the spatial configuration and the symmetry relation visually conspicuous. The phenomenological project is caught between the two other projects and thus has to face two tasks which are potentially in conflict with each other: it has to perceptually heighten the objective organizational relations, for the sake of efficient wayfinding, and it has to use its articulatory registers to perceptually heighten the semiologically active features and suppress everything else. Thus it seems that the orchestration of all three dimensions from the perspective of the total task, in line with architecture's societal function, requires an oscillating and iterative process rather than a linear progression from organization to phenomenological and then semiological articulation. Only a process that keeps all three dimensions in play throughout has a chance of finding the coincidence referred to above.

If the societal function of architecture can only be fully addressed by the semiological project, as is being argued here, then it seems as if the semiological project is the 'most architectural' of the three dimensions of architecture. This is indeed the consequence to which the theory of architectural autopoiesis points. The problem with this conclusion is that the semiological dimension in architecture is not only the dimension that is most difficult to grasp and control, but the semiological project, as conscious, theory-led design project, is also the least developed of the three projects that correspond to the three dimensions of architecture, despite the efforts made under the auspices of Postmodernism and Deconstructivism between 1970 and 1990. This state of affairs implies that the theory of architectural autopoiesis is pushing itself into a tight corner here. The theoretical conclusion implies that architecture's most salient capacity does not yet exist as a fully reflected and controlled competency. In emphasizing the semiological project, the theory seems to marginalize itself, it seems to distance itself from the very discourse and discipline it purports to speak for. However, there are sufficient points of connection within the 500-year discourse of architecture, not only in the period of 1970–1990 but also throughout the history of architectural theory. These points of connection are contained in the discussions of the role of decoration and ornament, as well as in the concepts of expression and character. These historical concepts have already been alluded to above.[308] Below, in the section on the self-descriptions of architecture, in particular on the classic treatises of architecture, more relevant points of contact will be revealed.[309] The reinforcement of such redundancies is important in order for the theory to establish its embeddedness within architecture's historical autopoiesis, to maintain the credibility of its allegiance to the rationality of the real, and thus to maintain enough plausibility and authority to push ahead. Still, it is within this section, as will become even more clear below, that the theory of architectural autopoiesis reaches its most risky and most speculative moment, with only minimal backing by established design theory and practice. The ambition of the theory to become architecture's most recent, most authoritative self-description exists in an inevitable tension with its simultaneous ambition to advance the autopoiesis of architecture along the lines of a coherent set of theoretical decisions. Whether this tension can be sustained and eventually resolved must, at this stage, remain uncertain.[310]

308 See chapter 6.2.1 *Organization and Articulation: Historical and Systematic*.

309 See section 10.3 *Classic Treatises*.

310 The success or failure of the author's own design efforts in this direction, within the contexts of the AADRL and Zaha Hadid Architects, might become a factor that bears on this question.

6.10.2 RELATIONSHIP BETWEEN ARCHITECTURAL LANGUAGES AND ARCHITECTURAL STYLES

The relatively circumscribed ambition of creating a self-enclosed, semiological project-world might be extended by proposing a general semiological heuristic that might serve to systematize a whole architectural style with a view to enhance its capacity to contribute to a unified architectural system-of-signification that is able to operate beyond single projects. However, before an enhanced semiological practice has been established, the formulation of a concrete semiological heuristic (beyond the reminders and pointers assembled above) is premature. The normative design heuristics of a style are ideally drawn from an emerging practice to further clarify and guide this practice. This is what the theory of architectural autopoiesis is able to do with respect to the general functional and formal heuristics of the maturing style of Parametricism.[311] However, what can and must be addressed here are questions concerning the conceptual relations set up within the general theoretical edifice proposed. In order to understand what relationships might exist between architectural languages and architectural styles, it is necessary to determine the theoretical relationship between the concept of architectural language and the concept of architectural style. The two concepts are set up as conceptually independent in the sense that neither of them enters into the definition of the other. The concept (category)[312] of architectural style has already been precisely defined within Volume 1 of *The Autopoiesis of Architecture*: an architectural style is a coherent and comprehensive design (research) programme, complete with both a functional and a formal heuristic. As this definition indicates, the concept entails more than what the concept of *architectural language* delivers. Thus an architectural language is *not, eo ipso*, a full blown architectural style, although it might be a component of a full-blown architectural style. On the other hand, the concept 'architectural style' does *not* demand the presence of an architectural language or system-of-signification. It does, however, not exclude it either.

Once more: what relationships might exist between architectural languages and architectural styles? An architectural language might be a component of an architectural style. Would this component belong to the formal or to the functional heuristic of the style? It would feature implicitly in both, but could not be fully formulated in either. Thus one

311 See chapter 11.2.2 *Operational Definition of Parametricism: The Defining Heuristics of Parametricism*.

312 The concept of style is a category within architecture (rather than mere concept) as it denotes a fundamental permanent communication structure within the autopoiesis of architecture.

should expect that a *semiologically enhanced style*, or *semiologically empowered style*, if explicitly reflected in a programmatic statement of its heuristics, would comprise the formulation of a semiological heuristic that provides both positive principles about as well as prohibitions on how to design systems-of-signification in coherence with the style. Similarly one might expect the evolving organizational and phenomenological competency of a maturing style to lead to the explicit formulation of additional heuristic principles that enhance or empower the style with respect to these dimensions.

Thus we must distinguish the ***core heuristics*** of a style, comprising its formal heuristic and its functional heuristic, from possible ***supplementary heuristics*** the style might encompass. There are three potential supplementary heuristics that can be identified on the basis of the conceptual scheme elaborated within the theory of architectural autopoiesis: organizational heuristics, phenomenological heuristics and semiological heuristics. However, the three supplementary heuristics *cannot* enter the set of necessary features required to define a style because then the concept of style would exclude both the most promising contemporary style and architecture's great historical styles. The phenomenon and concept of style constitute a pervasive category and permanent communication structure of architecture. To insist on hypothetical upgrades (too early) as definitory for the concept of style would result in a purely normative rather than a reconstructive definition. The concrete application of the concept would be made impossible as its extension would be empty. Rather than proposing utopian normative substitutions, the theoretical definitions of the theory of architectural autopoiesis are supposed rationally to reconstruct and thus explicate and systematize the real operating concepts and categories that structure architecture's ongoing autopoiesis in its currently most advanced manifestations. Thus the thesis remains that styles *might* be further empowered by additional heuristics, inclusive of the formulation of architectural languages. Here this notion can only assume the status of a programme for future design research with the long-term ambition of empowering the encompassing style/research programme which frames this research.

Could there be an architectural language that operates across several styles? This is possible and indeed happens within the spontaneous, index-based semiosis of the built environment. For instance, balconies index the residential function-type whether the design is Modern or Postmodern. A projecting canopy indicates 'main entrance' in various styles etc. Can this independence from the choice of style be maintained even in the case of the more elaborate, grammar-based architectural languages envisioned here? Although this possibility cannot be excluded on purely conceptual grounds it seems unlikely. The general hypothesis of the theory of architectural autopoiesis is that all variable communication structures are regulated under the auspices of a chosen style, ie, the default presumption is that any design is designed within a style, whether the architect/designer knows and acknowledges this or not. A style must be chosen. The kind of semiological project envisioned here will thus be launched within one of the styles available within contemporary architecture. There are only three distinct styles active today: Neo-Historicism, Minimalism and Parametricism. The formal registers of these styles are so different from each other that an elaborate architectural language that operates across the three styles seems implausible.

6.10.3 THE REQUISITE VARIETY OF ARCHITECTURAL ARTICULATION

Having unfolded the task of establishing architectural order in terms of the underlying organizational task, the precarious perception of complex order and finally the problematic of effective semiosis, we can formulate an ambition for contemporary architecture that advances beyond what is expected and achieved – even in the most accomplished segment of the contemporary avant-garde. This ambition can be given a precise theoretical formulation.

We are assuming that the organizational/articulatory task is – for all practical purposes – infinite. This task is infinite in the sense that the social, institutional task-domain – for instance a large corporate headquarters – is so complex and nuanced that the architectural design effort of organization/articulation can never fully exhaust the reservoir of social distinctions and relations that would deserve articulate spatial organization. Therefore we can say that the complex, contemporary social processes that challenge contemporary architecture are ***excessive*** with respect to the task of architectural articulation. Therefore, the spatial organization and articulation of the social life-process are always selective, engendering a reduction of the assumed social complexity. Social space is always ***under-articulated***. This means that the social processes that can be anticipated to unfold in the articulate spatial organization – for example, in the fully furnished headquarters building – will entail significant differentiations and affiliations that find no registration and receptacle within the designed environment. The ideal limit case here would be a fully articulated social space where all social distinctions and affiliations that are relevant to the respective social institution would have been registered and articulated by means of spatial, morphological and material features.[313]

This assumption of under-articulation allows for the fact that unforeseen and unaccounted for social/programmatic distinctions do indeed end up appropriating/utilizing found features of the environment that were intended to code for other social distinctions, or were simply 'random' features that had no programmatic counterpart. Excessive social distinctions might therefore be confronted with an abundance of unaccounted-for formal features. One might call such random features ***architectural excess***, ie, features that are not taken up within any semiological system. According to the three registers of architectural articulation we can distinguish spatial, morphological and material excess. Any architecture or space that contains excess is in this sense ***subsystematized.*** Some of this excess might later be semiologically systematized and interpreted by the accommodated social system with its distinctions and communication processes.

In the ideal limit case of a ***fully systematized*** space there would be no excess, no such 'random', or 'excessive' unaccounted-for features. Every detectable spatial, morphological or material difference would be accounted for in terms of a semiological system. However, this does not imply that every feature in such a fully systematized space is indeed significant in the sense of 'making a difference' to the social process that utilizes this space. Such a space would be a ***fully interpreted*** space. The systematized does not necessarily coincide with the interpreted. We might call this part of the formal material that has been semiologically systematized without being socially interpreted the ***architectural surplus*** within the system. (This idea of a semiological surplus presupposes that the syntactic layer of an architectural language can be identified independently of its semantic layer. This assumption is problematic. It is plausible only in so far as we assume here that most of the language's syntax is interpreted, and only partially under-interpreted.)

Such a fully systematized space could on the one hand still lack the requisite variety to fully register the complexity of the social process, while on the other features of the articulatory system remain

313 However, this is an unrealistic limit case. With respect to highly complex social institutions, the articulatory effort might run into the problem that the semiological system becomes too complex to be learned quickly enough by the more or less transient user groups in question. The average tenure of the respective user group is therefore a significant point of reference. There seems to be no immediate cognitive limitation with respect to the overall complexity of a semiological system for architecture. Language and writing systems demonstrate that if there is sufficient learning time, the cognitive capacity for semiological complexity reaches far beyond what might ever be expected with respect to an architectural language.

uninterpreted, leading to an ***under-interpreted*** space. Thus we can distinguish the following concepts to facilitate a nuanced and precise discussion:

- Under-articulated – relevant social content remains unregistered
- Substantially articulated – the most relevant social content has been articulated, ie, registered and matched by semiologically structured spatial properties or architectural features
- Fully articulated – all relevant social content has been articulated
- Sub-systematized – formal material remains semiologically unstructured
- Fully systematized – all formal material is semiologically structured (limit case)
- Under-interpreted – there remains a residue of structured but uninterpreted semiological offerings
- Fully interpreted space – all that is semiologically structured is socially interpreted

Usually we can expect a space to be sub-systematized, under-articulated and under-interpreted, ie, there are excessive social contents, excessive formal material and excessive semiological offerings. We might term the theoretical limit case where all these excesses are assumed to be absorbed and balanced a state of ***total articulation***, only to assert that there can be no totally articulated space. The reservoir of formal possibilities (differences) in a design project – differences that could be semiologically systematized and socially interpreted – is open ended. The world of social differences is equally open ended. Therefore there can be no exhaustive mapping between the two domains. The semiological system mediates between these two domains by means of a selective and systematized mapping which leaves both a residual reservoir of unaccounted formal material and a residual domain of social differences that are not yet articulated. However, the process of semiological systematization of the formal material usually produces a new surplus of semiologically structured spatial properties and formal features that have no equivalent in terms of the institutional or social differences that are to be articulated. This condition has been termed 'under-interpreted' here. This condition of under-interpretation produces an interesting effect: it constitutes an open invitation to the social life process to interpret this semiological offering. For instance, the semiological system has arranged a series of colours into a colour code representing functional domains or has structured a hierarchical series from the top floor to the lowest floor representing the levels in the social hierarchy. However, the number of colours distributed in the building exceeds the number of functional domains that have been institutionalized, and the number of floors exceeds the current number of levels in the social hierarchy of the respective client organization. In both cases these structural offerings might catalyze the social life-process into a further structuration. This kind of architecturally catalyzed process of social structuration does indeed occur all the time, at all scales, including the urban scale. As suggested above, we might speak of the *demiurge-like power of architecture*. This catalyzing power of architecture operates in two dimensions: virtuality and potentiality. Excess produces virtuality and surplus produces potentiality. We have defined ***architectural excess*** as random formal features that are not accounted for within the semiological system. These features provide unstructured raw material for future spontaneous semiosis. The way these features might be taken up later by the evolving social institution is not prescribed or prestructured by the semiological system. Therefore we speak of ***semiological virtuality*** to express the radical openness that is given in this case.

We have defined ***architectural surplus*** as systematized formal features that have no social-programmatic counterpart. These features provide well-structured empty places within the semiological system that are likely to be taken up later – in a prestructured way – by the evolving social institution. Thus architectural surplus provides ***semiological potential***.

The most pertinent ambition for architectural design can be formulated by means of the concepts elaborated here. The first task would be to register and absorb the most institutionally relevant social distinctions, striving to reach or approximate a state of substantial or even full articulation. However, since social institutions can be expected to evolve – probably in the direction of higher complexity – the designer should provide both *semiological potential* by means of architectural surplus and *semiological virtuality* by means of sufficient architectural excess. There is a balance to be struck here. The more excess there is in the system, the more might we expect the scene to be visually polluted. Too much excess might lead to overall visual chaos that defeats the articulatory effort and prevents swift orientation. Architectural surplus should also be kept within bounds. The majority of the semiologically systematized architectural features – configurational properties, morphological motifs and material textures – should be socially interpreted, ie, the interpreted features must dominate the uninterpreted features. Thus we can summarize that, in the case of highly complex, evolving social institutions, ambitious architectural design would have to aim for a substantially articulated space that contains moderate architectural excess offering sufficient semiological virtuality, as well as sufficient architectural surplus, to provide semiological potential and thus considerable demiurge-like power to catalyze the further social structuration.

Architecture's capacity to design substantially articulated territories in the sense promoted above is being augmented by the new design media. Design within the phenomenological dimension has already been augmented by new digital visualization techniques. Design within the organizational dimension has already been augmented by the techniques of space syntax as well as by crowd simulation techniques. Design within the semiological dimension might be augmented if current crowd simulation techniques could be extended and generalized – via multi-agent modelling – to encompass the simulation of patterns of occupation and social interaction in space. Such modelling would imply that the domain of the signified – the meaning of the designed territories – could be represented and worked on within the design medium of the parametric model. Both the function-type (for example, the different interaction types of a university such as lecture, seminar, workshop, tutorial etc) and the social-type (for example, students vs visitors vs staff within a university) could be represented and systematically correlated with the positional, spatial and morphological features of the simultaneously modelled territories. The (currently still utopian) dream of the semiological project would thus be a single parametric model whereby the signifying relation would be instantiated via scripted correlations between the signifier and the signified within the parametric associative model, or programmed agents would 'read' and respond to the system of designed semiological clues. Signification is nothing but systematic correlation, ultimately reducible to the systemic concatenation of communications.

7. The Design Process

It is the overall task of this part on the design process to elaborate a theoretical apparatus that allows the description and evaluation of design processes, and an assessment of the prospects of further design process developments within architecture. Like all components of the theory of architectural autopoiesis, this theoretical task can build upon prior theoretical efforts. It is indeed one of the methodological self-impositions of the theory of architectural autopoiesis that such a theoretical elaboration must connect to concepts that are already circulating within the autopoiesis of architecture. In the case of design process theory, this recuperation has to go back to a discourse that has been dormant for nearly 40 years. The form that this recuperation takes might best be characterized as a selective rational reconstruction. This is achieved via the integration of the recuperated material within the unified theoretical edifice that this book is trying to forge. Beyond this systematizing recuperation of prior theory there is the further task of the critical-functional explication of these prior theories in terms of the *raison d'être* of the prevalent design processes and design process conceptions described and formalized in these theories. This critical-functional explication will also extend to design process innovations that have not as yet received sufficient theoretical attention. Finally this critical-functional explication will also lead the theory of architectural autopoiesis to take a stance with respect to design processes and design process conceptions that are most promising with respect to the advancement of contemporary architecture. Thus, like all components of the unified theory, this part on the design process oscillates between a descriptive and a normative mode. This is an important general pattern of the theory elaborated here: before venturing into prescriptions and recommendations, the theory takes account of actual communicative practice. Only on the basis of observing, understanding and extrapolating the actuality of how the most impressive contemporary projects are being achieved can a normative agenda promoting further potentialities gain credibility.[1]

Design process reflection is as old as the discipline itself, ie, it begins with Alberti. However, the need for elaborate process reflection was limited because the variety of different tasks was so limited that the

1 This necessary dialectic between the descriptive and the normative mode of reflection has not always been sufficiently observed. Simple normative assertions often prevail within architectural theory.

presentation of exemplary solutions for all possible tasks was still possible, or at least conceivable. Durand is credited with having been the first to propose a specific method of design.[2] During the 1920s, attempts were made to assimilate the design process to the rigorous reasoning found in science. However, a veritable design process theory has only developed since the 1960s, utilizing theoretical resources from outside architecture, from a cluster of new disciplines including discrete mathematics, operations research, systems engineering/theory, cybernetics, decision theory and, most importantly, cognitive science (including artificial intelligence research). The prior design process theory that is being recuperated here stems mostly from this 'design methods movement'[3] of the 1960s and 1970s. It was during this period that, for the first time in the history of architecture, a sustained discourse on design processes emerged. The discourse flourished all through the 1960s and 1970s, only to disintegrate and virtually vanish from the architectural scene during the early 1980s.[4] This historical trajectory of the design methods movement can only partially be explained in terms of its internal exhaustion due to the fact that the applicability of formalized methodologies within architectural practice proved to be very difficult. This sobering realization and disillusionment within the movement cannot account for the disappearance of the whole discourse, because the discourse itself found a second lease of life precisely in working through how the complexity and openness of architectural design problems made the application of formalized methods difficult. The account of this difficulty led indeed to sophisticated theoretical reformulations of what process rationality can mean in the case of design problems.[5]

The thesis here is thus that the disappearance of this discourse does not imply its theoretical bankruptcy. It is instead historically explicable in terms of the crisis of Modernism that had reached its point of no return at the beginning of the 1980s. It makes sense that a sustained theory of the

2 His method was based on a combinatorial process of aggregating elements into parts and parts into wholes over a grid of regulating lines, always adhering to symmetry rules. The process opened up a versatile universe of possibilities while at the same time guaranteeing a certain type of order.

3 Nigel Cross (Ed), *Developments in Design Methodology*, John Wiley & Sons (Chichester), 1984.

4 In fact the discourse did not totally terminate. It lost its influence within architecture and thus vanished from the autopoiesis of architecture. However, it continued to live on as a purely academic field sustained by the academic journal *Design Studies* which was founded in 1983 at the University of Illinois at Chicago. Although the journal is not dedicated exclusively to methodological and design process issues, it carried on publishing a continuous stream of contributions to this field of research and reflection.

5 It is to these latest theoretical reflections within the problem-solving paradigm that the theory of architectural autopoiesis seeks connection.

design methods and processes emerged at a mature stage of a hegemonic style: Modernism. (It is one of the fundamental theses of the theory of architectural autopoiesis that design methods and processes in architecture should be expected to vary with architectural styles.) The stability of a mature, hegemonic style, in this case Modernism, is indeed a precondition for the painstaking description and critical-normative formalization of the design process. In line with the Modernist emphasis on the unprejudiced pursuit of functional prerogatives, the design methods discourse of the 1960s and 1970s was geared towards guaranteeing the best attainable rationality in terms of solving the design problem understood as meeting the functional requirements stated in the design brief. It is also to be expected that such a painstakingly elaborate discourse on process loses its significance if the hegemonic style is questioned. Modernism was radically questioned in its Functionalist foundations, as well as in terms of the specific functional values and priorities that it assumed. It should not surprise us if attention to process is suspended when the very values and purposes of architectural design are in question. At a moment when a longstanding paradigm has collapsed and the way forward is contested, philosophical rather than methodological orientation is called for. Also, the agendas of contextualism and the pluralism of individual expression that were emerging at that moment did not seem to lend themselves to a procedural formalization. The crisis of Modernism not only led to an initial turn to historical architectural forms – where else to look if the current repertoire seems inept – it also brought back older conceptions of the designer as intuitive artist. These developments are consistent with the theoretical thesis posited in the chapter on styles as research programmes, namely that the avant-garde segment of the discipline progresses through the alternation of cumulative and revolutionary periods. Here the further thesis can be added that a sustained design process theory should only be expected during cumulative periods.

If a systematic design process theory is once more promoted here, via reconnection to the forgotten discourse of the 1970s, it is because a new long wave of research and innovation has crystallized. The autopoiesis of architecture has indeed entered a new cumulative phase of design research, cohered under the auspices of a new hegemonic style: Parametricism.[6] The style has been maturing within the architectural avant-garde for more than a decade and is now making serious advances into the mainstream. Therefore the conditions are ripe for a new phase of sustained design process research and theorizing. It is being proposed

6 See section 11 *Parametricism – The Parametric Paradigm and the Formation of a New Style.*

here that this new discourse on the design process can be launched on the basis of a critical recuperation and augmented reformulation of the achievements of the 1970s' discourse. After an intermezzo of about 20 years during which – for very good reasons – avant-garde design processes remained intuitive and exploratory rather than systematic and strategic, ten years ago, a new cumulative design research began to gather momentum. Now the time has come when further advances are curtailed rather than opened up by the continued absence of a rigorous methodology. Without a strategically structured and methodologically controlled, rational design process the contemporary avant-garde will not achieve the enhanced credibility it needs to sustain its current claim for avant-garde hegemony, nor will it achieve the effectiveness it needs to gear up for its imminent launch into the mainstream. To this end, in what follows, a conceptual framework, a terminological apparatus, initial design process descriptions and a first tentative set of methodological principles are being proposed.

7.1 Contemporary Context and Aim of Design Process Theory

THESIS 35

Design process theories (with rationalizing methodological ambitions) make sense only during the cumulative periods of disciplinary advancement, under the auspices of a hegemonic style. The time has come for a new theoretical investment in design process theory with the aim of advancing contemporary design methodology under the auspices of Parametricism.

The reflection upon the design process has become a necessary, standard loop of reflection within the most advanced practices of contemporary architecture. The necessity for reflective guidance of the design process is primarily rooted in the increasing ***complexity*** of the posed design tasks. This complexity of the design task is a function of the general complexity, diversity and fluidity of social communication processes. Once more, thus, it is the ability to cope with complexity that is the pivot of our theoretical reflections.

The design process is a selection/decision process that must temporize the complexity of the problem.[7] This temporization of complexity succeeds via a stepwise, incremental approximation of the desired

7 The temporization of complexity is a general feature of communication processes (that rely on sequential processing). Compare Niklas Luhmann, *Zweckbegriff und Systemrationalität. Über die Funktion von Zwecken in Sozialen Systemen*, Suhrkamp Verlag (Frankfurt am Main), 1973, p 255.

performative complexity. The design process must transform the structural-performative complexity of a problem constellation into the temporal complexity of a process that exhibits a much reduced complexity at each moment, step or stage of the process. This implies that the rationality of the final artefact can only be analyzed and grasped during the design process. Although it is the final product that offers the real test of the design's social-performative capacity, it is comparatively opaque. It works well or not. It is difficult to unravel the factors that contribute to its success or failure. But, more importantly, rational evaluation requires the positing of alternatives, and it is only during the design process that all the ramifying possibilities of design alternatives are considered, compared and decided upon. The design process, a process that often takes many months, sometimes even years, is therefore the only point at which the rationality of a design can be queried, assessed and improved. It is the only effective lever, the moment of truth where general principles either gain their meaning by being effectively operationalized, or otherwise remain empty slogans.

The key focus here is on the question of how contemporary design practice can maintain a convincing concept of design process rationality. Design rationality is challenged by the increasing complexity of design tasks. It is also challenged by the increased expectation of continuous innovation. Innovation has become permanent. This means every design task is new and complex. This double challenge is now expected and routinely handled by contemporary architects. In particular, this double challenge is relished within the maturing style of Parametricism. It is necessary to investigate contemporary design processes, including the design processes of Parametricism, in terms of their methodological credentials as rational decision processes. This is important because Parametricism is pushing to become a mainstream force within world architecture.

The renewed interest in the design process is primarily due to the recent proliferation and fast evolution of digital design tool offerings that demand attention and exploration.[8] Accordingly, most contemporary design process reflection is concerned with new tools and techniques and with the formal/aesthetic effects that might be attainable with various digital techniques. Techniques are thus correlated with effects aiming at the expansion of the formal repertoire available to contemporary design. There is as yet no sustained reflection on how this expansion of the repertoire answers to societal challenges. The fascination with new

8 The reflection upon the design process thus includes reflection upon the various media of design as one of its moments. However, it encompasses much more.

techniques and new effects is linked to a general, healthy urge for socially transformative innovation. Ali Rahim, in his book *Catalytic Formations*, includes a chapter on techniques in which he emphasizes continuous innovation via the continuous introduction of new techniques. He warns against the 'risk of techniques becoming routine and static over time' and emphasizes that techniques are process driven, that they grow out of trial and error, and keep evolving. He celebrates the fact that 'new techniques destabilize existing practice'.[9] Although the author shares Rahim's insatiable thirst for the new in all its guises, the theoretical focus here moves nearly in the opposite direction. The theory senses and investigates a potential for normative stabilization within a maturing avant-garde design practice. It takes the recent proliferation of new techniques for granted, and asks to what extent the technique driven, contemporary avant-garde design practice can develop a methodological rigour that matches its increasing ambitions, and might help to prepare its pending inroads into mainstream practice. The presumption here is that the contemporary avant-garde is stabilizing into a new hegemonic style. If this is so, new routines are being established that need to be queried with respect to their rationality. As stressed above, the key focus is here on the question to what extent contemporary design practice can maintain a convincing concept of design process rationality.

Although the ambitions of Parametricism provide the background motivation for a deepened design process reflection, the theory of architectural autopoiesis must first lay down a general framework for an upgraded design process rationality that is able to give criteria that are independent of any particular style.

The complexity of the design task is initially given in the form of the complexity of purposes and performance requirements that should be met by the architectural artefact. The question is how the effective build up towards a final, required performative complexity can be ordered to increase the probability of succeeding in this complex task. The difficulty of this task is exacerbated if the task involves novel conditions that prevent reliance on precedent solutions. The difficulty the design process has to cope with thus hinges on two factors: the degree of performative complexity of the task, and the degree of unprecedented novelty or uniqueness of the task. A simple, straightforward task where the solution immediately presents itself in the form of an obvious precedent or typical solution hardly requires the problematization of the design process. A quick sketch hinting at the familiar precedent is here enough to set a

9 Ali Rahim, *Catalytic Formations – Architecture and Digital Design*, Taylor & Francis (London/New York), 2006, p 13.

readymade train in motion. While some mainstream practitioners might still be able to survive on the basis of such routine practice, the profession at large is faced with the double challenge of uniqueness and complexity. Therefore, the following question is to be posed: how is this double challenge of uniqueness and complexity reflected in the most advanced contemporary design processes? These processes need to be described and subjected to a critique that focuses on their rationality.

The rationality of the contemporary design process will indeed be the final focus of this part of the book. This rationality needs to be both reconstructed and projected forward. It will transpire here that this rationality proceeds in new, sometimes indirect, hidden ways, even in ways that initially appear irrational rather than rational.

7.2 Towards a Contemporary Design Process Reflection and Design Methodology

THESIS 36

At a certain stage within a maturing avant-garde style, prevalent processes have to evolve into self-critical methods. This requires the rational reconstruction of the prevalent processes rather than the invention of new processes, or the imposition of abstract ideals of rationality.

The design process is to be theorized as communication process. This is consistent with the general framework adopted by the theory of architectural autopoiesis. As proposed in the chapter on the elemental operation of architecture, the basic type of communicative operation that characterizes the autopoiesis of architecture is the design decision.[10] Design decisions, like decisions in general, are a special type of communication. Decisions are communications since decisions are only really (effective) decisions, if they are communicated as decisions. We can therefore say that the design process is a communication process that proceeds via design decisions. In observing sequences of design decisions, attention might first be placed upon their description, ie, which media they involve, their pattern of concatenation, how they move from the abstract/general to the concrete/particular, how they proceed to build up complexity, how they oscillate between formal and functional concerns etc. A second, further step in the analysis involves their reconstruction as episodes that follow a method. Here the question of rationality enters and demands of the theory a critical stance.

10 See Volume 1, chapter 3.3 *The Elemental Operation of Architecture.*

7.2.1 METHOD VS PROCESS

The architectural design process is both a generative process and an evaluative process – requiring generative and analytic theories respectively. The design process, at every stage of its progress, faces both a creative challenge – where or how to find candidate solutions; and an analytic-predictive challenge – how to assess whether the generated option is going to perform within the real world of social utilization. This assessment must be performed on the basis of a representation or simulacrum.

Due to the inevitability of building up the complexity of the final design in a lengthy, step-wise succession, the problem is further complicated: the difficulty is knowing – at each stage in the design process – which of the many possible next steps brings the simulacrum sustainably closer to the desired end-state. The restriction 'sustainably' is important because in sufficiently complex problem-constellations, the potential further trajectory of the chosen design path is largely opaque and might have many unforeseen problems in store. This means that a move which superficially brings the simulacrum closer to the desired end-state might have to be retracted later or paid for with a lot of downstream effort. Under such conditions, how can sustainable progress be identified? Does this difficulty imply that the design process is of necessity a cyclical or iterative process that backtracks nearly as much as it moves forward? What does this imply for the degree of rationality and objectivity that can be expected within the domain of architectural design? These are the kinds of reflections and questions that require us to distinguish questions of process and questions of method.

A complete design decision process completes a ***design project***. From the very outset, it is important to distinguish two dimensions according to which design projects and their decision processes can be investigated and assessed: the dimension of *method* and the dimension of *process*.[11] The dimension of ***method*** refers to the logic and rationality of the decisions within the design decision process, while the ***process*** dimension refers to the mechanisms of progression of the design decision process and its unfolding over time. These two dimensions can and should be conceptually separated. While the choice of a design method has implications in terms of what would be an appropriate process to realize the method, this determination is incomplete. A given design method might be instantiated by various design processes. Inversely, a

11 Unfortunately, this distinction is usually not explicitly clarified in the design method/process literature.

single design process might involve several design methods. Although a design project should follow an integrated and coherent set of methods, this is not always guaranteed in practice. The different parts or sub-routines of a given total process might be used for different ends, and in the context and service of rather different methods. This implies that methods and processes, although interrelated, vary independently across the spectrum of empirical design projects. There are design projects that share the same method but differ in process, and there are design projects that share certain process components while differing in terms of underlying method.

The concept of design method cannot be equated with the explicit methodological pronouncements of the designer. Such pronouncements might be taken as indications but they cannot be taken at face value. The concept of design method refers to the logical structure of the design project. It thus operates at a higher level of abstraction than the concept of design process. An empirical investigation of a given design project will have to start by describing the design process. The underlying design method, to the extent that there is a coherent method, will have to be inferred from the observation of the design process. We can thus say that the design process is open to observation while the design method is inferred, implicit. The recognition of methods requires the analysis of larger chunks of process, and ultimately the analysis of the overall process. The relationship between method and process can be stated as follows: the design process operationalizes the design method. Design method analysis is concerned with the principles and strategies that guide the design project and reflects on the control loops that assess interim results in the light of final objectives. The design process description is concerned with the moves, steps and operations through which the design project unfolds. It is concerned with the creation of interim results and their further forward projection. It describes the operations, as well as their sequencing, recursive looping and ordering into stages.[12] The distinction might thus be summarized as follows:

12 In order to further characterize the distinction, one might use the analogy of the distinction of the semantic vs the syntactic dimension of language: the dimension of method would map onto the semantic dimension and the process dimension would be parallel to the syntactic dimension. Although the distinction between method and process seems conceptually clear and productive it is difficult (and most probably impossible) to identify significant process units (rules) and their various derivations without already knowing their methodological import. Only a designer can analyze a design process, just as the identification of syntactic rules and their irregularities presupposes the linguist's prior understanding of the language being investigated.

Design method: The term method is here taken to refer to the logical structure of the design project. The term denotes a theoretical entity that is inferred rather than observed. It concerns the principles and strategies that guide the design project. The applicability of the concept of method is subject to the rationality constraints of goal-orientation and internal consistency. The identification of a process as constituting the execution of a design method thus depends upon its reconstruction as rational.

Design process: The term process is here taken to refer to the time structure of the design project. The term denotes an empirical entity that can be observed. It is concerned with the overt operational sequences, episodes and stages of the design project. The identification of a process as design process does not depend upon any successful rational reconstruction.

There is a second important distinction that needs to be made from the very outset. It is a distinction that operates on the meta-level of theoretical self-description: the distinction between *informative* and *normative* theory.

Informative theory: An informative theory of design is concerned with the *description* and *explanation* of actual design practice.

Normative theory: A normative theory of design is concerned with formulating *norms* or *recommendations* about how design ought to be conducted to succeed.

One might presume that the distinction should be aligned with the distinction between methods and processes, assuming that a concern with processes would lead to an informative theory while the concern with methods would lead to a normative theory. However, the distinction can and should be set up as an independent dimension that can be brought into an orthogonal rather than parallel conceptual configuration with the distinction of method vs process. There can and should be empirical investigations of the design methods that guide actual design projects leading to an informative theory of design methods. These investigations would proceed on the basis of logical analyses of observed design processes. On the other hand, it is perfectly conceivable, and indeed desirable, to proceed to construct a normative theory that not only posits a method in terms of guiding principles but then moves on to operationalize these principles via the elaboration of recommendations that specify (supposedly effective) design procedures.

The status of methods and methodological principles seems unproblematic when we are confronted with explicitly stated methodological norms, like for instance Christopher Alexander's insistence that a rational design process requires a *full* statement of all requirements, that these requirements must be stated negatively as the avoidance of *misfit,* and that the global set of misfit conditions needs to be *decomposed* in such a way that interdependent elements form subsets that are as independent from each other as possible. Here, the stated methods *motivate* certain procedures that are then enacted in order to follow the methodological norms stated. If a designer, perhaps the author of the norms himself, designs according to the stated rules, it seems as if the stated methods can serve to *explain* the observed design process. The explanation operates via the conscious goal-orientation of the designer. Conscious processes allow the 'final causes' (goals) that seem to operate against the arrow of time to be converted into antecedent causes. Nothing could be more common than this. But what status does this concept of method have in an informative theory where the design project under investigation might go on without stated rules? Is it legitimate to infer methods here? Is it also possible here that the merely *inferred* methods can serve to *explain* the observed processes? The method might be said to provide the *rationale* for the observed procedures. What does this mean in the absence of any explicit, conscious guidance? (This kind of explanation is clearly a functional rather than a causal explanation.) Do we have to posit unconscious mental processes that somehow constitute the reality of the inferred methods? Leaving this question suspended for a moment, and assuming that there *are* methods, then the methods themselves, in turn, can be explained by way of *their* rationale, ie, in terms of their power to ensure an effective design outcome. (Again, this kind of explanation is clearly a functional rather than a causal explanation.) The process rationale would thus be a derived rationale that ultimately depends on the effective design outcome guaranteed by the process of (unconscious) adherence to the inferred methodological rules. But is it not possible, and according to Ockham's razor advisable, to cut out the idea of method here and assume that the design process is directly explained – in analogy to the theory of evolution – by its capacity to procure an effective design outcome? No. Although the theory of architectural autopoiesis has no interest in investing time speculating about the mode of existence of hidden mental processes, the theoretical positing of an underlying method is a necessary level in the theoretical reconstruction of the design process rationale, whether there is a mental reality that corresponds to it or not. This is mandated by the fact that the overall functional effectiveness of the design project poses a certain set of general functional requirements that could be operationalized by many different process patterns. The rationality of the process requires a certain logical structure. In this sense the level or dimension of method is no more than a conceptual condensation of the manifold of processes into functional equivalence classes.[13]

For architectural theory, the importance of working with the concept of inferred methods lies in the fact that it facilitates the necessary theoretical trajectory from an informative to a normative theory of the design project. A sophisticated normative theory must be methodology before it offers process recommendations, and before a convincing normative methodology can be elaborated the most advanced and most effective actual design practices must be analyzed and theorized.

The two distinctions of *method vs process* and *informative vs normative* thus lead to the following roadmap for the construction of a convincing theory of the design project: the theory proceeds from a description of the actual, contemporary design process to the analysis of its underlying design method. A complete informative theory of an advanced contemporary design project would further include the functional explication of both process and method. On the basis of a rational critique of the thus analyzed and explicated design project, the theory might proceed with the elaboration of a normative design methodology, and finally formulate specific design process recommendations. However, before the work of design process description can commence, there is the need to establish a precise conceptual and terminological apparatus.

13 However, as alluded to in a footnote above, the very identification of process elements that might then be allocated into such equivalent classes of equally effective (or functionally equivalent) processes presupposes the analyst's knowledge on the level of method. (The abstraction 'functional equivalence' is the dimension 'method'.) A design process, except in its smallest components, is not a mechanical algorithm that can be followed through robotically. Therefore, it makes sense to assume that the successful, intuitive designer has at his disposal, although non-verbalized and non-reflective, some kind of understanding of the logic of what he/she is supposed to do, rather than assuming that he/she proceeds by blind process adherence. Blind process adherence would imply a level of vulnerability with respect to process contingencies that seems irreconcilable with the robustness of an experienced designer's ability to succeed. However, these are speculations that do not directly concern architectural theory. Their validation or refutation would be the business of scientific research. This kind of empirical research of designers' activities does indeed exist. To find such research one might consult the journal *Design Issues*.

7.3 The Design Process as Problem-solving Process

THESIS 37

Within a design process theory that intends to probe and enhance the rationality of design, the design process must be theorized as problem-solving process. Problem solving – especially at the level of such a complex endeavour as designing the built environment – can only be adequately theorized as accomplishment of an autopoietic communication system, geared up with its whole panoply of communication structures.

The design process is a specialized communication process that is geared towards solving design tasks. It can be described as a special type of problem-solving process. It proceeds via design decisions. Above, the design project was defined as complete design communication process. However, communication processes can only take place within social communication systems. Local communication systems might form as subsystems within larger communication systems. In this sense an architectural design ***project*** can be regarded as a communication system embedded within the autopoiesis of architecture (therefore the term 'design project' has two levels of meaning: as process and as social system of communications. Which meaning is implied can be inferred from the context). Project communications are regulated by the general communication structures of architecture, and by the more specific communication structures that regulate project work. Also, each individual project builds up its own unique communication structures within the course of its project history. Each project produces such structures that only insiders know and can rely upon in their communications.

A social communication system is an autopoietic system, ie, a self-referentially enclosed recursive network of communications that reproduces the communication structures it relies on within its ongoing communication process. The base units of communication processes/systems are communications. A communication entails three constitutive moments or selections: *impartation*, *information* and *understanding*.[14] It is possible to analyze the communication process and isolate its informational aspect. This is also possible with respect to a design project: the information-processing aspect can be isolated from the total design communication process. This affords the possibility of theorizing certain segments of the design process as information-processing processes. This possibility allows the theory to connect

14 Understanding here does not imply correct understanding. It includes misunderstanding, as long as the chain of communications continues, as long as *connectivity* is maintained.

to pertinent concepts from cognitive science and artificial intelligence research. The conceptual scheme originally proposed by Herbert Simon[15] and Allen Newell to analyze and simulate human problem solving is mobilized here in order to give a close account of the design process.

On the level of generality that the theory of architectural autopoiesis operates, an abstract, general conceptual apparatus and terminology must be adopted. The apparatus adopted here is the apparatus of the ***information-processing theory of cognition*** that was developed by Allen Newell and Herbert Simon during the 1960s in connection with their computational work on human problem-solving strategies. This conceptual apparatus will be introduced, adapted and deployed within what follows. However, a brief anticipation of the key concepts of this approach might be advanced here: the theory conceives the design process as a form of problem solving.[16] The process can be described as the successive transformation of so-called *problem states*. An *initial state* is operated upon and transformed via various *intermediate states* to reach a final, satisfactory *solution state* or *goal state*. The problem-solving process can now be conceptualized as a search for a solution within a ***problem space***, ie, the encompassing set of all problem states defined as a universe of possibilities that depends upon the initial problem representation and the full set of primitives and operations (transformations) that allow for the generation of new problem states out of given problem states. The problem space is searched via sequences of legitimate *state transformations*, starting from the initial state. Within architecture the initial state might be nothing more than the representation of the empty site plus schedule of accommodation, plus perhaps a topological diagram given within the design brief. Legitimate state transformations are all the design operations that are defined within the chosen medium of design.

7.3.1 THE DESIGN PROCESS AS INFORMATION-PROCESSING PROCESS

Herbert Simon and Allen Newell introduced a compelling conceptual framework for analyzing the cognitive processes involved in

15 The integration of Herbert Simon's concepts comes naturally to the theory of architectural autopoiesis. Niklas Luhmann appropriated Herbert Simon's insights among the fundamental building blocks of his whole theoretical edifice. Both intellectual careers started in the field of organization theory.

16 It will transpire that design problems are a special kind of problem. They have been classified as 'ill-defined problems' or 'ill-structured problems'. See Allen Newell, 'Heuristic Programming: Ill-Structured Problems', in: JA Aronofsky (Ed), *Progress in Operations Research*, Vol 3, John Wiley (New York), 1970.

problem-solving behaviour: *the information-processing theory of cognition*. The basic premise of their work is that human thinking processes, in particular problem-solving processes, might be investigated by means of computer simulations. The basic structure of a problem-solving process is therefore conceptualized by analogy to a computer program, ie, as information processing implemented as a sequential transformation of an initial information state into a goal or solution state via a series of intermediate states. This information processing is in turn characterized as a symbol manipulation process by means of physical symbol systems. The model of symbol manipulation posited by Newell and Simon was initially a rather rigidly constrained model in order to facilitate the study of information processing in symbolic systems in a precise, technical way. The model was 'hypothesizing in an extreme form the neatness of discrete symbols and a small set of elementary processes, each with precisely defined and limited behaviour.'[17] Newell and Simon justify this restriction as follows: 'This abstraction, although possibly severe, does provide a grip on symbolic behaviour that was not available before.'[18] The types of problem-solving processes Newell and Simon focused on were those that had been successfully treated by artificial intelligence (AI). This was important because only here was the requisite array of plausible mechanisms available that could model and simulate cognitive processes.[19] Newell and Simon conceptualize processes as being under the control of *methods*. The distinction made above between processes and methods is thus made here too: a method is a rational organization of processes, rational in relation to attaining a problem solution. General methods treated by Newell and Simon include sub-goaling-recognition methods, generate-and-test methods and heuristic search methods.

The severe restrictions imposed with respect to the parsimony and logical crispness of symbols and operations cannot be maintained when theorizing complex design tasks, although specific design sub-tasks or sub-processes might very well be analyzed with a rather restricted symbol set of the kind favoured by Newell and Simon. In any event, the basic conceptual apparatus of the information-processing theory of cognition

17 Allen Newell & Herbert A Simon, *Human Problem Solving*, Prentice-Hall International (London), 1972, p 5.

18 Ibid.

19 What makes the framework of Newell & Simon amenable to appropriation for our purposes is the fact that rather than venturing to pose specific physiological mechanisms that might correspond to the symbol manipulation processes, the processes are distinguished according to their problem-solving function. The idea is that operations with equivalent functions must be hypothesized in order to explain the achievements of human problem-solving intelligence.

can be adopted and developed to meet the particular requirements of theorizing the architectural design process.

Newell and Simon's information-processing theory of cognition became the adopted framework for many studies and computational simulations of problem-solving processes. In particular, it was also eagerly adopted within the design methods movement during the 1970s. Since Newell and Simon's book-length landmark publication, summarizing their work of the preceding 15 years, only appeared in 1972, the framework and conceptual apparatus entered the design discourse only in the 1970s. Theoretical adoptions within the field of architectural design include: Charles M Eastman's *Explorations of the Cognitive Processes in Design*, and Ömer Akin's *An Exploration of the Design Process*, as well as his book *Psychology of Architectural Design*. Key notions of William J Mitchell's *The Logic of Architecture – Design, Computation and Cognition* were also strongly influenced by Newell and Simon's information-processing theory of cognition.

The integration of this framework within the theory of architectural autopoiesis necessitates a fundamental conceptual transformation. This transformation requires that 'the human' (or the machine that simulates the human) is substituted by the social communication system as fundamental reference of the theory. The information-processing system – in Simon and Newell's work abbreviated to the acronym IPS – must be reconceptualized as the informational aspect of the social communication system that is the design project which in turn is embedded within the autopoiesis of architecture. The thinking human subject, as well as the AI computer, are reconceptualized as processing units that exist in the immediate environment of the communication system. Information processing and thus communication is certainly dependent on the complex mechanisms that take place within these processing units, but the underlying micro-mechanisms are not of interest to the theory of architectural autopoiesis.[20] It is the communication system that the theory ultimately credits with the design. The design process theory developed here is concerned with the communication processes of the design project, understood as structured social communication system. However, this system depends on and is constrained by the cognitive capacity of the enlisted human subjects as necessary but not sufficient condition.

20 What might be of interest within the context of a detailed design process reflection is the cognitive capacity of human subjects, *in as much as* this poses real limits to the information-processing capacity of the communication system.

This reconceptualization of the IPS is necessary in order to maintain the emphasis on communication systems rather than psychic, organismic or machine systems and their underlying micro-mechanisms. The direct, detailed engagement with issues of cognitive psychology, physiology or computer technology is thus avoided in favour of issues of communication (with the exception of the above-mentioned capacity constraints). The concept of information processing is sufficiently abstract to allow for the required conceptual transposition. Although Newell and Simon conceive their work as a part of psychology, it is possible to reinterpret and re-embed their conceptual apparatus within the social systems framework adopted here. Their abstract concept of information processing conceptualizes logical and heuristic operations that cannot only be realized by the behaviour of minds, brains or machines, but also by communicative actions within communication processes. In fact, it is only within social systems of communication that the kinds of intellectual problem-solving tasks Newell and Simon investigate (logic proofs, chess) can arise, be addressed and solved. Newell and Simon's concept of IPS abstracts from these conditions of its existence.[21] As Reitman observed: 'information processing theories ... emphasise the functional properties of thought and the things it achieves.'[22] This functional perspective is also the perspective of the theory of architectural autopoiesis.

The theoretical task here is to analyze design as problem solving and the design process as information processing in the sense conceptualized by Newell and Simon. Even though we are conceptually isolating the information process in order to closely analyze the informational fine structure of the design process, we must remain cognizant of the fundamental premise that the identity and meaning of these processes are constituted within the social communication system, ie, the design project embedded within the autopoiesis of architecture. The information-processing process that will be abstracted and analyzed below is only one moment within a larger process and system. The system

21 Although it cannot be denied that organisms and machines achieve a certain degree of intelligence or even rationality in the sense of behaviours that are somehow adaptive relative to an environment and relative to certain success or survival conditions, the kinds of complex problem-solving activities that are involved in design are still the exclusive preserve of society. Isolated human individuals, considered as mere organisms, or robots left without designed program, are hardly equal to the task. The necessary software design as well as the necessary socialization and education processes that are the precondition of the emergence of an AI expert system or a human designer will always be dependent on society, indeed on functionally differentiated society. The same applies to human designers. They can only evolve into the competent designers we know within social systems of communication.

22 Walter R Reitman, *Cognition and Thought – An Information Processing Approach*, John Wiley & Sons (New York/London/Sydney), 1965, p 1.

notion is important because the presuppositions and implications that give identity and meaning to any process are distributed across many processes, stretched across time and space. The crucial category here is the category of meaning. Only communication processes within social systems generate meaning. Information processes as such are just physical processes, for example, the information processing that goes on in an AI computer program, or in the brain of a human organism. In isolation such processes are literally meaningless. Neither organisms nor AI machines can generate meaning. Within the theory of social autopoiesis, human beings are revealed to be mere points of attribution within the ongoing communication process of the relevant social communication system.[23]

The conceptualization of information processes as embedded moments of social communication processes is coherent with Herbert Simon's reduction of information processing to a process of symbol manipulation enacted by means of physical symbol systems. Indeed, what happens right there and then when a drawing is generated, modified and elaborated is clearly just that: symbol manipulation within a physical symbol system.[24] The phenomenon of meaning emerges out of such processes. However, the phenomenon of meaning cannot arise from any such process in isolation. A single sequence of symbol manipulations cannot conjure up the phenomenon of meaning. It is the total rule-governed, rule-reproducing and rule-evolving traffic-pattern of such symbol manipulations – in short, the autopoiesis of the respective communication system – that constitutes meaning as a highly complex/condensed attribute of such symbol manipulations. The meaning of the symbol string is its use/role within the communication system that is nothing but the structured network of such strings.

Within the theory of architectural autopoiesis the design process remains a communication process. This stance will be valorized below, when the design process is specifically analyzed as a collaborative, discursive decision-making process that involves argument and critique as essential components that allow the full activation of architecture's highly evolved communication structures. Without argument and critique, and their anticipation, the highly evolved rationality of the discipline

23 The fact that the constitution of meaning is routinely attributed to human beings is a fact of communication that proves nothing except the fact of communicative attribution. The concept of 'subject' remains a mystification that must be reduced, dissolved and explicated within a theory of social communication systems. The subject is a communicative construct, a point of attribution and reference, which communication systems require to order their communications in practice.

24 Symbol systems are necessary components (not subsystems!) of communication systems.

cannot be brought to bear. However, for the precise description of the logical and procedural micro-structure of the design process, ie, for the analysis of what goes on when design drawings or models are evolving, Newell and Simon's conceptual set up seems to be adequate.

The design process can be classified as problem-solving process in which many small problem-solving episodes add up to an overall problem solution. This conceptualization of design as problem solving does not imply a neglect of aesthetic issues. The concept of problem solving is very broad. The aesthetic and formal issues that often preoccupy designers are considered here to be just further instances of problems to be solved. There are formal-aesthetic problems as well as functional problems to be solved. Both formal and functional aspects, ie, both beauty and utility, are pursued when work is progressing along any of the three dimensions of architecture's task, ie, when the design process is concerned with the organizational project, the phenomenological project or the semiological project.

Is there a general, abstract definition of the concept of *problem*? What does it mean – within the cognitive science research on problem solving – for an information-processing unit to have a problem? Perhaps the most convincing definition was provided by Walter Reitman in 1965: 'A system has a problem when it has or has been given a description of something but does not yet have anything that satisfies the description.'[25] The definition is as general as it is precise. The design problem or task is perfectly captured by this definition. As Reitman notes, this definition makes having a problem equivalent to having a task or having a goal. Problem solving thus equals task accomplishment and goal attainment. There is no requirement that the problem must be somehow difficult or non-trivial. As Reitman points out: 'even routine accomplishments appear to involve many steps integrated into complex sequences'.[26] Below, the particular character of design problems will be analyzed. However, before investigating design problems in particular, a conceptual apparatus for analyzing problem-solving behaviour in general is to be presented and theoretically integrated.

7.3.2 THE STRUCTURE OF INFORMATION-PROCESSING SYSTEMS

Newell and Simon's general model of problem-solving behaviour as information processing is being adopted and integrated here within the theory of architectural autopoiesis. According to this model, problems

25 Walter R Reitman, *Cognition and Thought – An Information Processing Approach*, p 126.
26 Ibid, p 1.

exist in the form of problem situations. The ***problem situation*** comprises two independent components: the ***task environment*** and the ***information-processing system*** (IPS).[27] The general characteristics of information-processing systems can be summarized succinctly. An information-processing system (IPS) is conceived as a system of functions that is required to process information. It comprises the following functional components:

- a ***processor*** operates on ***symbol structures*** by means of a set of ***elementary information processes*** (eip); the processor has a ***short-term memory*** (STM) to hold the input and output symbols of the current set of information processes; the processor also comprises an ***interpreter*** that determines the sequence of eips to be executed as a function of the symbol structures held in the STM
- a **(long term)** ***memory*** (LTM) capable of retaining symbol structures for later retrieval by the processor
- plus ***receptors*** and ***effectors*** to interact with an external environment

The listed functional components can be transposed to the design process situation as follows. The two poles of the problem situation – task environment and IPS – can be identified with the project (understood as internal communication system) taking the position of the IPS, and the client's life-process (understood as external communication system) taking the position of the task environment. The processor is the design team.[28] The symbol system can be identified with the chosen design medium. The symbol structures operated upon are the digital drawings/models that are employed to progress the design. The eips of the design process are the standard operations that are afforded via the tools of the chosen CAD system. The LTM resides in the accumulated explicit knowledge and the implicit collective intelligence of the design team, backed up by the information encoded in the communication structures of the discipline. The receptors and effectors that interact with the external environment reside in project meetings with the client or the client's representative.

27 This first distinction already raises the difficult question of whether a theory of problem solving is really a theory about the nature of the cognitive system or a theory about the nature of the problem domain. Newell & Simon state: 'The total system always includes both environment and organism.' Newell & Simon, *Human Problem Solving*, p 14.

28 The design team is comprised of individual designers. Within the theory of architectural autopoiesis, the underlying human beings remain black boxes, unanalyzed entities that exist in architecture's environment as an underlying condition. They enter the communication process only as points of reference and attribution.

Elementary information processes (eips) are also referred to as types of elementary operations. Information processes operate on symbol structures by taking a symbol structure as input and returning another symbol structure as output. *Elementary* here means that these processes are not further analyzed into yet simpler processes. The entire (internal) behaviour of the IPS is compounded out of sequences of eips. With respect to the set of eips, Newell and Simon demand that 'there must be a sufficiently general and powerful collection of operations to compose out of them all the macroscopic performances of the IPS. Furthermore, it is essential that these elementary processes be well-defined, ie, realizable by known mechanisms. Otherwise there is no point in taking them as primitive. For example, there is no point in taking solve-problem as eip. A system with such a primitive would tell us nothing about how problem solving is actually accomplished.'[29] Newell and Simon posited particular eips to cope with the specific AI task environments they investigated: logic proofs, mathematical puzzles and chess playing. Other elementary processes have to be assumed to explicate design within an architectural theory of the design process. They will not necessarily be tied to the requirement of being computationally implementable. Although computational realization is a desirable property, and in principle a healthy theoretical aim, it would be far too strong a stricture in the domain of architectural design. In particular, the analysis of the fine structure of early, conceptual design processes by means of freehand sketching must rely on positing elemental design operations that have not as yet been demonstrated to be machine implementable. Thus while a design process theory will add new elementary operations, it will also skip over many of the elementary operations featured in Newell and Simon which are too basic to be of much use and interest in the context of design, for example, the operation to find the item that follows on from a given item within a given list-structure, or the operation to test if two given symbol tokens are identical, ie, whether they are instances of the same symbol type.[30]

29 Newell & Simon, *Human Problem Solving*, p 29.

30 The distinction between ***symbol tokens*** as the concrete instantiations of ideal ***symbol types*** stems from Charles Sanders Peirce. The distinction seems trivial but leads into philosophical quicksand once we deal with ambiguous symbolic practices like sketching. Peirce explained the distinction of type vs token as follows: 'There is but one word "the" in the English language; and it is impossible that this word should lie visibly on a page or be heard in any voice, for the reason that it is not a Single thing or Single event. It does not exist; it only determines things that do exist. Such a definitely significant Form, I propose to term a *Type*. A single event *which happens* once and whose identity is limited to that one happening or a single object or thing which is in some single place at any one instant of time, such event or thing

Symbols are discrete, indivisible elements. They constitute the ***primitives*** of symbol systems.[31] Within design contexts the primitives of the symbol system are the primitives of the chosen CAD system. ***Symbol structures*** are defined as sets of (primitive) symbol tokens that are placed into certain syntactic relations. A symbol structure is said to ***designate***, or ***refer to*** an ***object.*** This relationship of reference is another philosophical quicksand. Newell and Simon, in sound reductionist manner, make this relationship dependent upon the availability of information processes. This works well if the designated objects are internal to the IPS, ie, if the objects referred to are themselves either symbol structures or information processes. However, designation becomes vague and simplistic in relation to objects in the external environment. The hint that receptors and effectors can achieve reference is clearly inadequate. However, since Newell and Simon are mostly concerned with 'central processes', they are primarily concerned with symbol structures that designate other structures within the IPS and are therefore 'concerned less frequently with symbol structures that designate external stimuli or responses, for at the time we deal with them, stimuli and responses in the external environment will already be encoded internally – designated by symbol structures'. This focus on internal designations also suits the analysis of the design process because most instances of referencing can be interpreted as internal references, for example, a wall section can be interpreted to refer to the corresponding wall object in the 3D master model rather than to the (non-existent) 'physical' wall yet to be constructed. Operationally the correctness of the section depends upon the 3D model.

7.3.3 PROGRAMMES

A ***programme*** is a symbol structure that designates an information process on the basis of a given input. The interpreter executes the designated

being significant only as occurring just when and where it does, such as this or that word on a single line of a single page of a single copy of a book, I will venture to call a *Token*. . . . In order that a Type may be used, it has to be embodied in a Token which shall be a sign of the Type, and thereby of the object the Type signifies. I propose to call such a Token of a Type an *Instance* of the Type.' Charles S Peirce, *Prolegomena to an Apology for Pragmaticism*, 1906, in: Charles S Peirce, *Philosophy of Mathematics – Selected Writings*, Indiana University Press (Bloomington/Indianapolis), 2010.

In line with their reductionist research programme Newell & Simon set the symbol token primary and let the symbol type emerge from the elementary process that detects and establishes symbol identity.

31 According to these definitions, in the symbol system of alphabetical writing, the letters of the alphabet are the primitive symbols, and the written words, sentences and texts are possible symbol structures.

process. Thus the symbol structures held in either the STM or LTM of the IPS are of two kinds: they are either ***programmes*** or ***data-structures***. Data-structures are thus all symbol structures that are not programmes. Thus there are three types of internal ***objects*** that might be referred to by means of symbol structures: programmes, data-structures and operations. Above we identified the eips with CAD tools. The concept of programme introduced here can be identified with rules guiding/instructing the specific use of CAD tools (output) on the basis of given design states (inputs). The concept of programme also comprises scripts that drive information processes on the basis of input data-structures.

Is there a fundamental set of necessary and sufficient eips that could account for and cover the totality of problem-solving behaviour? Or is it necessary to keep the set of eips open-ended in order to add new kinds of processes whenever a new problem domain poses a new task? According to Newell and Simon neither assumption is adequate: 'It is one of the major foundation stones of computer science that a relatively small set of elementary processes suffices to produce the full generality of information processing. The general purpose flexibility of the digital computer rests firmly on this foundation stone. On the other hand there turns out to be no *unique* basis. Rather there are many ways in which adequate sets of elementary processes can be chosen (in conjunction with corresponding schemes of composition).'[32] Similarly, albeit on a higher level of aggregation (compared with the basic eips of universal computation), all (currently) available design operations can be reduced to a set of elementary operations or tools. Again, there is no unique set of eips.

Newell and Simon defined the concept of ***programme*** as a symbol structure that designates an information process. This concept is expanded here in line with the prior use of the concept of programme within the theory of architectural autopoiesis. The programme consists of a set of rules that stipulate sequences of operations as a function of the informational context. We can think of a given IPS, involving a design-team-tool complex (including virtuoso Maya users), as being 'programmed' to tackle a particular type of design problem. We must analyze the 'programme' to understand how the IPS solves a problem. Because the programme is executed recursively, a finite programme delivers infinite communicative sequences. Conditional statements are a fundamental component of all programmes. Discriminations are made by carrying out a test or comparison and then branching to the step indicated by the conditional statement. Programmes also contain loops and loops within loops. Each loop must contain at least one conditional branch

32 Newell & Simon, *Human Problem Solving*, p 29.

process so that, when the condition is satisfied, the programme can branch out of the loop to terminate or continue further beyond the loop.

When observing a simple adaptive behaviour of an organism or mechanism within an environment it is not always easy to distinguish whether there is just a simple feedback mechanism or an IPS articulated with the specialized subparts of memory, interpreter and programme. The simple feedback model was underlying behaviourism. The limitations for such a model with respect to accounting for more complex behaviours led to the cognitive revolution in psychology. It was clear that human behaviour could not be reduced to an accumulation of conditioned stimulus-response mechanisms. Chomsky's point about the infinite variability of meaningful language production was a case in point. Hard-wired mechanisms alone are not enough to account for the flexibility of language responses. But even within a programmed IPS there must be some direct mechanisms. These mechanisms constitute the interpreter that mediates between programme and the execution of the elementary information processes. Newell and Simon: 'In analysing the behaviour of an information processing system, it is not always possible to draw a sharp boundary between the part of the system that is to be regarded as a simple mechanism and the part that is best viewed as governed by an interpreted programme. ... The important characteristic of an interpreter is that it replaces a large amount of mechanism by a small amount (the interpreter proper), plus a large amount of symbolic structure. Then, in spite of the simplicity of its interpreter, the behaviour that an IPS can exhibit is limited only by the complexity of the symbol structures that can be built up. ... The limitations of behaviour all reside in the content of the programmes stored in the IPS, and are not inherent features of the IPS itself. There are, of course, limits on the speed at which the IPS can accomplish complex endeavours, for these may require very long sequences of eips, and there may be no way of speeding up elementary processes.'[33]

It is this articulated structure of intelligence whereby a specialized subsystem receives or builds programmes within some kind of symbolic domain that accounts for the great flexibility and seemingly unlimited malleability of human intelligence. The fixed interpreter must unravel the variable programme statements into a sequence of elementary operations. It seems what happens when we 'understand' and respond to language can be described as interpreting a programme. However, what should always be remembered, and this in insufficiently reflected in Newell and Simon, is that the 'programmes' – the crucial site and source of

33 Ibid, p 34.

open-ended intelligence – are formed and elaborated by social communication systems on the basis of symbol systems like the spoken language, writing, mathematics, graphics, as well as the built environment and the world of artefacts in as much as they operate as semiotic systems and participate in the constitution of discursive formations. One might say that the programmes of rational behaviour are indeed condensed within these symbol systems. But this would still be an all too reifying conception, akin to Structuralist formulations. It is only the physical residues of these systems that exist in the straightforward way of being present and persistent. The full systems only exist in a distributed traffic pattern of the ephemeral communications that these physical systems participate within. The interpreter (as part of the processor) resides in the relatively fixed and simple organismic/psychic systems. However, although the organismic/psychic systems obviously have their fixed, genetically and physiologically determined base, they are also subject to transformation. Through socialization and learning, these biological/psychic processing units are drawn along with the overall socio-cultural (societal) evolution. These systems learn to speak, read, write, calculate, design etc. The variable and complex content for these basic interpretative processes is furnished by the total social process. Compared with the full complexity, flexibility and openness of the social communication system, the organismic/psychic systems remain simple and rigid.[34] As alluded to above, the design process theory developed here considers the design project (understood as communication system) to be the IPS. The designers – organisms operating a design medium – are the processors that operate on symbol structures via programmes. (The theory, for most of its discourse, leaves the designers and their cognitive processes behind as black boxes.) These programmes exist on multiple levels of aggregation and complexity. On the most basic level these programmes are simple conditional rules that condition/trigger the designer's specific use of CAD tools (eips), for example, a rule that instructs the designer to tessellate surfaces beyond a certain size. These low-level programmes can often be implemented via scripts.

If we take a step back from the minutiae of the design's progress and consider larger design steps, understood as design decisions involving evaluation within a discursive design deliberation within the project team, then the concept of programme elaborated here can be identified with the

34 The contribution of any single organismic/psychic system – even of the most original and proliferous individual – is next to negligible in comparison with the vastness of the total social system.

concept of style introduced in Volume 1 understood as communication structure that is necessary to programme the double code of utility and beauty. The concept might indeed be identified with the programmes that regulate the application of the code values functional vs dysfunctional and formally resolved vs formally unresolved. In this expanded interpretation that is required when we overview the design process more broadly, the programme constitutes the heuristic principles that define the style within which the design team works. The style is the programme that ultimately regulates the individual design decisions. In this case the interpreter of the programme is the self-socialized design team (consisting of pre-socialized designers) with its evolving, shared formal and functional biases and typical turns of argument and dispute resolution. This is the most involved and far-reaching understanding of the distinction between programme and interpreter. The programme on the level of style would, for example, demand that each new design step should involve a further gradient differentiation as well as further correlations as condition for the design's continued positive assessment as 'formally resolved'. This overarching programme might then be concretized via specific low-level programmes that implement the general demand of the style, for example, one specific programme/rule might instruct to tessellate all surfaces beyond a certain size relative to their curvature: the stronger the curvature, the finer the tessellation.

The problem here is that the general framework for design process analysis must remain abstract and general enough to allow for the fact that the analysis must move from the investigation of micro-processes to macro-overviews. The theory of architectural autopoiesis allows all the introduced concepts, including the concept of programme, to float between these two poles: the most myopic, detail-oriented analysis of design processes on the one hand, and the most overview- and principle-oriented analysis and critique on the other. In the first case the programme can be identified with a single CAD tool, or script, in the second case the programme must be identified with the chosen style.

This way of understanding programmes considerably expands Newell and Simon's concept. This is the consequence of the conceptual transformation of Newell and Simon's conceptual apparatus within a theory built upon the primacy of social communication systems. Newell and Simon have drawn the line between interpreter and programme within the IPS, understood as the thinking human being, and/or within the digital computer (supposedly) simulating human problem solving. Their theory offers no account of where and how the crucial programmes emerge. Another corollary of expanding the concept is that the operations that the programme conditions are less microscopic than those stipulated by Newell and Simon. The same goes for the set of elementary operations. (Newell and Simon themselves often find it convenient to take processes as primitive that can also be expressed in terms of still more primitive processes.)[35] The line between what is taken as a primitive operation versus what is taken as composed and therefore analyzable into more simple, underlying processes is considerably shifted towards higher order operations.

The theoretical transposition of Newell and Simon's conceptual apparatus is necessary due to the specific application of the apparatus within a theory of design with its own particular research agenda. Newell and Simon's theory is a constructive-explanatory theory of human problem solving (initially only tested in the domain of formal reasoning)[36] that aims to get at the internal cognitive processes within human subjects. In contrast, the theory developed here is only initially descriptive-explanatory. It soon becomes a normative theory of design that aims to describe, explain and then recommend certain design processes. There is no intention here to theorize the designer's base level cognitive processes, just as there is no intention here to look into the very base algorithms of the digital tools that the designer uses.[37] What concerns the theory of the design process are design specific information processes understood as design decisions (communications) that are progressed within certain design media (symbol systems) offering certain design moves (eips), and that are regulated by programmes.[38]

7.3.4 THE TASK ENVIRONMENT AND ITS REPRESENTATION AS PROBLEM SPACE

Rational or ***adaptive*** action might be defined as a behaviour that is 'appropriate to the goal in the light of the problem environment; it is the

35 Newell & Simon, *Human Problem Solving*, p 67.

36 In fact, it is a descriptive-explanatory theory that is aware of its limited ability to generalize, and therefore is explicitly stated as a theory of individual problem-solving cases. This is indeed a highly unusual stance for a scientific endeavour. To offer a theoretical model literally: 'for the behaviour of a single individual in a single task situation. Full particularity is the rule, not the exception. Thus, it becomes a problem to get back from this particularity to theories that describe a class of humans, or to processes and mechanisms that are general to all humans.' Ibid, p 10.

37 With these contrasts stated, one might wonder, why the theory starts with Newell & Simon's apparatus in the first place? The reason is twofold: first, despite the differences of intent and focus, the apparatus works very well as basis for a design process theory. This will transpire as the theory is being built up. Second, as mentioned in the historical overview above, the apparatus has already left its mark on architectural theory, and there are prior theoretical efforts, both empirico-analytical as well as normative, that can be taken into account.

38 This conceptual apparatus is supposed to facilitate design process descriptions. To assess the rationality of these processes, further concepts are required.

behaviour demanded by the situation'.[39] As Newell and Simon point out: 'if there is such a thing as the behaviour demanded by a situation, and if a subject exhibits it, then this behaviour tells us more about the task environment than about him'.[40] Economics is an approach that focuses all its analytical effort on the analysis of the task environment by assuming rational and omniscient economic actors with given utility functions. It was Herbert Simon's contribution to the field of economic theory to challenge unrealistic presumptions about rationality with the realistic concept of 'bounded rationality'[41] that recognizes the fact that the rationality of individuals (or business organizations) is constrained or bounded by the information accessible to them, their cognitive (computational) limitations and the finite amount of time they have to arrive at decisions. Decisions arrived at on this real basis obviously deviate from the abstract ideal of optimizing rationality. 'It is precisely when we begin to ask *why* the properly motivated subject does not behave in the manner predicted in the rational model that we recross the boundary again from a theory of the task environment to a psychological theory of human rationality. The explanation must lie inside the subject: in the limits of his ability to determine what the optimal behavior is.'[42] We therefore have to recognize that we observe *intendedly* rational behaviour. Its rationality is inevitably bounded rationality. These considerations lead to a 'two-bladed theory'[43] that can predict behaviour only if it combines an analysis of the structure of the task environment with an analysis of the limits of rational adaptation to task environments. These two aspects, the demands of the task environment on the one hand, and the cognitive constitution of the IPS on the other are, according to Newell and Simon, 'like figure and ground – although which is which depends on the momentary viewpoint'.[44]

The term ***task environment*** refers to the external environment of the IPS coupled with the goal, task or problem of the IPS, ie, only those aspects of the total environment are considered that are task-relevant. 'It is the task that defines a point of view about an environment, and that in fact allows an environment to be delimited.'[45] We have to ask whose point of

39 Allen Newell & Herbert A Simon, *Human Problem Solving*, p 53. Newell and Simon do not distinguish between behaviour and action.

40 Ibid.

41 Herbert A Simon, *Administrative Behavior – A Study of Decision-Making Processes in Administrative Organizations*, The Free Press (New York), 1945.

42 Newell & Simon, *Human Problem Solving*, p 55.

43 Ibid.

44 Ibid.

45 Ibid.

view is being referred to here? Who is describing the external environment with respect to the task posed? Once this question is raised it becomes clear that a distinction has to be made between the task environment as it is described by an external observer and the task environment as it appears to the information-processing system that is expected to solve the task. Newell and Simon reserve the term task environment for what is observed and analyzed by the external observer or theorist. For the task environment as it appears to the information-processing system, they propose the term ***problem space***. The IPS's problem-solving behaviour is described as taking place within the problem space. Newell and Simon use the term 'space' because an adequate description of problem-solving behaviour makes it necessary to describe not only actual actions, but the set of possible actions from which these were drawn, ie, the specific universe of possibilities in which the solution is to be found. The attempt to describe such a space amounts to 'constructing a representation of the task environment – the subject's representation in this case'.[46] The concept of problem space refers to how the IPS represents the problem internally. Whether and how a problem can be solved by the IPS depends on the system of representation through which the task environment is encoded to become the problem space for the IPS. The problem-solving system is confronted with a problem situation, for example, a design brief interpreting the client's ambitions and a set of graphical documents representing the site and context. Before starting with the problem-solving process proper, the IPS must 'encode these problem components – defining goals, rules, and other aspects of the situation – in some kind of space that represents the initial situation presented to him, the desired goal situation, various intermediate states, imagined or experienced, as well as any concepts he uses to describe these situations to himself'.[47] One might say that the issue of encoding is itself a crucial part of the problem, sometimes even the most crucial aspect and bottleneck of the whole problem-solving challenge. In certain formally definable problem domains like games there might be several different problem representations available that are logically equivalent, for example, an arithmetical versus a geometric representation, that make a difference in terms of efficiency of information processing for a given IPS. An IPS might have a choice of possible representations and thus problem spaces at its disposal. In this case one might take the conjunction of those problem spaces to be the overall problem space within which the IPS starts to operate. The availability of an adequate and powerful

46 Ibid, p 59.
47 Ibid.

medium is thus one of the key factors that determine the performance and success of any IPS.

At this point a philosophical blind spot appears that cannot be eradicated. Newell and Simon are aware of this point: 'In talking about the task environment we must maintain clear distinctions among the environment itself (the Kantian *Ding an sich*, as it were), the internal representation of the task environment used by the subject (the problem space), and the theorist's "objective" description of that environment. This is the classical problem in psychology of defining the effective stimulus.'[48]

This is the problem that lies at the very origin of the theory of autopoietic systems. The difficulty emerged in the late 1950s in the context of experiments in the psychology and biology of perception conducted by Lettvin, Maturana, McCulloch and Pitts.[49] It was Maturana who later inferred the key conceptual consequences. In a close examination of the frog's visual nerve under various stimuli, Lettvin et al were confronted by the difficulty to precisely correlate stimulus and response. It seemed to be extremely difficult to establish systematic correlations between the supposed stimulus and the responses of the frog's visual system as observed (via measurements conducted on the frog's optic nerve). The fundamental difficulty in determining *how* the frog's visual system discriminates is the uncertainty about *what* the visual system discriminates, ie, what of the manifold of the environment should be counted as effective input. Stimulus and response form a closed system that an outside observer cannot break into. No matter how resourceful the external observer is, no matter how sharp and how multiplicitous his/her arsenal of description and measurement, there are always further ways to observe, describe and measure the supposedly external 'input' to the frog's visual system. Maturana finally (later) shifted paradigm. He refused to assume that the external environment can be observed, described and measured in an 'objective' way that would be valid or relevant across species. Frog and researcher were juxtaposed as different closed systems, each constituting its own environment. He concluded that the units and features that are identified are always 'units of interaction'[50] of a specifically constituted observer/organism.

48 Ibid, p 56.

49 See JY Lettvin, HR Maturana, WS McCulloch, and WH Pitts, 'What the Frog's Eye tells the Frog's Brain', in: *The Mind: Biological Approaches to its Functions*, ed William C Corning & Martin Balaban, John Wiley & Sons (New York), 1968, pp 233–58.

50 Humberto R Maturana & Francisco J Varela, *Autopoiesis and Cognition – The Realization of the Living*, Reidel Publishing Company (Dordrecht), 1980.

Organisms/observers are self-referentially closed. What constitutes a relevant unit or, more broadly, an effective environment for an organism/observer depends on the constitution of the organism/observer. According to Maturana the very process of life always involves this kind of world-constituting cognition. This leads to a radically expanded and transposed concept of cognition and to the fundamental concept of living systems as autopoietic systems. The concept of autopoiesis is also fundamental for theorizing how a 'given' task environment is transcoded into the IPS's problem space. The task environment 'itself' (*Ding an sich*) is an empty, asymptotic concept. It vanishes in the uncontainable infinity of its potential representations. There are only problem spaces and their (observed) relations. An observer might attempt to construct mappings between various observed, attributed or postulated problem spaces.

In the case of modern and contemporary design processes, the organism as observer must be substituted by the social communication system as observer. The IPS that is being modelled here must be interpreted as such a social communication system. Niklas Luhmann has transposed the centre of reference for the concept of autopoiesis from organic to social systems. The theory of architectural autopoiesis follows this lead. This is also relevant and pertinent here in the context of a theory of the design process. Problem representation and problem solving – especially on the level of such a complex endeavour as designing the built environment – can only be adequately theorized as accomplishment of an autopoietic communication system, geared up with its whole panoply of communication structures.

The general concept of observing systems includes living systems, psychological systems and social systems. All these are autopoietic systems. When an observing system observes how other observing systems observe their respective environments, it reconstitutes these systems and their relationship to their environment as a function of its own constitution. The observing system – if it is sufficiently complex – can reflect this fact. This process of reflection utilizes new observational resources that must themselves remain unobserved at that moment. Here in lies the blind spot of all observation, cognition or thinking. Kant's philosophy of the subject tried to overcome the issue by assuming an effortless self-transparency of consciousness, and claiming that the 'I think' accompanies all apperceptions. Luhmann's insistence on the ineradicability of the blind spot recognizes that all cognition, taken as a process, takes time and is burdened by limited information-processing capacity. Although the 'I think', and any further reflection upon the a priori constitution of an observation, might be a possibility if the observing system has the respective cognitive/conceptual resources, it surely takes further effort and time. This is especially clear in the case of a communication process. Here an additional round of communications must be gone through. This new round of communications introduces new concepts that must be presupposed within this round, and the reflection of which would require a further round with further concepts etc. A blind spot remains. However, there is a crucial advantage in observing communication systems rather than organisms or the supposed mental processes of psychic systems: communication processes are not hidden in brains or minds. Although communications are complex relational entities, ie, their identity depends on distributed networks of communication events stretched out across time, they are in principle open to observation, rather than requiring hypothetical reconstruction via theoretical models.

Newell and Simon had already put their finger on the point that led Maturana to the concept of autopoiesis. Newell and Simon seem to have realized that it is impossible to maintain an objective notion of stimulus or environment: 'All sorts of alternative encodings are conceivable. ... To say, then, that a stimulus can be described adequately means that we can predict the vocabulary of elements and relations the subject will use in its initial encoding of it. The description no longer refers exclusively to the stimulus; it postulates something also about the first stages of processing that the stimulus will undergo as it is perceived by the subject. ... It need not be assumed, however, that the initial encoding of the stimulus will bear any close relation to the way in which it is represented internally in the subject's processing of it at some later stage. The stimulus may – and usually will – be subjected to further transformations as the subject seeks a convenient internal representation – one that he can process relatively easily.'[51] The differentiation between initial and further encoding is immaterial in what is at stake here: the need to bracket (if not abandon) the simplifying notion of a 'given' problem or task environment as touchstone for the various problem spaces that might be constructed and compared.

The conclusion we derive from this can be formulated as a set of premises for all further design process theorizing that follows:

- Instead of assuming objectively given task environments for architectural projects we assume the possibility of constructing multiple competing problem spaces. These problem spaces comprise three (semi-independent) subsystems: an interpretative ***conceptual system***

51 Newell & Simon, *Human Problem Solving*, pp 58–9.

(conceptual space), a generative ***modelling system*** (design space) and an immanent ***evaluation system*** (value space).
- The competing problem spaces and their underlying representational systems can be compared on a number of immanent counts: internal coherence, conceptual richness, information-processing capacity, ease of intuitive handling etc, without requiring reference to an assumed external task environment.
- The question of adequacy with respect to the external task environment leads the discussion beyond the concerns of any individual project. In general, reference to the external environment is mediated via the historically evolving communication structures of the autopoiesis of architecture. More specifically, the project's external reference is mediated via the functional heuristics of the chosen style. Therefore, in order to give guidance about how to move beyond immanent comparisons, the theory must turn normative to be able to propose a set of definite criteria that allows the evaluation of the environmental (societal) adequacy of any given problem space. For this purpose the notion of task environment is reintroduced as a necessary complement to the concept of possible problem spaces. This concept is made concrete within an explicitly normative outlook on the character of the tasks that confront architecture within contemporary society, theorized as Postfordist network society.[52]

The key problem that underlies the criteria for assessing task-environment adequacy is the problem of social complexity. A second key problem is the problem of task novelty. The design process theory must refer back to the theory of architecture's task developed in part 6, and evaluate design problem spaces (and then the design processes unfolding within these spaces) with respect to their ability to progress designs that can organize and articulate the required social complexity. The term 'task environment' should thus read 'relevant task environment as conceptualized within the normative task scheme proposed within the theory of architectural autopoiesis'. This normative task scheme is operationalized in the heuristics of Parametricism.[53] Before engaging with the particulars of Parametricism, the theory must initially remain more general, more abstract, without any explicit presumptions about the style that must be presupposed in any concrete project. The design

52 The theory is explicitly aligned with the specific contemporary style that is being promoted here: Parametricism. A normative understanding of Parametricism, ie, Parametricism as it should be rather than as it already is, is indeed the attractor and point of convergence and culmination of all theoretical strands that are woven together here.

53 Parametricism will be fully elaborated in the final part of this book.

process theory must first build up a general framework for describing design processes, and on this basis try to identify plausible criteria for evaluating design processes. The concept of problem spaces and the question of their task adequacy are central components of this general framework.

7.3.5 PROBLEM SOLVING AS SEARCH IN A STATE SPACE

In order to compare and assess the multiplicity of problem spaces, it is necessary to introduce a general conceptual schema that affords a formula for describing problem spaces. This schema must be sufficiently abstract and general to cover all empirical (and conceivable) problem spaces that have been (or might be) used within an architectural design project. The schema proposed here is the state space representation of problem spaces. This schema is once more drawn from Newell and Simon's work on human problem solving.

The ***state space schema*** for representing problem spaces, and for describing problem-solving processes, proposes that every problem, and thus every design problem, can be defined through the following components: ***initial state***, ***goal state*** and ***intermediate states***. Above we asserted with Reitman that a system has a problem when it has been given a description of something but does not yet have anything that satisfies the description. The 'given' (encoded) description points to the ***goal state***, the solution of the stated problem. Many problems, in particular all design problems considered here, do not allow for an instant, single-step positing of candidates for the goal state. A series of ***intermediate states*** is necessary. It is via these intermediate states that the goal state is approached. Initial states, intermediate states and goal states are symbol structures. The problem-solving process can then be conceptualized as an information-processing process that applies information-processing operators to ***transform*** the initial state into the goal state via an arbitrary number of intermediate states. State transformations might be compound (rather than elementary) operations.

A full description of the total problem-solving process would then comprise at least a description of the initial state, followed by a description of all intermediate states and of the goal state. It would also comprise the full sequence of operations. The sequence of states is called the ***solution path***. The sequence of operations is called the ***solution action sequence***. However, the mere description of solution path and solution action sequence would be insufficient to evaluate the rationality of a problem-solving process. Evaluation requires an account of the alternatives that were available and considered at each point in the sequence of state transformations, as well as the decision criteria brought to bear at each decision point. An interesting, informative account that would start to do justice to the problem-solving process as intelligent, rational decision process would further specify the rationale of selection at each point, ie, whether the selection of the next transformation was random or determinate, following some kind of rule or principle, or was perhaps a random selection from a systematically narrowed/constrained set of operational options etc. The process description thus has to advance to the identification of the underlying method. Further, such an account would also include a general characterization of the structure of the problem space as search space with particular topography and characteristics, ie, as structured universe of possibilities.

The problem space contains the initial state, all possible, satisfactory goal states, and all intermediate states that can be generated during the course of the design, whether they lead to a satisfactory goal state or not. All these states might be called possible ***problem states***. The problem space is then the total set of possible problem states. How are the terms of this apparatus to be applied to design processes? The goal state might be a complete set of construction documents that meets certain initially stated requirements for a building, or the goal state might be a desired concept design to be submitted to a design competition. In the latter case the ***initial state*** would be the set of competition documents including schedule of accommodation, adjacency diagrams and site plan. The intermediate states would be the various states of the digital design model through which the design is progressed, via state transformations. All these states have the required form of symbol structures, if we sufficiently expand the notion of symbol system[54] defined by Newell and Simon. In the discussion of state transformations in design processes, it is convenient to discuss compound rather than elementary operations, ie, multiple, integrated sequences of symbol manipulations that form a meaningful design step. Assuming a problem space with one privileged modelling system, for example, a particular CAD system, one might regard the set of CAD tools (operators/modifiers) as the primary set of elementary information processes (eip) available within the assumed problem space. Although the available toolset – in particular the availability of scripting – is an important aspect of the design world to be considered, the discussion of the design process might only rarely have occasion to refer to individual employment of specific modifiers. Scripts are a different matter – they might encompass considerable transformations in one computation, potentially condensing hundreds or thousands of individual

54 Vinod Goel's critique and formalized expansion of Newell and Simon's all too restrictive formal requirements for symbolic systems will be introduced and appropriated below.

elementary transformations. In fact, it seems appropriate to treat the creation of various scripts as an important design episode within the overall design process, setting its own sub-goal/subproblem and requiring its own sub-phases of conception and detailed decision making.[55] These initial reflections already show that the fineness or coarseness with which the design process is to be analyzed into intermediate problem states must be left open, and will depend on the specific focus of the respective analysis. There can be no one-fits-all definition that would allow for the individuation of intermediate states and state transformations.

Ömer Akin, one of the architectural theorists who has adopted Newell and Simon's state space concept, defines problem states as follows: 'A state is the totality of all information relevant to the problem solving process and available to the IPS at any given instance.'[56] He goes on to suggest that 'this information usually includes all dependent and independent variables of the problem, their values, criteria of evaluation, constraints of the problem, and the goals of the IPS'.[57] If one accepts this definition then the following questions can be posed with respect to any given or proposed problem space: how much of the ultimately relevant information is available within the early stages (states) of the design? And in which form is this information available, ie, how readily accessible is this information when design decisions are to be made by transforming the current into the subsequent state? How far should the definition of 'available information' be stretched? Does it include information stored in the design team's product library, or only the set of brochures pulled out onto the designer's desk for current inspection? Or should the definition of the state be restricted to digital product details and specs that are digitally referenced to the digital design model? To give a formalized definition is difficult here. It certainly seems artificial to restrict the state to a single integrated CAD or even BIM model. In particular, at the earlier design stages information is more scattered. Yet, the information seems to be there to the extent to which it is consulted and considered in the selection of the follow-on state. This means that one cannot readily detect and overview the informational extent of the state without observing what happens during the state transformation process. In any case, rather than trying to impose an operationally clean, formal definition – which would have to be rather restrictive – it might be

55 The final code-writing is left aside here as merely technical task – notwithstanding its high demands on skill and ingenuity. The ingenuity demonstrated here is not architectural ingenuity.

56 Ömer Akin, *Psychology of Architectural Design*, p 14.

57 Ibid.

possible to introduce the gist of the concept via illustrations and aid the description by further concepts, for example, by the concept ***degree of informational integration***. It surely makes a difference whether the designer (or design team) has to consult a collection of separate documents (separate plans, sections, elevations, structural documents, schedules of quantities) or whether most of the relevant information is integrated in a single model automatically cross-referencing the involved panoply of informations. Assuming the same total amount of information is available in both set ups, the second set up has a higher degree of informational integration. This comparative concept (ordinal, not quantitative) can then be used to compare and assess competing problem spaces. One might assume that a higher degree of informational integration increases the information-processing speed and reduces the risk of abortive work. However, neither a large amount of available information, nor a high degree of informational integration should necessarily be an advantage at all design stages. During the early design stages, both measures might overburden the designer and design team because too many aspects and criteria might have to be considered and/or defined in conjunction to make the next step. Design progress might thus be obstructed or blocked by too much information. Sometimes it might be better if the modelling system allows plans, sections and elevations to be considered separately, deferring the issue of their coordination.

To summarize, the following loose definitions are proposed. These definitions are here already tailored to the special case of problem solving in the domain of architectural design.

problem space — The problem space is the IPS's internal representation of the problem and task environment. All problem solving of the IPS is bound within the problem space. The problem space delimits the universe of possibilities that is being explored during the design process. It depends on the conceptual system, the modelling system and the evaluation system that are deployed by the problem-solving process. Thus we might distinguish the conceptual space, the design (modelling) space and the value space as aspects of the problem space. The problem space contains the total set of all *possible* problem states. This also includes non-feasible states. Everything is a possible state that can be reached via legitimate state transformations. The set of admitted transformational operators is entailed within the definition of a problem space. The definition of the problem space as set does not mean that the problem space is merely an unstructured collection. The problem space has a structure to the extent that problem states are located on possible paths. Although more than one path might exist that leads to a particular problem state, the assumption is that problem states cannot be jumped to. They can only be reached via certain sequences of transformations. Within the total problem space there is always a certain (relatively small) region that is the subset of all possible goal states, ie, the subset of all states that somehow satisfy the requirements and expectations associated with the design task and that therefore can be considered as solutions to the design problem posed. This solution subset might be a compact region within the problem space, or it might be fragmented and distributed across multiple zones.

problem state A problem state is the totality of all readily available information relevant to the problem-solving process at any given instance. Problem states are formulated via symbolic systems. In a complex design process, the formulation of each problem state usually requires the deployment of multiple symbolic systems. We must distinguish at least three symbolic systems corresponding to the conceptual, modelling and evaluation system. The actual problem states that the design process traverses can be categorized into three types: the initial state, the intermediate state and the goal state.

initial state The initial state is the internal problem space representation of the design task. The initial state comprises information about the broad requirements and expectations that define the design project. It further comprises both general constraints and conditions as well as a project-specific set of constraints and conditions that must be observed. Problems within the domain of architectural design are extremely information rich.[58] Therefore within this domain, problem requirements, expectations as well as constraints and conditions are only broadly stated at the initial state. The complexity and richness of architectural design problems imply that there can be no exhaustive statement of the totality of relevant project information at the outset. Even if the total information could be somehow stated, in which sense would such an immense volume of information be readily available to the IPS? How could such an immense volume of information be processed in a single state transformation? How can this information be funnelled into the first design move? The disaggregation of this information into a sequential process is inevitable.

intermediate state

All intermediate states are generated via state transformations from prior states. The intermediate states are all those problem states that are located on the solution path the design process is taking. This includes detours and backtracking, ie, the abortive branches of the path. Intermediate states exist within an ordered sequence. Within a design team, intermediate states might be decomposed into parts (sub-projects) that can be progressed in parallel, albeit without altogether losing communicative connection. In this case the notion of an overall problem state can still be maintained, although the degree of informational integration is reduced and the risk of abortive work increases. Within the domain of architectural design, the progression of intermediate states involves both a reduction in information that was potentially relevant as well as an increase in relevant information that is still relevant. General information is transformed into more specific information. As the design decision process narrows down the options, uncertainty is

58 In comparison mathematical problems, for example, the task to find/construct a proof for a given theorem on the basis of a small set of axioms and definitions, are extremely information poor.

absorbed and certain bodies of information that were required to make earlier design decisions recede into the background (although this induces the risk that criteria that were brought to bear on these decisions might be contravened at later, more detailed decisions). At the same time, both the required and the embodied information increase as the level of detail increases. More detail implies new conceptual information, as well as more modelled information and the need for much more evaluative information. Thus intermediate states are not informationally equivalent. There is both injection of new information as well as ejection of old information. Initially scattered information about requirements and contracts is converted into detailed information about the emerging solution/design.

goal state The actual goal state, also referred to as the solution state or terminal state, is the problem state at which the design process terminates because the requirements and expectations that were stated in the initial state, as well as all further, detailed requirements and expectations that transpired during the design process, are met reasonably well. In the domain of architectural design no problem has a unique, predetermined goal state. There are always multiple possible solutions or goal states that can be envisioned. These possible solutions might be radically dissimilar to each other. Architectural design competitions document this fact. This radical openness is a special characteristic of architectural design projects. With any non-trivial architectural design problem, there is little point in trying to anticipate the final form.

state transformations State transformations are the design moves by which the design process progresses towards the goal state. State transformations transform one problem state into the subsequent problem state. We might distinguish *lateral transformations* from *vertical transformations*. Via lateral transformations, the design process browses through alternatives. Via vertical transformations the design process builds up complexity and detail resolution. The design process oscillates between lateral and vertical transformations. According to the information-processing approach adopted here, state transformations are information processes that operate via the manipulation of symbol structures defined within symbol systems. Within a given modelling space it is possible to define state transformations on the elementary level of CAD tool operations. Depending on the particular focus of the analysis one might want to go even to the more elementary level of the micro-steps of the algorithms that implement the operations of the tools. Usually, the analysis will be much coarser than individual instances of tool operations. However, there is no stipulation here that state transformations necessarily involve design decisions. State transformations might be tentatively exploring potential solutions while suspending decision making. On the other hand, the concept of state transformation is kept abstract and open enough to condense a whole set of design decisions into a single transformation. This all depends on the focus of the particular analysis being conducted.

The conceptual apparatus is offered here as a general tool for the description and analysis of design processes. This apparatus seems especially apt with respect to the description of algorithmic design strategies. Indeed, Newell and Simon took problem-solving algorithms as their model for a general theory of human problem solving. Design via generative, recursive algorithms that explore a problem-space by iteratively approximating the parameters of a certain goal state fit this model very well. However, algorithms are best deployed for well-defined sub-goals, for example, layout optimizations or facade tessellations according to certain constraints and selection criteria. They might also be used for initial morphological browsing without any pre-set goals. In any case, algorithms – even a whole sequence of concatenated algorithms – can never constitute the totality of a design process. The problem aspects that architectural design processes have to address are just too multi-faceted to be fully formalized and brought under a seamless set of algorithms.[59] The conceptual apparatus presented here is therefore construed to be more general in scope, encompassing both computational processes and processes based on human step-by-step modelling guided by language-based reasoning. This reasoning might be intuitive or rule-based (computing without computer).

Thus *all* design processes can be described as solution action sequences resulting in solution paths that traverse the particular problem space that was constituted when a particular set of design media was chosen and the given design problem was initially interpreted. However, as hinted earlier the mere description of the solution path is of little inherent interest. The analysis must try to reconstruct this solution path as a strategic, goal-directed search within the problem space, ie, as an exploration and decision process that can be assessed in terms of its underlying rationality. Design processes might be compared with respect to their resource efficiency. For instance, one might compare the man-hours (and computer processing hours) consumed by different teams participating in a given architectural design competition. However, a mere efficiency comparison is insufficient. One might try to plot the solution path, in terms of graph theory, as search pattern, or ***search graph***. States would be represented as nodes and state transformations as directed links. Such an analysis would reveal the number and length of dead-end explorations. One can read such graphs whether the search explores the problem space in a ***depth-first*** or in a ***breadth-first*** pattern. A particular simplification of such a charted search graph is the effective ***decision tree***. Here, at each node (intermediate state) would be represented the alternatives considered and rejected at each point when a particular transformation is selected, without, however, showing all available options at each point (which would be impossible with respect to design problems) and without showing the dead-end depth-explorations that have occurred with some of the alternatives finally rejected. One could show how the path is split into parallel, global sub-explorations executed by different members of the design team, or according to sub-issues that can be progressed in semi-independence from each other. Such a plot, indexed with the time required for each state transformation, might give

59 This stricture also applies to genetic/evolutionary algorithms. Although the full formalization of design problems into a system of algorithms might be an aspirational regulating idea for a fully rationalized design process, it remains an infinite project. The formal a prioris that are inevitably presupposed in any computational set up cannot all be chosen by algorithms. Also, the oscillation between the code of utility and the code of beauty cannot be avoided or suspended. Both formal and functional criteria will have to be set as goal-state criteria of the algorithmic search processes. These selection and set up decisions exceed algorithmic treatment. However, they are captured by the general conceptual apparatus presented.

an indication of the relative difficulty of achieving progress at particular points, ie, when facing particular issues or subproblems. Newell and Simon suggest the metaphor of the problem space topography to help with the description of the structure of the problem space:

> An IPS, let us suppose, solves a problem by finding a path from A to G, via B,C,D,E, and F. . . . Perhaps getting from C to D was easy, but getting from D to E was very hard. With any particular node, say C, in such a search space, we can associate all the nearby nodes whose attainment is obvious, once they have reached C, to problem solvers of a specified level of intelligence. How they traverse these obvious sub-segments is often of little interest in explaining their overall behaviour. . . . The detailed topography of flat or slightly rolling hills will have little import. What will be interesting and significant is the location and detailed configuration of the mountain passes.[60]

The question might be raised here to what extent the encountered problem topography is due to the underlying task environment represented or to the system of representation that results in the particular problem space. In any case, once a certain system of representation has been chosen, constituting the problem space together with the external irritation of the client brief, the problem topography that must then be traversed assumes its own inevitability, and thus (apparent) objectivity. This 'objectivity' is inevitable only if the designer or design team has no access to other possible problem representations. If multiple constitutive problem representations are available then parallel explorations in different problem spaces might reveal that the difficulties are differently distributed. To the extent that correlative subproblem mappings between these spaces are possible – for example, between an integrated 3D design space and a space consisting of a cluster of 2D design spaces – one might find that what is relatively difficult in one space is relatively easy in the other and vice versa. Those regions where corresponding topographic features concur in all available problem spaces might be considered 'objective'. For instance, with respect to the design of a mixed-use tower, the design of the core (that needs to be finalized at the end of schematic design) represents a tall ridge within all known problem spaces, ie, whether you work in 2D or 3D, whether you work in a space privileging component aggregation or in a space privileging the subdivision of prior wholes into parts. However, there might be problem spaces that lie beyond this general impasse where this difficulty dissolves. For instance, there might be a problem space where

60 Newell & Simon, *Human Problem Solving*, p 85.

the framing conceptual system refuses to take readymade concepts like 'core' for granted, and instead insists on decomposing everything to the level of individual functions or performances. This 'iconoclastic' attitude was the attitude of 1920s' Radical Functionalism, and was given explicit theoretical backing by Christopher Alexander: 'The nature of the required form is uncertain. It may be given a name ... to make the problem specific, but one of the designer's first tasks is to strip the problem of the preconceptions which such names introduce.'[61] Richard Rogers' Lloyd's headquarters in London is a highly original solution of a tower without a core. In this design the functions usually condensed into the core are taken apart and distributed around the outer perimeter of the tower. One might presume that this decomposition alleviated the design difficulty by eliminating difficult problem-interpenetrations.[62] In this case the core as compact obstacle is dissolved into functional elements that might be tackled separately. The introduction of a new problem representation might be compared to Imre Lakatos' concept of 'problem shift' in science. The idea is that a shift opens a new perspective on a problem that suggests a new, often unexpected way to solve that problem. The solution space can now be searched in a different direction, exploring a hitherto unexplored region. The problem is no longer the same problem but rather a functionally equivalent substitution.

The mere description of an observed design process in terms of the pattern of its search graph, and in terms of the inferred problem space topography, is not yet concerned with the assessment of the rationality of the process as goal-directed search and decision process. The analysis has to move beyond process parameters to involve the concept of ***design method*** as defined above, and be juxtaposed to against the concept of design process. The distinction is also implicit in the way Newell and Simon introduce and emphasize the importance of the concept of problem-solving methods: 'The theory focuses on methods: a collection of information processes that combine a series of means to attain an end, or at least to attempt to attain an end. ... A method can only be understood in reference to its goal.'[63] Methods are 'rational organizations of processes'.[64] However, within the overall design project, as within many other complex problem-solving efforts, multiple methods will have to be

61 Christopher Alexander, *Notes on the Synthesis of Form*, Harvard University Press (Cambridge, MA), 1964, p 95.

62 Presumably, this solution did not become a standard solution because by taking away the difficult interpenetration of issues in a single, compact structure it also removed many opportunities for synergies, and concurring functional overlap.

63 Newell & Simon, *Human Problem Solving*, p 91.

64 Ibid, p 89.

brought to bear. Methods are defined relative to chosen problem spaces within which these methods organize the search/transformation processes. However, in complex problem-solving processes, it might be necessary to move between different problem spaces. In architecture this is the case. As the project progresses, the project moves through a whole sequence of different problem spaces, each potentially employing various methods. Therefore, in order for the whole process to assume a measure of rationality, one has to postulate the existence of a hierarchy involving an executive level organizing the selection, evaluation and sequencing of problem spaces and methods. Complex problem-solving processes are therefore often approached via a process planning space.

7.3.6 PLANNING SPACES

A ***project planning space*** is an abstract meta-space. It is a problem space where the design process itself becomes a problem. The project planning space is the space where the broad plan of an envisaged problem-solving process is mapped out, ie, the sequence of broad stages, problem spaces, methods and detailed processes. These project planning spaces must represent the design process, for example, as flow-chart, or as project schedule in matrix format, in order to work out and establish a viable project plan. The RIBA Outline Plan of Works offers a basic schema for the construction of an overarching process planning space. Smaller planning spaces, for more detailed project maps, are nested within this scheme.[65]

Newell and Simon are assuming that 'the IPS is fundamentally serial in its operation: it is a processor that evokes and activates one method at a time'.[66] However, in a complex design project advanced by a large design team, multiple problem spaces might be open simultaneously, with different methods of exploration pursuit in parallel. Thus an additional problem arises, the meta-problem of coordinating these parallel efforts and of integrating their results. These issues of coordination are also structured and solved within a project planning space. The establishment of a project planning space, a variant of second order observation, is thus a general feature that is required in all complex problem-solving efforts.

The concept of a project planning space is an extension of Newell and Simon's general notion of a ***planning space***, and the related notion of ***planning method***. Herbert Simon defines planning as a method that

65 The reality of this meta-level of design process planning as part of the ongoing design practice offers an opening, over and above mere theoretical discourse, through which the reflections offered here might be able to enter the ongoing autopoiesis of architecture.

66 Newell & Simon, *Human Problem Solving*, p 89.

proceeds by 'abstracting from the detail of a problem space, and carrying out preliminary problem solving in the abstracted (and consequently simpler) space'. This result of the problem-solving effort in the planning space is a plan. 'But the plan then has to be tested by trying to carry it out in the original problem space. The detail of the plan was thereby elaborated and its feasibility tested.'[67] We might complement Simon's notion of a ***planning space*** with the notion of ***execution space***, and note that these are relative concepts that lead to a hierarchy of nested spaces, each abstracting from further levels of detail in one direction and elaborating further levels of detail in the other direction. Thus we get a spectrum from the most abstract to the most concrete. A space picked out from the middle of this ordered sequence would be the planning space of the space below and the execution space of the space above. In a problem domain like theorem proving, it is quite clear what is the problem space of final implementation: the space where the actual symbol structures are processed that are finally transformed into the theorem set as goal state. In the case of architectural design, one might identify the construction documents as the final execution space where the terminal state of the design effort is reached when the full set of documents is submitted for tender. Or is one to consider physical construction, to some extent still supervised and directed by the architect, as the final problem-solving process progressing in a problem space constituted by the physical environment and the opportunities and constraints given by the construction industry? Is this the final execution space with all design work going on in planning spaces of various degrees of abstraction? This might be a way to view it, but this does not need to be decided here. In describing the design process of contributing to a

67 Herbert Simon, 'The Structure of Ill-Structured Problems', originally published in *Artificial Intelligence* 4 (1973), 181–200, reprinted in: Nigel Cross (Ed), *Developments in Design Methodology*, John Wiley & Sons (Chichester/New York), 1984, p 164. A sequential ordering of the problem-solving process exists, to some extent, on the macro-level of distinguishing the major stages that structure the overall design process. A strict sequential ordering exists on the micro-level of working through particular design problems within a specific modelling space. Here the process is confined within a single problem space, activating one method at a time to produce an integrated series of individual operations. The problem space is traversed by considering one state at a time. Analysis on the mesa-level, ie, the analysis of what goes on within each stage, leads to the identification of multiple parallel problem spaces, and multiple methods of exploring and advancing the various aspects of a design. These parallel efforts must be brought together according to a recurrent rhythm of design team meetings. There might also be a dedicated design vehicle that permanently tries to catch up with and integrate the different strands. Here inconsistencies are detected and communicated to minimize the risk that larger divergences develop. An efficient division of labour and a corresponding pattern of coordination are the problems to be solved within the project planning space.

design competition, one might choose to take the submission documents as the terminal goal state and the problem space of its elaboration as the final execution space. What is important here is the availability of the distinction of planning space vs execution space as a pair of relative concepts that can help to describe the structure of the architectural design process. It is indeed a fact of outstanding consequence that the architectural design process is subject to the nested hierarchy of levels of abstraction. The notion of ***levels of abstraction*** addressing respective ***levels of detail*** is important. There is a more or less definite, conventional stratification to be observed. Each problem space addresses a particular level of detail. Traditionally, these levels had been associated with particular scales to be addressed at particular work stages. More and more detail might be accumulated within a particular problem space, as long as these details operate on the same level of abstraction.

The hierarchical structure of nested problem spaces of increasing detail seems to be a fundamental feature of most architectural design processes. This planning method involves obvious risks. The execution of decisions taken in the abstract might turn out to be impossible on the next level, or might even be halted on any later level. To mitigate against this risk, key details that might block an idea later are considered early. As Nigel Cross points out: 'although there is a hierarchical structure of decisions, from overall concept to details, designing is not a strictly hierarchical process; in the early stages of design, the designer moves freely between different levels of detail.'[68] This early consideration of details cannot be comprehensive. It can only concern details somehow judged 'critical'.

The decision making and elaboration of intermediate states on one level of abstraction/detail have yet to be confirmed and executed (or might need to be overturned) on the next level of detail. Whether the two lines that describe a wall or a floor in a 1:200 section will be able accommodate all the required structural and mechanical elements yet to be specified remains uncertain until a detailed wall-section or floor build-up is elaborated in the 1:10 detail section that incorporates the respective information that has been received from the engineering specialists. With respect to such uncertainties, many design decisions remain preliminary. The more concrete and detailed the problem space, and thus the more advanced the design, the more predictive power is vested in the design. However, many issues can be investigated and fully

68 Nigel Cross, 'Natural Intelligence in Design', *Design Studies,* Vol 20, No 1, January 1999, in: Nigel Cross, *Designerly Ways of Knowing*, Birkhäuser (Basel), 2007, p 57.

settled in rather abstract spaces. Adjacencies, gross floor-areas and the basic volume of a building can be conclusively determined in schematic plans. Symmetries and proportions can be ascertained in rather abstract elevational diagrams. In this sense the various systems of drawing are perfect simulators and predictors of (selected) aspects of the final built projects. Everything to do with geometry and dimensional coordination of orthogonal buildings can be fully solved in the form of drawings. Concerning structures with non-orthogonal geometry, the 3D modelling space of CAD systems can fulfil this task. Complex geometry requires rather advanced systems but the principle is the same. All these systems allow for precise inferences concerning the geometric properties of the final physical structure. In fact, should a discrepancy occur between model and reality, it is the real building (rather than the model) that is presumed to lack precision. The truth of geometry resides in the model. Other inferences that might be made from a drawing are less certain. Crowd simulation software applied to the 3D model of a project might be trusted to predict circulation patterns. The visual appearance of a building can now be predicted with photorealistic visualizations that are sometimes hard to distinguish from real photos. Some inferences must wait for the final completion of the building to be fully verified. This goes for all the substantial functions for which the building is being designed. Whether a designed lobby space will work well as effective orientation space, and whether it will facilitate the envisaged encounters and informal communication events, is not easy to ascertain. Agent simulations, scenario planning and people animation might come close. The key point here is that each planning space is only as good as its predictive power over the next execution space and ultimately over the life-process of the building as frame for social communication. On the other hand, the design process in each problem/planning space is only as good as the simplification of the problem its abstractions achieve. These two criteria have contrary implications and need to be balanced.

7.3.7 HEURISTIC VERSUS EXHAUSTIVE PROBLEM-SOLVING METHODS

The problem space defines the set of problem states among which the solution states must be found. All problem-solving methods involve some form of sequential examination of problem states, one by one. In general, it makes a big difference whether the task is to find any satisfying solution or to find the best solution. The latter demand involves ***optimizing*** behaviour, while the former has been termed ***satisficing***[69] behaviour. In the domain of architecture, optimization is usually not applicable, certainly not for the whole design task of designing a building. Only with respect to well-defined and tightly circumscribed subproblems might optimization be applicable. In what follows we primarily assume satisficing only, ie, the problem space is searched until a problem state is encountered that satisfies the task requirements as defined within the problem space according to the IPS's explicit or implicit aspiration level. The difficulty of the search then depends, among other things, on the relative size of the solution space as subset of the overall problem space.

All problem-solving methods must incorporate at least one mechanism for each of the following two functions:

- ***Generating***: a mechanism for generating or obtaining problem states
- ***Testing***: a mechanism for examining whether the obtained problem state is a solution state

The most elementary method conceivable is the method whereby each and every element of the problem space is investigated in turn, either by a random trial and error process, or by a more systematic process that can guarantee that all states in the problem space are investigated. These basic methods that only incorporate the two fundamental functions of generation and testing are referred to as ***generate-and-test methods***. With respect to this kind of exhaustive process that searches through the entire space, the 'design time' needed is proportional to the ratio between the sizes of the problem space and the solution space.

There are at least three factors that determine the design time and effort required to solve a problem:

- the size ratio of problem space over solution space
- the effort required to generate a problem state
- the effort required to test the problem state against the solution criteria

Design methods should try to economize on all three counts. With respect to very small problem spaces the generate-and-test method might be most appropriate. For instance, if the task is to select dining chairs to complement a given dining table, with the additional requirement that

69 The neologism 'satisficing' was first introduced by Herbert Simon in his critique of the unrealistic presumption of optimizing behaviour in economics. Optimizing rationality is mostly outside the cognitive and computational capacity of economic agents. The fact must be recognized that economic agents satisfice, ie, they terminate their search once they hit upon a solution that meets their aspiration level. The same can be asserted for designers.

the chairs need to be selected from the same supplier as the table, then a full search of the catalogue and a one by one visual juxtaposition of chair and table seems to be the right method. There might be scope for upgrading the test method, for example, by switching the modelling space and creating Photoshop collages that depict the selected chairs set aound the table. One might stop as soon as a matching chair is hit upon. However, in this case it would also be conceivable, perhaps even expected, to conduct an exhaustive search for the sake of finding the best match. In a less constrained space, with two variables rather than with one constant and one variable, ie, where both table and chairs are to be chosen, and without the requirement of using the same supplier, the problem space is no longer small enough to suggest an exhaustive use of an exhaustive generate-and-test method. Assume the problem is to find a harmonious dining ensemble. Good match between table and chairs is the relevant criterion here. Assuming 50 conceivable table designs and 100 chair designs, the space to be searched for matching combinations would include 5000 problem states. No architect would ever consider literally going through all 5000 combinations via Photoshop collages, or indeed via any other examination method. In fact, in most architectural design problems the problem space is immense, encompassing literally billions of theoretically possible problem states, and thus a simple trial and error search is not only inconvenient, but inconceivable. In the case of the two variable searches considered here, a random trial and error process might be likely if the aspiration level is low: more or less anything goes. (After all there will be a table surrounded by chairs.) If this seems unacceptable a more structured approach is called for that somehow allows for the abbreviation of the search without giving up all semblance of rationality. 'The effect of more sophisticated methods can often be described as cutting down effectively the part of the space that must be explored in order to find a solution.'[70]

One strategy might be to introduce additional constraints that seem sensible. For instance, the imposition that the overall ensemble should be purchased from a single supplier. Assuming that there are 10 suppliers with five tables and 10 chairs each, this restriction reduces the search space from 5000 to 500 problem states, organized into 10 spaces to be investigated with 50 problem states in each. What could justify this enormous reduction of essentially 90 per cent of all principal options? First of all, an exhaustive search might simply be impossible. Here it would consume resources that are wholly out of proportion to the problem at hand. But a random cut of the domain would throw the

70 Newell & Simon, *Human Problem Solving*, p 94.

process back to the basic trial and error method with lower expectations or the risk of failing to find any solution. The justification for the move suggested above can be twofold. On the one hand, the likelihood of finding table-chair matches might be taken to be higher within suppliers than across suppliers. On the other hand, an extraneous advantage is gained that can be seen somehow to compensate for the reduction of options: the use of a single supplier reduces communication effort and transport costs etc. This introduction of new constraining criteria to reduce the scope of the search is a ubiquitous feature of architectural design rationality.

Even in this reduced space of what are now 500 problem states, a generate-and-test method might seem too taxing. The method is still too simple. The problem is to find a satisfying dining ensemble within a space of 500 possible ensembles. One strategy that is pervasive within architectural design is to decompose the problem into subproblems that might be solved sequentially. In this case the problem can be decomposed into two parts: the selection of the table and the selection of the chairs. There are two options here: select a chair and find a matching table or select a table and find matching chairs. If good match is the only criterion then this problem decomposing method leads to either five problem state examinations (randomly chosen constant chair, five variable tables from the same supplier) or to 10 problem examinations (randomly chosen constant table, 10 variable chairs from the same supplier), ie, it would lead to a drastic reduction of the search space, by 99 per cent or 98 per cent respectively, and in relation to the initial total space by 99.9 per cent and 99.8 per cent respectively. However, without the introduction of further criteria this process would be irrational. One might, for instance, narrow down the space by conducting a prior brand comparison, by applying a test to the 10 suppliers. Then, once more, a new criterion would have been introduced. This criterion would here take the position of a prior criterion, ie, effectively becoming the priority criterion. The problem has once more been redefined to make it more manageable without losing all semblance of rationality. If a brand testing mechanism is not readily available, the additional constraining criterion might be the quality of the individual table designs, or of the chairs, rather than just the harmony between the two designs. In this case the problem space is initially back to 250 problem states but decomposition and sequencing structure a path through the space that once more cuts down on the items that must be examined. A decision has to be made whether to consider the quality of the table or the quality of the chairs. Assuming that only the quality of the table matters, and stipulating that this becomes the primary criterion of the task, the problem has been structured to become manageable once more: assuming the best table (out of 50) is to be combined with matching chairs (10 from the same supplier) a maximum of 60 problem states would need to be generated and examined: 50 table examinations testing for quality (optimization), and 10 subsequent ensemble examinations testing for harmony. The space to be searched is now only 13 per cent and 1.3 per cent of the original spaces considered. The harmony of the ensemble is now a secondary, subsidiary criterion. Table quality has priority over ensemble harmony. Such a preference ordering of solution criteria is a ubiquitous aspect of design rationality and of rational decision making in general.

If both the chairs' and the table's quality is to be optimized then there would be no room left for considering harmony unless a more complex schema of relative weighting of the potentially conflicting aspects or criteria (quality vs harmony) is introduced.

The designer might lift the constraint on supplier correspondence and introduce a general, minimum quality level (satisficing) with respect to both tables and chairs, for example, rejecting the lower 90 per cent in each group. This would require a maximum of 50 quality checks on tables and 100 quality checks on chairs, and leave a pool of five tables and 10 chairs generating 50 ensembles. These might now be randomly scanned until a satisfying ensemble is encountered. Whether there is any such ensemble, and how many, depends on the aspiration level that is inbuilt in the testing mechanism that discriminates between harmonious and non-harmonious ensembles.

A method to optimize this problem (within the reduced pool of 50 ensembles) would be considerably more involved. There would be the need for a mechanism to measure or rank all ensembles according to harmony. If only binary comparisons can be plausibly achieved, 2500 comparisons would be required to produce a harmony ranking. Then there would be the need to rank all five tables and all 10 chairs for quality. Relative weights would have to be defined within a formula that would allow one to derive an overall score that somehow combines the three otherwise incommensurable ranking indices, the ensemble harmony index, the table quality index and the chair quality index. Such optimization procedures were suggested during the surge of the 1960s' design methods movement. (These methods were imported from operations research, mostly applied to multi-variable logistic problems.) However, the overall cumbersome nature of such procedures implied their impracticability, while the need for the arbitrary weighting of incommensurable measures, without fully overseeing the consequences of such weight allocations, made this optimization paradigm implausible. It never took root in architectural design practice.

All the processes described above uphold the qualification as rational decision behaviour. However, none of them, except the exhaustive generate-and-test method, can guarantee that a solution is obtained with respect to a prior stipulated test (assuming that the total problem space does contain at least one solution). Newell and Simon refer to methods that incorporate strategies that reduce the search task, while maintaining a good chance of arriving at a solution in a reasonable amount of time, as ***heuristic search methods***. The defining characteristic of a heuristic search in comparison with the simple generate-and-test method is that it breaks the generation of solution candidates into parts. Then, by successively operating on these partial solutions (which must somehow be recognized as such), the method approaches the final shape of the solution.

For instance, above, rather than directly generating full ensembles, there is a step-wise process of first selecting a preferred supplier (a partial solution), then selecting the best table from this supplier (a more elaborate partial solution) and finally selecting a matching set of chairs to arrive at a satisfactory solution. The example is, of course, an extremely simple and crude illustration in comparison to the task of designing a building, let alone a complex and innovative building. However, some general features of how a complex, multi-variable problem can be tackled with a heuristic search method are already discernible. Newell and Simon compare such a task to the attempt to find the code that opens a multi-dial safe. The combinatorial problem could only be solved if partial sequences were already to reveal that the search is on a promising track. 'Thus, information that tells us which solutions to try first, and in particular, information that allows us to factor one large problem into several small ones – and to know when we have successfully solved each of the small ones – reduces the search task tremendously.'[71]

How quickly problem spaces grow to an unmanageable size can be understood from the following example. Assume that the design of a building requires only 10 design decisions, each decision opening up a finite space of only 10 possibilities to select from. The total problem space counts 10^{10}, ie, 10 billion, possible problem states. Since in architecture there is never a unique solution, we assume further that for each decision only two out of the 10 options might possibly contribute to a satisfying solution state, while eight of the 10 possibilities available in each case lead to failure. The subset of all solutions is therefore 2^{10}, ie, 1024 problem states are solution states. The probability of hitting upon a solution by trial and error would therefore be only about one in 10 million cases (9,765,625). We assume here that the decision issues are

71 Newell & Simon, *Human Problem Solving*, p 98.

interdependent, in the sense that the question of which of the two options in each issue contributes to a solution depends on which choices are made for all the other nine issues. This means that when taking up any decision issue, it is unclear which choices are part of a solution. There is only a test mechanism for complete selections answering all 10 questions, ie, for fully completed problem states. It remains uncertain whether partial sequences are on the right track. Therefore, the generate-and-test method is the only available method here. However, the generate-and-test method is clearly non-feasible when faced with such improbabilities. If we assume that each cycle of generation and examination takes one minute, it would still take an average of 18 years for a solution to be discovered.

In this case everything hinges on whether there might be additional test mechanisms that could detect or predict a probability of success for partial answers. 'If gains over random search are to be attainable from a search method, then these gains must come from exploiting the additional information available – namely, from controlling the search at each step of the way in the light of what has been discovered and what remains to be done.'[72]

The example might be modified in a number of ways that make it more amenable to being tackled by a design method. If we assume that each decision can be separately decided on and tested, then we have 10 times a chance of two out of 10 to hit a partial solution. This would lead to an average of only 50 partial generation/examination cycles to find a total solution compared with the average of 10 million cycles necessary in the case posed initially. However, it might be more realistic to assume that there are dependencies that do not allow each individual decision to be taken by itself. Perhaps, however, it is possible to decompose the problem into four clusters: two clusters of three issues each and two clusters of two issues each. These clusters might be interpreted as components or subsystems of the overall design. If the problem could be structured like this, then the project could be solved in a total of four steps. Each of the three-issue clusters would require the designer to find one of eight partial solution states among 1000 partial problem states, requiring an average of 125 generation/examination cycles per cluster. The two-issue clusters would require an average of 25 (four over 100) examinations each. The total number of investigations required to hit a solution would then be 300, if the four clusters or subsystems were fully independent. The design work could be divided and worked upon simultaneously.

72 Ibid.

However, it might be more realistic to assume partial dependencies between clusters in the sense of conflicting decisions that transpire only when the clustered subsets of decisions (the designed components or subsystems) are to be conjoined. This would burden simultaneous working with the risk of abortive work. One of the four clusters, for example, subsystem 1 (structure), is arbitrarily chosen to begin the design with an average of 125 generate/test cycles. The stipulated dependencies would imply a reduction of the possible solutions available within the next chosen cluster, for example, subsystem 2 (envelope). For instance, one of the three decisions about the envelope loses one of its two options. This reduces the total number of possible partial solution states in this cluster from eight to four feasible options. However, that this is the case and which options fall away will only transpire as full subsystem states are generated and examined. Therefore 250 (four out of 1000) investigative cycles are now, on average, necessary to find a feasible subsystem 2 that fits the version of subsystem 1 that was discovered and retained in design step 1. (If more than one feasible option is encountered a choice/decision can/must be made.) Now one of the two remaining clusters is chosen, for example, subsystem 3 (internal space divisions). One of the two decisions that are required here might have a double dependency, depending both on subsystem 1 (structure) and on subsystem 2 (envelope). Perhaps one of the two options is made impossible by the discovered structure, and the other option is made impossible by the discovered envelope. At this point an impasse has occurred. One of the two subsystems has to be revisited. There is no guarantee here that a solution can be found by the method employed. Let's assume the second cluster is repeated. This time the impasse can be overcome. Subsystem 3 now has only one free variable leaving two solution states among the 100 problem states of this cluster thus requiring an average of 50 cycles. Finally, the fourth and last cluster is addressed. One of its variables might depend on, and is thus constrained/fixed by, the result of subsystem 3. Hence there remain two solutions within a pool of 100, on average requiring 50 cycles comprising generation and examination. The total information processing required in this overall four-step process, with one repeat step, thus amounts to 125+250+250(repeat)+50+50, ie, a total of 725 cycles to reach a solution in this near-decomposable problem constellation. This compares with 300 cycles required for a fully decomposable four-subsystem solution, 50 cycles for a fully decomposable 10 subsystem solution and 10 million cycles for a non-decomposable generation-test process.

Another, final variation of this example might be described as follows: the variables settled in the cluster that was first addressed and provisionally solved might narrow down the space that must be searched with respect to the follow on cluster, ie, it might be possible to narrow the search, on the basis of the additional information that resides in the fact that the first partial solution was discovered or chosen and thereby fixed. Thus we might presume that with each step not only the possible solution states decrease, but simultaneously it might be possible to focus the remaining search space. That might imply that all 10 decision options no longer have to be considered. Perhaps half might be eliminated with each of the steps resolving a subsystem. The initial openness of the process is thus closing down as the design approaches the last variables. It becomes clear that the space of manoeuvre is narrowing, until the last few decisions seem almost inevitable. Towards the end, the design progress gains an air of necessity.

In all the examples above the key advance of the method was its scheme of breaking the search into self-enclosed episodes. Obviously, this scheme requires that the problem is really, or nearly, decomposable. This implies that a partial solution must be recognizable as feasible subsystem solution. The method that capitalizes on this kind of decomposition can, after each episode, reduce a huge part of the overall search space. Further, it might be possible to use clues (information) within what has been achieved to guide the further search by eliminating possible problem states (with respect to further sub-tasks) from consideration. Such inferences must rely on the activation of prior knowledge or experience stored in the long-term memory (LTM) of the information-processing system (IPS). This problem constellation, where a problem is nearly decomposable and where partial solutions are both recognizable as (not certain, but highly probable) partial solutions and where, on the basis of prior knowledge, inferences can be drawn from this partial solution about the direction of the further search thus allowing the further search space to be narrowed down, is the typical constellation encountered in architectural design problems.

The total problem space can be depicted as a branching diagram or massively ramifying tree whereby branches represent design moves (generation-examination cycles) and nodes represent problem states. The simple illustrative example given above with 10 decision points offering 10 possibilities each quickly ramifies from a single point with 10 branches, each of which branches out in 10 directions etc, into a tree with 10 billion terminal branches/nodes. (Full graphic representation is obviously not to be expected.) A relatively small subset of these nodes represents the set of all possible solutions. Within this tree many more sub-trees exist that might theoretically represent particular design processes, showing all the problem states generated and examined

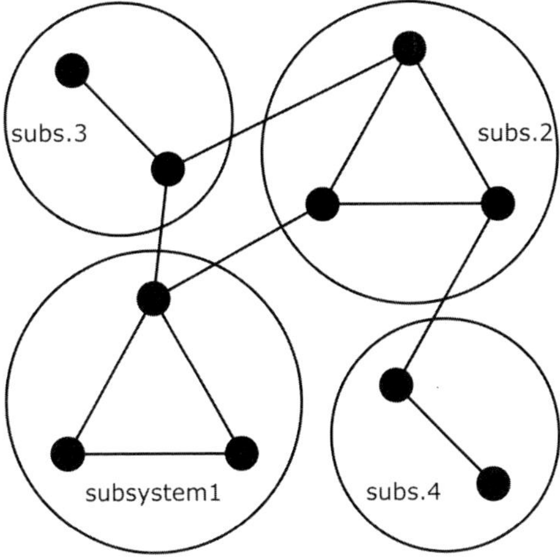

Figure 46 Nearly decomposable problem constellation with four subsystems

during the process. All paths through the problem space/tree that terminate in one of the solution nodes represent a completed design process.

Problem spaces might be depicted as triangles, or in 3D space, as pyramids. The apex of the expanding space indicates the initial state.[73] Figure 47 depicts a problem space that branches out from an initial state by opening up four design possibilities and again four further possibilities at each successive design decision point. Thicker lines indicate 'good' design moves that can lead to a terminal solution state. Here, 50 per cent of branches at each decision point are 'good' in this sense. After three branching steps, 64 problem states have been reached. Within this set of 64 states there are eight, ie, 12.5 per cent 'good' terminal branches or solution states.

It is impossible to draw an equivalent graph for the problem space that corresponds to the problem with 10 issues, each offering 10 options. This space branches into 10 billion problem states. Figure 48 can only offer an abstraction that hints at the space, and serves here as structural image for the purpose of structural comparison. In contrast to the immensity of the problem space of the non-decomposed problem, the

73 This is an idealization to the extent to which a design problem usually admits multiple different interpretations of what its exact requirements and constraints are. To depict this multiplicity of conditions one would simply have to start the diagram one layer inwards. The space would assume the shape of a truncated pyramid or trapezoid rather than a triangle.

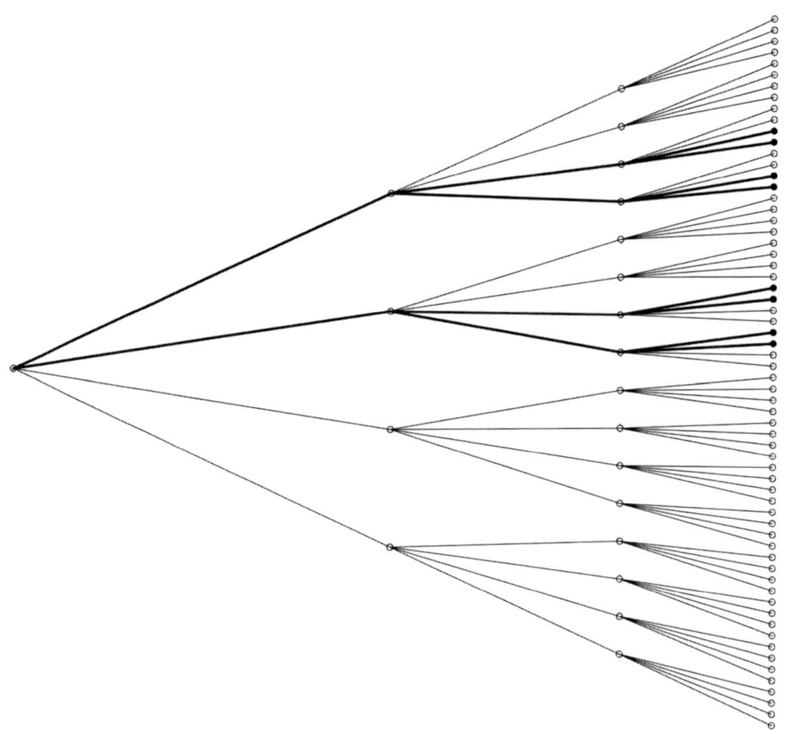

Figure 47 Problem space depicted as branching state space

problem space of the fully decomposed problem is rather tame and trivial. It can be fully depicted (Figure 49).

The (nearly) decomposable problem space is approximately depicted within Figure 50. Once more, it only allows for an abstracted depiction. (There are too many branches.) The four subsystems appear as a concatenated sequence of trees. Each tree represents a functionally independent design module. The sequence of the four modules is arbitrary. The assumption in this representation is that each subproblem/subsystem is closed before a new subproblem is tackled. This assumption is not quite realistic. Instead of fully decomposable problems, designers are mostly faced with nearly decomposable problems. Or rather, one might say, designers do not have to arrive at strict decompositions because they are able to take some dependencies into account and thus are also able to capitalize on the multifunctionality of components and synergies between components or subsystems. The most typical design problem constellation is the above-mentioned nearly

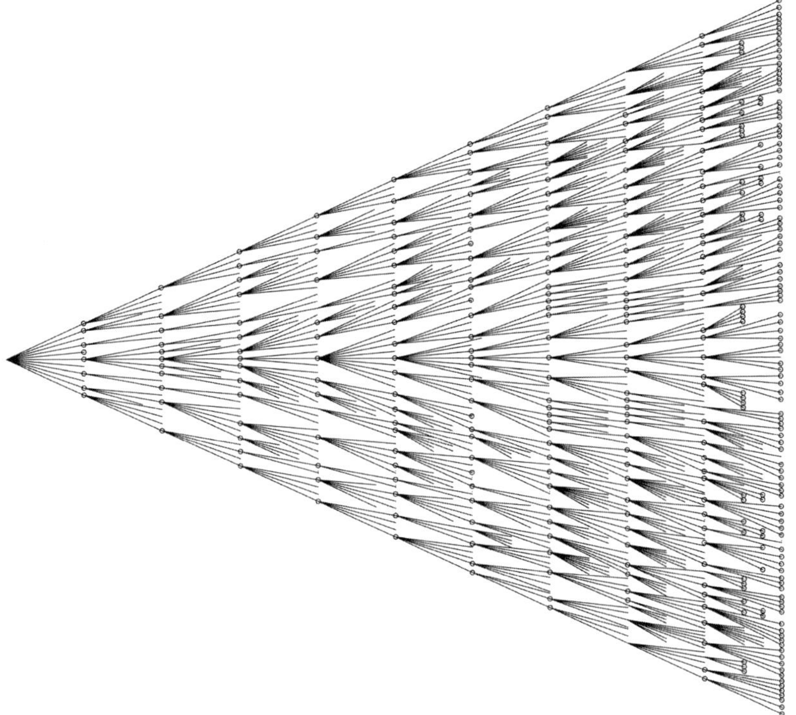

Figure 48 Expansively ramifying state space

decomposable problem. Vinod Goel talks about 'leaky modules', ie, modules that cannot altogether avoid interdependencies with other modules although they establish a strong difference between dense internal connections and sparse external connections. According to Goel, designers have 'two main strategies for dealing with these interconnections: they either (i) block the leaks by functional-level assumptions about the interconnected modules; or (ii) put the current

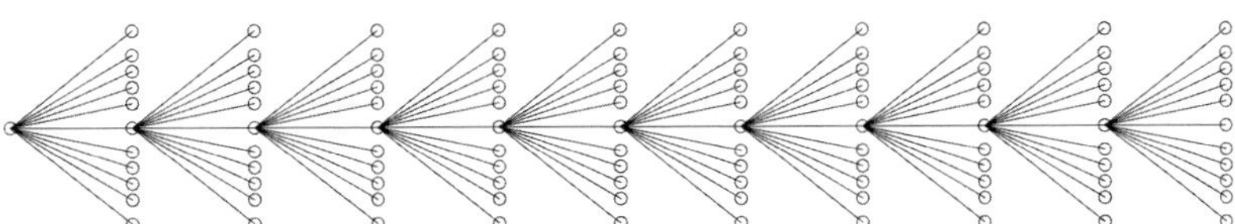

Figure 49 Fully decomposable problem space

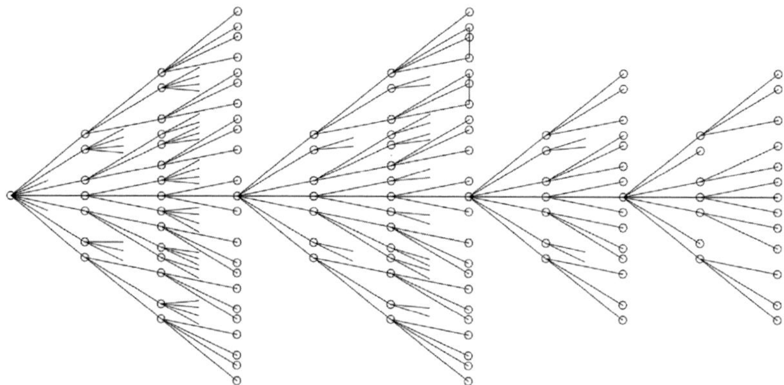

Figure 50 Decomposable problem space

module on hold and attend to an interconnected module.'[74] Putting modules on hold implies that interconnections can be assessed and resolved before modules are fully designed. This in turn suggests an oscillating or parallel processing of modules or subsystems. The strategy of blocking interconnections leads to a substandard rationality because it either gives up potential synergies or ignores interferences. This was the strategy of Modernism. Parametricism is able to overcome this limitation. The inherent adaptivity of parametrically constituted subsystems implies that mutual adjustments that can resolve interdependencies are possible deep into the detailed design. Furthermore, the strategy of Parametricism is to find synergies between subsystems. Both aspects, the avoidance of conflict and the garnering of synergies, can be worked upon via the establishment of systematic subsystem correlations.

One might assume that all processes eventually arrive at a solution node, but with different degrees of efficiency, ie, with different amounts of abandoned dead end pursuits. The capacity of a design method can then be described as the capacity to navigate the design process through the ramifying problem space with a path that is as streamlined as possible. In the words of Newell and Simon: 'The task of a problem solving procedure is to grow a tree of operator sequences that will not branch too luxuriantly, and will include at least one solution path.'[75]

74 Vinod Goel, *Sketches of Thought*, MIT Press (Cambridge, MA), 1995, p 103.

75 Newell & Simon, *Human Problem Solving*, p 100.

7.4 Differentiating Classical, Modern and Contemporary Processes

THESIS 38

Design via scripted rules is replacing design via the direct manipulation of individual forms. Scripts can uniquely enhance both the design process's generative power and its analytical power. The ability to combine the explorative potential for surprise discoveries with the guaranteed adherence to key criteria is the unique advantage of the new computational techniques. Through these techniques the design process simultaneously gains breadth and depth.

The characterization and illustration of various design methods in the previous chapter is rather abstract. But an initial set of insights can already be garnered on this basis. The illustrated methods, including the final, most 'realistic' variant, are heuristic because they cannot guarantee a result that satisfies pre-established criteria. Also, the final variant must make assumptions about how the problem might be dissected into (nearly) self-contained subproblems, implying assumptions about the near-decomposability of the possible solution state (the final building or action-artefact network), and making assumptions about where the most promising points for dissection lie. This might be unproblematic with respect to routine design tasks, but remains problematic in the case of the ambition to innovate, or with respect to addressing novel problems. The decomposition problem and the related issue of the subsystem hierarchy are key issues for any original avant-garde design effort. These issues bear directly on the sequence in which issues are to be tackled. Within the avant-garde segment of architecture we should not assume that the design sequence can be fully pre-planned. Rather, the sequence itself is the subject of experimentation. Sequence often determines hierarchy rather than vice versa. Without a prior design process plan, the design team must, at each stage, make uncertain inferences about the most promising further direction and focus of the further design investigation, both with respect to which issue to tackle next, and to which decision to take within the selected issue.

It might be noted here that within the isolated subproblems, and despite the achieved search focus, the basic generate-and-test procedure recurs. It remains the base process that has to be resorted to when the problem can no longer be further reduced or narrowed. The problem might be decomposed into very small parts where generate-and-test is quick and trivial, or the direct recognition of the solution from memory might be possible. With respect to routine design problems within the mainstream of architecture, direct recognition does not have to be confined to very small components. Although the 'recognition' of a full, readymade solution, ie, simply pulling a completed design project out of the drawer in response to a design task, is only a theoretical limit case within architecture, significant parts of a design task might be so handled within a mainstream practice. The case is rather different with respect to the avant-garde segment of architecture. Here problem solving by recognition is definitely excluded. Such a process would spell the exclusion of the respective design team from the avant-garde. With respect to small components, recognition will always be relied upon. 'Recognition is very often the way this last step is accomplished. We say "he reduced the problem to something he knew".'[76] Both generate-and-test and recognition remain the 'methods of last resort'.[77] 'If it were not for the existence of some weak but general-purpose methods such as this one, the basic strategy of reducing a single hard problem to a myriad of small subproblems might not be feasible.'[78]

If cycles of generation and examination remain the backbone of all problem solving in general and of all architectural design processes in particular, then a theory of the design process must look closer at the processes of generation and examination and at their relationship. 'The generality (and weakness) of the generate-and-test scheme lies precisely in the fact that the generation process and the test process are completely independent. Each has only to fulfil certain minimal conditions of its own. Conversely, the power (and specificity) of a method for the search formulation must lie in the dependence of the search process upon the nature of the object being sought and the progress being made toward it.'[79] Above, reference was made to the fact that a good heuristic method must be able to direct/focus the search by narrowing the search space. This can be done if the generator is tightened. For instance, in the case of designing a layout within an orthogonally constrained 2D modelling space with rectangles as primitives, any arbitrary configuration of such rectangles might be generated. Alternatively, the internal proportions of the rectangles might be preconstrained within certain limits. Or only rectangles are generated that have area values that match at least one of the spaces listed in the schedule of accommodation. In the case of freehand sketched layouts, such pre-constraints are built in only a very

76 Newell & Simon, *Human Problem Solving*, p 95.

77 Ibid, p 110.

78 Ibid.

79 Ibid, p 98.

approximate and uncertain fashion, if at all. However, in a digital drafting environment, the generation of solutions might be pre-constrained more precisely. One might pre-constrain the search for an adequate layout solution by representing the initial state as an arbitrary scatter of all required room-figures and define translation, rotation and area-conserving re-proportioning of the elemental rectangles as the basic operators within the problem space. Then every operation generates a new problem state that already secures some of the requirements that serve as criteria for identifying solution states. Further constraints might be incorporated, especially if the IPS is augmented with scripting techniques that allow the programming of such constraints. 'The solution generators of these programmes have, then, a great deal of built-in selectivity. Many irrelevant parts of the space of possible solutions are excluded from the search.'[80] To give the generation process a meaningful selectivity might come at considerable information-processing cost. The effort might very well be worth it as it focuses the search space and also saves on the side of the examination or testing mechanism. No testing is required for the property in question. The investigation of how the selective power of the generator might be enhanced should therefore be a central part of any attempt to devise a design method. However, there are clear computational limits to this kind of incorporation of solution properties as constraints within the generation process. The immediate generation of problem states that incorporate all the required properties that must be exhibited within a satisfactory solution state can only serve here as a theoretical limit case that is inconceivable with respect to architectural design problems. A full readymade generation would just imply the transfer of the design process into the generation process. Only with respect to some narrowly defined subproblem might this be the case when a specified subcomponent is simply drawn directly from a memory database readymade, or readily adapted with some basic algorithm hidden from the view of the designer. In all realistic cases it is only some of the solution properties that can be built into the generation process for new intermediate states.

The thought experiment with the limit case shows that making generators selective is equivalent to decomposing the original problem. If we assume that a design project has to satisfy three broad requirements or properties p1, p2 and p3, and we assume that either one or two of the required properties can be built into the generator while at least one variable must remain free to allow for the production of options that will later be exposed to the examination procedure, then there exist six

80 Ibid, p 117.

possible schemes for making the generator selective, three leaving one variable free and three leaving two variables free. Which variable will be incorporated as pre-constraint depends on the relative ease or difficulty of generating elements guaranteeing the property in question, as well as, on how difficult or easy these properties make the further search and examination process for the additional variables/criteria. Those properties must be incorporated into the generation of intermediate states that might be hard to obtain once other properties are already in place. In other words, properties that are rare in the overall problem space should be incorporated into the generator, if at all possible.

With respect to architectural design projects one might broadly categorize the major design criteria into three kinds of requirements: geometrical fit, functional fit and aesthetic fit. One might then ask which of these requirements can or should be pulled to the front end of the design process and, as it were, incorporated into the generator. Again, there are six possibilities of pre-constraining the generator. For instance, all intermediate design states, all the way through, adhere to the geometric and aesthetic criteria. Then these states are tested and selected for functional fit. One might call such a method form-to-programme method or form-to-function method. Then there is the possibility of starting with functionality and ascertaining that all intermediate design states, all the way through, adhere to functional requirement, while leaving the geometric coordination of the functional components as well as the aesthetic criteria for later selection from the proliferation of functional versions. This method might be called function-to-form method.

This is indeed the method of Modern Functionalism. This only works here because the constraints on the global form of a complex building are very loose. Each function can be accommodated in a different, separated part of the building. No strong aesthetic constraints, like proportional systems or symmetries, are imposed. The articulated character of Modern Functionalist designs like the Dessau Bauhaus implies that the need for geometrical coordination is minimized. The different parts, each with their own building depth, overall height, floor-to-floor height and fenestration system, are only connected by minimal, articulated joints. Functional issues posed the main difficulty. A whole new range of diverse social/institutional functions had to be accommodated. These issues had to be attended to first and could not be pre-constrained by aesthetic or geometrical concerns. In contrast, Classical architecture pre-constrained both geometry and aesthetics, leaving functional accommodation as a later selection criterion determining the final choice between readymade aesthetic-geometric states. However, functions were easily accommodated because they were simple and repetitive. The result generally presents a greater sophistication and cohesiveness in the appearance of Classical buildings when compared with Modern buildings. The case with the modern avant-garde is, however, different. Here there was plenty of formal research that was not burdened by difficult functional constraints. Examples include the various iconic villas of Modernism, like Rietveld's Schröder House or Le Corbusier's villas, and Expo pavilions like Mies' Barcelona Pavilion, as well as the various pavilions from Le Corbusier, Aalto and Melnikov. A new, rich, formal repertoire had to be created before the function-to-form method could be effectively deployed.

The contemporary avant-garde tends, once more, towards a form-to-programme method. Social functions are complex, but they are defined more loosely than they were in Modern Functionalism. Social communication patterns are too rich and fluid to be cast into highly specialized spaces. Contemporary architecture can no longer work by minutely fixing very definite functions. It offers richly differentiated spatio-morphological fields for self-organized, aleatoric appropriation. Demonstration of specialized functionality is not required to the same extent that it was required during the Modernist paradigm. As long as the spatial characteristics that in general facilitate contemporary life, ie, richness of diverse settings, gradient transitions between domains and the general intensification of connections between domains, are given, the self-organizing functional processes no longer call for detailed functional specification. It seems the contemporary style of Parametricism[81] translates this tendency into a preference for generating complex geometrical systems that are then selected on the basis of broad aesthetic criteria, before finally being tested with respect to functional affordances. The radicality of this form-to-function method might be due to the fact that Parametricism is still in its avant-garde phase without much penetration into the mainstream. However, due to the socio-institutional patterns of contemporary society hinted at above, this tendency might very well survive Parametricism's projection into the mainstream. This excursion into the history/future of architectural styles should provide here only a first hint as to how methodological biases might be seen to correspond to styles. These correspondences might be summarized in a table as follows. Difficult and 'rare' properties tend to be imposed by the generator while intermediate states tend to be examined for easily testable properties that are then selected. Which solution

81 See part 11 *Parametricism – The Parametric Paradigm and the Formation of a New Style.*

properties are difficult/rare and which are made easy depends upon the style and its mode of adaptation within its historical/societal context.

architectural styles solution properties	**Classicism**	**Modernism**	**Parametricism**
functional fit	*test*	*generate*	*test*
geometric fit	*generate*	*test*	*generate*
aesthetic fit	*generate*	*test*	*test*

The specific power of the new scripting-based design processes available to Parametricism lies in the capacity to devise systems of rules that regulate the interaction of large component assemblies. These rule-based systems are now the primary domain of intervention in contrast to the direct manipulation of form that marks all prior eras of architectural design. These rule sets are the essential, defining layer within each problem state. Rule sets, in conjunction with specific parameter inputs, generate complex geometric configurations that cannot always be fully anticipated. Sets of simple rules compute complex, sometimes surprising emergent patterns. Unexpected qualities might be discovered that can then be investigated with respect to their aesthetic power and functional potential. Despite their often surprising quality, these results are fully reproducible. Discovered qualities can be focused upon and refined and integrated into the expanding geometric-spatial repertoire. We might call this power to produce a wide variety of novel patterns and qualities the ***generative power*** of the thus deployed scripting techniques. In parallel the new scripting techniques afford a further profound advance: they allow for complex, multi-variable constraints to be built into the generative rule set. We might call this capacity to build in multiple constraints into a rule set the ***constraining power*** of the deployed scripting techniques. This strategy makes it possible for key solution criteria of the design to be guaranteed in advance while a fecund, generative process explores the space of possibility that is still open despite the inbuilt constraints. Generative and constraining power can thus operate together and complement each other. These computational techniques also exhibit a compelling ***analytical power***. Each result can be instantly measured. Component variations can be tied to a quantitative analysis (measurement) of underlying layers. This analytical power can be used to further enhance the rationality of the design process.

This ability to combine the explorative potential for surprise discoveries with the guaranteed adherence to key criteria is the unique advantage of the new computational techniques. Another, related point is that these techniques allow for the condensation of long, recursive sequences of elementary information processes into a single generative design act. Traditional design techniques would have to break each iterative run of the script into hundreds of transformative steps. This is practically impossible. There is a definite complexity barrier here for Classical and Modern design methods. Scripts work deep into a problem space by chaining many decisions into a forward trajectory. With each design step, the complexity of the model can be substantially enhanced. At the same time, series working is made easy by changing parameters or selected script components. This kind of series working gives breadth to the search. For those who still remember how design progressed in the old days, the pervasive reality of extensive series working, nearly all the way through the design process, is one of the most striking features of the contemporary design method in comparison with Modern design. Through these techniques, the contemporary process gains both breadth and depth simultaneously. Whether this contemporary design process, augmented by scripting techniques in the way indicated, is a veritable design *method* depends on the examination procedures that follow each cycle of generation, and on the decision criteria that are brought to bear on the progress of the design. The ability to build in constraints is certainly a feature that enhances the overall rationality of the process, if the constraints are selected in accordance with the guidelines suggested above. The proliferation of options is also an inherently rational move. However, as will transpire below, the rationality of the overall process within contemporary design is not an obvious matter.

To the extent to which these techniques are deployed according to criteria of rationality (to be further specified below), they become key components of a powerful contemporary design method. Parametricism is the contemporary style that is most vigorously advancing its design agenda on the basis of these techniques. To the extent that the label 'Parametricism' is here not only deployed as a descriptive, classificatory label that is applied to observed contemporary tendencies in architecture, but is also used with normative import outlining an agenda for contemporary architecture, we might call the process/method envisioned here the ***Parametricist process/method.***

To summarize: contemporary, scripting-based design processes allow for the establishment of a powerful design process/method, the Parametricist design process/method. The unique power of this process/method lies in its ability to combine otherwise conflicting trajectories:

1. The combination and simultaneous increase in both the ***generative power*** and the ***constraining*** power of each design cycle.
2. The combination and simultaneous increase in both the ***breadth*** and ***depth*** of the solution search in each design cycle.

Despite the ability to front-load functional constraints within generative scripts, the overall character of the Parametricist process/method remains a form-to-function heuristics. In particular, this is the case during the avant-garde phase of Parametricism. Here constraints are often treated abstractly, as formal-explorative devices that stand in for the real constraints that must later be chosen in terms of valid functional criteria.

7.5 Problem Definition and Problem Structure

THESIS 39

The architectural design process is self-determined. There are only very few, very general constraints that are accepted in advance. The design process then proceeds by continuous self-stimulation on the basis of its own intermediate states. This self-determination is a correlate of the autonomy of architecture as autopoietic subsystem of society.

The history of the 1960s' design methods movement was a history that went from over-enthusiasm to disenchantment and cynicism. This trajectory parallels the general trajectory of the 1960s from the technological optimism and euphoria that culminated in the moon landing to a general disenchantment and scepticism that hit the historical mood during the 1970s.[82] To some extent, however, this trajectory was inherent in the subject matter (as it would be with any new and promising discovery). Design methodology had swamped and usurped schools of architecture but there was virtually no positive evidence that the stringent and cumbersome methods proposed could be applied in actual design practice. Was the resistance to methodological rigour a case of natural obstinacy of a profession that would not upgrade its act as long as it could get away with its traditional, intuitive ways, or was the fault to be sought in the proposed methods that were simply not practical? Or was it still too early to pass judgement, and simply that more theoretical work was required? In the early 1970s a lot of the discussion centred on the peculiar character of design problems that seemed to make the transference of methodological models from other

82 The economy was in crisis and many promises and hopes – the student revolution, modernization/development of the former colonies – were frustrated.

problem-solving domains, like operations research (OR) and artificial intelligence (AI) research, into architecture difficult. The key point that became the point of departure for design process thinking was the thesis that design problems, and in particular architectural design problems, were ***ill-defined problems*** or ***ill-structured problems***. What this means and what consequences flow from this characterization of design tasks are the subject of this section.

7.5.1 WICKED PROBLEMS

The notion of so-called ill-defined problems was first introduced within the context of the information-processing approach to artificial and human problem solving. It was Walter Reitman who proposed classifying problems into well-defined vs ill-defined problems. The emphasis on the ill-defined nature of modern design problems was pushed furthest by the mathematician and design methodologist Horst Rittel. His position led to a radical scepticism with regard to the rationalization of design methods pursued in the preceding decade. According to Rittel, architectural and urban design/planning problems are inherently ***wicked problems.***[83] Rittel was Professor of the 'Science of Design' at the University of California in Berkeley when he published his seminal paper on the 'Dilemmas in a General Theory of Planning'. Although he had been teaching in various schools of architecture and his points cover urban planning issues, Rittel makes his point most cogently with reference to a much wider notion of planning in the context of large and complex social systems, with explicit references to issues of national social policy. This expansion of local design problems into comprehensive system problems was a typical trait of architectural and urban design methodology inspired by systems thinking. This expansive trait seemed to make sense in the era of comprehensive, state-sponsored modernization. The unusual expansiveness of the problems Rittel refers to goes a certain way towards accounting for the radicalism of his pronouncements. Architectural design problems cannot be considered as the most typical examples of wicked problems, but because Rittel's radically sceptical point was taken up within methodologically-oriented architectural theory, it is necessary to engage with his position.

Rittel's reflections emerged in the early 1970s, after the failings of post-war social policy programmes evidenced the intractability of the respective problems addressed. The failure of planned societal modernization was in particular made evident by the diverse protest

83 Horst WJ Rittel & Melvin M Webber, 'Dilemmas in a General Theory of Planning', *Policy Sciences* 4 (1973), 155–69.

movements that problematized the assumptions and methods of professional policy makers.

The abstract of Rittel's paper starts with the following bold assertion: 'The search for scientific bases for confronting problems of social policy is bound to fail, because of the nature of these problems. They are "wicked" problems, whereas science has developed to deal with "tame" problems.'[84]

Rittel considers ***goal-finding*** to be one of the central functions of planning. The initial task is to discover and formalize our latent purposes. However, there are usually multiple audiences or publics with diverging interests to be catered for. Professionalism has been understood to be one of the major instruments for perfectability. Based in modern science, each of the professions has been conceived as the medium through which the knowledge of science is applied. Rittel notes that in contrast to this conception experience should have taught us to think about the planning task in very different ways:

> We have been learning to see social processes as the links tying open systems into large and interconnected networks of systems, such that outputs from one become inputs to others. In that structural framework it has become less apparent where problem centers lie, and less apparent *where* and *how* we should intervene even if we do happen to know what aims we seek. We are now sensitized to the waves of repercussions generated by a problem solving action directed to any one node in the network, and we are no longer surprised to find it inducing problems of greater severity at some other node. And so we have been forced to expand the boundaries of the systems we deal with, trying to internalize those externalities. . . . As system boundaries get stretched, and as we become more sophisticated about the complex workings of open societal systems, it becomes ever more difficult to make the planning idea operational.[85]

This implies, according to Rittel, that the classical paradigm of science and engineering that has underpinned modern professionalism is not applicable to urban planning and planning in general in relation to the problems of complex societal systems. The problems of scientists and engineers are mostly 'tame' or 'benign'. In the case of tame problems, the problem-solving effort terminates when a solution has been arrived at. In the case of complex planning problems, it remains rather uncertain – even with clarified purposes – whether the problem has been solved or not. Furthermore, this question always remains contentious because of diverging purposes. As examples of such wicked problems, Rittel cites

84 Ibid.
85 Ibid.

the location of a freeway, the adjustment of tax rates, the reform of school curricula or the attempts to tackle crime.

Wicked problems, according to Rittel,[86] can be distinguished from tame problems by the following 10 traits:

1. *There is no definitive formulation of a wicked problem.* The information needed to *understand a* wicked problem depends on one's idea for *solving* it. Every textbook of systems engineering starts with an enumeration of these phases: understand the mission/problem, gather relevant information, analyze information, synthesize information and work out solution. For wicked problems there can be no such step-wise scheme. It is not possible to search for information without the orientation of a solution concept.
2. *Wicked problems have no stopping rule.* In solving a chess problem or a mathematical equation, the problem solver knows when he has done his job. There are criteria that tell us when a solution has been found. Because there is no end to the causal chains that link interacting open systems, there is no fixed point of termination in the problem solving effort.
3. *Solutions to wicked problems are not true-or-false.* There are no conventionalized criteria for objectively deciding whether the offered solution is successful. For wicked planning problems, there are no true or false answers. Normally, many parties are equally equipped, interested and/or entitled to judge the solutions.
4. *There is no immediate and no ultimate test of a solution to a wicked problem.* With wicked problems any solution, after being implemented, will generate waves of consequences over an extended – virtually an unbounded – period of time. Moreover, the next day's consequences of the solution may yield utterly undesirable repercussions which outweigh the intended advantages or the advantages accomplished hitherto.
5. *Every solution to a wicked problem is a 'one-shot operation'.* In the sciences and in fields like mathematics or mechanical engineering design, the problem solver can try various runs without penalty. With wicked planning problems, however, every implemented solution is consequential. It leaves 'traces' and irreversible effects. Every attempt to reverse a decision or to correct for the undesired consequences poses another set of wicked problems, which are in turn subject to the same dilemmas.

86 What follows is a compressed summary, an excerpt from: Rittel & Webber, 'Dilemmas in a General Theory of Planning', 155–69.

6. *Wicked problems do not have a finite set of potential solutions, nor is there a well-described set of permissible operations that may be incorporated into the plan.* There are no criteria that enable one to prove that all solutions to a wicked problem have been identified and considered. It may happen that *no* solution is found, owing to logical inconsistencies in the 'picture' of the problem. 'Anything goes' or, at least, any new idea for a planning measure may become a serious candidate for a resolution.
7. *Every wicked problem is essentially unique.* There are no *classes* of wicked problems in the sense that principles of solution can be developed to fit *all* members of a class. Despite seeming similarities among wicked problems, one can never be certain that the particulars of a problem do not override its commonalities with other problems already dealt with. Part of the art of dealing with wicked problems is the art of not knowing too early which type of solution to apply.
8. *Every wicked problem can be considered to be a symptom of another problem.* For instance 'crime on the streets' can be considered as a symptom of general moral decay, or permissiveness, or deficient opportunity, or wealth, or poverty. The level at which a problem is settled depends upon the self-confidence of the analyst and cannot be decided on logical grounds. There is nothing like a natural level of a wicked problem. Of course, the higher the level of a problem's formulation, the broader and more general it becomes: and the more difficult it becomes to do something about it. On the other hand, one should not try to cure symptoms: and therefore one should try to settle the problem on as high a level as possible.
9. *The choice of explanation determines the nature of the problem's resolution.* In dealing with wicked problems, the modes of reasoning used in the argument are much richer than those permissible in scientific discourse. That is to say, the choice of explanation is arbitrary in the logical sense.
10. *The planner has no right to be wrong.* It is a principle of science that solutions to problems are only hypotheses offered for refutation. Consequently, the scientific community does not blame its members for postulating hypotheses that are later refuted – so long as the author abides by the established rules of the game. In the world of planning and wicked problems no such immunity is tolerated.

Rittel asserts: 'We are thus led to conclude that the problems that planners must deal with are wicked and incorrigible ones, for they defy efforts to delineate their boundaries and to identify their causes. . . . The planner who works with open systems is caught up in the ambiguity of their causal webs. Moreover, his would-be solutions are confounded by a still further set of dilemmas posed by the growing pluralism of the contemporary publics, whose valuations of his proposals are judged against an array of different and contradicting scales.'[87]

The most interesting and challenging problems that contemporary society poses for architecture are indeed 'ill-defined' in Reitman's sense, and probably also 'wicked problems' as defined by Horst Rittel. However, the result of Rittel's analysis is largely negative.[88] He is not only blocking the analogy of planning and design with science and engineering, he is leaving the question of the rationality of design and planning suspended. Rittel's caution is to be heeded, namely that it is 'objectionable for the planner to treat a wicked problem as though it were a tame one, or to tame a wicked problem prematurely, or to refuse to recognize the inherent wickedness of social problems'.[89] However, a theory of the design process must go further than this and try to formalize the rationality that still prevails. Also, the theory of architectural autopoiesis disagrees with his conclusion that 'planning is a component of politics'.[90] At least with respect to design – including urban design – the theory of architectural autopoiesis insists that architecture has been differentiated as a *sui generis* system of communications that can be subsumed neither under politics nor under science.

7.5.2 THE STRUCTURE OF ILL-STRUCTURED PROBLEMS

The theory of architectural autopoiesis follows Herbert Simon in taking issue with the negative, residual nature of Rittel's concept of Wicked Problems. Simon's point of reference was Reitman's concept of ill-defined problems. Simon reluctantly accepts the existence of so-called 'residual concepts', ie, concepts that are defined negatively, by what they are not. A problem is ill-structured if it is not a well-structured problem. According to Simon such residual categories are 'tenacious' in the sense that they are hard to get rid of: 'The scope of a residual category can be narrowed progressively by explaining previously unexplained phenomena; it cannot be extinguished as long as a single phenomenon remains

87 Rittel & Webber, 'Dilemmas in a General Theory of Planning', 155–69.

88 However, Rittel has also drawn constructive conclusions from his assessment of complex design and planning problems. He developed a discursive, argument-based approach to planning.

89 Rittel & Webber, 'Dilemmas in a General Theory of Planning', 155–69.

90 Ibid.

unexplained.'[91] The task is thus to explore the structure of ill-structured problems. Here this means to understand the rationality of those actual processes that are indeed always already handling and resolving ill-structured problems. Herbert Simon's focus is narrower, ie, to explore 'whether the problems regarded as ill-structured are inaccessible to the problem-solving systems of artificial intelligence'. In particular, Simon is trying to 'show that there is no real boundary between WSPs (well-structured problems) and IPSs (ill-structured problems), and no reason to think that new and hitherto unknown types of problem-solving processes are needed to enable artificial intelligence systems to solve problems that are ill-structured.'[92]

The criteria that have been proposed to distinguish well-structured problems generally express characteristics of a problem domain in relation to characteristics of a problem-solving system. Simon gathered six such criteria that he takes to represent what has usually been proposed as characterization of well-defined problems within the problem-solving literature:

1. There is a definite test as to whether a proposed terminal problem state is indeed a solution to the problem.
2. There is a problem space that fully represents the initial problem state, all intermediate states and the goal states.
3. Attainable state changes can be represented as transitions from given problem states via well-defined operations.
4. Any knowledge that the problem solver acquires can be represented in the established problem space.
5. If the actual problem involves acting upon the external world, then the effect of the operators on the problem states accurately reflects the laws that govern the external domain.
6. All the information processes required to fulfil the above criteria require only practicable amounts of computation.

General Problem Solvers (GPS) developed within the artificial intelligence (AI) paradigm can take on problems that fit these criteria. Such a programme would need to have a set of terms to describe the problem states, and it would require a description of the solution state to test whether a solution was obtained. The system would further require a set of terms and tests to detect relevant differences between states and an

91 Simon, 'The Structure of Ill-Structured Problems', 145–66.

92 Ibid, p 146.

associated set of operators for reducing or removing the detected difference.

Wicked problems as characterized by Rittel and Webber violate all of the criteria listed above. What kinds of specific problem types fit those criteria? What are the typical examples of well-structured problems that ill-structured problems are usually contrasted with? Examples often referred to in the relevant literature expounding the essential difference between ill-structured problems like design problems and supposedly well-structured problems include precisely those problems the early AI researchers such as Herbert Simon and Allen Newell had focused on, namely problems such as proving logic theorems or succeeding in playing chess. However, Herbert Simon demonstrates that both types of problems are not well-structured according to the criteria put forward. For instance, with respect to finding or constructing a proof for a basic logic theorem, it might be necessary or opportune to step away from the direct manipulation of axioms via defined operations and instead analyze the problem and plan one's steps in a meta-language, or use experience with similar problems as a guide for finding a proof.[93] The characterization of well-structured problems does not admit the shifting of the problem space (criterion 2). It also does not admit that the problem-solving system introduces new operations and/or new knowledge during the problem-solving effort (criterion 4). These moves imply that the problem is being effectively restructured. The characterization of well-structured problems does not admit restructuring and instead demands that problem space, and the problem-solving resources like relevant knowledge and relevant information processes, are specified in advance. It follows that 'problems of discovering proofs in formal logic are not, for all problem solvers, well-structured.'[94] Also, with respect to criterion 6 – practicable computability – many theorem proof problems remain outside the scope of mechanical theorem provers. The other candidate for a well-structured problem that has been tackled by AI is playing chess to win. Its status as well-defined problem is equally suspect. Even if we only consider the problem of finding a good next move within a given chess constellation, the problem solver is soon confronted with a computational barrier. To be well-structured, the chess problem would have to be formalized

93 There are indeed AI systems that use meta-linguistic techniques in theorem proving. See: RD Kling, *A Paradigm for Reasoning by Analogy*, Proceedings of the 2nd International Joint Conference on Artificial Intelligence, British Computer Society (London), 1971.

94 Simon, 'The Structure of Ill-Structured Problems', p 149.

(redefined) as maximizing and testing some approximate evaluation function.

If a whole game rather than a single move is considered, the status of being well-defined has to be denied: the move in the real game is countered by a consequent move frequently different from what was anticipated. New, unexpected information has to be absorbed, and therefore playing a game of chess involves continually redefining what the problem is.

Simon's conclusion at this stage in the argument reads as follows: 'Definiteness of problem structure is largely an illusion that arises when we systematically confound the idealized problem that is presented to an idealized (and unlimitedly powerful) problem-solver with the actual problem that is to be attacked by a problem solver with limited (even large) computational capacities. . . . In general, the problems presented to problem-solvers by the world are best to be regarded as IPSs. They become WPSs only in the process of being prepared for problem solvers. . . . There are no WSPs, only IPSs that have been formalized for problem-solvers.'[95] Although Simon rejects the conclusion that the 'real' problem-solving activity thus resides only in the process of providing a problem with structure – because a lot of non-trivial information processing remains to be done after precise problem formulation – he admits that 'there is merit to the claim that much problem solving effort is directed at structuring problems, and only a fraction of it at solving problems once they are structured'.[96] There can be no doubt that this statement resonates with the author's experiences with architectural design.

After having thus deconstructed and nearly dissolved the demarcation between well-structured and ill-structured problems – in the sense of having shown that there are no inherently well-structured problems – Simon reverses the direction of the argument.

The usual argument had often been that there are two radically different kinds of problems demanding radically different methods: well-defined problems susceptible to the exact methods of optimizing algorithms, or algorithms that can guarantee a solution, and ill-defined problems that require heuristic approaches understood as intuitively handled rules of thumb. Herbert Simon is trying to dissolve this divide. On the one hand, he is showing that even the presumably well-structured problems cannot meet the criteria that would seem to be necessary for the application of fail-safe methods. On the other hand, he is emphasizing that these problems have nevertheless been successfully

95 Ibid, p 150.

96 Ibid, p 151.

tackled by AI. Since the problem domains that have been explored so far with well-understood mechanical techniques (AI) fail to meet the requirements of WSPs, he now goes on to ask 'how problem-solvers of familiar kinds can go to work even on problems that are, in important respects, ill-structured'.[97] Simon is approaching this question with reference to architectural design problems which he considers 'lie well toward the ill-structured end of the problem continuum',[98] in particular, 'if the architect is trying to be 'creative''.[99] If one confronts a typical architectural design problem with respect to the six criteria that characterize well-structured problems, it fails on all six counts:

1. There is initially no definite criterion to test a proposed solution.
2. The problem space is not defined in any meaningful way because its definition would have to encompass all relevant information and all kinds of structures the architect might at some point consider, in any modelling space whatsoever. Simon talks about the 'hopelessness of defining in reasonable compass a problem space that could not, at any time during the problem-solving process, find its boundaries breached by the intrusions of new alternatives'.[100]
3. Therefore it is not possible to ensure that attainable state changes can be represented as transitions from given problem states via well-defined operations.
4. It is not feasible to assume that all knowledge that the problem solver acquires can be represented from the start, in a single problem space. A lot of the required information is contingent upon the solution envisioned and becomes relevant only at a relatively advanced stage of the design process.
5. The modelling spaces used within architectural design fail to reflect many of the laws that govern the external domain. The building as it is actually used is something quite different from the building as represented. (However, contemporary simulation tools move in the direction of closing this gap.)
6. With respect to the issue of whether the architectural problem-solving team is equipped with the requisite computational power in order to compute expected information processes, there can be no general conclusion here. The point only serves as a reminder that the available information-processing capacity has to be considered when assessing whether the task is well-defined.

97 Ibid.
98 Ibid.
99 Ibid.
100 Ibid, p 152.

Having thus established that architectural design problems are not well structured in the demanded sense, Simon goes on the analyze design problems and how architects seem to solve them, in order to see how these processes can be formalized for the involvement of problem-solving mechanisms of the GPS type. His analysis is guided by a prior analysis conducted by Walter Reitman on the problem and process of composing a fugue. According to Reitman, creative tasks like musical compositions, although considered complex, include very few constraints as given: 'Here the main initial constraint, and it is an open constraint at that (ie, one that is incompletely specified), is that the end product be a fugue. All other constraints are in a sense supplementary, generated from one transformation of the problem to the next.'[101] The same lack of determinate constraints can be observed with respect to architectural design tasks. As Simon points out: 'The more distinguished the architect, the less expectation that the client should provide the constraints.'[102] We might add here that in the case of architectural design competitions, in particular in the case of international, high-profile competitions, there are even less determinate constraints than in any direct commission. In general one can say that the presence or absence of determinate constraints correlates with the distinction between avant-garde versus mainstream architecture. The avant-garde design process is in many ways marked by a strong sense of self-determination. This sense of self-determination is a direct correlate of the autonomy of architecture as autopoietic subsystem of society. One of the major open decisions that permeate the overall character of the design resides in the choice of the style within which the design is to be developed. This decision is usually not prefigured or constrained.

Simon suggests that the design task will evoke from the IPS's long-term memory (LTM) relevant information, issues and attributes that need to be addressed and specified at an early stage of the design. The task will also evoke some overall organization, or executive programme for the design process itself. 'Neither the guiding organization nor the attributes evoked from memory need at any time during the process provide a complete procedure nor complete information. ... The entire procedure could conceivably be organized as a system of productions, in which the elements already evoked from memory and the aspects of the design already arrived at up to any given point, would serve as the stimuli to evoke the next set of elements. ... The evocation of relevant

101 Reitman, *Cognition and Thought*, p 169.

102 Simon, 'The Structure of Ill-Structured Problems', p 153.

information and sub-goals from long-term memory can be sequential.'[103] In this way the design process progresses by means of self-stimulation. The design process usually starts with a global parti or 'primary generator'[104] and then progresses from global to local issues by means of progressive detailing. Simon is once more taking a cue from Reitman, who himself had taken his cues from Noam Chomsky's conception of a generative grammar conceived as proceeding from a global structure via a series of successively detailed substitutions on the basis of rewriting rules.[105] Above, Reitman was quoted as saying that the constraints that shape a composition are supplementary, generated from one transformation of the problem to the next. He then asked about the source of these supplementary constraints. His answer reads as follows:

'One important class of structural or syntactic constraints are those that appear in problem transformations which, to a first approximation, are analogous to the rewriting rules of structural linguistics. Just as "sentence" transforms to "subject plus predicate", and "subject" may transform to "article plus noun phrase", so "fugue" may be thought of transforming to "exposition plus development plus conclusion", "exposition" to "thematic material plus countermaterial", and "thematic material" to "motive plus development of motive".'[106] Reitman is talking about 'transformational formulas'[107] that control the processing sequence whereby subunits deriving from larger units are given. While here the idea of the design process as self-propelling series of successive, transformational substitutions – from the general to the specific – is brought into the architectural discourse via a second-hand analogy, Chomsky's idea has also had a direct influence via the work of Peter Eisenman, who utilized the idea to radicalize this aspect of procedural self-stimulation in his avant-garde practice. Perhaps it is Peter Eisenman's pervasive influence (that reaches all the way to the most contemporary avant-garde) that makes the analogy so convincing today. What makes such analogies productive is their high degree of abstraction. Simon's translation of the analogy into architecture is comparatively

103 Ibid, p 154.

104 Jane Darke, 'The Primary Generator and the Design Process', *Design Studies* 1, 1979, reprinted in: Nigel Cross (Ed), *Developments in Design Methodology*, John Wiley & Sons (New York), 1984.

105 Noam Chomsky, *Syntactic Structures,* Mouton (The Hague), 1957, Walter de Gruyter (Berlin), 2002.

106 Reitman, *Cognition and Thought*, p 169.

107 Ibid.

banal: 'house' transforms into 'general floorplan plus structure', structure is then further detailed into aspects etc. In fact any attempt to concretize the analogy within architecture exposes the fact that the schema of composition/decomposition within architecture is much less normalized than the grammatical composition/parsing of a sentence. Rewriting or self-substitution takes place but there is no normative, fixed hierarchy or scheme of substitution, and no stringent rewriting rules that would clearly demarcate the well-ordered from the dis-ordered design, ie, there is no direct equivalent to the linguistic demarcation between a grammatically correct sentence and a grammatical mistake. There is no general architectural grammar. Only within a given, well-established style do syntactic constraints approach a grammar-like condition. In particular, Modern and contemporary architecture seem to be much more open than the task of composing a fugue. (Contemporary music is again another matter.) Reitman acknowledges that even with respect to the composition of a fugue 'the coupling is very much looser than is the case with linguistic materials'.[108]

For Simon the essential aspect is that this scheme of successive substitutions allows the information to stream sequentially: 'The requirements that any of these components should meet can also be evoked at the appropriate times in the design process, and need not be specified in advance. ... Design alternatives can also be evoked in component-by-component fashion.'[109]

Thus the problem acquires structure via a self-determined process of successive detailing of hierarchically nested subsystems. This process is marked by a successive loading of additional information from the system's LTM. The system's long-term memory might be distributed between individual design team members, various expert consultants and various external data-banks that might be consulted as the need arises. The need is always triggered from within the evolving design itself, by the current problem state. The design process is inevitably sequential. Even if all the immense amount of relevant information were somehow there (where?), the sequential processing would still imply that information is loaded bit by bit. All cognitive processes are limited in terms of their short-term memory (STM) and can therefore only take up, consider and process a limited amount of relevant information. The medium of architecture – the drawing or digital model – is in fact a powerful STM enhancer. The density of simultaneously present information within a

108 Walter R Reitman, *Cognition and Thought*, p 169.
109 Simon, 'The Structure of Ill-Structured Problems', p 154.

detailed drawing, in view on a single sheet of paper, to be quickly glanced over, is enormous when compared with the amount of information that can be conveyed by the written or spoken word in the same unit of time. Digital models can activate and make simultaneously available even more information, ready for interactive engagement. This power is further enhanced by parametric models, dense with associative logics and embedded constraints.

An upgraded design medium is indeed necessary to cope with the informational richness of architectural design problems. However, despite such a powerful, specialized medium of communication, selectivity, ie, the concentration on priorities, is inevitable. As the process evolves, new concerns will be brought into play. Every episode concentrates on a new set of issues. This inevitably sequential mode of operation entails the risk that concerns and criteria that guided the design decisions at one stage of the design process are being lost sight of and contravened at a later stage when other issues occupy the foreground of attention. This problem exists despite the fact that the results of all prior design decisions are in view within the enhanced STM because only the results but not the reasons of all prior decisions are present. The complexity of the problem is unfolded over time. Special provisions would therefore be required to maintain the internal consistency of the design process in terms of the values and criteria brought to bear throughout. This risk is very real. It is indeed the personal experience of the author as participant, leader or critic of many design processes, both in professional and academic arenas, that the demand for internal coherence (consistency of criteria) is violated all the time. Contradictions abound, new criteria contravene old decisions, often without revisiting and unravelling those old decisions in terms of the new criteria discovered and brought to bear. Some measure of backtracking and iterative reworking is of course always happening, but the deep cutbacks that would often be required in any attempt to eliminate contradictions are usually dispensed with. Such inconsistencies put a serious dent in the rationality claim of any design process that is unable to provide remedial mechanisms. One possible mechanism whereby information-rich, multi-criteria design processes can be kept internally coherent is by means of design team organization, ie, by correlating issues with team members and thus giving social representation to all important criteria. This is happening. This also allows – to a certain extent – the move from sequential to parallel processing. With the introduction of social representation, the consistency problem now reappears as a coordination and integration problem. The new risk is now that parallel activities move into incompatible directions leading to abortive work.

Incompatibility is a much more severe issue than criteria-inconsistency. Incompatibility of subsystems spells product dysfunctionality. Criteria-inconsistency implies a lack of process rationality.

Problem solving in information-rich domains (like 21st-century architectural design) implies a gradual information- and criteria-loading. The informational enrichment of the process is self-induced. The interim result catalyzes further goals and criteria.

As a consequence there exists a certain degree of circularity between the problem and its solution, between what has become the problem and what has become its solution. The solution path – to a certain extent – specifies the problem. The problem is evolving together with the emerging solution. Only the final result allows for the full statement (reconstruction) of the problem. This formula does not cancel all possible claims towards rationality. It just poses a more complex form of rationality, a rationality that fully reveals and asserts itself only in retrospect.

7.5.3 AN INFORMATION-PROCESSING MODEL FOR INFORMATION-RICH DESIGN PROCESSES

The architectural design problem has been identified as very information rich, implying a gradual self-induced enrichment process. This correlates with Herbert Simon's conclusion that the key difference between well-structured and ill-structured problems might lie precisely in the amount of information required. However, Simon avoids talking of absolute measures of information but considers information relative to the simultaneous processing capacity of the information-processing system in question. Whether in relative or absolute terms, complex architectural design problems will always be on the information-rich end of the spectrum. Designs for complex buildings take many months, and no one should expect the issues to be compressed into a huge parallel process. Irrespective of Simon's over-emphasis on processing capacity, his conclusions are relevant here: 'Any problem solving process will appear ill-structured if the problem solver is a machine that has access to a very large long-term memory (an effectively infinite memory) of potentially relevant information and/or access to a very large external memory that provides information about the actual real-world consequences of problem solving actions. "Large" is defined relative to the amount of information that can direct or affect the behaviour of the processor over any short period of time; while "potentially relevant" means that any small part of this information may be evoked at some time during the problem solving process by recognition of some feature in the current problem state (the information available *directly* to the processor).'[110]

Simon's final, most condensed conclusion concerning the demarcation between well-defined and ill-defined problems reads: 'There may be nothing other than the size of the knowledge base to distinguish ISPs from WSPs.'[111] Simon's primary aim was to argue for the feasibility of a research programme that brings these 'ill-structured' problems into the frame of AI problem-solving mechanisms. His arguments achieve this much. However, as elaborated in the previous chapter, this difference in knowledge base has significant consequences for the character and rationality of the respective problem-solving process. Simon acknowledged this and has accordingly developed a specifically augmented information-processing model for the description of information-rich (ill-structured) problems like architectural design problems. This model is being adopted here within the theory of architectural autopoiesis. Once more the same theoretical transformation must be applied as it was with respect to the adoption of Newell and Simon's general theoretical apparatus: the focus on social communication systems[112] as 'subjects' of the problem-solving process has to be substituted for Simon's focus on the cognitive system of human subjects or their supposed machinic simulations.

The augmented model is a (considerably more complex) extension of the model introduced in the chapter on problem solving as search in a state space.[113] The model assumes a pattern of alternation between phases of problem solving in a locally well-structured problem space and phases of problem space shift (or problem space modification) induced by the retrieval of new information. This is necessary because of the serial character of the problem-solving system that simply cannot take in all information at once. 'If a large long-term memory is associated with a serial processor of this kind, then most of the contents of long-term memory will be irrelevant during any brief interval of processing.'[114] Recognition and retrieval processes are necessary to discover and provide the input the serial problem-solving processes need at the time they need

110 Simon, 'The Structure of Ill-Structured Problems', p 161.

111 Ibid.

112 The information-processing system is indeed an autopoietic, ie, self-referentially enclosed, system of communications involving all the currently active design team members. The shared project involvement does indeed create a unique set of concerns and a unique language, both verbal and graphic, that is only understood within the design team.

113 See 7.3.5 *Problem Solving as Search in a State Space*.

114 Simon, 'The Structure of Ill-Structured Problems', p 157.

them. 'There is no need for this initial definition of the problem space and task structure. All of the necessary information is potentially available, but distributed through long-term memory.'[115]

The problem-solving system must provide for two distinct information-processing capacities: first, the kind of information-processing system (IPS) described earlier, equipped with a set of operations – both generators and tests – that can traverse and navigate through a given problem space and, second, a recognition and retrieval system that might respond to certain problem states arrived at within the given problem space with the retrieval (from the LTM) of new information determining new sub-goals, and new constraints. The recognition/retrieval system scans the current problem states for clues and is capable of interrupting the ongoing processes in order to transpose the problem to a new problem space capable of receiving and handling the injection of new information now necessary. Thus a new problem space is defined and entered. Simon seems to assume that any new information/constraint/goal-criterion demands a change of the problem space. With respect to architectural design, one might distinguish between problem space modification, for example, the expansion of knowledge within one category of knowledge, and problem space shift when a whole new category of knowledge becomes relevant. One might thus rather couple the concept of problem space shift[116] to a more severe transposition that also involves a shift in the system of representation and thus a whole new way of working, with a whole new set of generators and tests. Below, the various systems of representation that are being employed within architectural design during its various design phases will be interrogated.

The adopted (and adapted) model or scheme for describing information-rich problem-solving processes, like architectural design processes, stipulates the necessity of the following systemic components:

- the information-processing system: the architectural project understood as an evolving autopoietic communication system involving all active design team members; the system is self-referentially enclosed within the unique problem space of the project (and its history) which is, however, in turn embedded within, and regulated by, the autopoiesis of architecture as discipline

115 Ibid.

116 Simon actually uses the term 'problem space modification'.

- a brief giving the initial outline of objectives that any goal state should meet
- a planning space in which the design process is strategized/plotted (for example, project schedule)
- a series of problem spaces, each with its specific conceptual space, value space and modelling space with respective types of states and operations (generators and tests) adapted to handle the currently relevant (embedded) problem formulation (issues, knowledge, constraints and criteria). In a parallel team process there might be more than one problem space operative at any time
- long-term memory: a vast reservoir of potentially relevant knowledge distributed between the various team members and various external consultants, data-banks, or other knowledge resources
- a recognition-and-retrieval system: a control system (represented by the design team leader) that overviews the evolving design states with respect to the new information that becomes relevant, guided by the project schedule and governed by the brief's objectives

The control system retrieves new information due either to a generic plan of staged increase of information depth, or to the specific trajectory the design process has taken. To the extent to which the unique trajectory of the project determines information relevance and thus problem reformulation, the design process is self-determined. At certain stages, again either pre-programmed or self-induced, the problem space is not only modified or expanded but suspended and replaced by a new, potentially radically different problem space. The problem then is transposed and substantially reformulated. New aspects come into view that demand a new way of working. The following steps in the evolution of a familiar design process represent stage-transitions which involve genuine problem space shifts, ie, each of the following familiar design activities opens up its own unique problem space:

- topological adjacency diagramming
- sketch design operating with freehand sketches to generate potential massing configuration
- translation of freehand sketches into rough 3D digital sketch models
- first attempt at hard-line, metric coordination of adjacency diagrams (CAD)
- 3D digital model coordinating sketch massing with metric plan layouts
- elaboration of visual articulation via renderings involving view angles, surface qualities, light etc (rendering software)

- integration of architectural concept with schematic engineering subsystems (BIM)
- integration of construction issues, build ups, subsystem interfaces, joints, tessellations etc (BIM)

These are typical design stages, each with its own set of issues, typical operations for the generation of alternatives and each with its own type of design decisions on the basis of its specifically relevant information and according to its own criteria. Each of these stages is operating within a different problem space with a different symbol system. This multiplicity of symbol systems is characteristic of design processes. Earlier we distinguished three subsystems that together characterize a problem space: the conceptual system, the modelling system and the evaluation system. The modelling system entails the system of representation and is the most tangible of the three subsystems, but the other two systems matter too. They prevent us from simply identifying problem spaces with software packages. The relevant knowledge base is linked in via the conceptual system and via the evaluation system.

The above list of stages represents a very familiar sequence. However, within each of these stages there remains the choice between rather different particular problem spaces and therefore design processes. For instance, within the topological diagramming stage, instead of intuitively browsing across some configurations that come to mind or evolve on the paper rather randomly, an optimization algorithm might be deployed that is able to search a constrained space of possibility exhaustively and to examine/rank alternatives according to a precise evaluation function. Within the stage of rough 3D digital sketch modelling, the problem space might be augmented by scripting and associative modelling techniques (MEL Script, Grasshopper). The respective conceptual system will thus include the key concepts of correlation, action-reaction, adaptation etc. During the next stages, when layouts are coordinated with 3D geometry, the process might involve a parametric modelling system like Digital Project (DP) that is able to translate the scripted associations of the sketch model while also allowing the register of the evaluation function of the topological layout tool as inbuilt constraints structuring the further design alternatives. We can notice here that the choice of certain problem spaces might have a bearing on the architectural style that is being employed. There is no simple determination from processes to styles. However, a style, in particular the current style of Parametricism, privileges and indeed depends upon being able to enter certain modelling spaces.

7.6 Rationality: Retrospective and Prospective

THESIS 40

The rationality of the specific characteristics, affordances and limitations of the various, radically different problem spaces a project typically moves through can be broadly aligned with the three fundamental dimensions of architecture's task: the organizational, the phenomenological and the semiological dimension.

The distinction of self/internal vs world/external reference exists in all modern function systems as the ***re-entry*** of the distinction of system and environment within the system. In the case of architecture this re-entry operates via the distinction between *form* (or space, geometry, composition, tectonics etc) on the side of self-reference and *function* (or programme, performance, purpose, activities etc) on the side of world-reference. The design communications that constitute the design process continuously oscillate between references to the functional aspects (world-reference) and references to the formal aspects (self-reference) of the evolving design. That is why the fundamental concept of the problem space cannot be reduced to the aspect of the modelling space within which solutions are generated. The aspects of conceptual set up and evaluation – concept space and value space – must remain equal foci of our reflective attention. Each problem space must allow for the oscillation between functional and formal aspects, and in each problem space both functional and formal evaluation must be possible. In what follows, the focus will be on the relative rationality of operations within problem spaces as well as on the relative rationality of problem space selection and sequencing. The double challenge of complexity and novelty implies that an ambitious design project will have to reckon with the fact that its rationality will to a large extent be ascertained only in retrospect rather than being fully plotted out and ascertained in advance.

It is important to understand that the design process, at the level of complexity that contemporary architecture has to deal with in its most ambitious projects, cannot be conceived as a predictable, linear sequence of steps that would start from the global function selecting a global form, then move to subsidiary functions with subsidiary forms etc, until all functions are matched with forms. Even if it were possible to decompose the global substantial function of the respective project into a simple tree-like hierarchy of functional subsystems – as the early Christopher Alexander had hoped – it would still be unrealistic to presume that the rationality of the process could be reconstructed as a series of unidirectional function-form determinations according to the formula: 'clarify and fix the functional requirement of a functional subsystem, then select appropriate form that best fulfills this function and then move to the next subsidiary level, once more clarifying/fixing functional requirements' etc. Such a procedure would indeed follow the ideal model of rationality where each design step is covered by an attendant rationale. If we observe closely, we find that the reality of our design experiences does not fit this model. Especially with respect to the design processes of the most advanced contemporary designs, this model of linear rationality cannot be maintained. Something else takes its place. It is this other process that delivers the best results in the face of novel tasks. Therefore it is this other process that deserves attention. The task is thus to describe successful design processes after the fact and to try to extract a new model of design rationality.

The double challenge of complexity and novelty implies that less stringently goal-oriented processes of exploration must be accepted as legitimate phases of an ambitious design process. The potential contributions, even the specific purposes of an architectural experiment, are often discovered only in retrospect. Goals are thus often outcome rather than the starting point of the design research. The acceptance of this logic is in fact implicit in the communicative practice of the contemporary architectural avant-garde. This 'logic' is indeed a logic in the sense that it can be explicated and justified as a productive component within an encompassing rationality. The positive reinterpretation of the concept of 'formalism'[117] as formal research can be understood in this context as the expansion of the formal repertoire as general solution space, as well as a project specific browsing through solution spaces in terms of a form-to-programme heuristic. In recent years the play with abstract forms has been augmented by the even more abstract play and playful exploration of computational logics. Here the suspension of functional and formal preconceptions is pushed even further. The process produces novel, unexpected results far beyond the architect's 'natural' geometric and compositional range, thus radicalizing Eisenman's idea of automatic formal processes. To illustrate this way of working one might cite one of Parametricism's key protagonists: 'There is no seminal idea to work from – only intuitions, and working knowledge of spatial transformations. These are more like abstract relations between sorts of given forms, and they are often expressed with mathematical

117 It was Jeff Kipnis who (in the early 1990s at the AA) turned the derogatory term 'formalism' into a positive slogan and programme of formal design research.

symbols. They produce effects of uniformity, non-uniformity, singularity, or any combination thereof. ... Exploring this topic is for me primarily a problem of notation, and for some time now I've chosen to approach it almost exclusively in writing ... through symbols and marks rather than figures and images.'[118]

The explicit recognition of such practices can also be found in the discourse of management and organization theory. James G March and Johan P Olsen developed a sophisticated critique of formal decision analysis involving a set of basic concepts that seems inevitable for the definition of rational action. The concepts of choice, decision, goal, reason, rule, experience, history etc are deconstructed in a text that can also be read as a challenge to engrained assumptions about the rationality of the design process. March and Olsen start their argument by analyzing what is presupposed in the concept of choice and identify the following three underlying assumptions: the pre-existence of purpose, the necessity of consistency and the primacy of rationality. These common-sense assumptions had been made the explicit axioms of decision theory. 'It is fundamental to those theories that thinking should precede action; that action should serve a purpose; that purpose should be defined in terms of a consistent set of pre-existing goals; and that choice should be based on a consistent theory of the relation between action and its consequences. Every tool of management decision that is currently part of management science, operations research or decision theory assumes the prior existence of a set of consistent goals. Almost the entire structure of micro-economic theory builds on the assumption that there exists a well-defined stable, and consistent preference ordering.'[119]

The reality of 'the fluidity and ambiguity of objectives'[120] that can be observed in contemporary practice – both within business practice and in design practice – can only be dismissed as deficiency within this theoretical framework. The systematic rift between ideals and reality allows us to employ the concept of ideology here. The ideology of decision theory imposes itself. 'Goals are thrust upon the intelligent man. We ask that he act in the name of goals. We ask that he keeps his goals consistent.' This insistence on prior and consistent goals as *conditio sine qua non* of all rationality is what must be questioned. However, March and Olsen do not simply negate goal-oriented rationality, they reconstruct its augmentation and upgrading to 'more complicated forms of

118 George Legendre, 'Excerpt: New Things', in: *GSD 08 Platform*, Harvard University Graduate School of Design/Actar (Barcelona), 2008, pp 9–11.

119 JG March & JP Olsen, *Ambiguity and Choice in Organizations*, Universitetsforlaget (Bergen), 1976.

120 Ibid.

consistency', ie, a more complex rationality which temporarily allows for vagueness, while being able to offer procedures ('plans') for the discovery/construction of new goals and values in the process. The reality of shifting goals seems to force us to 'choose now in terms of the unknown set of values we will have at some future time. ... This violates severely our sense of temporal order.'[121] Such a 'choice' is illogical according to the currently still predominant ideology of choice.

The crucial point to grasp here is that the processes that succeed in real life deserve recognition. There is no point in insisting on abstract ideals of rationality. The real is the rational. Rather than questioning the reality of fluid, retrospective goals, it is the ideology of rational choice that has to be questioned. So-called aleatoric design processes have precisely the warped time structure suggested by March and Olsen. This process involves the radical suspension of everything usually associated with 'design' as deliberate purpose-led activity. This was reflected in the reversal of the order of programme and form in the slogan 'Form to Programme'. In the aleatoric design method, the formal process is self-propelling and the social programme is read into it a posteriori, allowing for an innovative alignment of new form and new function. This seemingly irrational process is in fact the best way to push the expansion of the repertoire. With respect to business contexts one can say that this is the perfect strategy to create new markets instead of competing in old ones. The process involves a form of self-coercion in the sense of the designer's temporary submission to an arbitrary determination. 'Coercion is not necessarily an assault on individual autonomy. It can be a device for stimulating individuality.'[122] The aleatoric 'play' is an instrument of intelligence, not its negation or substitute. March and Olsen come to the same conclusion in relation to business strategy: 'Playfulness is the deliberate, temporary relaxation of rules in order to explore the possibilities of alternative rules. When we are playful we challenge the necessity of consistency. In effect, we announce – in advance – our rejection of usual objections to behavior that does not fit the standard model of intelligence. Playfulness allows experimentation. At the same time, it acknowledges reason. It accepts that at one point ... it will be integrated into the structure of intelligence.'[123] March and Olsen propose to treat 'goals as hypotheses'. The interim stage that a complex design for a novel task has reached might continue to be elaborated under the spell of new goals that were stimulated by the evolving design. These new

121 March & Olsen, *Ambiguity and Choice in Organizations*.
122 Ibid.
123 Ibid.

goals come with new evaluation criteria. Many aspects of the design might be up for reinterpretation. In fact all our prior work and experiences are subject to potential future reinterpretation. 'Experience can be changed retrospectively. By changing our interpretive concepts now, we modify what we learned earlier. ... Planning in organizations has many virtues, but a plan can often be more effective as an interpretation of past decisions than as a program for future ones. ... In an organization that wants to continue to develop new objectives, a manager needs to be relatively tolerant of the idea that he will discover the meaning of yesterday's action in the experiences and interpretations of today.'[124]

Within the design process one can find the same kinds of reversals when form inspires programme and goals are discovered during the design exploration. The state space schema for describing problem-solving processes assumes that initial states are transformed via interim states into goal states. However, due to the complexity and ill-structured nature of design problems, there are no pre-established solutions and no absolutely right or wrong answers. This always leaves room for the designer to change the problem parameters and criteria to align goal states and goal criteria with the qualities emerging in the interim states. Thus the direction of adaptation can, to a certain extent, be reversed.[125]

7.6.1 RATIONAL IN RETROSPECT: OBSERVING INNOVATIVE DESIGN PRACTICE

One might use UN Studio's (Van Berkel & Bos) project for Arnhem Central as a case study of contemporary forms of how functional reasoning is embedded in a differently patterned design rationality. The project formulates an infrastructural knot that comprises two bus terminals to be linked with a train station. The project is rather complex, both in terms of form and function. The process itself has a veritable complexity as it brackets ongoing formal experiments with a form-finding process based on the geometric and quantitative analysis of all traffic functions. The architects present the project and its design process as eminently rational. The claim is made that the project evolves through the spatial organization of the various required transfer flows. However, the real unfolding of this process is not reducible to the logic of linear functional determination. Neither is the design imposing a preconceived architectural figure. Rather it operates via the experimental creation of

124 Ibid.
125 Goel, *Sketches of Thought*, p 92.

new design options. Any determination is relative to a presupposed ontology, ie, a given 'design world' that opens and delimits a space of possibilities in which a certain optimization is definable. The jump into unexpected spaces of possibility will undercut any previous determination and set up another optimization cycle according to new rules. This happened in the case of the Arnhem project when the investigation moved from the world of two-dimensional planes into a three-dimensional single surface, ie, a layered space that multiplies the available transfer surface while avoiding the usual bottlenecks of trying to connect stacked floors. This solution could not have been derived within a linear process that operates within a given, well-formalized ontology. The a posteriori documentation and rationalization of this process become the medium to convert an explorative experiment – with all its leaps and loops – into a reproducible repertoire. Through such retrospective rationalization the project is able to legitimize itself as an effective solution to a given site as well as an innovative contribution to the culture of architectural research.

This process of project development and its final self-legitimization points towards a complex new logic of legitimate design speculation that requires to be elaborated in more detail. On this basis the pertinent process features can be systematized to constitute a valid method. This is, then, the aim of this chapter: to utilize the project and design process of UN Studio's Arnhem masterplan to clarify questions concerning the rationality of current research and practice in architecture.

In their contribution to *Any* magazine, Ben van Berkel and Caroline Bos express the uncertainty and vacillating mood of current avant-garde practices with respect to the question of rational principles that might guide and legitimize the work. They are among those struggling to define a practice that, on the one hand, assumes it to be 'natural and right that architects strive to be reasonable, responsible partners' in a cooperative process with clients, authorities and users, so that 'large investments can be safely entrusted to them', while on the other hand becoming increasingly sceptical with respect to the pressure of rationality and 'the demand to present the "right" solution, even when the contents of that concept have become very uncertain'.[126] Van Berkel and Bos are referring to the objectivity and rationality demanded by the client (and delivered by the architects) as a 'retrospective justification' or 'after-theory' that

126 Ben van Berkel and Caroline Bos, 'Diagrams – Interactive Instruments in Operation', in: *Any* magazine 23, *Diagram Work* (New Jersey), 1998, p 19.

'blocks the view of what went on behind it'.[127] They bemoan the lack of 'real' (vs post-rationalizing) architectural theory. They speak of the way their strategies react to their dependence on being selected for work and of the resultant fear of critically analyzing their internal discourse. This frank admission of being somewhat alienated from their own discourse marks a courageous step, yet raises the question of how a free and self-critical practice would proceed and present itself.

Prima facie UN Studio's Arnhem Project participates in the recent reorientation of Dutch avant-garde architecture towards a parameter-driven elaboration of spatial form. As a complex infrastructural project, ie, a transport interchange required to integrate train, bus, taxi, car, bicycle and pedestrian movement, it could well become a paradigmatic test-bed for the scope and validity of the method of parameter-based derivation of form. Such a method – the so-called 'datascape'[128] method – has been most explicitly proclaimed and practised by MVRDV. In its most ruthless guise, this approach considers the design process as an explicit optimization process guided by some (narrow) set of performance criteria. Viewed as such it would follow in the tracks of Hannes Meyer and the '60s and '70s efforts to resolve architectural design into a science.[129] Although important differences in 'sensibility' need to be registered, the continuities with historical

127 Ibid.

128 For an in-depth discussion of MVRDV's datascape concept see: Bart Lootsma, 'Ausblick auf eine reflexive Architektur', in: *Arch+* 143, October 1998; Bart Lootsma, 'Reality Bytes', in: *Daidalos* 69/70, December 1998/January 1999; Winy Maas, Jacob van Rijs, Richard Koek (Eds), *MVRDV FARMAX,* 010 Uitgeverij (Rotterdam), 1998.

129 Modern Functionalism in its purest form (H Meyer, L Hilbersheimer) tended to assume a linear determinism, proceeding from a coherent catalogue of needs, placed on a clean slate (tabula rasa) and posing the calculated optimization of solutions on the basis of known techniques. More comprehensive and further formalized systems of evaluation were developed in the 1970s – matrices of vertically ranked criteria crossed by ranked or measured sets of solutions. In order to 'calculate' anything here, ordinal relations have to be converted into number values despite the inherent incommensurability of criteria. This was a considerable drawback to any claim of objective optimization. However, the formalization achieved an increase in transparency and explicitness of the premises of any decision. The inevitable (although now explicitly identifiable) arbitrariness of the evaluation process, together with the very cumbersome tedium of the formalization process in the face of its rather meagre advance beyond intuitively available decisions, might have contributed to the demise of those formalized evaluation practices, which, in any case, existed more as academic research than as real world practices. Ultimately *these* particular efforts faltered on account of coming up against a complexity barrier: the operations of linear rationality demand a level of complexity reduction in stating the problem that is incompatible with convincing real-life solutions under conditions of Post-Fordist complexity, dynamism and ambiguity.

functionalism should not be denied. The datascape method is to be understood as the relativist heir to a realist functionalism. This is a tradition that deserves to be claimed. Attempts to pose and formalize systematic accounts of the design problem, design method and design result remain indispensable, even if such accounts will become ever more complex, transitory and relative.

The various presentations of the Arnhem project[130] tell a fairly systematic and straightforward story of functional determination: all required transfer routes are plotted out as required. The lines swell into volumes according to the respective circulation quantities. The account comes close to being thoroughly convincing, although from the outside real and rhetorical rigour are hard to tell apart. In order to trace the uncertainties and gaps in the design process that give its traditional format of presentation the sense of unease that van Berkel & Bos express in the *Any* article, it is required here not only to rehearse the design process, as it has been presented, but moreover to attempt a reconstruction according to the ideal schema of formalized decision analysis. On the basis of such a reconstruction it will be possible to appreciate the actual deviations from the ideal schema.

The rational justification of the Arnhem scheme usually takes the form of tracing its design *process* (and presenting this process as much as possible as a linear chain of function-to-form decisions). In the outlook of traditional decision analysis this is perfectly respectable. In the ideal schema of rationality one would expect that the hierarchy of *arguments* – from the overall system level to successive subsystem levels – that justifies the resultant scheme, would re-present the string of successive decisions, from major to minor decisions, by which the actual design or decision *process* did proceed. In this scenario the occurrence of post-rationalization would throw doubt on the rigour and certainty of both process and result. Behind the fact of post-rationalization lurks the accidental and therefore precarious nature of the supposed 'solutions'.

However, the direct translation between design process and legitimation no longer relates to recent practice. In architecture schools, post-rationalization has become a (legitimate) commonplace. Contemporary design process gropes, stumbles, backtracks and only then succeeds. The emergent rationality of this process, ie, a structured, reproducible method, can only be reconstructed retrospectively by cutting

130 The author attended presentations by Ben van Berkel as well as by the project architects Tobias Wallisser and Peter Trummer.

the dead ends, short-circuiting the loops etc. Innovative theory is always 'after-theory'. Therefore van Berkel & Bos' frustration with 'a posteriori rationalization' and 'after-theory'[131] must be interpreted as concerning the pretence that such after-theory is describing the actual process rather than being the result of post-rationalization.[132]

Before embarking on the concrete reconstruction (of some key aspects) of the Arnhem project we should visualize the most basic formal structure of a rational decision process. The process is structured as a decision path through a decision tree of the kind depicted in Figure 47. The process follows the ramifications of an initial decision in a linear fashion. It is analogous to navigation through a menu-structure. Each choice opens up a further finite series of dependent sub-choices. A decision, in order to qualify as rational, needs to be reconstructed as such a successive selection from evaluated sets of alternatives. The minimal requirement for any act to be worthy of being called a decision at all would thus be that it proceeded by comparison, ie, by comparative evaluation against at least one specified alternative. The ideal case of a rational process, combining the strongest claim with the simplest structure, would be defined through the following conditions whereby decisions are:

1. Hierarchical: the rational decision process is fully resolvable into a linear chain of discrete and self-sufficient decisions. This means that there is a clear hierarchy of decisions whereby a later ramification can never put previous decisions into doubt. (No loops and iterations are required.)
2. Ranked: the hierarchy of decisions presupposes a finite and stable list and ranking order of all objectives or performance criteria to be addressed.
3. Comprehensive: on each level or branching point of the decision tree, the menu or space of options is finite (or at least computationally exhaustible) and known to be comprehensive.
4. Decidable: at each level the space of solutions is measurable and unambiguously decidable relative to given performance criteria.
5. Coherent: a primary objective that provided the rationale for a primary decision cannot be sacrificed for another reason at a later stage without subverting the whole process.
6. Decomposable: in as much as there are parallel objectives (as well as objectives in an order of subsumption), those parallel objectives will be

131 van Berkel and Bos, 'Diagrams – Interactive Instruments in Operation', p 19.
132 Through the fact of post-rationalization shines the open-ended nature of research.

addressed in parallel decision trees. This requires the independence of those objectives and their solutions from each other.[133]

On the basis of this schema we can now investigate the deviations and complications encountered in the Arnhem project. The given situation and the first decision may seem simple enough: the major access road to the site runs parallel to the train tracks at about 120 metres distance. The project is wedged between those two edges.

The part of the project to be considered here – the most significant and formally the richest part – is the pedestrian zone of interchange that mediates between the major means of transport that meet on the site. This zone is framed by the train station (north); the pedestrian access from the city (east and south); the regional bus station (west); and the trolley bus station (south-east). To separate the latter two was the first major project decision that framed the further study of possible configurations. This way a central space was established in which the necessary transfer flows could be configured. This concentric figure has been established by comparison with (and elimination of) a figure according to which regional and city buses would have been butted against each other, and where the interchange/waiting space would have been the bulkhead instead of the centre of the system. This decision might seem self-evident but in order to be formalized and made transparent, the selection criterion would have to be stated, ie, the primary criterion of this primary decision. Also: the quality and credibility of the decision would be enhanced if the selection were to proceed from a greater number of configurational options. Ideally it would have to be shown that the offered alternative configurations exhausted the space of configurational possibility. Only then could we reach 'the triumphant conclusion that the particular design under discussion is the only objectively justifiable one'.[134] The simplest way to formally assure

133 In this respect it is important to notice that Modern design (and engineering) structured their solutions in a highly decomposed manner. The mechanical principle of linear decomposition which was the key to the productivity advances of the whole Fordist mode of production became also the key principle of Modern architectural rationality. The general mode of operation was segregative and specializing. Each function received independent treatment (building tract) with its own optimized articulation of geometry, dimensions and material. Each technical system (facade, structure, ventilation etc) in each part was rendered independent. Each system again was decomposed into individually calculable parts etc. See: Patrik Schumacher, 'Produktive Ordnungen' (Engl: 'Productive Patterns'), in: *ARCH+* 136, Your Office Is Where You Are April 1997 (Berlin), pp 28–33, pp 87–90.

134 The reference to the 'triumphant conclusion' is made in an ironic mode here. van Berkel and Bos, 'Diagrams – Interactive Instruments in Operation', p 19.

exhaustion of possibilities at any stage is to proceed by means of successive dichotomies. Concerning the missing explicit objective or selection criterion for the chosen centralizing configuration, any of the following might be proposed:

- the veto on any visual obstruction between any two means of transport to be linked
- the provision of a point of total visual orientation
- the maximization of such points
- the veto on any indirect (or chained) link between any two means of transport
- volumetric compactness (ratio of circumference to surface) of the transfer space
- the minimization of total length of transfer paths to be constructed
- the minimization of the average detour-factor imposed on any desired transfer link etc

Any of these criteria (or certain combinations) would privilege the selected alternative. We might even feel inclined to cite them all as so many good reasons to choose and start with the centralizing figure. But as, for example, the last two criteria are going to be placed in direct opposition when it comes to delineating the paths that run across the central space, the mere enumeration of good reasons at any point does not by itself qualify as a rational design process. Not all criteria are maintainable throughout and it makes a difference for the further elaboration of the scheme which criterion is implied as primary. In order to maintain *coherence,* the project's performance according to the postulated selection criterion (for example, orientation) would have to be protected from cancellation in the further development of the scheme. This obvious requirement is often violated in practice. Arguments that were used in earlier design decisions are left behind when other concerns come into the foreground. Later detail decisions might then spoil the very advantage that led to the original selection of one scheme over its alternatives. Such a process is evidently irrational if this later cancellation does not lead the designer to revisit and reconsider the original selection. Such a process is not irrational if new values and criteria (new goals) are discovered that place the resultant design on a new value basis. This is often the case with experimental design projects. Whenever this happens the design problem reveals itself to be an ill-structured problem.

The next two diagrams that UN Studio offer to describe the further elaboration of the scheme share the ubiquitous notation of network analysis (as exemplified in Figure 10). The first diagram states the necessary connections that have to be made between the various means of transport. The diagram is a weighted graph that represents the network topology, augmented by additional quantitative and ordinal information. (It is an all-lines graph like the top left diagram in Figure 5.) Each means of transport that needs to be connected through the central exchange space is represented as a node in the network diagram. The relative quantities of passengers that each means of transport brings to the system are represented by the relative size of the respective node. The links are differentiated by line thickness thus classifying and ranking (rather than quantifying) the respective binary transfer quantities. Spatial relations are represented topologically. The second diagram somehow translates the first one into a scaled plan representation. The density of originating pedestrian traffic as well as pedestrian transfer traffic density is now annotated by absolute quantities (cardinal numbers). This plan-diagram is, therefore, in certain respects, more concrete, in other respects, more abstract than the topological diagram. Both representations think of the problem – traffic interchange – in terms of nodes and links between nodes. This seems natural and straightforward enough. But in order to capture a key aspect of the new rationality that is evolving here – the proliferation of modes of representation (symbol systems) – we have to reflect upon the categorical imposition that any mode of representation effects.

Each type of diagram operates a different symbol system and thus opens a different problem space and solution space. Any analysis or design operation that proceeds via network graphs presupposes that the world consists (or should consist) of nothing but nodes and links, as well as higher order entities (networks) like rings, chains, trees, stars etc. Instead of speaking of the mode of representation we might speak of the 'design world'.[135] Each design world, ie, each diagramming technique, drawing type or software package, imposes its own brand of primitives, rules of manipulation and association, and thus opens/delimits a universe of speculation in which both problems and solutions are lodged. Each design world implies a quasi-ontology[136] and quasi-laws of nature. We might start to criticize them in terms of what they leave out. We can do this by reference to another design world that in turn has its own limits. The double-bind of revelation and blindness of any specific design world

135 William J Mitchell, *The Logic of Architecture*, MIT Press (Cambridge, MA), 1990, chapter 3: 'Design Worlds', pp 37–59.

136 This insight is captured in Heidegger's notion of revealing-concealing; see: Martin Heidegger, 'On the Essence of Truth', in: Martin Heidegger, *Being and Truth*, Indiana University Press (Bloomington), 2010. The book is based on Heidegger's lecture series delivered 1933–4.

is definable only relative to other design worlds. There is nothing self-evident, objective or compelling in the imposition of any design world. It remains an arbitrary imposition until it is rationalized by means of comparative evaluation against alternatives. But such alternative design worlds are not at hand at will. Below, we will sketch out what it takes to create a design world, ie, a recurrent social practice of communication. Also: different design worlds might well be incommensurable and can be compared only on the basis of an arbitrating meta-language. We lack an ultimate meta-position. All we can do is to experiment practically within various given symbol systems and hope that viable repertoires crystallize through competition in practice.

The standard scheme of rationality implicitly assumes that such a competition has already resulted in a stable and ranked selection of design tools: an appropriate tool for each specifiable task. This rationality thus assumes that progress and history have come to a standstill, at least as far as the evolution of design worlds is concerned.[137] This assumption is highly questionable in an era when the design medium is subject to continuous innovation. Contemporary design work is thus no longer (fully) covered by the standard schema of rationality. Each new system of representation, each new diagramming technique – in particular in its early stages as Deleuzian diagram[138] – not only expands the solution space in which solutions can be elaborated but is also prone to throw up new values and new goals.

During the past 25 years the architectural avant-garde has experimented with new types of diagrams, new types of drawings and more recently with many new digital tools. For hundreds of years the architect's design world has been a singular and stable system of hierarchically scaled line drawings. (Even the refoundation of the discipline in the 1920s did not change this.) From the scaleless (topological) sketch to the working drawings, this world distributes nothing but outlines and boundaries. Everything is about the distribution of horizontal and vertical planes. The meaning of each drawing resides in its position and role in the chain of translation from one drawing to the

137 This point may benefit from a comparison with scientific research: the traditional concept of rational research would only allow for a linear, cumulative progress that can be fully measured and defined on the basis of concepts and techniques that are available in advance. According to the historiography of science, since Thomas Kuhn, such linear progress can hardly account for scientific evolution. See: Thomas S Kuhn, *The Structure of Scientific Revolutions*, University of Chicago Press (Chicago), 1970.

138 Concerning Deleuzian diagrams see below. For a more detailed discussion see Volume 1, Chapter 4.2.2 *The Diagram*.

next (more detailed) drawing and from there to the construction process and the utilization of the building itself. Within this routinized practice of translation, from the abstract to the concrete, it is habitually known how each drawing constrains the next set of decisions, until the detailed lines finally translate into physical edges. (And we all have learned to perceive and inhabit space along those edges.) Only within such an order of routine practices can one speak of a well-defined representational system. The concept of a drawing that is firmly lodged in such routine practice is the model against which the Deleuzian 'diagram'[139] is defined. The difference does not reside within the object, but in the pattern of its use. The question here is whether or not (yet) it functions within a stable social practice of communication. The Deleuzian diagram does not yet know its place in a routine operation. It is creatively engaged in the formation of such a (potentially reproducible) practice. It therefore is worked upon without stable interpretation, without predetermined consequences. Work is assimilated to play.[140] At least since the mid-1980s virtually all design efforts at the AA, and soon after at most other schools in London, were conducted through 'diagrammatic' processes.

The reflection on the dependency of any design effort on the design world it operates in allows the discussion of the next crucial 'steps' of the Arnhem design process. 'Movement studies' are set to be 'the cornerstone of the proposal'.[141] Such movement studies could have taken many forms. Plotting a network graph is only one (rather economical) form such a study could take. Although the graph does constrain the further design moves, and thus is certainly not meaningless, a strict rule of translation from such a graph into a floor plan does not exist. The claim that the 'station emerges from these motion studies'[142] is therefore more anecdotal than rational. Without rule there is no determination. What can be rightfully claimed here, at least, is the negative implication that the main space of the station was not based on a preconceived (Platonic) figure or any known (Classical plaza) typology. Indeed, it seems to be the amorphous irregularity of the scheme which inclines us to grant credibility to the cited claim that the figure 'emerges' from movement studies.

The move from the plan-diagram to a second, more detailed plan-diagram implies, in terms of network or graph theory, an abrupt shift

139 For a detailed discussion of Deleuzian diagrams see: Volume 1, 4.2.2 *The Diagram.*

140 This shift is elaborated in: Patrik Schumacher, 'Arbeit, Spiel und Anarchie', in: Ed Herbert Lachmayer & Eleonora Luis, *Work & Culture – Büro.Inszenierung von Arbeit,* Ritterverlag (Klagenfurt), 1998.

141 Ben Van Berkel & Caroline Bos (UN Studio), 'Deep Plan', in: *AA files* 38, Architectural Association School of Architecture (London), 1999, pp 23–30.

142 Ibid.

from an all-lines graph, where every point is directly connected to every other point, to a branching graph. Another leap is the emergence of irregular curves in the next elaboration of the plan.

The leap from the all-lines graph to the branching graph is certainly not (yet) motivated by any known routine practice. The all-lines graph (showing all connections as direct connections) might be read as problem statement. The branching graph might then be considered as selected solution. A rational design decision would require that the posited branching diagram is the result of a selection from a set of (ideally exhaustive) alternatives (as shown in Figure 5) according to a criterion consistent with the design brief.

The next move introduces curvature. A parti is being developed that displays an organic complexity that became an architectural possibility only within the recent avant-garde. How this transformation was effected and how it can be motivated is not immediately obvious. (New information seems to have entered the discussion.) That does not mean that one could not, in the end, legitimately post-rationalize such a transformation and then routinize it by constructing a rule that would define the one figure as the regular translation of the other. In principle any anecdotal, initially intuitive connection might be reproducible and thus can be retrospectively elevated from a haphazard into a rational, methodical move.

What would motivate or justify the branching graph here? The centralization of control? The economy of paths? It depends. What we do know is that (according to formalized decision analysis) any motivation or justification would have to take the form of a criterion-based selection from a field of possible configurations that might include stars (star-shaped graphs), chains, spines, rings, grids or trees (branching graphs). But any such rationality is vulnerable to subversion when possibilities emerge that had not been in the original universe of selection. Van Berkel and Bos are talking about providing a hybrid between a centralized system and an all-lines system. The selection list above does not know of 'hybrids'. But once things called 'hybrids' have been admitted into this world, any analysis, decision or motivation based on the above list is obsolete. In this way all rational decisions are vulnerable to subversion.

UN Studio produce an arrangement of ramps that might be analyzed as an all-lines graph with a point of centrality that attracts and bends all lines towards a kind of empty centre of attraction without collapsing the individual lines. This deformational pull produces something that could be described as a hybrid between the two original diagrams. But as a unique, singular incident, this move gives us little certainty about how other, different hybridizations might be achieved. There is no general rule of hybridization. The presented 'hybrid' is also discussed as being inspired by the so-called Klein bottle, assuming transformational qualities in analogy to the spatial logic of the bottle. These moves are far from being well defined. One might be inclined to dismiss the introduction of the Klein bottle as an arbitrary graft. But then again, to refuse the bottle and rest with the usual a priori ontology of Platonic primitives would be even more arbitrary. The affordances of the Klein bottle would have to be compared with the affordances of other available diagrams.

In the next move, the project suddenly appears in the guise of a 3D computer model operating with smoothly bent cones. As these cones traverse the space they intersect, merge and branch. Yet another new design world has been opened, irreducible to any network graph. This world does not know of nodes and links between nodes whereas in turn the graph did not know of interpenetrations and fusions. Are these really cones? Are we looking at one, two, three, four or five components here? It is, in fact, impossible to unambiguously count the number of geometric elements to be distinguished. There are no discrete elements here and no clearly nameable spots and places. The project has leapt into a different world, a yet uncharted world. However, rules of translation back into a network graph might very well be definable. One could even construct translation-rules that would allow any network graph (perhaps with some additional information about peak time flows, and flow directions) to be transformed into such a 3D model. But those rules do not yet exist. At least they have not been made explicit. No performance criteria have as yet been specified. But again, it is never too late. We are never principally unprincipled. We might learn to trust our intuitions and expect that at least some of our creative moves will assume their principle retrospectively, against the arrow of time.[143]

The next iteration of the design announces a further transfiguration of the design process into yet another irreducible ontology and system of spatial manipulation: a single surface that peels and splinters smoothly into differential levels. This is the crucial moment where the project leaps from abstract 3D sketch diagrams to a model that can be interpreted as the literal to-scale modelling of the eventual architectural surfaces: floors, ramps and stair-ramps. (At this point the design also responds to and exploits the different existing levels of the site.)

This solution could not have been derived within a linear engineering process that would always be presumed to operate within a given,

143 On the back of Derrida's philosophy, contemporary architects have learned to inhabit this warped logic of time.

well-formalized ontology. No such fluid, spatial response was available to the discipline until fairly recently.[144] Once discovered, this possibility offers surprising advantages: a space is created that multiplies the available transfer surface while avoiding the usual bottlenecks (lifts or staircases) and the disorienting dichotomous segmentation of orthogonal, stacked space.

The design process described so far does, with respect to certain aspects, follow the augmented problem-solving model Herbert Simon presented for design problems in his article 'The Structure of Ill-structured Problems' discussed above. It follows the pattern of alternation between phases of problem solving in logically well-structured problem spaces and phases of problem shift or problem space modification. As Simon pointed out, the initiation of problem space shifts requires an additional information-processing capacity within the IPS. Simon refers to this capacity as a recognition-retrieval system that is able to recognize when design work within a given problem space has run its course so that new information about further requirements can be retrieved from the LTM. This new information is then used to determine new sub-goals and new constraints that can be explored/solved within a new problem space. The rationality of such a sequencing of problem spaces can only be established within an encompassing planning space that allows for the comparison of alternative sets of problem spaces and problem space sequences. In the case of the Arnhem project where new problem spaces are being invented as the project proceeds, such a rationality (or rational critique) is only available in a retrospective reconstruction, after several alternative potential design trajectories of the project have been compared, or after several similar design projects have become available to be compared and analyzed within a generalizing horizon of a general planning scheme.

The logic of design innovation is analogous to the logic of biological evolution. It goes through the necessary moments of mutation, selection and reproduction. Methodologically it is important to notice that the new formal universe of the single surface with its subtle distribution of gradients, ridges and sweeping cuts offers new, advantageous affordances that were neither available nor ever considered prior to the leap into this new morphology. Only on the back of the original leap into this world could the ambitions of a certain type of choreography be envisaged. A system of tunnels, lifts and travelators, which would have been a much more straightforward, linear elaboration of the initial network graphs,

144 The credit here has to go to Zaha Hadid who has been recursively exploring this particular formal universe since the 1980s.

could never have brought forward this discourse. Here we would have remained in the realm of mechanical traffic management. Throughout the design process new good reasons are being introduced. Those reasons will post-validate explorations that are not necessarily, at all times, covered by the strictures of the ideal schema of rationality. But even the result of a strict process might reveal unexpected qualities. In any such case, in order to recuperate the option of principled and rational conduct, one would have to admit the subversion of one's course of action, precisely because one has found more reasons than one had originally been looking for. Armed with those new values and criteria one would have to loop back and reinvestigate the design path travelled, and give a systematic account of the final result, on the basis of both well established and newly acquired knowledge. The attempt to reconstruct the Arnhem design process makes it abundantly obvious that the overall dynamic pattern of current design and design research can no longer, at all times, and in its totality, be cast into the mould of the ideal schema of rational conduct presented above. Nevertheless it deserves to be noticed that we are not demanding the abandonment of the schema. Rather we are witnessing its dynamization and complication. As a background definition from which the new practices deviate but ultimately around which they oscillate and gravitate, and to which they recursively return, if only in a relative and temporary mode, the ideal schema of a formalized decision process remains indispensable.

When we design today we will, overall, still be climbing up a decision tree, however much we will temporarily spread out laterally. We will still have to segment our process and follow instructions as the following: 'Pick up this task first and address another task later (and move from a first symbol system to a second system that can process further aspects and details).' We will try to identify a hierarchy and start with the most important decisions. Even if we find out later that the order of importance should have been otherwise, there should be, until further notice, always an order of importance to be considered. But we will have to give up the idea that we could know or take account of all options at each junction. New branches will sprout as we move up the tree. They also grow beside us from below. We might loop back or jump branches. There is rarely time to backtrack fully. A previously abandoned sidetrack might afford help. But for the next time round we know the straight line. A whole new tree might cast our whole path into the shadow. But it is too risky to jump and too late to go back to the root. But then the latest branches of the new tree might fall back onto the initial tree. Now several paths seem to converge rather than ramify further. The pursuits of parallel objectives get entangled. We will initially seek synergies but then cut as much as possible to keep the process manageable. The tree keeps mutating into a rhizome. We keep trimming it into a tree shape. This is not fundamentalism but a matter of economy. We are moving from the illusion of absolute rationality to 'bounded rationality' and 'good enough reason'.[145] As Herbert Simon often stressed, all information processes, especially in the context of practical rationality – and this includes design rationality – are subject to resource constraints. Design projects have to be completed within given time frames with given manpower and computational resources. Ideals of rationality always abstract from these capacity and resource constraints. This is their fundamental fallacy. Design is action under the burden of time and resource constraints. How can one assess the balance of investment in time and resources between design and execution? There is no answer outside experience. The competitive environment is the final court of appeal. It passes verdict on any course of action but without locating the moments of failure or success within it. We know we have won or lost the competition, but we are never told exactly on account of which factors. Innovative design practice, more than ever, means taking risks. That's why we need theory, not to eliminate risk, but to manage it: ante-theory, after-theory and meta-theory.

7.6.2 PROSPECTIVE RATIONALITY

As stated above, the double challenge of complexity and novelty of architecture's tasks implies that an ambitious design project will have to reckon with the fact that its rationality will, to a large extent, be ascertained only in retrospect rather than being understood in advance. However, this is a necessity rather than a virtue. Degrees of prospective rationality can be achieved in planning spaces that build on recent design experiences and build in provisions for coping with the consequences of complexity and novelty. A major aspect of this prospective rationality is the maintenance of reversibility deep into the design process.[146] Designers operate in a 'limited-commitment-mode'.[147] Although they rarely restart the design from scratch[148] they must always be prepared to backtrack and reverse or modify prior decisions. Tentatively developed design components are to be evaluated in multiple contexts according to multiple concerns. This way these contexts are probed. The making,

145 Herbert A Simon, *Models of Bounded Rationality*, MIT Press (Cambridge, MA), 1997.

146 See Volume 1, Chapter 4.2.3 *Specious vs Point-like Time: The Time Structure of the Architectural Project.*

147 Goel, *Sketches of Thought*, p 92.

148 Starting from scratch can be avoided because in design problems as ill-structured problems there are no absolutely right or wrong answers.

dissemination and propagation of provisional commitments is crucial. Propagated commitments deepen and gather detail resolution. The ability to maintain malleability and partial reversibility while progressing the design is critical. This is precisely the advantage of using media rather than operating in reality directly. This is also one of the key dimensions within which the various design media compete and progress, ie, the more advanced a medium the more can reversibility be combined with resolution. This is precisely the criterion that pinpoints the crucial advantage of associative-parametric design systems.[149]
Associative-parametric design focuses on systems of relations rather than the individual definition and placement of elements. The fundamental rationality of a design lies in the relationships it establishes between elements and their parameters, rather than in individual elements and parameters. This is true for all three aspects of architecture's project, ie, the organizational, the phenomenological and the semiological project. Hugh Whitehead pinpoints the essence of parametrics as: 'an attitude of mind that seeks to express and explore relationships'.[150] He continues as follows, alluding to the crucial ability to maintain malleability and reversibility while progressing the design: 'Embedded in this method of exploration is the idea of capturing *design history* and returning it in an editable form – that can be varied and re-played.'[151]

Another important aspect that has to be covered in a theory of prospective design rationality is the aspect of defining and sequencing pertinent problem spaces. Each problem space imposes an a priori framework – both a formal and a functional a priori – that constrains the solutions possible within its confines. Problem spaces – with respect to the modelling spaces they provide – also influence the ease of candidate generation, as well as candidate evaluation. (Some of these generation and evaluation processes might even be automated.) That is why contemporary design research must be supported by a continued foundational research into modelling spaces (design worlds). The relative rationality of any design project depends on the choice of its problem spaces. An attempt should be made to formalize a contemporary

149 Concerning the growing use of associative-parametric design systems see: David Jason Gerber, *The Parametric Affect – Computation, Innovation and Models for Design Exploration in Contemporary Architectural Practice*, Harvard Design School, Department of Architecture, Design and Technology Report Series 2009 (Cambridge, MA). Gerber speaks about the 'revolution' architecture is experiencing with the adoption of associative parametric design technology.

150 Hugh Whitehead, Forward in Robert Woodbury, *Elements of Parametric Design*, Routledge (London/New York), 2010, p 1.

151 Ibid.

state-of-the-art sequence of problem spaces as target for critique and vehicle for improvements.

What is important here is to grasp the rationality of the observed ***problem space multiplicity*** that characterizes advanced contemporary design processes. The specific characteristics, affordances and limitations of the various problem spaces through which a project typically moves must be analyzed. This theoretical task must begin with the elaboration of a conceptual apparatus for the analysis and comparison of the radically different problem spaces that are required within a single design project.

The different problem spaces the theory of architectural autopoiesis must distinguish and order can be broadly aligned with the three fundamental dimensions of architecture's task: the organizational, the phenomenological and the semiological dimension. However, although the theory of architectural autopoiesis chooses to focus on these aspects, this is not the full story. In the context of theorizing architecture's medium,[152] the theory of architectural autopoiesis has distinguished the following four projects that are potential referents of the design process and the documents it procures:

1. the ***architect's project***, ie, the task of designing in accordance with architecture's societal function
2. the ***client's project***, ie, the task of illustrating the design to clients, potential users or any other non-specialized interested parties
3. the ***engineer's project***, ie, the task of assessing the design's technical feasibility
4. the ***contractor's project***, ie, the task of facilitating construction

One might assume the external reference of the design process with its evolving network of drawings/digital-models to be the building. However, as was already pointed out, in the treatment of architecture's medium it is not quite that simple. First of all, the building does not yet exist. Second, any determinate reference and representation depend upon audience and purpose. The various parties involved – architects, critics, clients, consulting engineers, contractors, and the various types of workers on site – all focus on different points and aspects of the overall network of drawings. They each 'see' (perceive, evaluate and handle) the design drawings rather differently, ie, each is oriented to a rather different project. The various modelling spaces utilized within architecture have to cope with multiple concerns – each posing a

152 See Volume 1, part 4 *The Medium of Architecture*, in particular chapter 4.1.6 *Recursive Self-reference.*

different task or project – that are distinguished here by the four categories listed above. Only the architect's project is immediately relevant to the autopoiesis of architecture as a domain with its own exclusive medium, code and autonomous criteria of evaluation. It is with respect to the architect's project that the specific design processes have to prove their ability to create innovative action-artefact networks. The other tasks of the process/medium listed above are secondary and reside within the environment of the discipline of architecture, as inescapable constraints and stirring irritations, but they do not constitute its primary purpose. Thus, in what follows, the primary focus will be placed on the architect's project and its process structure. The attempt will be made to indicate a set of pertinent problem spaces and their relationships.

7.6.3 PROCESSING THE THREE TASK DIMENSIONS OF ARCHITECTURE

In part 6, three dimensions of architecture's task were distinguished: the organizational, the phenomenological and the semiological dimension. Accordingly, the architectural project was analyzed into three subsystems: the ***organizational project***, the ***phenomenological project*** and the ***semiological project***. How do these three projects feature within the (analysis of the) design process? The general sequencing of these three projects seems clear enough: organization comes before articulation. The organizational task is the first to be addressed. It involves the establishment of the parti of the project. What the sequencing of phenomenology and semiology should be is less clear. Above it was suggested that the semiological dimension must lead from behind. The phenomenological project makes the systematic differences that constitute the semiological project perceptually palpable and is thus a precondition of semiosis. The semiological project is the endgame of all architectural design. The semiological dimension is the leading dimension of architecture, whether this is always explicitly recognized in design practice or not. Architecture communicates via semiosis. Communication involves understanding and the distinction of information and impartation. This involves more than mere perception. Every sensitive designer operates within the domain of meanings, whether he/she is able to make this the explicit agenda of his/her design process and strategy or not. The handling of meaning involves more than making some features conspicuous. The question is which features are to be made conspicuous in which context. Which contrasts are to be constructed and which continuities are to be constructed by suppressing irrelevant differences? This question can only be answered from the vantage point of a system of distinctions that aspires to become a system-of-signification that can turn the built environment into an effective medium of communication. The theoretical reflection thus leads us to the logical priority of the semiological over the phenomenological project. However, logical priority does not necessarily translate into priority in terms of sequence of design elaboration. Design exploration has its own dynamics of creative generation as distinct from mere rationalization. Designers are not omniscient. They have to find, gather, compare, select and connect more or less randomly generated materials in a structured trial and error process. The structure of this process contains the moment of prospective rationality.

In some (but not all) respects the semiological project is also logically prior to the organizational project. The endgame of all organization should also be communication. However, this would translate into a full logical priority only if the totality of the built environment – or a fully self-sufficient project – could be designed as a single project. This is not a realistic assumption. All projects are engaging existing contexts. Therefore the spatial organization is preconstrained, at least with respect to the size and shape of the site and with respect to its contextual connections. The theory of architectural autopoiesis has identified the location type as a fundamental aspect of the signified of architecture's semiological project. To the extent to which locations are fixed prior to the new design project and thus deliver content to the process of semiological articulation, the organizational project is logically prior to the semiological project. The semiological project takes the articulation of such prior locational information as one of its objectives. The organizational project is also the site where aspects of physical efficiency and economy are irritating the architectural project. However, in spite of being thus preconstrained by site, context and aspects of physical efficiency, there remains a margin of freedom with respect to organization. The universe of possibilities is constrained but not foreclosed. Within the remaining space of manoeuvre, organizational decisions can and should be led by semiological concerns. A strict sequencing from organization to articulation is thus not possible. The orchestration of all three dimensions from the perspective of a full overview of the total task, in line with architecture's societal function, requires an oscillating and iterative process rather than a linear progression from organizational to phenomenological, and then semiological articulation. An ambitious contemporary design process should keep all three dimensions in play throughout the design.

More important than the aspect of sequencing is the aspect of defining pertinent problem spaces for the three dimensions of the architectural project. The three projects are to be pursued in three different problem spaces, each with its own conceptual space, value space and (set of) modelling space(s). The conceptual space of the organizational project is concerned with functional distribution involving relations of grouping, separation, adjacency and access. This conceptual space should be augmented by the conceptual apparatus of network theory.[153] Accordingly, the organizational project can initially be pursued via Venn diagrams (Figures 6, 7, 8) and network diagrams (Figures 10, 11, 12). In search of organizational diagrams, most designers browse the space of configurational possibilities via freehand sketches. These sketches might be understood as Venn diagrams, ie, as being primarily concerned with topological relations. As the initially fluid sketches solidify they go beyond mere topology and gradually start to fix geometric and dimensional aspects. At a certain point the design transitions into a new modelling space, the space of hard line, scaled plan diagrams. In this space exact dimensions and surface areas can be controlled and evaluated against the area requirements and site constraints. The whole traditional set of orthographic projections is geared to the organizational project (as well as to the engineer's and contractor's project). This set of 2D line drawings cannot support the phenomenological project. Traditionally, the phenomenological project had been supported by perspective constructions and graphically built up elevations with constructed shadows, washes and textures to indicate plasticity and materiality. Today the phenomenological project is pursued within the space of detailed 3D digital modelling, augmented by rendering engines taking into account materials, textures and variable lighting conditions. Evaluation involves the intuitive, experiential control of the design via rendered perspectives and walk-through animations to assess the perceptual effect of the design. In the context of an ambition to articulate complexity, the primary criterion of evaluation would be the visual legibility of the elaborated spatial order. The critical question to be tested here is how complex a scene can get without collapsing into visual chaos. How will a complex scene be cognitively decomposed into territories? A further agenda that might be explored concerns visual ambiguities leading to potential Gestalt-switches that might be instrumentalized to cater for multiple audiences with different requirements and expectations.

The semiological project should build upon and in turn steer both the phenomenological and the organizational project. Its conceptual frame of reference as well as its criteria of evaluation were elaborated above.[154] So far no dedicated semiological modelling space has been developed within

153 See above, section 6.4 *Supplementing Architecture with a Science of Configuration.*

154 See section 6.9 *Prolegomenon to Architecture's Semiological Project.*

architectural practice. Although every designer is intuitively navigating the space of architectural meanings, so far there are no examples of systematic semiological design efforts. Designers are seeking out particular connotations while avoiding others. For instance, a design for an opera house might aim for a sense of festive elegance, while the design for a hospital might aim for a sense of cleanliness, sober rationality and efficiency. The respective morphological features that transport these connotations are socially given and continue to evolve within the spontaneous social process of semiosis. Designers might try to deploy already coded features in slightly new ways to give new nuances to these meanings. An avant-garde designer might be keen to avoid any such standard connotations via a strategy of making strange. The above-mentioned strategies are pursued in parallel with the phenomenological project, within the same modelling space of 3D modelling and rendering. None of these strategies amounts to a systematic semiological project. The semiological project envisioned here demands that the project is conceived as an initially self-sufficient system-of-signification. This requires that the system of distinguished spatial and morphological features is correlated with a co-constituted system of differences in the domain of the signified. This might be facilitated by a special modelling space that utilizes agent-based crowd simulations to correlate behaviours with the features of the designed territories. Thus the domain of the signified can enter the model.[155]

7.7 Modelling Spaces

THESIS 41

A historically well-adapted style is a necessary precondition of any credible design process rationality.

The theory of architectural autopoiesis analyzes architectural design projects by distinguishing various sub-projects. The *architect's project* is distinguished from the *client's project*, the *engineer's project* and the *contractor's project*. In turn the architect's project has been further analyzed into the *organizational*, the *phenomenological* and the *semiological* project. These projects require different modelling spaces. For instance, the contractor's project requires detailed, annotated and dimensioned working drawings, quantities and written specifications. None of this is helpful to develop any of the three architect's projects.

155 The author is currently conducting a semiologically focused design research project at the University of Applied Arts in Vienna.

Also, none of this means anything for the client here understood as the final user of the building. Further, within the architect's project the progression of the design moves through several different modelling spaces, starting with diagrammatic freehand sketches and moving to progressively detailed hard line drawings and 3D digital and physical models. All along verbal communications are involved, constituting the different conceptual and evaluation spaces, as well as supplementing the various modelling spaces via descriptive clarifications. Questions thus arise concerning these modelling spaces with respect to their peculiar characteristics and affordances as modes of representation and design media.

In what follows, a set of pertinent distinctions – a conceptual apparatus – is being introduced that can facilitate the analysis of the information-processing capacity of the various modelling spaces that come into play during the design process. The conceptual apparatus introduced and integrated here stems from Nelson Goodman's general theory of symbols as developed in his books *Languages of Art*[156] and *Ways of Worldmaking*.[157] Goodman elaborates an intricate apparatus that allows us to navigate the world of symbol systems including natural and technical languages, notational systems, diagrams, renderings and physical models. He allows us to distinguish denotation from expression and exemplification, description from depiction and within depiction the diagrammatic from the pictorial. Goodman's conceptualization states that 'nothing depends upon the internal structure of a symbol, for what describes in some systems may depict in others. Resemblance disappears as a criterion of representation.'[158] It was Vinod Goel[159] – in the theoretical context of cognitive science – who first applied Goodman's conceptual apparatus to the analysis of the modelling spaces involved in design processes. Goel's introduction of Goodman's scheme is used here for the sake of pertinence and brevity.

Symbols are entities that ***refer*** to other entities. Goodman distinguishes three modes of reference: ***denotation*** vs ***exemplification*** vs ***expression***. The three concepts build on each other in that sequence. ***Denotation*** is the unanalyzed base concept here. It might be introduced as follows: a symbol denotes an object if it refers to the object. How this is

156 Nelson Goodman, *Languages of Art – An Approach to a Theory of Symbols*, Hackett Publishing Company (Indianapolis/Cambridge), 1976.

157 Nelson Goodman, *Ways of Worldmaking*, Hackett Publishing Company (Indianapolis/Cambridge), 1978.

158 Goodman, *Languages of Art*, p 231.

159 Goel, *Sketches of Thought*, 1995.

achieved is left open here.[160] A symbol might exemplify rather than denote. ***Exemplification*** implies that certain properties or predicates the symbol possesses are being referred to by the symbol within a given system of symbolization. If the symbol belongs to a system in which it is denoted by the predicate, then the symbol exemplifies this predicate. Reference thus runs here in the opposite direction of a simultaneously presupposed denotation. Goodman gives the following example: 'Consider a tailor's booklet of small swatches of cloth. These function as samples, as symbols exemplifying certain properties. But a swatch does not exemplify all its properties; it is a sample of color, weave, texture and pattern, but not of size, shape, or absolute weight or value. . . . Exemplification is possession plus reference. . . . If possession is intrinsic, reference is not; and just which properties of a symbol are exemplified depends upon what particular system of symbolization is in effect.'[161] Strictly speaking it is labels or predicates rather than properties that are exemplified. While anything may be denoted, only labels/predicates may be exemplified.[162] There is another restriction that limits exemplification. Exemplification is a motivated use of symbols because the symbol must possess the property it refers to, ie, the exemplifying symbol cannot be as arbitrary as the merely denoting symbol. Exemplification implies reference between the two parts of the relation in both directions. Exemplification includes the referential operation of diagrammatic and pictorial symbol systems – for instance a drawing exemplifies labels like 'circle', 'square', 'orthogonal', 'curvilinear', or exemplifies (and thus symbolizes/refers to) the relative position of the circles and squares, for example, 'east of', 'west of' or 'inside' etc.[163] However, exemplification is

160 Naturally Goodman understands (as much as Saussure and Luhmann) that a symbol's reference functions only via the social use of symbol systems within systems of communications.

161 Goodman, *Languages of Art*, p 53.

162 In Goodman's terminology predicates are a special type of label, namely labels from linguistic systems. According to Goodman, labels from other symbol systems – gestural, pictorial, diagrammatic etc – may be exemplified as well, even if we have no corresponding word or description for it. See Goodman, *Languages of Art*, p 57.

163 The concept of exemplification is supposed to undercut the standard explanation of the difference between linguistic and pictorial symbol systems, namely that pictures function via resemblance to what they symbolize. As Goel points out: 'any two objects resemble each other in any number of ways (or share as many properties as you like), thus resemblance or sharing of properties cannot be the basis of reference. . . . Resemblance or sharing of properties is neither necessary nor sufficient for reference.' Goel, *Sketches of Thought*, p 160. According to Goodman, pictorial representations are active rather than passive, a matter of classifying objects rather than of imitating them, of characterizing rather than of copying. Goodman, *Languages of Art*, p. 31.

not restricted to either diagrammatic or pictorial modes of reference. It is much more general.

Expression is a special type of exemplification. Here the expressed/exemplified label applies only metaphorically. An object (symbol) that is metaphorically denoted by a predicate thereby expresses that predicate. Expression is thus metaphorical exemplification. It is a mode of reference often used in the arts.[164] The diagrammatic and pictorial symbol systems or modelling spaces used within the architectural design process operate with all three modes of reference. They 'not only denote spatial and non-spatial properties but also exemplify and express such properties as relative size, shape, location, elegance, formality, rigidity, and certainty'.[165]

Goodman distinguishes three modes of reference: denotation, exemplification and expression. All three function within symbol systems. Goodman has developed a set of criteria for characterizing symbol systems. These criteria are organized around the question of whether a symbol system is a ***notational system*** or not. Notational systems are a special class of symbol systems. They include writing systems and, for instance, the system of musical notation. The concept also covers (and thus clarifies) the standard system of technical drawings in architecture. However, the significance of Goodman's 'theory of notationality' goes beyond the definition and characterization of notational systems because his set of criteria, by contrast, also serves to illuminate the specific characteristics of non-notational symbol systems like the symbol system or modelling space of the designer's practice of freehand sketching.

Before going into any further detail here a point of terminological clarification is required. The conceptual apparatus and terminology imported here from Goodman and Goel are at odds with the conceptual apparatus and terminology introduced above in the context of theorizing the semiological dimension of architecture's task. The two conceptual-terminological systems can co-exist as long as the domain of application remains segregated. Above, the sole focus is on how the built

164 One of Goodman's examples is a painting of trees and cliffs by the sea, painted in greys, expressing sadness. Obviously the picture is not sad in the same way as it is grey. While the picture literally belongs to the class of grey things, it only metaphorically possesses sadness or belongs to the class of things that feel sad. The painting expresses the label 'sadness', or perhaps 'loneliness'. This is not an intrinsic achievement of the painting via its excitement of such feelings. For this to occur a symbol system, grounded in social system of communication, is required that allows for such paintings to express (metaphorically exemplify) such labels as 'sad' or 'lonely'.

165 Goel, *Sketches of Thought*, p 192.

architectural artefacts can be conceived and launched to operate as system-of-signification within architecture's societal environment. Here, by contrast, the sole focus is on architecture's internal media of communication and how they function as design media in the form of modelling spaces. What is here called 'symbol system' is the equivalent of what is above called 'system-of-signification'. The decision has been made *not* to unify or condense the two conceptual-terminological systems because the two systems operate in two contexts and indeed help to keep the two contexts apart and easily distinguished. This decision also allows the theory of architectural autopoiesis to maintain a stronger connection to its respective theoretical sources. There are further terminological duplications: what above was called the 'domain of the signifier' is now called the 'symbol scheme' or 'scheme domain'. What was called the 'domain of the signified' is now called the 'field of reference'. A symbol system consists of a symbol scheme with a field of reference. What above was called 'signification', ie, the link between signifier and signified, is now called 'reference link' or 'compliance link', understood as relation of compliance. Following the distinction originally introduced by Peirce, Goodman splits the scheme domain into 'characters' or 'types' versus 'inscriptions' or 'tokens'. The field of reference is articulated into 'compliance class' versus 'object'. Whatever is referred to (denoted) by a symbol is said to *comply* with it. 'Compliance is with an inscription. In a given system, many things may comply with a single inscription, and the class of these constitutes the compliance-class of the inscription.'[166]

Goodman's theory of notationality formulates five logically independent criteria for the concept of notational system. Two of these criteria are syntactic and three are semantic. The syntactic criteria are *syntactic disjointness* and *syntactic finite differentiation*. The semantic criteria are *semantic unambiguity*, *semantic disjointness* and *semantic finite differentiation.* A symbol system is a ***notational system*** only if it satisfies all five criteria. The five criteria can be formulated as follows:

syntactic disjointness	This criterion builds on the distinction of character (type) and inscription (token). The criterion demands that the characters of a notation are disjoint sets of (character-indifferent) inscriptions.

166 Goodman, *Languages of Art*, p 144.

(Disjointness between sets excludes both set inclusion and set intersection.) All inscriptions of a character belong to an equivalent class. The binary relation of being a syntactically equivalent inscription (that holds between any two inscriptions of the same character) must be symmetrical and transitive. 'Being instances of one character in a notation must constitute a sufficient condition for marks being "true copies" or replicas of each other, or being spelled the same way. . . . For if the relation of being a true copy is not thus transitive, the basic purpose of a notation is defeated. Requisite separation among characters – and hence among scores – will be lost unless identity is preserved in any chain of true copies.'[167] Disjointness implies that no inscription can instantiate more than one character.

syntactic finite differentiation

This criterion demands that characters are finitely differentiated or *articulate*, ie, it must in principle be possible to distinguish characters by (perceptually) discriminating between their inscriptions. 'The more delicate and precise the stipulated differentiation between characters, the harder will it be to determine whether certain marks belong to one character or another.'[168] It must also be possible to distinguish a character from marks that are not characters of the notational scheme at all. Of course error cannot always be excluded but errors should at least be theoretically avoidable. Together the two syntactic requirements 'ensure a

167 Ibid, p 132.
168 Ibid, p 134.

one-to-one mapping between inscriptions and characters, and thus enable *the collapse of the distinction between inscription and character*'.[169]

unambiguity

The criterion is a semantic criterion. It demands that every inscription must have the same, single compliance class (meaning) in each instance, irrespective of context. 'A mark that is unequivocally an inscription of a single character is nevertheless *ambiguous* if it has different compliance at different times or in different contexts.'[170] Goodman's control example for a working notation is the musical score. Its purpose is to define and preserve the identity of the musical composition. The criterion of unambiguity must be fulfilled, otherwise 'identity of work will not be preserved in every chain of steps from performance to covering score and from score to compliant performance'.[171]

semantic disjointness

The criterion demands no two characters have any compliant in common. It imposes the disjointness of all compliance classes in the system. All characters of the system are semantically segregated. This excludes relations of inclusion and intersection between compliance classes of different characters, ie, it prevents the symbol system from containing terms that relate in an order of subsumption like 'European' and 'German', or includes overlapping terms like 'female' and 'immigrant'. These are severe restrictions. However, semantic disjointness does not exclude that a

169 Goel, *Sketches of Thought*, p 164.
170 Goodman, *Languages of Art*, p 147.
171 Ibid, p 149.

compliant of one character might be a part of a compliant of another character, ie, a notation might simultaneously include symbols for 'apartment' and 'kitchen' (because no apartment is a kitchen and no kitchen is an apartment). Any intersection of different compliance-classes defeats the purpose of notation. 'A chain from compliant to inscription to compliant will thus lead from a member of one compliance-class to something outside that class.'[172] Strictly speaking the system must also be free of character redundancy, ie, each compliance class should be symbolized by only one character. (However, redundancy in a notational system is relatively harmless and can be fixed by discarding redundant symbols.) The redundancy requirement is entailed in the requirement that no two characters have any compliant in common.

semantic finite differentiation

The criterion demands that the compliance classes that are symbolized by the system are finitely differentiated, ie, it must always be possible to assign a given object to a single class. This implies that the field of reference of the system must be articulated into discrete entities. As Goodman points out, this criterion appreciably narrows further the class of symbol systems that qualify as notational. For instance, it excludes any system of measurement that does not set any limits on what counts as a significant difference, ie, that does not granulate its measures.

172 Goodman, *Languages of Art*, p 150.

Goodman's five very general criteria give just the minimal set of logical requirements that all notational systems must adhere to in order to function as notations. There might be other, more pragmatic requirements that could be listed here, like a finite, manageably small set of atomic characters, the legibility of inscriptions, their mnemonic efficacy, their reproducibility and their manoeuvrability etc. Goodman's criteria are theoretical conditions that pertain to symbol systems rather than to individual symbols. The fruitfulness of these criteria is not limited to the identification of notational systems but 'other important types of symbol systems are distinguished by violation of certain combinations of these conditions'.[173] All discursive languages, whether natural or scientifically precise jargons, violate some (but not all) of the five criteria of notationality. They adhere to the syntactic criteria but violate the semantic criteria. Many of their terms are ambiguous, they allow for compliance classes that include and intersect each other and their field of reference is not always articulated into discrete units. There are further concepts that Goodman has defined in order to characterize other symbol systems as distinct from notational systems: *density,* and in relation to this *analogue* versus *digital* symbol systems, and *repleteness*.

syntactic density	A symbol scheme is syntactically dense if it provides for infinitely many characters so ordered that between each two characters there is a further character. If such a scheme has no gaps it is called *dense throughout*. In a dense scheme, the criterion syntactic finite differentiation is violated, because here no mark can be determined to belong to one rather than to many other characters.
semantic density	A field of reference is semantically dense if between any two referents there is a third. A semantically dense symbol system is not notational because the criterion of semantic finite differentiation is violated.
repleteness	Repleteness is a syntactic characteristic that is concerned with how many features of a character are constitutive of the character versus how many of its features can be disregarded as irrelevant. 'Unlike the notationality criteria and density criteria, repleteness is a matter of degree. A scheme in which little can be ruled out as contingent is called replete. A scheme in which much can be ruled out is

173 Ibid, p 156.

considered *attenuated*.'[174] Goodman explains the difference by comparing an electrocardiogram with a Hokusai drawing of Mount Fuji. 'The black wiggly lines on white backgrounds may be exactly the same in the two cases. Yet the one is a diagram and the other a picture. What makes the difference? ... The difference is syntactic: the constitutive aspects of the diagrammatic as compared with the pictorial character are expressly and narrowly restricted. The only relevant features of the diagram are the ordinate and abscissa ... For the sketch, this is not true. Any thickening or thinning of the line, its color, its contrast with the background ... none of these can be ruled out, none can be ignored.'[175] Although both the diagrammatic and pictorial scheme are dense (not articulate), they differ radically with respect to repleteness. The pictorial scheme is relatively more replete, the diagrammatic scheme more attenuated.

analogue vs digital A symbol *scheme* is analogue if syntactically dense; a *system* is analogue if syntactically and semantically dense. 'A system of this kind is obviously the very antithesis of a notational system.'[176] A digital scheme is discontinuous throughout; and in a digital system the characters of such a scheme are one-to-one correlated with a discontinuous set of compliance classes. To be notational a digital system would also need to be syntactically and semantically disjoint, as well as unambiguous. 'The real virtues of digital instruments are those of notational systems: definiteness and repeatability of readings. Analog instruments may offer greater sensitivity and flexibility. ... the analog instrument is likely to play its chief role in the exploratory stages, before units of measurement have been fixed; then a suitably designed digital instrument takes over.'[177]

174 Goel, *Sketches of Thought*, p 168.
175 Goodman, *Languages of Art*, p 229.
176 Ibid, p 160.
177 Ibid, pp 161–2.

Goodman's conceptual apparatus can now be employed for the analysis of the various symbol systems utilized within the architectural design process. The engineer's and contractor's projects require precise, annotated, technical drawings that allow for an unambiguous translation into calculations (engineer's project) and for a one-to-one translation into instructions to fabricate and build (contractor's project).[178] These purposes demand a notational system that prescribes the onwards activities with the same degree of reliability and precision with which a musical score prescribes the performance of a work of music. Musical notation is Goodman's paradigmatic instance for his concept of notation. He therefore calls all complete notational inscriptions ***scores.*** The design team's construction documents should function as a score in this sense, the score of the building.

Construction documents do indeed fulfil all the criteria that define notational systems. This assessment is confirmed by Vinod Goel: 'The final output of the design process are the contract documents. They consist of the specifications and blueprints. Both are largely denotative and notational. The specifications are written in a subset of a discursive language that tries to approximate notationality, by avoiding ambiguous, intersecting, and densely ordered expressions. There are conventionalized forms, expressions, and contexts agreed to by the community and the courts that facilitate unambiguous interpretation.'[179] The theory of architectural autopoiesis does not consider the contract documents to be the final output of the design process. In fact they are marginal to the central tasks of architecture in the light of its societal function and *raison d'être*. However, it is still of theoretical value here to follow Goel's analysis of the construction documents as a point of comparison and contrast with the other symbol systems employed within architectural design processes. Goel continues his assessment as follows:

> The contract drawings or 'blueprints' ... approximate a notational system. The linguistic labels used on blueprints are generally an unambiguous,

178 A notation (one-to-one translation) does not preclude that what is being denoted has more complexity than the notation. This additional complexity/information can be revealed in another description. Alphabetic writing notates speech without taking account of stresses; musical scores denote pitch and tempo, sometimes indicate phrasing, but do not denote the sonic qualities of timbre and texture. Scores are thus subject to multiple interpretations with respect to these dimensions. This does not imply ambiguity. All performances are performances of the composition according to the score; and all performances can be written down again resulting in the same musical notation. In the same way the information notated in drawings will be inflated by the translation to the next level of detail, or by translation into a constructed physical reality. This is coherent with the concept of a notational system.

179 Goel, *Sketches of Thought*, p 178.

> semantically disjoint, and differentiated subset of natural language. The system of drawing itself is not a notational system, but the full system is not in effect in the case of blueprints. Contract drawings indicate only, (and very roughly) relative size, shape, and location. Each drawing is clearly marked with the warning 'Do not scale'. Measurements ... are indicated in Arabic numerals, which are syntactically disjoint and differentiated ... but have densely ordered semantic fields. However, since accuracy of measurement is limited by convention to discernible limits (for example, one-sixteenth of an inch) the classes of lengths to which the numbers refer are not densely ordered. The linguistic labels used on blueprints are generally a notational subset of natural language. The specialized symbols or icons (for example, water closets, electrical outlets, doorways), although they look 'diagrammatic', on closer inspection have more in common with ZIP Codes and telephone numbers than with sketches and do constitute a notational system. Thus the constitutive properties of the blueprints are specified in a (near) notational system.[180]

Goel's assessment echoes Goodman's, who also considers blueprints issued for construction to be notations despite the fact that 'a plan is a drawing, with lines and angles subject to continuous variation'.[181] According to Goodman, 'the particular selection of drawings and numerals in an architectural plan counts as a digital diagram and as a score'.[182] As evidence Goodman cites that 'a rough and distorted version, with the same letters and numerals, qualifies as a true copy of the most precisely drafted blueprint, prescribes the constitutive properties as rigorously, and has the same buildings as compliants'.[183]

In order to structure the further analysis, the symbol systems utilized within the design process are laid out in a table. Here and in what follows only the architect's project is considered, leaving out the client's, the engineer's and the contractor's project. The architect's project is conceived as a double design effort whereby the project of articulation runs parallel to the project of organization. (The analysis abstracts from the further differentiation of the project of articulation into a semiological as well as a phenomenological project.) Each of the two aspects of the design project is structured broadly as a three-phased process. Thus we get two parallel strands, each involving its own three consecutive modelling spaces, resulting in an overall set of six modelling spaces. A seventh modelling space is proposed here in as much as the third and

180 Goel, *Sketches of Thought*, p 178.
181 Goodman, *Languages of Art*, p 218.
182 Ibid, p 219.
183 Ibid.

last stage of the architect's project might be pursued by an integrating design tool that can simultaneously service both the organizational and the articulatory project and feed into the more specialized modelling spaces on either side.

designing organization	designing articulation
Venn diagram, network diagram via freehand sketching	compositional/massing diagram via freehand sketching
↓ schematic drawings via set of 2D CAD files	↓ 3D geometric model, quick renders via 3D digital model (Maya)

detail drawings via 2D CAD files	← comprehensive, detailed 3D model via 3D parametric model (DP, Revit) →	photorealism via renderings

As will transpire, not all of the symbol systems coming into play here are notational systems. However, as Vinod Goel stresses: 'non-notational symbol systems are not weak, substandard, or defective in any sense. They are extremely powerful and productive, and much of their power comes from the very fact that they are nondisjoint, ambiguous, dense, replete, and so on. They have an important role to play in human cognition, and they may lie at the root of human creativity.'[184] According to Goel sketching is such a non-notational system, furthest removed from the strictures of a notational system. The same thrust can be found in Goodman. Goodman compares the relationship of a painter's sketch for a painting with the relationship of a score to a musical work and insists on the 'crucial difference in their status'.[185] In the painter's sketch, 'none among the pictorial properties of a sketch can be dismissed as irrelevant. ... Thus, whereas a true score picks out a class of performances that are the equal and only instances of a musical work, a sketch does not determine a class of objects that are equal and only instances of a work of painting. Unlike the score, the sketch does not define a work. ... No pictorial respects are distinguished as those in which a sketch must match another to be its equivalent, or a painting match a sketch to be an instance of what the sketch defines. And no magnitude of difference in any respect is set as the threshold of significance. Differences of all kinds

184 Goel, *Sketches of Thought*, p 189.
185 Goodman, *Languages of Art*, p 192.

and degrees, measurable or not, are on an equal footing.'[186] One might ask here whether all, some or none of the architect's sketches are like the painter's sketches in these respects.[187]

While Goodman's contrast is between scores and a painter's sketches, Goel contrasts the architect's working drawings or contract documents with the architect's early design sketches, assuming that the latter always follow the model of the painter's sketch. However, the term 'sketch' is not yet sharply enough defined. The theoretical characterization of sketches depends on the symbol system and thus on the communicative practice within which they acquire their meaning. In the table above, two types of modelling spaces have been distinguished with respect to the first phase of the design process, ie, the modelling spaces of Venn diagrams and network diagrams on the one hand and the modelling spaces of compositional diagrams and massing diagrams on the other hand. Both types of modelling spaces proceed via freehand sketching. However, it can be argued that the first practice of sketching is largely digitial, even notational, while the second type of sketching practice is largely non-notational, ie, analogue, ambiguous, dense and replete. To the extent to which the meaning of organizational freehand sketches can be equated with either Venn diagrams or network diagrams – just as the meaning of handwriting can be equated with printed type – the practice of organizational freehand sketching constitutes a notational system. These sketches are diagrammatic rather than pictorial. Both Venn diagrams and network diagrams fulfil all the criteria of notational systems with the exception of semantic disjointness. However, semantic disjointness is only violated by a harmless redundancy of characters, ie, there are always many ways in which a particular set-theoretic relation or a network-theoretic relation can be graphically spatialized. There is a many-to-one projection from graphic spatialization to topological relation. However, this redundancy of spatialization that characterizes both Venn diagrams and network diagrams is also precisely the point of difference between the meaning of organizational sketches and pure Venn diagrams and network diagrams. For instance, Venn diagrams are, strictly speaking, only meant to notate the set-theoretic (logical, topological) relations of inclusion, disjointness, intersection and complementarity. They are extremely attenuated. The architect's organizational sketches always imply more than purely logical (topological) relations. They 'mean' to be

186 Ibid, pp 192–3.

187 One might further ask whether all a painter's sketches can be characterized in that way. However, that is no longer the concern of architectural theory.

already specific spatializations of (topo)logical relations. However, what they share with pure Venn/network diagrams is that they abstract from exact shape, dimensions and proportions. They certainly abstract from the variable properties of the lines, such as linearity, curvilinearity, variable thickness etc. It is clear here which aspects of the sketch are relevant and which aspects are irrelevant. All this contrasts with the painter's sketch where (supposedly) none of these aspects can be dismissed as irrelevant.

What a sketched architectural bubble diagram was meant to imply becomes clear in its further translation into schematic drawings via 2D CAD files. The basic organizational parti is preserved while new information has entered via additional decisions about the exact geometry of the project's spatial organization. The modelling space of this next phase of the design process can be theorized here as constituting the field of reference of the notational symbol system of freehand organizational sketching. A notation (one-to-one translation) does not preclude that what is being denoted has more complexity than the notation. This additional complexity/information can be revealed in another description. Alphabetic writing notates speech without taking account of stresses; musical scores denote pitch and tempo, sometimes indicate phrasing, but do not denote the sonic qualities of timbre and texture. Scores are thus subject to multiple interpretations with respect to these dimensions. This does not imply ambiguity. All performances are performances of the composition according to the score; and all performances can be written down again resulting in the same musical notation. In the same way, the information notated in drawings will be inflated by the translation to the next level of detail, or by translation into a constructed physical reality. This is coherent with the concept of a notational system.

Which evaluation criteria are being brought to bear on the organizational sketch? Prima facie it seems that functional criteria, ie, relations of convenient adjacency and access between functionally designated territories, are the primary concern and selection criteria here. This is indeed so. However, this does not imply that the code of beauty can be dispensed with here. Questions of formal choice and formal resolution are brought to bear here too, otherwise the design decision task would be indeterminable. The topological relations alone cannot determine a single spatial layout. Each set-theoretic arrangement (and each network-theoretic pattern) has many (potentially infinitely many) spatial translations. Formal choices are necessary to terminate this initial design stage. The formal heuristics (biases, dogmas) of the architect's chosen style act as guidelines here, for example, by privileging a symmetrical over an asymmetrical parti. At the next stage of translation, where the exact geometry of the parti is being determined, formal biases once more help to make the necessary selections. At this stage certain rules about privileged proportions might programme/condition the application of the code value 'formally resolved'.

The modelling space of compositional massing diagrams is the first stage in the development of the project's articulation. One might presume that the practice of compositional sketching – oriented towards articulation and thus to the perceptual and semantic expression of the design – is more akin to the painter's sketching practice as characterized by Goodman as analogue, ambiguous, dense and replete. This is indeed so. When sketching in this mode – whether it is a freehand sketch on paper, a clay model, or a rough digital sketch model – it remains open which exact formal aspects of the sketch are relevant. No aspect can be dismissed in advance. The variable intensity and thickness of the outlines, the sharpness or softness of corners, the apparent proportions of the indicated bodies, the symmetry or asymmetry of the sketch, none of these aspects has to mean something but none of these aspects can be discarded as irrelevant. Architectural sketching thus displays a high degree of repleteness. The same applies to the less tangible qualities like the composition's sense of openness vs seclusiveness, compactness vs dispersement, massiveness vs lightness, hierarchy vs heterarchy etc. All this matters or might matter in terms of the architect's task to find pertinent Gestalt characteristics that are able to appropriately articulate the chosen organizational parti. Slight variations in the degree of outline curvature, or in the relative proportions, relative similitude of compositional elements or in the sense of lightness of the composition might make a significant difference in terms of the perceived decomposition and then comprehension of the scene. In this sense compositional sketches are densely ordered, ie, the respective symbol system is (syntactically and semantically) dense rather than finitely differentiated. This gives this modelling space great sensitivity to explore the nuances of figuration.

Both organizational sketches (spatialized Venn diagrams or network diagrams) and articulatory sketches (compositional massing sketches) involve all three referencing modes distinguished by Goodman: denotation, exemplification and expression. The field of reference of the sketch is the set of follow-on modelling spaces into which the sketch is to be translated, and ultimately the built spaces into which the sketch is to be translated via these modelling spaces. While a written symbolic system for set-theoretic or network-theoretic relations would operate purely in a mode of denotation, the spatialized Venn diagram and network diagram operate via exemplification. Relations like enclosure, intersection, adjacency, relative size (if intended) etc are relations[188] that hold between the spatial elements of the sketch that exemplify precisely those relations that should equally hold between the equivalent (denoted) spatial elements of the hard-line CAD drawings, and indeed with respect to the denoted spatial elements of the final built organization. Annotations like room names/numbers, the arrows in directed network diagrams or the weightings in weighted network diagrams are denotations.

In the case of the articulatory sketch, the field of reference is ultimately the anticipated/simulated perceptual experience and semantic reading of the designed project. Both objective geometric aspects of the sketch like curved vs sharp corners, rough vs smooth texture and the perceived qualities of the sketch like its sense of closed compactness are operating via exemplification. Qualities that might be ascribed to the sketch only in a metaphorical sense are referential in the mode of expression. For example, the sketch's sense of casual informality might be discovered and intended to persist all the way to the photorealistic renderings and in the final experience of the constructed building. This assessment is confirmed by Vinod Goel: 'The symbol systems used by designers not only denote spatial and nonspatial properties but also exemplify and express such properties as relative size, shape, location, elegance, formality, rigidity, and certainty. ... Our perceptual system is set up to deal with these properties in the world at large. If our representations of the world can preserve these properties, we can deal with them directly rather than having to decode a purely denotational system.'[189] The advantage of these modes of reference – exemplification and expression – is that they allow designers to manipulate the relevant properties and relations directly within their medium of design. This immediacy of intuitive manipulation makes these modelling systems very effective. The same applies to the difference between a set of 2D drawings which together define a three-dimensional geometry that is only accessible via inferential decoding on the one hand and, on the other, the immediate availability of the three-dimensional geometry in 3D digital sketch models or physical sketch models that allows for the direct manipulation of the geometry.

Which criteria of evaluation are brought to bear on the articulatory sketch? It is not the sketch itself but rather the design developed via the

188 Relational predicates rather than properties.

189 Goel, *Sketches of Thought*, p 192.

sketch that is being evaluated.[190] The functional criteria brought to bear here are the criteria of successful articulation, ie, the intelligibility of the design as architectural order. This intelligibility has two aspects, the perceptual recognizability (palpability, conspicuity) and the semantic legibility (comprehensibility) of the design's spatial organization and distribution of functional designations. However, intelligibility is not the same as beauty or elegance. Thus the code of beauty brings to bear a second set of criteria concerned with the formal resolution of the project's articulation. A given spatial organization and distribution of functional designations might be articulated in many different ways that might claim to be equally intelligible. Again, the design decision process must be terminated by appealing to the formal principles of a chosen style. This aesthetically driven completion of the design decision process does not introduce an irreducibly irrational element into the design process. The dogmatism of the style is a required asset in any concrete design decision situation. Without it, the design process would involve too much arbitrary fiat or paralyzing indecision. While a style as well as many further formal and conceptual a prioris that are embedded in deeper, more permanent layers of the discipline, are presupposed in any concrete design process, these presuppositions are thereby not irrational. The historical formation of a mature style is an evolutionary process that ensures the viability and thus rationality of its prescriptions. In the case of avant-garde styles which as yet lack historical corroboration, theoretical arguments might be put forward that explain the advantages and the overall historical rationality of its heuristics.[191] A historically well-adapted style is thus a necessary precondition of any credible design process rationality. Further specificity with respect to the rationality of design processes is thus better gained and elaborated within the context of a specific contemporary style. The specific rationality of any given or proclaimed style depends upon its pertinence with respect to the dominant societal problematics and exigencies of contemporary world society.

190 Occasionally a sketch or rendering might be judged on its merit as sketch or rendering independently of the implied design, for example, a rendering might be criticized for misrepresenting the design. The implication is then that the rendering is to be changed without implying a change in the design. This distinction between sketch/rendering and design can only be made if the design has an independent registration in another representation, for example, in other sketches/renderings or in a set of plans and sections or in a 3D digital model.

191 An example of theoretical arguments explicating the historical rationality of a style can be found in part II *Parametricism – The Parametric Paradigm and the Formation of a New Style*.

8. Architecture and Society

Wherever communication takes place, social systems are produced or reproduced. All communications and all local system formations take place in the global discursive horizon provided by society. Society can be defined as the autopoietic social system that encompasses all other social communication systems and thus the totality of all communications.[1] The overall social communication process that today spans the world constitutes an effective world society.[2] This global societal communication process evolves within the global spatial environment that is planet earth. This natural space is differentiated geographically, climatically as well as in terms of the biosphere. This global organization of the human habitat is the natural substrate upon which the complex metabolism of human world society plays out, with its world-spanning infrastructures (engendering differential time-space compressions), and with its territorializing political structures that – like all social structures – order and constrain the free flow of communications.

The metabolism between humankind and the rest of nature is always problematic. The global environmental problematic implies the danger of unbalancing the world-ecosystem, and the life-process of every individual organism is confronted with the vicissitudes of physical nature. However, it is a hallmark of our modern civilized condition that the problematic metabolism with nature that confronts the modern world citizen is *mediated* by social systems of communications. All problems we might face as organisms within the material world (hunger, cold, disease) confront us as problems of communication. The sustenance of each of our basic needs is mediated by the social communication process and transposed into a need to communicate effectively according to regulating social structures like the economy, the political system and the legal system. Accommodation and framing is provided within purpose-designed buildings, patterned according to the concepts, categories and spatial organizations provided by the discipline of architecture. Even if nature

1 As the system of all communications, society is self-referentially enclosed within an environment that comprises the physical and organic world as well as human organisms and psychic systems.

2 Within Luhmann's social systems theory, the concept of society as the encompassing system of communication is strictly distinguished from the concept of the state that pertains to the political subsystem of society.

strikes brutally with natural disasters, the problem instantly transforms into a problem of effective social communication: we need to apply for relief, claim insurance payments, redeem medical insurance provisions, rely upon police protection, legal rights and expert designed shelters allocated by registered, charitable organizations etc.

Human society exists and reproduces within a material world. However, all difficulties and bottlenecks in this reproduction process appear as problems of communication. Material production depends upon the communication processes of the economy, taking up the results of the communication processes of science. Individuals rarely encounter the underlying physicality of their existence. Usually they exist in the safe bubble of a well-tempered, technologically augmented environment that delivers all required comforts via social communication. There are some rare moments, such as in the case of accidents and disease, where we might encounter the raw materiality of life. However, even here, beyond the first shock, all problems transform into issues of social communication: has the ambulance been called? Is traffic congested? Will the health insurance cover this medical condition? Another example: if I want to travel 10,000 miles to a desired destination, my primary problems and inconveniences are of a social rather than a material nature. Do I have enough money to afford the air ticket? Are there delays due to congestion? The main inconveniences are security controls etc. This general condition, whereby issues of social communication are always *the* critical issues in comparison with challenges posed by the material world, justifies the theoretical foregrounding of communication, abstracting from the materiality of the world. This abstraction is a real, ongoing abstraction effected by the ongoing communication processes.

This massive, evolving man-nature metabolism – that is at the same time the structured communication process of world society – is sustained and carried forward by the evolution of the man-made physical environment. Many aspects of this man-made physical environment remain outside the purview of architecture and urban design: for example, regional planning, certain overarching aspects of city planning, the overall planning of the utilities networks and transport infrastructures. Architecture and urban design thus make a particular contribution to the advancement of particular layers and aspects of the man-made physical environment that sustains world society. In Volume 1, part 5 – *The Societal Function of Architecture* – 'framing' was identified as the societal function of architecture and design. Thus architecture and urban design are concerned with the innovation of those layers and aspects of the man-made physical environment that contribute to the framing of communicative interaction. Everything that functions as frame or interface – everything conspicuous in our shared visual field – belongs to architecture/design's domain of competency.[3] The theory of architectural autopoiesis reserves the term *built environment* to these particular layers that are within architecture and urbanism's purview. The built environment is thus defined functionally as a framing system constituted through organized and articulated spatial and morphological relations. Architecture is the societal function system that is responsible for the continuous development and innovative adaptation of the built environment as society's frame. Architecture has to reflect its ongoing framing contribution to a changing society. Its development is embedded within the total developmental process of world society. It coevolves with the other subsystems of society. In its own way it reflects, works through and contributes to these changes.

As explicated in Volume 1 of *The Autopoiesis of Architecture*, according to Niklas Luhmann, modern society is most profoundly characterized as *functionally differentiated society*. Luhmann's general theory of society is a theory of *modes of societal differentiation*. This category of *modes of societal differentiation* takes the place of Marx's category of *modes of production* as the primary characterization that distinguishes types of society as a basis for historical periodization. Where Marx distinguishes slaveholding, feudal and capitalist societies as successive modes of production, Luhmann distinguishes segmentary differentiation, centre-periphery differentiation, stratification and functional differentiation as successively dominant modes of differentiation that determine the historical character of the respective society. In contrast to Marx's characterization of capitalist society as class society, Luhmann, without denying the existence of classes, argues that stratification is no longer the primary mode of societal differentiation. Society – and Luhmann argues that there is only one society, ie, world society – is differentiated into autonomous subsystems, each claiming a monopoly with respect to a specific function within the overall social process: the world political system (with its national subsystems), the (only partially globalized) world of legal systems, the world economy, world science, the world education system, world art, the world mass media. The theory of architectural autopoiesis adds world architecture to this list. Social inclusion in these systems is no longer premised on a given position in a presumed hierarchical order of stratification.[4] In principle, every citizen is participating in each of these

3 The invisible technical infrastructures belong to the domain of engineering.

4 Although a strong sense of stratification still persists, it is no longer institutionalized. Stratification is no longer the dominant mode of ordering social communication. For instance,

function systems.[5] Everybody has an equal right to vote, has access to the legal system, the freedom to engage in economic transactions in the market, to engage in science; everybody has the opportunity to go to school, read newspapers, write blogs, enjoy/criticize art, and everybody uses designed spaces and artefacts, can comment on their functional and formal merits and in principle everybody can hire an architect to commission a work of architecture.

8.1 World Architecture within World Society

THESIS 42

Contemporary architecture exists as a single, unified world architecture.

Within Luhmann's social systems theory, the concept of society is defined as the encompassing system of all communications. This concept is strictly distinguished from the concept of the state that pertains primarily to the political subsystem of society. While the world remains divided into many independent states, most types of communications flow freely across state boundaries. In particular, the great function systems of society are communicating globally. Therefore the different societies of the past have evolved and fused to become effectively a single world society. The attendant reality of world architecture is as evident as the world economy and the worldwide communication system of science. The existence of a worldwide mass media system, a world education system and the beginnings of a world political system are also evident.

We might speak of world architecture in analogy to world literature or world cinema. The assumption here is that the writers and film-makers of this world know of each other's work and thereby influence each other. National traditions in architecture have faded into insignificance much more so than in literature or cinema where the different languages still constitute semi-insulated national domains. In architecture, world integration is thus stronger than in literature and cinema. It is not merely a matter of circulating influences. Especially within the avant-garde segment, for every ambitious, self-conscious architect the primary audience is the global community of architects. While it takes time for books to be translated, shipped and read, every avant-garde design is

legitimate political power no longer automatically yields economic strength, legal rights, claims towards beauty, scientific truth or public opinion.

5 Although universal inclusion is a systemic principle, the inclusion of all in all systems is not everywhere a reality. The fact that any concrete exclusion raises the spectre of corruption and is a potential scandal demonstrates that the principles of functionally differentiated society are universally accepted as indisputable. All exceptions are treated as problems to be solved.

instantly available and influential via the World Wide Web. There exist no national architectures any more within the contemporary autopoiesis of architecture. While the political process and the legal system largely operate with a national or regional focus – because of the close connection these two function systems have with the nation state – architecture has no such ties. Architecture nearly reaches the same level of worldwide discursive integration that can be observed with respect to science (where failure to be aware of the global production of one's specific field spells irrelevance).

While it seems rather obvious that there are no autonomous architectural domains in terms of region or nation, we might ask whether there might be different architectures that are discursively separated by approach or style. The answer to this question is probably also negative. Especially since the advent of the Internet – more than ever before – the autopoiesis of architecture is effectively an integrated worldwide discourse. The plurality of styles, arguments, ideologies and theoretical approaches remains embedded within a single system of communications. The different approaches recognize each other and argue with each other.

The ongoing integration of all architectural communications into a single, unified autopoiesis takes place on the basis of a non-hierarchical, self-organizing network of communications without any stable centre. Contemporary world architecture is therefore misconceived if it is still treated like the invasion or imposition of supposedly 'Western' (American/European) models onto the rest of the world. Discursive focal points might crystallize in cultural centres like London, New York, Tokyo or Beijing but without any national identification.

The material foundation of world architecture is being laid by the process of economic globalization that reached effective and unmistakable pre-eminence in the 1980s. This process of economic globalization had been prepared by a long history of world trade, was enhanced by the expanding colonialism of the 18th and 19th centuries and reached its first peak at the end on the 19th century during the epoch of imperialism – the culmination and crisis point of colonialism. The key European powers had succeeded in carving up the totality of the world by integrating all lands and peoples into their respective empires. This period of colonialism/imperialism produced two rather different avenues of architectural globalization:

1. The forced introduction of the architectural models of the imperialist powers (Great Britain, France etc) into their respective territories –

primarily in the form of government buildings that served to project imperial power.
2. The importation of the world's cultural heritage into the centres of the imperialist powers.

The architectural presence of Great Britain in India – Calcutta, Bombay and New Delhi – might act as a typical example of the first avenue of architectural globalization. The Royal Pavilion in Brighton might serve as a typical example of the second avenue of architectural globalization that led to the integration of diverse influences into the stylistic repertoire of eclecticism, the European precursor of world architecture. However, the regime of imperialism could not foster the conditions of a full-blown world architecture in which influences and contributions flow freely, unencumbered by political prerogatives.

The decisive step forward towards a truly globalized architectural culture came during the 1920s. One of the compelling factors was the ideological thrust of Modern Functionalism. The universalization of building tasks worked against the privileging of representational government palaces that had projected a one-sided and forced dissemination. Second, Modern Functionalism rejected tradition and ornament and therefore eliminated the primary traditional insignia of local origin. This set the stage for an international style that was radically new and could in principle receive equally relevant contributions from anywhere in the world. Early original contributions from South America (Niemeyer) and Japan (Tange) testify to this world openness.

Modernism also produced the first truly world-spanning careers. Most notably Le Corbusier's oeuvre that spans many countries and continents, including work in France, Germany, Italy, Brazil, Uruguay, Algeria, the USA, India, Russia and Japan.

However, Le Corbusier's international career remained an exception that was followed by only a rather small group that reached a similar standing. This group included Walter Gropius, Mies van der Rohe, Alvar Aalto and Oscar Niemeyer. Also, these figures still had a home territory that provided for the majority of their works and their excursions abroad remained exceptions, unlike today's leading architects who have often totally transcended any notion of home territory, for example, Foster, Renzo Piano, OMA, Zaha Hadid Architects, Coop Himmelb(l)au and Herzog & De Meuron.

During the reign of Modernism's International Style (1920–70) there were still local heroes and national clusters of architects that operated alongside the small group of world-spanning figures. It was these local heroes who could expect to gain all the significant projects within their domain. Now, every medium-sized city is aspiring to employ a world renowned architectural brand. During Modernism – despite its global reach as International Style – it still made sense to talk of national sub-groupings with their own nuances, like Czech Cubism, Russian Constructivism and Italian Rationalism. There are no equivalent, locally identifiable phenomena within contemporary architecture.

A certain backlash against the supposed global homogeneity of the International Style came in the form of *Critical Regionalism*. The idea of adaptation to local climatic and cultural conditions could be integrated within the paradigm of Modern Functionalism. This idea emerged as the International Style spread into new and different territories. Critical Regionalism is about the local adaptation of architecture on the basis of universal principles that inherently allow for such adaptation. This notion of Critical Regionalism has nothing to do with a return to parochial isolation. It does not challenge the existence of a single, unified architectural autopoiesis. Parametricism's claim to world architectural relevance matches Modernism's claim in this respect. However, the principles of Parametricism are more conducive to local (climatic and cultural) adaptation. Due to its malleability, its globalizing thrust is much more robust. Thus it is under the auspices of Parametricism that architecture will truly become world architecture. This is to be endorsed. No region should be excluded from participating in the benefits of a global state-of-the-art mode of developing built environments and no region should be excluded from contributing to its progress.[6]

8.2 Autonomy vs Authority

THESIS 43

The autonomy of architecture implies its discursive authority but lacks the power to impose its authority. Within a polycontextual societal environment architecture needs to sustain its autonomy precisely to be able to respond to all the disparate challenges of the different societal subsystems. However, its proposed solutions are no longer backed up by power.

Contemporary society relies upon the provision, adoption and application of ever advancing/improving architectural design services (as much as it relies on, for example, an ever updated system of legal regulation, or an

6 This globalization of best practices can also be observed in the other great function systems of society. Science is the most obvious case. There can be no regional science. The same applies to the economy. Here best practice procedures, best practice regulatory frameworks etc are spreading inevitably.

ever improving education of the population). The most advanced design potency – afforded by the most advanced contemporary architectural style – is a definite form of specialized societal potency, like the advancing knowledge provided by the sciences, updated legal regulations, educational provisions etc. Whether the internally most compelling avant-garde style is being accepted by architecture's societal environment, for example, in terms of being considered marketable, economically feasible, or politically viable, is obviously decided elsewhere, external to architecture, in the other autopoietic systems of society.

All societies have always been dependent upon their built environments – in the sense of a relatively permanent, artificially constructed environment – for the ordering and stabilization of their social systems of communication. This still holds true today. The theory of architectural autopoiesis proposes that architecture constitutes one of the indispensable function systems of contemporary society. Certainly, contemporary society can neither function without buildings, nor without the ongoing provision of ever more buildings. The same immediate, existential dependency, however, does not hold for the avant-garde discourse of architecture. It should be remembered that the theory of architectural autopoiesis places the avant-garde segment in a privileged position with respect to acting in the name of architecture. It is here that architecture's autonomous discursive authority originates.[7] However, there is no guarantee of the relevance and acceptance of the specific urban and architectural innovations which the autonomous, academic discipline of architecture proposes. It is necessary to distinguish between the societal requirement for replacement construction and quantitatively expansive construction on the one hand and the societal requirement for innovative, better adapted built environments on the other. The indispensability of architecture as autonomous academic discipline – articulated into avant-garde and mainstream – only pertains to the extent to which contemporary society can only survive on the basis of permanent evolution.[8]

It is the accelerated evolution of society, rather than its immediate existential reproduction, which depends upon the advancing autopoiesis of architecture. In periods of accelerated societal transformation, a

7 The relationship between avant-garde and mainstream in architecture is similar to the relationship of the advancing sciences as distinct from well established knowledge.

8 In the short term, simple stable-state reproduction could theoretically suffice. Practically, however, cut-throat international competition prevents this possibility.

situation might occur where the established solutions of mainstream architecture are failing to satisfy the new societal needs while the avant-garde discourse is not able to offer new, pertinent solutions. In this case the authority of the discipline is challenged and clients might abandon architecture in favour of ad hoc adaptations. Architecture is becoming irrelevant, and lacks the social power to impose its fading expertise. This will impact initially via the withdrawal of resources. This perturbation might then irritate the autopoiesis of architecture and lead to the internal reinterpretation of its tasks and to the exploration of new concepts, repertoires, methods and values, on the basis of an analysis of those vital ad hoc adaptations that emerged in the built environment in violation of the standard architectural wisdom. The spontaneous adaptations of the built environment outside architecture might be superior to the bankrupt solutions of architecture (in terms of the most urgent requirements), but they should not be assumed to provide sustainable solutions that can satisfactorily integrate the many more nuanced, long-term requirements that an advancing society might have. Retroactive manifestos are never one-to-one translations of the contemporary vernacular. Theory-led experimentation is required to elaborate a new, adaptive pertinence. There is no guarantee that this adaptive effort will succeed. Autonomy is required to develop a specialized discourse that is able to deepen architecture's expertise. Architecture's autonomy implies that it is independent from political power and, in turn, cannot use power to succeed.

This situation is paralleled within science. The immediate, ongoing reproduction of society requires consolidated knowledge, while the advancing sciences offer potentials for accelerated evolution. A certain shared, well-established knowledge has always been constitutive of all societies. Yet precisely the most advanced expert knowledge that is evolving within the operationally closed autopoiesis of modern science can be relatively indifferent to the reproduction or immediate crisis management of society. The ongoing (crisis) management of society cannot afford to consult the latest research. This new/advanced knowledge would socially be too risky and controversial. Society is dependent upon this scientific autopoiesis *only* with respect to its further evolution. Ordinary, ongoing communication remains indifferent to the advances of science and avant-garde architecture, until its respective mutations are selected, confirmed and filtered down into the mainstream processes of ongoing reproduction.

Niklas Luhmann has observed the peculiar fact that scientific knowledge must simultaneously 'stand its ground and take itself back; it must continue to produce new achievements and, at the same time, it must refrain from defining the world for society'.[9] Luhmann continues: 'To be sure, no one seriously doubts the descriptions of the world furnished by science, insofar as science itself trusts them. Nonetheless, the effect is virtually non-binding as far as other systems of communication are concerned.'[10] The same ambivalent status might be observed with respect to advanced architecture. Even though architecture has an exclusive and autonomous hold over its disciplinary domain – it does not submit to any outside dictates – it has in turn no chance to force itself upon society at large. As a specialized societal function system, architecture does indeed enjoy a certain privilege (and responsibility) of 'first bidding' in respect of the proposition and promotion of innovations. However, this privilege does not entail the absolute exclusivity of a guaranteed monopoly. The tendencies that gain the upper hand within the intense exchanges of avant-garde communications usually find enough early adopters to press forward towards the mainstream, but there can be no guarantee of society-wide success. In turn, sustained innovations might indeed crystallize outside and against architecture – and are discovered, sublimated and recuperated into architecture only later by means of retroactive manifestos. Such efforts at recuperation are important adaptations – important for the ongoing vitality of architecture and ultimately for its survival, precisely because architecture has lost its authority to impose its achievements onto society at large. In former times – within stratified societies – architecture's authority was imposed by the top of the social hierarchy. It therefore lacked autonomy.

Just as modern science, in comparison with the metaphysics that preceded it, has lost its authoritative power as the normative explication of a cosmic order, so contemporary architecture has lost its authoritative power to dictate a unified physiognomy to society. The Baroque style – in its time pervasive across the Western world – represents the last unambiguous instantiation of the (since lost) authoritative power of architecture. This power of architecture depended upon architecture being closely tied to the centre of a hierarchically stratified society.[11] In contrast, the contemporary potency of architecture lies in its autonomy, as the generally recognized (more or less exclusive) provider of architectural innovations, that in turn are taken up by society or not.

9 Niklas Luhmann, 'The Modernity of Science', in: *New German Critique*, Winter 1994, Issue 61, Telos Press (New York) pp 9–16.

10 Ibid.

11 It was the essential characteristic of traditional stratified society that at its apex political, moral, economic, technological and aesthetic power were converging, concentrated in one hand or closely knit group.

Another consequence of this new arrangement is that the potency of architecture is very much dependent on the pace of societal evolution. If this analysis has a measure of veracity, we should expect the vitality and prestige of architecture to be at risk in periods of rapid societal transformation, precisely at the moment when its contribution is most required.[12] Architecture usually gains status during periods when conditions have settled into a new societal formation (for example, Fordist mass society, Post-Fordist network society) and avant-garde architecture has settled into a new style (for example, Modernism, Parametricism) within which to advance design research cumulatively with the prospect of generalizing its advances into a new, pertinent mainstream practice.

Architecture is one of society's great function systems with an exclusive and comprehensive competency for the innovation of the global built environment. The effective monopoly status of the autopoiesis of architecture requires, in turn, a non-hierarchical network pattern of internal communication that knows no internal boundaries and protected turfs. Otherwise this privilege would very soon be lost through a lack of adaptive versatility. The radical internal openness of patterns and opportunities of communication is therefore the necessary internal correlate of operational closure and monopoly-style exclusivity in its externally assumed responsibility. As established above, there is no guarantee that internal discursive success within the avant-garde segment translates into a viable mainstream practice that can secure and reproduce external acceptance. Therefore, the internal discourse must take the experience (or absence) of external validation into account and self-regulate its criteria accordingly, otherwise architecture as a whole becomes irrelevant. The responsibility of finding innovative solutions and viable evolutionary pathways is the sole responsibility of the autopoiesis of architecture as self-referentially closed system of communications. There can be no direct outside guidance or instruction. The tasks are too complex to allow clients or politicians to suggest or dictate solutions. All clients can do is either to reject or accept a presented solution; or select from a given menu of competitively offered designs, without being able to fully rationalize their decision, and with no guarantee that the selected design will really satisfy their needs later. How can the architectural discourse set out and ascertain a viable, long-term strategy – the investment in a new long-term style – on the basis of this kind of raw

12 Recent history corroborates this: the 1970s was a period of socio-economic stagnation and architectural denigration. Since the 1980s, architecture has grown in prestige along with the momentous socio-economic transformations that have been theorized under the heading of Post-Fordist restructuring.

feedback? Although empirical feedback is important, a blind empirical trial and error approach would hardly have a chance to succeed here. What is required is a comprehensive architectural theory that can relate formal possibilities to functional performances. The theory of architectural autopoiesis, in particular Part 6 on architecture's task[13], is making steps to upgrade architecture's theoretical capacity to do this. These specific theories of form-function relations must in turn be embedded in a general understanding of architecture's societal function.[14] While this understanding is relatively timeless (long term – as long as functionally differentiated society persists), the translation of this general understanding of architecture's societal function into concrete task formulations and design research agendas is historically more specific (medium term – as long as a style remains valid). These more concrete task formulations must be periodically updated with respect to the most prominent and most relevant developmental tendencies within contemporary world society. Such a medium-term architectural theory is thus required to make sense of the empirical feedback the discipline receives via its successes and failures within its societal environment. What is therefore required is that architecture develops and periodically updates a pertinent conception of society.

8.3 Architecture's Conception of Society

THESIS 44

Architecture must periodically adapt and upgrade its internal representation of society. To do this it must draw on external theoretical resources.

The relationship between architecture and society might be decomposed into a series of two-way relationships of mutual dependence between architecture and the various other subsystems of society. Part 8 is dedicated to exploring some of these relationships, reflecting the way in which the autopoiesis of architecture depends upon, is irritated by and responds to specific conditions and communication structures it encounters within its societal environment. The first dependency of architecture on other societal systems to be reflected here is the dependency of architecture's autopoietic self-regulation on outside theoretical resources from the social sciences. Architecture must develop and periodically update its conception of society with respect to which it re-defines and reasserts its societal function and relevance. Here is thus

13 See part 6 *The Task of Architecture.*

14 See Volume 1, part 5 *The Societal Function of Architecture.*

an occasion for the theory of architectural autopoiesis to reflect its historical status as aspiring self-description for contemporary architecture, its dependency on outside theoretical sources and the historical, discursive pertinence of these resources.[15]

All function systems develop their own specific perspective on society and must define their respective role within it. There are quite a few general theories of contemporary society that can serve as possible points of departure for the description and observation of society. Accordingly, contemporary society might be characterized as *globalized society, late capitalist society, the society of the spectacle, the era of empire, post-colonial society, post-industrial society, Post-Fordist society, information society, network society, multicultural society, post-socialist liberal society, risk society, functionally differentiated society* etc. These catchphrases are making both competing and partially complementary claims. Their attendant theories originated mostly within the social sciences or in the reflection theories[16] of the political system and/or economic system. From these points of origin, the most successful theories and slogans were picked up and disseminated by the mass media to become part of the general world view shared within society.[17] The fact that this diversity of possible theoretical characterizations circulates within society at large implies that a diversity of competing points of departure for self-explication is available within each separate function system. Accordingly, there is neither a reason to expect a unitary theoretical account of society *across* the different function systems, nor is there a reason to expect a unitary theoretical account of society *within* any of the function systems of society. The role-defining societal account of society is a contested ground within each function system. What is contested is thus also the fundamental societal self-location and

15 The resources include Niklas Luhmann's social systems theory as general framework, Luhmann's theory of functionally differentiated society as long-term theory of world society, and finally the theory of Post-Fordism (Post-Fordist network society) as a theory describing the latest epochal transformation of world society since the 1970s.

16 The theoretical self-steering efforts of the great function systems – political theory, economics, jurisprudence, pedagogy, art theory, architectural theory etc – are not sciences. Luhmann uses the term 'reflection theory'.

17 Architectural theory also contributed a catchphrase – the Postmodern – that became available for general usage far beyond its architectural origin. It was picked up within cultural theory, media studies, the art system and philosophy. The characterization of the transitional style of Postmodernism inspired a general characterization of contemporary culture and society as 'the condition of Postmodernity'. See: Charles Jencks, *The Language of Post-Modern Architecture* (1st edition 1977), 5th edition, Rizzoli (New York), 1987; David Harvey, *The Condition of Postmodernity: An Enquiry into the Origins of Cultural Change*, Blackwell Publishers (Cambridge, MA/Oxford), 1990.

self-definition of each function system. This self-definition guides the discursive self-regulation of the respective function system.

According to the theory of architectural autopoiesis, architecture is one of the great function systems within functionally differentiated society.[18] This raises the serious question of how the unity of the function system's autopoiesis can exist in the presence of contesting theories of society. The unity of architecture is indeed one of the axiomatic presuppositions of the theory of architectural autopoiesis. It requires that architecture operates with a unitary conception of society. How can this contradiction be dissolved? The first thing to point out here is that the specific theoretical/explanatory differences that mark out the different theories of contemporary society listed above are not necessarily differences relevant to architecture and its responses. Which theoretical differences make a difference depends upon the context within which the theories are received. What distinguishes the (originally) Marxist theory of Post-Fordism from the neo-liberal theory of *post-socialist liberal society* makes a big difference in terms of politics but with respect to the concerns of architecture their relevant descriptions of what happens in terms of socio-economic restructuring seem to be converging. To the extent to which there remain different architecturally relevant societal diagnoses, as well as different philosophical world views and epistemologies, the key to dissolving this contradiction can be found in the distinction between implicit conception and explicit theory, together with two central distinctions by which the theory of architectural autopoiesis denotes two fundamental structures within the autopoiesis of architecture, ie, the distinction of avant-garde versus mainstream as two simultaneously operating subsystems within architecture's autopoiesis on the one hand, and the distinction of revolutionary versus cumulative periods of design research on the other. The latter distinction structures the architectural discourse in the time dimension and leads to the related distinction of transitional versus epochal styles in architecture.

To the extent to which the self-regulation of the function system is always already operative, we should assume that there is an implicit, ongoing self-conception of the function system and of its role within society. However, this condition pertains only with respect to the mainstream of architecture. The mainstream operates implicitly on the

18 The fact that the theory of architectural autopoiesis bases itself on one of the various circulation theories of society does not prevent it from recognizing the fact that other, competing (potentially influential) theories are available. However, the discursive success of the theory of architectural autopoiesis is one of the conditions of its validity. Failing to achieve hegemony implies a refutation of its claims. This unusual effect, not unlike the case of Marxism, marks the autological structure of the theory.

basis of a theoretical self-explication that achieved hegemony within the previous cycle of innovation. This is reflected in the fact that the explicit attempts at self-definition usually take the form of critique. These explicit, critical attempts at self-definition take place within the avant-garde segment of the discipline, during periods of revolutionary research, often leading to new transitional styles. As a new hegemonic style emerges[19] from the competition between rival attempts to update a discipline in crisis, a style that is able to shift the avant-garde from revolutionary to cumulative research, a new explicit self-definition is being advanced, embedded in a new, broad understanding of the societal environment. Once the emerging hegemonic avant-garde style has accumulated sufficient strength, confidence and competency it might be able to conquer the mainstream of architectural production, thus becoming the new epochal style. As time passes, the ideological controversies of the revolutionary transition period are forgotten and the general conception of society that underlies and justifies the new mainstream practice is implicit rather than explicit. It becomes explicit once more only if new challenges and problems inspire a new wave of theoretical questioning and criticism within a newly emerging avant-garde tendency. With the exception of relatively short and intense, revolutionary transition periods – contained within architecture's avant-garde segment – the autopoiesis of architecture can be presumed to operate on the basis of a unitary, largely implicit, unquestioned, underlying conception of society.

It is within the implicit horizon of such a broad understanding that architecture comprehends its societal function. This function and *raison d'être* of architecture are explicitly reflected in the comprehensive theoretical treatises (self-descriptions) that have accompanied and participated in the evolution of architecture's autopoiesis throughout its history. What does this imply for the current conjuncture? Currently the mainstream professional discourse is operating with a unitary, underlying conception of its societal function to the extent to which it still operates on the basis of the Modernist world view. The current avant-garde has emerged from an extended period of ideological debates and controversies. These debates have succeeded in thoroughly discrediting the Modernist world view that has been underpinning architectural Modernism. On the basis of Post-Structuralism, in particular the philosophy of Deleuze and Guattari, as well as via the reception of complexity theory, avant-garde theory and practice have experienced a powerful convergence in recent years. Modernization theory – together

19 The hegemony of a new avant-garde style results from the competition of transitional styles.

with its positivist epistemology – has been superseded by a new outlook and epistemological horizon. This new post-structuralist epistemological horizon has been absorbed and then applied implicitly rather than via the explicit endorsement of a philosophical system. The contemporary tendency of Parametricism can be understood as drawing the practical conclusions from the theoretical critique and reorientation of recent years. The theory of architectural autopoiesis is further augmenting these tendencies – trying to give them an explicit theoretical expression – on the basis of Luhmann's conducive work. The theoretical resources that are brought to bear here include Niklas Luhmann's social systems theory as general framework, Luhmann's theory of functionally differentiated society as long-term theory of world society and, finally, the theory of Post-Fordism (Post-Fordist network society) as a theory describing the latest epochal transformation of world society since the 1970s. The underlying epistemology is Luhmann's epistemology of Radical Constructivism.[20]

8.3.1 THE CRISIS OF MODERNISM'S CONCEPTION OF SOCIETY

During the era of Modernism there was indeed a unified representation of society within architecture that was guiding the orthodox, mainstream architect in the prioritization of his/her concerns. For half a century, from the early 1920s to the early 1970s, Modernist architecture understood itself as contributing to a global project of technological and social modernization based on the principles of Fordist mass production delivering economies of scale and leading to an unprecedented, universal consumption standard. Human progress was understood to be based on this model of mass industrialization, secured by a national welfare state. Within architecture, CIAM was involved in formulating a unified and authoritative stance with respect to a modern world society. Modern world society was understood along the lines of a universalizing modernization theory, as a community of industrial, democratic welfare states. This extrapolation of the Western European and US post-war experience offered an outlook that initially seemed reasonable in relation to the general developmental tendencies of the time. However, this linear developmental trajectory mutated and took an unanticipated turn that ultimately eroded the Modernist understanding of society. Although the 1950s and 1960s witnessed promising processes of industrial and social modernization in many countries beyond the confines of the so-called First World, this process faltered during the 1970s and 1980s. The

20 The discussion of Radical Constructivism would take us beyond what can be contained within an architectural theory. Here it suffices to note that Radical Constructivism is broadly consistent with the insights of Post-structuralism.

underlying developmental model encountered many difficulties, contradictions and resistances in the Second and Third Worlds. The envisioned global modernization did not materialize. Even the industrial heartlands of the First World were shaken by crises, leading to the erosion of the welfare state. The experience of social and economic contradictions as well as the experience of environmental degradation and presumed shortages in natural resources led to a questioning of modernization theory, even putting the very meaning of human progress and prosperity into question. The socio-economic development model of Fordist modernization was bankrupt.

At the same time, as part of the overall process of disillusionment with the prior ideology of modernization, architectural Modernism experienced its own crisis and rejection. What Modernist architecture had to offer in terms of urbanism and architectural solutions was rejected. New towns with remote sleeping silos and isolated greenfield sites for industrial mass production were fast becoming the dysfunctional dinosaurs of a bygone era.[21] The vital and innovative social and economic processes literally abandoned Modernist architecture and instead sought out and moved to the spaces offered by the historical cities. To regain its relevance architecture had to shift its discourse and reinvent itself. This also involved an intellectual reorientation, in terms of conceptualizing society, its values and potential developmental trajectories. Further, it involved the absorption of various radical critiques that tried to come to terms with how the previous theories, assumptions and expectations could have been so wrong. The following philosophical critiques had gained prominence during the 1960s, 1970s and 1980s: originally enlisted to support the modernization process, anthropology and sociology, for example, in the shape of ethnomethodology, started to question the modern belief in a unitary developmental trajectory, emphasizing instead the diversity of cultures, values and world views. The idea of an unproblematic, shared concept of human progress that had underlain modernization theory was undermined. From the perspective of complexity theory, on the basis of the discovery of non-linear dynamics and self-amplifying feedback processes etc, the idea of planning and prediction in the arena of global development was put into question. Post-Structuralism and the philosophy of Deconstruction emphasized the dependency of all knowledge and values on language and cultural systems. Cultural systems (including language) are based on historical social practices that are ultimately arbitrary, contingent and continuously evolving. On this

21 The most vital and dynamic regions of the Modernist era – for example, Detroit, Ruhrgebiet etc – became problem zones (rust belts). See Patrik Schumacher & Christian Rogner, 'After Ford', in: Georgia Daskalakis, Charles Waldheim & Jason Young (Eds), *Stalking Detroit*, Actar (Barcelona), 2001.

account all claims to objective, universally valid knowledge were undermined, as well as the modern idea of individual agency and authorship.

Both Postmodernism and Deconstructivism – the transitional architectural styles that had challenged and replaced the Modernist style – had started to import the new intellectual tendencies into architecture, somehow trying to use these theories to respond to the new, complex, multifarious challenges that architecture had been facing. For Postmodern architecture, the respective response involved the celebration of diversity and hybridity via playful bricolage and eclecticism, broken by an ironic pose. Deconstructivism radicalized bricolage and hybridization and abstracted these principles from the historical material with which Postmodernism had been invested. By these means Deconstructivism was trying to turn architectural design itself into a form of philosophical critique. The aim was to expose and violate the notions of stable order which architecture had been previously exemplifying and to subvert social institutions by disrupting their routinely expected spatial configurations. As these responses indicate, the avant-garde work of this period was highly experimental, engaged as much in critique and creative destruction as in the discovery of new spatial/formal possibilities. There was as yet no attempt to formalize and promote a new, constructive path for architecture that might be generalized across the various programmes and territories of world society. In fact, such an ambition would have been inherently antithetical to the spirit of Postmodernism and Deconstructivism and anathema to the philosophical resources by which these architectural tendencies were inspired. The theorizing that was absorbed during this period was primarily negative, proclaiming the end of the hegemonic modernization theory and, in general, the end of all 'grand narratives'.[22] Within this intellectual milieu there was no intention of forming a consensus about the essential positive characteristics of the new, emerging system of society. There is no explicit, systematic, Post-Structuralist theory of society that could have been used as premise for the redefinition of architecture's societal function.

8.3.2 SOCIAL SYSTEMS THEORY AND THE THEORY OF ARCHITECTURAL AUTOPOIESIS

Against the panorama of primarily negative theories concerning architecture's position within a transformed society, the theory of architectural autopoiesis stands out in its attempt to formulate a positive,

22 Jean-François Lyotard, *The Postmodern Condition: A Report on Knowledge*, University of Minnesota Press (Minneapolis), 1984, original French by Les Editions de Minuit (Paris), 1979. In the introduction Lyotard writes: 'I define postmodern as incredulity toward metanarratives'.

instructive self-positioning of architecture on the basis of a systematic theory of society. It is obviously beyond the scope and capacity of architectural discourse to develop a theory of society from within its own resources. The way forward must be to initiate a theoretical communication nexus within the avant-garde of the discipline that starts to experiment with the importation and integration of theories of society that are available outside. This book is such an initiative. It draws on a particular theoretical resource, works through a first round of implications for architecture, and on this basis offers the outlook that architecture can regain an appropriate representation of society and of its own place and purpose within it.[23]

Niklas Luhmann's social systems theory and theory of functionally differentiated, polycontextual society is the first compelling attempt to construct a systematic, comprehensive theory of society that is able to absorb and answer all the challenges that were formulated by Post-Structuralism and Deconstruction. Social systems theory builds upon the insights and theoretical resources of complexity theory (systems theory, cybernetics, chaos theory, theory of autopoiesis) that had gathered into a powerful new scientific paradigm during the second half of the 20th century. These primarily constructive rather than critical/Deconstructive theoretical approaches have already been very influential within the architectural avant-garde, especially since the early 1990s.[24] Thus Luhmann's theory of contemporary society is uniquely placed to become architecture's theoretical reference of choice with respect to updating its self-description and the definition of its societal function.[25] There is no credible alternative theory of society that could connect equally well to contemporary architectural design thinking while at the same time being able to absorb all the critical challenges of Post-Structuralist philosophy.[26] Therefore, if the theory of architectural autopoiesis proposes Luhmann's theory of society as architecture's current conception of society, it can pick up and connect to many

23 Here is thus, once more, a point reached where the theory of architectural autopoiesis – autologically – reflects its own status and ambition.

24 The great philosophical influence of this period was Deleuze and Guattari's *A Thousand Plateaus,* itself heavily influenced by the new sciences of complexity. However, Deleuze and Guattari never advanced a systematic theory of contemporary society.

25 The theory of architectural autopoiesis is the first to take up Niklas Luhmann's theory of functionally differentiated society as encompassing theory of society to provide the theoretical framework for the required self-positioning. The unique scope and depth of Luhmann's theory are attracting ever more worldwide attention as his major works are successively being translated. This fact might further contribute to the potential fruitfulness of the theory of architectural autopoiesis.

26 Luhmann's theory is also, by far, the most comprehensive and elaborate social theory circulating today.

theoretical tropes and threads that lead into the heart of architecture's contemporary self-conception. Luhmann's key problematic – complexity – is also the key problematic of contemporary architecture's most vital avant-garde tendency. Thus the (necessary) selection of a viable, encompassing theoretical framework for architecture's self-location within contemporary society was not based on an arbitrary, personal bias. It was based on the informed bias of an active participant within contemporary avant-garde design culture. This choice is congenial to this culture. The hope is therefore justified that it is on the basis of social systems theory that a broad but unitary, coherent understanding might be built that can sustain the unity of architecture during the forthcoming period.

Both Luhmann's social systems theory in general, based on the centrality of the concept of communication, and his theory of contemporary society as functionally differentiated society in particular, have been presented and extensively applied to the analysis of architecture in Volume 1 of *The Autopoiesis of Architecture*. These analyses are presupposed and further developed here within Volume 2. There is no point in repeating these premises and analyses here.[27] The point here has been to establish and reflect that architecture must, in each new historical era, redefine and re-ascertain its place and role within society, and that architecture's efforts in this respect depend upon theoretical resources that originate outside architecture's autopoiesis.

8.4 Architecture in Relation to Other Societal Subsystems

THESIS 45

Architecture coevolves with all the other major autopoietic subsystems of society in relations of mutual facilitation and irritation.

Society is differentiated into autonomous subsystems. These subsystems depend upon each other – each relying on the performance of all the other function systems. The modern economy in general presupposes a legal system as well as a reliable science. Both modern science and the modern legal system in turn presuppose a stable economy. Modern

27 Functional differentiation is the dominant mode of societal differentiation within contemporary society. Functional differentiation implies that each subsystem assumes *exclusive and universal competency* with respect to its respective social function. Architecture can only be produced by expert architects. The innovation of the built environment as societal frame is the exclusive domain of the disciplines of architecture. The vernacular can no longer deliver anything but transitory emergency measures in pockets of underdevelopment. In particular, since the Modern Movement of the 1920s, architecture is advancing as avant-garde architecture with a (more or less sophisticated) sense of its historical mission.

architecture too relies on a stable economy, a peaceful political order and legal security etc. Over and above these general mutual presuppositions, there are specific inter-system communications, which take the form of specific provisions: an architectural project requires an initial economic investment decision; it also requires certain political decisions (for example, planning permission); it further requires the provision of certain legal services in relation to the various contracts upon which all the design and construction work depends; furthermore science is providing specific knowledge required to calculate and ensure the technical performance of the design. In return, architecture provides the spatial layout and design for the construction of all the necessary buildings upon which the ordering of all economic, legal, political, educational and scientific activities depend. All of these systems make necessary contributions to the overall success of society on the basis of their own self-regulated criteria.[28] Besides the great function systems, there are further types of social systems that play important parts within the overall ordering of the total societal autopoiesis: families, friendship circles and all sorts of formal organizations (operating within one or across several of the great function systems) like the various state organizations, business firms, professional bodies, organized interest groups, charitable organizations etc. All of these social systems make a necessary, inextricable contribution to the overall social life-process that is world society, and each of these social systems comes with its own peculiar logics, constraints and needs. All these systems also act as clients for architecture.

The societal service of architecture is far from trivial. It is not merely a physical provision of shelter or an external shell containing the workings of the various social institutions. Rather, architecture contributes to the organizing logic and articulation of those complex social processes. Architecture participates in the ongoing innovation of those institutional patterns via the innovation of their spatial frame. Spatial patterns are inextricably involved as indispensable substrate of social memory upon which the complex patterns of communication in question are inscribed. A lot of these mechanisms are non-discursive and operate beyond the level of well-understood and consciously applied design features. In this sense the built environment achieves more than has as yet been

28 Therefore the economic subsystem cannot – as Marxism claims – be the ultimate ruling system even if its function (securing material reproduction) is arguably the most basic function, most urgently tied to the basic condition of survival. The promotion of 'economic performance' as most fundamental selection criterion of all social structures makes little concrete and specific sense because the respective economic consequences of social institutions are far too indirect to allow the concrete, effective use of this fundamental criterion.

incorporated into the knowledge base of architecture. Therefore some of these provisions, to the extent that they are side effects that remain hidden, are *stricto sensu* not provisions of the discipline of architecture – not until a retooled architectural theory can identify, trace and systematize those provisions.

Social order is supported by spatial order. Architecture, urbanism and design contribute to the build up of societal complexity by means of spatial organization and articulation. This is true with respect to social relations on many scales and levels of social aggregation – from simple family relations to complex corporate structures, from stable institutional arrangements to quick encounters and short-term interaction systems, from the local integration of communities to the global, society-wide articulation of status groups. All processes of social communication require spatial settings that are located within an overall system of territorial organization and morphological articulation. In this sense all social systems feature as architecture's clients. For instance, the economy features via the spaces of production, trade, banking and consumption. Its logic is represented by organized social systems (business organizations) that act as the clients of specific architectural projects. Furthermore, the logic of the economic system features in all architectural projects, whether they serve as spaces for economic activity or not. The design and construction of family homes, of churches, of museums for the art system etc are also mediated by economic communications and thus must take economic criteria into account. The same goes for the spaces that are designed and built for the political system, the legal system, the education system, the mass media etc. All architectural projects are at the same time their client's investment projects, and the architect's services are at the same time deliverables traded within the economy. Similarly, legal communications are involved in all of architecture's deliverables, and political communications are often involved as many (large-scale) construction projects become politicized. Thus one might distinguish three types of relationships that can hold between architecture and other social systems within its environment:

1. The service relation whereby another social system acts as architecture's client. Here architecture provides structuration to the client's communication processes via designed spatial frames.
2. The reverse service relation whereby architecture receives structuration of its own communication processes, for example, the economic, educational, legal and political structuration of architecture's autopoiesis.

3. The relation whereby architecture's services to its clients are constrained by the ubiquitous logics and regulations of the economy, the legal system, the political system, the mass media etc.

The point here is not to give an exhaustive account of all these types of relations that hold between architecture and all the other function systems.[29] Rather, in what follows some key relationships will be explored and provisionally theorized in order to set the scene for future research in this area.

8.4.1 ARCHITECTURE IN RELATION TO THE ECONOMIC SYSTEM

Like all function systems, the economic system partially relies on spatial order both to distinguish and separate itself from its societal environment and to support and stabilize its internal communication structures. Places for economic activity – like markets and places of work/production – are spatially marked out against other, non-economic activities like spaces of rest, private intimacy, leisure, religious service or political debate etc. Architecture and urbanism support the distinction, arrangement and connection between the key components of economic reproduction: production, administration, distribution and consumption. The internal division of labour within, for example, an administrative business organization is framed by respective spatial divisions and architectural articulations. In order for architecture to do this innovatively and thus to contribute to the further evolution of the economy, it must develop an updated understanding of the dynamics operating within the most advanced sectors of contemporary world economy. Contemporary business processes might thus become a topic for architectural design research trying to explore the kinds of organizational patterns and spaces these new business processes might best flourish within. The author was involved in such a design research project at the Design Research Lab of the Architectural Association in London.[30] For avant-garde design

29 An exhaustive account of architecture's environmental relations would also have to go beyond architecture's relations with the other great function systems and include architecture's relations with many other types of social systems, especially many types of organizations. Organizations constitute a special type of social system that is very widespread within modern society. Organizations are hierarchical systems that operate by regulating membership and by setting up conditions for continued membership that allow the communications of the organization to be governed via the writing of general rules and the authorization of individual instructions. All great function systems – although themselves not organized – utilize organizations, for example, firms in the economy, political parties in the political system etc.

30 See Patrik Schumacher, 'Research Agenda: Spatializing the Complexities of Contemporary Business', in: Brett Steele (Ed), *Corporate Fields – New Office Environments by the AADRL*, AA Publications (London), 2005, pp 74–82.

research, the key criterion is the exploration of new principles with a potential for high performance/productivity rather than the concrete performance/productivity or the economy (cost side) of the project itself. In the context of this research an attendant architectural theory was developed that tried to relate new forms of spatial organization and architectural articulation to new forms of business organization and management as expounded in the respective reflection theories of the economic system, ie, economic theory (Post-Fordism) as well as organization and management theory.[31]

This much should suffice here to indicate aspects of the first type of relation between architecture and the economy, ie, architecture's contribution to the innovative functioning of the economy. In the following chapter, the third type of relation will be explored, ie, the relation whereby architecture's services to its clients are constrained by the pervasiveness of economic criteria.

8.4.2 THE ECONOMY AND THE DESIGN-PRINCIPLE OF ECONOMY OF MEANS

The economy is one of the most important societal environments to which the system of architecture has to adapt and respond. Every architectural design depends upon specifically related communications from within the economic system that formulate the economic criteria for the project. The relevant economic criterion that irritates most architectural design projects concerns the profitability of the client's or developer's investment. This profitability depends upon the competitive, economic value of the designed architectural artefact in relation to the cost of its design and construction. It is the client (rather than the architect) who plans, measures and controls the project's economic viability. Economic criteria obviously influence the design of most projects. Accordingly the discipline of architecture has long since instituted its own principle of 'economy'. The principle of an 'economy of means' has long been a

31 Within the last 25 years a fundamental socio-economic transformation has been identified. This transformation has been theorized under the label of Post-Fordism. Post-Fordist socio-economic restructuring involves significant shifts in the organizational patterns that structure work and business relations. These real shifts are anticipated, reflected and extrapolated by the current revolution in concepts of management and organization theory. Proceeding from these discourses we can explore their spatial and architectural implications. The investigation of contemporary trends in corporate organization and management theory revealed a striking coincidence of terms and a parallelism of principles with respect to the emerging style of Parametricism. See Patrik Schumacher, 'Productive Patterns – Restructuring Architecture', Part 1, in: *architect's bulletin*, *Operativity*, Vols 135–6, June 1997, and Part 2, in: *architect's bulletin*, Vols 137–8, November 1997, Slovenia, also: Patrik Schumacher, 'Business – Research – Architecture', in: *Daidalos* 69/70, December 1998/January 1999.

necessary (if not sufficient) condition of beauty. This aspect was radicalized within Modern Functionalism of the 1920s. One might recall Hannes Meyer's famous pronouncement: 'everything in this world is a product of the formula: function x economy'.[32] However, the notion of economy internal to architecture cannot be correlated one to one with the criteria that operate within the economic system under the code of profitability. The architectural 'economy of means' is a different notion that nevertheless somehow mediates and represents the strictly economic measures and demands within the architectural design project. Architectural designs are always constrained but never determined by economic criteria and decisions made within the economy. The architectural principle and value of an 'economy of means' – demanding that a design must achieve its aims by maximizing its performance with a minimum of material and formal means – is both a functional and a formal issue, relating to both the code of utility and the code of beauty. Adherence to these principles is presumed to produce both efficiency and elegance. It might seem that this principle of economy is specific to Modernism and its recent revival as Minimalism. However, this principle is more widespread, even universal within architecture. Renaissance and Neo-Classicism do not pose any problem for this claim. How about the Baroque, or the current style of Parametricism? The author believes that the principle still applies here too. To understand this, one must realize that the economy-of-means principle provides a relative rather than an absolute criterion. The means must be measured against the effects aimed for. The Baroque set itself the task of visually drawing large ensembles together into a unified whole. Parametricism sets itself the task of organizing and articulating a new level of social complexity without allowing the scene to descend into visual chaos. In both cases the economy principle might be fruitfully applied. Thus the hypothesis might be put forward here that the functional/formal principle of an economy of means is architecture's way of representing the demands of the economy within architectural discourse, on the terms of architecture's double code of utility and beauty. The principle – in its very abstraction – is a permanent feature of architecture's code. It needs to be concretely interpreted within each architectural style. However, this principle only moves towards the recognition of the fundamental scarcity constraint of the economy. It cannot be identical to economic values proper. (This would imply the economic subjection of architecture.) Obviously, if a design project overruns its allocated monetary budget it might be either

32 Ulrich Conrads (Ed), *Programs and Manifestoes on 20th-Century Architecture*, MIT Press (Cambridge, MA), 1971, p 110.

cancelled or subjected to a so-called 'value engineering' process. Cancellation is always possible. This does not destroy architecture's autonomy because it implies merely that no architecture is being produced here. The value engineering process is a redesign process where the designer is once more in charge and called upon to decide on useful and beautiful solutions that meet the externally set budget constraints. How these constraints are met must be left to the architect who acts under the guidance of architecture's values (made concrete by the adopted style). Should the client's representative try to micro-manage the value engineering process then the project is expelled from the domain of architecture. Again, no architecture has been produced in this case. Within architecture, the selection/dismissal of a certain design proposal can never be based solely on economic criteria, indifferent to the double code of utility and beauty. Economic criteria are not able to determine the architectural merit of the design. The architectural merit or status only emerges within the autonomous discourse of architecture itself. Obviously, architectural discourse – in the long run – has to adapt its discursive criteria to the developing economic conditions in order to remain relevant. This process is the collective, discursive process of style formation. In doing so, architecture has to use its autonomy to mediate and integrate the demands of all the other function systems as well, not only the demands of the economy. It has to recognize science, engineering, the law and political criteria as much as it has to recognize economic concerns.[33] That is why architecture needs its autonomy. That is why it cannot be subjected to the unconditional imperatives of the economy or of any other function system that might develop the ambition to control and determine architecture. Within modern, functionally differentiated society such unilateral control has become untenable. All function systems are equally uncontrollable and irreplaceable. There is no longer any control centre.[34]

Architecture and architectural theory reflect the polycontextual force-field of society. They respond and adapt to the force-field of different 'irritations' – political, economic and scientific irritations – and develop their *themes* accordingly. Any attempt to order these *external references* in terms of stable hierarchies of importance is bound to fail. Instead one observes (and should expect) an oscillation between these various concerns according to the urgency of the respective external

33 The concerns of these function systems have to be recognized over and above architecture's primary task, namely to provide for the framing requirements of the social systems that are to be accommodated in the designed spaces.

34 There is only the (uncontrollable) coevolution of parallel subsystems, all equally autonomous and equally dependent upon each other.

irritation. However, this urgency/intensity of irritation is only partly given externally. Irritations are always co-constituted by environment *and* system. What registers as irritation depends upon the system's general constitution as well as on its current state. In order to be at all irritated by certain environmental changes, the system needs to have a respective general sensitivity. For instance, architecture is sensitive to changes in society's mode and intensity of social differentiation. It is less sensitive to changes in the relation between the sexes (as witnessed in the second half of the 20th century). Architecture is also highly sensitive to advances in construction technology. It is less sensitive to advances in medicine or aviation. Architecture's current state might heighten or blunt its particular sensitivities. For instance, whether a certain change in the environment irritates the system depends on whether the change in question had been ignored for a long time so that pressure to adapt had been building up, or whether a fairly recent response to a similar change has provided a reserve capacity that can now absorb the new (otherwise irritating) environmental changes. Failure to adapt and satisfy societal demands will lead to criticism, and ultimately to abandonment. Every system is sensitive to the withdrawal of economic resources. If social imperatives are not met, resources are eventually withdrawn. If the immediate economic imperatives of the client (cost control) are not met, resources are withdrawn immediately. However, how the client's immediate economic imperatives are met and squared with all the other imperatives that need to be accommodated can only be answered within the autopoietic system, with the help of the accumulated wisdom that is embedded within its evolving communication structures. That's why there can no longer be any viable alternative to autopoietic closure and self-determination.

The 1920s was a period where changes, irritations and responses were violent on many fronts simultaneously: the economy pushed for new Fordist production processes – architecture responded with the programme of an industrialized architecture and with the aesthetic promotion of asymmetry, seriality and stretched proportions. At the same time, Modern architecture responded to the new political system of social democracy by putting the question of affordable workers' housing at the top of its design research agenda. Architectural theory – for a relatively short period – acquired strong political overtones. The period of post-war reconstruction narrowed and focused the agenda on the question of economical mass housing provision. The radical politicization of the late 1960s irresistibly re-politicized architectural discourse. In the 1980s the resurgence of competitive capitalism once more led to the foregrounding of economic value as paramount environmental factor for architecture.

This time the focus was on market value via product differentiation and brand image, rather than focusing on the economic rationalization of a well-established standard as was the case during the 1950s and early 1960s. The historical macro-oscillation between different foci of irritation/adaptation – economy, politics, law, science etc – is paralleled by an analogue micro-oscillation within each design project.

8.4.3 ECONOMIC CONDITIONS OF ARCHITECTURAL DISCOURSE

The economic conditions of architectural discourse comprise, at the most immediate level, the architect's fees and the salaries of the architect's staff, as well as the livelihoods earned by the academically based contributors to the discourse. Obviously, the economic reproduction of the various players within the discourse, individuals as well as organizations, needs to be guaranteed at any moment in order for communication to continue. This implies that all those players are simultaneously acting in the economy. This in turn means that virtually every architectural communication or event also features as an economic event. It is either paid for by clients or at least enhances the future fee-earning potential of an architect, or it confirms and advances the academic career of a design professor, lecturer or architectural writer. (This career advancement implies future earning potential.) This implies that every architectural communication is potentially over-determined by economic motives. All participants learn to understand that such secondary motives play a role and have to be reckoned with. Everybody is able to read between the lines. However, the communication about these motives and conditions terminates the discussion about architectural concerns and shifts the conversation into a different domain. Concerning an architectural design project one can either discuss the architectural merits of the project or the profitability of the project for the architectural firm. These two discussions do not connect. They belong to different, incommensurable systems of communication and need to be kept apart.[35] Yet, it is undeniable that a relationship of conditioning is operating here: the higher the fees the more manpower is available to push the quality of the design. Original, design-intensive avant-garde work requires more manpower and thus higher fees than the routine

35 Those who fail to navigate their communications along those lines of demarcation are not fit to participate in the discourse. Successful participation in architecture – as in any of the other function systems of modern society – places considerable demands upon the intellectual capacity, socialization and general education of the individual participant, over and above his/her professional training. Such a high level of socially evolved, communicative competency cannot be taken for granted. In this respect all the modern function systems rely on the provisions of the education system as well as on more diffuse mechanisms of socialization.

reproduction of standard mainstream solutions. The same is true with respect to construction budgets. Original avant-garde projects require higher construction budgets than standard mainstream solutions, not only because a higher level of performance is aimed for but primarily because solutions are novel or unusual and therefore cannot benefit from well-established construction processes. Avant-garde designs also pose much higher economic risks for all participants, ie, for clients, architects, engineers and contractors. There are not only risks on the cost side. There are further risks on the revenue side reflecting risk in terms of the project's social performance. The prospective end users might not accept the product and the sales effort might fail. This non-acceptance of the project leads to its economic failure. At the same time, the project's failure to satisfy its destined users directly irritates the autopoiesis of architecture. How the project's failure to find acceptance (and its attendant economic failure) are interpreted within architecture and which reactions or adaptations are being developed will emerge in the autonomous discourse of the discipline.

8.4.4 ARCHITECTURE AND EDUCATION

The education system is one of the great function systems of society. It comprises all formal teaching that takes place in schools and universities, inclusive of all local communications between educators, as well as all general expert debates about education.[36] As all function systems, the education system maintains its own self-reflective discourse, the theoretical discipline of pedagogy[37] with all its publications, conferences etc. The education system provides an important service to society that is indispensable for the reproduction and further evolution of our increasingly sophisticated civilization. The various types of knowledge and skill required in the different arenas of societal communication make formal education necessary.[38] Specialized, formal education is also a societal precondition for the ongoing autopoiesis of architecture. This raises the question of where the university is to be positioned within the theoretical map elaborated here. Does what goes on in university

36 The education system also includes the socialization within the family in as much as it is increasingly guided and monitored by specialized publications and expert advice.

37 The theoretical self-descriptions that guide the function systems from within are not sciences. Luhmann introduces the term 'reflection theories'. Both pedagogy and architectural theory are reflection theories rather than sciences. The same applies to jurisprudence, political theory and media theory.

38 The societal function of the education system might be defined as socialization and selection. Its concrete tasks are to teach and test. See Volume 1, *Appendix 1: Comparative Matrix of Societal Function Systems*.

architecture departments belong to the education system or to the autopoiesis of architecture?

Some of the communications that go on within architectural schools are exclusively educational communications, for example, the enrolment documents, assessments, marks, certificates etc. Many communications that take place within architecture schools belong to both architecture and the education system.[39] The content (rather than the form) of the curriculum is drawn from architecture, and the students learn and exercise to communicate architecturally. Student projects are discussed and evaluated on the basis of their architectural merit. However, the educational forms of exercises, tests and design thesis submissions imply that the discussions and evaluations are also guided by the code of the education system – pass vs fail – and by concerns of the individual student's educational career, ie, whether there is a learning curve etc. Thus, for instance, a student's project presentation can be followed by an architectural comment on certain design features of the project presented, or by an educational comment on the student's presentation skills. The communication about conditions of failing or passing terminates the discussion about architectural concerns and shifts the conversation into a different domain. The protagonists of the respective communication episode are both competent educators, conversant with the discourse of education, and competent participants within the autopoiesis of architecture. Within a review or tutorial situation the communication might indeed switch between these two modes. This implies that two incommensurable systems of communication overlap here. Competent communication requires the ability to distinguish between these two layers of the communicative event. These two discussions do not connect. They belong to different, incommensurable systems of communication and need to be kept apart.[40] Yet, it is undeniable that a relationship of conditioning is operating here: the communicated identification of architectural merit will influence the educational assessment. However, there is no one-to-one translation from architectural merit to success in the terms of the education system.

39 The general conceptual scheme promoted here has the advantage of focusing on the communicative process and the communications themselves, and not on the participants, be they individuals or organizations. Both architecture and education, as communication systems, are made up of communications, and not people. Individual communications can participate in multiple systems. Thus, while the communications that take place within architecture schools might belong either to education or to architecture, many of them might very well belong to *both* architecture *and* education.

40 Those who fail to navigate their communications along those lines of demarcation are not fit to participate within the discourse.

The degree to which the architectural or the educational communication nexus predominates depends on whether the respective architecture school is merely training future architects in standard, mainstream design skills that are fixed in institutionalized curricula, or whether they involve the teachers and students in innovative, published avant-garde work. In the first case what goes on in the respective architecture school is largely enclosed within the education system. Although it picks up and enacts architectural communications, it does not contribute to the larger autopoiesis of architecture. In the second case what goes on in a school of architecture might make a significant contribution to architecture's ongoing autopoiesis and evolution.

We do not expect first-year undergraduate students to make significant contributions to the autopoiesis of architecture, but certain diploma and master degree programmes undoubtedly contribute. Indeed, certain key schools of architecture have long played a crucial role in the furthering of the repertoire and discourse of architecture. The Bauhaus was carrying architecture forward in the 1920s. The Architectural Association in London has played its part ever since the early 1960s. Columbia University was crucial during the 1990s. During the second half of the 20th century, the AA in London went furthest in converting the architectural school from a place of professional training into a place where the resources allocated to education are re-directed to promote original avant-garde work. The vehicle for this reorientation was the so-called 'unit system' that was first introduced around 1980 and remains in use today. In the absence of any central, formal curriculum, the students are placed at the free disposal of the autonomous unit masters (young ambitious architects), who can impose their experimental agenda, working methods and evaluative criteria. The unit masters are thus able to guide their allocated student body for a whole year, utilizing their time and energy as the extension of their own creative ambitions. This autonomous, creative freedom of the unit is disciplined only via two framing institutions: the market-like institution of choice at the beginning of the academic year, when the students can choose the unit they would like to join, and the collective assessment institution at the end of the year, when the final validation of the results is conducted via peer-group evaluations, whereby the results of each unit are judged by a panel made up of other unit masters.

This unit system made such an impact that it was copied in many other architecture schools. In its most extreme instantiation, at the AA itself, it allows even the first-year student to escape the logic of education and enter the autopoiesis of architecture, mediated via critical public review sessions, exhibitions and salient publications, albeit only within the shadow of his/her unit masters. This phenomenon of the unit system is only the most extreme case of a general tendency: certain educational institutions[41] are more and more drawn into the role of quasi-research institutions. This phenomenon is especially prominent in architecture, because of the otherwise total absence of dedicated research institutes within architecture. The schools have to bridge this gap. This tendency also reflects the general fact that the stable canon of confirmed knowledge and methods that could serve as a shared curriculum has been dissolving.

The total usurpation of architecture schools for the purposes of avant-garde design research compromises the educational function of the respective institutions. Students might fail to receive the knowledge and skills required and expected within the mainstream segment of the discipline. Therefore this total institutional usurpation of the whole of a student's educational career must remain the exception rather than the rule. The model cannot be universalized across all schools. It remains the preserve of an exclusive subset of schools.

8.5 Architecture as Profession and Professional Career

THESIS 46

Architecture no longer tolerates that the bearer of architectural reputation has any outside ambitions.

Architecture, like many of the other function systems, is instituted as a profession. Architecture, the law and medicine are classical professions. The education system has also developed into a profession. Although science, art, politics, the mass media and the economy have good reasons to resist being instituted like the classical professions, there can be no doubt that all these systems have undergone a process of professionalization. Neither artists, nor politicians will ever insist on being treated as expert professionals, nor will there ever be licensing professional bodies for artists or politicians. The same applies to scientists and entrepreneurs. However, the reality is that in all these vocations a pertinent university education and a seamless, function-system-specific *career* have become necessary preconditions for succeeding in these fields. The concept of 'the professions' with its complementary concept of 'domain of professional competency' is the commonsense registration of the theoretical concept of 'function system'.

41 Only the most prominent schools of architecture are geared up to contribute to the avant-garde segment of the autopoiesis of architecture.

The transition from this commonsense concept to the theoretical concept of 'societal function system' was prepared by Talcott Parsons. Parsons emphasized the professions' orientation towards rationality as distinct from traditionalist orientations. This indicates the innovative thrust within all autopoietic function systems. The second moment that Parsons emphasizes is the fact that professionals are able to claim authority, albeit only within the bounds of their specific expertise. 'Professional authority, like other elements of the professional pattern, is characterized by specificity of function.'[42] This aspect of functional specificity also points in the direction of identifying the professions with the autopoietic function systems of society. Luhmann's theoretical concept of 'autopoietic function system' involves much more than is captured by the idea of a profession. The concept of a career, however, is already connected with the commonsense, empirical idea of a profession. All professionals, including all architects, are defined through their careers. Careers start at school (university) and continue within organizations (studios), or via published contributions to the discourse. Anybody's career, at any moment in time, is registered by the individual's current curriculum vitae. Careers produce professional identities as reference points for the attribution of communicative contributions. The construction of an advancing career is the necessary precondition and the result of contributions communicated within the autopoiesis of architecture. The fact that successful innovations are the surest means of advancing one's career indicates once more that all autopoietic function systems are geared towards innovation.

8.5.1 AUTHORSHIP, REPUTATION, OEUVRE

The autonomous self-constitution of architecture is confirmed by the fact that an architect's ***architectural reputation*** is gained (and lost) within the self-referential discourse of architecture. Who is and who is not recognized as a 'great architect' results from the discourse internal to architecture. Architecture is thus able to project its internally processed system of reputations onto society at large, however not without further selective filtering and attendant loss of information. How is this possible? Shouldn't popular acclaim by the general public determine what great architecture is? Is the capacity/confidence of the general public to recognize architectural reputations too limited? The fact is that the great architects who are recognized by society at large have first been recognized within architecture: Norman Foster, Frank Gehry, Rem

42 Talcott Parsons, 'The Professions and Social Structure', in: Talcott Parsons, *Essays in Sociological Theory*, The Free Press (New York), 1954, p x.

Koolhaas, Zaha Hadid etc. How is this possible? What needs to be understood is that the 'general public' is a fiction or abstraction that is construed within the function system of the mass media. General societal reputations exist in the form of the mass media construction of celebrity. The most prominent of the internally constituted reputations are transposed into the domain of mass media communications by the writings of architectural critics.[43] A certain time lag with respect to the societal (mass media) dissemination of architectural reputations has to be conceded. The general societal recognition often comes too late, ie, after the respective architect has already been overshadowed within the discipline by a new generation of avant-garde protagonists. However, the important point here is that the autopoiesis of architecture is autonomous in the allocation of the architect's general reputational status, both within and without architecture.

Another general, structural fact is that extraneous social factors like birth, wealth and power have no relevance in terms of architectural reputation, both as concerns reputations within the discipline of architecture and as concerns architectural reputations within society at large. Architectural reputations are not hereditary – even if architectural firms are. Within a comparative sociological and historical perspective these seemingly obvious facts are not to be taken for granted. They are to be accounted for as aspects of the differentiation of architecture as self-referential social system. That there is at all something like an architect's public reputation, implying respect for the architect as creative individual, is to be understood as part of the overall increased societal valuation of the individual within modern functionally differentiated society, where birth/family can no longer be relied upon.

There is another curious fact that needs to be noted here: a strong reputation in a neighbouring field like art or engineering no longer gives a head start for the pursuit of architectural career ambitions. On the contrary, such external reputations are a liability or hindrance to being taken seriously within architecture. This fact bears witness to the depth to which the systemic distinctions of functionally differentiated society

43 Architectural critics are architecturally socialized writers – often educated as architects – working for national/international newspapers. The institution of architectural criticism is a specialized interface institution (structural coupling) that manages the information flow and mutual irritations on the boundary between architecture and the mass media. The critic picks up the result of the internal architectural evaluation process and supplies this result with a new set of reasons satisfying the values and criteria of mass media communication. Since these critiques are also read by architects – irritating the architectural discourse – aspects of these external evaluations might lead to adaptations within the autopoiesis of architecture. See section 10.5 *Architectural Criticism*.

are ingrained in general. In particular, this fact underlines the extent to which architecture has been severed and differentiated from both art and engineering.

The architect's career as a clearly categorized and *uniquely focused* professional is a necessary condition for participation only in the 20th-century. Earlier many great architects and architectural theorists were polymath: Alberti (poet, social philosopher), Michelangelo (painter, sculptor), Bernini (sculptor), Perrault (medical doctor, biological researcher), Guarini (theologian, mathematician), Wren (astronomer, mathematician-physicist), Balthasar Neumann (artillery engineer), Laugier (Abbé), Schinkel (painter), von Klenze (painter), Ruskin (social/moral philosopher), Morris (political philosopher), Behrens (graphic artist, industrial designer) etc. We also find valid contributions from figures, like Leonardo and Raphael, whose primary reputations lie outside architecture.

Architectural reputations are attributes of individual architects. Although all designs are in fact the collective work of an architectural design team, the ***authorship*** of projects is usually attributed to an individual, namely the principal of the architectural studio or firm. While within architecture's internal discourse publications often feature full credit lists, within the mass media this attribution is exclusive, ie, only the principal is mentioned. In the case of partnerships, authorship is usually attributed to one of the names only, the name considered most prominent. Collective identities are sometimes possible but are not preferred within the mass media. Examples are Coop Himmelb(l)au with Wolf Prix as primary author, or OMA with Rem Koolhaas as primary (sole) author. One might speculate about the factors that contribute to this phenomenon: the power that comes with the ownership title held by the principal for the firm's products within the economic system, his/her copyright within the legal system, or the ideology of the genius as exceptional creative talent. Although these factors might play a role, they are not necessary to make sense of the phenomenon. As motivation for this practice of authorship attribution, it suffices to point to the convenience of single authors' names in terms of referencing works in a condensed and recognizable way within the architectural discourse. Thus we can understand this (fictional) attribution pattern in its functional rationality. The same argument applies – even more prominently – in the case of mass media communication. (The mnemonic advantages of individual attribution are of even higher importance here because the general capacity for the recognition of architectural reputations is much smaller.) The author's name dominates the project's name because it allows for a further condensation of discursive references, assuming that an architect/author displays a certain stylistic consistency. This allows the author's name to become a shorthand reference for the discussion of the respective stylistic tendency he/she comes to represent. This latter communicative convenience is further reinforced by the insistence that the vehicle of an architectural reputation must be the build up of a consistent ***oeuvre***. Singular works (that are not embedded within an oeuvre) and their authors rarely achieve a high standing within the autopoiesis of architecture. Great works are always crucial parts of the oeuvre of a great architect. This insistence on the development of a consistent oeuvre as a precondition of attributing importance or greatness to an architect (and, by implication, to an architectural studio) has its own rationality. It makes sense in terms of the need for value to be placed on innovations that can be generalized on the basis of principles that could be (as much as possible) universally applicable. All great architects are radical innovators. Greatness in architecture contains originality as one of its necessary components. This implies that (in the 20th and 21st centuries) architectural reputations can only be acquired within the avant-garde segment of architecture's autopoiesis. The societal task of architecture involves the continuous innovation (adaptive upgrading) of the built environment. The rationality of tying great architectural reputations to an original, evolving oeuvre lies in the necessity to pursue the innovation of general principles rather than singular solutions. The concept of oeuvre embodies the pursuit of a coherent design research project across various concrete designs. Such a design research project should lead to or inspire a general design research programme, ie, a new architectural style. Indeed, it can be observed that the greatest architects (the most outstanding architectural reputations) have always been members of a pioneering group involved in the founding of a new style.

8.5.2 CENTRE-PERIPHERY DIFFERENTIATION WITHIN ARCHITECTURE

The autonomy of architecture is confirmed on the level of the profession by means of its independent bodies of professional representation and self-governance: the architectural chambers. In most countries these institutions administer the protected title 'architect', monitor architectural education and formalize the standards of architectural professionalism. A characteristic problem which all the modern function systems have to solve is how to maintain their unity in the face of increasing complexity.[44] Most function systems resort to the formation of

44 Compare: Niklas Luhmann, *Die Politik der Gesellschaft*, Suhrkamp Verlag (Frankfurt am Main), 2000, p 251.

a central organization which is able to centralize the resolution of key issues that would otherwise threaten to fragment the system. These central organizations are organized hierarchies that are thus enabled, with respect to certain issues, to speak and act in the name of the system as a whole, without ever being able to fully control the network of communications that is the real life of the system.

Niklas Luhmann describes this formation of central hierarchies as the internal ***centre-periphery differentiation*** of the function systems. The periphery is obviously not hierarchically integrated. Here segmentary differentiation allows for a much more free and fluid, but also rather fragmented and divergent pattern of communications, with no guarantee of speaking in unison. This centre-periphery differentiation is the differentiation of different modes of differentiation: hierarchy (at the centre) vs segmentation (at the periphery).[45] This combination of two types of differentiation allows for the combination of their respective advantages. The hierarchy allows for decisive action, while the open network furnishes the sensitivity to changes in the environment, the ability to experiment and thus to respond creatively. The discursive process filters out the promising tendencies that emerge from those experiments and responses. Only the distributed periphery has the information-processing capacity to observe the environment in all its facets. The periphery processes and reduces the environmental complexity to the point that the hierarchical centre can take on particular issues that require an organized response. In relation to the global discipline of architecture this hierarchical centre is still rather weak and regionally fragmented. The UIA and its annual conference can hardly claim a central position for the world system of architectural communication. The national professional chambers are only taking on a narrowly defined mandate that is solely concerned with architecture as professional service, ie, its concern is to regulate the interaction of architecture with the other modern function systems: primarily with the economy (correlating fee scales and scopes of services), and with the law (contract law, copyright, legal protection of the professional monopoly), with the education system, by providing expert validation of educational results, and finally with politics, where the formation of the relevant legal framework is negotiated. The interaction of architecture with the education system concerns the education system's continuously upgraded supply of well-trained future architects/designers required by professional

45 The relationship between centre and periphery itself is not hierarchical. Neither can we assume that the centre ranks higher in terms of importance. In the case of the profession of architecture and its central body of professional representation rather the reverse has to be assumed.

architectural firms. The central, representative bodies of the discipline interact with the education system by trying to set skill and knowledge standards for architectural degrees. Such attempts succeed only partially.

The regulation of inter-subsystem relations that can be decided and administered by the central bodies constitutes only one side of the interface between architecture and the other functional subsystems of society, namely the extent to which economy, law, politics and education concern the needs of architecture as profession. Concerning architecture's service to the other function systems – in terms of the provision of building designs for the various function systems like the design of public buildings for the political, legal and educational institutions – the central professional bodies can only regulate the professional form of the provision or delivery. The substantial content is being generated, evaluated and selected within the distributed communication process, ie, within the extensive 'periphery' of the system.

Luhmann's analysis focuses on the political system of modern society as the paradigmatic case of such centre-periphery differentiation: the modern state apparatus is the hierarchically organized centre that relies on the network of 'peripheral' organizations – such as the multitude of political parties and organized interest groups – to generate, filter out, test and prepare political issues for the decisions of the state apparatus. The equivalent centre of the legal system is the hierarchically integrated system of the courts, surrounded by the peripheral network of law firms, lawyers, legal theorists etc. In the economy it is the organized banking system, headed by the central bank, that operates as a comparable centre within an otherwise open network (market) of economic agents. Again, it is only selected key aspects that can be regulated in this way. Overall control of the economy is out of the question.

Similarly, the central, hierarchical organizations that speak in the name of architecture – such as the Royal Institute of British Architects (RIBA) and the Architects Registration Board (ARB) in the United Kingdom or the American Institute of Architects (AIA) and the National Council of Architectural Registration Boards (NCARB) in the United States – cannot control what is going on in architecture, as if all architects were somehow subordinated to the functionaries of those organizations. These organizations are far from directing the autopoiesis of architecture. But the reverse assumption is equally fallacious: the central organization is not just a straightforward expression of the *volonté générale* of the architects. The formation of this central organization/representation does imply an emergent new quality within the autopoiesis of architecture. One should neither overestimate nor underestimate its impact. The AIA and NCARB might seem weak and even irrelevant to most concerns of the discipline, but they have not been without effect. These organizations were crucial for the introduction of formal academic training, the formulation of guidelines towards a unified curriculum, the establishment of a single accredited degree, the national certification and registration/licensing that protects the title 'architect', and that guarantees the exclusive right to submit planning applications (building permits), the codification of the status and role of the architect in relation to the client and to the contractors, the general definition of the architect's scope of work, responsibilities and standard codes of professional conduct, the demarcation of the professional turf against the related consultants and engineering professions, and the contribution to the regulation of the architect's relation (as lead-consultant) to the other collaborating professionals. Whether one agrees with these definitions and regulations or not, these are effective rules that help to preserve the unity of architecture and continue to shape the autopoiesis of architecture. However, the contribution of the central bodies has been to formalize rather than to create the regular communication structures listed above. This regulating activity cannot be wilful and there is going to be little patience with utopian zeal. It can only channel and unify tendencies already well under way. Any central regulation can only be effective if it is rooted in a realistic assessment of both the demands of the environment and the capacity of the system.

Regulation only succeeds if the vital experiences of the architects have somehow been gathered, filtered and evaluated within an open discourse. These experiences are changing. Some of these changes are linked to general changes within overall society as well as to changes in the construction industry as one of the more immediate environments of architecture. These changes also concern changes in the social status the architect used to enjoy as professional. Carl Sapers, the former president of the American College of Construction Lawyers, talks of the 'denigration of the professions', as a general social phenomenon that concerns all professions, not only architects: 'Years ago, in a less educated, more class-ridden society, the professions constituted a middle force between the working and the capitalist classes, . . . calling on resources not within the competence of non-professionals.'[46] Professionals stood aloof from ordinary tradesmen. 'The English barrister's robe had a crepe envelope affixed to the back, so that the grateful client could deposit pounds sterling in its opening without distracting the barrister from his lofty

46 Carl Sapers, 'Losing and Regaining Ground: A Jeremiad on the Future of the Profession', in: William Saunders (Ed), *Reflections on Architectural Practices in the Nineties,* Princeton Architectural Press (New York), 1996, p 86.

contemplation of the law.'[47] The architect enjoyed a similarly exalted status. 'Issues were settled on the job site by the architect's ruling. ... All parties assumed that the architect would rule fairly. ... That special role of the professional has all but disappeared.'[48] In America, some of the achievements of the central representative professional bodies have been undone within recent decades. 'In the last three decades the rules against competitive bidding, supplanting, and advertising, which had been found in most professional codes, were wiped away. Recommended fee schedules were ruled illegal. Shorn of these protections, the professional's practice came to look more like that of the tradesperson; the old distinctions were blurred.'[49] Although such changes are evident, the societal recognition of the distinctive and autonomous authority of architecture remains intact. In fact, increasing specialization remains a general tendency within functionally differentiated society. This can only serve to enhance architecture's status as exclusive expert discourse. However, this also implies that the architect's professional services require the support of an ever greater crescent of subsidiary, specialist consultants. Although the factors these specialists advise on need to be considered within the architect's design, these specialist consultants belong to the domain of science/engineering rather than to architecture.

8.5.3 THE ABSORPTION OF UNCERTAINTY

The function of an architect as professional is the confident absorption of uncertainty with respect to the exclusive responsibility that architecture holds within the complex societal division of labour. The logic of institutionalized expertise is specific to functionally differentiated society. The architect is a certified professional expert. This is in line with the typical modern mechanism to cope with uncertainty by means of regulating the process of *how* and by *whom* this uncertainty is to be processed. Every decision fills an information gap and therefore involves risk-taking as well as the taking of responsibility. Decisions are never based on complete information; at best they might be based on the best information available at the time. But decisions have to be made, uncertainty has to be bridged, otherwise there is vacillation and blockage. Niklas Luhmann follows Herbert Simon and James March when he characterizes the achievement of the decision as an ***absorption of***

47 Ibid, pp 86, 87.
48 Ibid.
49 Ibid, pp 86, 88.

uncertainty. Simon and March coined and developed this concept in the context of their theory of the business firm. Within the corporate organization, this problem of processing decisions is tackled by means of allocating/distributing positions of decision-making competency and responsibility. The holder of such a position is expected to decide issues within his/her domain of competency. He/she *has to* leap over the inevitable information gap. It is expected – a necessary fiction – that the required expertise exists at this appointed position. The next operative within the chain of decision-making receives the decision as an unquestioned premise for further decisions, ie, further action is based upon the received decision without the requirement or ability to check the correctness/rationality of the decision that was handed down the chain.

Within society at large the emergence of specialized function systems with their respective professional experts offers a comparable structure of uncertainty absorption. Again, the assumption of competency, here in relation to the certified professional experts such as medical doctors, lawyers, scientists etc, is a useful fiction that prevents societal paralysis. In the same way the architect, as a professional expert, is expected to know everything that concerns the domain of architecture. He has to absorb enormous amounts of uncertainty, load up huge responsibilities, with a straight face. Vacillations, worries and uncertainties about the necessary design decisions cannot be expressed in front of the client. The uncertainty has to be absorbed and a solution has to be presented with confidence. The expression of doubt, ie, the refusal to absorb uncertainty, would inevitably disqualify the architect. That is what the client pays the architect for: to take on and carry this responsibility. Of course, the architect is not left alone with his/her burden. The available design repertoires, techniques and values of the discipline guide the individual architect.[50] The architect in turn can offload some of his/her burden of uncertainty absorption and responsibility onto his/her sub-consultants, ie, further experts like structural engineers, services engineers and cost consultants. Within the architect's professional office, the responsibility is delegated to the variously allocated professional staff within an overall division of labour. Uncertainty is absorbed both when instructions are handed down and when information is reported upwards. Instructions (decisions) are followed without re-analyzing all factors that led to the instruction/decision. Information is taken up without re-examining the evidence.[51]

50 And if all else fails there is indemnity insurance – at least for the basic functional risks.

51 Later design decisions build upon earlier design decisions without questioning the rationality of all earlier decisions at every step.

8.5.4 THE ARCHITECTURAL DESIGN STUDIO AS ORGANIZATION

Formal organization as a well-defined type of social system is ubiquitous in modern society. Organizations are social systems where membership is granted and formally established via co-optation and can be revoked at any time. The rewards of membership are exchanged for the member's willingness to allow him/herself to be regulated and instructed according to the centrally set purposes, rules and programmes of coordinated action. Organizations are very effective social machines without which modern society could not function. All modern function systems operate via formal organizations. The legal system depends on the various law courts and law firms, the economy depends on the business organizations as economic agents, the system of the sciences depends on organized research institutes, the education system operates via schools and universities, the mass media via public or private news corporations etc.

With the exception of the most trivial design problems, the (more or less) formal organization is also the universal type of social system through which architectural work is produced. The individual architect as effective unit of architectural design does not exist. All design work is performed by teams operating from within organizations. However, the individual architect as identifiable author seems to be a necessary fiction, an indispensable reference point within the autopoiesis of architecture as discursive system. Stylistic positions require authors as reference points.[52] The real social process of architectural design work is a different matter. Although these realities of organized design work are changing, they impact the autopoiesis of architecture only indirectly. They are not part of this autopoiesis because they are not communicated within the discourse of architecture. However, as one of the most immediate environmental conditions of the autopoiesis of architecture they deserve treatment here. Architectural design studios are formal organizations. Even loose networks of collaborating individuals – like OCEAN or SERVO – are organizations as defined here. Membership is explicit and requires determinate commitments. The architectural studio has to reproduce itself as individual economic agent within the economic system of society. This imposes effective constraints and manifests manifold consequences. The architect's design organization has to survive as a business organization, which implies a minimum level of

52 Obviously the market of potential clients also requires brand names, but this is a different matter which concerns the economy rather than the autopoiesis of architecture as discipline.

profitability, which in turn constrains the design time that is – on average – available to the design team.[53]

The architectural design studio is the effective unit that produces a particular oeuvre. This oeuvre is recognized and referenced within the autopoiesis of architecture by the name of the studio or by the name of the founding architect-owner of the studio. Within these recognized units, individual designs or projects are produced by dedicated design teams. Teams are usually more or less hierarchically structured units headed by a lead designer or project architect. These units are recognized within the architectural design studio, but they remain largely invisible to the larger discourse outside the studio. Although the publication of the respective designs/projects often prints credit lists featuring the members of the design team, these credit lists are never referenced within the further discourse. The internal organization of the architectural design studio thus constitutes a backstage arrangement that is never thematized in printed publications. However, via Internet based communication media like blogs, a new layer of previously obscure (backstage) players is creating communication networks and informal discourses that more and more partake in the overall autopoiesis of architecture. The creative work of those many backstage players has long been contributing to the discourse without being recognized and specifically attributed. Attribution now starts to happen in mostly localized (but potentially fully public) communication platforms.

However, the capacity of the overall autopoiesis in terms of the sheer number of circulating focal reference points that can serve to orient the overall autopoiesis is naturally limited. Therefore we can expect backstage names – although no longer strictly hidden – to be swamped and swallowed by the names of the studios within which they work.

The general societal transformations that affect architecture's task domain are also affecting architecture at its point of production in the design studio. These transformations have been theorized under the heading of Post-Fordist socio-economic restructuring.[54] The professional architectural consultancy is indeed one of those realms prone to Post-Fordist restructuring. There seems to be evidence that this process

53 This applies as well to those studios that are producing losses that are financed from their members' outside sources of income. The losses that they can afford to accumulate are highly constrained.

54 See the following articles: Patrik Schumacher & Christian Rogner, 'After Ford', in: Georgia Daskalakis, Charles Waldheim & Jason Young (Eds), *Stalking Detroit*, Actar (Barcelona), 2001; Patrik Schumacher, 'Productive Patterns', in: *architect's bulletin*, Vols 135–6 and Vols 137–8; German: 'Produktive Ordnungen', in: *ARCH+* 136, *Your Office Is Where You Are* (Berlin), 1997.

is gathering pace. The open question here, as everywhere, is how the challenge of increasingly differentiated and fluid societal demands can be met, ie, which forms of work organization will be able to deliver under the given societal conditions and within the progressing technological framework. Although these forms will indeed be manifold, there is no guarantee that the professional office, as unitary organization figureheaded by ***the*** architect, will survive this restructuring process. One new form of organization that can be observed within architecture is the loosely coupled network. This organizational form first emerged during the 1990s within the avant-garde segment of the discipline. This form involves a group of young architects (mostly architectural researchers with teaching positions in different locations) trying to pool opportunities, resources and publications to make a mark within the world of architecture. Examples are OCEAN and SERVO. Both networks are spread out between Europe and America. This form of design studio organization was made possible by the vastly increased technological means of communication that have become available in recent years. The progressing design elaborated within the new digital design media can be shared via the Internet.

The new design technologies require a continuous upgrading of skills. This often implies that the principals of larger design studios are no longer able to design personally. They cannot keep up with the progressing digital skills. This often implies a subtle empowerment of the most recent graduates in the design team, ie, of those who have had the opportunity to develop mastery over the latest design techniques. In general, the increasing complexity of design tasks imposes an increasing level of specialization on the architectural design team. This implies the tendency for functional rather than stratified forms of differentiation to become more prevalent within the design team.

8.6 The Built Environment as Primordial Condition of Society

THESIS 47

Architectural figures offer the archetypical paradigm of any concept or order. The emergence and stabilization of any social order require that the spatial traces of social interactions ossify into a sedimented social memory that acts both as an organizing framework and as system of signification.

The evolution of society depends on architecture's continued innovation of the built environment. The development of the built environment is understood as an indispensable material substratum of any socio-cultural evolution, from society's very beginnings to its contemporary and future life-process. This section goes into prehistorical depths and touches on the role artificial built environments must have played in human society's emergence from the animal kingdom. The built environment, together with the world of material artefacts, provides *Homo sapiens* with a cumulative social memory that allows for the gradual build up and reproduction of societal complexity. It is, as it were, the DNA of the cultural evolution. The point of departure of the above thesis is the fact that no human society has ever evolved without the simultaneous emergence of spatial frames. The coevolution of society and its built environment is a universal feature of all human history. The modern constellation whereby the built environment is steered by architecture as autopoietic function system that coevolves with several other such function systems constitutes only the latest mode of this universal feature of human history.

8.6.1 THE BUILT ENVIRONMENT AS INDISPENSABLE SUBSTRATE OF SOCIAL EVOLUTION

Society can only evolve with the simultaneous ordering of space. The elaboration of a built environment, however haphazard, precarious and based on accident rather than purpose and intention, seems to be a necessary condition for the build up of any stable social order. The gradual build up of a social system must go hand in hand with the gradual build up of an artificial spatial order. Social order requires spatial order. The social process needs the built environment as a plane of inscription where it can leave traces that then serve to build up and stabilize social structures that in turn allow the further elaboration of more complex social processes. The evolution of society goes hand in hand with the evolution of its habitat understood as ordering frame. The spatial order of the human habitat is both an immediate physical organising apparatus that separates and connects social actors and their activities *and* a mnemotechnic substrate for the inscription of an external 'social memory'. These 'inscriptions' might at first be an unintended side effect of the various activities. Then given spatial arrangements are functionally adapted and elaborated. Then they are further marked and underlined by ornaments which make them more conspicuous. The result is the gradual build up of a spatio-morphological system of signification. Thus emerges a semantically charged built environment that provides a differentiated system of settings that help social actors to orient themselves with respect to the different communicative situations that constitute the social life-process of the community. The system of social settings as a system of distinctions and relations uses both the positional identification of places (spatial position) and the morphological identification of places (ornamental marking) as props[55] for the social communication process. Indications for this formative nexus between social and spatial structure abound within social anthropology, attesting to the crucial importance of cross-generationally stable spatio-morphological settings for the initial emergence and stabilization of all societies. In the analysis of the social structure of primitive societies, the drawing of the village plan often serves as the most succinct summary and point of reference.[56]

Appropriately designed places regulate social communication by helping to define the situation, reminding the actors about who they are, ordering the actors into their appropriate relative position, for example, the place at the head of the table for the focal communicator of the group etc. The semiological dimension of the built environment is already coming into play here. As the built environment develops from the state of vernacular tradition to the state where it is advanced by the autopoiesis of architecture, the task of conscious semiological articulation arises.[57]

The importance of the spatio-morphological setting as defining frame for social communication has also been recognized within sociology and social psychology. Erving Goffman, for instance, was very much aware of the need for frames and 'assemblages of sign-equipment'[58] that structure social communication: 'First there is the "setting", involving furniture, décor, physical layout, and other background items which supply the scenery and stage props for the spate of human action played out before, within, or upon it. A setting tends to stay put, geographically speaking, so that those who would use a particular setting as part of their performance cannot begin their act until they have brought themselves to the appropriate place and must terminate their performance when they leave it.'[59] The built environment remains a powerful tool of organization, sorting and ordering people and their activities. It is important to grasp that the ordering capacity of spatial arrangements and the specific order

55 Prop here means both support structure and stage equipment for the staging of communication.

56 A good example is the chapter on 'Social Organization' in: Claude Lévi-Strauss, *Structural Anthropology*, Basic Books (New York), 1963, pp 101–63.

57 See section 6.8 The *Semiological Dimension of Architectural Articulation*.

58 Erving Goffman, *The Presentation of Self in Everyday Life*, Anchor Books (New York), 1959, Penguin Books (London), 1990, p 33.

59 Ibid.

provided are not independent, objective properties of the respective built spatial arrangement, but crystallize only in the patterns of utilization that it catalyzes. The built environment plus the more mobile artefacts such as furnishings, tools, clothing etc together engage in the staging of social interaction processes which unfold within system of communications. As the built environment develops from the state of vernacular tradition to the state of architecture, the task of conscious semiological articulation arises. Architectural settings are to be designed as framing communications, as permanent broadcasts that function as constraining/enabling premises for all further communications that are to be expected within the respective space. Architectural settings are communications that help to define and structure social institutions.

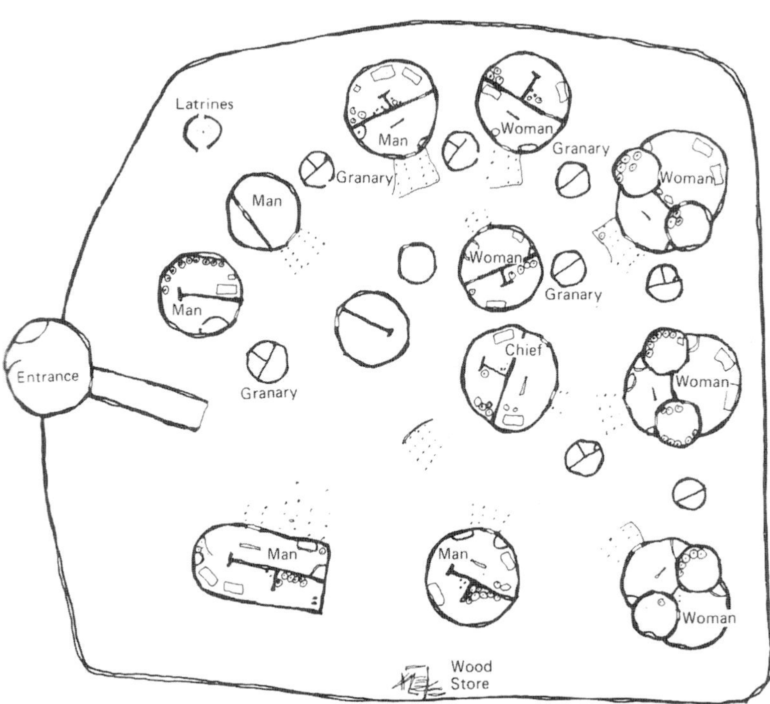

Figure 51 Enclosure and partition as fundamental operations constituting spatial, social and conceptual order: compound in Cameroon. From Hillier & Hanson, *The Social Logic of Space*, 1984

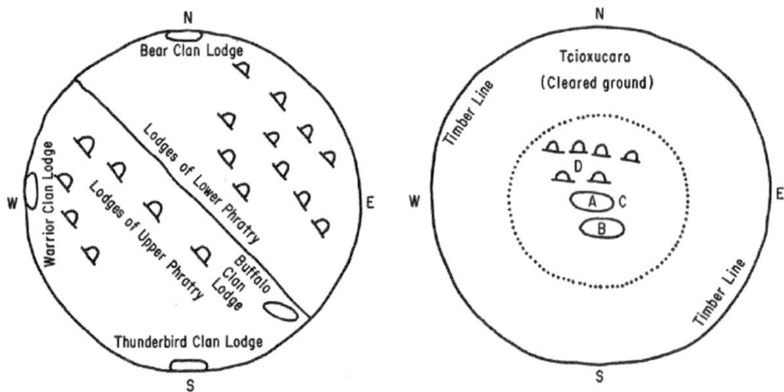

Figure 52 Enclosure and partition as fundamental operations constituting spatial, social and conceptual order: Winnebago Village. From Claude Lévi-Strauss, *Structural Anthropology*, 1963

8.6.2 FROM SPATIAL ORDER TO CONCEPTUAL ORDER

In the previous chapter the built environment was understood to be involved in the structuration and stabilization of social systems. The current chapter focuses on a further power of the built environment: its involvement in the formation and dissemination of our most fundamental conceptual schemata of abstract thinking. The various observations, reflections and speculations offered here resist placement within the taxonomy of academic disciplines. The thesis of the built environment's contribution to abstract thinking utilizes ingredients from epistemology, logic, history, cognitive science, sociology and architectural theory. The premises as well as implications of this thesis transcend the domain of architecture conceived as a discipline controlled by architects. 'Architecture'[60] here inflates to indicate a profoundly formative aspect within the ongoing evolution of humankind. 'Architecture' is at the root of intellectual order and a primary source for the apparatus of abstract, conceptual thinking. ***Architectural figures offer the archetypical paradigm of any concept or order.*** The built environment provides the historical/material conditions for the emergence and transformation of those deep-seated conceptual 'architectures' that are constitutive of our abstract thinking in general. Elevated to the status of general intellectual

60 This more general use of the term 'architecture' goes beyond the sharply defined concept otherwise presupposed within the theory of architectural autopoiesis, namely the concept of architecture as self-conscious, autopoietic system of communications since the Italian Renaissance.

principles, these patterns of order also feed back into the architect's design thinking and thus prefigure his/her 'creative' interventions in the built environment.

The thesis proposed here insists that the formation of the built environment is not only a necessary substrate for social evolution but also for intellectual evolution and, more specifically, for the formation of logic. Indeed it is the order of the built environment that sponsored the most general operations of logic: the primary and primordial device of architecture – the wall as demarcation/separation device as well as collecting/grouping device – is paralleled by the primary and primordial device of thinking: ***distinction***. Our world is ordered by us, via the distinctions we make. Distinctions distinguish (separate) and classify (group). Logic is a technique for navigating configurations of multiple distinctions. The classical logical forms and inferences are modelled on the navigation of spatial configurations built up via spatial demarcations. To fully grasp the depth of the thesis unfolded here we need to rehearse some of the insights of 20th-century philosophy.[61] These insights finally broke the stranglehold of certain long ingrained ideas about the human mind, and offered approaches and steps towards stripping the veil of mystery from this most extraordinary phenomenon. The human capacity to think was finally naturalized and integrated into the domain of ordinary reality. Thinking could finally be analyzed as a material process that depends on systems of signification that evolved within practically situated systems of communication.

Plato had postulated an other-worldly existence for the contents of human thinking, a separate cosmos of eternal ideas, where the soul receives its knowledge before it is born into the ordinary world. Descartes postulated a strict dualism of minds and bodies. In the dominant idealist and rationalist traditions, thinking seemed to be this immaterial, effortless activity that can imagine anything at will without being subject to the constraints (friction and inertia) of the material world.[62] Constraints, supposedly, only pertained in as much as truth was aimed for.

61 These insights might be widely acknowledged, but they are very hard to fully internalize/operationalize, ie, even those who have fully grasped these insights find it difficult to hold them active so as to avoid the lapse back to the prior ingrained notions at the first turn of further thinking.

62 Locke and Hume had suggested that the contents of thinking are received via the senses and that thinking is restricted to the recombination of those contents. More doubts were raised by Marx and Engels who opposed the prevailing idealism which gave unconstrained creativity and power to ideas. Instead their *historical materialism* suggests that material life determines consciousness.

The breakthrough towards an understanding of thinking as a social-material process came with the so-called *linguistic turn* in philosophy. There is neither space nor occasion here to elaborate on all the precursory steps and ingredients which made this breakthrough possible. A few hints must suffice. Marx's historical materialism as well as American pragmatism gave important early pointers. The following crucial contributions ushered in our contemporary understanding: Ludwig Wittgenstein's late work in the Anglo-Saxon context, Ferdinand de Saussure's work and reception within French-speaking philosophy, and Martin Heidegger's work in Germany. All three contributions recognized thinking's fundamental dependence on language and in turn understood language as a social process which produces rather than receives meaning. Those three philosophical traditions overlapped in their central insight which was later confirmed, reinforced and elaborated on many fronts: the theory of evolution, cognitive science, computer science, artificial intelligence research, cybernetics, complexity theory, Constructivist epistemology, Jacques Derrida's Deconstruction, Michel Foucault's archaeology of knowledge and Niklas Luhmann's social systems theory. Foucault's concept of ***discursive formation***[63] is especially instructive here. The concept denotes the ever present, implicit conceptual horizon that structures all human thinking. The concept includes not only language and institutionalized social practices but also the built environment as well as the artefacts that are involved in processes of communication/thinking. For instance, medical thinking (the discourse on medicine) depends as much on the institution of the hospital – inclusive of the spatial order of its buildings, its practices and instruments – as it depends upon the language that coevolves with those practices, buildings and instruments.[64]

Logic is abstracted architecture. Architecture lends its figures to abstract thinking: it 'distinguishes', 'classifies', 'relates'. These supposedly mental activities first gain shape and regularity on the basis of architectural operations. 'A vision of the world is a division of the world, based on a fundamental principle of division which distributes all things of the world into two complementary classes. To bring order is to bring division, to divide the universe into opposing entities, those that the primitive speculation of the Pythagoreans presented in the form of "columns of contraries" (*sustoichiai*). The limit produces difference and the different things "by an arbitrary institution", as Leibniz put it,

63 Michel Foucault, *The Archaeology of Knowledge*, Routledge (London), 1989, French: *L'Archéologie du savoir*, Éditions Gallimard (Paris), 1969.

64 This insight bears strongly on architectural theory.

translating the *"ex instituto"* of the Scholastics.'[65] Architecture operates by means of boundaries and connections. Walls prefigure the logical operation of distinction. 'The cultural act *par excellence* is one that traces the line that produces a separate, delimited space, like a *nemus*, a sacred wood apportioned to the gods, the *templum*, a precinct delimited for the gods, or simply the house which, with the threshold, *limen*, a dangerous line where the world is reversed and all signs are inverted, provides the practical model of all rites of passage.'[66] The logic of subsumption is based upon successive enclosures within enclosures, prefiguring classification. The most basic trope of logical inference – the Aristotelian syllogism – is directly analogous to the transitive relation of enclosure. If one interprets concepts as classes or sets, and spatializes sets as spatial enclosures, then it transpires that the logic of the syllogism might indeed be based on the transitivity of the enclosure relation. The fact that all classical logical operations can be spatially represented by the Venn diagrams of set theory serves as a powerful indication here. Classification starts with sorting. Sorting is a concrete material process before it becomes an abstract mental process. As a material process, classification is supported by the architectural operation of the wall, sorting objects, plants and domestic animals by means of spatial devices like boxes, fences/fields, cages, stables, barns and their subdivisions. Such basic, practical devices developed together with language to create an initial conceptual universe. The moment of architectural abstraction via an emerging self-conscious discipline of architecture coincides with the development of the sciences during the same period. Building was paralleled with drawing and collecting was paralleled by written or diagrammed classification systems. Here too the built environment was involved by providing buildings for the establishment of scientific collections. Physical tables, shelves and cabinets were as much involved as their equally physical (albeit dematerialized) abstractions: lists, printed tables, filing systems etc. The principle of enclosures within enclosures is the dominant conceptual structure of all abstract thinking and diagramming. However, there is a second formalism for abstract thinking and information processing, the formalism of path systems. The structure of a path (or of a system of paths) is the analogical source of thinking in terms of sequences such as chronological sequences of events, means-ends relationships, causal chains, flow diagrams and branching diagrams like decision trees or genealogical trees. The underlying formalism of all these conceptual structures might also be derived from

65 Pierre Bourdieu, *The Logic of Practice*, Polity Press (Cambridge), 1990, p 210.
66 Ibid, pp 210, 211.

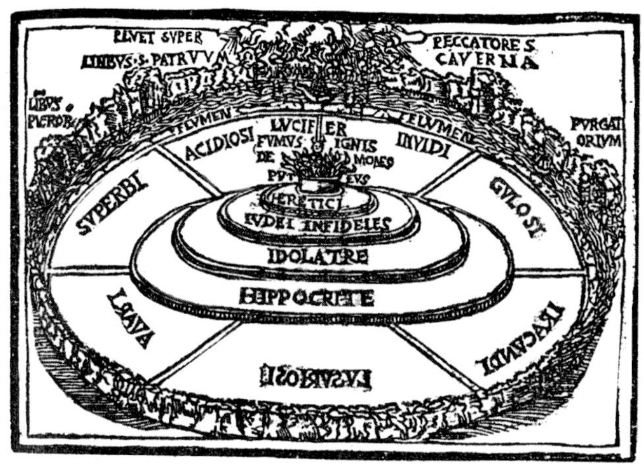

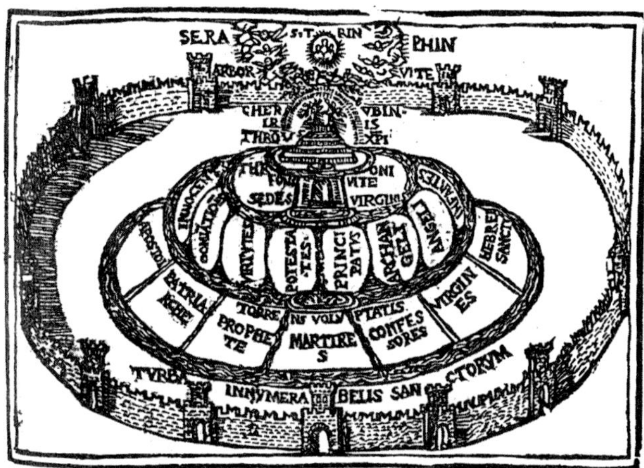

Figure 53 Spatialized conceptual orders: system of vices and system of virtues, Cosmas Rossellius, *Thesaurus Artificiosae Memoriae*, Venice, 1579

the originally spontaneous formations of the built environment: in this case from the circulation system of the built environment.

The two diagrams depicted in Figure 53 are trying to conceptualize the moral universe of vices and virtues. The diagrams construct an abstract conceptual order. Diagrammatic conceptualizations became prevalent during the Renaissance and continued to be prominent until the end of the 18th century. However, there was but one schema for such conceptualizations: the organizational schema of the ideal city. This schema of an ideal city as a concentric order was itself abstracted from the prior material reality of the unplanned, medieval walled city. Thus at the root of this universal conceptual structure – the classificatory pyramid – lies the spontaneous, evolutionary morphogenesis of the concentrically growing walled city.

The Classical architectural canon that developed following the rebirth of architecture in the Italian Renaissance served as the source domain for the transference of analogies of order within all domains of abstract, conceptual thinking, including the most sophisticated philosophies of the Enlightenment. Symmetry – natural to simple balanced structures – has been made the norm in Classical architecture. Conceptual symmetries inform all Classical conceptual formalisms within science and philosophy up to the end of the 18th century: for instance the Kantian table of categories is marked by an insistence upon symmetric order – signifying completeness. This insistence on symmetry, which was for Kant an unreflected a priori of his theory, strikes us today as an irrational formalism. Modernism had since established the possibility of designing architectural orders without symmetry. While symmetry was once a necessary ingredient of order, it now raises the suspicion of following an empty formalism.

The spatial order of the built environment constitutes one of the primary analogical source domains for schemata of thinking. This pertains most strikingly to the earliest emergence of human society, the

1.
Quantity of Judgments
Universal
Particular
Singular

2.
Quality
Affirmative
Negative
Infinite

3.
Relation[b]
Categorical
Hypothetical
Disjunctive

4.
Modality
Problematic
Assertoric
Apodictic

Figure 54 Formal a priori: symmetry and completeness, Immanuel Kant, Table of Judgments – *Critique of Pure Reason*

initial, precarious build up of social complexity, ie, long before we can speak about architecture as a specific societal discourse. However, this phenomenon is not restricted to prehistoric times, but remains an active force all along. The permanent possibility and immediacy of architectural/spatial analogies as resource of our thinking are reinforced and confirmed through our daily navigation of architectural orders. Order might still be defined as 'everything in its place and a place for everything'.

'Architecture' is still at the root of most of the conceptual schemata we rely on today: sequences, branching graphs, grids, concentric nesting etc. This deep-seated power of architectural tropes, embedded in the most general operations of logic and language, poses a formidable barrier to radical innovation. The transcendence of these tropes is so difficult because the very patterns of conception (clear and distinct thinking) are locked within these tropes. An architecture that today is self-conscious of its formative role within the domain of conceptual order should be able to challenge deeply ingrained patterns of thought by effective spatial intervention. The conceptualizations of the various institutions that call for architectural translation into buildings are themselves already dependent on ancient conceptual 'architectures' that were originally abstracted from the built environment within which the original formation of these institutions unfolded in the first place.

Every brief issued to the architect is already an abstract piece of 'architecture': it displays a well-structured list of contents, an en-suite series of chapters, each a well ordered composition of paragraphs disposed on the space of the paper, and finally with a schedule of accommodation plotted as array of boxes within boxes. Relations of exclusion, inclusion, subsumption and subdivision, as well as lists and sequences, mean that abstracted architectural tropes are recycled back to concrete architectural construction. Deconstructivism was trying to cut this knot. It was the vehicle by which philosophy returned to its roots in architecture in an effort to break this vicious circle of repetition through direct action in space. Deconstructivism did indeed violate longstanding conceptions of clear and distinct order. Initially this work was limited to the creative destruction of order, producing gestures of disruption and disorder. However, a new repertoire of ordering principles emerged that was able to increase the capacity of architecture to organize and articulate complex life-processes and social institutions. For instance, Deconstructivism elaborated a capacity for spatial overlap and interpenetration of domains. This capacity recognizes a salient trend in contemporary social institutions whereby conditions of multivalency become more and more widespread.[67] The main point here is to increase the repertoire of both conceptual and spatial ordering principles and to upgrade their capacity to structure complexity. The contemporary style of Parametricism is well prepared to continue the Deconstructivist project of expanding architecture's repertoire of conceptual and spatial ordering.

One especially pertinent arena in which to explore the power of architecture as spatio-conceptual ordering system is the task domain of exhibition design. Exhibition design is enlisting space directly in the task of articulating knowledge/information as spatial structures. These spatial structures are supposed to follow the conceptual structures that order the content of the exhibition. What can be observed here very clearly is the 'pre-established harmony' between traditional spatial structures and the most prevalent conceptual structures. Traditionally, exhibitions and museums operate with a handful of very simple ordering devices – suggested by the palace architectures appropriated or imitated for the installation of a museum collection. In most Classical museums, the central symmetry axis is enlisted to establish a basic dichotomy within the museum: a natural history museum typically bifurcates into the animal kingdom on the left and human ethnography on the right. An art historical museum might bifurcate into Ancients vs Moderns. Usually rooms are taken to establish groupings or classes of objects. Each wing of the building might represent a larger grouping encompassing the rooms as so many subsumed subgroups. The en-suite sequence of rooms – offering a linear path – is utilized as the basis of ordering such groupings into a chronological sequence. Klenze's Munich Glyptothek can serve as the paradigmatic example here, articulating the sequence: Archaic, Classic, Hellenistic. This small set of ordering devices – dichotomous distinction, grouping/subgrouping and linear sequence – is in fact all there is and has been within the traditional repertoire of spatial ordering of knowledge in museums and exhibitions. It is no accident that the primary organization of books – as summarized by the list of contents – follows exactly the same logic: a sequence of chapters and subchapters.

Parametricism can be applied here in a similar way to how it is applied to the ordering of social institutions. Parametricism allows exhibitions to pursue an increased level of narrative complexity implying the intensification of relations between the content elements of the

67 For instance, as industrial production and services are more and more oriented towards permanent innovation, the division of labour needs to be continuously reorganized and collaborative task forces emerge that operate at the intersection of departmental domains. As domains of competency interpenetrate, so should the spatial territories allocated to the respective departments.

exhibition. Contemporary exhibition strategies require ordering strategies over and above the Classical or Modern paradigm of simple linear (for example, chronological) sequences or simple orders of classification and subclassification. Parametricism suggests the introduction of gradients and of simultaneous interpenetrating orders of reference with overlapping domains. Intensive networks of cross-reference can be spatialized and articulated. Such tropes and features imply a new organizational and articulatory repertoire for the spatialization of complex, contemporary information structures. The resultant exhibition designs are more layered and able to set up more alignments and cross-references between the elements of the exhibition. The same principles could be applied to graphic design with the same aim of increasing the simultaneously legible amount of information. These principles – geared to the legible organization and articulation of more complex, information-rich scenes – also induce a new aesthetic sensibility. Complexity must appeal rather than repel.

8.6.3 BEAUTY AND THE EVOLUTION OF CONCEPTS OF ORDER

Aesthetic values encapsulate condensed, collective experiences within useful dogmas. Their inherent inertia implies that they progress via revolution rather than evolution. This thesis has been put forward within Volume 1, in the section on the rationality of aesthetic values.[68] There the focus was on the operation of aesthetic values within the autopoiesis of architecture and the emphasis was put on the historical transience of aesthetic values and concepts of beauty. However, it was also noted that the aesthetic values that operate within the advanced communication system of architecture are ultimately rooted in the visceral responses that are a basic characteristic of all cognitive creatures. Aesthetic appreciation is a socially mediated sublimation of the organically rooted, (pre-)cognitive mechanism of conditioned reflexes. Conditioning as a basic psychological mechanism is always involved when it comes to individual aesthetic responses, even in the case of aesthetic appreciation on a highly cultured level. Aesthetic responses are conditioned responses. Thus the very category of beauty can be anthropologically grounded. The discrimination of the beautiful versus the ugly is a culturally overdetermined instantiation of the fundamental biological mechanism of attraction versus repulsion. The behaviour of organisms is well adapted if they are attracted to what serves their survival/reproduction and repulsed by what impairs or threatens their survival/reproduction. Thus the pervasive fact of aesthetic sensibilities and the attendant category of

68 THESIS 17, Volume 1, section 3.8 *The Rationality of Aesthetic Values.*

beauty can be explained in terms of evolutionary theory, comprising both the biological and the cultural evolution. To the extent to which the appeal of beauty implies the immediate sensory identification of the functional, the respective aesthetic sensibility is operating according to an underlying rationality. Thus the distinction between emotional and rational responses does not necessarily imply that emotional responses are irrational. They might follow an underlying rationality. This insight is encapsulated in the term 'emotional intelligence'. Aesthetic sensibility – the discrimination of the beautiful versus the ugly, and in more general terms: appeal versus revulsion – is a constant, universal feature of all human behaviour and action. The same kind of sensibility that facilitates the intuitive navigation of the environment also facilitates the designer's intuitive selections during the design process. This facility is not specific to art or design. It is much more general. However, which concrete phenomena appeal, which phenomena are deemed attractive or beautiful, often depends on who is judging. Responses are *not* uniform across individuals, generations, societies, cultures.

What is beautiful? Whatever appeals at first sight. Being impressed by beauty is a gut reaction, triggered by a perceptual encounter. This immediate gut reaction operates according to an underlying rationality. The recognition of beauty within a built environment is the recognition of the vitality of this environment, on the basis of its mere appearance, prior to a more in-depth experience and verification of its functionality. This works due to the extent to which subjects are conditioned by prior experience. However, as society evolves what was once vital might have become dysfunctional. Aesthetic sensibilities have to be adapted via aesthetic revolutions. New vital societal processes might be unduly constrained by the established order of beauty. They break out of this order and the environments they find or bring forth appear ugly. Their aesthetic rejection becomes a fetter on their further progress. A contradiction develops that can only be solved by an aesthetic revolution. Sensibilities need to be (periodically) brought in line with the morphological conditions of the most vital social life-processes.[69] In this sense beauty keeps changing its physiognomy.

But is the category of beauty really devoid of any features that persist across its different, concrete historical manifestations? If this were so we would not be able to see the beauty of earlier styles. However, contemporary society – inclusive of contemporary architects – is still

69 A similar logic applies to the evolution/revolution of moral values and sentiments. Here too each new historical epoch with new vital patterns of social communication requires a revaluation of values.

touched by the beauty (filigree order) of the Gothic, by the beauty (simple elegance) of the Renaissance, by the beauty (intense plasticity) of the Baroque etc. Contemporary architects recognize the beauty of past eras (although they would not find it appropriate to use any of these older styles to frame contemporary institutions). Is it possible to identify an invariant characteristic, a universally applicable condition that must be met by all environments, and even by all phenomena, that is recognized as beautiful? Yes, there is an invariant aspect that guides all discriminations of beauty versus ugliness: the sensation of beauty is always bound to a sense of ***order*** as distinct from ***chaos***. Order as the ***universal and invariant*** aspect of beauty has been alluded to by many classical definitions of beauty. For instance Leon Battista Alberti's famous definition reads as follows: 'Beauty is that reasoned harmony of all the parts within a body, so that nothing may be added, taken away, or altered, but for the worse.'[70] The positive principle of harmony/order is emphasized by reference to an 'integral body' and contrasted with a mere agglomeration: 'The harmony is such that the building appears a single, integral, and well-composed body, rather than a collection of extraneous and unrelated parts.'[71] The same point is further explicated by negating its opposite which might thus be taken as the implicit definition of the ugly: a composition should be 'neither jumpy, nor confused, nor disorganized, nor disconnected, nor composed of incongruous elements, . . . nor too disjointed or distant from the rest of the body.'[72]

Alberti references order via the phrase 'harmony of all the parts'. However, his insistence on completeness, ie, that nothing may be added, taken away or altered, is specific to Classical architecture and can no longer be considered a universal and invariant feature of beauty. Alberti's concept of an organic whole, with symmetry and strict rules of proportion, with a state of completeness or perfection that tolerates neither additions nor subtractions, describes a general ideal of beauty that remained in force from the Renaissance until the Historicism of the 19th century. The restrictions of symmetry, proportion and wholeness/completeness were abandoned within 20th-century Modernism. Instead, order was maintained via the order of the module, the grid and via the order of dynamic equilibrium. In addition features like simplicity and lightness were pursued, further specifying the Modernist sense of beauty. The formal heuristics of Parametricism call for order via lawful differentiation

70 Leon Battista Alberti, *On the Art of Building in Ten Books*, translated by Joseph Rykwert, Neil Leach & Robert Tavernor, MIT Press (Cambridge, MA/London), 1988, p 156.

71 Ibid, p 24.

72 Ibid, p 163.

and correlation.[73] These concepts are implemented via rule-based (algorithmic) design processes. A sense of order as distinct from chaos is maintained in all historical concretizations of the code of beauty. Order vs chaos is thus the invariant criterion of beauty. However, the criterion of order vs chaos is insufficient to give an operational definition of beauty that could fully guide the concrete application of the code values beautiful vs ugly. The order vs chaos criterion is still too abstract and leaves too many possibilities open. There can be many different forms of ordering, of relating non-arbitrarily.[74] Order is a necessary but not a sufficient condition of beauty.[75]

Being attracted to order and repulsed by chaos might be a biologically hardwired response, ie, the rationality of this response might be based on biological evolution rather than on cultural evolution or on conditioning on the basis of individual experience. Chaos, the absence of any perceived order, is disorienting and thus threatening, especially if the whole environment lacks order. If the environment is partially ordered and partially configured randomly, then it makes sense that attention is drawn towards the ordered aspects, ignoring the less ordered or accidental configurations. The probability that a random configuration of entities constitutes an interrelated, functioning assemblage is very low. Where entities are configured into an order, the presumption is justified that these entities somehow add up to a unit of interaction. Ordered configurations are thus more likely to constitute a force than random configurations, a force that should be reckoned with. Complex order inspires curiosity and awe, random configurations – like a heap of garbage or the disarticulated agglomerations of suburbia – are usually taken no notice of, except negatively for their ugliness and thus absence of interest. All natural systems are ordered in some way. However, the complexity of many natural phenomena prevented the recognition of their order and beauty in earlier times.[76] Animal forms (and animal formations like flocks) are more organized than plant forms. Attention to animals is of higher evolutionary importance than attention to plants. Cultural

73 See Chapter 11.2.2 *Operational Definition of Parametricism: The Defining Heuristics of Parametricism.*

74 For the definition and theoretical elaboration of the concept of order see: section 6.2 *Order via Organization and Articulation.*

75 There might be an exception to this rule: in periods of crisis or transition when old norms have become anachronistic and can no longer identify the most vital as the most beautiful, or where the established code of beauty promotes the dysfunctional, the absence of any order might be preferred over the wrong order. An example is the Deconstructivist aesthetic of the early Frank Gehry, and the early Coop Himmelb(l)au.

76 The beauty of natural landscapes was appreciated only after the chaotic urban developments of early industrial capitalism revealed their relative order.

evolution further confirmed the privileging of order over disorder. The more ordered appearance of the early city-based civilizations (Babylon, Maya Civilization etc), compared with village-based clan societies, correlates with the superiority of these civilizations. The effort to give order to the built environment has been a constant feature of the process of civilization, both before and after the inauguration of architecture as self-conscious discipline.

9. Architecture and Politics

In pre-Modern times, fortresses, palaces and other major monuments were constituents of the political system as were religion, the law and the economy. In Modern times, according to the theory of architectural autopoiesis, architecture and politics are separate autopoietic function systems. As such they are incommensurable systems of communications, each with its own self-referentially closed system of distinctions, codes and programmes. This raises the question of their proper relationship, their mutual observation, engagement and adaptation.

The thrust of this section is in one important respect decisively negative: the widespread conception of architecture as a site of political activism must be repudiated. Architecture is *not* inherently political. The slogan 'everything is political' was born and spread in the late 1960s during a general revolutionary period. In 1968, politics was no longer contained within the boundaries of the institutionalized political system. Generally, during a revolutionary period,[1] all aspects of social life do indeed become political. Nearly everybody becomes involved in a multi-faceted political discourse and struggle that questions all institutions, communication structures and modes of interaction. However, revolutionary periods are exceptional periods that cannot continue for very long. Revolutionary periods subside or escalate into a full-blown revolution. In any event, society must eventually move back into a situation where politics is contained within a separate political system that works through some but not all aspects of social life. The revolutionary period of the late 1960s peaked in 1968 and receded in the following years. However, the slogan 'everything is political' continued to circulate in intellectual circles that found it difficult to accept that the intoxicating ferment of the revolutionary situation had in fact vanished.[2] The slogan lives on but runs idle without any real meaning within architecture or anywhere else in society.

This section tries to give an operationally tenable account of architecture's relationship to politics within modern liberal democracies.

1 A revolutionary period is a historical period that might last from a few months to a few years. It might or might not develop into a full-blown social revolution.

2 Revolutionary periods are the intellectuals' great moment of exceptional influence and power.

9.1 Is Political Architecture Possible?

THESIS 48

The notion of a political architecture has transformed from a tautology to an oxymoron.

To the extent that Classical architecture was not yet claiming universal competency and relevancy with respect to the totality of the built environment, but was instead addressing itself exclusively to special buildings of public significance – such as churches, palaces and other public institutional buildings – to this extent all architectural projects had immediate political significance. During the reign of the great Classical styles of architecture – Gothic, Renaissance and Baroque – all architecture was commissioned and directly controlled by political power. The notion of a political architecture would have been a tautology.

An architecture of progressive political engagement was possible only to the extent that the most progressive segment of society had seized power. The political masters of society were at the same time the sole clients of architecture (understood as academically supported discipline transcending mere building).

This situation changed when the client base broadened and architecture started to claim universal responsibility for all new buildings that were to be built. This implied that a lot of what was to be built was politically indifferent, and not prone to invite any particular political reading. But it also implied that architecture now started to project many voices, with the potential to express different ideologies. Architecture was faced with the fact that some private projects, without political intentions, were nevertheless bound to gain a particular political significance. Architecture, to some extent, became a contested field and thus also a way to stake out political claims. Architectural projects had gained the potential to be conceived as part of a political manifesto. The model socialist industrial communities of the 19th century can serve as early examples, for instance Robert Owen's New Lanark (1800–25) and New Harmony (1825–9), and Charles Fourier's Phalanstère (1832–6). Although architectural designs were a central part of the conception, promotion and implementation of these ideologically motivated model communities, there was little architectural distinctness and therefore little lasting impact within the history of architecture. The apparent social and economic success of Robert Owen's New Lanark were, together with Owen's writings, generating more resonance within the political system of society. Although further attempts to put Owen's or Fourier's ideas of utopian community into practice were made in the 19th and early 20th centuries by various experimental groups in Europe and the US, all these were localized and relatively short-lived experiments which ultimately remained marginal.

The paradigmatic period for politically engaged architecture was the 1920s. A significant series of avant-garde projects displayed a clear alignment with the social democratic labour movement: for instance the famous Karl Marx Hof in Vienna, or the work of Ernst May in Frankfurt. Another arena for political architecture opened up in the early Soviet Union. Here architecture, like all the other function systems of society, was concerned with the revolutionary reconstruction of society.

The follow-on period of fascist and Stalinist clamp-down in Germany and Russia implied the total suspension of the autopoiesis of architecture in those territories. Architecture – in the sense defined and theorized within the theory of architectural autopoiesis – ceased to exist under the condition of totalitarian usurpation.

The architecture of the 1950s and early 1960s was characterized by political muteness. However, the potential for politically relevant architecture still existed. That the muteness of the 1950s and early 1960s was only a temporary phenomenon became evident when radical, left-wing political tendencies were surging in the mid-1960s, culminating in the events of Paris 1968. This revolutionary period witnessed a wave of architectural projects with explicit political intentions, comparable to the early 1920s. However, the character of the political ferment as a primarily student-based movement meant that the 'politics' that was projected was much more radical and utopian in character, without any material backing. It was also more short-lived, and no significant translation into built architecture was achieved. Politically radicalized student groups produced written manifestos and radical manifesto projects. The intellectual level, ambition and seriousness of commitment of the student protagonists were indeed impressive. The depth of the theoretical embedding of architecture within an overall agenda for societal reconstruction was unprecedented, and has never been repeated since. The radical avant-garde architecture of that time was participating in a general revolutionary movement. The failure to achieve a lasting, radical transformation of society resulted in a gradual dissipation of the revolutionary ferment and of its architectural reflection.

9.1.1 POLITICAL VACUUM

The political radicalism of the late 1960s shook up all aspects of modern society, including architecture. Since then no further exciting and plausible political projects have emerged. But ever since, the echoes of this shockwave return to inspire, haunt and embarrass the discipline. Calls for a 'political architecture' are raised again and again. However, these calls characteristically fail to specify the desired politics. Instead of offering a political position and programme, the respective authors lament the lack of a vigorous political dimension within the architectural discourse. This nostalgic lament is usually expressed via a series of vague phrases that serve as little more than non-committal gestures towards a vaguely progressive politics. They mark the absence of real politics rather than vigorous engagement. For instance, according to Roemer van Toorn, architecture should 'project alternatives', offer 'critical resistance' and 'social directionality'. Architects are to look for 'open works' and 'radical democracies' and 'aim at a systematic understanding of architecture as a political palimpsest for alternative social and political hypothesis while itself reanimating architecture as an instrument of social and political invention'.[3] All this is well put and the underlying desire commands sympathies. The missing ingredient is the plausible, concrete political project, backed up with sufficient political power. The anti-globalization movement is perhaps the only more recent outburst of political energy that might be cited. However, this political protest movement lacks a positive political identity that could give a positive direction to architectural research. As long as these movements remain mere protest movements without an organization that could command far-reaching commitments, such forces lack constructive power. They remain limited to temporary outbursts and disruptive gestures.

But it seems authors like Roemer van Toorn do not search for real political force. They say that they want to 'resist the tameness and mediocrity of social democracy'.[4] This means to stay away from actual political decision-making processes. Instead: 'Like Chantal Mouffe I am looking for a politics beyond the triumph of moralizing liberalism.'[5]

It transpires that van Toorn's political sympathies closely follow those of Ernesto Laclau and Chantal Mouffe, involving the notions of 'radical democracy' and 'agonistic pluralism'. Mouffe and Laclau are theorists rather than politicians. There is no political force that has formed under the banner of 'radical democracy'. Political theory might help architectural theory to interpret the political system, but it cannot serve as substitute for real politics when architecture wants to identify a viable political agenda with which to align. Political theory contributes to the

3 Roemer van Toorn, *Hunch* 5, Berlage Institute, N/A Publishers (Amsterdam), 2002, pp 166, 167.

4 Roemer van Toorn, 'Dirty Details', in: Zaha Hadid & Patrik Schumacher (Eds), *Latent Utopias*, Springer Verlag (Vienna/New York), 2002, p 77.

5 Ibid.

self-observation of the political system. This is especially true for some of the other authors Roemer van Toorn refers to and rehearses, such as Ulrich Beck, Anthony Giddens and Scott Lash. These authors address a wide readership, but they are also read and referred to within political circles, party think tanks etc. Anthony Giddens, in particular, is closely connected with the UK Labour Party. He is now Lord Giddens, a Labour peer. Giddens is the author of *The Third Way: The Renewal of Social Democracy* which came to be associated with the politics of Tony Blair and New Labour, as a kind of unofficial New Labour manifesto. Ulrich Beck was a member of the Commission for Future Questions of the Free States of Bavaria and Saxony. However, both remain academic figures. Neither is a political leader or politician. The efforts of architectural theorists like Roemer van Toorn to scan and filter social and political theory for the sake of 'irritating' architecture (and thus allowing architecture to reorient itself) are crucial contributions to the ongoing viability of architecture's autopeisis. But van Toorn is eager to 'do more than simply report from and on the field of modernization' and asks: 'Is it enough to surf the contemporaneity of late capitalism?'[6] To do more requires more than theoretical re-description. However, this cannot be done within architecture.

A political project that could give political meaning to architecture cannot originate within political theory, neither can it originate within architecture. Architecture itself cannot offer political direction, or project political alternatives. Here powerful external stimulation is required – *powerful* in the most literal sense. A second precondition for a politically engaged architecture is then the clear alignment with such a powerful political position. Vague anti-capitalist allusions to the 'smooth circuit of production and consumption'[7] obviously do not suffice to get this off the ground. Such phrases merely paper over the underlying political vacuum and disorientation. They stand in for the missing political dynamic. They symbolize the desire to be energized by a political position without risking the embarrassment of real political alignment. It seems authors like van Toorn either have no clear political allegiance, or they sense that outing such an allegiance would not really be productive within the architectural discourse. To offer an isolated, marginal political opinion, or an academic analysis from the domain of political theory, however compellingly presented, does not help to inject political vitality into architecture.

6 'Equipping the Architect for Today's Society: the Berlage Institute in the Educational Landscape – Dialogue between Wiel Arets and Alejandro Zaera-Polo', moderated by Roemer van Toorn, in: *Hunch – the Berlage Institute Report*, No 6/7, 2003, chapter 'Architecture or Politics', p 33.

7 Roemer van Toorn, *Hunch* 5, pp 166–167.

Architecture can only react with sufficient unanimity and collective vitality to political agendas that already have the real power of a tangible political force behind them.

Alejandro Zaera-Polo's recent contribution to the topic of politics within architecture provides an impressive and stimulating tour de force through recent political theory. Admirably, he tries to inject a measure of concreteness into the discussion by probing the political potential of various building types ordered according to the dimensional proportion of their respective envelopes. His 'political critique' tries to identify the architectural envelope as the primary site where architecture might regain 'effective political agency'.[8] However, Zaera-Polo's text is also locked in the contradiction between his desire for a politically engaged architecture and his inability to state any viable alternative political position. Paradoxically, he is even trying to turn this absence of a position into a virtue and positive strategy that attempts to avoid alignment with both the staus quo and its opposition. He argues for a 'political discourse of architecture with the capacity to produce effects that may actually destabilize political regimes rather than functioning as mere representations of politics, whether of the status quo or the resisting parties'.[9] Instead of political alignment Zaera-Polo is proposing to somehow (how?) follow certain conceptual moves promoted within recent political theory as points of departure for investing architecture with a renewed political agency. Reference is made to Peter Sloterdijk's *spherology* and his notion of *explicitation,* to Bruno Latour's *object-oriented politics of things,* to Ulrich Beck's notion of *micro-politics,* and to a practice of the *politically incorrect* as inspired by Karlheinz Stockhausen's bizarre provocation that 9/11 was 'the greatest work of art imaginable'. Although it remains vague how these notions can be turned into architectural-political strategies, one thing seems certain, as Zaera-Polo is willing to admit: these strategies (or subterfuges) lead us away from – rather than towards – what one might be able to call a coherent political project.

Again, Zaera-Polo's intellectual engagement, like Roemer van Toorn's, remains with political theory, rather than moving on to real politics. This is indeed a frequent drawback in attempts to revitalize architecture's political significance: in the absence of a new and inspiring politics, architects all too often look for inspiration in political theory. Neither Beck, Latour, Sennett and Sloterdijk, nor Hardt and Negri, can stand in

8 Alejandro Zaera-Polo, 'The Politics of the Envelope – A Political Critique of Materialism', in: *Volume*, Archis (2008), #17, p 79.

9 Ibid.

for relevant political leaders effectively representing real political forces.[10]

Zaera-Polo's explicit refusal of concrete political positioning, just like van Toorn's implicit avoidance, cannot be put down to mere individual disorientation, cowardice or lack of imagination. It reflects the general character of the political within functionally differentiated society on the one hand, and the particular inertia within the current period of global politics on the other. While the global political mood and constellation of forces might shift abruptly, the very much settled, general character of the political system in the most advanced countries implies that any new wave of political activism or shift in political power will have less immediate impact on the other function systems than in previous historical eras. Politics no longer rules the overall movement of society.[11] Instead politics irritates the other function systems, and the other function systems each find their own way to absorb those irritations. This also applies to architecture. How architecture might react to shifts in the political landscape cannot be predicted. Perhaps a dedicated discursive subset termed 'political architecture' might emerge to absorb the most immediate impact and to experiment with potentially generalizable adaptations. However, it seems that such a 'political architecture' can only emerge within a political landscape that offers sufficiently sharp contours and contrasts to allow architects to take a side and make this decision conspicuous. If there are no conspicuous sides to take then there can be no 'political architecture', not even in this insulated sense of a discursive subset within architecture.

9.1.2 NORMAL VS REVOLUTIONARY POLITICS

The paradigmatic examples from the early 1920s and the late 1960s that give meaning to the notion of politically engaged architecture were born in the exceptional condition of social revolution (or pending social revolution). During such periods everything is politicized: the law, the economy, education, architecture and even science. The autonomy of the functional subsystems of society is temporarily suspended. It is during such a period that Le Corbusier's famous dictum 'architecture or

10 What we can expect from political theorists is a general assessment of the modes, conditions and limitations of contemporary politics, and perhaps clues towards the modes, conditions and limitations of architecture's relationship with such a politics. Such clues are more likely to be forthcoming if, as is the case with Niklas Luhmann's political theory, such a political theory is embedded in a comprehensive and systematic theory of contemporary society.

11 This thesis of a muted impact is only valid as long as there is no genuine social revolution. However, a social revolution cannot be classified as a political phenomenon. Revolution implies the meltdown of these distinctions and their underlying differentiation.

revolution' was coined: 'It is a question of building which is at the root of the social unrest of today; architecture or revolution. . . . Society is filled with a violent desire for something it may obtain or may not. Everything lies in that: everything depends on the effort made and the attention paid to these alarming symptoms. Architecture or Revolution. Revolution can be avoided.'[12] This kind of condition can recur, but it is not the normal state of affairs that is theorized by Luhmann's social systems theory.

The past 30 years have witnessed a consolidation and expansion of the so-called 'liberal democracies'. The term denotes a condition with the following ingredients: national capitalist economy, welfare state, rule of law and multi-party representative democracy. Representative democracy is the form the political system tends to take in the most advanced nation states within functionally differentiated world society. Representative democracy professionalizes politics and regularizes the channels of political influence, negotiation and (collectively binding) decision making. The specialized, well-adapted channels of political communication absorb and bind all political concerns. Art, science, architecture, education and even the mass media are released from the burden of becoming vehicles of political expression. The more this system consolidates, the longer this division of labour within society works smoothly, the more false and out of place rings the pretence of 'political architecture'. Political architecture finally becomes an oxymoron – at least until the emergence of the next revolutionary situation, when a new socio-political upheaval re-politicizes all aspects and arrangements of society. At *that* stage – within the throes of a genuine social revolution – we can expect the meltdown of these distinctions and their underlying differentiation. Then we are no longer concerned with politics in the narrow sense that this term currently denotes.

During normal times architecture and politics are separated as autonomous discursive domains. The hegemony of a particular architectural style emerges from within the autopoiesis of architecture and is not a political issue. The political usurpation of architectural autonomy would spell the termination of the autopoiesis of architecture.

Political orientation from within the autopoiesis of architecture is always possible and might be expected under conditions of irritation or stimulation from the political system. However, it seems as if architecture is not sufficiently sensitive to politics to register and respond to normal political occurrences like the usual power-transfer from a centre-left to centre-right coalition after democratic elections. The political

12 Le Corbusier, *Towards a New Architecture*, Dover Publications (New York), 1986, reprint. Original English translation published: John Rodker (London), 1931, pp 269–89.

lead-distinction of politically progressive (left) vs politically conservative (right) has no regular architectural correlate. Is the opposition between Minimalism and Parametricism politically aligned with left vs right? The answer is that no such alignment exists. Is this a shortcoming? Should architecture transmute political distinctions and programmes into architectural research programmes or styles? This last question might be answered in terms of the general requirement of adaptive innovation that confronts all societal function systems. There is no need – and most probably no plausible possibility – to translate nuanced political distinctions and party programmes into architectural programmes before these political agendas have reached the point of democratically empowered implementation. Only then is there indeed the requirement to adapt to the relevant, collectively binding decisions that are the net result of the political process.

One fundamental difficulty here is the fact that the autopoiesis of architecture is a world system (global communication system) while the relevant political decisions, like, for example, social housing programmes, urban planning rules or policies of hertitage/identity preservation, are formulated locally or nationally. This severely limits their registration within world architecture. This means that the resolution of architecture's political responsiveness is rather coarse. World architecture can only react to global political trends. For instance, the intensifying political formation of ecological concerns in green parties and the resultant ascendancy of green politics leading to respective collectively binding decisions that are widespread across the advanced countries. This in turn engenders an increasing weight of ecological agendas within the discourse and design research efforts of architecture. A worldwide politicized focus on poverty and class might equally stir (but never steer!) the autopoiesis of architecture. A general intensification of political activism and a persistent world political focus on issues such as poverty or class would engender a considerable stimulation/irritation within architecture, perhaps shifting the focus of architectural research once more to industrialized low-cost mass accommodation. In contrast to a national electoral shift from centre-left to centre-right or vice versa, a more profound, global political shift would sooner or later be registered and worked through within architecture. Failure to respond would threaten architecture's societal standing and continuation. But today such speculations are rather academic. A viable political architecture must wait for the arrival of a viable new politics.

The key thesis that must be emphasized here is that it is *not* architecture's societal function to actively promote or initiate political agendas that are not already thriving in the political arena. Architecture is no viable site for such initiatives. It cannot substitute itself for a missing political agenda. Instead of furthering speculation about 'potentials' for political vitality, we should try to understand how the relationship between architecture and politics operates today.

9.2 Theorizing the Relationship between Architecture and Politics

THESIS 49

To respond to hegemonic political trends is a vital capacity of architecture. It has no capacity to resolve political controversy. Political debate within architecture overburdens the discipline. The autopoiesis of architecture consumes itself in the attempt to substitute itself for the political system.

9.2.1 THE INCOMMENSURABILITY OF ARCHITECTURE AND POLITICS

According to the theory of modern, functionally differentiated society adopted here, the relationship between architecture and politics is the relationship between two autonomous, self-referentially enclosed systems of communication. Both politics, understood as the system of political communications, and architecture, understood as the system of architectural communications, are very special types of social system. They both belong to the group of the great function systems of society. Each function system sustains its own autopoiesis, each treating all the other social systems within society as a constraining environment rather than as a contribution to a common concern. Each is differentiated on the basis of taking exclusive responsibility for a distinct, necessary societal function. The societal function of the political system is the ordering of social communication via the provision of *collectively binding decisions*. Architecture's societal function is the ordering of social communication via the provision of *spatial frames*. The thesis of autopoietic, self-referentially enclosed systems of communication entails the recognition of a fundamental incommensurability between the different communication structures of the distinct social systems. This thesis also holds for the great function systems of society. The great function systems of society differ with respect to their preferred types of communicative operations, as well as with respect to their constitutive communication structures, including their codes and media.

Codes and media are very special communication structures that have evolved in all modern function systems: each function system has its own unique code and unique medium of communication. It is the communications' commensurability with these codes that marks and confirms the system-reference of the communications in question. Luhmann has developed several versions for the code of politics: progressive (left) vs conservative (right), government vs opposition, and ruler vs ruled.[13] The theory of architectural autopoiesis has identified the following codes as operating within architecture: *functional* vs *dysfunctional* (code of utility) and *formally resolved* vs *formally unresolved* (code of beauty). A third code, *original* vs *conventional* (code of novelty) has been identified for the avant-garde segment of architecture. The specific medium of architecture is the drawing (or digital model). Codes are asymmetric, binary schemata that claim universal relevance within their respective communication systems. Any communication that purports to participate in the autopoiesis of the respective system must be able to answer a code-based probing – otherwise its participation within the system cannot be sustained, ie, only communications that accept the relevance of the code belong to the system. The code is thus the touchstone of the system's differentiated identity. All supposedly political communications can be queried with respect to their alignment on the *left* vs *right* dimension, or on the *affirmative* vs *oppositional* dimension. Communications that refuse such alignments cannot be regarded as political communications. All supposedly architectural communications must relate to both the code of beauty and the code of utility, ie, all concretely design-related communications can be queried with respect to their position on the functionality and formal resolution of the design in question, and all more general communications (like communications within architectural theory) can be queried about the import of their pronouncement with respect to the general criteria of functionality and beauty. This means that the autopoiesis of architecture cannot enter into political arguments. It can only relate to given political agendas as 'irritating' premises for its own architectural thinking. These premises are merely irritating premises, rather than regular, logical premises, because there is no ingrained logic within architectural thinking that would allow architects or architectural theorists to draw regular conclusions from those premises.

13 Niklas Luhmann, *Die Politik der Gesellschaft*, Suhrkamp Verlag (Frankfurt am Main), 2000, pp 88–102. Luhmann never resolved this ambiguity. The distinction ruler vs ruled is the code formula for pre-democratic times. The other two distinctions remain pervasive and it seems impossible for the theory to eliminate one in favour of the other. The distinction of progressive vs conservative (left vs right) seems to be the most general characterization of any possible political attitude. The distinction of government vs opposition is also always relevant in any democratically constituted political system. This distinction is explicitly tied to power as the specific medium of the political system.

9.2.2 ARCHITECTURE RESPONDS TO POLITICAL AGENDAS – THREE SCENARIOS

Since the codes of the political system are different from the codes of architecture, it follows that political and architectural communications are mutually incommensurable. They cannot connect to each other in the same way that communications with the same system-reference can connect to each other. For instance, when a political communication, ie, the proclamation of the political demand that all means of large-scale industrial production are to be nationalized, is taken up by an architect or by an architectural theorist the following question arises: under what conditions can such a political position be made productive as a premise for the architect's design work, or as a premise for the architectural theorist's architectural propositions?

To answer this we have to distinguish between the case of the practising architect and the case of the architectural theorist:

1. It is clear that for the architect's practical design work it could only form a premise if this political demand had already been successfully implemented. Then it would be a real premise for certain types of architectural design work. The proclamation would no longer have any political charge. It would be a mere statement of the fact that a political decision has resulted in a new legal and economic condition. For the practising architect this condition would, with respect to, for example, the task of designing a factory complex, imply a new type of client with new institutional expectations demanding an architectural response for which the architect might or might not be adequately prepared. While the political decision to nationalize was identifiable as a left-wing position, it makes no sense within architecture to discuss particular architectural responses in terms of left vs right. The adequate architectural translation of a left-wing political intention is not itself left-wing. Within the autopoiesis of architecture there can be no *left-wing architecture*, neither can there be *oppositional architecture*. ('Affirmative architecture' is therefore equally meaningless, or at best an empty tautology.) A building or design might become effectively associated with these political categories only if a politician chooses to do so within the political communication system.
2. If the political proclamation is still a demand only, but its political success and implementation might be expected or at least are a real possibility, then it might be a worthwhile task for an architectural theorist to think through the general implications of its eventual success for the methods and values of architectural design that might

have to be brought to bear on certain types of design tasks. Both analytic and generative architectural theorist would thus anticipate the kind of adaptive responses required in terms of architecture's concepts, methods and organizational-articulatory repertoire. At that point it might make sense for design projects (paper architecture) to try possible design translations of the respective theoretical propositions.

The following question arises at this point: is the respective political proposition – taken as premise of a theoretical anticipation of its architectural consequences – a genuine political statement posited within architectural discourse? The answer is no, because within the autopoiesis of architecture the political proposition is best treated as hypothetical thought-experiment rather than as demand, so that the specific architectural intelligence of the discipline is able to focus on the question of whether the form-function relationships have been thought through convincingly and the criteria/programmes for the code values have been reformulated in a convincing way etc. What if the argument takes the form of a manifesto starting with the demand for nationalization and then proceeding to a demand for an architecture that takes account of this demand in a particular way, for example, via the most rigorous modularization? This form of presentation would not be able to prevent its reception along the lines of inquiry just sketched out above: form-function relations etc. The architectural discourse might ignore the fact that the theorist's ideas are presented in the form of a political demand and instead choose to focus on the architectural (formal and functional) aspects of his ideas. A discussion of the fundamental merit of the political proposition, its multiple ramifications within society, the political chances of and conditions for its eventual success etc would soon lose traction and resonance within the autopoiesis of architecture. Architects are not called upon to resolve such questions. They can at best be irritated and inspired by such questions, by taking such propositions as hypotheses.

Thus, within architecture no effective political statements can be made. Political positions can only be rehearsed hypothetically. Political statements belong to the political communication system. Only here can all the different ramifications of a proposed political decision be gathered and discussed. All citizens can participate in the political system of society, by communicating in the specific medium of the political system – the medium of power – via voting in political elections. However, their voices only mean something after they have been coalesced behind a party or candidate. To make effective political statements within this communication system requires a certain position of political power – parliamentarian, party leader, trade union leader or speaker of a certain political pressure group etc.[14] Only a voice backed up by power can gain attention within a political debate. The political opinion of an architect means nothing within the political system. Equally, it means nothing within architecture.

Above, two principal scenarios for architecture's engagement with political propositions were distinguished. Neither scenario leads us to a point where we would be able to say that architecture has become political. Neither the architect, nor the architectural theorist, acts politically. Neither's communications were able to come through as political communications. For architects to act politically they have to participate within the political process of the political system as citizens. How can architects, as architects, participate in the political process? Via the mass media publication of paper architecture?

This scenario hinges on the theoretical use of the design medium of the drawing (digital model). Speculative architectural and urban designs might be convincingly elaborated on the basis of a (counter-factual) political hypothesis. Such designs might depict new urban and architectural possibilities that could be realized if certain political decisions were carried through. Such designs might be published in magazines and exhibitions. This is the genre of utopian (or dystopian) designs. Their form of engagement – addressing the general public – works in principle like the 'political' messages that are issued by politically engaged art or cinema.[15] There is a potential here for 'political' agitation. However, according to Luhmann's theory of functionally differentiated society, these kinds of messages are not *stricto sensu* political. The theory of architectural autopoiesis follows this categorization.

The efficacy of this kind of private agitation within the public domain has to be questioned. That's why the theoretical decision not to include engaged art within the domain of politics makes sense. This kind of agitation can only become effective if it is picked up by a serious political force, by a player with political credibility and power, for instance by a political party. *Then* such a message does indeed become a political

14 In this sense it might only be a representative figure like the president of the RIBA who could – not so much as architect but as representative of the collective social power of the profession – make political interventions and thus enter the political arena.

15 In this connection it is noteworthy that Roemer van Toorn chooses examples from art and cinema when he tries to exemplify how his key political concept of And/Otherness might be translated within architecture. See Roemer van Toorn, 'Dirty Details', in: Zaha Hadid & Patrik Schumacher (Eds), *Latent Utopias*, Springer Verlag (Vienna/New York), 2002, p 88.

message. This political message is then attributed to the respective political party. An example of this is the integration of Constructivist designs in the agitprop[16] campaigns of the early Soviet Union. Another example is the politically charged, utopian architectural imagery that emerged during the 1960s, morphing from initial techno-utopias (Metabolism, early Archigram) to counter-culture utopias (Constant, Yona Friedman) and ideologically charged dystopias (Superstudio). The alignment with real political players was far less clear here – although one might say that the whole counter-culture movement represented a form of diffused, quasi-political power that finally irrupted during the student revolutions of 1968. In Germany a relatively short-lived, so-called extra-parliamentary opposition (APO) was formed. However, the final political articulation of these movements was realized indirectly via the channels of the political system, ie, via the first post-war election victory of the German Social Democratic Party. At this stage, the radical utopian visions had already receded.

The scope for this kind of involvement, or rather for the enlistment of architecture within politics, has been diminishing ever since. The historical experiences of the 20th century, with their respective exaltations and disillusionments, have left a mark of scepticism on the potential audience for this type of quasi-political message.

9.2.3 SERVICE PROVISIONS BETWEEN ARCHITECTURE AND POLITICS

Critical theory[17] is trying to politicize architecture in the same way it is trying to politicize all phenomena of social life. That everything that goes on in society has potential political significance is recognized and explained within the theory of functionally differentiated society. That anything within society has 'potential political significance' here means that anything that goes on in society can be made topical within the political system of parliamentary and party politics. This is an effect of the universal scope of all modern function systems. This universal scope does not only pertain to politics. For instance, it pertains equally to the legal system: every act or communication that takes place within society can be queried with respect to its legal status, all the way from domestic communications to economic exchanges or even philosophical disputes

16 Agitprop stands for *otdel agitatsii i propagandy*, ie, *Department for Agitation and Propaganda*, which was part of the central and regional committees of the Communist Party of the Soviet Union.

17 Some of the theoretical groundwork concerning the relationship between architecture and politics has been covered in Volume 1, Chapter 1.3.6 *From Deconstruction to the Programme of Critical Theory*.

where, for example, copyright issues might be implied. The same goes for the economy: nearly every act or communication has an economic aspect and can be measured in monetary terms. The same goes for architecture and the design disciplines within modern society. Since Modernism, architecture and design claim universal competency with respect to the organization and articulation of all spaces and all artefacts of modern civilization; and since literally all social communications take place within designed settings – with the only (unlikely) exception of nudists encountering each other in the wilderness – all social communications are framed by means of architecture and design.

Just as much as every building and every architectural design feature has economic value and might become a legal issue, every architectural design might potentially have political significance in the sense that it might be made into a political issue, within the political communication system. This is a rather common phenomenon.[18]

But the theory of architectural autopoiesis – in line with Luhmann's theory of functionally differentiated society – avoids drawing the conclusion that all architectural communications must therefore be (explicit or implicit) political communications. Such a conclusion would lead to the collapse of the distinction between architecture and politics, and if 'everything is political', indeed to the collapse of all distinctions between discursive domains.

Instead of observing the progressive fusion of discursive domains, social systems theory observes their progressive differentiation. The relationship between these differentiated, discursive domains is theorized on the one hand as a relationship of potential mutual *irritation*, and on the other as a relationship of *structural coupling*.

The relationship of structural coupling is the relationship of regularized mutual dependencies and service provisions, whereby the different, autonomous communication processes have reached a relationship of mutual adaptation. It is important to understand that this relationship excludes the interpenetration of discursive domains desired by the critical theorists. There can be no deep communicative connections between architecture and politics because the respective discursive structures (lead-distinction, codes and media) are very different. The effect is that any attempted penetrating communication,

18 The kind of landmark public buildings we are designing at Zaha Hadid Architects are often made the occasion for political debate by the local opposition party. For instance, this was the case with respect to our train-station project in Innsbruck which played a pivotal role in the mayoral election contest. Similarily, our design for a new Guggenheim museum in Taichung (Taiwan) was a point of political dispute. In both cases we presented our design to the city parliament.

for instance, when a politician uses a quote from an architect, would immediately denaturalize, because the new context is unable to honour its inherent intent and logic. The meaning of a communication never resides simply within the utterance itself, but always in the extensive network of communications that are actually or potentially connected with the communication in question. Meaning means connectivity. What happens with a communication when it tries to cross system boundaries is rather unstructured and therefore unpredictable. The notion of irritation captures this sense of looseness and unpredictability. A communication that is picked up on the other side of a discursive border is like a chemical radical that requires reinterpretation and reintegration into a new network if it is not to be stillborn. Such efforts to digest the essentially indigestible – because the appropriate digestive system is not available – lead to irritations that might in turn lead to productive mutations in the receiving system.[19]

Another matter, in contrast to the 'irritating' pseudo-communicative stray bullets, are the exchanges between autopoietic systems that have been regularized in terms of structural coupling. What is important to understand here is that structural coupling happens on the periphery of autopoietic social systems via the final, crucial output communications of each function system. Structural coupling often involves institutions that facilitate the regular service transmission from one function system to another. For instance, as stable forms of structural couplings between the economic system and the legal system, Luhmann mentioned the institutions of contract and ownership.[20] Contracts (and civil court rulings) are the crucial, final provisions that the legal system provides to the economy. However, the ongoing interpretation of the contract and the handling of the contract provisions in the case of dispute remain the prerogative of lawyers communicating according to the code of the legal system.

In the case of the political system these crucial communications are the collectively binding decisions (political decisions) that the political system issues as its service to all the other social systems. All social systems – including the autopoiesis of architecture – rely on the provision of such collectively binding decisions. Within the political system these final political decisions are only one – albeit focal/pivotal – set of political communications. It is via these final political decisions that the political system fulfils its societal function. Families, corporations and all sorts of other social systems – not least the other great function systems of

19 The general theory of autopoietic systems recognizes such irritations as a factor of evolution.
20 Luhmann, *Die Politik der Gesellschaft*.

society – rely on political decisions to regulate their own communications and expectations.

Architecture's focal/pivotal communications are the completed designs and finally the finished buildings that constitute architecture's service to so many social systems, again including families, business organizations etc. All the great function systems rely on their respective specific provisions of architecture's service – and this includes the political system which requires appropriately organized and articulated government quarters, buildings, spaces and interior furnishings. It is via these final built communications that architecture fulfils its societal function of *framing*: the societal function of architecture is to order social communication processes via the continuous innovation of the built environment as a system of frames.

Architecture provides a direct service to the political system via the design of the buildings and spaces that accommodate/frame the political institutions of the political system of society: parliament buildings, party headquarters, ministries etc. Does this in itself imply that architecture enters 'politics'? Are such designs/buildings 'political'? Potentially, but not necessarily! In principle, such designs/buildings have the potential to become an issue of political debate just as any other communication that occurs within society: the internment of a refugee, a controversial divorce case, the latest unemployment statistics or the publication of the latest genetic research. The unveiling of the design for a new parliament building is also likely to become a political issue to which further political communications connect. Such a debate might refer to specific architectural features as welcome or questionable political statements that are now queried with respect to the code of the political system, interpreted as either right-wing or left-leaning or, less divisively, as politically progressive or conservative. Specific features as well as the overall atmospheric effect of the design might have been the topic of detailed consultations between the architect and his political client. Although the architect is recognized as the design's author, the resultant political statement will certainly be attributed to the political client: the majority party in power, or the bipartisan parliamentary committee that might have been formed. Political responsibility can only be taken and communicated within the political system. It is the client who controls the political message, and it is the client to whom the political message is attributed.

We should not necessarily expect such designs/buildings to engender fierce and sustained political debate. One might rather assume that such a debate would remain rather mellow, circulating around generalities, like democracy and national identity, prone to subside fairly quickly. Many less prominent designs/buildings for political institutions might never excite the political arena, and in this sense remain apolitical.

Within Luhmann's theory of the political system, the notion of the political is reserved for communications that connect within the political communication system of society. The term 'political' should be limited to those communications that participate within the communication processes that finally lead to the provision of collectively binding decisions. Luhmann's notion of the political is thus sharply defined and precisely positioned within his overarching theory. It is therefore much narrower than the under-defined notions that abound within the critical academic literature that is being received at the theoretical margins of architecture. The theory of architectural autopoiesis follows Luhmann's lead and much prefers to work with precisely defined concepts.[21]

Political action or engagement is a matter of participating in the (largely but not exclusively) public communications of the political system. Although architecture cannot formulate political agendas, it can certainly *serve* political agendas formulated and empowered within the political system; for instance, by being enlisted within political campaigns (agitprop), or by designing appropriate architectural frames for the central political organs. In these cases architectural expertise and talent can even be enlisted to articulate what might be appropriately termed a political statement.[22] Architecture can and has been used with political effect by political institutions – especially by nation states. In former times, architecture was often called upon to give government buildings an outward expression prone to instil a sense of solemn respect for tradition and authority or, conversely, within contemporary democracies, is often asked to imbue the institutions of government with a sense of understatement and approachability.[23]

Architecture's enlistment within political agendas formulated and empowered within the political system is by no means confined to the

21 The overall complexity of the communication patterns that have to be grasped is such that conceptual rigour is an absolute precondition for any theoretical orientation.

22 There are quite a few books dedicated to this topic of the architectural representation of political power. For instance: Adrian Tinniswood, *Visions of Power: Ambition and Architecture from Ancient Rome to Modern Paris*, Mitchell Beazley (London), 1998, or: Deyan Sudjic, *The Edifice Complex: How the Rich and Powerful Shape the World,* Penguin Books (New York), 2005.

23 The political utilization of the representational capacity of architecture is often viewed with a suspicion that is motivated by a distrust of power in general and of state power in particular. The author does not share this generalized suspicion but considers political power a necessary mechanism for social synthesis. Parliamentary democracy is considered to be the most appropriate currently available form of political constitution. The presumption of parliamentary democracy is the implicit default premise in the author's discussion of the relations between architecture and politics.

architectural accommodation/framing of political institutions. Architecture might serve political agendas with respect to other forms of state provision, for example, the provision of public housing. This is not just a case of material provision. Urban and architectural design contribute via the organization and articulation of space in ways that might be perceived to have ideological overtones. The semiotic dimension of architecture comes into play, and the design might become a political communication, if it is engendering political responses. The architectural frame has then become a political statement, albeit one that is fraught with an inherent vagueness. The building is indeed a statement *only* to the extent to which it is recurrently interpreted, ie, to the extent to which it is embedded in a network of further communications. It is a political statement *only* to the extent to which this network of further communications is linked to the medium of power, and structured by the code of politics.

These built political communications are communications within the political communication system of society. They are attributed to the client, ie, to political institutions and their exponents rather than to the architects in question. The discussions that such designs might engender within architecture will have a different focus from the political debates that might simultaneously ensue. The architectural discussions should be means-oriented rather than ends-oriented. The ends – whether political ends or any other ends that architecture might be asked to further – are set by the client, and merely interpreted by the architect.

The question that must be clarified at this point is: to what extent can or should these two discourses – the discourse of politics and the discourse of architecture – overlap, if at all? To what extent can and should politics and the political discourse of society be received and discussed within architecture? To answer this question it is best to initially bracket the thorny issue of radical political *critique* and *critical architecture*. Thus initially we are only considering mainstream politics. Furthermore, the presumption of parliamentary democracy serves here as the default premise in the discussion of the contemporary relations between architecture and politics. Developments within the political system are an important aspect of architecture's societal environment. It is the task of the avant-garde segment of architecture, supported by architectural theory, to continuously innovate the disciplinary resources in line with the demands of society. Relevant here are the real demands actually posed by contemporary society via clients knocking on architects' doors rather than demands as formulated within high-flying academic theories. It is one of the vital contributions of Rem Koolhaas that he surreptitiously subjected the architectural avant-garde and architectural theory to such a reality check. He refused to feed his theory from theoretical sources only and exposed the danger of what one might call the academization of architectural theory.

The task of architectural theory is to contribute to the adaptive upgrading of architecture's capacity to fulfil its societal function. The task of adaptive upgrading includes architecture's capacity to adequately respond to emerging political agendas. The establishment of the social democratic welfare state and the attendant nationalization of large-scale industry in post-war Europe was a political challenge architecture responded to. The privatization drive of the 1980s was another challenge. The ascendancy of the political agenda of environmental protection is also a good example in this respect. The demand for environmentally conscious design can no longer be denied. In Europe every architectural competition for a public building now demands a demonstration that this concern has been taken on by the design team. The discipline responded resourcefully, both in terms of organization (envelope-configuration, apertures, passive systems etc) and in terms of articulation via 'green' aesthetics, in order to signal the underlying environmental concern of the framed institution. Architecture's adaptation to hegemonic political trends naturally requires the reception of the related dominant political concepts within architecture. These concepts must be received as premises rather than being debated and questioned. However, the architectural interpretation of these concepts is a matter of debate within architecture. The restriction to hegemonic trends and dominant concept is important. The real political process must be sufficiently resolved before it can productively irritate architecture. Otherwise the debate is bound to continue within architecture without a chance to be settled. That is why the introduction of marginal political agendas within the architectural debate leads to an unproductive overburdening of the discourse, with a tendency to consume a disproportionate amount of communication time. The autopoiesis of architecture would consume itself in the attempt to substitute itself for the political system.

9.3 Architecture Adapts to Political Development

THESIS 50

Architecture responds to resolved and thus depoliticized politics. To bind architectural positions to an ongoing political polemic is counterproductive. The intransigence of political positions operating in the medium of power leads to communicative dysfunction within the architectural discourse.

Historically, the most striking example of architecture's adaptive response to political change was the case of the Modern Movement responding to the socio-political revolutions that transformed Europe (and Russia) in the aftermath of the First World War. The autopoiesis of architecture responded with a radical transformation: the rebirth of architecture as Modern architecture.[24] Progressive architecture was aligned with progressive politics, because the new, democratic authorities were architecture's most prominent clients. This adaptive alignment was guided by architectural theory. The theories of Constructivism, Rationalism and Functionalism, together with the variously proclaimed new conception of space, correlated well with the new, democratic political agenda. Together they constitute architecture's answer to the challenges posed by the new politics (and by the related new economy). However, it is notable in this connection that the accompanying architectural theory – including the early sweep of manifestos – is virtually devoid of political statements. Typical examples of the kind of programmatic pronouncements and theoretical statements of this period are Adolf Behne's Functionalist statement from 1923 that 'architecture is no more than a fixed and visible structure of the final organization of every movement, every occupation, every purpose and use of the building',[25] or Gabo and Pevsner's 1920 Constructivist statement that 'we reject the closed spatial circumference ... and assert that space can only be modeled from within outward in its depth, not from without inward through its volume'.[26]

With respect to the architectural programmes and theories of the Modern Movement, we might speak of an essentially non-political, problem-solving spirit in the architectural translation of the new political agenda.

There are two notable exceptions to this absence of direct political reflections and demands, namely the 1919 declaration of the 'Work Council for Art'[27] and the agitation of the ABC group, representing two forms of explicit engagement with the political system. The CIAM

24 See Volume 1, Chapter 2.2.2 *The Refoundation of the Discipline as Modern Architecture*.

25 Adolf Behne, *The Modern Functional Building*, Getty Research Institute for the History of Art and the Humanities (Santa Monica), 1996.

26 Naum Gabo & Antoine Pevsner, 'Basic Principles of Constructivism', in: Ulrich Conrads (Ed), *Programs and Manifestoes on 20th-Century Architecture*, MIT Press (Cambridge, MA), 1971, p 56.

27 The Work Council for Art was intended as a national initiative directed by Walter Gropius, César Klein and Adolf Behne in Berlin, and had enlisted leading avant-garde architects and artists under its agenda. The 1919 statement of the Work Council for Art was entitled 'Under the Wing of a Great Architecture' and was a condensed and clarified version of Bruno Taut's 1918 *Program for Architecture*.

declarations (CIAM I–IV, 1928–33) represent a third exception, presenting a combination of those two types of engagement.

9.3.1 MODERN ARCHITECTURE CALLS ON POLITICS

The March 1919 statement of the Work Council for Art is indeed an explicit statement of political demands. However, these are not general demands concerning social justice, the regulation of the economy or the constitution of the state. The proclamation and the formulated demands have the character of architecture's (and art's) alignment with the political revolution[28] and its interpretation of the new social and political values in terms of the domains of architecture, design (crafts) and the visual arts. To a certain extent they can also be read as architecture's request for political regulation/deregulation of its affairs. The Work Council for Art poses as a quasi-representative body, as a kind of political pressure group, voicing the interests of architecture and art and calling upon the political system to deliver appropriate, collectively binding decisions, as well as the allocation of public funds. In the introductory paragraph, the declaration identifies the 'conviction that the political revolution must be used to liberate art from decades of regimentation' as the motivation for forming the council. The proclamation then formulates its guiding principles: 'Art and people must form a unity. Art shall no longer be the enjoyment of the few but the life and happiness of the masses. The aim is alliance of the arts under the wing of a great

28 The German Revolution started with the Sailors' Revolt in the naval ports of Germany, spread across the whole country within days and led to the proclamation of a republic on 9 November 1918, followed by the abdication of Kaiser Wilhelm II. Elections for a National Assembly (to be convened in Weimar) took place in December 1918, but were boycotted by the Communist Party. The Assembly was formed without the Communists.The further-reaching goals of socialist and communist revolutionaries failed after a popular workers' uprising in Berlin was defeated by a military clampdown ordered by the SPD leadership in January 1919. In February, the National Assembly elected the leader of the Social Democratic Party (SPD) as President of Germany. Thus by March 1919 the outcome of the revolution had already been settled in favour of the reformist Social Democratic Party to become a capitalist republic. However, political volatility prevailed. In 1920, the government was overthrown by a coup and a nationalist government was briefly in power, until a general strike by the trade unions and mass workers' demonstrations forced the regime out of power and helped to reinstate the elected government, a centre-left coalition government including the SPD. The SPD left the coalition in 1923. After elections in 1924 the centre-right coalitions dominated. However, the fact that the SPD remained a strong opposition party, together with the existence of a trade union movement, implied that conditions were favourable for public investment in social infrastructures like public housing.

architecture.'[29] The declaration then proceeds to list six demands, as follows:

1. Recognition of the public character of all building activity, both State and private. ... Unitary supervision of whole urban districts ... Permanent experimental sites for testing and perfecting architectural effects.
2. Dissolution of the Academy of Arts, the Academy of Building and the Prussian Provincial Art Commission ... Replacement ... from the ranks of the productive artists themselves. ...
3. Freeing of all training in architecture, sculpture, painting, and handicrafts from State supervision. ...
4. Enlivenment of the museums as educational establishments for the people. Mounting of constantly changing exhibitions ... State funds for the acquisition of old and new works.
5. Destruction of artistically valueless monuments. ... Immediate cessation of work on the war museums proposed for Berlin and the Reich.
6. Establishment of a national centre to ensure the fostering of the arts within the framework of future lawmaking.[30]

From the general political transformation, the declaration tries to draw premises for the transformation of architecture,[31] and in turn raises its own demands for the political regulation of architecture's internal affairs. No general political demand or argument can be detected here.

9.3.2 THE ABC GROUP: POLITICAL AGITATION WITHIN ARCHITECTURE

The only true manifestation of a general political agitation from within the architectural discourse comes from the ABC group. As a pertinent document we might cite its 1928 declaration 'ABC demands the dictatorship of the machine'.

The title already alludes both to the communist slogan of the 'dictatorship of the proletariat' and to Marx's materialist conception of history, using reference to the machine as cipher for the historical

29 'Work Council for Art, Under the Wing of Great Architecture', in: Ulrich Conrads (Ed), *Programs and Manifestoes on 20th-Century Architecture*, p 44.

30 Ibid, pp 44, 45.

31 However, no specific consequences for the methods and repertoires of design have as yet been formulated here.

dominance of the means of production. The group, arguing from a Marxist perspective, starts with a general premise and a historical positioning:

> The machine is nothing more than the inexorable dictator of the possibilities and tasks common to all our lives. ... As a leader of the masses, who are inescapably bound up with it, it demands more insistently every year the transformation of our economy, our culture. ... Under its pressure we have evolved the new methods of mass-production. Because of it we have had to place greater and greater organizational powers in the hands of the State. ... We have taken the first step: the transition from an individualistically producing society held together *ideally* ... to a capitalistically producing society *materially* organized in response to the need for industrialisation.[32]

From this general analysis of the historical context the authors of the manifesto move on to implicate their architectural colleagues: 'The thinking of our professional romantics ... has not followed even this step. They have ceased to understand elemental, vital facts because they think exclusively in terms of morality and aesthetics. And because they fear the worst for the future of our ideal goods, namely, that they themselves will be out of work, sheer idealism makes them either become the bodyguard of reaction or take flight into sectarianism.'[33] Further we read that in contrast: 'the Leninist architect is not an aesthetic lackey, and unlike his colleague in the West, not a lawyer and custodian of the interest of the capitalist ruling class there. ... For him architecture is not an aesthetic stimulus but a keen-edged weapon in the class struggle.'[34]

The manifesto then moves on to the level of general politics and expounds that 'we have to take the second step: the transition from a society that is *compelled* to produce collectively but is still individualistically oriented to a society that *consciously* thinks and works collectively'.[35]

The political position expounded within the manifesto was decisively aligned on the left of the political spectrum, ie, with the Communist International and its various national affiliates. Communism represented a credible political position during the 1920s, given the example of the

32 'ABC Demands the Dictatorship of the Machine', in: Ulrich Conrads (Ed), *Programs and Manifestoes on 20th-Century Architecture*, p 115, original: 'ABC fordert die Diktatur der Maschine', in: *ABC – Beiträge zum Bauen 4* (1927–8).

33 Ibid.

34 In 1932 Hannes Meyer published 'Der Architect im Klassenkampf' (The architect within the class struggle). The article was published in *Der Rote Aufbau* #5 (Berlin), 1932. Meyer was thus trying to directly engage the political communication system.

35 'ABC Demands the Dictatorship of the Machine', p 116, original: 'ABC fordert die Diktatur der Maschine', in: *ABC – Beiträge zum Bauen 4* (1927–28).

Soviet Union, and given the fact of sizeable European communist parties.[36]

With respect to most of the other Modern architects, we do not know their specific political views because they did not volunteer them. We might therefore assume that they were rather apolitical or, given the predominantly public character of their commissions, perhaps vaguely oriented towards social democracy. The communist political position dealt as harshly with social democracy as with any other political party. The sharp political divide was revolution vs reform, ie, the dictatorship of the proletariat vs the dictatorship of capital. Are general political differences of this kind really differences that make a difference within architecture, with respect to the general principles (methods and criteria) of design, or with respect to the concrete design decisions, for example, concerning the design of a housing estate, school building, train station or market hall?

In terms of its architectural design work, the ABC group was fully aligned with the Functionalism of the Modern Movement – a few years later canonized as the International Style. Even such stark distinctions between general political programmes such as the opposition between socialist revolution (left, KPD) vs capitalist reform (right, SPD, DDP[37]), do not have any clear equivalents to map onto with respect to the programmes that determine the application of the code values within the other function systems (with the exception of the economy). This difficulty also applies to any attempt to map political programmes onto architectural styles, ie, the programmes of architecture. To illustrate this difficulty we might refer to one of the most prominent state-sponsored commissions of the period: the Weissenhof Colony in Stuttgart, an avant-garde residential estate that was completed under the auspices of the German Werkbund in 1927, the very year the aforementioned ABC manifesto was written. Here the designs of politically 'bourgeois' architects Walter Gropius and Mies van der Rohe, among others, form a formal and functional whole together with the designs of the communist ABC member Mart Stam. Hans Schmidt, another expressly communist

36 The German Communist Party (KPD) was, together with the USPD (Independent Social Democrats) and the mainstream SPD (Social Democratic Party), one of the major left opposition parties represented in parliament within the Weimar Republic during the 1920s. The SPD left government in 1923. From then the government was led by a coalition between the Catholic Centre Party and the liberal parties DDP and DVP. All three left parties were represented in the German Reichstag. The SPD entered a coalition government once more in 1928–1930.

37 The DDP (German Democratic Party) was a middle-class party, supported by the professions, civil servants and small industry.

ABC protagonist, even designed the apartments within Mies' apartment block, all operating coherently within the same style: Modernism.

Bourgeois city governments in Berlin and Frankfurt, both DDP, empowered Modernist architect-planners like Martin Wagner (Berlin) and Ernst May (Frankfurt) to direct extensive city planning investments encompassing social housing projects that Wagner and May either designed themselves or distributed to their Modernist colleagues, including communist ABC protagonist Mart Stam. The implication here is that the selectivity of macro-political positions with respect to architectural styles often lacks the appropriate resolution that could make the close integration of specific macro-political arguments productive within the discussion of architecture.

Perhaps, if we look closer we might still characteristics that systematically distinguish ABC architecture within 1920s' Modernism. There are indeed two features that might serve to distinguish the group architecturally within the European avant-garde:

1. Formally it was the strong expression of structural members and the exalted articulation of aspects of the circulation system, as exemplified in Meyer and Wittwer's 1926 project for the Petersschule in Basel, or in their 1927 project for the League of Nations competition. In fact, these features were inspired by the Soviet Constructivist projects that El Lissitzky had brought to the attention of the later ABC protagonists in 1922.
2. Theoretically it was the absolute rejection of all aesthetic considerations for the sake of a supposedly exclusive concern for function and economy. It seems that this stance was deemed to be the logical conclusion from Marxist materialist philosophy.

However, neither of the two characteristics is necessarily restricted to architects on the political left. Further, the two characteristics do not require each other. Indeed, there is a distinctive tension, if not contradiction, between the theory of Radical Functionalism and the exalted articulation efforts of Constructivist design. The Russian projects that had inspired ABC had a decisively compositional self-consciousness, describing their design agenda as formal studies in terms of qualities like solid and void, mass and equilibrium, dynamism and rhythm etc. While utilizing the compositional research of Russian Constructivists, Meyer rejects composition,[38] declaring that art is composition and thus

38 Hannes Meyer, 'bauen', in: *Bauhaus* Year 2, No 4, Bauhaus (Dessau), 1928.

contradicts function, while life is function and thus is anti-artistic.[39] Meyer uses deliberately brutal phrases like: 'all things in this world are a product of the formula: (function times economy)', and: 'building is a biological process, building is no aesthetic process'.[40] ABC's absolute rejection of aesthetic concerns seems to be rooted in a rather crude understanding (or an inadequately provocative presentation) of historical materialism.[41] In fact, that the rejection of the idealist-formalist stance of traditional architecture should not lead to a rejection of the legitimacy of a discourse concerning form and aesthetics was argued at the time (1923) by Leon Trotsky: 'Materialism does not deny the significance of the element of form, either in logic, jurisprudence or art. Just as a system of jurisprudence can and must be judged by its internal logic and consistency, so art can and must be judged from the point of view of its achievements in form. ... The methods of formal analysis are necessary, but insufficient.'[42]

However, the theoretical validity of ABC's position with respect to Marxism is not the primary concern here. The primary point of contestation here is the fact that the alignment of such an architectural position with a strong political polemic is counterproductive for the progress of architecture.

9.3.3 THE VICISSITUDES OF POLITICAL POLARIZATION

While architectural arguments against aesthetes, both of the unworldly and the cynical kind, were a necessity at that time – and still are today[43] – the political polemic was disruptive. The polemic could be misdirected against fellow Modernists like Mies and Corb. In fact, in 1930, after Mies van der Rohe had become the new director at the Bauhaus, he was promptly attacked by the organ of the communist

39 The theory of architectural autopoiesis has developed a conceptual system that allows such contradictions to be resolved: the distinctions between avant-garde and mainstream, as well as between formal proliferation and functional selection give room to formal research. Further, the elaborated notion of function involves organizational as well as articulatory and semiotic dimensions that all contribute to the architecture's adequate framing of communication.

40 Meyer, 'bauen'.

41 In 1931 Meyer was working on a text entitled 'Thesen über marxistische Architektur' (Theses about Marxist architecture), unpublished manuscript.

42 Leon Trotsky, 'The Social Roots and the Social Function of Literature' (1923), in: Leon Trotsky, *Art and Revolution: Writings on Literature, Politics and Culture*, Pathfinder (Atlanta), 1992.

43 The theory of architectural autopoiesis insists that the framing of social functions is the final purpose and meaning-horizon of all architectural communication. However, the theory also explicitly recognizes the contribution of formal research within the division of labour that has emerged in contemporary avant-garde design research. The formalist outlook might be tolerated as the necessary, false consciousness of the most productive formal innovators.

student organization, in a tone reminiscent of Meyer's rhetoric[44] denouncing Mies as an 'individualist who has lost all contact with the world'. The pamphlet goes on as follows: 'With which legitimation does Mies van der Rohe use the phrase "we"? Does he mean the unworldly artists when he says "we"?'[45]

One wonders what would have been left of the innovative force of Modernism, if such politically inspired attacks had succeeded in discrediting Mies, Corb, Gropius and all the other 'bourgeois aesthetes' who contributed to the refoundation of architecture as Modern architecture.

That Mies van der Rohe's position as protagonist of Modern architecture should be subject to denunciation on the grounds of a quasi-political argument demonstrates the counterproductivity of such polemics launching oppositional politics within architectural discourse. This thesis does not depend on any assessment as to whether the communist political agenda itself was a sensible and viable political agenda at that time.[46] Two aspects are relevant here:

1. Communism was not in power. Communism was a political minority position that was operating as political opposition within the political system of the Weimar Republic.
2. The ABC group aligned itself with communism and charged their architectural discourse with a radically oppositional, general political critique and polemic.

The ABC protagonists thus effectively bound their architectural arguments to their political polemic and thus poisoned their architectural points with the intransigence of political opposition (operating in the medium of power).

That this strategy was counterproductive within the autopoiesis of architecture was soon discovered by the ABC protagonists themselves. Their stark, antagonistic stance hindered their affiliation with progressive organizations like the German and Swiss Werkbund. Adjustments to their

44 Meyer, the Bauhaus director preceding Mies, had encouraged the formation of a politically vociferous communist student group.

45 'Der neue Direktor! Der neue Kurs?', in: *Bauhaus, Sprachrohr der Studierenden*, No 3 (1930), reprinted in: Hans M Wingler, *Das Bauhaus 1919–1933 Weimar, Dessau, Berlin und die Nachfolge in Chicago seit 1937*, 3rd edition, Verlag Gebr Rasch & Co (Wiesbaden), 1975, p 176.

46 It is indeed my opinion that the communist opposition was not only sensible and viable, but the Communist International was indeed the most advanced political force at the time. In this sense all communists of the time – including Hannes Meyer and the other communist ABC protagonists – have my respect and admiration for their political foresight. ABC also deserves appreciation for their achievements in architectural design. But all this is irrelevant for the question discussed here.

strategy soon followed which allowed their Swiss ranks to expand and their practical work to finally flourish.

Political strife at the Bauhaus continued. Meyer had initiated a lecture series covering philosophy, sociology and psychology. Most speakers were Marxists. Mies continued these programmes but exchanged the phalanx of speakers. In a later edition of the *Bauhaus Sprachrohr,* an article entitled 'Politik am Bauhaus' complained about the 'apolitical teaching' that was 'arranged so that right-wing to centre-right bourgeois guest-lecturers would be able to achieve their intended lulling, soporific effect . . . no marxist was allowed to speak.'[47] Again, my point here is not to judge the merit of the different political philosophies that were given voice at the Bauhaus. My point here is that the introduction of the political code as primary code of the debate, and the alignment with positions still struggling for power, easily usurps the debate. Once the political controversy itself, rather than the architectural translation of political positions, is given space to unfold, there is little hope of finding the way back to architectural matters until the controversy is resolved in the medium of power. However, such resolution cannot be expected within architecture while the power struggle is still waged outside. One might (with hindsight) argue that towards the end of the Weimar Republic, with the spectre of rising fascism, political battle had to come before all else. Then the communist students at the Bauhaus were right. But we need to be clear that such an attitude implies the (temporary) abandonment of architecture for politics. When a political power struggle comes to a head, all spheres of life might indeed get involved in the battle, battling out the political direction before resuming their respective detailed work. Under non-revolutionary circumstances, in a society with a functioning political system, political power struggles are to be kept at bay, outside the boundaries of the other function systems, rather than allowing them to pervade and usurp all specialist communications.

This discussion of the costs of burdening architecture with a general, oppositional, political critique are a matter of contemporary relevance. Although powerful oppositional politics of the force and prospects of the Communist International in Europe in the 1920s are not available within the environment of contemporary architecture, some critical architectural theorists are all the more vociferous in their denunciatory polemics, conducting themselves as if a decisive political power struggle were coming to a head.

47 'Politik am Bauhaus', in: *Bauhaus, Sprachrohr der Studierenden*, No 3 (1930), reprinted in: Hans M Wingler, *Das Bauhaus 1919–1933 Weimar Dessau Berlin und die Nachfolge in Chicago seit 1937*, 3rd edition, Verlag Gebr Rasch & Co (Wiesbaden), 1975.

Reinhold Martin might be given as an example here. Martin is trying to develop his architectural critique from the perspective of a (rather vague) 'utopian realism' that is – as it were – aligned with an (equally vague) 'party of Utopia'. Again, political sympathies are not the point of contestation here. What is highly problematic and ultimately counterproductive is Martin's tactic of political denunciation. For instance, he accuses architectural theorist Michael Speaks of: 'championing the jargon and techniques associated with right-wing think tanks and the CIA',[48] without any further engagement with Speaks' arguments. Martin's politically motivated rejection of the architectural competition for the World Trade Center site led him to the following denunciation of all participating architects: 'By responding obediently to the call for architectural "vision" while remaining utterly blind to the violence of the package served up, these architects and others put themselves in a position of docile compliance with the imperatives of a nation at war.'[49] Special contempt was reserved for United Architects supposedly pandering to a 'kinder, gentler imperialism' and for 'switching sides in the ongoing culture wars'.[50] In another article Martin calls on architecture to 'refuse its assigned role in a vast coverup',[51] in parenthesis implying Frank Gehry's Bilbao museum as a paradigmatic example of such a cover-up role. What exactly is covered up here remains as obscure as how architecture could become revelatory instead. There is but one hint given: 'It would seek to make visible those deaths that occur on a daily basis in the name of sovereign "freedoms" and by way of fake plans (perhaps in the form of reverse memorials, monuments not to the past but to futures betrayed).'[52] Martin's revulsion at American "imperialism" might be a sentiment shared by many, but this is not the point here. That Martin's proposed example project operates in the domain of engaged art rather than architecture is indicative of an inherent problem within his position. However, this is not the primary point here either. The key point here is Martin's communicative dysfunction: his decision to bind his judgements within architecture to his revulsion against American "imperialism" is counterproductive in its impact on the autopoiesis of architecture. To theorize mainstream architecture as 'vast

48 Reinhold Martin, 'Critical of What? Toward a Utopian Realism', in: William S Saunders (Ed), *The New Architectural Pragmatism,* University of Minnesota Press (Minneapolis/London), 2007, p 151.

49 Ibid, p 157.

50 Ibid.

51 Reinhold Martin, 'Moment of Truth', in: *Log*, Vol 7, Winter/Spring 2006, Anyone Corporation, p 20.

52 Ibid, p 18.

coverup', and to denounce key protagonists of contemporary avant-garde architecture as operating from a position of 'docile compliance' disrupts rather than facilitates productive discourse in architecture.

9.4 The Limitations of Critical Practice in Architecture

THESIS 51

The vitality of architecture depends on its ability to register and address the political agendas empowered within the political system. Those forms of theoretical politics that can merely be desired or hoped for cannot become productive within architecture.

9.4.1 GENERAL POLITICAL CRITIQUE AND MACRO-POLITICAL AMBITIONS

Does architecture need to wait for external political challenges? Or can it try to anticipate political programmes before their real political power is manifest? Can architecture even actively contribute to the formation of such a political process? This seems to be the ambition of what is sometimes referred to as 'critical architecture'. However, within architecture, the engagement in political speculation must remain unproductive. Such speculative discourse – by its very nature – is extremely volatile. It must find its clues among the myriad of alternative political voices and try to enter such political debates. This is an interminable endeavour. Instead, architecture should be drawing relevant architectural conclusions from a real political movement that has already filtered and forged multiple perspectives into a coherent programme. Productive, politically oriented architectural research can come into play only after a political programme has reached hegemony on the basis of identifiable positions and collective decisions. In contrast, 'critical architecture' is eager to enter an open-ended, free-wheeling debate. In order to draw its architectural consequences it must somehow itself try to conclude this debate. Thus critical architecture must either operate within the political system, or substitute itself for the political system. The latter is what usually happens under the banner of critical architecture. Such a move fundamentally contradicts the principles of functionally differentiated society. The protagonists of critical architecture consume themselves in this substitution effort and hardly ever reach the point of formulating the architectural consequences of their political arguments. These efforts overburden the communicative capacities of the discipline and run up against an inherent complexity barrier. There is little hope that the 'critical architect' can deliver realistic and reliable anticipations of the global political potentials. The political process itself, ie, the vast range and extent of appropriately resourced communications within the political system, has to explore, filter and resolve such potentials. There can be no shortcut across this complexity barrier, nor any simulation or substitution that would be in any way credible. This is the fundamental reason why the efforts of a politicizing critical theory and practice within architecture must remain marginal. The marginal, and indeed untenable status of 'critical architecture' is further exacerbated by the fact that, by definition, its prospects of built realizations are highly precarious: critical architecture must rely on a clandestine subversion of the client's agenda.

Another reason for the precarious, marginal status of these critical architectural efforts is their inevitable tendency towards internal splintering. Arguments are not sufficiently constrained. Only an already formed political force would be able either to align or weed out and silence, all the possible trains of thought that might spring up within a debate. Politically oriented architectural thinking and design have no chance of reaching architectural hegemony without a firmly established political hegemony. Only unambiguous political facts on the ground can deliver sufficiently robust premises for architectural work to build a sufficiently coherent momentum to succeed. In the absence of a real political force, self-consumption and splintering imply a marginal existence. Critical architecture – as a small subset of the architectural avant-garde – can therefore hardly hope to usurp architectural hegemony. The architectural avant-garde as a whole can never indulge in such pursuits without self-dissolution. To the extent to which the architectural avant-garde moves into the critical mode, its very viability is threatened. Thereby architecture's vital ability to register and confront the real irritations, challenges and tasks that the real and effective political trends (rather than those that are merely desired and hoped for) represent to the ongoing autopoiesis of architecture would be threatened.

This much concerns the productivity of critical, macro-political debate within the autopoiesis of architecture. The result is largely negative. Macro-politics is debated and decided within its own proper domain, the autopoietic function system of politics. Architecture responds by taking up the democratically sanctioned political agendas as premises for its own specific societal responsibility: the framing of social communication. That's how far architecture's political agency stretches. It cannot substitute itself for the democratic political process.[53] It seems at this point, paradoxically, that in order to keep macro-political debate at bay

53 Does the refusal of such a substitution deserve the label of 'docile compliance'?

within the autopoiesis of architecture, the theory of architectural autopoiesis has to make its own implicit political premise explicit: the theory of architectural autopoiesis presupposes an affirmative orientation towards functional differentiation as primary mode of societal differentiation, and considers contemporary forms of representative democracy as the most advanced type of political communication system available today. This pointer is not more than this. It should certainly not be taken as invitation to engage the author in a political debate. Quite the opposite: those who want to debate architecture should keep their political convictions to themselves.

For those who think that the critical bottleneck of all further (architectural) progress is politics, the practical conclusion can only be to enter the political system. All political agendas must be pursued in the political system. This also applies to any politics concerning the built environment. Those who want to argue politics should enter politics proper.[54]

9.4.2 ARCHITECTURE'S 'MICRO-POLITICAL' AGENCY: MANIPULATING NON-POLITICAL POWER

How then do we theorize what has often been described in phrases like 'the socio-political potency ... of architectural possibility'.[55] There might be another notion of the political implied here. In recent years architectural theory has promoted the notion of micro-politics[56] as appropriate arena for 'architecture's political agency'. The notion seems to go back to Michel Foucault who had called for 'a plurality of autonomous struggles waged throughout the microlevels of society, in the prisons, asylums, hospitals, and schools. For a modern concept of macropolitics where clashing forces struggle for control over a centralized source of power rooted in the economy and state, Foucault substitutes a postmodern concept of micropolitics where numerous local groups contest diffuse and decentred forms of power spreading throughout society.'[57] It seems it is this notion of micro-politics and micro-power

54 This conclusion is coherent with the theory of functionally differentiated society. One might also interpret this statement as a modest political statement, a political statement backed by today's political consensus. It is consistent with the political system's due expectation within representative democracy, and it is both the first and the last political position offered within the theory of architectural autopoiesis.

55 David Cunningham, 'Architecture as Critical Knowledge', in: Jane Rendell et al (Eds), *Critical Architecture*, Routledge (London), 2007, p 32.

56 As will be clarified below what is often called 'micro-politics' is no real politics at all, ie, it does not belong to the political system. It should rather be termed 'micro-power'.

57 Steven Best & Douglas Kellner, *Postmodern Theory: Critical Interrogations*, Macmillan and Guilford Press (London/New York), 1991.

that is often implied when architects talk about the political dimension of architecture. It is also often the underlying understanding of 'politics' in the discussions concerning 'critical architecture'. In a recent article intended to reinvigorate architecture's 'effective political agency'[58] architect Alejandro Zaera-Polo raises the question: 'Political, social and economic factors shape architecture;[59] the question is whether architecture can in turn alter the distribution of power.'[60] Again, it seems that he refers to power and politics more in the sense of such micro-levels, rather than in the sense of big politics.

This so-called level of 'micro-politics' refers to the local, everyday power struggles in which urban spaces and buildings, as well as the territories and spaces within buildings (for example, work environments), are often so hotly contested pawns. To the extent that most of those power negotiations remain below the threshold of political visibility and are therefore not addressed within the political communication system, they are, according to our definition, non-political. There are many such forms of social power that resist or escape politicization.[61] Such forms of social power, and the often silent struggles that surround them, are not political at all, although, in principle, they could be drawn into the political arena (by properly equipped political agents). It is important to distinguish those forms of power that are made politically visible from those that are not. Even very small and local issues might become political within the proper arena of local democratic politics, including any local political protest that addresses itself to this arena. These protests are political issues because they are addressed within a political process that aims for resolution via collectively binding decision. If we distinguish like this there is indeed no need for any notion of 'micro-politics'. Instead, we should rather distinguish two types of social power: political power vs non-political power. However, since the notion of micro-politics is rather well established we maintain the usage here, albeit confined to the case of non-political power. Thus we can define

58 Alejandro Zaera-Polo, 'The Politics of the Envelope – A Political Critique of Materialism' *Volume*, Archis, 2008, #17.

59 Strictly speaking, Zaera-Polo's premise that political and economic factors *shape* architecture must be reformulated: neither the economy, nor the political system of society can shape architecture. Developments in these domains can only irritate architecture, which remains autonomous in its manner, means and timing of its adaptive responses.

60 Zaera-Polo, 'The Politics of the Envelope – A Political Critique of Materialism', p 80.

61 Total politicization of all forms of social power is an unattainable utopian dream. In this sense Luhmann's theory of functionally differentiated society opposes Foucault's idea that political progress can switch to a diffused mode of 'micro-politics' when the path forward in the arena of macro-politics lacks dynamic.

'micro-politics' as the negotiation of non-political social power.[62] The distinction between political power and non-political power is sharply defined, but it is not to be assumed that the extensions of the two categories are immutable. What is currently a non-political form of social power can be made political by making this form of power an issue within the political communication system. This possibility is obviously subject to cost-benefit estimates on the part of those who might consider such a move, as well as subject to the overall communicative capacity of the political system. After these clarifications we may formulate as follows: the fact is undeniable that there is, below the threshold of macro-political regulation of power within the political system, an urban 'micro-politics', a family 'micro-politics', the 'micro-politics' of the workplace etc, where the organization and articulation of space are a charged manifestation that often becomes the contested arena of (non-political) power distributions and power articulations.

9.4.3 WHO CONTROLS THE POWER-DISTRIBUTING CAPACITY OF DESIGN?

The organization and articulation of space are, according to the theory of architectural autopoiesis, the concrete task through which architecture fulfils its societal function: the framing of communicative interactions. The theory of architectural autopoiesis recognizes that this task of spatial organization and architectural articulation encompasses 'micro-politically' sensitive operations that are indeed able to constrain, facilitate, co-structure, or prestructure the distribution of (non-political) power within the occupying social communication system (client body) in question.

There can be no doubt about this power-distributing capacity of architectural design. However, it is important to clearly distinguish this capacity from the effective, communicative control over the employment of this capacity. It should be clear that it cannot be the architect's prerogative to determine what the 'micro-political' distribution of power within the accommodated social system should be. This is both an empirical fact and an eminently rational principle: the spatial 'micro-politics' of a social institution is a matter for the client, however constituted, to determine. Our general, contemporary ethos as professionals has internalized this principle. For an architect to force his 'micro-political' agenda on his client – public or private – is a wholly

62 Thus we are left with the unhappy notion of a 'micro-politics' that is by definition non-political. In order to handle this terminological monster, its usage is always marked with quotation marks.

unreasonable and inherently unacceptable imposition. However, the central idea of 'critical architecture' is precisely such an imposition. Mark Wigley, for instance, in an interview entitled 'Architectural Weaponry', states that 'we have not interrupted enough. We have reinforced patterns; we've not interrupted them'.[63] Of course, the architect might do as much critical 'interruption' as he can get away with without getting caught. In order to *argue* for such an interruption or imposition, the argument would have to go further and question the legitimacy of the client's control over his allocated social power. The issue would have to be politicized within the proper political arena. This would immediately expand the argument beyond the confines of the individual case into a generalized political contest that would be difficult to contain. Architecture would thus have to enter the arena of macro-politics, even on occasion of any 'micro-political' contest. The particular project in question would have to wait for these arguments to play out. The impossibility of such a scenario is obvious and explains why all this remains armchair speculation about vague notions of architecture's potential for 'progressive political agency' etc. Aware of this obvious problem, the armchair promoters of a critical architecture often seem to suggest clandestine operations instead. Another 'solution' for those whose urge to politicize seems irresistible would be to move on, as Alejandro Zaera-Polo suggested in an interview, a few years prior to his renewed passion for politicizing architecture from within architecture: 'My friends who became more involved in political action are no longer architects today. They became politicians or developers.'[64]

Within contemporary society a practice that tried to systematically pursue such a 'critical' pattern of imposition – whether by stealth or backed up by intimidating rhetoric – would be wholly unsustainable for any profession, or subsystem of societal communication. Every architectural design is subject to 'micro-political' readings and sensibilities of the kind Zaera-Polo identifies. However, the definition and control over this aspect must remain with the client. There is no expert knowledge involved in sensing 'micro-political' nuances that are – deliberately or inadvertently – expressed in the design of a building. The architect is expected to use his expertise to translate the client's desired sensibility into a spatial composition and morphology that elicits the sought-after effect. Indeed, I have yet to come across any practising

63 Mark Wigley, 'Architectural Weaponry', Interview, bldgblog.blogspot.com/2007/04/architectural-weaponry.

64 'Equipping the Architect for Today's Society: the Berlage Institute in the Educational Landscape – Dialogue between Wiel Arets and Alejandro Zaera-Polo', moderated by Roemer van Toorn, in: *hunch – the Berlage Institute Report*, No 6/7, 2003, chapter 'Architecture or Politics', p 34.

architect who would not be eager to detect and translate the client's 'micro-political' sensibilities. That is a systemic bias that is fully internalized within the professional ethos of the practising architect. How could it be otherwise? The immediately felt impossibility – if one could picture such a scenario – of succeeding with the imposition of an ideology that is alien or contrary to the client's self-image discourages any such attempts, even before they are formulated. This goes for competitions nearly as much as for direct commissions.

The universal truth of the practising architect's experience with clients is that – we just need to picture the scenario – the attempt to confront the client with a controversial political argument would spell instant self-destruction as both professional and person. It should follow logically that a scenario that projects a position of absolute social-communicative impossibility in the case of the concrete practice of the architect must be rejected in the domain of architectural theory. Architectural theory claims to guide architectural practice. Can an architectural theory that pushes architectural practice towards a strategy of oppositional political engagement contribute to the ongoing vitality of the autopoiesis of architecture? The answer is no! What is excluded within practice should not gain ground in theory.

The practising architect's role is to try to understand the client's intentions and expectations, also with respect to the client body's micro-political sensitivities, and to appropriately frame the respective social institution by translating its intentions via effective patterns of organization and articulation. His/her task is to utilize the organizational and articulatory resources that are being elaborated internally within architecture so that the framing is successful, assessed according to architecture's code of utility. Although the immediate criteria of *architectural* success are set and applied internally, within the autopoiesis of architecture, there are always external criteria of success that sooner or later produce a backlash if architecture's provisions fail to satisfy. This kind of backlash, which is very immediate for the practising architect who fails to satisfy fundamental expectations of his clients, will sooner or later become an impacting irritation for the discipline as a whole, if such experiences are recurring. In consequence of such recurring failings, the applied organizational and articulatory repertoire will be questioned within the autopoiesis of architecture. The issue must then be worked through with respect to the internal resource development of the discipline. Should this be a matter of fundamental reorientation – as was the case during the crisis of Modernism – the avant-garde segment of architecture is likely to shift from its problem-solving gear into a revolutionary gear. A period of fundamental questioning and competing paradigms ensues. Consolidation around one of the competing paradigms finally initiates a renewed process of style formation, updating both the programme for the code of beauty and the programme for the code of utility. The period of revolutionary questioning within the function system often coincides with rapid, and frequently confusing, changes in the societal environment. It is during these periods that political debate – to a certain extent – diffuses into and penetrates the various subsystems of society eager to grasp and adapt to the emerging conditions. It is during these revolutionary periods that the strictures against political speculation within the different function systems are loosened. These strictures might be loosened within the avant-garde segment of the discipline, while remaining intact with respect to mainstream practice.

For the client body, especially for the end-user, the 'micro-political' impact of a design is viscerally evident, sometimes very concretely as a frustration with an individual loss of position, with respect to specific threshold anxieties that certain architectural features produce, or only vaguely, in terms of the oppressive or uplifting atmosphere of the allocated spaces. The presence of 'political effects' is certainly not identified in the rarefied, speculative domain of a theoretical discourse. The risk for theoretical speculation to systematically mis-ascribe such effects might be significant without empirical, post-occupation studies. How the project operates 'micro-politically' is finally experienced within the ongoing social communication processes themselves.

The capacity to predict these effects requires the further build up of the analytic-predictive capacity of architectural theory. In the meantime, empathetic immersion into photorealistic renderings and animations might be a viable complement or substitute. After all, a sophisticated, contemporary social sensibility with respect to the distribution of social power should be a universal capacity of all subjects navigating the contemporary social world. Perhaps, especially on this aspect of 'micro-political' sensitivity, intuitive judgement might for a long time be a more reliable guide than any theoretical apparatus. However, empathetic immersion into renderings can only guide the designer, together with a sufficiently intimate knowledge of the client's social constitution and communication patterns. It can only complement, but not substitute for, such knowledge.

9.4.4 PUBLIC COMPETITIONS AS STRUCTURAL COUPLING BETWEEN ARCHITECTURE AND POLITICS

Theoretically at least, public competitions – with politicians usually as members of the jury – are an opportunity for critical architects to present 'micro-politically' charged designs. There is even the theoretical opportunity to go further by trying to make the involved social power negotiations politically visible. It is at these rare moments that Mark Wigley's high-spirited invocation of the architect as public intellectual might become a plausible scenario:

> Architecture is a set of endlessly absorbing questions for our society rather than a set of clearly defined objects with particular effects. Architects are public intellectuals, crafting forms that allow others to see the world differently and perhaps to live differently. The real gift of the best architects is to produce a kind of hesitation in the routines of contemporary life, an opening in which new potentials are offered, new patterns, rhythms, moods, sensations, pleasures, connections, and perceptions. The architect's buildings are placed in the city like the books of a thoughtful novelist might be placed in a newsstand in a railway station, embedding the possibility of a rewarding detour amongst all the routines, a seemingly minor detour that might ultimately change the meaning of everything else. The architect crafts an invitation to think and act differently.[65]

While this kind of transformative engagement – which might very well also include the critical, politicizing engagement with hitherto non-political 'micro-political' routines – might indeed be posited as worthy aspiration for architecture, it must in all probability remain a rather rarefied occasion within the global autopoiesis of architecture. Rem Koolhaas' (unsuccessful) contribution to the MoMA competition of 2002 might have been such a rare moment. Zaha Hadid Architect's 2001 winning competition scheme for the One-North Masterplan in Singapore might perhaps be construed as a further such moment.

The institution of public architectural competitions, now a globally recognized mechanism for soliciting and selecting architectural solutions for public projects, is as old as the autopoiesis of architecture itself. Architectural competitions date back to Ancient Greece and were common during the Renaissance. For instance, the competition announced in 1418 for the Dome of Florence was a totally open, public competition inviting 'whoever desires to make any model or design'.[66] Shortly after the French Revolution, architectural competitions were organized by the Comité de Salut Public (Committee of Public Safety) for a triumphal arch, a Temple of Equality, a primary assembly, a public bath etc. According to Sigfried Giedion, the 1927 international competition for the League of Nations Palace at Geneva was of particular importance

65 Mark Wigley, 'The Future of the Architect', Dean's Statement, website of GSAPP, Columbia University.

66 Quoted after Ross King, *Brunelleschi's Dome: How a Renaissance Genius Reinvented Architecture*, Vintage Random House (London), 2008.

for the breakthrough of Modern architecture, because 'it unexpectedly forced high officials from everywhere in Europe to consider seriously a kind of architecture which they had always dismissed as aesthetic trifling'.[67] The significance of the public competition system as platform to launch and test architectural innovations has been growing ever since.

Within the systematic, conceptual scheme that the theory of architectural autopoiesis elaborates, on the back of Niklas Luhmann's general theory of social systems, we can identify the global institution of public architectural competitions as the dedicated mechanism that has been differentiated for the ***structural coupling*** of the autopoietic function systems of architecture and politics. This mechanism has been operative ever since the respective function systems were differentiated during the Italian Renaissance, at the dawn of modernity, in line with the general shift from stratification to functional differentiation as the primary mode of societal differentiation.

As dedicated mechanism for the structural coupling between the two domains of architecture and politics, public architectural competitions are a primary avenue for the autopoiesis of architecture to irritate the political system.

This institutionalized platform of the public competition is the only mechanism by which architects could, legitimately and effectively, launch a provocative initiative, open up a critical, alternative perspective upon certain public institutions, or even politicize aspects of such institutions that are usually taken for granted. Here, and only here, the theory of architectural autopoiesis is thus recognizing and appreciating the possibility of a politically (or 'micro-politically') transformative intervention. Public competitions are the only viable vehicles for such pursuits.

However, this possibility only concerns the opportunity to launch such communications. With respect to the potential content of such critical initiatives, everything said earlier about the inherent constraints on making oppositional political agendas topical within architecture remains valid. This, of course, cannot prevent determined and politically minded individual architects from launching their critical projects. Competitions are constituted as a forum where such ideas might be tested, and a politicization could be provoked. However, such individuals should not expect the autopoiesis of architecture to be able to engage with the political agenda of the project. Also, this window of critical opportunity that is given with this institutionalized mechanism of structural coupling

67 Sigfried Giedion, *Space, Time and Architecture – The Growth of a New Tradition*, 5th edition, Harvard University Press (Cambridge, MA), 1967, p 430.

cannot be sustained if it were ever to be pushed too much as a one-way street for tendentious critique. Obviously, this danger is not imminent – quite the opposite – but some authors write as if architecture is only worth as much as its critical edge, and that all architecture worth its name must be dedicated to a radical, political or 'micro-political' critique, and everything else is to be written off as 'docile compliance'.

The significance of public architectural competitions is broader than offering architecture an opening for politicizing critique. The agenda of tendentious critique cannot be the primary function of this institution. Its primary purpose is to test the general adaptive up-to-dateness and in-tuneness of the current avant-gardist design research by sharing an institutionalized forum of discussion with the empowered representatives of the political system, from the municipal to the national level. It is from the ranks of architects that most members and the head of the jury are recruited. Architects are also being commissioned to write the competition brief in collaboration with the respectively empowered political authorities. This mechanism of structural coupling will only be able to sustain itself and expand if it remains a two-way mechanism that allows the political system to observe and participate in the deliberations concerning the selection of the politically most significant architectural manifestations within society. The initial setting of the project agenda originates within the political system. Its articulation into a workable competition brief is prepared by architects and approved by the political representatives. The shortlisting of competitors is usually a negotiation between the system of current architectural reputations as it emerges from within the autopoiesis of architecture on the one side, and the system of public architectural reputations that has escaped internal architectural control on the other. The presentations to the jury, the jury deliberations and the final decision-making process constitute a specialized platform of discursive interchange between the two systems. On most public juries in Europe, the architects on the jury can usually assert their leadership, playing on their expert authority, albeit not without being sensitive to the core concerns of the political clients.

The competing projects need to be spoken for, but to a certain extent a compelling project is able to speak for itself in architectural competitions. Thus public architectural competitions represent a unique platform for architecture's own, unique, non-discursive form of social speculation.

There is also potential to build up a collective force here. For instance, if most of the contributions to an important public competition are working in the same emerging style, then the new style is prone to claim victory, usurp the occasion and attract public attention. This opportunity that a collective thrust might be brought to bear on a competition theoretically also includes the (far-fetched) possibility of a general usurpation of a public project by a unified political front of all participating architects, if such a front could ever be constructed. What is much more likely is that oppositional or critical intentions might become a mildly transformative layer articulating 'micro-political' nuances of a particular public project, rather than initiating a revolution in public sensibility.

The prospect of transformative nuances being grafted onto certain focal buildings, effecting slight 'détournements', punctuations, hesitations and mild interruptions of habitual routines revealing latent 'micro-political' tensions, even daring to project subtle alternatives, and hoping to create a clearing for emancipatory communications, to initiate a progressive becoming etc etc, in the vein outlined above by Mark Wigley, and called for by Roemer van Toorn, Alejandro Zaera-Polo and many others, might indeed be the most appropriate form of political or 'micro-political' agency that can be legitimately and effectively pursued via the public competition system, and most probably *only* via this very special mechanism of structural coupling. The pursuit of such strategies might indeed 'animate architecture as an instrument of social and political invention', it might even be considered the spice of architectural life, if convincing examples where such strategies are succeeding in built form could finally be put forward. (The author remains rather sceptical in this respect.) The ability to interpret built projects as successes with respect to such strategies constitutes a necessary touchstone for the credibility of this whole approach. It is to Roemer van Toorn's credit that he tried to deliver on this expectation. His touchstone architectural project – offered in parallel to the movie *Festen* by Thomas Vinterberg – is OMA's competition-winning public museum, the Rotterdam *Kunsthal.* It is convenient that virtually every active participant within the autopoiesis of architecture (and thus every potential reader) has a first-hand experience of this building. Here is Roemer van Toorn's account in condensed form:

> The Kunsthal by Rem Koolhaas in Rotterdam . . . enables different conventional positions of the museum to confront each other in an open manner full of antagonism. The policy of the 'neutral' exhibition room . . . is foiled in many ways in this art gallery. In different places in the building all sorts of programmes meet. The monumental entry, common to most museums, is replaced by a cross passage that relates everything and everyone in an unexpected manner and releases one repeatedly from a preoccupied perspective. The museum and the city constantly move

> alongside each other. ... It is the opposite of the museum as a temple ... Koolhaas breaks the autonomy of the neutral isolated exhibition rooms. The work of art and the public sphere confront each other as an open work ... In order to be liberated, the development of a progressive becoming can only occur when there is still a certain stammering or alienation present in the positioning or interpretation of the specific programme. ... To activate progression one must build a deliberate absurdity or friction ...The tree as a column introduces such a 'détournement' ... The white box concept is consciously broken and provided with comment ... unmasking meaning systems without exploding or denying them ... provoked by an absurd aesthetic intervention you can never fully comprehend. ...The Kunsthal tries to communicate with banal middle class culture ... Commodification is clearly the basic condition here for creating a deeper social value. The margin is not sought to locate resistance; instead the museum is put right in the middle of our pleasure museum culture ... it seeks to activate another creative potential right in the middle of the mesh, in coexistence with mass culture. It makes clear that the old notion of critical distance is outmoded, even impossible. ... The walkway breaks the museum open and the exhibition and lecture space relates to the city ... Koolhaas uses the technique of displacement and alienation to provoke the speechless to speak again. The Kunsthal thus frames a politics of speechlessness. ... The Kunsthal communicates with the masses and creates dialogical conditions within the mesh of the multitude. ... Koolhaas creates a genuine two-way street and feedback ... the contradictions from within everyday (banal) society allow and energize other voices ...[68]

It will have to be left to each reader to consult van Toorn's full text and to assess how much these descriptions and ascriptions convince and retrospectively resonate with everybody's individual experience and memory of the building in question, and to what extent this kind of 'micro-political' engagement satisfies or whets the reader's appetite for 'political' architecture.

The theory of architectural autopoiesis can leave these questions for the reader to answer, because this kind of critical spice is not the primary task and *raison d'être* by which the autopoiesis of architecture – one of the great function systems of society – sustains itself. Architecture's societal function – the provision of the necessary ordering and articulating spatial frames of social communication – is discharged by the construction of types (for example, white box) rather than by their deconstruction, by the placement of ordering distinctions rather than by their displacement, by achieving smooth operation rather than friction, by

68 Toorn, 'Dirty Details', pp 77–93.

the facilitation of routines rather than via their interruption, by the establishment of adjacency-expectations rather than by confronting users with the unexpected, by elaborating rather than unmasking meaning systems, by achieving identification rather than alienation, by framing the stage for those able and empowered to speak rather than by prompting the speechless etc etc.

My emphasis on construction rather than deconstruction does not imply a dismissive attitude towards the intentions of contributors (Wigley, van Toorn, among others) who are searching for architecture's agency along critical lines. The theory of architectural autopoiesis is taking account of this contribution as much as it is taking account of the contributions of other factions such as the devout Formalists (Eisenman, Kipnis, among others) who are focusing on innovating architecture's formal repertoire, and those who upgrade architecture's medium (Lynn, Spuybroek, among others), or those who seek to upgrade architecture's analytic rigour (Steadman, Hillier, among others), and finally those who synthesize all these parallel researches in their projects (OMA, ZHA among others). Critical deconstruction can indeed play a role in architectural innovation, via the initiation of productive mutations, but it can never carry the weight of architecture's societal responsibility.

10. The Self-descriptions of Architecture

All function systems must reflect their own constitution and societal function in order effectively to steer themselves in the absence of authoritative directives from outside. Theoretical self-descriptions facilitate this necessary reflection. As one of the great, autopoietic function systems of modern, functionally differentiated world society, the autopoiesis of architecture must continue to reflect its own unity and guide its own development by means of updated, sufficiently complex self-descriptions.

Comprehensive theoretical treatises are the most adequate form this necessary reflection should take. In what follows, three key treatises that have been seminal in the historical evolution of architecture's autopoiesis have been selected and subjected to a detailed, parallel analysis: Alberti's treatise from 1485,[1] Durand's treatise of 1802–5, and Le Corbusier's treatise from 1923. These treatises are confident, comprehensive accounts of the discipline, each reflecting architecture's societal function and arguing for certain principles, methods and repertoires that should guide the discipline in discharging its function. Each of these texts has been seminal in inaugurating or representing one of the epochal styles of architecture: the Renaissance, Neo-Classicism and Modernism respectively. The analysis of these three texts has been structured by the conceptual grid that underlies and organizes *The Autopoiesis of Architecture* itself, thus directly confronting the theory of architectural autopoiesis with these prior attempts at providing architecture with an authoritative self-description. Here then arises another occasion of autological self-inclusion for the theory of architectural autopoiesis: an occasion for the theory to analyze and historicize itself as an attempt to provide architecture once more with an authoritative self-description, this time expounding the emerging epochal style of Parametricism.

1 Alberti's *De re aedificatoria* was written in 1450. It first circulated as a hand-copied manuscript and was then published in 1485 as the first printed book on architecture.

10.1 Theoretical Underpinnings

THESIS 52

Architecture, as a self-reflective system of communications, is trying to steer itself via theoretical self-descriptions that attempt to theorize and define architecture's role within society. The complexity and sophistication of the contemporary societal environment demand increasingly complex and sophisticated architectural self-explications. Convincing autological self-inclusion is now one of the indispensable conditions that any serious candidate for architectural self-description must fulfil.

The necessity for architectural theory has already been presented at the beginning of this book.[2] There it was stated that the primary function of architectural theory is to compensate for the lost certainty of tradition. In the case of traditional building, the appropriateness and functionality of buildings – the accommodating and *framing* capacity – were guaranteed by the fact that the new buildings consisted in nothing but the faithful repetition of long evolved and surreptitiously corroborated models. Under conditions of innovative architecture, architectural theory had to step in to assure and convince both the architect and his clients that beauty and utility were maintained and even enhanced despite the novelty of the proposal.

All that is required to postulate the necessity of architectural theory is the demonstration that it functions as a means of communicating potentially innovative deviations from traditional practice. To ascertain the necessity of theory, it is not even necessary to assume that architectural theory had evolved a real, effective problem-solving capacity, since it might fulfil its task of persuasion by whatever means necessary, by appeals to cosmic order, or even by arguing that the proposed deviations are in fact deeply rooted in tradition. Thus the theory of architectural autopoiesis distinguishes a *communicative* or *rhetorical function* and a *problem-solving function* of architectural theory. With respect to the problem-solving function, the theory in turn distinguishes ***problematizing theories***, ***generative theories*** and ***analytic theories***, in reference to the difference between problem statement, the generation of potential solutions and the informed selection of solutions, and as distinct from merely rhetorical theories.

At the advanced stage of the theory that has been reached here, it is time explicitly to reflect a further function of architectural theory: the function of providing architecture with a comprehensive ***self-description***

2 See Volume 1, chapter 1.3.1 *The Function of Architectural Theory.*

that allows architecture to observe, navigate and reflectively adjust its position and role within society. Architectural theories that fulfil this function might be termed ***reflection theories*** or ***reflective self-descriptions.*** Architecture, like all the great function systems of society, has entertained such self-descriptions or reflection theories throughout its 500 year history.

The various architectural self-descriptions that have come to prominence during the history of architecture might be classified as follows:

- *Humanist self-descriptions* presume to find the essential purposes of architecture enfolded in the nature of man and see the task of architecture as to serve and perfect man's natural constitution.
- *Modernist self-descriptions* identify the task of architecture within a presumably objective account of mankind's progressive development or *modernization.*
- *Post-Structuralist self-descriptions* presume that architecture's purposes are a matter of its own discursive self-definition, often formulated as critique of society's wider discursive formation.
- *The evolutionist-constructivist self-description* – the description proposed here, within *The Autopoiesis of Architecture* – understands architecture's purposes to be the result of architecture's continuous, adaptive self-steering, via its very self-descriptions, within the coevolution of society's functionally differentiated subsystems.

The theory of architectural autopoiesis thus offers *itself* as a reflection theory and comprehensive self-description of architecture. It establishes an evolutionist-constructivist self-description of architecture. The theory of architectural autopoiesis defines itself as a ***domain specific super-theory***[3] and thus locates itself *within* the autopoiesis of architecture. Full autological self-inclusion is a turn of reflection that goes beyond what one might traditionally have expected from an architectural self-description, although – as we shall see below – a certain level of self-reflectiveness can be found in earlier theoretical accounts of architecture. However, autological self-inclusion, and thus critical self-probing, is becoming a theoretical necessity in an era where the diversity of theoretical perspectives – not only within architecture but society wide – has made meta-theoretical loops of reflection a necessary commonplace. Meta-theoretical reflections concern themselves with prior, philosophical and methodological premises. They engage in

3 See Volume 1, chapter 1.3.5 *The Theory of Architectural Autopoiesis as Domain-specific Super-theory.*

controversy with alternative methodologies and philosophical perspectives. However, it is the conviction of the author that foundational arguments cannot arbitrate the contest between divergent perspectives. Ultimately, it can only be the richness and coherence of the results of a theory that set the scene for the contest. One aspect of this contest must be the ability of the respective theory to theorize and historicize itself within its own account of architecture. The test of autological self-inclusion and self-historicization is to be posed as a necessary test for any contemporary contender for a pertinent self-description. A theory that cannot adequately theorize its own role, and the conditions of its efficacy, can no longer convince, and should be struck off the list of relevant contenders. For instance, theories that emphasize the return to straightforward performance issues should be disqualified because they implicitly reject the need for a platform for the critical investigation and continuous re-statement of the conceptual, formal and medial conditions of architecture's performative efficacy.

Further, theories without a self-conception within the historical lineage of architectural theory must be disqualified. Without historical self-location, no architectural theory can count as pertinent self-description of architecture. However, when the history of architectural theory is explicitly reflected and the respective self-description includes itself within its story, paradoxes might arise that disqualify the respective account. This is, for instance, the case with the 'phenomenological' approach to the self-explication of architecture, exemplified in the architectural theory of Christian Norberg-Schulz. Norberg-Schulz fails to distinguish architecture from vernacular building and suggests that architecture is the art of place making within the life-world. Norberg-Schulz does indeed place his own theory within a historical summary of architectural theory since Vitruvius. However, for Norberg-Schulz, most historical, architectural theory indexes a progressive alienation of architecture from the world of life. For instance, Durand's Neo-Classicist theory of composition is characterized as 'formalistic atomism'[4] with 'no roots in the world of life',[5] and Modernism, although initially with the good intention to design for life, fails due to the prevailing 'spirit of abstraction and quantification'.[6] With respect to more recent architecture, Norberg-Schulz states that 'many architects fell victim to the deterioration of the profession, with the

4 Christian Norberg-Schulz, *Architecture: Presence, Language, Place*, Skira Editore (Milan), 2000, p 24.

5 Ibid.

6 Ibid, p 26.

proliferation of many new "isms" ... culminating in "deconstructionism", as a nihilistic negation of all meaning.'[7] In contrast, Norberg-Schulz's own 'phenomenological method for understanding architecture'[8] leads to the proselytizing call 'of returning to the basic structures of the world of life'.[9] His whole enterprise is a nostalgic battle against an ongoing, alienating process whereby 'places have lost and continue to lose their identity, both in terms of demarcation and character'.[10] The approach holds fast to the concept of place, trying to reverse these inevitable developments (instead of adapting architecture's conceptual and formal repertoire to operate productively beyond clear demarcation and unitary character). The phenomenological method is intended as 'a tool with which to penetrate into an understanding of place'.[11] Norberg-Schulz's account of architecture, just like Christopher Alexander's, proposes vernacular building as architecture's lost ideal. Architectural theory is seen to be implicated in this loss. Thus, the phenomenological theory of architecture is conceptualizing itself as undoing the alienation wrought by architectural theory. Paradoxically, more theory is posited to eliminate the effects of theory. This 'phenomenological' conception of architecture suffers from being grossly ahistorical, despite its engagement with traditional building, historical architecture and architectural theory. A theory of architecture that regards most of the discipline's achievements as forms of deterioration surely cannot grasp the adaptive progress within the discipline's history, and thus fails to grasp the rationality of the real. And moreover, in undermining not only all prior architectural theory but also the very institution of guiding architecture via rational theorizing, the theories undermine and annihilate themselves.

The historical account that the theory of architectural autopoiesis offers could not be further removed from such ahistorical pessimism. The theory of architectural autopoiesis places itself within the historical lineage of architectural theory understood positively as a crucial component within the discipline's adaptive (and exaptive) progress. At the end of this part, the theory of architectural autopoiesis will re-present itself as a new, condensed self-description of architecture, as a (temporary) point of culmination in the ongoing, historical chain of successive self-descriptions. The autological structure of the theory of architectural autopoiesis will thus, once more, be made evident and productive.

7 Ibid, p 9.
8 Ibid, p 26.
9 Ibid, p 27.
10 Ibid, p 31.
11 Ibid, p 61.

10.1.1 REFERENCE AS SELF-REFERENCE

The notion of reflective self-descriptions as moments within the autopoiesis of advanced social systems is a rather specific concept that Niklas Luhmann has defined within an intricate network of related distinctions. Like all of Luhmann's key concepts that have been utilized here, the general concept of the reflective self-description of a social system allows us to compare the architectural instances of this concept with instances that Luhmann has elaborated in connection with his analyses of the other great function systems of modern society.

The concept of reflective self-description is systematically embedded within an encompassing, general theory of social system. Luhmann's fundamental premise is that all social systems are self-referentially closed systems of communication. A reflective self-description is a special, advanced form of self-reference. It is important to remember here that Luhmann deliberately avoids talking about mental operations and focuses on observable communications instead – although he does not deny the underlying necessity of psychic systems and their internal operations. Communicative operations include gestures, drawings, verbal or written communications, as well as all forms of electronically supported communications. Referencing is a basic function of all communicative operations. References indicate something according to an assumed distinction. The utilized distinction is an emergent product that results from prior communications. Thus references can only emerge within a nexus or network of related communications that, in this sense, require each other and refer to each other. Individual communications cannot, by themselves, refer to something out there in the world. Neither can they, by themselves, in isolation, refer to themselves. They are never self-sufficient. They always rely on connections to prior as well as later follow-on communications. Communications are connected via relations of *anticipatory recursivity*.[12] Such relations are constitutive of the very meaning of each communication.[13] In this sense we can say that all communication, and thus all reference, is self-referential, namely in the sense all communications refer back to communications. Luhmann calls this basic condition *basal self-reference*. By basal self-reference what is implied here is not 'pure' self-reference whereby a single communication

12 Niklas Luhmann, *Social Systems*, Stanford University Press (Stanford, CA), 1995, p 447.

13 Luhmann gives the following example: 'A man offers a woman his seat on a crowded bus: part of the meaning of this action, part of it being a correct and successful action, is being rewarded and confirmed by the woman's taking the seat. (One can check this by imagining a deviant course of events: the woman does not accept the seat but puts her handbag on it!) The appropriate, expected consecutive action also belongs to the meaning of the action; finally the woman can now sit down.' Luhmann, *Social Systems*, p 446.

refers to itself as in 'this sentence contains five words'. The concept of basal self-reference indicates the general, basic condition that *all* communications rely on and refer back (and forward) to their own kind: to prior and further communications. More specifically, under enhanced communicative conditions sustained by a sufficiently complex language, a specific communication, for example, an elaborate argument, might, during its extended course, refer back to itself. This is still different from the above example whereby a single communication exclusively refers to itself and to nothing else. Rather, a certain part of a long communication refers to itself, and reflects an aspect of itself, for example, intercepting itself with the proviso that the argument is to be taken as no more than a tentative proposal. This moment of self-reference occurs while the communication primarily refers to matters beyond itself. 'The self-reference needed for autopoiesis is only *accompanying self-reference.*'[14] Luhmann calls this the 'theorem of accompanying self-reference'.[15] Accompanying self-reference whereby communications frame, limit, further clarify, or apologize for themselves is a ubiquitous phenomenon in many forms of social communication. However, to understand the specific status and significance of architectural self-descriptions as an advanced and ambitious form of self-reference we have to follow Luhmann in distinguishing different levels of (accompanying) self-reference.

10.1.2 LEVELS OF SELF-REFERENCE

Every enduring social system stabilizes and guides itself by giving itself a name to describe and distinguish itself explicitly.[16] As explicated earlier,[17] every social system distinguishes self-reference and world-reference. The distinction of form (the architectural artefact) vs function (the accommodated social institution) is the distinction of self-reference vs world-reference. It is also the distinction of the system (architecture) versus its environment (society) as it is processed *within* the system of architectural communications. Every stable, complex social system requires and achieves such a 're-entry'[18] of the

14 Luhmann, *Social Systems*, p 446.

15 Ibid, p 447.

16 One might refer to Émile Durkheim's study of Totemism as presenting the most simple, precarious/unstable social formations known, ie, the clan structures of Australia.

17 See Volume 1, chapter 3.4.3 *The Double Reference of the Design Disciplines.*

18 Luhmann picked up this theoretical figure of 're-entry' from the mathematician George Spencer-Brown. See: George Spencer-Brown, *Laws of Form*, Allen & Unwin (London), 1969. Re-entry implies that a distinction is (re-)applied to one of the two terms distinguished. Luhmann's use of the concept here focuses on the fact that systems operationally distinguish

system/environment distinction within the system. This kind of self-reference *on the level of the system* is a special, advanced form of general, communicative self-reference. Luhmann calls this system-level of self-reference *reflection,*[19] or reflectivity. Reflectivity is the most ambitious of the three levels of self-reference that Luhmann distinguishes.

Luhmann's general theory of social systems distinguishes three forms of self-reference: ***recursivity*** (***basal self-reference***), ***reflexivity*** and ***reflection*** (or reflectivity). Recursivity refers to connected *operations*, reflexivity refers back to the specific encompassing communication *process*, and reflection refers to the *system*. The principle of distinction – the unity of the distinction – here is the question of which of the following three *further* distinctions determines the 'self' of self-reference: the distinction between *element and relation*, the distinction between *before and after* in a process, or the distinction between *system and environment.* The distinction between the three levels of self-reference might be further elaborated as follows:

Recursivity: Recursivity, or basal self-reference, is defined by Luhmann as the form of self-reference whereby the communication (the 'self') that is referred to is an elemental communication that is identified and distinguished as one element (operation) in relation to other elemental communications. Social systems operate ***recursively*** – every elemental communication *connects* to others. Connection involves selection among options. This selection must be in some way consistent with the prior communication that the new communication connects to, for instance, it must continue in the same mode, for instance the mode of argument, and focus on the same topic. It thus demonstrates understanding and confirms aspects of the prior communication. In this sense, Luhmann uses the term self-reference in connection with recursivity as the most basic form of 'self'-reference that is presupposed in all communication: ***basal self-reference*** here means reference to another, similar communication, as distinct from the simultaneous reference to the event or

themselves and maintain their distinctness within their environment. The reflective operation of the system recognizing and communicating its identity in differentiation from its environment becomes a necessary stabilizing moment within the system's capacity to maintain its identity/distinctiveness.

19 Luhmann, *Social Systems*, pp 442–8.

object that is being talked about. In this sense basal self-reference is only an accompanying self-reference. 'Basal self-reference is the minimal form of self-reference, without which autopoietic reproduction of temporalized systems would be impossible.'[20] This self-referentiality, as exact opposite of self-sufficiency, has already been demonstrated above with respect to architectural drawings and digital models.[21] This participation in (or reliance upon) related elemental communications is always implicit. They become explicit in explicitly self-referential communications such as 'I did not say this, but that ...' etc. The possibility of communicating about communication resides in and always accompanies communication, regardless of whether one resorts to it or not.[22]

Reflexivity: In addition to this basal self-reference (that is always presupposed) communications might be ***reflexive***, ie, sometimes certain communications explicitly thematize/problematize other communications as being part of and regulated by a certain communication process or episode. All communications are communications within a specific communicative process. The social communication process monitors and steers itself via explicit, reflexive self-reference. Reflexive communications might be used to remind the participants of a communication episode, for instance a debate, about the theme of the debate, or within a design process about the particular aim of the particular design session. Reflexive self-reference, or reflexivity, always refers to the process within which the respective reflexive communication is embedded. This might be a single operation like 'stay with the topic', or it might extend to an intermediate process that undertakes to 're-introduce the process into the process'.[23] Such reflexive processes are sometimes especially differentiated for this function. For instance, within a disintegrating design session, a whole intermediate discussion trying to clarify the aim of the

20 Ibid, p 443.

21 See Volume 1, part 4, *The Medium of Architecture*, in particular in section 4.1.6 *Recursive Self-reference*.

22 Luhmann, *Social Systems*, p 446.

23 Ibid, p 451.

design session might have to be inserted before going on with the design session proper. Reflexivity 'gives the unity of the process value within the process'.[24] *Reflexivity* is the form of self-reference whereby the implied 'self' is the ongoing communication *process* – constituted by the distinction of before and after – within which the respective communication is embedded. Reflexivity is thus achieved when within 'the course of a communicative process one can communicate about that communicative process'.[25] Luhmann therefore also talks about 'processual self-reference'.[26] Reflexivity enables communication processes to guide and control themselves. This possibility is not always to be taken for granted. For a communication to be reflexive it has to remain embedded within and continue the process it tries to refer to. It therefore must adhere to (rather than disrupt) the respective conditions of process continuity. While every parliamentary debate is full of process-oriented self-references, within a church service such reflexivity is unattainable. Ritualization, as well as routinization, is the antidote of reflexivity. However, nothing stands in the way of architectural design processes to achieve full reflexivity. Mainstream design routines would be disrupted and therefore avoid reflexivity. But avant-garde processes tend to be inherently reflexive. The contemporary autopoiesis of architecture offers manifold conceptual resources that support design process reflexivity, and a high level of reflexivity or processual self-reference has been a hallmark especially of recent avant-garde design processes.[27]

Reflectivity: Over and above reflexivity, social systems tend to be ***reflective***, ie, they refer to their own ***unity*** on the level of the system as the whole. ***Reflection*** (reflectivity) is the form of self-reference whereby the implied 'self' is the communication *system* within which the reflective communication is located. 'Only in reflection does self-reference exhibit the characteristics of system

24 Ibid.

25 Ibid, p 443.

26 Ibid.

27 Permanent self-evaluation and self-criticism concerning the design process as a whole, in its global characteristics as a process, are particularly pronounced in the design studios of most advanced architectural schools.

reference. . . . The self is the system to which the self-referential operation attributes itself. It is an operation by which the system indicates itself in contrast to its environment.'[28] The underlying distinction that allows the reflective identification of the system from within the system is thus the distinction between system and environment. Luhmann speaks of a higher layer of control that is attained when social systems orient themselves to themselves as different from their environments.[29] The surest indication that a social system has attained a reflective capacity is that it has given itself a name by which it can refer to itself as distinct from its environment and the other systems in its environment. Clans and families are an obvious example. For instance, the use of a family name guides and demarcates communications as family communications. The same goes for all modern organizations like business firms or political parties. Scheduled social events that are announced are another category of examples. However, this special form of self-reference is neither required nor can it be expected from every social system. Many casual interaction systems like pub conversations or tourist groups constitute self-referentially closed systems without reaching the moment of reflection. (Spatial co-presence can sometimes function as functional equivalent for the self-reflective efforts of boundary maintenance. Framing architectures are effective in this way.) Friendships are self-referential systems of communication that sometimes continue without either spatial frame or built-in reflection. Conflicts represent another category of social system that often continue without reaching reflection. A conflict or an undeclared friendship without reflection leaves its continuation and developmental trajectory to chance. Outside chance conditionings might strongly impact upon such systems where the latent double contingency of all communication is not controlled by reflection. In contrast to the volatility of chance determinations, reflection stabilizes. The use of the term 'architecture' regulates and demarcates architectural communications within the

28 Ibid, p 444.
29 Ibid, p 455.

social communication system of architecture, via interventions such as '*this budgetary argument has nothing to do with architecture*' or '*an architecturally ambitious project cannot afford to ignore the question of originality*'. Reflection is thus used to demarcate the communication system and to steer communication via reminders about the essential, defining communication structures of the system in question.

To summarize: Luhmann distinguishes three levels of self-reference. These levels of self-reference – recursivity, reflexivity and reflectivity – are correlated to individual communications, communication processes and communication systems:

- Recursivity involves basal self-reference on the level of operations as general condition of all communication. Individual communications connect to further (prior or later) communications.
- Reflexivity denotes the self-reference of the communication process, ie, reflexivity is instantiated where the ongoing communication process refers back to itself as process.
- Reflectivity involves reflection upon the unity and demarcation of the specific autopoietic system in question.

Recursion is always presupposed, but we cannot take the possibilities of reflexive and reflective self-reference for granted.

Reflexivity is a special performance that is only possible under certain conditions (sufficient communicative complexity) and that are only required under certain circumstances. The need for reflexive episodes, increases with the level of ambition of a communication process. It also increases in line with the degree of innovation that is expected and embarked upon. Thus we should expect that the level of reflexivity increases historically, and that this levels is much higher within the avant-garde than in the mainstream segment of the architectural autopoiesis.

Architecture is a self-reflective system of communications that, at any time, is able to reflect (communicate about) itself as a unitary discourse or *system* of communications.[30] Reflectivity facilitates adaptive innovation, in dialectic interplay with the stabilization of a coherent identity. Reflectivity is also an important moment in the consolidation of

30 It is interesting to note here that if one observes this most advanced form of self-reference, ie, the occurrence of statements such as '*the essence of architecture is. . ., true architecture requires. . ., this is a milestone within the history of architecture, because . . .*' etc, one usually observes the oscillation between functional and formal concerns.

an avant-garde movement leading to the formation of a new style. To succeed a style has to give itself a name and reflect its distinctiveness within a competitive environment. (That motivates the term 'active-reflective styles'.)

10.2 The Necessity of Reflection: Architectural Theory as Reflection Theory

THESIS 53

Like all other great function systems, architecture tries to unify and orient itself via self-descriptions that reflect/define its *raison d'être* and identify/define its tasks within its societal environment. Although necessary, these self-descriptions, like all descriptions, are fallible and risky self-simplifications. The fact that these descriptions might become influential, and thus might indeed seem to shape the reality of what they describe, does not vitiate the prior fact that the reality of architecture's autopoiesis always already exceeds its simplified descriptions.

Self-descriptions are a special, elaborate form of re-usable system-reflection, ie, a semantic artefact that indicates the system's unity and to which further communications can repeatedly refer. Such self-descriptions are only possible on the basis of writing. Self-descriptions 'can be performed orally, but this presupposes a textual model developed on the basis of writing, in particular, long, disciplined texts whose understanding is largely independent of the situation. When in the context of such self-descriptions the participants speak of "we" or give their connection a name that can be spoken of in other contexts, this has entirely different consequences than when a self-observation is merely reproduced or an impression of presence is, so to speak, collectivized.'[31] For self-descriptions to be truly reflective in the sense defined above they must produce a semantics that can represent the relationship between system and environment within the system. Alberti achieved this for architecture by contrasting the abstracted and erudite domain of design, handling pure lines and angles (in the mind or on paper), with the immediate environment of physical construction as the domain of the building crafts. Like all self-descriptions this involved a radical self-simplification. Self-simplification, ie, the reduction of complexity, is a necessary condition of all self-observations and self-descriptions. Such self-simplifications focus and thus reduce the scope of alternative courses of action that might be considered and

31 Luhmann, *Social Systems*, p 456.

selected. That is their function. The historical role of self-descriptions is an undeniable fact of architecture's 500 year history. That this reflective layer of self-description is necessary for the stabilization and continuous adaptation of architecture as vital societal function system can be evidenced via the concrete historical influence of the various dominant self-descriptions from Alberti to Le Corbusier. However, as the thesis above states, this influence – the apparent efficacy of a given self-description – is itself no guarantee that the reality of architecture's autopoiesis coincides with its dominant self-description. The communicative reality always exceeds any (necessarily selective) description. This note of caution is necessary to avoid the idealist fallacy that presumes (accepted) theoretical orientation to be equal to determination. All we can assume is a bracketing, channelling, constraining etc of the ongoing autopoiesis. This note of caution is further relevant here since it prepares the ground for the (continuous) retrospective reinterpretation of architecture's history in the light of its present concerns.

As Luhmann points out, it has been a distinctive feature of European modernization that the written, reflective self-descriptions of the emerging political, legal and economic systems assumed the particular form of ***theory***, or more specifically the ***theoretical treatise***. This, perhaps with a slightly lesser degree of sophistication, also pertains to architecture since Alberti. When the reflective self-descriptions assume the form of theory, Luhmann speaks of reflection theories (or theories of reflection) –*Reflektionstheorien*. Luhmann defines a reflection theory as a 'theory of the system within the system'.[32] These theories reflect the unity of the respective system within its environment. Luhmann elaborates: 'One can speak of *theories* of reflection if a system's identity is not only indicated in distinction to the environment (so that one knows what is meant) but also conceptually worked out so that comparisons and relations can enter.'[33] However, the scope of these comparisons is constrained through the abstractions that emerge from within the system.

Although all modern function systems produced self-descriptions or theories of reflection in the form of comprehensive theoretical treatises, there is no guarantee that such self-descriptions are readily available and readily renewed as required. One can observe historical stretches where a unifying, orienting self-description is not available. In architecture, for

32 Ibid, p 478. The most literal translation of *Reflektionstheorie* would be reflection theory understood as 'a theory that reflects'. Thus we might also translate this term as 'reflecting theories'.

33 Ibid, p 457.

example, such a comprehensive, shared self-description has been lacking ever since the crisis of Modernism. Under such conditions the autopoiesis is threatened with fragmentation. Economics as the reflection theory of the economy is another example that might be cited. Here too such a fragmentation of efforts was observed. In 1962 Murray Rothbard lamented the absence and disappearance of comprehensive economic theory in the form of 'the old-fashioned treatise on economic principles'[34] and the splintering of the discipline into conflicting or unrelated specialized pursuits. According to Rothbard, previously 'the standard method, both of presenting and advancing economic thought, was to write a disquisition setting forth one's vision of the corpus of economic science. ... The author ... carved out of economic theory an architectonic – an edifice.'[35] Rothbard continues: 'This type of treatise has disappeared from economic thought, and economics has become appallingly fragmented, dissociated to such a degree that there hardly *is* an *economics* anymore: instead we find myriad bits and pieces of uncoordinated analysis.'[36] The same might be said with respect to architectural theory.

Insight into the value, and perhaps even 'necessity', of a principled treatise is a first step towards a cohering self-description. The second step is the construction of an edifice that does indeed cohere many (if not all) of the myriad advances that were made in the interim since the last attempt at self-description succeeded. The third step would be the success in dissemination and persuasion of such a unified theory.[37] Close attention and even immersion into what actually goes on within the autopoiesis of architecture are critical. An overly idealistic approach that merely tries to proclaim what should be going on is fruitless. The rational has to be detected, selected and extrapolated from within the real.

It is important to distinguish theories that emerge as self-reflections within an autopoietic system from theories that are produced by an outside observer like a social scientist or philosopher. Theories of reflection are not scientific or philosophical theories but theories that are formulated from within the system by engaged participants. Theories of reflection are 'bound to their object through loyalty and

34 Murray N Rothbard, *Man, Economy, and State – A Treatise on Economic Principles*, Scholar's Edition, 2nd edition, Ludwig von Mises Institute (Auburn, AL), 2009, p li.

35 Ibid.

36 Ibid, p lii.

37 Murray Rothbard's grand attempt to reintegrate economics failed with respect to his mainstream influence. However, he succeeded to re-vitalize/refound Austrian economics as a cohesive, vibrant, growing heterodoxy.

affirmation'.[38] The *raison d'être* of theoretical self-descriptions is to reflect upon, clarify and confirm the societal function – the *raison d'être* – of the respective system as a whole. 'Only formulas related to function could actually operate as self-descriptions, that is, could be fed into the system and its ongoing communication.'[39] Then, on the basis of having identified the societal function that marks the very identity and *raison d'être* of the respective function system, such theories address the central problems and challenges that the system faces at its respective historical junctures. The most profound approach to understanding these self-descriptions is thus by trying to interpret them in terms of their primary problem orientation.

The emergence of such reflecting theories, as theoretically elaborate, functionally oriented self-descriptions, can be identified as a crucial factor in the development of all modern function systems since the 17th and 18th centuries. Luhmann cites the political system, the legal system, the economy, science and finally the education system as primary examples where reflecting theories became prominent. Concerning the political system, the guiding problem was how to reconcile the need for an ultimate authority that can resolve all conflicts with the need to restrain the arbitrary use of such sovereign power. 'The result is the theory of the modern constitutional state which functionalizes its parts, such as the separation of powers, democratic representation, or protection of basic rights, in terms of this problem.'[40] For the legal system, the critical problem was how to reconcile the need for continuous, adaptive legislation with the need to preserve the dignity and authority of the law that was previously underpinned by the idea of natural law. The solution was the theory of positive law. In the domain of economic theory, the problem was to gauge the degree of freedom that should be given to economic agents and their relations. Adam Smith's theory of the inherently rational 'invisible hand' of unfettered play of economic relations produced an important reference point for the development of European capitalism. The sciences struggled with the problem of reconciling the need for firm, reliable validity with the need for continuous progress and development. Epistemologies were developed that tried to cope with this problem by variously conceptualizing the relation between knowledge and its object. The initial rationalist and empiricist competitors were first synthesized in Kant's transcendental

38 Niklas Luhmann, *Die Gesellschaft der Gesellschaft*, Suhrkamp Verlag (Frankfurt am Main), 1998, p 965.

39 Luhmann, *Social Systems*, p 465.

40 Ibid, p 458.

conception of an empirical science structured by inviolate, system-constituting principles. The education system had to resolve the problem of whether to emphasize the need for particular, instrumental skills or the open development of general capacities. Was the goal of education usefulness or perfection? In Germany, pedagogy sided with the latter under the high-minded slogan of 'Bildung'.

The examples cited all focus on the first consolidated (and consolidating) results in the pursuit of theoretical self-descriptions in each of the great, modern function systems. Although in the meantime further reflection theories have produced successive re-descriptions, in each evolving subsystem such an initial, important point of culmination can be identified. It was around 1800 that most of these initial, anchoring reference points were established and available to guide and consolidate the further differentiation of the great function systems for the subsequent century. The following figures might be regarded as best representing these early points of theoretical culmination that provided a solid point of reference and departure for the further development of their respective function systems: Baron de Montesquieu's constitutionalism[41] for the political system, Jeremy Bentham's positivism[42] for the legal system, Adam Smith's economic liberalism[43] for the economic system, and Immanuel Kant's resolution of the opposition between empiricism and rationalism in his transcendental epistemology of scientific experience.[44] The culminating achievements of these figures – formulating seminal self-conceptions for their respective modern function systems – dominated the 19th century and are still recognized as relevant points of reference today.[45]

Is it possible to identify a comparable, early point of theoretical culmination within the history of architecture? As plausible candidates to fill this (theoretically constructed) position within the autopoiesis of architecture one might propose Jean-Nicolas-Louis Durand's typological

41 Charles de Secondat, Baron de Montesquieu, *The Spirit of the Laws*, 2 vols, Crowder, Wark & Payne, 1777, original French: *L'esprit des lois*, originally published anonymously in 1748, also: *Montesquieu: The Spirit of the Laws*, Cambridge University Press (Cambridge), 1989.

42 Jeremy Bentham, *An Introduction to the Principles of Morals and Legislation*, Dover Publications (New York), 2009, originally published in 1781.

43 Adam Smith, *An Inquiry into the Nature and Causes of the Wealth of Nations,* University of Chicago Press (Chicago), 1976, originally published 1776.

44 Immanuel Kant, *Critique of Pure Reason*, Cambridge University Press (Cambridge), 1998, original German *Kritik der reinen Vernunft*, first published in 1781.

45 However, the emphasis on a few canonic authors is a necessary self-simplification that every system produces when it reflects itself historically. In reality, the work of each of the authors above was embedded in a dense network of similar prior and later works.

proto-functionalism[46] as the most compelling, early self-description of architecture that framed the autopoiesis of architecture during the whole of the 19th century.

The establishment of these early, proto-modern key frameworks of self-description – political constitutionalism, legal positivism, economic liberalism, scientific empirico-rationalism, architectural functionalism – did serve to stabilize and orient the further coevolution of the respective autopoietic function systems. However, within and against these broad frameworks the reflective discourse continued. During the 20th century, these frameworks were radically questioned, and the field of self-descriptions was opened up in all function systems, including architecture. In particular since the 1960s, ie, since the crisis of Modernism, the theoretical discourse has been so diverse and fluid that no self-description emerged with the capacity to assert itself as compelling, hegemonic framework for architecture's self-orientation. In architecture there circulate humanist, historicist-progressivist, Radically Functionalist, Phenomenologist and Post-Structuralist versions of the story of architecture, each with its own primary concerns and directives. Nothing of significance has been added in the last 25 years. Now the theory of architectural autopoiesis adds its own evolutionist-constructivist story of architecture. Each of these potential self-descriptions of architecture requires architects to reflect and decide upon the character and flavour of the ongoing autopoiesis of architecture they would like to be part of.

10.2.1 CONTINUITY VS CONSISTENCY

The architectural self-descriptions that have been circulating and evolving throughout the history of architecture are constitutive parts of a single historical machine, namely of the autopoiesis of architecture, that calls itself architecture and has continuously been trying to describe and re-describe itself since its second inception during the Renaissance. Even this term of historical self-location employed here – 'the Renaissance' – is a product of architecture's self-differentiating self-description. The trail of connotations that is evoked by the term 'Renaissance' (and by the related term 'Classical architecture') remains an ineradicable heritage or trace – as both resource and burden – that has been allied to this term during its long circulation within the autopoiesis of architecture.

The explicit reflection upon the theory-dependency of architecture, together with the recognition of the long gestation of the self-descriptive

46 Jean-Nicolas-Louis Durand, *Précis des leçons d'architecture données à l'École royale polytechnique* (Paris), 1802–5, English translation by David Britt, published by The Getty Research Institute (Los Angeles), 2000.

resources of any architectural theory, has important consequences for the manner in which we should go about the further development of architectural theory. Previous theories cannot simply be dismissed as false. They are involved in the constitution of the conceptual resources and the very object of current architectural theory. They remain persistent moments of architecture. These moments cannot be purged all at once. There is no way of starting from scratch. This necessary ladenness with historically evolved terms that have attained the status of near-inevitability is also evident throughout the theory of architectural autopoiesis set out in this book. Architecture – inclusive of its theories – is a *non-trivial, historical machine*[47] with its own dynamic/inertia and evolution. The starting point for any serious self-description must be the respectful acknowledgement of this historical machine, by means of finding points of connections and inscribed tracks to follow and to follow on from. The new apparatus of distinctions that has been superimposed on the theoretical heritage here is identifying, redescribing and reordering the most vital and continuously relevant of those inherited discursive resources.

The defining task of all architecture remains the production *and demonstration* of new viable form-function relationships. This aspect of demonstration distinguishes the self-conscious discipline architecture from mere (vernacular) building. This had already been hinted at in Vitruvius' chapter on the education of the architect: 'The architect should be equipped with knowledge of many branches of study and varied kinds of learning, for it is by his judgement that all work done by the other arts is put to the test. This knowledge is the child of practise and theory. Practise is the continuous and regular employment where manual work is done with any necessary material according to the design of a drawing. Theory, on the other hand, is the ability to demonstrate and explain the productions of dexterity on the principles of proportion. It follows therefore, that architects who have aimed at acquiring manual skills without scholarship have never been able to reach a position of authority.'[48] Practice is here clearly subordinated to theory. Although theory is here unduly limited to the theory of proportions, the insistence that theory and scholarship distinguish the architect is very clear.

47 The distinction between trivial, and non-trivial, historical machine stems from the systems theorist Heinz von Foerster. While a trivial machine converts inputs into outputs according to a fixed algorithm, a non-trivial machine is historical in the sense that each input-output sequence changes the underlying mechanism of the machine, ie, the machine evolves via the accumulation of experiences. Living systems are historical machines in this sense. If you (try to) kick the dog a second time its reaction will be different from the first time.

48 Vitruvius, *The Ten Books on Architecture*, Dover Publications (New York), 1960, p 5.

Architectural theory – like architectural design – operates under the requirement of producing innovations. This implies the production of new statements, and possibly the elaboration of new concepts. All theory and self-reflection are required to catch up with the latest developments on the operational level of the system. That this is not trivial and cannot be taken for granted is demonstrated by the recurrent appearance of retroactive manifestos. Better still would be the anticipation of future trends. The best bet here would be to produce a self-fulfilling prophecy by way of influence. However, whether this can succeed depends as much upon the constraining environment as upon the internal conditions of discursive connectivity.

Self-descriptions are very special theories. The theoretical self-descriptions of the discipline constitute the most fundamental internal formulations of architecture's societal function. This self-conception of architecture's societal function is the point of departure for the unfolding of architecture's most fundamental problems, principles and values. The historical sequence of fundamental self-descriptions of the discipline is tied to the progression of the styles (research programmes) of the discipline. Thus the self-conception of architecture is reformulated with each epochal style. Each attempt at the reformulation of architecture's fundamental self-conception requires a sufficient degree of redundancy in relation to the established, hegemonic self-description. This is necessary in order to maintain the self-identity of the discipline throughout its various transformations. Strong internal communicative connectivity requires continuity in terms of the crucial problematic of the discipline. If this condition is violated, the attempt at reformulation degenerates into an escape from the discipline. The result is a failed mutation, ending in mutual rejection. Examples are Hermann Finsterlin's Expressionist architecture and Leon Krier's Ultra-Historicism.[49]

Connectivity does not require continuity in terms of approaches and solutions, ie, there is no need for theoretical consistency across different theoretical offerings. Quite the opposite is the case: polemical opposition often achieves the highest levels of communicative connectivity. The attempt to maintain or construct theoretical consistency across the succession of self-descriptions is futile and counterproductive. We have

49 It is no accident that such extremely aberrant attempts emerge during periods of crisis and transition. What characterizes these stillborn attempts at radical transformation in comparison with serious contenders that also emerge during transition periods is the sense of fantastic aberration and total communicative disconnection. Alternative contenders often coexist as rival strands within a new hegemonic era. For instance, the Organic trend of Frank Lloyd Wright and Hugo Häring during Modernism.

to learn to live with the fact *and expect* the different self-descriptions and research programmes by which the discipline evolves to be not only different, but indeed incompatible. However, as contributions to the autopoiesis of architecture they should never be incommensurable.[50] Paradigm shifts are marked by progressive problem shifts. But the fundamental problematic of the discipline's societal function must remain. And the theoretical quest remains: to formulate this function with sufficient generality so that all of architecture's past, present and future achievements/tasks are covered, and then to identify the most vital, current/future tasks in order to guide contemporary architectural research.

Thus we have to distinguish architecture's invariant ***problematic*** from its variable, historically specific ***problems***. The continued relevance of ***the classics of architectural theory*** is based on this stability of their underlying problematic while the more particular historical problems and solutions that have been formulated within these theories are no longer applicable. This distinction between an invariant problematic that is directly related to the societal function of architecture on the one hand, and the variably re-formulated specific problems and solutions promoted in each historical era on the other, explains why all classics of architectural theory are self-descriptions. Only this theory type explicitly addresses and interprets the underlying problematic of architecture. Partial theories that are only concerned with programming the codes or with the expansion of the organizational and/or articulatory repertoire of architecture become outdated as soon as a new style and research programme engenders a problem shift. Such theories are therefore not entering the evergreen canon of the classics of the discipline.

10.2.2 CATEGORICAL VS VARIABLE STRUCTURES OF COMMUNICATION

How can the distinction between variable problems and an invariant problematic be drawn and recognized? The operational maintenance of this distinction is an ongoing achievement of the autopoiesis of architecture. It cannot be defined and fixed in advance of the ongoing historical evolution. Communications either connect and find recursive sustenance, or fall into a void. This also applies to ambitious communications like comprehensive theoretical self-descriptions. Instead of chasing an illusory general definition of the eternal essence and identity of architecture, the theory of architectural autopoiesis observes and reflects the 500 year long history of architecture.

50 Truly incommensurable theories might be unmasked and expelled as escapes from architecture: escapes into art, engineering, science or politics.

All concepts that emerged within the long history of architecture can be classified according to the following two classes:

1. Invariant *categories* indicating the permanent constituents of the autopoiesis of architecture.
2. Variable *concepts* indicating the temporary, historically specific components that are attributable to one or another style.

The first class of invariant categories comprises the permanent structures of architectural communication that have been the core content of this book. We might call these communication structures the ***categorical structures*** of architecture. The use of the term categorical is not to suggest that the respective communication structures are absolutely immune to historical transformation. They are indeed products of historical evolution. They are significant evolutionary achievements. The distinction of categories versus concepts should indicate that there is a definite hierarchy of structures, whereby the categorical structures provide the relatively stable skeleton for their variable conceptual articulation. The term category – as distinct from concept – should indicate that it is a more abstract schema that can be differently filled out and concretized by the historically variable conceptual structures. The categorical, permanent structures of architecture include:

1. the reflection upon the societal function of architecture
2. the distinction between avant-garde and mainstream
3. the demarcation of architecture against art and engineering
4. the lead-distinction of form and function
5. the code of utility
6. the code of beauty
7. the code of originality
8. the progression of the discipline via styles as research programmes
9. the double task of organization and articulation
10. the design process
11. the utilization of a specialist design medium

The theory of architectural autopoiesis introduces the concept of self-description into architecture and defines self-description as a comprehensive reflection and theoretical description of the discipline that is taking as its point of departure the formulation of architecture's societal function. As we shall see below, such self-descriptions have existed throughout architecture's 500 year history, ie, this new concept 'self-description' can be empirically validated. Reference to the societal function is the only determination that is made a part of the concept's definition here. The reflective thematization of all the other invariant determinants listed above is asserted here on the basis of historical observation. The historical persistence of these determinants might very well be disputed on the basis of historical research. They might also be challenged and pushed aside by eager iconoclasts. Until such endeavours succeed, the theory of architectural autopoiesis maintains that any attempt at self-description that tries to deny or abandon the structures identified in the 11 points above is bound to fail. Such attempts failed in the past and we might therefore expect them to fail in the future.

There have indeed been plenty of attempts to reformulate the foundations of architecture in violation of the invariant structures identified here:

1. A specific concept to address the category of the societal function of architecture is given with every major architectural theory or self-description. Usually this category is expressed in phrases like 'the aim (goal, purpose) of architecture is ...'. Sometimes, however, this concept is not made so explicit. Since the second half of the 19th century, the societal function of architecture might be reflected in relation to an attempt at positioning architecture within a general history of human civilization. Since then, more and more architectural self-descriptions have come along with an account of architectural history embedded within a broad schematization of general history. This is the case with Gottfried Semper's architectural theory, and with all self-descriptions of Modern architecture from Friedrich Naumann, via Le Corbusier to Sigfried Giedion. This necessary historical positioning was lacking in most self-descriptions before the 20th century, with some notable exceptions like Semper. However, relapses into an ahistorical essentialism still occur.[51] Also, there have indeed been (failed) attempts to set architecture free from any societal function or responsibility. This is, for instance, the stance of Formalists such as Peter Eisenman and Jeffrey Kipnis. This position also correlates with the attempt to assimilate architecture to art.
2. There have been numerous failed attempts to overcome the dialectic of avant-garde and mainstream by declaring all architecture to be either all mainstream or all avant-garde. We can cite Venturi and Koolhaas on the one side, denying the vitality of the avant-garde, and Jeff Kipnis on the other, denying that architectural discourse could ever escape the reclusiveness of a bohemian demi-monde.

51 For instance John Pawson's *Minimum*, Phaidon (London), 2006.

3. There have been many failed attempts to overcome the demarcation of architecture against either art or engineering. These attempts are closely related to the abandonment of either form or function.
4. There have been many failed attempts to abandon the lead-distinction of form and function in favour of elevating either one or the other to hold exclusive sway over architecture. We might cite the Radical Functionalism of the ABC group on the one hand and the Radical Formalism of Peter Eisenman on the other. Neither approach could succeed, and indeed both claims were rightly rejected as outlandish.

   The triple code of utility, beauty and originality has been challenged on all fronts:
5. Eisenman and Kipnis denied the relevance of utility.
6. Hannes Meyer, Winy Maas and others denied the relevance of beauty.
7. Blondel, Loos, Mies and others denied the need for originality.
8. The relevance of the concept (category) of style was explicitly denied at the beginning of the Modern Movement only to be reasserted 10 years later with the announcement of the International Style. The category was again under attack during the heyday of Deconstructivism. Today the category seems rather muted and it is indeed the theory of architectural autopoiesis that is trying here to reinvigorate the category once more. We might hypothesize that the concept of style is under attack in revolutionary periods of paradigm shift and tends to re-emerge in periods of paradigm consolidation.
9. The double task of organization and articulation has been challenged as well. In particular the semiotic dimension of the task of articulation has been under attack in recent years under the slogan of performativity versus representation. Once more, it is the theory of architectural autopoiesis that is defending this category. However, this defence is not an artificial rearguard action. The semiotic dimension of architecture has been recognized by many as one of the fundamental invariants of architecture in relation to its societal function.
10. The design process is listed above as an invariant communication structure in the sense that every epochal style is correlated with rules concerning the design process. Design always proceeds under the auspices of rules that structure the design process as proper, due process. This fact is not always visible or made explicit. The regular design process has traditionally been taken for granted without critical reflection. The design methods movement of the 1960s and 1970s put an end to this dogmatic slumber. Towards the end of the 20th century, the proliferation of experimental design processes led

to an intensification of design process reflection. However, this situation also led to the illusion that 'anything goes', ie, to a kind of design process agnosticism, or even design process anarchy, that explicitly or implicitly denies the idea of a rule-governed, regular design process.

11. That the reliance upon a specialized, architectural design medium is a general, invariant fact of the autopoiesis of architecture is perhaps easier to see than the case of the (regular) design process. However, the predicament of the category of the design medium in the reflection theories of the discipline is similar to that of the design process. The utilization of a particular design medium has traditionally been invisible, or has simply been taken for granted without reflection. Then came the explosion of means of representation in the second half of the 20th century. Design medium reflection took off. Especially since the micro-electronic revolution entered the discipline in the 1980s and digital design tools fully pervaded the discipline during the 1990s, the reflection on the impact and meaning of the new, powerful design media is perhaps the primary theme of most architectural theorizing. However, there are still theorists who try to deny or belittle the constitutive relevance of architecture's medium by maintaining that the design medium is no more than a convenient tool.

All self-descriptions of architecture reflect the societal function of architecture. They vary with the progression of styles. If all the above categories are invariant, constitutive moments of architecture, what scope is there left for the reformulation of architecture's self-conception? For once, each new substantial self-description re-theorizes architecture's societal function, reconceptualizes the way the form-function relationship is supposed to be handled, re-defines the programmes for the double code of beauty and utility, and reflects the new, emergent rules for the regular design process etc.

Effective self-descriptions need to be as assertive to serve their function. The points that each new comprehensive architectural self-description has to address can be summarized as follows:

1. reassert the societal function of architecture
2. reformulate the stance of the avant-gardist historical orientation[52]

52 Since Modernism, every comprehensive architectural self-description must explicitly articulate a historically argued future orientation for the discipline. In line with this requirement, all self-descriptions can be expected to align themselves with a contemporary avant-garde trend.

3. re-establish the most urgent demarcation lines between architecture and its neighbouring systems
4. re-state the directives towards the general handling and integration of form-function relations
5. reformulate the programme for the application of the code of utility
6. reformulate the programme for the application of the code of beauty
7. reformulate the programme for the application of the code of originality
8. identify the avant-garde movement that can evolve into a new hegemonic style
9. guide the expansion of the repertoire for spatio-architectural organization and articulation
10. in relation to an updated formulation of architecture's task, give methodological and design-process guidance
11. in relation to an updated formulation of architecture's task, identify the most effective design media
12. demonstrate self-reflectiveness via autological self-inclusion

These 12 requirements are posited here as the general requirements that are expected to be addressed by any theoretical treatise that aspires to become a comprehensive, orienting self-description of architecture within architecture. These 12 requirements might also be used to analyze all prior self-descriptions that have become manifest within the 500 year history of architecture's autopoiesis.

10.3 Classic Treatises

THESIS 54

All classics of architectural theory are self-descriptions. Only this theory type explicitly addresses and interprets the general, underlying, permanent problematic of architecture. The continued relevance of the classics of architectural theory is based on this stability of their underlying problematic even when the more particular historical problems/solutions that have been formulated within these theories are no longer applicable.

The autopoiesis of architecture took off at the historical point when the reliance on craft traditions in the determination of (key aspects of) the built environment was replaced by a conscious, creative practice whereby new ideas were speculatively elaborated in the abstracted realm of the drawing, apart from and in advance of construction. Moreover, this practice of innovative design via drawings was from the very outset supported by a theoretical practice whereby the new design ideas were thought through and argued for in writing. This simultaneous emergence of innovative drawing and theorizing was the big bang of architecture. Its ex post facto historical justification lies in the momentous acceleration of the development of the built environment that went hand in hand with its successive subordination to the autopoiesis of architecture.[53]

Since its decisive point of origin within the Italian Renaissance – which had already furnished architecture with its first powerful self-description – the autopoiesis of architecture has evolved (or better: coevolved with the other emerging function systems as well as with total society) via a progressive series of epochal styles. Each epochal style features at least one decisive architectural self-description or key text that not only reasserts the societal function of architecture with respect to the new historical challenges of the epoch but also addresses the consequences that are to be drawn in terms of a pertinent re-conceptualization of many (if not all) of the categorical communication structures[54] that together prestructure the evolving system of architectural communications.

If this general characterization of the historical sequence of self-descriptions is valid, it should be possible to reconstruct the series as a canon of classical texts that are tied together by the shared fundamental problematic, via successive relations of ***polemic continuity***. It should further be possible to align this series with the progression of styles that constitutes the 500 year history of architecture. What follows is the attempt to give a (highly condensed) summary of this sequence of classics – in each instance focusing on the moment of polemic continuity.

The period after the Italian-led Renaissance, from the 17th to the 19th centuries, witnessed the formation of nation states leading to a certain split of the architectural discourse along national lines. This condition was exacerbated by the demise of Latin as pan-European medium of writing. The discourse split into French, German and English strands. However, the most important works from each national strand were eventually translated into the other relevant languages. This phenomenon served to focus attention upon the key works that were translated and disseminated across Europe.

Key authors/works that might be picked out as contributors of classic self-descriptions within the autopoiesis of architecture are: Leon Battista Alberti, *De re aedificatoria*, 1450/1485; Andrea Palladio, *I quattro libri dell'architettura*, 1570; Nicolas-François Blondel, *Cours d'architecture*, 1675; Guarino Guarini, *Architettura civile*, 1737; Marc-Antoine Laugier,

53 This should serve as a reminder against all too one-sided 'materialist' interpretations of history.

54 The idea here is that the categorical, permanent communication structures receive re-articulation via historically changing variables.

Essai sur l'architecture, 1753; Jean-Nicolas-Louis Durand, *Précis des leçons d'architecture,* 1802–5; Gottfried Semper, *Der Stil in den technischen und tektonischen Künsten*, 1861–3; Hermann Muthesius, *Stilarchitektur und Baukunst*, 1902; Le Corbusier, *Vers une architecture*, 1923; Sigfried Giedion, *Space, Time and Architecture,* 1941.[55] These names provide (some of) the major classics of the discipline, selected from our contemporary vantage point. The above list of requirements, ie, the catalogue of issues that must be addressed by any self-description of the discipline, can now serve as a comparative grid (below) for a point by point analysis of (three of) the considered classics:

1. the societal function and the task of architecture
2. avant-gardist orientation
3. disciplinary demarcations
4. form-function relations
5. programme for the code of utility
6. programme for the code of beauty
7. programme for the code of originality
8. implied style
9. expansion of the repertoire
10. design-process guidance
11. design medium
12. self-reflectiveness

In what follows, these 12 headings will in turn structure the examination of three selected classic texts, the texts of Alberti, Durand and Le Corbusier, representing highly influential architectural self-descriptions during the Renaissance, Neo-Classicism and Modernism respectively. The presentation of the three texts proceeds to a large extent on the basis of ordering and stringing together extensive quotations[56] rather than cloaking everything into paraphrases. Commentary and analysis are thus clearly distinguishable from original formulations.

10.3.1 ALBERTI'S *DE RE AEDIFICATORIA*

Alberti's *On the Art of Building in Ten Books* is the inevitable point of departure in the story of architecture's self-descriptions. In turn, Alberti's point of departure and reference point was the penultimate classic of architectural theory, Vitruvius' *Ten Books on Architecture*

55 For the period since the crisis of Modernism one might pick out, among others, Alexander (1964, 1965), Venturi (1966), Frei Otto, Koolhaas (1978, 1995), Lynn (1992) and Kipnis (1993). However, none of these latter names provides a full-blown self-description of architecture.

56 Translated from Latin and French respectively.

(*De Architectura)* written in the first century BC. Like Vitruvius' work, Alberti's was organized in 10 books covering more or less the same subject matter. As Joseph Rykwert notes in his introduction to his new translation of *De re aedificatoria*, while Vitruvius had written a record of a bygone epoch, codifying the Greek building theories and practices that had flourished before Vitruvius' time, without paying much attention to the advances of his own time (such as concrete vaulting), and without any sense of the vast achievement of Roman imperial architecture that was to come, 'Alberti was, on the contrary, consciously setting out on a fresh enterprise'.[57] Rykwert continues: 'The essential difference between Alberti and Vitruvius is therefore that the ancient writer tells you how the buildings that you may admire as you read him were built, while Alberti is prescribing how the buildings of the future *are to be* built.'[58] Alberti's book did much more than this. As architecture's inaugural self-description, it opened a new epoch, effectively inaugurating architecture as autopoietic system of communications that would soon evolve to become one of the great function systems of modern, functionally differentiated society.

Leon Battista Alberti's *De re aedificatoria* was the first treatise on architecture since antiquity. In 1485 it was posthumously published as the first printed book on architecture. Handwritten manuscripts were circulated much earlier, since Alberti had presented his treatise to Pope Nicholas in 1450. The specific content of the work was developed on the basis of Alberti's detailed survey and study of the ancient monuments in Rome.

Alberti's practice as designing architect took off only after he had completed his theoretical treatise. His practice was informed by the principles and values stated in his treatise. Before *De re aedificatoria,* Alberti had already completed a series of noted literary works including, among others, a treatise on the advantages and disadvantages of literary studies (*De commodis litterarum atque incommodis*, 1429), a treatise on the family (*Della famiglia,* 1432), a treatise on painting (*De pictura*, 1435) and a treatise on the law (*De iure*, 1437). It is significant that an outstanding man of letters dedicated himself to architecture and in doing so helped to lift the profession from the stage and status of a craft to the status of a learned discourse that proceeds on the basis of precepts and arguments that have been elaborated, rehearsed, criticized and advanced on the basis of writings.

57 Leon Battista Alberti, *On the Art of Building in Ten Books*, translated by Joseph Rykwert, Neil Leach & Robert Tavernor, MIT Press (Cambridge, MA), 1988, p ix.

58 Ibid, p x.

In what follows, Alberti's text will be analyzed according to the comparative grid introduced above:

1. societal function and the task of architecture
   At the very beginning of his treatise, in the prologue, Alberti vigorously spells out the importance of architecture for society. He attributes the very existence of society to architecture. 'Some have said that it was fire and water which were initially responsible for bringing men together into communities, but we, considering how useful, even indispensable, a roof and walls are for men, are convinced that it was they that drew and kept men together.'[59] This quote contains a rather remarkable insight concerning the depth of architecture's involvement in the formation of human community and society. There is indeed no human society that exists or has existed without 'coming together' and ordering itself and its affairs via the establishment of an artificial spatial order. There is even a hint of understanding that architecture provides social stability in the dimension of historical time: 'How many respected families, both in our own city and in others throughout the world would have totally disappeared, brought down by some temporary adversity, had not their family hearth harbored them, welcoming them, as it were, into the very bosom of their ancestors?'[60] One might presume that Alberti is here not only alluding to physical protection but also to the maintenance of customs, roles and thus social order. This presumption might be warranted given the fact that Alberti had earlier written a treatise *On the Family* examining, in dialogue form, how to maintain and advance the demographic health and good fortunes of a large family. Alberti's *Della famiglia*[61] treated topics widely discussed in humanist writings on moral and social questions such as the purpose of marriage, spousal relations, child rearing and education.[62] Alberti is also explicit about architecture's role in representing and stabilizing political power by referring to the 'imperial authority and fame that the Latins got by their buildings'[63] and to Thucydides' insight that the Ancients used their buildings 'to

59 Alberti, *On the Art of Building in Ten Books*, p 3.

60 Ibid.

61 Leon Battista Alberti, *Opere volgari*, ed C Grayson, Laterza (Bari), 1960–73, III, p 156.

62 Anthony Grafton, *Leon Battista Alberti – Master Builder of the Italian Renaissance*, Penguin Books (London), 2002, p 157.

63 Alberti, *On the Art of Building in Ten Books*, p 5.

give the impression of having far greater power than they really had'.[64]

The first remarkable aspect of Alberti's theoretical treatise is its comprehensive scope. It covers the whole of the built environment including the location and layout of cities, down to the details of building construction and (exterior as well as interior) decoration, as well as the whole world of human artefacts and devices. With respect to urbanism and architecture, Alberti's approach to the subject is most profound: he links his detailed discussion back to architecture's fundamental societal function, namely to order and frame social communication. For Alberti, architecture must relate to society's structure, in his terms: the 'divisions within society'. Alberti thus starts his discourse on public buildings (Book 4) by surveying the different kinds of social order that have been observed and described (by the Ancient authors). Alberti suggests that one should try to relate the diversity of building traditions in different times and countries to the respective socio-political constitutions of the respective societies. Alberti expresses this as follows: 'When we look around at the quantity and variety of buildings, it is easy to understand that ... the range of different works depends principally on the variation within human nature. If we wish to give an accurate account of the various types of buildings and of their constituent elements, our whole method of investigation must open and begin here, by considering human variety in greater detail; since buildings arose on man's account, and for his needs they vary; so that they may be dealt with more clearly by distinguishing their characteristics.'[65]

In order to determine the societal premises of architecture, any competent self-description of architecture must consult the established social theory of its time rather than venturing itself unguided into this domain. In the case of Alberti, the most advanced social theory was still contained in the writings handed down from Classical antiquity. Alberti continues: 'We shall consult therefore the experienced men of antiquity who founded republics and laid down their laws, to find out what they had to say about divisions within society, since they devoted zeal, diligence, and care to questions of this nature, and their conclusions have drawn much praise and admiration.'[66] Alberti then refers to the writings of Plutarch, Caesar, Thucydides and Diodorus, among others, to give a brief overview of

64 Ibid, p 5.
65 Ibid, p 92.
66 Ibid.

how societies were ordered into social classes: in Theseus' Athens, in Solon's Athens, in Romulus' Rome, then in Gaul, Britain, Egypt and India, as well as in Hippodamos' ideal city. He also refers to the theoretical constitutions of Aristotle and Plato respectively. Alberti's underlying premise here is that the order of society will have to be reflected in the layout of the city and in the differentiation of building types: 'These brief extracts I have digested from the many writings of the ancients. And from them I draw this lesson: that all the above are different parts of the state, and that each should be designated a different type of building.'[67] Alberti then offers his own brief sketch of how a good society should be ordered hierarchically into functional strata and which characteristic features and abilities the members of each stratum should possess. Alberti considers four strata, each with its own function. At the top stand those with the highest power of reason responsible to set up laws, devise policies, regulate justice and administer religion. The second group are those with skill and practical experience. They should be entrusted with the execution of the policies. The third group is thought to be a group of economic leaders (landowners and merchants) who are providing the funding for the operations of the state. 'All other citizens should, within reason, owe allegiance to and respect the wishes of the leading group.'[68] However, in the further detailed examinations of the various building types, this proposed four-tier order of society does not find any application. The detailed architectural teachings refer instead to real institutional arrangements, past and present. The utopian sketch remains idle.[69]

In the concluding remarks of his prologue, Alberti emphasizes once more that architecture is indispensable, and that the architect deserves the greatest honour and recognition for his inventions and his service to society. He then closes as follows: 'To conclude, then, let it be said that the security, dignity, and honor of the republic depend greatly on the architect: it is he who is responsible for our delight, entertainment and health while at leisure, and for profit and

67 Ibid, p 93.

68 Ibid, p 94.

69 Alberti's normative political sketch has been included here because it reflects the recurring temptation within architecture to cross its boundary and venture into politics. The boundary or distinction that needs to be observed is the distinction between reflecting and addressing architecture's societal function in order to innovate architecturally in relation to the reality of socio-political development on the one hand, and the attempt to speculate about utopian possibilities on the other. In the latter case, architectural and political issues fuse and architecture attempts to substitute itself for the political system.

advantage while at work, and in short that we live in a dignified manner, free from any danger.'[70]

2. avant-gardist orientation
   Since Modernism, every comprehensive architectural self-description must explicitly articulate a historically argued forward orientation for the discipline. However, when Alberti was writing there was as yet no clear concept of the total historical transformation of society. What is clear, however, is that Alberti emphasized invention and design innovation, as can already be gathered from the few quotes given above. He also had an understanding of the historical progress of (Ancient) architecture from Egypt, via Greece, to Rome. However, this history was a history of perfection rather than a history of adaptation with respect to the dynamic of total social transformation.

3. disciplinary demarcations
   Every comprehensive architectural self-description must try to re-establish architecture's most urgent demarcation lines against its neighbouring systems. The crucial demarcation which is emphasized at the very beginning of Alberti's treatise is the inaugural demarcation between architecture and the building trade: 'Before I go any further, however, I should explain exactly whom I mean by an architect; for it is no carpenter that I would have you compare to the greatest exponents of other disciplines: the carpenter is but an instrument in the hands of the architect. Him I consider the architect, who by sure and wonderful reason and method, knows both how to devise through his own mind and energy . . . what can be most beautifully fitted out for the noble needs of man. . . . To this he must have an understanding and knowledge of all the highest and most noble disciplines. This then is the architect.'[71] The architect designs rather than builds. The same point is once more brought home towards the end of the treatise, in the last pages of Book 9 after having explored the subtleties of creating beauty as the architect's task beyond the mere pragmatics of building: 'To make something that appears to be convenient for use, . . . is the job not of the architect so much as the workman. But to preconceive and to determine in the mind and with judgement something that will be perfect and complete in its every part is the achievement of such a mind that we seek. Through his intellect he must invent, through

70 Alberti, *On the Art of Building in Ten Books*, p 5.

71 Ibid, p 3.

experience recognize, through judgement select, through deliberation compose ... based on prudence and mature reflection.'[72]

In both quotes emphasis is laid on mind, reason, method and knowledge, as tools to create a perfect design in advance of construction. The carpenter or workman representing the construction trade is excluded from the lofty realm of architecture and relegated to the position of mere instrument of execution. This is exactly the arrangement that still operates today. However, no demarcation was as yet possible between architecture and engineering. The invention and engineering of technological devices and methods was included in the compass of architecture.

The architect/engineer designs rather than builds, and he designs the building fully and precisely before construction starts. This affords a new level of control and foresight in contrast to the methods of the masterbuilder. Alberti advises the architect as follows: ' ... before embarking on the work, weigh up the whole matter ... reexamine every part of your proposal ... from the roots to the uppermost tile there is nothing, concealed or open, large or small, for which you have not thought out, resolved, and determined, thoroughly and at length, the most handsome and effective position, order, and number.'[73] According to Alberti, 'a prudent man would act like this: ... he would set out everything, and leave nothing without some form of rule or measure.'[74] Noting that large buildings often fail to be completed within a single man's lifetime, he still insists that the creation is a complete design and that the original design should be honoured by the later executioners. 'I feel that the original intentions of the author, the product of mature reflection, must be upheld.'[75] This, once more, marks a decisive departure from the previous practice, before Alberti's inauguration of architecture. Architecture is conducted by architect-authors creating a perfect design according to reasoned theoretical principles.

4. form-function relations
Architecture's lead-distinction of form vs function, and the double code of utility and beauty it sponsors, determines the very structure of architecture's inaugural self-description. The first half of the treatise – Books 1 to 5 – treats architecture in its functional aspects, while the second half – Books 6 to 9 – treats architecture's formal

72 Ibid, p 315.
73 Ibid, p 313.
74 Ibid.
75 Ibid, p 319.

aspects. (Book 10 covers the restoration of buildings.) There are strong symmetries between the functional half and the formal half of the book: each half is structured according to the same sequence starting with a general discussion ordered by a series of six topics (location, site, compartition, roof, walls, openings) and then moving on to a more specific discussion of first public and then private buildings.

Time and again Alberti juxtaposes utility and beauty as two cooperating, indispensable requirements of architectural quality. Alberti demands a 'harmonious work that respects utility, dignity, and delight. . . . Each member should therefore be in the correct zone and position; it should be no larger than utility requires, no smaller than dignity demands.'[76] He remarks approvingly of the Ancient Roman architects that 'they found that grace of form could never be separated or divorced from suitability for use'.[77] We can observe the typical oscillation between concerns of utility and concerns of beauty. In the first half of the treatise, we find formulations that seem to give precedence to utility over beauty, while the order of importance is reversed in the second half, with explicit formulations. However, at no point is one of the two concerns denied for the sake of the other. The moment of functional priority is articulated as follows: 'Each part should be appropriate, and suit its purpose. For every aspect of building, if you think of it rightly, is born of necessity, nourished by convenience, dignified by use; and only in the end is pleasure provided for, while pleasure itself never fails to shun every excess.'[78] In the same vein, at another occasion, Alberti criticizes the ostentatious foregrounding of luxurious decoration found in the buildings erected under the direction of Nero: 'I cannot approve of them, and much prefer someone who gives the impression that he will always make utility and frugality his primary concern in anything.'[79] In contrast to these statements, the moment of formal priority is articulated as follows: 'Of the three conditions that apply to every form of construction – that what we construct should be appropriate to its use, lasting in structure, and graceful and pleasing in appearance – the first two have been dealt with, and there remains the third, the noblest and most necessary of all.'[80] This statement

76 Ibid, p 23.
77 Ibid, p 158.
78 Ibid, p 24.
79 Ibid, p 317.
80 Ibid, p 155.

was placed close to the beginning of Book 6, introducing the primary concern of the second half of the treatise (Books 6–9). Alberti continues: 'Most noble is beauty, and it must be sought most eagerly. . . . What remarkable importance our ancestors, men of great prudence, attached to it is shown by the care they took that their legal, military, and religious institutions – indeed the whole commonwealth – should be much embellished; and by their letting it be known that if all these institutions, without which man could scarcely exist, were to be stripped of their pomp and finery, their business would appear insipid and shabby.'[81] It is important to note that Alberti here refers beauty back to the fundamental function of architecture in society. He further calls on the authority and example of nature to underpin his point about the necessity of pursuing beauty: 'Nature herself, as is everywhere plain to see, does not desist from basking in a daily orgy of beauty – let the hues of her flowers serve as my one example.'[82]

Thus Alberti is at pains to express the absolute necessity of both utility and beauty, ie, is enforcing the double code of utility and beauty, the simultaneous co-presence of both concerns, with the utmost stringency. Again, this double commitment leads necessarily to the oscillation of emphases as the juxtaposition of the following two quotes once more demonstrates. On the one hand Alberti states that 'to have satisfied necessity is trite and insignificant, to have catered to convenience unrewarding when the inelegance in a work causes offense', while on the other hand he states that 'even if everything has to be done for the sake of ornament, we should furnish the building in such a way that you would not deny that utility was the principal motive'.[83] The thesis posed here with respect to Alberti's double claim is that architecture, in the 21st century, remains committed to this double claim. Alberti's apodictic statements ring as true and compelling as ever. They point to the defining, permanent communication structures of the discipline. In the terminology of the theory of architectural autopoiesis, this implies that the discipline is submitted to the organizing thrust of its binary lead-distinction – form vs function – and the attendant double code of utility and beauty.

81 Ibid.
82 Ibid.
83 Ibid, p 317.

5. programme for the code of utility

In order to function as a comprehensive architectural self-description, an architectural theory must formulate a programme for the application of the code of utility,[84] ie, utility must be defined so that guidance is attained for the concrete application of the code values – functional/useful vs dysfunctional/useless – in any given design decision situation. The theory must offer guidance on how to understand, address and fulfil the functional requirements that architecture sees itself confronted with in each concrete building task (within a particular society and historical era). As elaborated above in the paragraphs on the societal function of architecture, for Alberti architecture must relate to the divisions that order society by a corresponding urban structure and by 'designating a different type of building' to the 'different parts of the state'.[85] 'Some buildings are appropriate for society as a whole, others for the foremost citizens, and yet others for the common people. Then again for the foremost citizens those presiding over domestic councils require different buildings to those involved in executing decisions or those engaged in accumulating wealth.'[86] Thus Alberti frames his discussion of utility in architecture by the broadest possible functional classification of societal groups and their functional requirements with respect to architecture.

Alberti structures his discussion of the functional aspects of architecture's task by first considering the location and overall layout of the city. Next he considers places and buildings that are public in the sense of being fully accessible to all members of society. Then he treats buildings that serve the state but are of restricted access. These include senate houses, courthouses etc, as well as the ruler's palace, and the private residences of the leading households in general. The location and design of cities are treated as an aspect of nation building. 'Everyone relies on the city and all the public services that it contains. ... Surely, the most thorough consideration should be given to the city's layout, site, and outline.'[87] Alberti gives detailed functional considerations to various locational possibilities (coast, river, hilltop etc), to the design of walls, to public infrastructures like harbours, approach roads, gates, streets, bridges

84 See Volume 1, chapter 3.5.2 *Utility and Beauty as the Double Code of Architecture.*

85 Alberti, *On the Art of Building in Ten Books*, p 93.

86 Ibid, p 94.

87 Ibid, p 95.

and large squares to be used as marketplaces and places for military exercise etc, each underpinned by ancient examples and elaborated with technical expertise. After this discussion of general considerations that are considered universally valid for all cities, Alberti engages in a discussion of city design with respect to questions of social order and social control. Alberti's premise here is that the principles and features of city design must be specifically differentiated with respect to the political constitution of the state (city-state). Alberti distinguishes, and in turn discusses, the urban and architectural requirements of monarchies, tyrannies and republics, without apparent prejudice or preference. He starts with the location and design of the palace or seat of government.[88] 'Let us begin with the more exalted. The highest of all are those entrusted with supreme power and judgement; this may be entrusted to several individuals or just to one. The one who alone rules over others is he who should have the greatest honor. Let us therefore consider what is appropriate in his particular case.'[89] Then Alberti introduces the importance of considering the type of regime: 'Above all it is important to establish ... whether he is the sort who governs reverently and piously over willing subjects ... or one who would wish to control the political situation so that he could remain in power even against the will of his subjects. For each building and even the city itself should differ when under the rule of those called tyrants, as opposed to others who take up their command and care for it like a magisterial office conferred to them by their fellows.'[90] This political distinction leads – in the case of the tyrant – to the need for internal control and defence rather than merely defence against outside enemies. To these requirements of internal control Alberti pays considerable detailed attention. The autopoiesis of architecture adapts its discourse and service provisions to the requirements of the political system of society. Alberti refers to the example of the city Carrare in Egypt where: 'prudently their princes had so divided it up with water conduits ... to reduce the fear of any large-scale popular uprising'.[91] He also mentions that 'Servius Tullius ordered all the patricians to live in a district where any rebellion could be instantly

88 This is treated at the beginning of Book 5, 'On the Works of Individuals', since 'Public Works' only comprises works accessible to all.

89 Alberti, *On the Art of Building in Ten Books*, p 117.

90 Ibid.

91 Ibid.

put down from a hilltop.'[92] The siting of the palace within the city differs with respect to the difference between kings and tyrants: 'A royal palace should be cited in the city centre, should be of easy access . . . but that of a tyrant, being a fortress rather than a house, should be positioned where it is neither inside nor outside the city. Further, whereas a royal dwelling might be sited next to a showground, a temple, or the houses of noblemen, that of a tyrant should be set well back on all sides from any building.'[93] With respect to a republic, Alberti suggests that the temple, senate house and courthouse should be placed together in the centre of the city, for the convenience of the state officials. 'Not only that, but should ambassadors or legates from some foreign country arrive to request an audience with the senate, it is well to have somewhere worthy of both guest and city to receive them while they wait.'[94] Thus Alberti's programme of utility operates more via detailed description and consideration of social activities than via the mere dogmatic insistence on established types. With respect to the surroundings of the temples, Alberti insists that 'nothing unclean or indecent, which might offend the elders, matrons, and virgins who arrive for worship, should be seen near it, or distract them from carrying out their religious duties.'[95] Even in a republic, social and political control remains an issue that architecture must address and provide for: 'The entrance to the senate house must be well fortified . . . not least to prevent a reckless band of revelers within the crowd, incited by someone of mischievous intent, from having the freedom to break in at will and disturb the elders.'[96]

Concerning the larger spatial organization of the city, with respect to society's overall order into two primary social classes (nobility/patricians vs commoners), Alberti makes an original proposal: 'The best means of dividing the city is to build a wall through it. This wall should not run diametrically across the city but should form a circle within a circle. For the wealthy citizens are happier in more spacious surroundings and would readily accept being excluded by an inner wall, and would not unwillingly leave the

92 Ibid, p 118; Servius Tullius was the second king of the Etruscan dynasty and reigned 578–535 BC. He was the sixth king of Ancient Rome, and the first to accede without being elected by the Senate.

93 Alberti, *On the Art of Building in Ten Books*, p 122.

94 Ibid, pp 130–1.

95 Ibid, p 126.

96 Ibid, p 131.

stalls and the town-center workshops to the marketplace traders; and that rabble ... of poulterers, butchers, cooks and so on, will be less of a risk and less of a nuisance if they do not mix with the important citizens.'[97]

A similar concern with social divisions and the life-processes that they are engaged in informs the organization of the large houses of the foremost citizens. First of all, Alberti recommends for state officials like priests, senators and judges that 'each of the above should have two separate types of abode, one for official business, the other a place to retreat with his household'.[98] The same classification that structured the discussion of the city is now applied to the house:

> In houses, as in towns, some parts are public, others restricted to the few, and others for single persons. The portico and the vestibule... are for citizens of all ranks. ... Within the house the corridors, yard, atrium and salon ... are intended for general use, rather than solely for those who live there. There are clearly two types of dining room, one for free men and one for slaves; then there are bedrooms for married women, young girls, and guests, almost all being single rooms. In the first book we dealt with the distribution of these parts in general terms. In their lineaments, number, size, and positioning they must be laid out in a manner appropriate to their respective uses. We shall now deal with them individually.[99]

The organization as well as the individual spaces of the private houses of important citizens are described in close connection with the prevailing patterns of social communication. 'The atrium, salon, and so on should relate in the same way to the home as do the forum and public square to the city: they should not be hidden away in some tight and out-of-the-way corner, but should be prominent with easy access to the other members. It is here that stairways and passageways begin, and here that visitors are greeted and made welcome.'[100] According to Alberti, each house should have one primary entrance, a back entrance for deliveries, and 'a more private side door, for the master of the house alone, to enable him to let in secret couriers and messengers, and to go out whenever the occasion

97 Ibid, p 118.
98 Ibid, p 125.
99 Alberti, *On the Art of Building in Ten Books*, p 119.
100 Ibid.

and circumstances demand, without the knowledge of the household.'[101] Once more, detailed attention is given to the expected life and communication processes. Issues of social control demand attention, not only with respect to the organization of the city but also in terms of the organization of individual households. With respect to the different dining rooms on the one hand, and the service rooms on the other, Alberti insists: 'They should be kept separate, lest excessive contact between guests and attendants detracts from the dignity, comfort, and pleasure of the former or increase the insolence of the latter.'[102] Other forms of social engineering operate positively by proximity rather than negatively by separation: 'The young men over seventeen should be accommodated opposite the guests, or at least not far from them, to encourage them to form an acquaintance'. Thus architectural organization is not always a question of accommodating and protecting communicative interactions but also of the stimulation and prompting of communications.

The functional perspective remains prevalent in all of Alberti's explanations in the first half of his treatise (Books 1–5). This also applies to his account of the next level of details that must be considered, the typical elements of a building like roofs, walls, doors and windows etc. However, rather than simply taking stereotypes for granted he seeks to explain them in terms of their functional rationality. For instance, instead of simply naming windows and doors as naturally given elements, Alberti starts with a functional distinction: 'There are two types of opening, one for light and ventilation, and the other to allow man or object to enter or leave the building.'[103] He then postulates: 'Each individual chamber then, should have windows, so to admit light and to allow a change of air; they should be appropriate to the requirements of the interior and should take into account the thickness of the wall, so that their frequency and the light they receive are no greater or less than utility demands.'[104] References back to utility – understood in terms of the life-processes to be accommodated – accompany all discussions.

According to the theory of architectural autopoiesis, organization and articulation are two necessary dimensions of the task of

101 Ibid, p 120.
102 Ibid, p 119.
103 Ibid, p 28.
104 Ibid.

architecture.[105] Although at first sight it may seem as if organization is concerned with function, judged according to its utility, and as if articulation is concerned with form, judged according to its beauty, the theory of architectural autopoiesis resists this latent alignment, and insists instead that the distinction organization vs articulation cuts orthogonally across architecture's lead-distinction of form vs function. Both the organization and the articulation of a space/building involve both form and function. Both can and should be judged according to beauty *and* utility. Articulation operates via appearance and atmosphere. It orients the users, both in terms of their wayfinding and in terms of prompting and preparing them with respect to the communicative situations that are to be expected in a given space. On this count articulation certainly contributes to the effective functioning of the built environment. In all pre-Modern architecture, ornament was a crucial medium of articulation. We should not allow ourselves to be deceived by the fact that Alberti uses the term 'Ornament' as title in all the books (Books 6–9) in which he develops his theory and programme of beauty. Ornament *functions* with respect to architecture's task and is discussed in this respect within Alberti's treatise, both within the sections treating utility, *and* within the sections primarily dedicated to beauty. Ornamentation is subjected to the code of utility and Alberti's programme of utility includes suggestions about the proper use of ornament. The concept of propriety is central here. Another pertinent category is the category of character. For instance, in his discussion of the proper location and arrangement of the royal palace, Alberti does not fail to include concerns of articulation: 'A royal palace ... should be gracefully decorated, elegant, and refined, rather than ostentatious.'[106] In his description of the citadel, physical and atmospheric attributes fuse: 'The citadel should be threatening, rugged and rocky, stubborn and invincible.'[107]

105 Organization is concerned with the physical distancing, separation and connection of domains and is thus *framing* communication physically, by physically channelling movement and communication. Articulation is concerned with orientation and is framing communication cognitively. Articulation is channelling movement and communication via atmospheres, and perceptual as well as semiotic clues. Organization recognizes and operates via social communication's dependency on human beings as mobile bodies in space, while articulation recognizes and operates via social communication's dependency on human beings as perceiving/comprehending systems. See section 6.2 *Order via Organization and Articulation.*

106 Alberti, *On the Art of Building in Ten Books*, p 121.

107 Ibid, p 123.

Ornament was to be regulated according to the social character of the respective building, effectively resulting in a semiological system: 'It is quite clear that each building does not require the same ornament. With sacred works, especially public ones, every art and industry must be employed to render them as ornate as possible: sacred works must be furnished for the gods, secular only for man. The latter, being the less dignified, should concede to the former, yet will be ennobled with their own details of ornament.'[108] Private buildings should not be seen to compete with or outshine public buildings. 'Not that precious materials should be completely renounced and banished; but they should be used sparingly in the most dignified places. ... The severest restraint is called for, in the ornament to private buildings, therefore, although a certain license is often possible.'[109] The licence referred to here is not a licence for ornamental opulence but rather the licence to stray from strictly regulated ornamental systems: 'Indeed, sometimes it might be more delightful to stray a little from the dignity and calculated rule of lineaments, which would not be permitted in public works.'[110] There are also distinctions to be observed concerning town house versus country villa: 'The ornament to a town house ought to be far more sober in character, whereas in a villa the allure of license and delight are allowed.'[111] The deployment of ornament should not only differentiate *between* buildings (of different social purpose and social standing), but should also differentiate zones and uses *within* a single building. The public reception rooms are to be emphasized by decorations while other areas should remain unadorned. Ornamentation is also to be deployed to give different social settings a different character, 'so that some display gravity and majesty, others gaiety and festivity'.[112]

In summary, according to Alberti's programme of utility, functionally resolved are those designs that frame, ie, organize and articulate, the pertinent patterns of social communication of the social institution in question. The argument reconstructs and stabilizes given typologies on the basis of functional analysis with respect to the life/communication processes accommodated. The

108 Ibid, p 244.
109 Ibid, p 293.
110 Ibid.
111 Ibid, p 294.
112 Ibid, p 314.

taken for granted *formal a priori*[113] of all discussed organizing efforts is the assumption that the spatial organization for each considered institution proceeds via closed off cellular (mostly rectilinear) spaces that are arranged into a compact, overall array under a single roof. This unreflected premise was first questioned 450 years later, by Modernism.

6. programme for the code of beauty
   In order to function as a comprehensive architectural self-description, an architectural theory must formulate a programme for the application of the code of beauty, ie, beauty must be defined so that guidance is attained for the concrete application of the code values – formally resolved/beautiful vs formally unresolved/ugly – in any given design decision situation. Alberti starts with his famous, rather abstract and general definition of beauty: 'Beauty is that reasoned harmony of all the parts within a body, so that nothing may be added, taken away, or altered, but for the worse.'[114] He distinguishes beauty from ornament: 'Ornament may be defined as a form of auxiliary light and complement of beauty. ... Rather than being inherent, it has the character of something attached or additional.'[115] As noted above, Alberti honours the double code of utility and beauty by going twice through the various steps of the design process that are necessary to cover all the aspects of a design project: first with respect to utility, and second with respect to beauty. These steps/aspects are location, site, compartition, roof, wall and openings. In both sequences, most emphasis is placed on compartition, ie, the parti or organization of the whole into parts. When Alberti addresses compartition the second time, in the context of elaborating an operational definition of beauty, he still cannot avoid referring back to utility. The oscillation between the two codes continues. 'In terms of its nature, utility, and methods of operation, everything should be so defined, so exact in its order, number, size, arrangement, and form, that every single part of the work will be considered necessary, of great comfort, and in pleasing harmony with the rest. For if the compartition satisfies these conditions completely the cheerfulness and elegance of the ornament will find the appropriate place and will shine out; but if not, the work will undoubtedly fail to retain any dignity.'[116] The demand for proper

113 See Volume 1, chapter 3.8.4 *Formal A Priori, Idiom and Aesthetic Values.*
114 Alberti, *On the Art of Building in Ten Books*, p 156.
115 Ibid.
116 Ibid, p 163.

compartition is simultaneously a functional and a formal demand. In any case, neither utility nor beauty allows us to consider the individual parts and elements of an architectural work in isolation. According to Alberti the whole regulated the parts: 'The entire composition of the members, therefore, must be so well considered, conform so perfectly with the requirements of necessity and convenience, that this or that part should not give as much pleasure separately as their appropriate placing, here or there, in a particular order, situation, conjunction, arrangement, and configuration.'[117]

The same general idea is expressed time and again throughout Alberti's treatise. Here is another formulation taken from the final reflections in Book 9: 'All should be composed with such method and order that not only do they vie one with another to ennoble the work, but one could not exist on its own, nor maintain its dignity without the other.'[118] The same point is also reinforced via negative formulations. A composition should be 'neither jumpy, nor confused, nor disorganized, nor disconnected, nor composed of incongruous elements, ... nor too disjointed or distant from the rest of the body'.[119] Again the positive principle is reinforced and further explicated by negating its opposite: 'The harmony is such that the building appears a single, integral, and well-composed body, rather than a collection of extraneous and unrelated parts.'[120] Once again, positive and negative heuristics cooperate: 'The mistake is [to be] avoided of making the building appear like a monster with uneven shoulders and sides. Variety is always a most pleasing spice, where distant objects agree and conform with one another, but when it causes discord and difference between them, it is extremely disagreeable.'[121] One might presume that these negative injunctions were not just a rhetorical device but had a real target: they might be read as a polemical rejection of the agglomerative patterns of construction typical in medieval building practice. Alberti's insistence on a well-ordered whole is informed by the examples of Ancient Greece and Rome, and corroborated and further reinforced by analogy with the human body, or more generally with the animal organism: 'Just as the head, foot, and indeed any member must correspond to each other and to all the rest of the body in an animal,

117 Ibid, p 163.
118 Ibid, p 314.
119 Ibid, p 163.
120 Ibid, p 24.
121 Ibid.

so in a building, and especially a temple, the parts of the whole body must be so composed that they all correspond one to another, and any one, taken individually, may provide the dimensions of all the rest.'[122] The concept involves the idea of fixed types: 'Every body consists entirely of parts that are fixed and individual; if these are removed, enlarged, reduced, or transferred somewhere inappropriate, the very composition will be spoiled that gives the body its seemly appearance.'[123] This concept of an organic whole, with symmetry and strict rules of proportion, with a state of completeness or perfection that tolerates neither additions nor subtractions, remained in force throughout the Renaissance, Baroque and Neo-Classicism. The rationality of this rigid notion of order relies on the uniformity and fixity of institutions. It started to be challenged only in the 19th century, in the Neo-Gothic style, within Eclecticism, and then Art Nouveau. It was fully and finally abandoned only with Modernism.

Alberti distinguishes three kinds of aesthetic effect that architectural works might produce – dignity, grace and admiration – and he attributes these effects to three aspects of architectural form – composition, ornament and material – which in turn are attributed to three factors – intellect, craft and nature as follows: 'The intellect is responsible for choice, distribution, arrangement, and so on, which give the work dignity; the hand is responsible for laying, joining, cutting, trimming, polishing, and such like, which give the work grace; the properties derived from Nature are weight, lightness, density, purity, durability, and the like, which bring the work admiration.'[124] There is a clear hierarchy operating here, privileging the contribution of the intellect: 'A common material skillfully treated will be more graceful than a noble one piled up in a disorderly manner.'[125] Although the refined techniques of art, applied to uncommon gifts of nature, like a rare stone, contribute to the effect of a building, according to Alberti, 'they will look worthless unless their composition is precisely governed by order and measure'.[126]

After moving through the formal aspects of location, site, parti, roof, walls and openings (Book 6), Alberti gives detailed descriptions and explanations of the organization, dimensions, construction details and ornaments of many ancient buildings, often related in

122 Ibid, p 199.
123 Ibid.
124 Ibid, p 159.
125 Ibid, p 164.
126 Ibid.

connection with the social institutions and life-processes within which these buildings participated. Alberti ordered his discourse according to the distinction of sacred (Book 7), secular public (Book 8) and private buildings (Book 9). At the end of Book 9 he returns and deepens the more general, theoretical discussion of beauty he had started at the beginning of Book 6. He sets out to theorize the essence of beauty, assuming beauty to be a single essential entity in all its manifold manifestations. He states the problem his 'extremely difficult inquiry'[127] must solve as follows: to identify that 'one entity ... [that is able] ... to tie and bond several elements into a single bundle or body, according to a true and consistent agreement and sympathy'.[128] Alberti insists that many very different things can be equally beautiful, whether in architecture or in nature. Another premise is that aesthetic judgement is universally shared and thus must be based on an inborn mental faculty. 'For within the form and figure of a building there resides some natural excellence and perfection that excites the mind and is immediately recognized by it. I myself believe that form, dignity, grace and other such qualities depend on it, and as soon as anything is removed or altered, these qualities are themselves weakened and perish.'[129] The question is 'what arouses and provokes such a sensation in the mind'.[130] Thus the theoretical riddle is posed.

The solution is first set down in general terms, then argued for by appealing to the study of nature, and finally elaborated in operationally applicable detail. Alberti introduces a special, theoretical term to denote the identified essence of beauty: *concinnitas*. The Latin term derives from *concinnus* meaning skilfully put together. In Alberti's treatise it takes on the meaning of perfect harmony. According to Alberti, it requires the cooperation of three constituent components: *numerus* (number, quantity), *finitio* (measured outline) and *collocatio* (relative position): 'The three principal components of that whole theory into which we inquire are number, what we might call outline, and position. But arising from the composition and connection of these three is a further quality in which beauty shines full face: our term for this is *concinnitas*. ... It is the task and aim of *concinnitas* to compose parts that are quite separate from each other by their nature, according to some precise

127 Ibid, p 301.
128 Ibid.
129 Ibid, p 302.
130 Ibid.

rules, so that they correspond to one another in appearance.'[131] It is the final task of Alberti's theory precisely to specify these rules or criteria to make the code of beauty operational. However, before he engages with the level of operational detail, he tries to ground his theory by referring to nature to underwrite his 'law' of *concinnitas:* 'Everything that Nature produces is regulated by the law of *concinnitas.*'[132] His definitive, summary statement of his theory of beauty makes this grounding in nature clear once more: 'Beauty is a form of sympathy and consonance of the parts within a body, according to definite number, outline, and position, as dictated by *concinnitas,* the absolute and fundamental rule in Nature. This is the main object of the art of building, and the source of her dignity, charm, authority, and worth.'[133]

Alberti credits the ancient study of nature with these insights: 'All that has been said our ancestors learned through observation of Nature herself; ... not without reason they declared that Nature, as the perfect generator of forms, should be their model. And so, with the utmost industry, they searched out the rules that she employed in producing things, and translated them into methods of building.'[134] On the basis of this general principle – emulating nature – Alberti moves on to the concrete rules discovered: 'Taking their example from Nature, they never made the bones of the building, meaning the columns ... odd in number – for you will not find a single animal that stands or moves upon an odd number of feet. Conversely, they never made openings even in number; this they evidently learned from Nature: to animals she has given ears, eyes, and nostrils matching on either side, but in the centre, single and obvious, she has set the mouth.'[135] Alberti also motivates a general law of perfect symmetry: 'Look at Nature's own works: ... if someone had one huge foot, or one hand vast and the other tiny, he would look deformed. ... so natural is it that right should match left exactly. We must therefore take great care to ensure that even the minutest elements are so arranged in their level, alignment, number, shape, and appearance that right

131 Ibid.

132 Ibid, pp 302–3.

133 Ibid, p 303. So-called 'part to whole relationships' are still considered crucial within contemporary architecture. The author is instead calling for elements to integrate into differentiated *subsystems* and for the scripting of *correlations* between these subsystems. The concept of system and of relations between subsystems avoids the connotation of completeness or even perfection that attache to the concept of the whole.

134 Alberti, *On the Art of Building in Ten Books*, p 303.

135 Ibid.

matches left, top matches bottom, adjacent matches adjacent, and equal matches equal.'[136] Next to the insistence on perfect symmetry, the second key component of Alberti's operational theory of beauty as *concinnitas* is the theory of proportions. It refers to both individual members such as columns, their spacing, as well as to whole rooms. The system of proportions is again assumed to be derived from nature. Alberti refers to 'a certain correspondence between the lines that define the dimensions ... taken from those objects in which Nature offers herself to our inspection and admiration'.[137]

Alberti aligns his discourse with the Pythagorean metaphysics of cosmic harmony as demonstrated in the simple whole number relations of musical harmonies: 'I affirm again with Pythagoras: it is absolutely certain that Nature is wholly consistent. ... The very same numbers that cause sounds to have that *concinnitas,* pleasing to the ears, can also fill the eyes and mind with wondrous delight. From musicians therefore who have already examined such numbers thoroughly, or from those objects in which Nature has displayed some evident and noble quality, the whole method of outlining is derived.'[138] Alberti is then rehearsing 'the varying harmonies which the ancients have classified into set numbers corresponding to the relationships between consonant strings'.[139] Alberti is going through the following musical proportions: 2 : 3 (*diapente* or *sesquialtera*), 3 : 4 (*diatessaron* or *sesquitertia*), 1 : 2 (*diapason*), 1 : 3 (*diapason diapente*), 1 : 4 (*disdiapason*), and 7 : 8 (*tonus*). 'Architects employ all these numbers in the most convenient manner possible: they use them in pairs, as in laying out a forum, place or open space, where only two dimensions are considered, width and length; and they use them also in threes, such as in a public sitting room, senate house, hall, and so on, when width relates to length, and they want the height to relate harmoniously to both.'[140] Thus it seems that the system of harmonic proportions is giving a set of formal constraints within which the final selection is determined by considerations of utility. When working in three dimensions, all ratios between the three coordinated dimensions must be harmonic, for instance a space with the dimensions 2, 3 and 4 would fulfil the rule as it involves only the above-named harmonic binary relations, namely 2 : 3, 3 : 4 and 1 : 2. Alberti gives a few examples of how a group of

136 Alberti, *On the Art of Building in Ten Books*, p 310.
137 Ibid, p 305.
138 Ibid.
139 Ibid.
140 Ibid.

three numbers can be arrived at so that each pairing is harmonic. He also allows for a further set of methods for deriving admissible proportions: 'Rules for the composition of outlines in three dimensions may be derived from other sources, apart from harmonies. ... There are several methods of three-dimensional composition that are particularly suitable; these are not only drawn from music and geometry but also arithmetic. ... The philosophers have called these *means*.' Alberti defines the three principal methods to determine means, the *arithmetical*, *geometrical* and the so-called *musical* mean, 'whose object is to find, given two other numbers, an intermediate one, which will correspond to the other two by a fixed rule'.[141] Again examples are given together with the procedure: 4 : 6 : 8 (arithmetical mean), 4 : 6 : 9 (geometric mean), and 30 : 40 : 60 (musical mean). Again, within the formal limits thus imposed, functional considerations can be accommodated: 'Thus in three dimensions, whatever numbers are judged most suitable for the work are drawn from the above list.'[142] Alberti is then using his theoretical apparatus further to derive and explain the proportional systems that govern the three Classical orders, the Doric, Ionic and Corinthian orders, explaining the Ionic column proportion 1 : 8 as arithmetical mean between the two possible proportions suggested by the human body, 1 : 6 as the ratio of human height to width and 1 : 10 as the ratio of human height to depth. 'The ancients may have built their columns to such dimensions, making some six times the base, others ten times. But that natural sense, innate in the spirit, which allows us ... to detect *concinnitas* suggested to them that neither the thickness of the one nor the slenderness of the other was suitable. ... They concluded that what they sought lay between the two extremes.'[143] The relative heights of the Doric and Corinthian columns were then derived as mean between the Ionic height on the one hand and the rejected extremes on the other hand, ie, with the ratios 1 : 7 and 1 : 9 respectively.

Wholeness and harmony, operationalized in terms of symmetry and proportion, are the primary aesthetic values of Alberti's theory of beauty. However, there is a further aesthetic value that must be mentioned here: variety. Alberti explicitly encourages variety in the composition; however, he couples this with an immediate stricture against discord. 'I would not wish all the members to have the same

141 Ibid, p 308.
142 Ibid, p 307.
143 Ibid, p 309.

shape and size, so that there is no difference between them: it will be agreeable to make some parts large, and good to have some small, while some are valuable for their very mediocrity. It will be equally pleasing to have some members defined by straight lines, others by curved ones, and still others by a combination of the two, provided of course that the advice on which I insist is obeyed, and the mistake is avoided of making the building appear like a monster with uneven shoulders and sides. Variety is always a most pleasing spice, where distant objects agree and conform with one another, but when it causes discord and difference between them, it is extremely disagreeable.'[144] Once again, positive and negative heuristics cooperate. Again music is cited as source of corroborating analogy: 'Just as in music, where deep voices answer high ones, and intermediate ones are pitched between them, so they ring out in harmony, a wonderfully sonorous balance of proportions results, which increases the pleasure of the audience and captivates them; so it happens in everything else that serves to enchant and move the mind.'[145] Nature is also drawn in once more to support Alberti's insistence on the value of variety. Again, he attributes this insight to the Ancients: 'By studying in Nature the patterns both for whole bodies and for their individual parts, they understood that at their very origins bodies do not consist of equal portions, with the result that some are slender, some fat, and others inbetween; and observing the great difference in purpose and intention between one building and another, ... they concluded that, by the same token, each should be treated differently.'[146] Thus the aesthetic value is understood to correlate with a performance value. In the same vein Alberti also theorizes and justifies the parallel existence of the three Classical orders: 'Following Nature's own example, they also invented three ways of ornamenting a house. ... One kind was fuller, more practical and enduring: this they called Doric. Another was slender and full of charm: this they named Corinthian. The one that lay in between ... they called the Ionic: they devised these for the body as a whole.'[147] Alberti even allowed for the three Classical orders to be combined in a single building, one on top of the other as exemplified in Rome's Colosseum.[148] Variety is also recommended specifically in relation to

144 Ibid, p 24.

145 Ibid.

146 Ibid, p 303.

147 Ibid.

148 Alberti employed this device in his Palazzo Rucellai, Florence 1452–70. The building was designed after Alberti had completed his treatise.

ornament: 'I would not make everything uniformly ornate and rich in ornament – variety is as useful as quantity. ... Items varying in importance and not quite similar in character may be skillfully contrasted, so that some display gravity and majesty, others gaiety and festivity.'[149] Again aesthetic concerns support and fuse here with the functional aspects of articulation. The theory was thus – for its time – a convincing guide to how architecture should discharge its task: the organization and articulation of social complexity.

In summary one might note that Alberti's theory and programme of beauty are able to offer operational criteria and rules for the application of the code values (and thus for a methodical advancement of the design process), while at the same time not only leaving sufficient room for manoeuvre to address and satisfy rich and nuanced functional concerns, but beyond this also offering a compelling degree of coincidence between the promoted formal values and the functional concerns considered appropriate to the societal context within which Alberti's generation was working. All this was packaged into a mnemotechnically compact theoretical apparatus and supported by a metaphysical superstructure that was able to give both the apparatus and the operational recommendations that were formulated through it sufficient force to unify and stabilize the emerging discipline.

7. programme for the code of originality
Alberti seems to have had a rather balanced view about how to navigate the line between redundancy and novelty. He indicates that in architecture 'all the power of invention, all the skill and experience in the art of building, are called upon'.[150] He further suggests that the architect should 'follow the methods sanctioned by those who are experienced: to contravene established customs often detracts from the general elegance, while conforming to them is considered advantageous and leads to the best results'.[151] However, he immediately continues to emphasize that the architect should also exercise his original creativity: 'Although other famous architects seem to recommend by their work either the Doric, or the Ionic, or the Corinthian, or the Tuscan division as being the most convenient, there is no reason why we should follow their design in our work, as though legally obliged; but rather inspired by their example, we

149 Alberti, *On the Art of Building in Ten Books*, p 314.
150 Ibid, p 23.
151 Ibid, p 24.

should strive to produce our own inventions, to rival, or if possible, to surpass the glory of theirs.'[152] From these remarks one might reconstruct Alberti's programme for the code of originality as follows: strive for original innovations on the basis of experience and knowledge of prior achievements; avoid arbitrary novelty; avoid slavish dependency on prior models. At another occasion, Alberti once more expresses his dialectical approach to redundancy and novelty: 'I would approve of any new invention that incorporates the established rules of ancient buildings, as well as the ingenuity of modern contrivance.'[153] This accords with his demand that the architect should strive to innovate, but only on the basis of a full acquaintance and understanding of the great Ancient works. In this respect, Alberti compares the architect with the writer: 'I would have him take the same approach as one might toward the study of letters, where no one would be satisfied until he had read and examined every author, good and bad, who had written anything on the subject in which he was interested. Wherever there is a work that has received general approval, he should inspect it with great care, record it in drawing, note its numbers, and construct models.'[154] Alberti continues: 'But above all he must inspect each building for the rare and precious artifice it might contain, the result of some considered and recondite artistry or of remarkable invention; . . . and should he find anything anywhere of which he approves, he should adopt and copy it; yet anything that he considers can be greatly refined, he should use his artistry and imagination to correct and put right; and anything that is otherwise not too bad, he should strive, to the best of his ability, to improve.'[155] What emerges here is the spectre of a critical, rational, competitive discourse that is neither constrained by traditional dogma nor by undue reverence towards authority but instead values creativity where it delivers real innovation, albeit without making a fetish of novelty. This general characterization of architecture as a rational discourse with innovative forward thrust can still – over half a millennium later – serve as valid formula within a pertinent self-description of the autopoiesis of architecture.

8. implied style

The inauguration of architecture as theoretically led discipline of design that based itself on the erudite and empirical recovery of the

152 Ibid, p 24.
153 Ibid, p 316.
154 Ibid, p 315.
155 Ibid, p 316.

lost architectural repertoire and expertise of Ancient Rome was much later, in the second half of the 19th century, theorized as part of a larger cultural-epochal phenomenon christened *Renaissance*.[156] As an architectural/artistic style it was identified in contrast to the medieval/Gothic that had preceded it, and to the Baroque style that followed.

9. expansion of the repertoire
   Every pertinent and forward-looking self-description of architecture should guide the expansion of the repertoire for spatio-architectural organization and articulation. Alberti recovered the full repertoire of Ancient Roman architecture and urbanism, both in terms of the variety of organizational types and of the possibilities for differentiated tectonic articulation. Compared with the Gothic proto-architecture, this entailed an immense expansion of the repertoire. At the same time, the idea of design, together with the concept of *concinnitas* and the systematic use of proportions, gave a much increased sense of precision and predictability to the built environment.

10. design-process guidance
   Alberti insists on a principled, methodical, coherent process, based on a clear purpose: 'nothing is begun without establishing a procedure to an end in view, nothing raised except according to the principles on which it was begun'.[157] Beyond this general insistence, and the overall sense that design should proceed via careful, rational deliberation, and via the conscientious application of the rules of symmetry and proportion, there is no explicit, operational discourse on method or design process. However, there is a definite sequence by which Alberti proceeds in introducing the aspects of the design task that must (in turn) be considered, namely: location, area, compartition, roof, wall, openings. It seems plausible to interpret this sequence as the sequential steps by which a rational design process should proceed.[158] This sequence occurs twice, first under the auspices of the concern of utility, and then under the auspices of the concern of beauty. The sequencing of these two concerns (that make up the double code of architecture) in the book might suggest an

156 The seminal work that firmly established the term/concept of the Renaissance was Jacob Burckhardt's *The Civilization of the Renaissance in Italy*, published in 1860. With respect to the contrast of Renaissance and Baroque art/architecture, Heinrich Wölfflin's *Renaissance und Barock* (1888) was seminal.

157 Alberti, *On the Art of Building in Ten Books*, p 164.

158 The first three steps also order the design of cities.

ordering in terms of the design process, at each step: address utility first (albeit constrained by an implicitly assumed formal a priori), then formalize with respect to the criteria of beauty.

11. design medium
The much increased level of completion and precision that Alberti demands with respect to the design in advance of construction requires a much enhanced design medium with a much increased capacity for the elaboration, anticipation and control of the intended building project. The great advancement in the capacity of representation during Alberti's time was the invention of linear perspective. The invention – or better re-invention since antiquity – was attributed to Brunelleschi. It was Alberti, however, who wrote the first systematic introduction on perspective representation: *De pictura,* in the mid 1430s. However, the book was not immediately concerned with architecture and design. It was concerned with painting. The book was, indeed, 'the first modern manual for painters, the first systematic modern work on the arts ... the first artistic manifesto of the modern world'.[159] As Anthony Grafton suggests, Alberti set out to transform painting from a traditional craft into a learned art by offering systematic principles on the basis of theoretical discussion. The construction of perspective via a specific set of geometric techniques based on the laws of optics allowed painting to achieve a new, convincing level of veracity. According to Alberti, this new technique gives painting the power to 'make the absent present'.[160] The same techniques and effects were applicable to Alberti's enhanced ambition for architectural design. Accordingly, Alberti insists that the educated architect requires sufficient expertise in two further arts: 'Of the arts the ones that are useful, even vital, to the architect, are painting and mathematics.'[161] Hinting at his prior book, Alberti then further qualifies: 'Let it be enough that he has a grasp of those elements of painting of which we have written.'[162] Mathematics is not only required for perspective construction but also for the application of the comprehensive, coordinated system of proportions that Alberti expected to be implemented. The use of drawings other than perspective, as well as the use of scale models was required to achieve a fully coordinated,

159 Anthony Grafton, *Leon Battista Alberti – Master Builder of the Italian Renaissance*, Penguin Books (London), 2002, pp 113–14.

160 Leon Battista Alberti, *Opere volgari*, C Grayson (Ed), Laterza (Bari), 1960–73, III, pp 44–5.

161 Alberti, *On the Art of Building in Ten Books*, p 317.

162 Ibid.

detailed design. Alberti explains on the basis of his own design experience: 'I have often conceived projects in the mind that seemed quite commendable at the time, but when I translated them into drawings, I found several errors. ... When I pass from the drawings to the model, I sometimes notice further mistakes in the individual parts, even over the numbers.'[163] Alberti explicitly recommended the use of scaled models, 'to avoid any hesitation, change, or revision after the commencement of the work, and so that we may form a concise overall picture of the whole'.[164]

12. self-reflectiveness

Alberti's *De re aedificatoria* is a self-conscious effort to elaborate a comprehensive theory of architecture that would be able to guide the practice of architects on the basis of theoretically grounded principles. Alberti is explicit: 'Anyone who builds so as to be praised for it – as anyone with good sense would – must adhere to a consistent theory; for to follow a consistent theory is the mark of true art.'[165] While Alberti states his case for a theory-led practice with confidence, he also reflects that others have argued against this possibility: 'This particular part concerning beauty and ornament, being the most important of all, must depend on some sure method and art. ... Yet some would disagree who maintain that beauty, and indeed every aspect of building, is judged by relative and variable criteria, and that the forms of buildings should vary according to individual taste and must not be bound by any rules of art.'[166] However, he attributes this scepticism to ignorance: 'A common fault, this, among the ignorant – to deny the existence of anything they do not understand.'[167]

Alberti is not insisting on a rule- and knowledge-based practice blindly, as it were, merely accepting established wisdom and consensus. His reflection inquires into the processes through which the attained theory was able to develop: 'The arts were born of Chance and Observation, fostered by Use and Experiment, and matured by Knowledge and Reason.'[168] These reflections demonstrate an astonishing depth of insight. Alberti continues: 'Thus medicine, they say, was developed by a million people over a

163 Ibid.
164 Ibid.
165 Ibid, p 156.
166 Ibid, p 157.
167 Ibid.
168 Ibid.

thousand years; sailing too, as almost every other art, advanced by minute steps.'[169] Thus Alberti's respect for the inherited achievements of antiquity is based on an understanding of how their rationality emerged from a long, cumulative process of development.

Alberti's self-conception with respect to his theoretical endeavour is rather mature and sophisticated. He is clear that he must build his expertise upon the recovery of the superior architectural culture of Ancient Rome. But he doesn't rate the Roman achievements just on account of their impressiveness. Alberti understands the achievements of Roman architecture as the culmination of a long process of historical development and traces the main steps or milestones of this development. The story starts in Asia, then moves to Greece, and culminates in Rome. About the Greek architects Alberti writes: 'They began by examining the works of the Assyrians and the Egyptians, from which they realized that in such matters the artist's skill attracted more praise than the wealth of the king: for vast works need only great wealth; praise belongs to those with whom experts find no fault. The Greeks therefore decided that it was their part to surpass through ingenuity those whose wealth they could not rival.'[170]

Alberti thus finds in his historical reconstruction of the discipline's historical origin an admirable ethos and values that are still precious today, and worthy to be heeded. Further, he is trying to understand how the Greeks were able to reach their admirable level of achievement: 'As with the other arts, so with building, they sought it in, and drew it out from the very bosom of Nature, and began to discuss and examine it thoroughly, studying and weighing it up with great incisiveness and subtlety. They inquired into the differences between buildings that were admired and those that were not, overlooking nothing. They performed all manner of experiment, surveying and retracing the steps of Nature. ... They continued to consider each individual part in the minutest detail, how right agreed with left, vertical with horizontal, near with far. They added, took away, and adjusted, greater to smaller, like to unlike, first to last, until they had established the different qualities desirable in those buildings intended to endure for ages.'[171] Obviously these demystifying reflections on the way past achievements were reached are intended to inform and inspire contemporary efforts.

169 Ibid.
170 Ibid, pp 157–8.
171 Ibid, p 158.

In the description of Rome's achievements, Alberti applies his own most precious concepts: 'As for Italy, their inborn thrift prompted them to be the first who made their buildings very like animals. ... They realized that where the shape of each member looked suitable for a particular use, so the whole animal itself would work well in that use. Thus they found that grace of form could never be separated or divorced from suitability for use.'[172] Alberti continues: 'But once they had gained dominion over the world, they were so obviously eager to embellish their city and property as the Greeks had been. ... The empire had sufficient resources to supply anything needed to provoke astonishment. ... In spite of all this, they preferred to temper the splendor of their most powerful kings with a traditional frugality, so that parsimony did not detract from utility, nor was utility sacrificed to opulence.'[173] In these passages Alberti is presenting and indeed rationally reconstructing the source of his own expertise and values, the ancient heritage, as a vital inheritance that can and must continue and prosper.

Indeed, Alberti saw his treatise as an effort of retrieving and securing a cultural treasure and knowledge base that was in danger of being lost. This at least was his original motive to commence his work on architecture: 'The very reasons that first induced me to embark on it ... encouraged me to continue. For I grieved that so many works of such brilliant writers had been destroyed by the hostility of time and of man, and that almost the sole survivor from this vast shipwreck is Vitruvius, an author of unquestioned experience, though one whose writings have been so corrupted by time that there are many omissions and shortcomings. What he handed down was in any case not refined.'[174] This barely veiled criticism of Vitruvius is at the same time Alberti's justification for writing a new treatise that should surpass and supersede Vitruvius. Alberti continues to express his concern about imminent loss of a cultural treasure and vital resource: 'Examples of ancient temples and theaters have survived that may teach us as much as any professor, but I see – not without sorrow – these very buildings being despoiled more each day. ... As a result of all this a whole section of our life and learning could disappear altogether. ... As I was exploring this matter, many noble, useful things, vital to the existence of man, came to my notice, which I decided not to neglect in writing. Moreover, I felt it the duty of any

172 Ibid.
173 Ibid.
174 Ibid, p 154.

gentleman or any person of learning to save from total extinction a discipline that our prudent ancestors had valued so highly.'[175] The discipline of architecture had to be saved by being re-inaugurated anew, a discipline with a vital societal function.

Alberti reflects on his own process of discovery and learning: 'No building of the ancients that had attracted praise, wherever it may be, but I immediately examined it carefully, to see what I could learn from it. Therefore I never stopped exploring, considering, and measuring everything, and comparing the information through line drawings, until I had grasped and understood fully what each had to contribute in terms of ingenuity or skill.'[176] Then he goes on to state where he saw his main challenge and, by implication, his main achievement, namely, 'to collate material from sources so varied, heterogeneous, and dispersed, ... to arrange [it] in a proper order, to articulate [it] precisely and explain [it] rationally'.[177] Thus, there can be no question of a blind following of results. Alberti's project was the inquisitive and critical recuperation of the rationality of the great achievements of the past in order to innovate once more on the basis of such an understanding. Alberti characterizes his own process of theory formation as a dialectical back and forth between empirical investigation and experimentation on the one hand, and philosophically informed, theoretical reflection that attempts to abstract and ground general principles on the other. 'Through the example of our ancestors, therefore, and through the advice of experts and constant practice on our part, thorough understanding may be gained on how to construct, and from that understanding well-proven principles may be deduced. ... These we must set down, as was our undertaking, and explain to the best of our ability.'[178] Alberti continues to classify these principles into two kinds: 'These principles either direct every aspect of beauty and ornament throughout the building or relate individually to its various parts. The former are derived from philosophy, and are concerned with establishing the direction and limits of this art; the latter come from the experience of which we spoke, but are honed, so to speak, to the rule of philosophy and plot the course of this art.'[179]

175 Ibid.
176 Ibid, p 155.
177 Ibid.
178 Ibid, p 159.
179 Ibid.

10.3.2 DURAND'S *PRÉCIS DES LEÇONS D'ARCHITECTURE*

Jean-Nicolas-Louis Durand's *Précis des leçons d'architecture*[180] might be posited here as the second milestone in the theoretical strand of architecture's evolution. That Durand's *Précis* might deserve to be classified as a self-description of the discipline can already be gleaned from the preface which ambitiously promises to present 'accurate ideas as to the nature of the art; its purpose, means, and general principles'.[181]

The work is indeed a classic in terms of its ambition, original innovative thrust, its extraordinary success and its enduring problematics. Durand's *Précis* was first published in two volumes in 1802 and 1805. Three further editions, in 1817–19, 1823–5 and 1840, testify to the success of the work. The importance of Durand's *Précis* in its own time – the 19th century – is also indicated by the fact that it was translated into German influencing Leo von Klenze,[182] Karl Friedrich Schinkel and, in turn, the entire German *Klassizismus*. As Antoine Picon testifies, Durand's influence had been sustained for a considerable stretch of architectural history: 'Durand's writings offer one of the earliest formulations of the concepts of composition and type that were to guide the teaching of the Beaux-Arts until it collapsed under the onslaught of Modernism.'[183]

Like all classics of the discipline, Durand's work is as much connected to its contemporary design culture as it is deeply embedded in the total theoretical tradition it challenges. In particular Durand builds on a string of French theoretical contributions that originated in the 16th century with Jean Martin's translation of Alberti's *De re aedificatoria*, published in Paris as *L'Architecture et art de bien bastir* in 1553. This series of theoretical works includes among others Roland Fréart de Chambray's *Parallèle de l'architecture antique et de la moderne* (1650), Claude Perrault's annotated translation of Vitruvius (1673, 1684), Nicolas-François Blondel's *Cours d'architecture* (1675, 1683) as the first academic textbook for the Royal Academy of Architecture founded in 1671, Claude Perrault's *Ordonnance des cinq espèces de colonnes selon la méthode des anciens* (1683), Charles Perrault's *Parallèle des anciens et des modernes* (1688), Jean-Louis de Cordemoy's *Nouveau traité de toute l'architecture* (1706, 1714), Marc-Antoine Laugier's seminal *Essai*

180 Jean-Nicolas-Louis Durand, *Précis des leçons d'architecture données à l'École royale polytechnique* (Paris), 1802–5, English translation by David Britt, published by The Getty Research Institute (Los Angeles), 2000.

181 Ibid, p 73.

182 Leo von Klenze had followed Durand's lectures in Paris.

183 Antoine Picon, 'From "Poetry of Art" to Method: The Theory of Jean-Nicolas-Louis Durand', in: Durand, *Précis des leçons d'architecture*, p 2.

sur l'architecture (1753), Julien-David Le Roy's *Les ruines des plus beaux monuments de la Grèce* (1758, 1770), Jacques-François Blondel's nine-volume *Cours d'architecture* (1771), Nicolas Le Camus De Mézières' *Le génie de l'architecture* (1780), Antoine C Quatremère de Quincy's *Encyclopédie méthodique: architecture* (1788), Étienne-Louis Boullée's *Architecture – essai sur l'art* (1794), and Claude-Nicolas Ledoux's *L'architecture considerée sous le rapport de l'art, des moeurs et de la législation* (1802). This rather extensive (but far from exhaustive) sample of antecedent texts is listed here to emphasize that Durand's *Précis* builds upon a rich discourse. This discourse was full of controversial arguments rather than a seamless lineage of instruction. The controversies concerned the origin, purpose, principles and values, as well as readily applicable rules for architecture. Durand's *Précis* includes explicit references to Vitruvius, Laugier and Le Roy. Both Vitruvius and Laugier are quoted at length in order to be refuted and superseded.

1. the societal function and the task of architecture:
   In his introduction to the *Précis*, Durand immediately homes in on the importance of correctly identifying the societal function of architecture as starting point for an instructive theory of architecture. 'To succeed in anything, one must have a tangible and rational aim. ... From this, once established, we shall naturally deduce the general principles of architecture.'[184] Durand is stressing the necessity of a unifying point of departure for architectural theory. Durand would like to build his architectural teachings on the clear formulation of architecture's fundamental purpose. He wants to start with a unifying point of departure rather than starting with the traditional division of the field. Durand reflects upon his own theoretical enterprise and emphasizes: 'the more general remarks that we have prefixed to our successive particular observations; ... what architecture is, why we practice it, and how to practice it'.[185] Durand continues his reflections: 'We therefore deemed it necessary to address ourselves, first of all, to the nature of the art, the purpose to which it tends, and the means that it must embrace, in order to extract some general principles on which all the particular principles might securely rest.'[186]

184 Jean-Nicolas-Louis Durand, *Précis des leçons d'architecture données à l'École royale polytechnique*, p 78.
185 Ibid, p 132.
186 Ibid.

In an implicit reference to Jacques-François Blondel's *Cours d'architecture,* Durand criticizes those courses of architecture that start by dividing architecture into the three distinct parts of *decoration*, *distribution* and *construction*. Durand disputes the general relevance of these categories and demands ideas that 'would have to be entirely general, affording elevated vantage points from which to embrace the art as a whole before descending to survey the whole range of particulars'.[187] Durand finds all prior self-descriptions of architecture defective as they 'fail to supply any such general idea, . . . which would be the source of all those particular ideas that must guide us in the composition of all buildings'.[188] Durand recognizes that a division of the domain into subdomains of study is indeed necessary, but he insists that 'far from pitting particular ideas against each other in mutual opposition, as often happens, it must be a division that binds them together through a simple and natural order.'[189]

Before fully explicating what he presumes to be the principal purpose (societal function) of architecture, Durand engages in a critical debate with what he considers to be a predominant misconception: 'Most architects take the view that architecture is not so much the art of making useful buildings as that of decorating them. Its principal object, accordingly, is to please the eye and thereby arouse delightful sensations; an object that, like the other arts, it can attain only through imitation.'[190]

It is in relation to this fundamental debate at the very beginning of his theory that Durand engages Laugier and Vitruvius. Laugier proposed the primitive hut as object of imitation, while Vitruvius proposed the proportions of the human body as model. Durand presents long quotes from both, and then rejects the idea that architecture's rationale can be decoration founded on imitation. Specifically, Durand argues: 'that the Greek orders were not an imitation of the hut at all; and that, if they had been, this imitation would have been utterly imperfect. . . and if the human body can never have served as a model for architecture; and if . . . the orders are not an imitation of either, the necessary conclusion must be that these orders are not the essence of architecture, . . . that such

187 Ibid, p 77.
188 Ibid, p 78.
189 Ibid.
190 Ibid, p 79.

decoration is itself a chimera'.[191] Durand refers to the fact that Greek architecture often remained unadorned. 'Of course, care and purity are apparent in its execution; but is not care essential for solidity? ... Is it not clear that such ornaments are not essential in architecture?'[192] This double challenge, ie, the challenge of the Classical theory of imitation that brings architecture under the general concept of art as mimesis and the challenge of the importance of decoration, marks Durand's book as a radical innovation right from the start.

Durand explicitly states his understanding of the societal function of architecture as follows – hinting that he is even willing to sacrifice the categorization of architecture as art: 'Whether we consult reason or examine the monuments, it is evident that pleasure can never have been the aim of architecture; nor can architectural decoration have been its object. Public and private utility, the happiness and the protection of individuals and of society; such is the aim of architecture. Whether it be accorded or denied the name of art, it will nonetheless deserve to be practiced.'[193] This is a remarkably enlightened and mature point of departure for an architectural self-description at the beginning of the 19th century. These premises state principal theoretical underpinnings of architectural theory that reach beyond the confines of the Neo-Classicist style and lay the foundation of Modernist architectural theory. Durand is even offering a deep, anthropological (utilitarian) underpinning for his fundamental tenet about the aim of architecture: 'in all ages and in all places, all of men's thoughts and actions have sprung from two principles alone: love of comfort and dislike of all exertion'.[194] This reference to the utilitarian, materialist world-view indeed anticipates the philosophical foundations of Modernism. This utilitarian reasoning leads him to posit the societal necessity of architecture: 'architecture, of all the arts, was the one whose productions exacted the most trouble and the most expense, ...it was, nevertheless, the art most generally practiced in every age'.[195] Durand continues his argument: 'men are naturally hostile to all forms of exertion as they are desirous of comfort; ... they would never have practiced architecture so generally and so constantly as they do, if it had not been of great advantage to

191 Ibid, pp 82–3.
192 Ibid, p 84.
193 Ibid.
194 Ibid.
195 Ibid, p 133.

them.'[196] Durand stresses the utilitarian benefits of architecture and indeed claims that architecture is essential for society's very existence and survival: 'it is to architecture that the human race owes its survival, society its existence, and all the other arts their birth and their development'.[197] He concludes his argument as follows: 'if instead of all these inestimable benefits, architecture had offered no more than the frivolous advantage of delighting the eye, it would soon have been eclipsed by painting and sculpture, ... in consequence, the purpose of architecture cannot be pleasure but utility'.[198]

2. avant-gardist orientation
   Since Modernism, every comprehensive architectural self-description must explicitly articulate a historically argued forward orientation for the discipline. However, Durand is writing at the end of the 18th and the beginning of the 19th centuries, when historical orientation and forward projection were not yet the inevitable and pervasive frame of world-orientation they have since become. Although there are innovations, they are not made with a full consciousness of their originality and transformative power. Architectural innovations are still presenting themselves as discoveries (or re-discoveries) of eternal truths.

   For instance, after stating his radically innovative notion that architecture must avoid all decoration and that fitness and economy must serve as the penultimate principles of architecture demanding the utmost simplicity and forbidding absolutely anything that is not strictly necessary, Durand dissimulates his innovation: 'Such are the general principles that must have guided reasonable men everywhere and in every age, when they came to erect buildings; and such are the principles that governed the design of the most universally and justly admired of ancient buildings.'[199]

3. disciplinary demarcations
   Bernard Huet notes that 'The *Précis* is the first architectural treatise to take as its subject architecture itself, architecture without

196 Ibid, p 133. This turn of reasoning already anticipates the materialist-functional explanations of history later systematized by Marx and Luhmann.

197 Ibid.

198 Ibid.

199 Ibid, p 85.

reference to the art of construction.'[200] Although this is not strictly so, the gist of Huet's remark is valid. While Durand's work – like all prior architectural treatises – does still include a lot of technical details, it is fair to say that Durand's *Précis* has a clearer architectural focus if compared with the works of his predecessors. What is important is the way the technical detail is integrated into the overall theory. The theory treats construction issues under the heading of 'The Elements of Buildings' and treats them in view of their bearing on composition. Technical issues are also connected to the value of 'economy' and the related aesthetic values of 'character' and 'variety'. Thus there is a sense that the architectural aspects start to separate from and guide the merely technical aspects of construction.

The full separation of architecture and engineering as incommensurable systems of communication took place later. What we can find at the beginning of the 19th century, however, is an awareness of two disciplines that seem to be competing around the same societal function. The emergence of engineering was a result of the bourgeois/industrial revolution that brought about an enormous expansion of construction tasks. Some of those were naturally taken up by architecture, for instance the buildings for the expanding political administration, urban tenement buildings, or the private houses for the aspiring bourgeoisie. Many other, more utilitarian and infrastructural buildings were involving engineers. Durand was in fact lecturing at the École Polytechnique rather than at the architectural academy. In his preface to the *Précis* he alludes to the two professions as follows: 'Architects are not alone in being required to erect buildings: so, frequently, are engineers, both civil and military. ... engineers ... have more opportunities to carry out large undertakings than do architects proper. The latter may well build nothing but private houses all their lives; but the former ... find themselves professionally required to construct hospitals, prisons, barracks, arsenals, magazines, bridges, harbors, lighthouses: a host of buildings of the first importance.'[201]

The École Polytechnique was founded in 1795 as school of public works (École Centrale Des Travaux Publics) as the world's 'first training centre for engineers and architects with an institutionalized

200 Bernard Huet, 'Les trois fortunes de Durand', in: Werner Szambien, *Jean-Nicolas-Louis Durand 1760–1834: De l'imitation à la norme*, Picard (Paris), 1984, p 10.

201 Durand, *Précis des leçons d'architecture données à l'École royale polytechnique*, p 73.

teaching programme and with modern training goals'.[202] The school provided a general scientific and technical curriculum as stepping stone and necessary precondition for further higher education leading to government posts. It was dominated by scientists, primarily chemists and mathematicians. In 1797 Durand was engaged as *Instituteur d'Architecture* to lead the polytechnic course in architecture. He himself had studied at the Académie d'Architecture in the studio of Étienne-Louis Boullée until 1782. However, the Revolution had abolished the academies of the arts and sciences and the École Polytechnique was the first re-institutionalization of state education. Following Napoleon's takeover, the school became a major device for the bureaucratic instrumentalization of science and engineering for the centrally set purposes of the state, including its military tasks.[203] All public buildings were to be designed by state functionaries trained according to scientific principles. This societal context, as well as Durand's immediate academic context, explain why Durand aligns architecture with science and separates it from art. Later, after Napoleon's final defeat in 1815, the development of the French educational system gave more prominence to the École des Beaux-Arts. Although Durand's writings were also influential within the École des Beaux-Arts, the architectural self-consciousness of the 19th century in general continued to maintain architecture's close affiliation to art.

As we shall see below, Durand was clearly differentiating architecture from painting and sculpture, both in terms of function (utility instead of pleasure) and in terms of its means (fitness and economy instead of imitation). However, Durand is not willing to demarcate between architecture and science. The opposite is rather the case, ie, he is trying to assimilate architecture to science. He explicitly states that 'Architecture is at one and the same time a science and an art.'[204] Durand emphasizes the rational sequence by which he builds up his 'science and art' of architecture. Part I gives the *elements* of buildings, 'the way in which they are to be

202 Ulrich Pfammatter, *The Making of the Modern Architect and Engineer, The Origins and Development of a Scientific and Industrially Oriented Education*, Birkhäuser (Basel), 2000, p 17.

203 In 1804, the school was effectively militarized: 'Towards the middle of 1804 Napoleon awarded the "École" military status, designated a governor responsible for the school, ordered the students to be placed in barracks, and organized into military corps. Individual professors took on ministerial posts.' Pfammatter, *The Making of the Modern Architect and Engineer*, p 34.

204 Durand, *Précis des leçons d'architecture*, p 131. The word 'art' used here has a much broader meaning than merely the practices we now comprise under the concept of art.

employed, ... the forms and the proportions that can be applied to each element',[205] Part II treats *composition in general*, ie, it examines 'how to combine them (these elements) and how to dispose them relative to each other',[206] and Part III is concerned 'in a more specific manner with the composition of every kind of building in particular'.[207] Durand emphasizes the methodical nature of his presentation and procedure in contrast to those who refuse methods in the name of genius: 'The sequence ... is no different from the course that is followed in all the sciences and in all the arts: it consists in a progression from the simple to the composite, from the known to the unknown; one idea always prepares the mind for that which follows, and the latter always recalls that which precedes it. We do not believe that in the study of architecture it is possible to follow any other sequence – still less to dispense with one altogether, as do many architects, who say that rules and methods are the shackles of genius. ... reason may dispense with genius, but genius can only go astray unless led and illuminated by reason.'[208]

Above we have already seen that Durand was – for the first time – willing to separate architecture from art. Even if architecture remains to be classified within the 'arts', Durand is explicitly stressing the uniqueness of architecture: 'Architecture is an art of a kind unique to itself, and its object is the composition and execution of buildings, both public and private.'[209] These words are placed at the beginning of the recapitulating section of the *Précis'* introduction. Durand returns again to the topic of architecture's distinction and relation to the other arts in the final paragraph of Volume 1 of the *Précis*. After dismissing the idea that architecture and architectural theory should focus on drawing in order to be associated with the noble art of painting, Durand restates his notion that architecture has its own important purpose and principles: 'In view of architecture's importance for humanity, let it be treated in accordance with its true principles. Then, perhaps, far from needing to advance it to equality with any other art, we shall find no other that can justly be placed on

205 Durand, *Précis des leçons d'architecture*, p 131. The word 'art' used here has a much broader meaning than merely the practices we now comprise under the concept of art.
206 Ibid, p 132.
207 Ibid.
208 Ibid.
209 Ibid, p 87.

a level with it.'[210] This is indeed the concluding sentence of Durand's *Précis* Volume 1. The strategic placement of Durand's demarcation efforts is significant. He starts his introductory recapitulation with an insistence upon architecture's uniqueness and he closes his first volume with a related point. It is clear that Durand is placing some emphasis on the fundamental definition and demarcation of architecture as unique discipline. Above we saw that Durand clearly demarcates architecture from painting and sculpture by reference to its distinct purpose: utility rather than mere pleasure and delight for the eye.

It is typical of the period that questions of demarcation or distinction immediately enter into questions of placement within a ranking order. For Durand it is not enough to state architecture's difference and independence; he insists on architecture's supremacy. This kind of insistence on rank is alien to us at the beginning of the 21st century. His preoccupation with the establishment of priority within a ranking order betrays Durand as remaining steeped in a mentality that belongs to the historical era dominated by stratification as primary mode of societal differentiation. It took the whole of the 19th century to complete the transition from stratified societies to functionally differentiated societies. Only in the 20th century – with some delay due to the inherent inertia of ideas – does the obsession with ranking subside. Now the statement of differences suffices to structure communication. There can no longer be any question of ranking different function systems.

4. form-function relations

Under this heading we expect directives towards the general handling and integration of form-function relations. Durand conceptualized the relationship between form and function by means of the concepts of *fitness* and *economy* on the side of function, and *simplicity* and *regularity* on the side of form. Having absorbed the sober, materialist sensibility of the Enlightenment, Durand is one of the first architectural theorists to rigorously bind form to function. Function for him is the essential motivating force or determinant of architectural form. Function rules form, both in terms of the human uses that need to be accommodated, and in terms of the demands of effective, durable construction. After going through the various construction materials, in terms of their properties, and techniques

210 Ibid, p 127.

of preparing them for effective utilization within the various elements of construction, Durand generalizes as follows: 'The union of these materials naturally gives rise to forms and proportions.'[211] Function determines form. However, Durand is not pursuing this notion in abstract radicality. He recognizes custom or tradition as another force that has to be reckoned with and that must perhaps be accommodated. He is further – significantly – considering the human apprehension of architectural forms. Durand realizes that forms cannot simply be derived from functions because there remains a considerable degree of underdetermination that implies the need for other guiding criteria in order to arrive at the final definition of architectural form. That's where the concerns of human perception and the adherence to tradition come into play to guide the final articulation of architectural form. Durand demonstrates here a rare level of insight and an impressive sophistication in the theoretical elaboration of these insights. The particular passage is therefore worth quoting at length:

> Forms and proportions may be divided into three categories: those that spring from the nature of materials, and from the uses of the things they serve to build; those that custom in a sense made necessary to us, such as the forms and proportions of the buildings of antiquity; and finally, those simpler and more definite forms and proportions that earn our preference through the ease with which we apprehend them. Of these, only those in the first category are essential; but they are not so firmly defined by the nature of things that we cannot add to them or subtract from them, so that there is no reason not to combine them with those of the second class, derived from ancient buildings. Since these vary considerably ... one is at liberty to select the simplest, ... the best suited to satisfy both the eye and the mind.[212]

Durand thus sets out a clear hierarchy of the determinants of architectural form: the primary factor is the function, in terms of human utility, technical performance and economy; the second factor is custom in the form of the inherited architectural tradition; the third determinant is easy comprehensibility.

211 Jean-Nicolas-Louis Durand, *Précis des leçons d'architecture données à l'École royale polytechnique* (Paris), 1802–5, English translation by David Britt, published by The Getty Research Institute (Los Angeles), 2000.

212 Ibid, pp 108–9.

The function of buildings is the primary concern. To make this general concern concrete within his treatise, Durand must distinguish the various function-types current in (French) architecture at the beginning of the 19th century. Accordingly, Part III, by far the longest part of the book, is dedicated to the exploration of the various function-types. Part I is entitled *Elements of Building*, Part II is entitled *Composition in General* and Part III is entitled *Examination of the Principal Kinds of Building*. Durand lists 44 different functional types, each treated with a dedicated chapter, and arranged into three sections: *The Principal Parts of Cities*, *Public Building* and *Private Buildings*. That Durand is really concerned with establishing a functional classification (rather than merely treating traditional building types) is evident in his anticipation of the section on public buildings at the beginning of Volume 2: 'we reviewed the principal public buildings necessary for government, education, subsistence, commerce, health, pleasure, security, and so on'.[213] This list of functional categories does indeed read like a comprehensive classification of all aspects of social life.

5. programme for the code of utility
Every comprehensive architectural self-description must try to re-formulate the programme for the application of the code of utility. Antoine Picon asserts in connection with Durand that 'In the second half of the 18th century, the issue of the utility of architecture was thrown into prominence by the nascent rivalry between architects and engineers.'[214] This might be so, in terms of emphasis, but the issue of utility is undeniably a constituent of the autopoiesis of architecture from its very inception. What changes from one self-description to the next – and from one style to the next – is the programme that operationalizes architectural utility.

Durand analyzes utility in two primary aspects: fitness and economy. He derives these primary aspects of utility from his utilitarianist-anthropological insight already quoted above that, 'in all ages and in all places, all of men's thoughts and actions have sprung from two principles alone: love of comfort and dislike of all exertion'.[215] Durand continues to explain: 'Accordingly, whether

213 Ibid, p 132.

214 Antoine Picon, 'From "Poetry of Art" to Method: The Theory of Jean-Nicolas-Louis Durand', in: Jean-Nicolas-Louis Durand, *Précis des leçons d'architecture données à l'École royale polytechnique*, p 18.

215 Ibid, p 84.

building their own private dwellings in isolation, or erecting public buildings in society, men inevitably sought (1) to derive from their buildings the greatest possible advantage, consequently making them as fit as possible for their purpose; and (2) to build them in the way that would in early times be the least laborious and later – when money had become the price of labor – the least costly.'[216] Durand concludes his argument by asserting that 'thus, fitness and economy are the means that architecture must naturally employ, and are the sources from which it must derive its principles: the only principles that can guide us in the study and exercise of the art'.[217]

Fitness is then further analyzed into three independent, necessary sub-aspects or requirements: solidity, salubrity and commodity. Solidity is concerned with the structurally appropriate choice of materials, with foundations, disposition of structural members and so on, ie, with what has since been differentiated as the specialist domain of the structural engineer. Salubrity is concerned with issues such as protection from the elements, lighting, ventilation and so on, ie, with matters that have since been differentiated as the specialist domains of building physics engineers and services/environmental engineers. The third component of fitness for purpose is the one that remains within the core competency of the discipline of architecture: commodity. Commodity is identifying what we today still recognize as architectural fitness for purpose. In the terms of the theory of architectural autopoiesis, the requirement of commodity, as defined by Durand, can be identified with the architectural task of *organization*. Durand defines a building as commodious 'if the number and size of all its parts, their form, situation, and arrangement, are in the closest possible relation to its purpose'.[218] This issue of commodity/organization that Durand systematically positions within his discussion of fitness encompasses what the French architectural tradition before Durand had addressed under the heading of distribution. Durand's notion of commodity has general applicability in architecture, while Durand denies this generality to the traditional concept of distribution which, according to him, only relates to residential buildings. 'By distribution, nothing more is meant than the art of disposing, in accordance with our present-day customs, the different parts that make up a building

216 Ibid, p 84.
217 Ibid.
218 Ibid, p 85.

intended for habitation: for no one speaks of the distribution of a temple, a theatre, a courthouse, and so on.'[219]

Despite this generalizing thrust, so far, with respect to his notion of fitness, Durand's theory of architectural utility just systematically re-states what was considered to be self-evident throughout the architectural tradition. However, his uncompromising emphasis on economy as fundamental principle that is supposed to regulate the application of the code value constitutes a radical innovation. Durand boldly states that 'economy demands the utmost simplicity in all necessary things, it absolutely forbids all that is unnecessary'.[220] In Durand's terms economy implies geometric simplicity, which in turn entails regularity and symmetry. Thus the primary formal characteristics of Classical (and Neo-Classical) architecture are derived from the principle of economy as sub-principle of the principle of utility. Durand explicates: 'If a given area demands less length of perimeter when bounded by the four sides of a square than when bounded by those of a parallelogram, and less still when bounded by the circumference of a circle: it will be readily supposed that the more symmetrical, regular, and simple a building, the less costly it becomes.'[221]

6. programme for the code of beauty
Durand's privileging of utility as the primary origin of all architectural principles does not lead to a total rejection of the notion of beauty.[222] Instead, Durand's theory establishes a clear, hierarchically ordered relationship between utility and beauty. He is clear in his insistence that beauty and aesthetic pleasure cannot be the purpose of architecture. According to Durand, the achievement of beauty should therefore not be the aim of architectural design, but he admits that aesthetic pleasure is a noteworthy effect of architecture. Rather than allowing the pursuit of beauty as a secondary aim, Durand argues that it is the inevitable result of the rigorous pursuit of utility.[223] Thus the

219 Ibid, p 78.
220 Ibid, p 85.
221 Ibid.
222 The total rejection of all concerns with beauty was finally argued for by the Radical Functionalists of the early 20th century.
223 This conception of the relationship of utility and beauty was very influential and was indeed the conception that was adopted wholeheartedly within Modernism, more than 100 years after it was so eloquently stated by Durand.

relation between utility and beauty is theorized as a relationship of cause and effect. Durand states: 'Far from denying that architecture can give pleasure, we maintain that it cannot but give pleasure, where it is treated in accordance with its true principles.'[224] Durand then reconnects this claim with his fundamental anthropological thesis: 'Has not nature associated pleasure with the satisfaction of our needs, and are not our keenest pleasures the satisfactions of our most pressing needs?'[225] He then goes on to address the aesthetic pleasure of enjoying beauty and demonstrates how a series of recognized aesthetic values is related to fitness and economy:

> Certainly, the grandeur, magnificence, variety, effect, and character that are observed in buildings are all beauties, all causes of pleasure that we derive from looking at them. But where is the need to run after such things, if a building is disposed in a manner fitted to its intended use? Will it not differ sensibly from another building intended for some other use? Will it not naturally possess a character – and, what is more, a character of its own? If all of the parts of the building, being intended for different uses, are disposed as they should be, will they not inevitably differ? Will not the building afford variety? And if the same building is disposed in the most economical, that is to say, the simplest manner, will it not appear as grand and as magnificent as it is possible to be? Undoubtedly, it will, because the eye will embrace the greatest number of its parts in one glance.[226]

So beauty – magnificence, variety and character – is an inevitable side effect of fitness and economy. There is, according to Durand, no need 'to chase after all these partial beauties'.[227] But that is not all; there is a tragic irony in the pursuit of beauty: 'Indeed, such a pursuit is harmful even to decoration itself. For if, smitten with the effect of certain beautiful features in one building, you attempt to transfer them to another, where they are out of place; or if, where such beauties are naturally present, you seek to amplify them further than the nature of the building permits: is it not plain that they will disappear; and worse still, that they will be transformed into

224 Durand, *Précis des leçons d'architecture*, p 85.
225 Ibid.
226 Ibid.
227 Ibid.

faults?'[228] According to Durand such transferrals and artificial enhancements can only lead to monstrous absurdity. Durand also implies that anything that is aesthetically displeasing must be either badly disposed or superfluous.[229] Later, in connection with the basic principles of construction, Durand gives a more specific hint about the origin and appropriate use of (beautiful) decoration, saying that decoration is to be produced by making the construction evident.[230] In contrast, the direct pursuit of decoration as an end in itself leads to 'the appearance of an imaginary construction – which not being the real construction of the building, falsifies the latter, and detracts from its character instead of enhancing it – by an arbitrary decoration made up of an assemblage of unnecessary objects that can never give pleasure but only fatigue the eye, outrage common sense, and displease in every way.'[231]

He concludes his discussion of beauty and its relationship to utility as follows: 'Disposition must therefore be the architect's sole concern – even if he were a lover of architectural decoration, even if he wished only to please – since decoration cannot be called beautiful or give true pleasure, except as the necessary effect of the most fitting and the most economical disposition.'[232]

Thus Durand's *Précis* specifies and operationalizes the application of the code values beautiful versus ugly. Beauty can be pursued via the aesthetic values of grandeur, magnificence, variety and character, by adhering to the concerns of fitness, giving different forms to different functions within and across buildings (variety and character), and by adhering to the concerns of economy by optimizing the design in terms of simplicity, regularity and symmetry (grandeur and magnificence), and by allowing the construction to become evident. Durand's notion of beauty – as elaborated with his notions of variety and character – is indeed driving towards the concept of articulation, understood both as the articulation of social functions and as tectonic articulation. Variety becomes an aesthetic value to the extent to which it expresses functional differentiation.

228 Ibid, p 86.

229 Ibid, p 121.

230 There is a nuance here that deviates from his most radical formulation that mere concern with utility produces beauty. 'Making evident' (Durand's words) does imply an extra special effort towards beauty. See Durand, *Précis des leçons d'architecture*, p 108. This notion of 'making evident' seems to anticipate an aspect of the notion of *articulation* as it is being defined by the theory of architectural autopoiesis.

231 Durand, *Précis des leçons d'architecture*, p 108.

232 Ibid, p 86.

Durand describes the design of a palace: 'It will be observed that this building requires some rooms of considerable size, the height of which must in consequence be greater than that of a number of others, whose area is less, and that the differences in height naturally give rise to a certain movement in the elevation of the building ... thus giving the building all the variety of which it is capable.'[233]

Decoration is invoked with the stricture to avoid anything arbitrary or imitative: 'the true decoration resides in the appearance of its construction'.[234] Durand elaborates further: 'if the disposition is as fit for its purpose and as economical as it can be, it will naturally give rise to an architectural decoration of a different kind, one that is truly calculated to please because it shows us a true image of the satisfaction of our needs: a satisfaction to which nature has attached all our truest pleasures'.[235] It is evident here that Durand is indeed recuperating and operationalizing the Classical notions of beauty and decoration within his new theoretical system. His functional analysis of aesthetic values (decoration, beauty) comes close to the analysis proposed within the theory of architectural autopoiesis, albeit without the awareness of the historical transience of aesthetic values. The insistence on economy is further operationalized in terms of the concrete values simplicity, symmetry and regularity.[236]

The verdict of ugliness (displeasing, absurd, monstrous) is to be applied to designs that – in the name of a misunderstood beauty – either falsify construction, misplace otherwise useful architectural features, try to amplify features beyond what fitness suggests, or in any other way add arbitrary and superfluous elements. Durand summarizes his understanding at the beginning of Volume 2 of his lectures: 'When a building has all that it needs, and nothing but what it must have; and when everything necessary is disposed in the most economical – which is to say, the simplest – manner, then that building has the kind and degree of beauty appropriate to it; ... to seek to add anything but the ornaments of painting and sculpture is to weaken and sometimes to obliterate its style, its character, and, in a word, all the beauties that are desired for it.'[237] These strictures

233 Ibid, p 156.
234 Ibid, p 116.
235 Ibid, p 134.
236 Ibid.
237 Ibid.

that allow for nothing that cannot be argued for in terms of functional or structural necessity lead to the following concrete conclusions relative to the Classical tradition: the rejection of Ionic as well as Corinthian capitals as 'absurd'. The same negative conclusion is arrived at for the triglyphs, as well as the bases under the columns. What thus remained was the Doric order. However, Durand emphasized that the antique examples must be studied: 'with the eyes of reason, rather than ... by an appeal to antique authority'.[238] Durand explicitly follows Le Roy in his suggestion: 'that the Greeks themselves did not recognize those distinct orders in which the moderns see the essence of architecture and the principle of all beauty and decoration; and that those nations saw nothing in what we call the *orders* but supports and parts supported: useful objects, which they proportioned, not in imitation of anything whatever, but in accordance with the eternal principles of fitness'.[239]

Durand tries to tie the pursuit of beauty to the primacy of utility. However, he is aware that forms cannot be strictly derived from function. Function does not determine form fully. He classifies forms and proportions into three categories: 'those that spring from the nature of materials, and from the uses of the things they serve to build; those that custom has in a sense made necessary to us, such as the forms and proportions of the buildings of antiquity; and finally, those simpler and more definite forms and proportions that earn our preference through the ease with which we apprehend them'.[240] The third category, reflecting upon easy apprehension, might be interpreted as an anticipation of the concern of articulation. However, it might also be interpreted as a hint towards the concern with formal resolution independent of all concerns with performance, be it organizational or articulatory performance. The second category might be interpreted as hinting towards the inherent inertia of all aesthetic values. Durand considers only the first category to be essential. However, he says that these forms and proportions are never so firmly defined by the nature of things as to prevent their modification. Thus the other two moments – custom and easy apprehension – are allowed to overdetermine architectural form. Durand thus anticipated

238 Ibid, p 136.
239 Ibid.
240 Ibid, p 108.

our insight that function is insufficient to determine form fully. According to the theory of architectural autopoiesis, it is this impossibility of comprehensive functional determination that underlies the need for a second code: the code of beauty.

7. programme for the code of novelty/originality
   The code of novelty was not as yet very far developed during Durand's time. Theorists were still more likely to argue against the dangers of arbitrary invention than praise originality. Accordingly Durand's *Précis des leçons d'architecture* is mute on this point. Rationality as established during the Enlightenment was seen to be an absolute, timeless achievement.

8. implied style
   Durand's design works – a lot of which serve as illustrations within his theoretical treatise – are Neo-Classical. This stylistic classification is a retrospective classification.[241] The classification of architectural works according to their style, whereby styles are understood in relation to architecture's historical development, emerged only during the 19th century.

   However, Durand's advocacy of attention to need, fitness and economy, as well as his insistence on an efficient, rational design process, led to designs which have their own characteristic physiognomy that starkly contrasts with the prior Baroque period. The following passage from Durand's *Précis* can be best understood if it is interpreted as a polemic against the Baroque and Rococo (or perhaps against French Classicism following the Baroque): 'It is by decorating – that is to say, by piling up the useless upon the useless, the meaningless upon the meaningless, at enormous expense, and by sacrificing every requirement of fitness to decorative absurdity – that the moderns have presumed to excel the ancients in the composition of their temples.'[242] In line with his rejection of imitative ornamentation, Durand positively emphasizes simplicity, symmetry and regularity. So much for the formal heuristics – both negative and positive – of Durand's active Neo-Classicism. The functional heuristics of Durand's Neo-Classicism builds upon his functional classification of building types.

241 The early Neo-Classicism of Laugier and Durand is therefore an active style but not yet active-reflective. See Volume 1, section 3.6 *Architectural Styles*.

242 Durand, *Précis des leçons d'architecture données à l'École royale polytechnique*, p 152.

9. expansion of the repertoire
   Like every forward-looking self-description of architecture, Durand's writings expand the repertoire of architectural design. Durand's first book, *Recueil et parallèle des édifices en tout genre, anciens et modernes,* which he started to publish in 1799, contains a rich variety of architectural examples from different eras and cultures, both ancient and modern. Durand provided plans, sections and elevations, and he combined several buildings on a single page or double spread. All examples were drawn at the same scale. This panorama of all previous architecture can be seen as inspiration and challenge to Durand's system of architectural composition. The emphasis on plans indicates his focus on composition as organization rather than decorative motifs and details. In fact, in terms of decorative motifs and details, Durand's Neo-Classicism does indeed imply a constraint upon the repertoire. However, in terms of plan organization, Durand's system of architectural composition implies a massive expansion of the repertoire of architecture. This large expansion of the organizational repertoire matches Durand's perceptive understanding of his era as an era marked by a challenging variety of societal demands both in terms of the variety of building types and in terms of the individual variations that must be accommodated in each design project. Durand talks about the 'near-infinite variety of classes of buildings', each in turn 'susceptible of an infinity of modifications' because 'the particular requirements of any one building might be varied by places, times, persons, sites, costs, and so on'.[243]

10. design-process guidance
    Durand proposes a definite design process that is coherent with his utilitarian conception of architecture's primary purpose. Disposition (organization) lies at the heart of the matter. The functional and economical disposition of the building is to be achieved via the composition of a (rich but discrete) set of architectural elements. Durand is concerned with the rationality and efficiency of design as a process of composition. He was perhaps the first to introduce a diagrammatic process within architecture. Durand proposed a 'mechanics of composition'[244] made easy and efficient by using gridded paper upon which a series of basic elements like walls and columns could be combined – following the rules of alignment,

243 Ibid, p 140.
244 Ibid, p 196.

regularity and symmetry – to form standard building parts like porches, vestibules and rooms which in turn could be combined into various whole buildings, again following the rules of alignment, regularity and symmetry. Both elements and parts were familiar. To further rein in the results of the compositional process, from the very start Durand proposed a procedure of decomposition or successive division starting from global geometric forms like squares or rectangles. Even with these top-down restrictions the introduction of diagrammatic composition implied an unheard-of variety of results: 'there is no telling how many different compositions this host of combinations can produce'.[245]

From the results of this diagrammatic process, the rest of the design (including all the familiar Classical detail) followed automatically. The diagram was translated into the primary floor plan, and from the plan follow sections and elevations. Durand distinguished 'between two kinds of disposition: horizontal, as presented by plans; and vertical, as presented by sections and elevations'.[246] Durand describes a design process that starts with the establishment of a grid and forces everything within the design to follow the order of this grid: 'Once we have set out parallel and equidistant axes, and drawn other axes at identical intervals to intersect them at right angles, the walls are set down on the axes, as many interaxes apart as is considered appropriate, and the columns, pilasters and so on, are placed on the intersections of those same axes; then the interaxes are bisected to create new axes that serve to define the positions of the doors, windows, arcades, and so on.'[247] One should note here that the order of the grid replaces the concept of proportions. This substitution gives more freedom while maintaining order. As Durand suggested above: 'the walls are set down on the axes, as many interaxes apart as is considered appropriate'. However, there are further restrictions that have to do with simplicity/economy as one aspect of utility in juxtaposition/opposition to fitness: 'The exterior walls, which are designed to close off the building, must pass directly from one corner to the other, the straight line being the shortest distance between two

245 Ibid, p 126.
246 Ibid, p 119.
247 Ibid, p 120.

points; and the partition walls, which not only divide the interior into several parts but also link the outside walls with each other, must, as far as fitness permits, run to the whole length or width of the building. ... Windows and doors not only serve to establish communication between the various parts of a building and to afford the pleasure of seeing exterior objects, but they also permit air and light; they must therefore correspond to each other as much as possible.'[248] The design process thus encapsulates a functional rationality in its formal-procedural strictures. Hence we can say that Durand was able to elevate his design process into a proper design method.

The method was strictly linear. In accordance with the emphasis on utilitarian disposition, the design had to start with the plan. The horizontal disposition was set out first and constrained the vertical disposition that followed. 'Without exception, the vertical (combinations) are naturally derived from the horizontal. But, since any given horizontal disposition is capable of giving rise to several vertical dispositions, the latter are infinitely more numerous.'[249] Durand is explicitly warning against deviating from this method: 'Otherwise, there would be a danger of succumbing to the attraction of one or another of those decorative ensembles and composing in the manner of those who, because they see nothing in architecture but decoration, start a project with the facade and then make shift to fit their plan and section to the elevation: a way of composing that runs counter ... to the aim of architecture.'[250] It is important to note how Durand links his distinctive process strictures back to his distinctive understanding of the purpose of architecture. He goes even further in his argument claiming that his process is also better able to serve beauty than the direct pursuit of decorative ensembles. Durand states that this superficial way of composing with decoration as primary aim also runs counter 'to the very aim an architect has in mind when he sets out to decorate. All buildings and designs devised in such a spirit are more or less alike, and despite their great number they offer no more than three or four different combinations; whereas those composed in the natural order – that is to say, in which the plan is considered first, then the section, and in which the elevation is no more than the result of these two – offer such variety that the

248 Ibid, p 120.
249 Ibid, p 121.
250 Ibid.

same decorative effect is never found twice.'[251] According to Durand the elevation had to be 'the visible reflection of the internal disposition'.[252] The design process that he proposed operationalized this idea.

Durand was emphasizing the power of his method of design for the generation of a large solution space. In the introduction (preliminary discourse) to Volume 2 of the *Précis* – which in effect provides a summary of the results of Volume 1 – Durand describes how his hierarchical system of composition with its many possible general dispositions, each collecting elementary combinations into many more 'super-combinations', which in turn allow for a further multiplication by all the possible vertical combinations, finally creates 'an incalculable number of architectural compositions'.[253] As hinted at above, Durand recognizes that this powerful process pertinently confronts a 'near-infinite variety of classes of buildings', each in turn 'susceptible of an infinity of modifications' because 'the particular requirements of any one building might be varied by places, times, persons, sites, costs, and so on'.[254] This confrontation of the combinatorial rationality of the process with the inherent variation of the societal requirements turns the process into an appropriate method that is rationally adapted to the societal challenges of the time. As Durand states at the end of his Volume 2 introduction: 'with the mechanism of composition, it would be possible to execute with facility, and even with success, the design of any building whatever, even without having previously done any other'.[255] (Durand seems to be anticipating the claim of universal competency that became one of the hallmarks of the refoundation of architecture as Modern architecture.) Durand continues: 'One would merely have to inquire as to the particular requirements of the building in question, since one would already possess every possible means of worthily filling the commission.'[256]

11. design medium

Any ambitious architectural self-description should try to identify the most promising avenues for the development and advanced

251 Ibid, p 121.
252 Ibid.
253 Ibid, p 140.
254 Ibid.
255 Ibid.
256 Ibid, pp 140, 141.

deployment of the specialized design medium in relation to an updated formulation of architecture's task.

Durand has made an effort to reform the manner of drawing of his time. His agenda was a purification of the medium in line with his Neo-Classicist focus on the essential architectural aspects of shape and arrangement without distraction by rich ornament. 'We have been economical in our use of drawing. We have more or less reduced it to a single line, drawn to indicate the shape and arrangement of objects; and if we had recourse to wash, this has simply been in order to distinguish solids from voids in our plans and sections.'[257] Durand is talking about 'the abuse of geometric drawing in architecture', whereby an attempt is made to produce an effect in the geometric elevation leading to the adding of 'unnecessary parts'.[258] Durand is effectively promoting a clear functional differentiation of drawing types: simple line orthographic projections are utilized to objectively define the shapes and arrangements. Perspective projections are utilized to test the subjective effect. 'Perspective alone might give a true idea of the effect of the building.'[259] Durand tried to mute the image character of the drawing. One might describe his plans as diagrams rather than as drawings. Durand's compositional process operates on a historically new level of abstraction. His plans are abstract diagrams. The power of Durand's process to quickly proliferate a large number of options depends on its high level of abstraction. The downstream translation of these diagrams into detailed designs is routinized via the standard parts and elements.[260] Having freed the orthographic projection from its image character he can go on to innovate by introducing the efficiency of allowing multiple coordinated drawings to share the same regulating axis: 'Not only have we reduced drawing to its simplest terms, but we have also tried to place on a single sheet the largest possible number of objects, so that, most of the lines that represent them are being shared, a considerable number of them can be drawn in no more time than it would have taken to draw any one of them separately.'[261]

257 Ibid, p 75.

258 Ibid.

259 Ibid, p 74.

260 According to the classification of diagrams introduced in Volume 1, Durand's diagrams have to be classified as metric-ordinary diagrams. See Volume 1, chapter 4.2.2 *The Diagram*.

261 Durand, *Précis des leçons*, p 75.

12. self-reflectiveness

Full autological self-reflectiveness in the form of an incorporated theory of architectural theory should not yet be expected here.[262] But a certain measure of general self-reflection had been institutionalized at the time Durand was writing. The book-length treatise is the general form all self-descriptions of society's function systems take. As examples one might cite, for the political system, Jean Jacques Rousseau's *The Social Contract or Principles of Political Right* (1762), or, for the economy, Jean-Baptiste Say's *A Treatise on Political Economy,* or his *Production, Distribution and Consumption of Wealth* (1803). This form of the treatise provides institutionalized devices for self-reflection: the preface and the concluding remarks, sometimes even a dedicated epilogue. The instances of Durand's self-reflection quoted below are taken from both the *Preface* and from the concluding remarks found on the final two pages of Volume 1 of the *Précis*, as well as from the *Preliminary Discourse* that fronts Volume 2.

The *Précis* starts with positing the necessity of architectural theory, ie, its own necessity. The opening remarks of the preface hint at the societal importance of (well-grounded) architectural knowledge (theory). Durand relates its importance to the universality of building and to the large expense that construction imposes on society. 'Whatever the object and the purpose of architecture, it is certain that of all the arts this is the most generally practiced and the most expensive. There are few countries in which there are no private dwellings for individuals or public buildings for society at large. It is extremely costly to erect large buildings, and costly enough even for buildings of the least account. It follows that those who intend to devote themselves to architecture must possess the necessary knowledge and talents.'[263] On the first page of Volume 2, Durand writes: 'Architecture is at one and the same time a science and an art. As a science, it demands knowledge; as an art, it requires talents.'[264] He goes on to define talent on the basis of knowledge thus making knowledge the central category: 'Talent is accuracy and facility in the application of knowledge; and such accuracy and facility can be acquired only through sustained practice and repeated

262 This demand can only be made in the wake of *The Autopoiesis of Architecture*.

263 Durand, *Précis des leçons d'architecture données à l'École royale polytechnique*, p 73.

264 Ibid, p 131.

application.'[265] Even if practice is required, knowledge is considered primary.

Durand's *Précis des leçons d'architecture* is aimed at students of architecture and engineering. This should not deceive us with respect to Durand's ambition. The *Précis* stands in the tradition of one of those comprehensive theoretical treatises that took the shape of a textbook. Throughout the 19th century – not only in architecture but in all academic disciplines – the original texts that advanced the discipline also functioned as textbooks in the universities and academies. The most ambitious, original contributions to the field often involved the full reformulation of the field in the form of a comprehensive treatise. Thus despite being presented as a lecture course for students, the *Précis* is very different in ambition to a pure textbook in the contemporary sense understood as mere compilation for students without original ambitions. The distinction between original treatise and merely educational textbook had not yet occurred.

The knowledge that Durand posits as the crucial point of departure of all architecture is conceived as systematic, well-grounded knowledge in the philosophical tradition of rationalism rather than empiricism. Durand conceives of architecture in analogy to a deductive science, where everything is logically deduced from first principles. 'To succeed in anything, one must have a tangible and rational aim. Otherwise, success would be purely a matter of chance. ... From this, once established, we shall naturally deduce the general principles of architecture; and once these are known, it will only remain for us to apply them.'[266] Durand professes to start with 'accurate ideas as to the nature of the art; its purposes, means, and general principles.'[267] These general principles 'may generate all those specific ideas'[268] that comprise the teachings of architecture. Durand continues: 'To avoid fatiguing the attention or overcharging the memory, we have sought, first, to make those general ideas as simple and as few as possible, and second, to associate them with each other and with the specific ideas so that a first leads to a second, and the second infallibly recalls to mind the first.'[269] Besides reflecting itself as deductive system, the *Précis* reflects itself

265 Ibid, p.131
266 Ibid, p 78.
267 Ibid, p 73.
268 Ibid.
269 Ibid, p 74.

here also in terms of its mnemotechnic merit. A theory's mnemotechnic performance is indeed an important factor in its ability effectively to guide the discipline.

10.3.3 LE CORBUSIER'S *VERS UNE ARCHITECTURE*

Le Corbusier's *Vers une architecture* was first published in French in 1923. It was put together from a series of articles that Le Corbusier had published in the preceding years in his own avant-garde magazine *L'Esprit Nouveau*. The German translation *Kommende Baukunst* appeared in 1926 and the English translation *Towards a New Architecture* in 1931, based on the 13th French edition. The book was by far the most widely read and influential treatise on Modern architecture and might very well be regarded as the central manifesto of Modernism. However, it was not without precedents. Two prior treatises that had already formulated most of the ideas put forward by Le Corbusier should be mentioned here: Otto Wagner's *Moderne Architektur* (1895) and Hermann Muthesius' *Stilarchitektur und Baukunst* (1903). Further components of Le Corbusier's arguments had been articulated in Friedrich Naumann's small book *Die Kunst im Zeitalter der Maschine* (1904). Within these three works, among others, the whole theory of Modern Functionalism was fully formulated nearly 20 years before the publication of Le Corbusier's book. However, the striking new look of Modernist architecture was only developed in the early 1920s. It was the visual shock of the new style that suddenly brought prominence to Modern Architecture (Modernism) and its theory. Le Corbusier's treatise is a mature work of systematic theoretical synthesis building on over 20 years of explicit prior discourse, which in turn was based on the systematic radicalization of ideas that had been in gestation for much longer. Published in 1923, although theoretically mature, the book stands at the beginning of the development of Modernism as decisive avant-garde style. There can be no doubt that in 1923 the principles of the Modernist style were fully formed and demonstrated by the early designs of Le Corbusier, Walter Gropius and Mies van der Rohe. Some of Le Corbusier's early designs and drawings are represented within the book. It also features an early design by Walter Gropius. However, *Vers une architecture* was published in advance of the iconic paradigm works that soon came to define Modernism: Gerrit Rietveld's Schröder House (1924), Walter Gropius' Bauhaus Dessau (1926), Le Corbusier's Villa Stein in Garches (1927), Le Corbusier's Villa Savoye (1929) and Mies van der Rohe's Barcelona Pavilion (1929).

Vers une architecture was the decisive treatise of the 1920s and of the whole era of architectural Modernism. Its scope and ambition are comprehensive and deep enough to be regarded as one of architecture's Modern self-descriptions. Several further treatises followed. Moisei Ginzburg's *Style and Epoch* (1924) reads nearly like a translation of Le Corbusier's treatise. Adolf Behne's *Der Moderne Zweckbau* (1926) adds new aspects to the discourse but with less messianic zeal. Bruno Taut's *Modern Architecture* (1929) finally delivers the *architectural* illustrations[270] that were still rather sparse in *Vers une architecture.* Henry-Russell Hitchcock and Philip Johnson's *International Style* made its mark in 1932 and in 1941 followed Sigfried Giedion's voluminous *Space, Time and Architecture.* All of these works can be regarded as veritable self-descriptions of architecture. However, none of these later treatises reached the same level of prominence that was enjoyed by Le Corbusier's *Towards a New Architecture.* Le Corbusier's treatise remained without rival, the decisive self-description of architecture throughout the 50-year history of architectural Modernism.

1. the societal function and tasks of architecture
   The fact that Le Corbusier was both the most influential architectural theorist and the most successful architect was no coincidence. Le Corbusier had a clear, historically well-attuned sense of architecture's societal function: 'We are living in a period of reconstruction and of adaptation to new social and economic conditions.'[271] This consciousness of the need to adapt architecture to a new historical era permeates all parts of Le Corbusier's *Towards a New Architecture.* Le Corbusier is aware of the fact that modern life and modern technology demand a new architectural sensibility. 'Architecture has for its first duty, in this period of renewal, that of bringing about a revision of values, a revision of the constituent elements of the house.'[272] *Towards a New Architecture* expresses a strong sense of urgency: 'The problem of the house is a problem of the epoch. The equilibrium of society today depends upon it.'[273] Le Corbusier saw the historical problem of society that architecture was

270 A lot of the illustrations within *Vers une architecture* illustrated the machine age via its manifestations outside architecture: industrial structures such as silos and factories, as well as the latest technological wonders of the age such as ships, automobiles and aircrafts.

271 Le Corbusier, *Towards a New Architecture*, Dover Publications (New York), 1986, unaltered republication of English translation of 13th French edition, published by John Rodker (London), 1931, p 63.

272 Ibid, p 6.

273 Ibid.

to address as a social problem: the universal provision of a new standard of living. 'Industry on the grand scale must occupy itself with building and establish the elements of the house on a mass-production basis.'[274] Le Corbusier understands that 'new needs have arisen'.[275] His claim that society's equilibrium depends on architecture's capacity to adequately serve the new needs of society must be understood in the historical context of the wave of socialist/communist revolutions that had swept Europe in the aftermath of the First World War. This is the context in which to make sense of Le Corbusier's famous phrase 'architecture or revolution'.

The first chapter of *Towards a New Architecture* titled 'Argument' closes with this famous phrase: 'This machinery of Society, profoundly *out of gear*, oscillates between amelioration, of historical importance, and a catastrophe. . . . The various classes of workers in society today *no longer have dwelling adapted to their needs; neither the artisan nor the intellectual*. It is a question of building which is at the root of the social unrest today: architecture or revolution.'[276] This sense of historical urgency is backed up by a more general anthropological grounding of architecture's societal importance: 'Architecture is one of the most urgent needs of man for the house has always been the indispensable and first tool that he has forged for himself.'[277] Le Corbusier also emphasizes the anthropologically creative aspect of architecture: 'Architecture is the first manifestation of man creating his own universe.'[278] Beyond the recognition of architecture's general anthropological importance and beyond the political urgency of satisfying current social demands, there is the recognition that architecture should be adapted to the new social life engendered by a new technological era: 'A new epoch is replacing a dying one. Machinery, a new factor in human affairs, has aroused a new spirit. An epoch creates its own architecture.'[279] Technological change is linked up with spiritual and social change. Together these factors challenge architecture. 'Our external world has been enormously transformed in its outward appearance and in the use made of it, by reason of the machine. We have gained a new

274 Ibid.
275 Ibid, p 8.
276 Ibid.
277 Ibid, p 13.
278 Ibid, p 73.
279 Ibid, p 90.

perspective and a new social life, but we have not yet adapted the house thereto.'[280] A lot of the illustrations within *Vers une architecture* were illustrating the machine age via its manifestations outside architecture: industrial structures such as silos and factories, as well as the latest technological wonders of the age such as ships, automobiles and aircraft. Throughout the treatise, Le Corbusier refers back to the new historical situation and to architecture's new societal tasks. In the section on the plan he writes: 'The great problems of tomorrow, dictated by collective necessities, put the question of "plan" in a new form. Modern life demands, and is waiting for, a new kind of plan both for the house and for the city.'[281] Both architecture and urbanism require adaptive upgrading. Le Corbusier analyzes the maladaptation of cities: 'The great towns have become too dense for the security of their inhabitants and yet they are not sufficiently dense to meet the new needs of "modern business".'[282] He understands that with respect to these strategic adaptations architecture cannot wait to be instructed by clients. He realizes that it is architecture's own responsibility to identify society's architectural and urban needs and to upgrade its adaptive pertinence by reforming itself.

2. avant-gardist orientation
Since Modernism, every comprehensive architectural self-description must explicitly articulate a historically argued forward orientation for the discipline. The avant-gardist orientation of Le Corbusier is evident throughout *Towards a New Architecture*. It follows directly from his very urgent, historically specific understanding of architecture's societal function. A new architecture for a new society. For Le Corbusier there is no doubt that architecture has to adapt to a radically new era. 'We do not appreciate sufficiently the deep chasm between our own epoch and earlier periods.'[283] Le Corbusier refers to the 'transformation of domestic economy that demands a new type of plan for dwelling houses, and an entirely new organization of services corresponding to modern life in a great city'.[284] He is very much aware of the avant-gardist, experimental and therefore risky character of his endeavour: 'A period of 20 years is beginning, ... a period of

280 Ibid, p 17.
281 Ibid, p 45.
282 Ibid, p 57.
283 Ibid, p 271.
284 Ibid, p 61.

great problems, a period of analysis, of experiment, a period of great aesthetic confusion, a period in which a new aesthetic will be elaborated.'[285] There are new tasks and new means of construction. 'Construction has undergone innovations so great that the old "styles", which still obsess us, can no longer clothe it.'[286] Although Le Corbusier is definitely a keen innovator, aware of the fact that architecture has to advance along the general developmental lines of the machine age, his attitude towards architectural history is rather different from the radical, open iconoclasm of the Futurists. His position with regard to novelty versus tradition is rather ambiguous. Le Corbusier tries to tie his work into a revered architectural tradition as much as he tries to overturn tradition. This dialectic of renewal and return is expressed in formulations like the following: 'The new horizons before us will only recover the grand line of tradition by a complete revision of the methods in vogue and by the fixing of a new basis of construction established in logic. In architecture the old bases of construction are dead. We shall not rediscover the truths of architecture until new bases have established a logical ground for every architectural manifestation.'[287] Here is another proclamation that reveals a tension between the readiness to take on novel tasks and materials on the one hand and a sense of returning to eternal principles: 'There is so much novelty in the forms and rhythms furnished by these constructional methods, such novelty in arrangement and in the new industrial programmes, that we can no longer close our minds to the true and profound laws of architecture which are established on mass, rhythm and proportion: the "styles" no longer exist, ... if they still trouble us, it is as parasites.'[288]

Le Corbusier's book has been translated as *Towards a New Architecture*. However, as Reyner Banham points out, 'the original title of Le Corbusier's treatise *Vers une architecture,* simply says "Towards an Architecture", and implies, from internal evidence in the book, an absolute or essential architecture, which had always existed and had merely been mislaid. ... It was precisely this rediscovery of the old in the new, this justification of the revolutionary by the familiar, that ensured the book its enormous readership, beyond that of any other architectural work published in

285 Ibid, p 64.
286 Ibid, p 286.
287 Ibid, pp 63–4.
288 Ibid, p 286.

this century to date.'[289] Although Le Corbusier, rightly, was looking for continuities with the past achievements of architecture, he cannot be accused of overemphasizing tradition. He believed in progress and was scathing about the backwards orientation of the established mainstream architecture of his time: 'There is one profession and only one, namely architecture, in which progress is not considered necessary, where laziness is enthroned, and in which reference is always to yesterday.'[290]

Le Corbusier provides a compelling insight into how progress can be achieved only after the collective research has converged on a basic standard solution. His insights can be related to Thomas Kuhn's distinction of revolutionary versus normal science. The theory of architectural autopoiesis transfers Kuhn's distinction into the domain of architecture by distinguishing revolutionary from cumulative design research. Both are necessary aspects of progress. 'Once a standard is established, competition comes into play. It is a fight; in order to win you must be better than your rival *in every minute point*. ... Thus we get the study of minute points pushed to its limits. Progress. A standard is necessary for order in human effort.'[291] The theory of architectural autopoiesis extends this insight to the necessity of avant-garde styles as collective design research programmes.

3. disciplinary demarcations
Every comprehensive architectural self-description must try to re-establish architecture's demarcation lines against its neighbouring systems, ie, against those systems that architecture is most likely to be confused with. While the theory of architectural autopoiesis demarcates architecture both against art and engineering/science, Le Corbusier tends to align the architect with the artist to clarify the contrast with the engineer. The demarcation of architecture against engineering does not imply a relative devaluation of engineering. The engineer is admired for his pursuit of logic and economy. The engineer's work is conceived as a necessary ingredient or antecedent of architecture's task. Architecture builds on engineering. However,

289 Reyner Banham, *Theory and Design in the First Machine Age*, The Architectural Press (London), 1960, p 246.
290 Le Corbusier, *Towards a New Architecture*, p 109.
291 Ibid, pp 134–5.

architecture must go beyond mere engineering.[292] The difference and relationship between architecture and engineering is one of the major themes that runs through the whole of the treatise. The first sentence of *Towards a New Architecture* reads: 'The Engineer's Aesthetic, and Architecture, are two things that march together and follow one from the other: the one being now at its full height, the other in an unhappy state of retrogression.'[293] This asynchrony between the development of architecture and engineering is no historical accident. The architect's artistic refinement comes after the logic and economy of the engineer have established robust, functional standards. The machine age is still new and raw. However, now the time of architecture has come. Le Corbusier juxtaposes the engineer and the architect as follows: 'The Engineer, inspired by the law of Economy and governed by mathematical calculation, puts us in accord with universal law. ... The Architect, by his arrangement of forms, realizes an order which is a pure creation of his spirit; by forms and shapes he affects our senses ... he wakes profound echoes in us, he gives us the measure of an order which we feel to be in accordance with that of our world.'[294] The unity of the difference is 'accord', the accord with universal law versus the accord with *our* world. It is the sensation of this latter, spiritual accord that Le Corbusier identifies with the sensation of beauty. Le Corbusier emphasizes that architecture is a 'pure creation of the mind'. Below the eponymous paragraph heading, Le Corbusier emphasizes the demarcation between architecture and engineering: 'Contour and profile are the touchstone of the architect. Here he reveals himself as artist or mere engineer. Contour is free of constraint. There is here no longer the question of custom, nor of tradition, nor of construction nor of adaptation to utilitarian needs. Contour and profile are a pure creation of the mind; they call for the plastic artist.'[295] Here the alignment of architecture and art is once more explicit.[296] The same

292 This contrasts with the theory of Radical Functionalism that emphasized the alignment, even identity, of architecture and engineering while proposing a radical demarcation against art and the pursuit of aesthetic values.

293 Le Corbusier, *Towards a New Architecture*, p 1.

294 Ibid.

295 Ibid, pp 5–6.

296 This seems to contrast with the thesis that architecture and art separated during the 1920s. However, we have to remember that Le Corbusier's text was written before 1923. At this time the Bauhaus was still trying to synthesize the different art forms under the umbrella of architecture. Le Corbusier was painting Purist paintings. However, the voices that wanted to distance architecture from art became stronger during the second half of the 1920s. Also, the

alignment is emphasized again and again: 'Architecture is a thing of art, a phenomenon of the emotions, lying outside questions of construction and beyond them. The purpose of construction is to make things hold together; of architecture to move us.'[297] The question of purpose – of societal function – is indeed the key to understanding the differentiation of function systems.

4. form-function relations
Under this heading we expect directives towards the general handling and integration of form-function relations. Modern Functionalism is presumed to be defined by Louis Sullivan's famous formula 'form follows function'. Le Corbusier does not discuss this formula. Le Corbusier's own famous formula 'A house is a machine for living in'[298] also conveys the credo of Functionalism that architectural form should be based on function. The analogy with the machine implies that the architect should go wherever the required function leads him, without sentimental attachments to traditional forms. However, there is a second, equally famous formula within the pages of *Towards a New Architecture*: 'Architecture is the masterly, correct and magnificent play of masses brought together in light.'[299] Le Corbusier is proposing a two-step approach to design. First the functional necessities of the modern, industrial age have to be addressed. A basic solution (form) is found. It becomes a standard solution/form that is gradually improved. Le Corbusier talks about 'solutions which spring from a problem that has been clearly stated'.[300] He uses the modern ship, the aeroplane and the motor car as examples for functional design. 'The form and appearance are in no way preconceived, they are a result; they may have a strange look at first sight. Ader made a "Bat", but it did not fly; Wright and Farman set themselves the problem of sustaining solid bodies in air, the result was jarring and disconcerting, but it flew.'[301] The second step is the artistic refinement that treats the functional form in terms of massing, proportion, light and shadow. Le Corbusier distinguishes the first condition as responding to a need from the 'higher factors of

ideological and rhetorical affiliation to art have to be distinguished from the actual integration or separation of the evolving discourses.

297 Le Corbusier, *Towards a New Architecture*, p 19.

298 Ibid, p 95.

299 Ibid, p 29.

300 Ibid, p 103.

301 Ibid, p 138.

harmony and beauty'.[302] Both are necessary to produce good architecture. This two-step approach is only viable if the satisfaction of the functional requirements constrain the form only partially so leaving sufficient room for manoeuvre for the final artistic determination. Le Corbusier thus underwrites two sets of criteria, functional criteria and formal criteria. Both sets of criteria can be stated independently, leading to independent programmes for the code of utility and the code of beauty. However, Le Corbusier is echoing Durand when he detects something like a pre-established harmony between the useful and the beautiful. Within Le Corbusier's account, this coincidence between the useful and the beautiful remains a mystery. The great utilitarian structures of the industrial age, such as factories and grain stores, satisfy Le Corbusier's concept of beauty demanding primary geometric forms.

According to the theory of architectural autopoiesis, aesthetic values must be adapted to the historical functional requirements. Le Corbusier did this intuitively. However, in his own theory he sets his aesthetic values as eternal and absolute. This stands in direct contradiction to his acute awareness of the new, specific functional requirements of his time. Le Corbusier cannot resolve this contradiction. But he offers an explanation for the coincidence between what satisfies functional criteria and what satisfies (independently defined) formal criteria. However, this explanation leaves no room for historical specificity: 'Not in pursuit of an architectural idea, but simply guided by the results of calculation (derived from the principles which govern our universe) and the conception of a *living organism*, the engineers of today make use of the primary elements and, by co-ordinating them in accordance with the rules, provoke in us architectural emotions and thus make the work of man ring in unison with universal order. Thus we have the American grain elevators and factories, the magnificent first fruits of the new age.'[303] The contradiction is right here, in the juxtaposition of the eternity of the universal order and the historicity of the new age. There is, however, a kernel of truth in Le Corbusier's explanation of the coincidence of functionality and beauty. This kernel of truth is taken up by the theory of architectural autopoiesis. It can be

302 Ibid, p 111.
303 Ibid, p 31.

integrated with a coherent account of the historical variability of aesthetic values by positing that this variability is constrained. Aesthetic values adapt to the formal features of contemporary, high performance morphologies. However, all high performance morphologies share the general, abstract feature of being law-governed rather than random. That is what Le Corbusier hints at with his notion of order. Within the theory of architectural autopoiesis, the distinction of *order* vs *chaos* marks the permanent, universal aspect of beauty. The sensation of beauty is always bound to a sense of order as distinct from chaos. Order attracts, random configurations are ignored or rejected. 'Where order reigns, well-being begins.'[304] The rationality lies here in the low probability that a random configuration of entities constitutes a functional unit. Where entities are configured into an order the presumption is justified that these entities somehow add up to a unit of interaction.[305] That Le Corbusier had grasped that rule-governedness is the general condition that accounts for the deep convergence of utility and beauty is evident in the following formulation: 'The creations of mechanical technique are organisms tending to a pure functioning, and obey the same evolutionary laws as those objects in nature which excite our admiration.'[306] However, the simple, primary forms Le Corbusier celebrates, ie, cubes, cylinders and pyramids, are certainly not the only rule-based forms, they are not the only organized morphologies that are 'governed by economy and conditioned by physical necessities'.[307] They do *not* deserve eternal devotion.

5. programme for the code of utility
   In order to function as a comprehensive architectural self-description, an architectural theory must formulate a programme for the application of the code of utility. The Modernist programme of utility, as it was emphatically formulated within Le Corbusier's *Towards a New Architecture*, states the tasks of architecture in terms of universal, standard function-types. Le Corbusier talks about *the* house, *the* dwelling, *the* city. He is expecting, in analogy to *the* motor car, a single, optimized solution that serves everybody and that can

304 Ibid, p 54.

305 Being attracted to order and repulsed by chaos might be a biologically hardwired response, ie, this response might be based on biological evolution rather than on cultural evolution or on conditioning on the basis of individual experience.

306 Le Corbusier, *Towards a New Architecture*, p 102.

307 Ibid.

be made the object of industrial mass production. 'Architecture is governed by standards. Standards are a matter of logic, analysis and precise study. Standards are based on a problem which has been well stated. . . . Standardization is imposed by the law of selection and is an economic and social necessity.'[308] One of the primary function-types that Le Corbusier considers to be exemplary is the house. The code of utility covers both practical and constructive criteria. This corresponds to the distinction of substantial vs subsidiary functions introduced within the theory of architectural autopoiesis.[309]

'The standard of the house is a question of a practical and constructive order.'[310] The first aspect responds to the new (social-democratic) mass society. The second aspect responds to the new construction technologies of steel and concrete as well as to the ambition to subject residential construction to a factory-based mass fabrication process. 'Eradicate from your mind any hard and fast conceptions in regard to the dwelling-house and look at the question from an objective and critical angle, and you will inevitably arrive at the "House-tool", the mass-production house, available for everyone.'[311] The phrase 'house-tool' and the formula 'the house is a machine for living in' emphasize practical utility but also allude to the use of contemporary technologies of construction. In the machine age the house is a machine built by machines. It is conceived, perfected and produced as a universal standard dedicated to a well-specified use. It is the same for everyone. 'Industry on the grand scale must occupy itself with building and establish the elements of the house on a mass-production basis.'[312] The fact that Le Corbusier thinks of a new universal standard dwelling that is well adapted to the conditions and resources of the modern industrial age is also evident in that he offers a 'Manual of the Dwelling'. He stipulates the required rooms on the basis of distinguishing essential types of activities that must be separated as follows: 'One for cooking and one for eating. One for work, one to wash yourself in and one for sleep. Such are the standards of the dwelling.'[313] There are further detailed

308 Ibid, pp 145–8.

309 See chapter 6.1.2 *Substantial versus Subsidiary Functions*.

310 Le Corbusier, *Towards a New Architecture*, p 141.

311 Ibid, p 163.

312 Ibid, p 6.

313 Ibid, pp 114–15.

instructions, for instance concerning the bathroom: 'One wall to be entirely glazed, opening on to a balcony for sun baths; the most up-to-date fittings with a shower-bath and gymnastic appliances.'[314] Further, he suggests the following: 'Demand bare walls in your bedroom, your living room and your dining room. Built-in fittings to take the place of much of the furniture. ... Demand concealed or diffused lighting.'[315] The suggestion of fitted furniture and diffused lighting enhances the drive towards total standardization, driving out all haphazard individuality. Le Corbusier is explicit: 'Buy only practical furniture and never buy decorative "pieces". ... Keep your odds and ends in drawers or cabinets.'[316] The insistence on universal standards for a mass society also includes the mechanically reproduced cultural products that can now enter the standard dwelling. Mechanically reproduced music guarantees a standard quality and is to be preferred over the vagaries of live performance: 'The gramophone or the pianola or wireless will give you exact interpretations of first-rate music, and you will avoid catching cold in the concert hall, and the frenzy of the virtuoso.'[317] Today the very idea of a standard manual for the modern dwelling seems out of touch with contemporary culture.

The functional heuristics of Modernism, the Modernist programme of utility, demands functional separation, functional specialization and the mass repetition of standard solutions. The principle of strict functional zoning is evident in Le Corbusier's urbanism as expounded and illustrated in his book *Urbanisme*.[318] Within the pages of *Vers une architecture*, Le Corbusier alludes to the principle of functional separation in the discussion of Roman architecture and urbanism. He points out that Rome provides the first example of Western planning on a grand scale. According to Le Corbusier, Roman architecture and planning are exemplary in terms of 'unity of operation, a clear aim in view, and classification of the various parts'.[319] He goes on to elaborate as follows: 'A clear aim, the classification of parts, these are a proof of a special turn of mind: strategy, legislation. Architecture is susceptible to these aims, and repays them with

314 Ibid, p 122.
315 Ibid, p 123.
316 Ibid, p 123.
317 Ibid, p 123.
318 Le Corbusier, *Urbanisme. Collection de 'l'Esprit Nouveau'*, Les Éditions G Crès & Cie (Paris), 1925, English translation: *The City of Tomorrow and Its Planning*, Dover Publications (New York), 1987.
319 Le Corbusier, *Towards a New Architecture*, p 158.

interest.'[320] The Modernist programme of utility based on functional separation, specialization and mass repetition remained in force for nearly 50 productive years, leading a global transformation of world society's built environments. However, this programme experienced a severe crisis during the 1970s. The transition from Fordist mass society to Post-Fordist network society implies the need for a new programme with new principles.

6. programme for the code of beauty
   Le Corbusier underwrites two sets of criteria, functional criteria and formal criteria, the code of utility and the code of beauty. Both sets of criteria are stated independently. However, Le Corbusier sets out the following relationship between utility and beauty: utility is a necessary but insufficient condition of beauty. Beauty is impossible without utility. It is the first condition. Without it, 'it is not possible that the higher factors of harmony and beauty enter in'.[321] However, utility is not enough. Le Corbusier explicitly rejects the idea – which he acknowledges to be a 'commonplace' among the young architects of his time – of simply identifying the beautiful with the functional. 'When a thing responds to a need it is not beautiful; it satisfies only one part of our mind, the primary part, without which there is no possibility of richer satisfaction.'[322] However, Le Corbusier is assuming that the useful is somehow already en route to becoming the beautiful. Le Corbusier introduces the term 'harmony' as intermediate step between mere utility and beauty. 'Harmony' is attributed to the useful, rational, well-engineered. It is not yet beauty but like utility it is considered to be a precondition of beauty. Beauty builds upon utility and harmony. Harmony can be reached by means of rational engineering on the basis of physics and economy. 'Our engineers ... employ a mathematical calculation which derives from natural law, and their works give us the feeling of HARMONY.'[323] Beauty presupposes economic/mathematical harmony. 'The emotion will not be aroused unless reason is first satisfied, and this comes when calculation is employed.'[324] But the achievement of beauty requires more than objective logic and calculation, it is a 'pure

320 Ibid, p 158.
321 Ibid, p 111.
322 Ibid, p 110.
323 Ibid, p 15.
324 Ibid, p 241.

creation of the mind'[325] and requires the creative sensibility of an artist. Beauty is the 'animation that the artist's sensibility can add to severe and pure functioning elements'.[326] Le Corbusier talks about 'beautiful things in which economic law reigns supreme, and mathematical exactitude is joined to daring and imagination'.[327] Then he adds: 'That is what you do; that, to be exact, is Beauty.'[328] The architect as artist 'gives us the measure of an order which we feel to be in accordance with that of our world, he determines the various movements of our heart and of our understanding; it is then that we experience the sense of beauty'.[329] Beauty is the highest aim of architecture. 'Architecture is the art above all others which achieves a state of platonic grandeur, mathematical order, speculation, the perception of harmony which lies in emotional relationships. This is the AIM of architecture.'[330]

Besides the conceptual definition and theoretical position concerning the concept of beauty, Le Corbusier's *Towards a New Architecture* also delivers a straightforward operational programme of beauty, a set of criteria that guides the application of the code values beautiful and ugly. According to Le Corbusier's apodictic pronouncements, the most beautiful forms are the primary, geometric forms like cubes, cylinders and spheres. These should remain unadorned and are to be set into simple, clear relations. Le Corbusier accepts that the surfaces of the primary volumes must be divided up due to utilitarian and construction needs. However, he rejects the punching of holes (doors and windows) into the volumes. 'These holes are often the destruction of form.'[331] Le Corbusier also rejects giving relief to the walls. 'To model the plain surface of primary and simple form is to bring into play automatically a rivalry with the mass itself.'[332] Instead of the imposition of holes or mouldings, Le Corbusier insists that all necessary dividing lines should be generated on the basis of the geometry of the volume. Le Corbusier refers to those lines as 'the generating and accusing lines of these forms'.[333]

325 Ibid, p 6.
326 Ibid, p 7.
327 Ibid, p 18.
328 Ibid, p 18.
329 Ibid, p 1.
330 Ibid, p 111.
331 Ibid, p 39.
332 Ibid, p 41.
333 Ibid, p 40.

With respect to cubes, this implies the imposition of a regular grid. Le Corbusier illustrates this point with images of American factories:[334] large, simple, rectilinear volumes with ruthlessly gridded facades, and without any further articulation. 'These accusing lines are in practice the chessboard or grill – American factories.'[335]

In terms of composing and relating volumes into a larger whole or ensemble, Le Corbusier recommends rhythm, repetition, symmetry and balance. As with the beauty of the primary geometric forms, he seems to consider these laws of composition to be universal and eternal. His use of historical examples suggests as much. 'Rhythm is a state of equilibrium which proceeds either from symmetries, simple or complex, or from delicate balancing. Rhythm is an equation; Equalization (symmetry, repetition) (Egyptian and Hindoo temples); compensation (movement of contrary parts) (the Acropolis at Athens); modulation (the development of an original plastic invention) (Santa Sophia). So many reactions ... in spite of the unity of aim which gives the rhythm, and the state of equilibrium.'[336] Le Corbusier also gives us the negative heuristics here, the definition of the ugly: 'Without the plan there can be neither ... rhythm, nor mass, nor coherence. Without the plan we have the sensation, insupportable to man, of shapelessness, of poverty, of disorder, of wilfulness.'[337]

Towards a New Architecture not only tells us how to operationalize beauty, how to identify beautiful things. It also contains a theory of beauty that tries to explain why the beautiful is perceived. It tells us about the meaning and advantage of our sense of beauty as defined above. 'Our eyes are constructed to enable us to see forms in light. Primary forms are beautiful forms because they can be clearly appreciated.'[338] Clarity allows for comprehension and orientation, prevents ambiguity, confusion, disorientation. 'Light and shade reveal these forms; cubes, cones, spheres, cylinders or pyramids are great primary forms which light reveals to advantage; the image of these is distinct and tangible within us and without ambiguity. It is for that reason that these are *beautiful forms, the most beautiful forms*.'[339] The same explanation/justification is given with respect to

334 There is also a photograph of Walter Gropius' *Fagus Werk*, Alfeld an der Leine, Germany 1911–13.
335 Le Corbusier, *Towards a New Architecture*, p 41.
336 Ibid, pp 50–1.
337 Ibid, p 48.
338 Ibid, p 23.
339 Ibid, p 29.

the most beautiful surface treatment: 'The generating and accusing lines of masses: ... clear and limpid, giving rest to our eyes and to the mind the pleasure of geometric forms.'[340] These formulations nearly seem to functionalize the laws of beauty in terms of articulation for the sake of comprehension/orientation. However, Le Corbusier appears to believe in a more exalted role for beauty. As for Alberti, for Le Corbusier beautiful architecture somehow connects us to the order of the universe. At least such an exalted idea is allowed to shine through from behind the more straightforward discourse of comprehension/orientation.

> Architecture, which is a matter of plastic emotion, ... should use those elements which are capable of affecting our senses, ... plastic elements, forms which our eyes see clearly and which our mind can measure. These forms, elementary or subtle, tractable or brutal, work physiologically upon our senses (sphere, cube, cylinder, horizontal, vertical, oblique, etc), and excite them. ... Certain relationships are thus born which work upon our perceptions and put us into a state of satisfaction (in consonance with the laws of the universe which govern us and to which all our acts are subjected), in which man can employ fully his gifts of memory, of analysis, of reasoning and of creation.[341]

Le Corbusier is indeed willing to indulge in metaphysics here: 'Proportions which we feel to be harmonious ... arouse, deep within us and beyond our senses, a resonance, ... an indefinable trace of the Absolute which lies in the depth of our being. ... This is indeed the axis on which man is organized in perfect accord with nature and probably with the universe. ... This could afford an explanation of the cause of the satisfaction we experience at the sight of certain objects.'[342]

How does Le Corbusier's programme of beauty fit with his programme of utility? His attempts at theoretical integration can no longer convince us. In practical terms there is a good fit. Simple, unadorned forms, grids, repetition, clear, unambiguous distinction of volumes – all this fits rather well with the idea of establishing

340 Ibid, p 41.
341 Ibid, pp 16–17.
342 Ibid, pp 203–12.

universal standards for distinct function-types. Both programmes together make sense with respect to the requirements and opportunities of a society based on Fordist mass production. That's why Le Corbusier's double programme became the defining programme of the epochal style of Modernism that changed the physiognomy of the global built environment in the 50 years that followed the publication of *Towards a New Architecture*. Le Corbusier had the right intuition: 'Everything tends to the restoration of simple masses: streets, factories, large stores, all the problems which will present themselves tomorrow.'[343] His attempt to exalt and eternalize the historically specific aesthetic of Modernism is theoretically unsatisfactory. But it may have helped to win the necessary ideological/aesthetic battles and thus it made practical sense.

7. programme for the code of originality
   Le Corbusier was certainly aware that originality was required (and thus had to be valued) in order to successfully address the task posed to architecture by the machine age. Le Corbusier acknowleged that 'new needs have arisen'[344] that demand new solutions. 'Architecture has for its first duty, in this period of renewal, that of bringing about a revision of values.'[345] Innovation implies creative destruction. Originality implies the courage to reject established dogmas. 'Religions have established themselves on dogmas, the dogmas do not change; but civilizations change and religions tumble to dust. . . . The cult of the house has remained the same for centuries. The house will also fall to dust.'[346] Le Corbusier promotes progress without any sentimental attachment to architectural forms that no longer sustain life. 'We throw the out-of-date tool on the scrap-heap. . . . This is a manifestation of health, of moral health, of *morale* also.'[347] The marvels of modern technology – the steam-ship, aeroplane and motor car – are taken as inspirations for architecture to break free from an 'age-long but contemptible enslavement to the past'.[348] Modern business organizations lead the way in terms of the new spirit required: 'Intelligence lies behind every initiative, bold

343 Ibid, p 41.
344 Ibid, p 8.
345 Ibid, p 6.
346 Ibid, p 14.
347 Ibid, p 13.
348 Ibid, p 103.

innovations are demanded. The morality of industry has been transformed: big business is today a healthy moral organism. If we set this new fact against the past, we have a Revolution in method and in the scale of the adventure.'[349]

The invention and design of the aeroplane is taken as an example for architecture: 'The airplane mobilized invention, intelligence and daring: *imagination* and *cold reason*.'[350] One key to original inventions is the clear statement of the problem. Problem focus goes hand in hand with the elimination of stereotypes and all preconceptions. The rejection of all fixed preconceptions is the key for any heuristics of originality: 'We eliminate from our hearts and minds all dead concepts ... and look at the question from a critical and objective point of view.'[351] Again, the invention of the aeroplane indicates what it takes: 'The airplane shows us that a problem well stated finds its solution. To wish to fly like a bird is to state the problem badly, and Ader's "Bat" never left the ground. To invent a flying machine having in mind nothing alien to pure mechanics, that is to say, to search for a means of suspension in the air and a means of propulsion, was to put the problem properly: in less than ten years the whole world could fly.'[352] Again, Le Corbusier emphasizes the rejection of preconception and the willingness to accept unexpected results that violate the established aesthetic values. 'The form and appearance are in no way preconceived, *they are a result*; they may have a strange look at first sight. ... Wright and Farman set themselves the problem of sustaining solid bodies in the air, the result was jarring and disconcerting, but it flew.'[353] Le Corbusier foresees 'a period of great problems, a period of analysis and experiment, a period also of great aesthetic confusion, a period in which a new aesthetic will be elaborated'.[354] It is not easy to see how this fits with Le Corbusier's insistence on a handful of primary forms and a set of compositional rules. Perhaps, if the forms and rules are abstract enough then there remains sufficient room for unprejudiced exploration. A certain formal a priori is always necessary for any

349 Ibid, p 284.
350 Ibid, p 109.
351 Ibid, p 6.
352 Ibid, p 113.
353 Ibid, p 138.
354 Ibid, p 64.

exploration. Also, even after a functional form has been found, there remains further room for the final formal (aesthetic) refinement. According to Le Corbusier, this final artistic refinement is also a matter of creative genius. Beauty too requires originality. 'And beauty? This is an imponderable which cannot function except in the actual presence of its primordial basis: the reasonable satisfaction of the mind (utility, economy); after that, cubes, spheres, cylinders, cones, etc (sensorial). Then the imponderable, the relationships which create the imponderable: this is genius, inventive genius, plastic genius, mathematical genius, this capacity of achieving order and unity.'[355]

8. discourse on style
   In contrast to the other two prior architectural self-descriptions analyzed here, Le Corbusier's *Towards a New Architecture* is full of explicit statements involving the concept of style(s). Le Corbusier assumes that each epoch should develop its own characteristic style. With this thesis Le Corbusier connects to an ongoing discourse that had been initiated by Heinrich Hübsch[356] in 1828, was picked up by, among others, Gottfried Semper[357] during the 1860s and had been gathering pace around the turn of the century, especially with the founding of the German Werkbund in 1907. Since, according to this discourse, the 19th century failed to develop a style for the modern era and instead indulged in recycling prior styles, Le Corbusier distinguishes the need for a genuine *style* (singular) from the superficial existence of *'styles'* (plural, in quotation marks).[358] The distinction of style vs 'styles' is introduced on page 3: 'The "styles" are a lie. Style is a unity of principle animating all the work

355 Ibid, p 143.

356 Heinrich Hübsch, *In What Style Should We Build?*, German original from 1828: *In welchem Style sollen wir bauen?*, excerpt in: Harry Francis Mallgrave (Ed), *Architectural Theory*, Blackwell Publishing (Oxford), 2006.

357 Gottfried Semper, *Style in the Technical and Tectonic Arts, or Practical Aesthetics*, Getty Publications (Los Angeles), 2004, original German: *Der Stil in den technischen und tektonischen Künsten oder Praktische Aesthetik: Ein Handbuch für Techniker, Künstler und Kunstfreunde*, Verlag für Kunst & Wissenschaft (Frankfurt am Main), 1860. See also: Gottfried Semper, *Über Baustile* (1869), extracts reprinted in: Gottfried Semper, *Wissenschaft, Industrie und Kunst*, Neue Bauhausbücher, Florian Kupferberg Verlag (Mainz/Berlin), 1966.

358 Compare: Hermann Muthesius, Style-Architecture and Building Art: Transformations of Architecture in the Nineteenth Century and its Present Condition, University of Chicago Press (Chicago), 1994, original German: *Stilarchitektur und Baukunst : Wandlungen der Architektur im XIX. Jahrhundert und ihr heutiger Standpunkt*, Schimmelpfeng (Mülheim-Ruhr), 1902. Muthesius contrasts the art of building with an architecture that imitates old styles.

of an epoch, the result of a state of mind which has its own special character.'[359] According to Le Corbusier, the new style has been taking shape unconsciously, outside architecture, through the agency of modern engineering and industrial machine production. 'Our own epoch is determining, day by day, its own style. Our eyes, unhappily, are unable yet to discern it.'[360] The new style has already arrived, except in architecture. This conception of a genuine style as an inadvertent byproduct of industrial life rather than conscious stylistic effort was not original. This was Semper's conception as well as the conception of William Morris and Hermann Muthesius. However, this understanding of styles involved a certain degree of subversion with respect to the idea of style as artful or artistic phenomenon that had become the primary commonplace conception of the term 'style'. Le Corbusier rejects the common identification of the concept of style with decoration. 'The specialized persons who make up the world of industry and business and who live, therefore, in this virile atmosphere where indubitably lovely works are created, will tell themselves that they are far removed from any aesthetic activity. They are wrong, for they are among the most active creators of contemporary aesthetics. Neither artists nor businessmen take this into account. It is in general artistic production that the style of an epoch is found and not, as is too often supposed, in certain productions of an ornamental kind, mere superfluities.'[361] This assessment is in line with the use of factories and grain elevators as examples of the new style.[362] Only in architecture had this new style not yet been manifested, because architecture remained imprisoned by the traditional 'styles'. 'We shall learn that "styles" no longer exist for us, that a style belonging to our own period has come about.'[363] Steel and concrete imply that 'the old codes have been overturned'.[364] Le Corbusier sets his generation the task of manifesting the new style within architecture, of createing a new architectural style for the machine age. However, he has no name for it.

359 Le Corbusier, *Towards a New Architecture*, p 3.
360 Ibid, p 3.
361 ibid of English translation of 13th French edition, published by John Rodker (London), 1931, p 89.
362 The use of these examples was also not original. Walter Gropius had used images of American grain elevators earlier, in an essay in the *Jahrbuch des Deutschen Werkbundes* of 1913.
363 Le Corbusier, *Towards a New Architecture*, p 7.
364 Ibid.

9. expansion of the repertoire

The advent of Modernism implies the most striking expansion of architecture's repertoire since architecture's inception in the 15th century.[365] Modernism's repertoire expansion was made possible by the radical rejection of the historical styles with their adherence to fixed typologies, symmetry, Classical proportions and ornamental-tectonic motifs. The organizational repertoire of all pre-Modern architecture was to a large extent constrained by traditional construction technologies. This became evident once Modernist architects like Le Corbusier made the conscious effort to take full advantage of the modern construction technologies afforded by steel, reinforced concrete and flat-roof technology. The conceptual shift from edifice to space[366] and Modernism's close connection to abstract art promoted the liberation and expansion of the formal repertoire. The radical abstraction implied by the concept of space together with the embrace of asymmetry and unconstrained proportions meant that organization was set free. However, initially the concept of dynamic equilibrium (Le Corbusier's idea of 'balance') and orthogonality (Le Corbusier's privileging of the right angle), as well as the maintenance of some form of proportional system (Le Corbusier's 'regulating lines') constrained this new freedom, at least during most of the 1920s. The white, orthogonal Modernism of the 1920s was already a massive repertoire extension. Hans Scharoun soon broke the restriction of orthogonality.

The early Modernist expansion of the repertoire was primarily an expansion of the repertoire of organization. Despite the stated ambitions to reveal the interior on the exterior one might argue that the early, white Modernism did not deliver an increase in architecture's repertoire of articulation. The total abandonment of ornamentation and the reduction of all surfaces to glass or white plaster spelled an impoverishment. The social rationality behind this might be the fact that the articulation of social status was no longer required or desired. This initial articulatory impoverishment was overcome in later stages of Modernism, in the subsidiary styles of Brutalism, Structuralism, Metabolism and High-Tech. Le Corbusier's later work made crucial contributions to Brutalism and Structuralism. Some of these subsidiary styles, namely Structuralism and

365 Only the shift from Modernism to Parametricism (via Deconstructivism and Folding) implies an even more radical expansion.

366 See Volume 1, chapter 2.2.5 *The Switch from Edifice to Space.*

Metabolism, also contributed to a further expansion of architecture's organizational repertoire.

Despite Modernism's evident repertoire expansion there is no explicit reflection of this fact within the pages of *Towards a New Architecture.* Perhaps the emphasis on the reduction to pure, primary forms clouded Le Corbusier's intellectual grasp of this expansion. Also, although the concept of space had already been hailed in the early 1920s,[367] ie, before the publication of *Towards a New Architecture,* Le Corbusier does not explicitly refer to the concept of space here. He has too much invested in the promotion of primary solids. There is perhaps too much emphasis on plasticity and on the architect as supposed plastic artist. However, the concept of plasticity is as abstract as the concept of space. In principle, this concept could be as conducive to a liberated repertoire as the concept of space. Le Corbusier's limitation here is thus primarily his insistence on primary forms.

Although the term space is absent, the switch from edifice to space does not totally elude Le Corbusier. In the chapter 'The Illusions of Plans', Le Corbusier emphasizes that the plan proceeds 'from within to without'[368] and that 'the exterior is always an interior'.[369] Here we also find phrases that seem to suggest that Le Corbusier had grasped the relation between abstraction and (organizational) repertoire expansion: 'The plan is the generator, it is the determination of everything; it is an austere abstraction, an algebrization.'[370]

10. design-process guidance
Le Corbusier assumes a collective, competitive process that involves the following stages: the clear stating of the problem, analysis, experimentation, the establishment of a type or standard, and finally the artistic perfection of the form for the purpose of moving our intellect and emotions. This final effort of formal refinement is no longer based on logic, calculation or performance experiments. It is a 'purely human creation'.[371] To begin with the explicit statement of

367 See Naum Gabo & Antoine Pevsner, 'Basic Principles of Constructivism'; and DeStijl, Manifesto V; both in: Ulrich Conrads (Ed), *Programs and Manifestoes on 20th-Century Architecture*, MIT Press (Cambridge, MA), 1971.
368 Le Corbusier, *Towards a New Architecture*, p 180.
369 Ibid.
370 Ibid.
371 Ibid, p 148.

the design project as specific problem, as a set of requirements, is trivial, self-evident to us today. One hundred years ago when the organization, form and appearance of a house were taken for granted, this was a revolutionary move, ie, to turn the house into a problem in search of a new solution, to call for a 'machine for living in', to treat the house like a motor car. 'The actual needs of the dwelling can be formulated and demand their solution. ... henceforth the problem is in the hands of the technical expert: we must enlist the discoveries made in industry and change our attitude altogether. ... A house as serviceable as a typewriter.'[372]

'We must aim at the fixing of standards in order to face the problem of perfection. The Parthenon is a product of selection applied to a standard. Architecture operates in accordance with standards. Standards are a matter of logic, analysis and minute study: they are based on a problem which has been well "stated". A standard is definitely established by experiment.'[373] Standards are based on experiment and analysis. 'The establishment of a standard involves exhausting every practical and reasonable possibility, and extracting from them a recognized type conformable to its functions, with a maximum output and a minimum use of means.'[374] As Le Corbusier observes, all motor cars have the same essential arrangements.[375] 'When once a standard is established, competition comes at once violently into play. ... In order to win you must do better than your rival *in every minute point*.'[376] These quotations indicate that Le Corbusier clearly understood the competitive and thus collective nature of design research. The precondition of intense, focused competition is that a large number of designers work on the same problem. The theory of architectural autopoiesis further insists that problems can only be sharply posed within the framework of a shared paradigm. This is the significance of the insistence upon styles as shared design research programmes.

There is a second important design process recommendation found within *Towards a New Architecture.* The principle to 'proceed from within to without'.[377] This design process principle has become

372 Ibid, pp 240–1.

373 Ibid, p 131.

374 Ibid, p 137.

375 Here we find indeed a singular, ultra-stable standard which has so far lasted another 90 years since Le Corbusier made this observation.

376 Le Corbusier, *Towards a New Architecture*, p 134.

377 Ibid, p 181.

one of the most widespread mantras of Modernism. It is further operationalized by the insistence to start with the plan rather than with the exterior elevations. 'The plan is the generator, the plan is the determination of everything; it is an austere abstraction, an algebrization. ... It is a plan of battle. ... A plan proceeds from within to without, for a house or a palace is an organism comparable to a living being.'[378] The principle finds its most stark formulation in the simple assertion: 'The exterior is the result of an interior.'[379]

11. design medium
Modernism expanded architecture's design medium in two ways. The first expansion was the introduction of abstract organizational diagrams, able to express programmatic and spatial relationships without yet fixing architectural form. The second expansion was the introduction of axonometric projections. *Towards a New Architecture* made extensive use of axonometrics in the chapter on mass-production houses. Axonometric projections are used here to depict large urban layouts, individual blocks, as well as the organization of the standard dwelling unit. Here Le Corbusier uses cut-away axonometrics in order to reveal the interior spatial organization of the dwellings in three dimensions. No abstract diagrams appear in the pages of *Towards a New Architecture.*

There is very little explicit reflection on drawing as the design and communication medium of architecture. There is only Le Corbusier's insistence that the plan must be the generator of organization and the warning against succumbing to the 'illusions of the plan'.[380] This warning or stricture requires the architect to resist designing plan patterns which cannot be perceived from the eye-level perspective of architecture's users. 'In actual fact a bird's-eye view such as is given by a plan on a drawing board is not how axes are seen; they are seen from the ground, the beholder standing up.'[381] In this context Le Corbusier uses perspective sketches.

12. self-reflectiveness
Le Corbusier's *Towards a New Architecture* certainly does not display the autological self-reflectiveness that we might expect from a

378 Ibid, p 180.
379 Ibid, p 181.
380 Ibid, pp 179–98.
381 Ibid, p 187.

comprehensive treatise today. Indeed, there is no explicit reflection on the role of theory in architecture at all within *Towards a New Architecture.* This might be due to the fact that the book was not written as a systematic treatise but was collated from a collection of essays Le Corbusier had published in his magazine *L'Esprit Nouveau.* These essays were written in the assertive tone of a manifesto rather than in the reflective style of a theoretical treatise. The book offers neither a preface nor an author's introduction. Instead the book fronts the seven chapters (essays) with an eight-page summary termed 'Argument' that draws together the main slogans and arguments under their respective chapter headings. The slogans are again pulled out on to a single page, highlighted in italic font, in front of every chapter. This device reinforces the manifesto-style proselytizing (rather than reflective) character of the book. The manifesto was indeed a widespread literary form in the first half of the 20th century. Intense polemical debate was a necessary hallmark of Modernism's ascent to architectural hegemony. The theoretical depth of these debates in terms of relating architecture's progress to the social and technological progress of modern, industrial civilization was unprecedented. However, within these debates the universal value and power of Enlightenment rationality were taken for granted. This was the era of positivism. The lack of theoretical self-reflectiveness was a general streak of Modernist architectural theory.

10.3.4 *THE AUTOPOIESIS OF ARCHITECTURE*

The self-inclusion of *The Autopoiesis of Architecture* within this section on architecture's classic self-descriptions is not only intended to indicate the author's hopes concerning the future status of his work. Rather, this self-inclusion reflects the autological character of *The Autopoiesis of Architecture*. The statement that the theory of architectural autopoiesis, *qua* published architectural theory, becomes itself a part of the autopoiesis of architecture is a simple consequence of the theory's basic definitions. More than this, as a theory that critically engages with the question of architecture's societal function, the theory recognizes itself as a *self-description* of architecture. As a comprehensive theory of architecture (understood as theory-led system of communications), it recognizes its own autological structure and theorizes itself as *domain-specific super-theory*.[382]

382 See Volume 1, chapter 1.3.5 *The Theory of Architectural Autopoiesis as Domain-specific Super-theory*.

Self-inclusion has been posited here as a requirement of any comprehensive theory of architecture that wishes to convince in our post-metaphysical and post-positivist times. Thus, as autological theory, the theory of architectural autopoiesis cannot afford to pass over any opportunity to reflect and expose itself. The comparative context of the analysis of three important historical self-descriptions is therefore a welcome opportunity that affords another autological loop of reflection. *De re aedificatoria*, *Précis des leçons d'architecture* and *Vers une architecture* delivered seminal self-descriptions of architecture that were respectively aligned with the epochal styles of the Renaissance, Neo-Classicism and Modernism. Within this context *The Autopoiesis of Architecture* theorizes itself as a new self-description aligned with the style of Parametricism.

The analytical grid that structured the analysis of the three classic texts was based on a posited catalogue of issues that *must* be addressed by any architectural theory that aspires to serve as self-description of the discipline. The fact that this probing grid of issues delivered substantial results from all three classic texts validates the imposition of the catalogue. The grid/catalogue is no abstract axiom any more. In fact this grid was derived from the main theoretical body of the theory of architectural autopoiesis as comprehensive discourse analysis of the discipline. It can now be deployed once more for a point by point comparative self-analysis of *The Autopoiesis of Architecture* in the context of the three classics. What follows might therefore also serve as yet another partial summary[383] of the theory of architectural autopoiesis.

1. the societal function and tasks of architecture
   The theory of architectural autopoiesis introduces the concept of 'societal function' as a meta-concept imported from Luhmann's social systems theory. The societal function of a function system acts as evolutionary attractor of system formation. This meta-theory has been validated here, in the context of architecture, by the fact that all the architectural self-descriptions (reflection theories) analyzed did indeed take the reflection upon what they considered to be architecture's societal function as the fundamental starting point (and point of return) of their respective theories.

   The meta-theory presupposed here demands that *the* societal function of any function system is singular and exclusive to each

383 Further summaries contained within *The Autopoiesis of Architecture:* the most condensed summary of the theory can be found in Volume 1, *Concluding Remarks*, in conjunction with *Appendix 1, Comparative Matrix of Societal Function Systems*. The compilation of 60 theses (24 theses in Volume 1, 36 theses in Volume 2) might serve as another summary.

function system. Accordingly, the theory of architectural autopoiesis is decisive in stating *the* societal function for architecture as the ***framing of communicative interaction***. More precisely, the societal function of architecture is to order/adapt society via the continuous innovation of the built environment as a system of spatial frames. This has been the defining societal function of architecture since its very inception in the Renaissance. The tasks of architecture that follow from this have been posited as ***organization and articulation***. The latter has in turn been elaborated in the terms of phenomenology and semiology. Although never stated so sharply, anticipations of this understanding of architecture's societal function and attendant tasks can be found in all major self-descriptions of architecture.

2. avant-gardist orientation
   There is no other architectural theory that promotes a more decisive avant-gardist orientation than the theory of architectural autopoiesis, perhaps with the sole exception of Futurism. However, this avant-gardist forward orientation does not inspire a blind theoretical iconoclasm. Innovation must be distinguished from mere novelty. Innovation, in order to enhance architecture's adaptive rationality, must understand and build upon the intelligence that architecture and architectural theory have accumulated over several centuries. Innovation has been identified as the *raison d'être* of architecture's autonomization and establishment as autopoietic function system. The differentiation of an avant-garde subsystem set against the mainstream has been explained and explicitly promoted as an institution that is necessary for the ongoing vitality of the autopoiesis of architecture.

   Every comprehensive architectural self-description must entail a historically argued forward orientation for the discipline. The theory of architectural autopoiesis has identified the specific, epochal challenges and opportunities posed by Post-Fordist network society, inclusive of the opportunities afforded by the micro-electronic revolution, as the primary, productive irritations that architecture must register (and respond to) in its societal environment.

3. disciplinary demarcations
   Every comprehensive architectural self-description must try to re-establish architecture's most urgent demarcation lines against its neighbouring systems. The theory of architectural autopoiesis places a unique, unprecedented emphasis on the question of systemic demarcation. The demarcation of architecture has not changed since

the refoundation of the discipline as Modern architecture in the 1920s, although the demarcation lines that were first drawn during that decade have since become much sharper. This concerns ***the demarcation of architecture from both art and engineering***. The respective discourses have since become truly incommensurable. In fact during the 1920s these issues of demarcation were argued about without having been resolved and settled in theory. As is evident in the above analysis of *Towards a New Architecture*, Le Corbusier tried to align architecture with art while demarcating it from engineering. The Radical Functionalists tried to assimilate architecture to engineering/science. In reality, both art and engineering developed their own very distinct discourses that could no longer be reunited as aspects of a single discourse. The theoretical understanding and acknowledgement of these realities lagged behind for most of the 20th century.

4. form-function relations
The theory of architectural autopoiesis posits the distinction of form vs function as the lead-distinction of the discipline. It represents the system-environment distinction within the system. 'Form' denotes architecture's internal reference. 'Function' denotes architecture's external (world) reference. Form and function can be distinguished as aspects of an artefact. The distinction of form and function poses the question of their effective correlation. The unification of these aspects becomes problematic. All presumed essences are dissolved. Functions are posed as problems. Forms are probed, selected and elaborated as solutions to problems. The distinction of form vs function marks the inauguration of architecture as rational-reflective discipline, as a precondition of innovation. Only the distinction of form vs function allows the framing of social interaction – a necessary dimension of all social evolution – to become a subject of critique and innovation. The task of architecture can thus be cast in terms of architecture's lead-distinction: ***to give form to function***. According to the theory of architectural autopoiesis, both forms and functions are communications. ***Forms are framing communications, functions are framed communications.*** The theory of architectural autopoiesis distinguishes substantial versus subsidiary functions and suggests substantial functions be explicated in terms of action-artefact networks. The functions of architecture are those communicative interactions and communicative event scenarios that are framed by architecture's forms. All design is ultimately communication design.

5. programme for the code of utility
   In order to function as a comprehensive architectural self-description, an architectural theory must formulate a programme for the application of the code of utility. Whether this is made explicit in the respective architectural theory or not, any programme for the code of utility – as well as any programme for the code of beauty – implies the positing of an active style. *The Autopoiesis of Architecture* is explicit in its (theoretically argued) commitment to Parametricism. The programme for the code of utility is therefore explicitly formulated in the context of the exposition of Parametricism.[384] In fact, a style is operationally defined by its programmes. Parametricism's programme for the code of utility – with its code values functional (useful) vs dysfunctional (useless) – can be identified with Parametricism's functional heuristics, ie, with the principles that guide the interpretation of the brief and the functional elaboration and evaluation of the design.

   Functional heuristics (programme of utility): avoid rigid functional stereotypes, avoid segregative functional zoning; all functions are parametric activity/event scenarios, all spaces/activities/events communicate with each other.

6. programme for the code of beauty
   In order to function as a comprehensive architectural self-description, an architectural theory must formulate a programme for the application of the code of beauty. The programme for the code of beauty must coincide with the formal heuristics of an active style. Here this style is made explicit: Parametricism. The formal heuristics of Parametricism give the operative as well as evaluative criteria for the application of the code values of the code of beauty, ie, formally resolved (beautiful) vs formally unresolved (ugly).

   Formal heuristics (programme of beauty): avoid rigid forms, avoid simple repetition, avoid collage of isolated, unrelated elements; all forms must be malleable, all systems must be differentiated, all systems must be correlated.

   The formal heuristics or programme of beauty also defines the aesthetic values that are most pertinent to contemporary life.

7. programme for the code of originality
   The Autopoiesis of Architecture recognizes and confirms that originality is a highly prized value within the autopoiesis of

384 See chapter 11.2.2 *Operational Definition of Parametricism: The Defining Heuristics of Parametricism.*

architecture. This can be explained and justified with reference to architecture's societal function and *raison d'être*: the adaptive *innovation* of the built environment. However, the theory of architectural autopoiesis observes and confirms that the value of originality operates as code – original (new) vs conventional (old) – only within the avant-garde segment of architecture's autopoiesis. Within the avant-garde the third code does indeed become prevalent. This additional code facilitates the formation of the avant-garde as a recognizable subsystem within the autopoiesis of architecture. This code imposes the relevance and recognition of the code values original vs conventional on all avant-garde communications. Mainstream architectural communications are not subject to this limitation. The code of originality (novelty) cannot impose itself here. Originality is – to a certain extent – valued within the mainstream but it does not function as code here, ie, it does not operate as indispensable precondition of communicative participation. (This makes sense because the mainstream must guarantee state of the art results. The mainstream cannot afford to take risks. Also, the mainstream is ill prepared to venture into the new.) Novelty requires special conditions for its successful production. Only in the (academic) avant-garde segment do these conditions exist, ie, the time and resources to experiment with brand new ideas.

What counts as original depends on the contrast with the conventional, established mainstream practice. However, this in itself, as a purely negative statement, does not suffice. In order for a design contribution to be recognized as an original contribution it must be recognizable as a contribution to a certain shared problematic. This, in turn, requires that the contribution is located within a paradigm or research programme, ie, it must be recognizable as a contribution to the development of a given or emerging avant-garde style. Only in very rare cases, during revolutionary periods, can a single contribution establish its own paradigm. But even then it must be recognizable as a re-problematizing contribution at a certain contemporary conjuncture or impasse. An original contribution cannot exist in isolation. In order to communicate it must combine novelty with redundancy. It must be part of a shared endeavour. Otherwise it would just be a bizarre curiosity.

Accordingly, here the programme for the code of originality must, once more, be tied to the research programme of Parametricism. The programme thus calls for *new* forms of elemental malleability, *new* forms of system differentiation and *new* forms of subsystem correlation, on the basis of *new* parameters, framing *new* parametric event scenarios that are connected to each other in *new* ways etc.

8. promoted style
   The Autopoiesis of Architecture contains an elaborate theory of styles. It distinguishes *passive, active* and *active-reflective* styles. It theorizes avant-garde styles as design research programmes and distinguishes *epochal* from *subsidiary* and *transitional* styles. The particular style that is being explained, justified and promoted within *The Autopoiesis of Architecture* is made abundantly explicit: ***Parametricism*** is being recognized here as today's most prevalent avant-garde style that has already established the conditions of a sustained, cumulative design research (drawing in more and more young designers globally). Further, Parametricism is being theorized as the most promising candidate to take on the mainstream to become the new global, epochal style after Modernism. The potential scope of the style is unlimited: it has the potential to take command over all design disciplines including architecture and urbanism. Parametricism is ready to transform the physiognomy of the world's artefacts and built environments in the 21st century, just as Modernism did in the 20th century.

9. expansion of the repertoire
   Every pertinent and forward-looking self-description of architecture should guide the expansion of the repertoire for spatio-architectural organization and articulation. This expansion of architecture's repertoire is most evident within the illustrated pages of part 11: *Parametricism – The Parametric Paradigm and the Formation of a New Style.* Within this part it is especially chapter 11.2.5 *Agendas Advancing Parametricism* that offers original contributions that entail a strategic expansion of architecture's repertoire. The subheadings there read as follows: *Parametric Inter-articulation of Subsystems, Parametric Accentuation, Parametric Figuration, Parametric Semiology, Parametric Responsiveness, Parametric Ecology, and Parametric Urbanism.* Further clues towards the expansion of architecture's repertoire are given in part 6: *The Task of Architecture.* Here, the three general agendas for upgrading architecture's intelligence (along the three dimensions of organization, phenomenological articulation and semiological articulation) also contain suggestions for an expansion of architecture's design repertoire, independent of any immediate stylistic alignment. Especially sections 6.4 *Supplementing Architecture with a Science*

of Configuration and 6.7 *The Phenomenological Dimension of Architectural Articulation* should be useful in this respect.

10. design-process guidance
The Autopoiesis of Architecture provides a prolegomenon for a contemporary design process theory that intends to probe and enhance both the creative productivity and the ***rationality*** of contemporary design processes. Accordingly, the design process is being theorized as ***problem-solving process***. (The aesthetic and formal issues are also understood as problems to be solved.) Problem-solving processes – on the level of complexity displayed by contemporary architecture and urbanism – can only be adequately theorized as accomplishment of an autopoietic communication system, geared up with its whole panoply of communication structures.

The design process is a specialized communication process that proceeds via design decisions that are posited and argued for within the communication systems of the ***project***, on the basis of incomplete, uncertain information. The theory of architectural autopoiesis connects back to the design methods movement of the 1960s and 1970s and adopts the conceptual apparatus of the *information-processing theory of cognition*. It has to be remembered that the analysis of the design process as information-processing process is only one abstracted moment within a larger process and system. Within the theory of architectural autopoiesis, the design process remains a communication process, a collaborative, discursive decision-making process that involves argument and critique as essential components that allow the full activation of architecture's highly evolved communication structures. Without argument and critique, and their anticipation, the highly evolved rationality of the discipline cannot be brought to bear. However, for the precise description of the logical and procedural micro-structure of the design process, ie, for the analysis of what goes on when design drawings or models are evolving, *information-processing theory* seems to be adequate.

Information processing is nothing but symbol manipulation within a physical symbol system. Symbols are discrete, indivisible elements. They constitute the *primitives* of symbol systems. *Symbol structures* are defined as sets of (primitive) symbol tokens placed into syntactic relations. Symbol structures are either *programmes* or *data-structures*. A data-structure *designates* an *object*. A *programme* is a symbol structure that designates an information process. If we take a step back from the minutiae of the design's progress and consider larger design steps, understood as design decisions involving evaluation within a discursive design deliberation within the project team, then a generalized concept of *programme* might indeed include the programmes that regulate the application of the code values, ie, the heuristic principles that define the style within which the design team works. The style is the programme that ultimately regulates the individual design decisions, ie, the Parametricist instructions 'differentiate' and 'correlate' are broad programmatic instructions that are then implemented via the concrete information processes that are executing a respective (differentiating or correlating) script. In this way *The Autopoiesis of Architecture* connects design process theory to the theory of style(s).

Instead of assuming objectively given task environments for architectural projects, the theory of architectural autopoiesis assumes the general possibility of constructing multiple competing ***problem spaces***. These problem spaces comprise three semi-independent subsystems: an interpretative *conceptual space*, a generative *modelling space* and an evaluative *value space*. The key problem that underlies the criteria for assessing the presumed task environment adequacy of problem spaces is the problem of social complexity. Ultimately, any specific design process assessment must refer back to the normative task scheme developed in part 6 in terms of the organization and articulation of complexity, and finally operationalized in the heuristics of Parametricism. To further advance the conceptual tools of such an assessment, the general design process theory proposed here analyzes the design process as a ***search*** in a ***state space***. The *state space schema* for representing problem spaces, and for describing problem-solving processes, proposes that every problem, and thus every design problem, can be defined through the following components: *initial state*, *goal state* and *intermediate states*. The design/problem-solving process can then be conceptualized as an information processing that *transforms* the initial state into the goal state via an arbitrary number of intermediate states. Design processes can now be described as series of state transformations (solution action sequences) resulting in *solution paths* that traverse the particular problem space that was constituted when a particular set of design media was chosen and the given design problem was initially interpreted. One might try to plot the solution path, in terms of graph theory, as search pattern or *search graph*. States would be represented as nodes and state transformations as directed links. (*The Autopoiesis of Architecture* offers illustrations to this effect.) Such an analysis would reveal the number and length of dead-end explorations. Although in itself revealing, the mere description of the solution path is insufficient. The analysis must try to reconstruct this solution path as a strategic, goal-directed search within the problem space, ie, as an exploration and decision process that can be critically assessed in terms of its underlying rationality. The question must be raised to what extent the observed search pattern is due to the underlying task environment represented or to the system of representation that results in the particular problem space. If multiple constitutive problem representations are available then parallel explorations in different problem spaces might reveal that the difficulties and impasses are differently distributed depending on which problem space or modelling space is used, ie, what is relatively difficult in one space might be relatively easy in the other space and vice versa.

The focus on rationality calls for the distinction of methods vs processes. *Methods* are rational organizations of processes. Design methods are defined relative to chosen problem spaces within which these methods organize the search/transformation processes. However, in complex problem-solving processes it might be necessary to move between different problem spaces. In architecture this is the case. As the project progresses, the process moves through a whole sequence of different problem spaces, each potentially employing various methods. Therefore, in order for the whole process to assume a measure of rationality, one has to posit the existence of a hierarchy involving an executive level organizing the selection, evaluation and sequencing of problem spaces and methods. Complex problem-solving processes are therefore often approached via a *process planning space*.

All problem-solving methods must incorporate at least one mechanism for ***generating*** or obtaining problem states and one mechanism for ***testing*** whether the obtained problem state is a solution state, or somehow approaches the solution space.

The most elementary method conceivable is thus the method whereby each and every element of the problem space is investigated in turn, either by a random trial and error process or by a more systematic process that can guarantee that all states in the problem space are investigated. These basic methods that only incorporate the two fundamental functions of generation and testing are referred to as *generate-and-test methods*. With respect to this kind of exhaustive process that searches through the entire space, the time needed is proportional to the ratio between the sizes of the problem space and the solution space. There are at least three factors that determine the design time and effort required to solve a problem: the size ratio of problem space over solution space, the effort required to generate a problem state, the effort required to test the problem state against the solution criteria. Design methods should try to economize on all three counts. Methods that incorporate strategies that reduce the search task while maintaining a good chance of arriving at a solution in a reasonable amount of time are *heuristic search methods*. The task of a problem-solving procedure is to grow a tree of operator sequences that will not branch too luxuriantly, and will include at least one solution path. But how can the problem dependent search space be reined in? Only through the decomposition of the global problem into relatively self-contained subproblems. Full decomposition is unrealistic and leads to weak results. The design process must be geared towards the elaboration of nearly decomposable systems, ie, systems with leaky modules or subsystems that cannot altogether avoid interdependencies with other subsystems. In principle, designers have two main strategies for dealing with these interconnections: they either block the leaks or they put the current subproblem on hold and attend to an interconnected subproblem. Putting subproblems on hold implies that interconnections can be assessed and resolved before subsystems are fully designed. This in turn suggests an oscillating or parallel processing of subsystems. The strategy of blocking interconnections compromises rationality because it either gives up potential synergies or ignores interferences. This was the strategy of Modernism. Parametricism is able to overcome this limitation. The inherent adaptivity of parametrically constituted subsystems implies that mutual adjustments remain possible while details progress. Furthermore, the strategy of Parametricism is to find synergies between subsystems. Both aspects, the avoidance of conflict and the garnering of synergies, can be worked upon via the establishment of systematic subsystem correlations.

The designer must make assumptions about how the problem might be dissected into self-contained subproblems, implying assumptions about the near-decomposability of the possible solution state (the final building or action-artefact network), and making assumptions about where the most promising points for dissection lie. This might be unproblematic with respect to routine design tasks, but remains problematic in the case of the ambition to innovate, or with respect to addressing novel problems. The decomposition problem and the related issue of the subsystem hierarchy are key issues for any original avant-garde design effort. These issues bear directly on the sequence in which issues are to be tackled. Within the avant-garde segment of architecture we should not assume that the design sequence can be fully pre-planned. Rather, the sequence itself is subject of experimentation. Sequence often determines hierarchy rather than vice versa. The rationality of the process can then only be reconstructed in retrospect.

A good heuristic method must be able to direct/focus the search by narrowing the search space. This can be done if the generator is tightened or constrained by a built-in selectivity so that every operation generates a new problem state that already secures some of the requirements that serve as criteria for identifying solution states. This is an essential technique of parametric modelling (*constraint modelling*). However, this might come with considerable information-processing cost, not only in terms of computational power/time but also in terms of design thinking time/effort. The immediate generation of problem states that incorporate all the required properties that must be exhibited within a satisfactory solution state can only serve here as a theoretical limit case that is inconceivable with respect to architectural design problems. A full readymade generation would just imply the transferral of the design process into the generation process. In all realistic cases it is only some of the solution properties that can be built into the generation process for new intermediate states. Only with respect to some narrowly defined subproblem might this be possible. Making generators selective is thus equivalent to decomposing and sequencing the original problem. With respect to architectural design projects one might broadly categorize the major design criteria into three kinds of requirements: requirements of geometrical fit, requirements of functional fit, and requirements of aesthetic fit. Which requirements/aspects can or should be pulled to the front end of the design process, and incorporated into the generator? The theory of architectural autopoiesis distinguishes Classical, Modern and Parametricist design methods depending on which of the three aspects is preconstrained. Methodological biases thus can be seen to correspond to styles.

The specific power of the new scripting based design processes available to Parametricism lies in the capacity to devise systems of rules that regulate the interaction of large component assemblies. These rule-based systems are now the primary domain of intervention in contrast to the direct manipulation of form that marks all prior eras of architectural design. These rule sets are the essential, defining layer within each problem state. Rule sets, in conjunction with specific parameter inputs, generate complex geometric configurations that cannot always be fully anticipated. Sets of simple rules compute complex, sometimes surprising, emergent patterns. Unexpected qualities might be discovered that can then be investigated with respect to their aesthetic power and functional potential. Despite their often surprising quality, these results are fully reproducible. Discovered qualities can be focused upon, refined and integrated into the expanding geometric-spatial repertoire. This power to produce a wide variety of novel patterns and qualities is the ***generative power*** of the deployed scripting techniques. In parallel the new scripting techniques afford a further profound advance: they allow for complex, multi-variable constraints to be built into the generative rule set. This capacity to build in multiple constraints into a rule set is the ***constraining power*** of the deployed scripting techniques. This strategy makes it possible for key solution criteria of the design to be guaranteed in advance while a generative process explores the space of possibility that is still open despite the inbuilt constraints. Generative and constraining power can thus operate together and complement each other. These computational techniques also exhibit a compelling ***analytical power***. Each result can be instantly measured. Component variations can be tied to a quantitative analysis (measurement) of underlying layers. All three powers potentially enhance the rationality of the design process. This ability to combine the explorative potential for surprise discoveries with the guaranteed adherence to key criteria is the unique advantage of the new computational techniques.

These techniques become key components of a powerful contemporary design method. Parametricism is the contemporary style that is most vigorously advancing its design agenda on the basis of these techniques. To the extent that the label 'Parametricism' is here not only deployed as a descriptive, classificatory label that is applied to observed contemporary tendencies in architecture but is also used with normative import outlining an agenda for contemporary architecture, we might call the method that organizes the parametric processes according to the rationality criteria elaborated here *the Parametricist method*.

11. design medium

The Autopoiesis of Architecture emphasizes the fundamental importance of the medium. The medium is revealing and concealing aspects of reality. In terms of design output it opens and delimits a universe of possibilities. In particular, *The Autopoiesis of*

Architecture theorizes architecture's design medium of the *model* as a specialized *success medium* in Luhmann's sense of the term, parallel to *money*, *power* and *truth*.[385] The model (drawing) has been developed as a medium of speculation that is able to depict an uncertain future state with a very convincing degree of internal consistency and detail. Only via the medium of the model is it possible to *succeed* in communicating radical innovations to clients and committing a large number of people around a new complex endeavour requiring long chains of coordinated activity, whose results lie in the relatively distant future.

The evolution of architecture's autopoiesis involves the evolution of its specific medium. The introduction of the medium established the capacity to progress the architectural project while maintaining reversibility. Each further step in the development of the medium increased this crucial capacity to combine design progress with the preservation of adaptive malleability. The medium of the model, just as money and power, has been able to upgrade itself on the basis of the micro-electronic revolution, ready more effectively to meet the increasing challenges of society.

Architecture's design medium has been radically transformed since Le Corbusier's treatise. The medium's advancement during Modernism was minimal (compared with the advancement of the last 20 years). The diagram and the axonometric projection are modern additions to a medium that has otherwise remained virtually unchanged for 500 years, since Alberti. Le Corbusier did not have to learn a single new design medium during his career which spanned over 50 years. Today every avant-garde architect has to continuously upgrade his/her design medium literacy. Every year new powerful tools enter the scene.

The shift from paper to CAD was the first step in this transformation. Then the deployment of generative, intelligent computational processes (scripting) started to replace design via the direct manipulation of individual forms. This engendered a paradigm shift in the very conception of design as an intellectual endeavour. Thinking in terms of elements and their unique composition has been replaced by thinking in terms of the correlation of systems of parametrically malleable components. The new ontology depends on the new medium. Although the phenomenon of Parametricism cannot

385 Luhmann refers to these media also as 'symbolically generalized' media. See Volume 1, chapter 4.1.1 *Symbolically Generalized Media of Communication*.

be reduced to the increasing use of the new medium, it was inspired by it and remains dependent upon it.

12. self-reflectiveness

    The Autopoiesis of Architecture aspires to a new level of self-reflectiveness, especially in comparison with the three classic treatises analyzed here. Contemporary intellectual culture and the challenge to navigate a poly-perspectival world make this indispensable.

    The theory of architectural autopoiesis comprises an integrated theory of architectural theory in general as well as a theory of architectural self-descriptions in particular. On this basis, the theory formulates its autological self-inclusion. It positions itself as domain-specific super-theory.[386] Through the general concept of architectural self-description, the theory of architectural autopoiesis theorizes itself in terms of its own role and pertinence as disciplinary steering device with respect to architecture's societal contribution and continued relevance. As a post-metaphysical and post-positivist theory, the theory sets itself contingent and offers itself as one of many possible self-descriptions that might be advanced to guide the complex and multi-faceted discipline and profession that calls itself architecture. The theory does this explicitly in the historical context of prior key texts that have reflected architecture in terms of its societal function. This historical comparison is summarized in Appendix 3: *The Autopoiesis of Architecture in the Context of Three Classic Texts*.

10.4 Architectural Historiography

THESIS 55

Architectural historiography is always committed historiography. It is an integral part of architecture's self-description. It is a reflection theory rather than a science. Its organizing principle and coherence can only be derived from a principle that identifies a particular historical problematic and task for contemporary architecture.

As architecture discovers itself it also discovers its own history. The two phenomena go hand in hand. The construction of origins and histories is a characteristic move within the autopoiesis of social systems: family histories, tribal histories, national histories, disciplinary histories etc.

386 Concerning the concept of super-theory see Volume 1, chapter 1.3.4 *Super-theories*, and chapter 1.3.5 *The Theory of Architectural Autopoiesis as Domain-specific Super-theory.*

In effect each architectural theory constructs its own appropriate architectural history. The first significant theoretical self-description of architecture since antiquity – Alberti's *De re aedificatoria* – already contains a clear schema for an architectural historiography, dividing the history of architecture into three phases as steps in a progression towards perfection: the Egyptian phase, the Greek phase and the Roman phase. In this historical schema, Alberti already takes account of the role of theory in the perfection of architecture. The phases of development of architecture are thus also understood as phases in the emerging self-consciousness of architecture as a discipline: Alberti writes that Egyptian architecture was 'begot by chance and observation', that Greek architecture was 'nursed by use and experience' and that Roman architecture was 'filed and perfected by the principles of philosophy'.[387] It is quite obvious that this account of history is consistent with his own agenda of reinstating the canon of antique Roman architecture as well as with his own involvement as a man of letters and his particular 'philosophical' style of theorizing architecture.

Other famous examples of 'histories' (or rather the construction of an origin) are Laugier's account of the origin of architecture in the context of the promotion of Neo-Classicism, or the rather sophisticated historical reconstructions and schemas proposed by Gottfied Semper in *Der Stil in den technischen und tektonischen Künsten*.[388] For the Modern Movement it was – famously – Sigfried Giedion's *Space, Time and Architecture* that provided the appropriate history of architecture leading up to the advent of the Modern Movement. Giedion was conscious of the fact that history is always inspected and reconstructed anew, according to the latest interests and questions of contemporary architecture. This is indeed a condition of historiography's relevance. 'The Historian, the architectural historian especially, must be in close contact with contemporary conceptions. ... History is not simply the repository of unchanging facts. ... The backward look transforms its object: every spectator at every period – at every moment, indeed – inevitably transforms the past according to his own nature.'[389] Manfredo Tafuri made the same point when he insisted on 'an unstable dialectic in

387 Alberti, Book 6, pp 113–15, quoted in David Smith Capon, *The Vitruvian Fallacy – A History of the Categories in Architecture and Philosophy*, John Wiley & Sons (Chichester, West Sussex), 1999.

388 Gottfied Semper, *Der Stil in den technischen und tektonischen Künsten*, Vol 1, Verlag für Kunst und Wissenschaft (Frankfurt am Main), 1860, Vol 2, Bruckmann Verlag (Munich), 1863.

389 Sigfried Giedion, *Space, Time, and Architecture*, 5th edition, Harvard University Press (Cambridge, MA), 1967, p 5.

history, . . . an unresolvable multiplicity of meanings and directions' that 'matches the need to make its meanings operative'.[390]

In the context of the theory of architectural autopoiesis proposed here, the reconstruction of the history of architecture might take two distinct forms: the first historiographical effort concerns architecture's successive autonomization and the historical evolution/elaboration of its internal communication structures (in relation to internal and external challenges). This historiography has yet to be written. *The Autopoiesis of Architecture* only offers a sketchy outline of this history of architecture's formation as a self-conscious discipline. The second type of architectural historiography is closer to what has commonly been understood to be the history of architecture. This historiographical effort builds upon the familiar history of architectural styles. It is trying to give an account of the history of architectural styles as architecture's response to systemic changes in its societal environment. A brief sketch of this form of architectural historiography is given below, embedded within part 11 on the style of Parametricism rather than here within the general reflections on the role of architectural historiography. Here the task is to give a general characterization of the two types of architectural historiography.

10.4.1 HISTORY OF ARCHITECTURE'S AUTONOMIZATION AND INTERNAL STRUCTURATION

The historiography of architecture's successive autonomization and evolving internal structuration has two related parts. First, there is the attempt to trace the phases of architecture's formation as a self-conscious discipline. The task here will be to identify those key moments within architecture's crystallization as a self-referential discourse and practice, when lines of demarcation were drawn and its peculiar criteria of self-evaluation were first asserted. The second part of this historiography would attempt to give an account of the evolving, internal differentiation of architecture's communication structures. This historiography would chart the historical development of architecture's specialized medium. It would include a history of the avant-garde's emergence as subsystem within the autopoiesis of architecture. It would also include a history of the increasingly important role of architectural theory, as well as the emergence of architectural historiography itself during the 19th century. Both parts of this (inherently autological) historiography will have to be written within the context of a general history which describes the broad

390 Manfredo Tafuri, *Theories and History of Architecture*, Harper & Row Publishers (New York), 1976, p 152. Tafuri, however, also warns against reading history from the point of view of an architecturally committed position.

outlines of societal development as a transformation of society's primary mode of differentiation from stratification to functional differentiation. The schema for this overall history is given in Niklas Luhmann's *Die Gesellschaft der Gesellschaft*.[391] It underlies and links all his separate accounts of the various function systems of modern society. The underlying schema of architectural historiography is thus established in advance, as a consequence of the decision to follow Luhmann and link the whole theoretical project to his overarching theoretical system.

The success (or failure) of the attempt to sketch out the key steps in the emergence of architecture as autopoietic function system within modern society will be one more measure of the fruitfulness of the theoretical adventure embarked upon here. The crux will be whether this schema, on the one hand, allows for a plausible interpretation of the familiar historical material, even making new and compelling sense of events already considered significant, and whether, on the other hand, it succeeds further in foregrounding, illuminating and rationalizing features within the history of architecture (and architectural theory) that hitherto seemed aberrant and meaningless.

In any event, the historical sketch offered here is obviously only one among many possible histories. Like all other histories, its distinctions and concerns not only offer to make sense of the present, but are also prone to be projected into the future – either in the sense of an extrapolation of the tendencies identified, or as an occasion to mobilize resistance.

It should be clear by now that the historiography proposed here must be a history of the discipline and its discursive structures coevolving with its societal environment. This history is closer to a history of ideas than to history conceived as causal chain of events. This history also reflects the various historical self-descriptions that are involved at each stage. The paradigm that guides the historiography proposed here is the theory of evolution rather than a traditional history of ideas concerned with tracing influences across time. The evolutionary paradigm is mostly concerned with the question why certain discursive structures are selected and how they are incorporated and made to function for the respective autopoietic system within a certain given environment. Such an evolutionist historiography always aims for a functionalist history based on the fundamental question of how a system continues to function within its environment. Such a functionalist history of 'ideas' and discursive

391 Niklas Luhmann, *Die Gesellschaft der Gesellschaft*, Suhrkamp Verlag (Frankfurt am Main), 1998. This book presents the final keystone of Luhmann's theory of modern society. It has yet to be translated into English.

structures does not claim that it can always explain the origin of the respective discursive structures. The origin of the features and structures that seem so well – fitted for their purpose in the case of living organisms usually lies outside the functional agenda they end up serving. The features and structures that are selected are rarely made to purpose. They are drafted in for certain purposes by utilizing their latent capacities or affordances. The same applies in the case of concepts, tropes, media and turns of argument etc. They are the product of a prior evolution based on superseded system requirements. Only their selection has a rationale. Their provision is always serendipitous. Their latent capacities are only revealed at the moment of being selected into the evolving system.[392] The whole point of the functionalist explanation of the discursive structures of the discipline is to understand why certain discursive structures (concepts, principles, repertoires) are selected, persist, propagate and conquer the domain of architecture during a certain historical period.

Although various historiographical sketches have been interlaced in the text all the way through, the *theory* of architectural autopoiesis is not the appropriate site to provide a full *historiography* of architecture's 500 year autopoiesis. However, the theory can give reference points for historical research. The following list suggests key areas for further historical research into architecture's evolving internal structuration as autonomous system of communications:

- the history of societal differentiation that produces architecture as autopoietic subsystem of society
- the historical development of architecture's primary distinctions, categories and codes
- the historical development of architecture's media of communication
- the history of the emergence of an architectural avant-garde
- the history of the increasing importance of architectural theory
- the history of architecture's increasing historical consciousness

10.4.2 HISTORY OF ARCHITECTURAL STYLES AS RESPONSES TO EPOCHAL SHIFTS IN THE SOCIETAL ENVIRONMENT

Architectural history contributes to architecture's ongoing self-reflection with the aim of guiding future practice. It is thus a part of architecture's self-description or ***reflection theory***. Niklas Luhmann's insistence that reflection theories belong to their respective function systems, rather than

392 The selected features and structures of any evolutionary process are always pre-adaptive advances, ie, they have either been previously selected for other purposes, due to other capacities, or they have been fallow side effects of other functional capacities. What is selected from what is given is made to fit, and put to work.

belonging to the separate function system of science, carries an important implication. Architectural history in this sense can only be coherently written from a theoretical position that is broadly committed to a contemporary style or avant-garde tendency. Architectural history must make a difference with respect to contemporary controversies about how best to operationalize the architectural codes of utility and beauty. A historiography that insists on the code of truth as the only relevant criterion – rejecting all normatively relevant conclusions about the plausibility and probable future success of competing tendencies – operates outside architecture, within the domain of pure science. In this sense a committed architectural historiography – written from within the autopoiesis of architecture – has to be distinguished from scientific architectural historiography as part of the science of history. What relationships exist between the two? Committed historiography utilizes scientific historiography to answer its practically motivated questions. Scientific historiography might use contemporary commitments as research questions in its investigative work. The concept of an utterly uncommitted historical science is a chimera. There can be no scientific work without prior guiding questions. Such guiding questions can only come from arenas of practical engagement. This applies to architectural historiography as much as it applies to political and socio-economic history. Nevertheless, it is possible to distinguish between the various histories that are written from within the various function systems as part of their respective reflection theories on the one hand and historical research that is regulated by the communication structures of science on the other. In the latter category original work of retrieving sources as evidence is done according to the standards of the science of history. The underlying research questions of the science of history, however, must be drawn in from the various other function systems and their attempts at historical self-reflection, ie, from the political system, from the legal system, from the economic system, from architecture etc, or else they might be drawn from another social science like sociology. These research questions might be rather broad and the historical research is often multifunctional in terms of its further utilization within the various specific function systems. To make such general historical work relevant to the problems discussed within a specific function system thus requires function-system-specific appropriation and interpretation.

Architectural history has never been at the centre of attention of the science of history. Only with respect to earlier civilizations where written records are rare did the remains of their built environments receive attention and analysis as record of these civilizations. More recent architectural phenomena have been studied within the context of art history, which gained recognition as an independent field of historical inquiry without being subsumed within the art system. Art history comprises the study of artefacts, buildings and art works of all eras, before as well as after the differentiation of an autonomous art system. Therefore we can distinguish (more specifically than above) between an architectural historiography written from within the autopoiesis of architecture and an architectural historiography written as part of the academic discipline of art history. An example of an architectural historiography written from within architecture is Sigfried Giedion's *Space, Time and Architecture*. An example of an art-historically framed architectural historiography is Heinrich Wölfflin's *Renaissance und Barock*. This close relationship between architectural historiography and the historiography of art works became the more misleading the more art and architecture separated. Perhaps this accounts for the fact that in recent years most architectural history has been written by architects rather than art historians. What is required now is historical research that would contextualize architectural history within a broad overview of the history of world society understood as the historical coevolution of all the important societal function systems. More detailed research questions would have to be developed with a view to addressing the specific challenges and opportunities faced by contemporary architecture as reflected in current controversies.

It is from the vantage point of the intuitions or hypotheses of contemporary architectural theory about future architectural possibilities and their probable societal effectiveness that history must be investigated and probed. This kind of committed historiography has nothing to do with aligning famed historical exemplars as precedents in order to dignify one's own current agenda. The probing of the historical material should be open with respect to the potential refutation of a proposed hypothesis and agenda. As example of a fruitful research question for historical research one might consider the question of architecture's semiological efficacy with respect to its different styles and with respect to its different societal environments. This research question is directly inspired by the contemporary agenda of the semiological project as formulated within part 6 of *The Autopoiesis of Architecture*.[393] The theory of architectural autopoiesis could spawn quite a few fruitful questions and hypotheses for historical research. For instance, research into the historical context of the development of architecture's specialized communication medium, or

393 See sections 6.8 *The Semiological Dimension of Architectural Articulation*, 6.9 *Prolegomenon to Architecture's Semiological Project,* and 6.10 *The Semiological Project and the General Project of Architectural Order*

historical research into the phenomenon of transitional styles, or into the phenomenon of subsidiary styles, as defined within the theory of styles put forward in Volume 1 of *The Autopoiesis of Architecture*.[394] These particular research questions come out of a particular, committed architectural theory/self-description. These questions also link up with contemporary design agendas that are ultimately intended to serve the upgrading of a specific contemporary avant-garde tendency: Parametricism. According to the theory of architectural autopoiesis, Parametricism is best (although not exclusively) placed to incorporate an upgraded semiological project. It is also best placed further to advance and benefit from the development of architecture's medium. It is also most likely to spawn new subsidiary styles within its epochal framework and best placed to recognize Postmodernism and Deconstructivism as transitional styles in order to recuperate their advances without any danger of backtracking. On the basis of the identification of such connections between historiographical research questions and contemporary design ambitions, the thesis is put forward that the most coherent and fruitful architectural history might be written from the vantage point of the coherent agenda posed by a contemporary style.

That is why the (very brief) illustrated history of architectural styles has been placed within the section on Parametricism, in order to make its logical dependence on a contemporary agenda unmistakably explicit. This logical dependency does not imply that architectural history can or should be studied only after a clear architectural position has been fully formulated. Browsing historical study goes hand in hand with the trial and error formation of a new design approach leading to a new style. The study of history plays its role in most new style formations. What the thesis of logical dependency implies is that historical research can become much more strategic and focused after a contemporary position has been formulated as clearly articulated hypothesis. The thesis implies that at a certain stage within an architect's evolving self-description a mature position might be reached that allows him/her to confirm his/her contemporary commitments in terms of a historiography that locates his/her commitments within an encompassing historical rationality.

On the most general level of abstraction, the key principle for probing architectural history within the framework of the theory of architectural autopoiesis is the principle of adaptive pertinence. This principle concerns both the historical pertinence of architecture's communication structures in general and the historical pertinence of architecture's styles in particular. The succession of styles delivers the most prominent

394 See sections 3.6 *Architectural Styles* and 3.7 *Styles as Research Programmes*.

periodization of architecture's autopoiesis with respect to both internal and external observers. The task of architectural historiography with respect to architecture's succession of styles is to explain this succession as a series of successful adaptations to changes – irritations in the form of new challenges and opportunities – in architecture's societal environment. The heuristic-theoretical premise is that the major styles of architecture respond to systemic shifts in the order of society.

The theory of architectural autopoiesis has identified architecture's societal function as the continuous, adaptive re-ordering of the total system of social communicative interaction via spatio-morphological frames. This societal function translates into the tasks of spatial organization and morphological articulation of the total system of social institutions. The simultaneous dynamization and increasing complexity of this system of institutions are being identified as the primary challenge of contemporary architecture. The maturing style of Parametricism has been identified as the most pertinent response to this challenge within contemporary architecture. The problematic of the organization and articulation of increasing societal complexity and dynamism might therefore be proposed as organizing principle for a coherent historiography of recent architecture. One might also attempt to generalize this principle across the whole span of architectural history since the Renaissance. It can indeed be argued that the very emergence of architecture in the 15th century can best be explained by the new demand and opportunity for rapid, innovative restructuring of the built environment in the context of a dynamized overall societal process. The further developmental stages (styles) are also involved in respective increases in architecture's ability to handle increased societal complexity. However, this general dimension of progress must be further articulated with respect to the specific features of the various epochal styles in relation to the specific features of the various societal epochs. The fact that architectural history is articulated into distinct styles correlates with the fact that the overall historical evolution of society displays distinct stages rather than a smooth, gradual progression. The envisioned historiography of architectural styles as adaptive responses to societal shifts thus relies on a general historiography of stages of societal development. A brief outline of such a historiography and a first sketch of how the succession of architectural styles – including the style of Parametricism – fits into and contributes to such an encompassing historiography will be presented below, in the part on Parametricism.[395]

395 See section 11.1 *Parametricism as Epochal Style, chapter 11.1.1 Historiographical Sketch: The Epochal Alignment of Styles*.

10.5 Architectural Criticism

THESIS 56

Architectural criticism provides the interface (structural coupling) between architecture and the mass media. The results of architecture's internal evaluation processes are supplied with a new set of reasons satisfying the values and criteria of mass media communication. Therefore architectural criticism can neither share in nor convey architectural intelligence. Instead it can productively irritate this intelligence.

The autonomous self-constitution of architecture is confirmed by the fact that an architect's architectural reputation is gained (and lost) within the self-referential discourse of architecture. Who is and who is not recognized as a 'great architect' results from the discourse internal to architecture. Architecture is able to project its internally processed system of reputations into society at large, however not without further selective filtering and attendant loss of information. How is this possible? Should not the popular acclaim by the general public determine what great architecture is? Is the capacity/confidence of the general public to recognize architectural reputations too limited? The fact is that the great architects who are recognized in society at large have first been recognized within architecture: Norman Foster, Frank Gehry, Rem Koolhaas, Zaha Hadid etc. A certain time-lag with respect to the societal dissemination of architectural reputations has to be conceded. The societal recognition often comes too late, ie, after the respective architect has already been overshadowed within the discipline by a new generation of avant-garde protagonists. This kind of delay can also be found with respect to the mass media recognition of scientific reputations. Artistic reputations seem to spread faster. In architecture the construction time of a building – often between five and 10 years in the case of important buildings – imposes a further delay.

Still, the fact remains that architectural reputations are made nowhere else but within the autonomous autopoiesis of architecture, despite the fact that buildings are visible within the public domain. How is this possible? What needs to be understood is that the 'general public' is a fiction or abstraction that is construed within the function system of the mass media. General societal reputations exist in the form of the mass media construction of celebrity. The most prominent of the internally constituted reputations are transposed into the domain of mass media communications by the writings of ***architectural critics***. Architectural critics are architecturally socialized writers – often educated as architects – working for national/international newspapers. The institution of architectural criticism is a specialized interface institution (structural coupling) that manages the information flow and mutual irritations on the boundary between architecture and the mass media. The critic picks up the result of the internal architectural evaluation process and supplies this result with a new set of reasons satisfying the values and criteria of mass media communication. It is therefore not to be expected that architectural criticism provided by critics operating within the mass media can directly contribute to the accumulated intelligence of architecture, neither do these kinds of writing share in or convey architectural intelligence. Since these critiques are also read by architects – irritating the architectural discourse – aspects of these external evaluations might lead to adaptations within the autopoiesis of architecture. The importance of the institution of architectural criticism for producing signals for architecture's self-steering efforts should not be underestimated. It produces a major type of irritation, second only to the direct irritation supplied by the immediate clients of architecture. All ambitious architects are sensitive to their mass media presence. Although architectural reputations can only be initiated within the autopoiesis of architecture, mass media promotion produces significant multiplier effects with important consequences for the architect's chances of securing high value work. This, in turn, gives the architect the chance – however without guarantee – to further enhance his/her reputation within architecture. Architectural reputations can be multiplied, inflated and destroyed by architectural criticism circulating within the mass media.

11. Parametricism – The Parametric Paradigm and the Formation of a New Style

There is a strong, global convergence in recent avant-garde architecture that justifies the enunciation of a new style: *Parametricism*. Its most conspicuous outward characteristic is a complex and dynamic curvilinearity accentuated by a swarm-like proliferation of continuously differentiated components. Beyond such obvious surface features one can identify a series of new concepts and methods that are so different from the repertoire of both traditional and modern architecture that one is justified in speaking of the emergence of a new paradigm within architecture. The shared concepts, formal repertoires, tectonic logics and computational techniques that characterize this work are indeed engendering the formation of a new style. Parametricism is the great new style after Modernism. Postmodernism and Deconstructivism have been transitional episodes that ushered in this new, long wave of research and innovation. Modernism was founded on the concept of space. Parametricism differentiates fields. ***Fields*** are full, as if filled with a fluid medium.[1] Instead of the Classical and Modern understanding of design as the composition of a handful of simple parts, according to Parametricism design involves the scripting of dynamic fields that encompass myriads of malleable components organized into differentiated and mutually correlated subsystems. New design tools play a crucial part in making this possible, establishing a whole new design process and methodology. This new way of working has been both radicalized *and* refined over the course of recent years. Parametricism is thus dependent on the adoption of sophisticated computational techniques. However, as a style rather than as a mere panoply of new techniques, Parametricism is characterized by its new distinctive values and sensibilities that started to emerge even before the computational methods were ready to hand.

1 See Volume 1, chaper 5.4.4 *From Space to Field.*

As elaborated in Volume 1, section 3.7 *Styles as Research Programmes,* avant-garde styles might be interpreted and evaluated in analogy to new scientific paradigms, sponsoring a new conceptual framework and formulating new aims and methods. Styles are design research programmes.

Innovation in architecture proceeds via progressing within a style as well as progressing from style to style. Styles thus represent cycles of innovation. They gather design research efforts into a collective endeavour. Avant-garde design projects are best understood as hypotheses, formulated within a certain style. The style serves as a research programme that allows for a *systematic series* of design experiments. Stable self-identity is here a necessary precondition of directed evolution. The style might initially be defined: all elements and systems are parametrically malleable in order to intensify internal and external associations. However, an operational definition – in terms of a pertinent design heuristic that can reliably guide the design process – is crucial for advancing the style as collective design research effort. Styles understood as design research programmes must guide both the understanding/handling of functions as well as the corresponding elaboration of forms. The operational definition of Parametricism must thus comprise both a functional as well as a formal heuristics:

Functional heuristics of Parametricism

Negative principles (taboos):	avoid rigid functional stereotypes avoid segregative functional zoning
Positive principles (dogmas):	all functions are parametric activity/event scenarios all spaces/activities/events communicate with each other

Formal heuristics of Parametricism

Negative principles (taboos):	avoid rigid forms (lack of malleability) avoid simple repetition (lack of variety) avoid collage of isolated, unrelated elements (lack of order)
Positive principles (dogmas):	all forms must be soft (intelligent: deformation = information) all systems must be differentiated (gradients, thresholds, singularities) all systems must be interdependent (correlations)

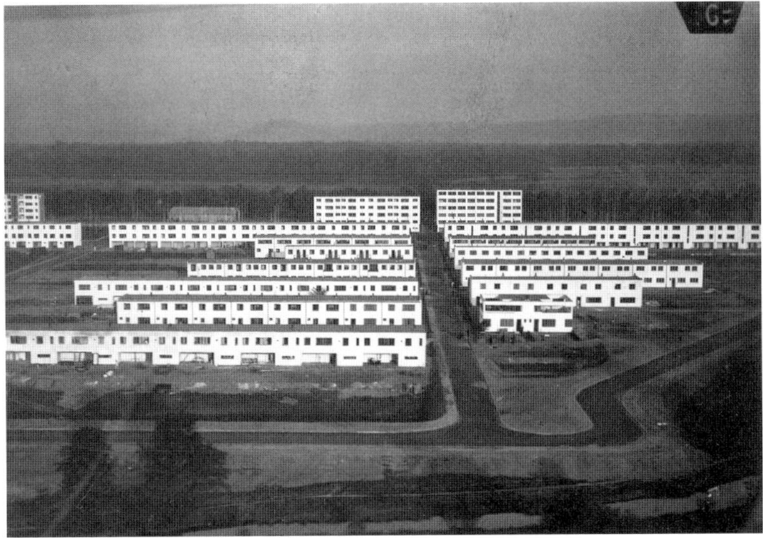

Figure 55 Modernism, Walter Gropius, Mustersiedlung, Karlsruhe, 1929

Avoidance of the taboos and adherence to the dogmas deliver complex order for complex social institutions. The consistency of the style as a collective design research programme depends upon the unfailing adherence to these strictures and impositions. Although the style has been proclaimed and explicitly defined only recently, it has developed over the last 15 years. A fast expanding generation of young architects is joining the movement, vigorously adhering to the general strictures formulated above – whether they explicitly proclaim allegiance to the style or not. The style – maturing over the last 15 years – is now claiming hegemony within avant-garde architecture. It has already established a long wave of systematic innovation. It is now gearing up to go mainstream to finally succeed Modernism in changing the physiognomy of the global built environment. The style finally closes the transitional period of uncertainty that was engendered by the crisis of Modernism and that was marked by a series of short-lived episodes including Postmodernism, Neo-Historicism and Deconstructivism.

The morphological results of Parametricism appear like (organic or inorganic) natural phenomena that are the result of processes of self-organization and evolution. The work of Frei Otto is the only true precursor of Parametricism. He used physical processes as simulations and design engines to 'find' form rather than to draw conventional or invented forms. The inherent lawfulness of the engaged physical processes produced a combination of complexity, rigour and elegance

Figure 56 Postmodernism, OMA, City of the Captive Globe, 1978

Figure 57 Deconstructivism, Daniel Libeskind's Berlin City Edge, 1987

Figure 58 Parametricism, Zaha Hadid Architects, Soho City, Beijing, 2003

that was otherwise unattainable. The power and beauty of this approach was striking. However, the fact that this design process was bound to physical models limited its potential to be generalized across the discipline. It required the easy availability of computational simulations to allow Frei Otto's pioneering work to gain the widespread influence and significance it has today.

Contemporary Parametricist design harnesses digital simulation and form-finding tools that are inherently open to artificial modulation. Not only can parameters be shifted out of natural ranges but wholly new, artificial forces and their defining laws and logics may be defined. Any parameter (property or relation) of any object (geometry, position, colour, transparency etc) may be associated with any parameter (property or relation) of any other object (or group of objects). An artificial, second nature can be conjured via scripted, quasi-natural laws, rich in internal and external ***correlations***. The notion of correlations is crucial for the Parametricist concept of architectural order. Correlations are either internal to the design or they obtain between the design and its context. Internal correlations include the interdependencies that obtain between the various subsystems that constitute the design as well as the

Figure 59 Frei Otto & Bodo Rasch, soap film model for a tent

interdependencies between the component elements that together make up each respective subsystem. External correlations are contextual adaptations and affiliations. Such contextual adaptations have been an a priori demand within the autopoiesis of architecture for quite a while. The heuristics and techniques of Parametricism lift the theme of contextualism to a new level of intensity.

11.1 Parametricism as Epochal Style

THESIS 57

Avant-garde architecture and urbanism engage in an ongoing cycle of innovative adaptation – retooling the discipline in order to elaborate its capacity to adapt the architectural/urban environment to the demands of the socio-economic era of Post-Fordism.

The contemporary avant-garde tendency that has recently been christened 'Parametricism' might be misunderstood as mere fad or fashion. The very act of christening it as an 'ism' might invite or reinforce this misunderstanding despite the fact that the intention of giving a name to the tendency was rather the opposite: to identify it as an epochal event. The insistence that what currently goes on within the contemporary avant-garde of world architecture should be interpreted as the formation/maturation of a new (potentially epochal) style requires that the concept of style(s) – which had been trivialized in recent decades – is reconstructed anew as profound key category of architectural self-description. This theoretical work has been accomplished with the integrated theory of style(s) presented in Volume 1 of *The Autopoiesis of Architecture*: styles are the necessary programmes that operationalize architecture's double code of utility and beauty. At the same time they serve as avant-garde architecture's design research programmes, a necessary precondition for collective/cumulative design research.

The emergence and worldwide expansion of Parametricism is an epochal event. What does this mean?

The theory of style(s) expounded in Volume 1 distinguishes epochal, subsidiary and transitional styles. The key category is the category of epochal style(s). The concept implies the alignment of architectural styles with general societal epochs. The concept thus presupposes a theory of society/history that establishes a general periodization, ie, a theory that distinguishes societal epochs. All periodization schemes assume that society develops via distinct stages rather than as an even, continuous process/progress. This assumption is consistent with the fundamental idea of society as a *system* understood as an entity where elements and subsystems are functionally integrated and thus mutually interdependent so that their individual variation is constrained. This in turn implies that these elements and subsystems are mutually stabilizing. It also implies that if some key elements or subsystems do change and manage to break out of the normal operation of the system, then the other elements/subsystems are likely to be disrupted and thus forced to change as well. Thus the pattern of evolution of well-integrated systems should be expected to be uneven, oscillating between periods of relative stability and periods of accelerated change. With respect to the evolution of life's ecology, this phenomenon has been observed and theorized under the concept of punctuated equilibrium. Thus the history of overall society as well as the history of each of its subsystems is articulated by stages. Within the architectural subsystem of society these stages are the epochal styles of architecture.

Traditionally theories distinguishing the broad stages of societal development have been the domain of philosophy – the philosophy of history – with key contributions from Vico, Hegel, Spencer and Marx. Marxism developed by far the most sophisticated discourse of historical periodization. Although the theory of architectural autopoiesis is built upon Niklas Luhmann's theory of society which has developed its own compelling principle of periodization, some of the more detailed historical analyses that were developed within the Marxist framework cannot be fully dispensed with here. Thus, in what follows, the attempt has to be made to reinterpret and integrate some pertinent Marxist concepts within the overarching framework of Luhmann's theoretical system. Luhmann's framework establishes the key category of 'predominant mode of societal differentiation'. This category replaces Marx's category of fundamental 'modes of production' as key to the individuation of historical epochs. Luhmann distinguished four modes of differentiation and placed them in the following sequence:

1. segmentation
2. centre-periphery differentiation
3. stratification
4. functional differentiation

Marx distinguished four modes of production in sequence as follows:[2]

1. primitive communism
2. slavery
3. feudalism
4. capitalism

Primitive communism – the communal sharing of many (not all) resources – was the economic institution of tribal societies. The primary mode of differentiation at this stage of the development is segmentary differentiation. The clans that made up the tribe operated parallel to each other, as equal segments, without hierarchical integration or division of labour.[3] The same principle of equal segments dominated relations between clan members. Both slavery and feudalism are possible economic forms of societies in which stratification is the primary mode of societal differentiation. It is thus not possible to align the two sets in a one-to-one mapping because both slaveholding and feudal societies are stratified societies. However, if we narrow the historical focus to the last 1000 years and thus only consider the major epochal transition that started about 500 years ago (often referred to as the advent of modernity), then an alignment is possible. The transition from stratified to functionally differentiated society is at the same time the transition from feudalism to capitalism. Luhmann's categories intend to be more

2 Marx also predicted a further stage: world communism.

3 The distinction between segmentary differentiation and functional differentiation captures Durkheim's distinction between mechanical and organic solidarity. Functional differentiation is more complex and more organized. It allows for the integration of much larger societies. One might compare this distinction to the distinction between a primitive organism like a segmented worm on the one hand, and a mammal with many functionally specialized organs on the other. On the basis of the latter principle, organisms can (and must) usually become much larger. In a segmented organism or society, the segments are much more autonomous and might be able to survive and reproduce if cut off from the encompassing organism or society.

general than Marx's in the sense of avoiding singling out the transition in the economic sphere as decisive/defining. The transition from a feudal to a capitalist economy is just one of several transitions that took place in parallel in the various coevolving subsystems of society.

These transitions might also be characterized as mutually amplifying processes of domain autonomization establishing the major autopoietic functions systems from domains that were previously not yet clearly separated but instead fused together under a single authority. Luhmann's concept of *modern functionally differentiated society* describes the result of this process of separation and autopoietic closure. The important point to make here in comparison to Marx is that Luhmann's theory is symmetrical with respect to the different domains. He refuses to privilege any one of them. There is no hierarchy that orders the interplay between the autonomous function systems. The interplay between the political system, the legal system, the economy, science, the mass media etc is like an ecology of mutually interdependent species. For Marx, in contrast, the economy clearly dominates all other domains of social life. His distinction of base and superstructure attests to this. As soon as we suspend this distinction and – with Luhmann – treat the economy and its systemic stages of development as one dimension of a multi-dimensional process, then it is possible to speak of the transition from feudalism to capitalism within the framework of Luhmann's theoretical system. The transition from feudalism to capitalism is then just one moment of the transition from stratification to functional differentiation.[4] By extrapolation it is then equally possible to introduce and integrate further concepts of Marxist provenance in order to enrich the conceptual apparatus for the identification of societal epochs that might be used to align and illuminate the architectural styles to be identified and explained within architectural historiography.

Two key concepts of Marxist provenance that are especially useful here are the concepts of Fordism and Post-Fordism. This enrichment of Luhmann's discourse is necessary in as much as Luhmann has not offered further, detailed periodizations within the overarching epoch of functionally differentiated society. Luhmann's theory of the transition from a society primarily built upon stratified differentiation to a society primarily built upon functional differentiation only delivers the transition from tradition-bound building to architecture as self-consciously innovative autopoiesis. Further subdivisions within the great era of the emergence and evolution of functionally differentiated society are

4 Another important moment of this transition was the emergence of science as the emancipation of knowledge and learning from its dependence upon political power.

required to account for the styles of architecture. Luhmann's concept of functionally differentiated society – as a society where functional differentiation is the primary mode of societal differentiation – seems most pertinent with respect to the first half of the 20th century. The era of Fordism when most corporate and state institutions were organized by means of rigid, functional hierarchies, was perhaps its most paradigmatic instantiation.

During the last 30 years, new organizational tendencies and patterns of communication have emerged that imply more fluid forms of differentiation. Functional specialization continues but it is becoming more temporary, continuously redefined, redistributed and re-associated in fluid networks. Domains of competency are sometimes fuzzy and temporarily interpenetrating. The Post-Fordism discourse, as well as the recent discourses in management science, has emphasized these new tendencies. It is these new tendencies that Parametricism recognizes and responds to. The key term that has captured and condensed most of these new phenomena is the term 'network'.[5] Therefore the theory of architectural autopoiesis uses the phrase 'Post-Fordist network society' to describe the current (and coming) societal epoch. It is an epoch that is still in its early stages of formation. In many ways its new dynamics and patterns of communication are fuelled by computational power and the digital communication media. Luhmann's schema of distinguishing societies in terms of their primary mode of differentiation remains in place. The premise of the theory of architectural autopoiesis is that Post-Fordist network society is still a version or sub-period of functionally differentiated society. Perhaps the next society will move from functional differentiation to a new primary mode of differentiation. Perhaps this mode of differentiation might be called network differentiation. Concerning Luhmann-inspired speculations about the next society we can consult Dirk Baecker who insists that the next society can only be imagined as networks of selective, risky and surprising associations.[6] Social systems theory remains the overarching framework for the theory of functionally differentiated society, its network version, and for the theoretical speculation about the next society.

On the basis of Luhmann's system of periodization presupposed by the theory of architectural autopoiesis, world society continues to be

5 See Manuel Castells, *The Rise of the Network Society: The Information Age: Economy, Society, and Culture,* Vol 1, 2nd edition, John Wiley & Sons (London), 2010; also: Jan van Dijk, *The Network Society: Social Aspects of New Media*, Sage Publications (London), 2006.

6 Dirk Baecker, *Die nächste Stadt: Ein Pflichtenheft*, unpublished paper 2009/2010, www.dirkbaecker.com. See also: Dirk Baecker, *Studien zur nächsten Gesellschaft*, Suhrkamp (Frankfurt am Main), 2007.

characterized as functionally differentiated society as long as the autopoietic function systems Luhmann identified persist. This is certainly the case for the foreseeable future.[7] Even if the new network form of differentiation/communication starts to dominate many organizations and many processes *within* the great function systems, the demarcations *between* these function systems exhibit no signs of dissolution. That is why Post-Fordist network society must be theorized as the current evolutionary stage of functionally differentiated society. Architecture – upgrading itself to meet the demands of Post-Fordist network society by embracing Parametricism – remains one of world society's great function systems,[8] upgrading its operations and variable communication structures on the basis of the same (permanent) communication structures that have been distinguishing architecture since the Renaissance.

11.1.1 HISTORIOGRAPHICAL SKETCH: THE EPOCHAL ALIGNMENT OF STYLES

The evolution of the built environment starts haphazardly, via trial and error, like a quasi-biological, material process. Enclosures tend to be circular because any other shape is less efficient and less stable. Medieval fortresses became the circular nuclei for cities by way of concentric extension. Another self-asserting geometry is the geometry of rectilinear cells, best suited for the tight packing of differently sized enclosures. No intelligent insight needs to be assumed to explain the patterns exhibited by pre-architectural environments. Stable performance

7 The author judges that the significance of certain Postmodern cultural phenomena like the dissolution of artistic genres, the emergence of interdisciplinary research projects etc is being misinterpreted as a general tendency towards the dissolution of functionally specialized domains. In contrast, the theory of architectural autopoiesis hypothesizes the ultra-stable persistence of the function systems. The dissolution of national state competencies within a globalized world is coherent with this general tendency towards functional (rather than segmentary or stratified) differentiation.

8 The author also expects the emergence of further function systems as an aspect of the ongoing, general tendency of functional specialization. For instance, one might expect the growing profession of counselling psychology to establish itself as autopoietic function system. As social relations become more complex, dynamic and demanding for everybody, counselling might become a universally demanded service akin to the permanent utilization of medical services. The communication structures that are currently crystallizing within this professional domain seem to be susceptible to a Luhmannian systemic analysis: counselling psychology demarcates itself explicitly from the medical model of psychiatry. It engages with 'clients' rather than 'patients'. Its lead-distinction is 'presenting problem vs action plan' rather than medicine's 'diagnosis vs treatment', its code is 'coping vs not coping' or 'adaptive vs maladaptive' rather than 'healthy vs ill', its programmes are the various counselling approaches (Cognitive-Behavioural, Person Centred, Psychodynamic, Systemic), its specific medium is conversation or talk therapy, and its societal function is the individual's adaptation to the complexity of societal demands and opportunities.

Figure 60 Castle as origin of concentric medieval town, from Leonardo Benevolo, *The History of the City*, 1980

criteria, trial, error and time suffice to account for all architectural prehistory. The evolution of the built environment progressed very slowly. Stable reproduction was a precondition of incremental improvements. This was the prehistory of architecture, the era of tradition-bound building. This started to change about 550 years ago with the birth of architecture (as distinct from building) in the Italian Renaissance, together with the birth of science and early capitalism. The medieval, so-called Romanesque style is only a passive style, ie, it is a style only according to retrospective classification by later outside observers. The Romanesque period is still locked in the pattern of tradition-bound building. The Gothic style can be interpreted as a first major step from tradition-bound building towards architecture. The Gothic style is aligned with the rise of the free cities within the bosom of feudal society. The stunning, innovative achievements of the Gothic make it difficult to exclude it from the concept of architecture. However, within the theory of architectural autopoiesis the decisive factors of architecture's full-blown emergence are the systemic separation of design from construction, supported by the specialized medium of graphic representation, as well as a specialized theoretical discourse, supported by printed books combining drawings and arguments in the promotion of architectural innovations. Not before the Renaissance did an individual author-architect claim full responsibility for a design project. Not before the Renaissance was an architectural project fully designed and visualized on paper. Therefore, only since the Renaissance could the autopoiesis of architecture progress

Figure 61 Palmanova – ideal city as rationalized medieval town

via purely theoretical projects. These factors have been decisive for the accelerated evolution of the built environment ever since. The Renaissance marks the big bang of architecture. In terms of socio-economic alignment, Renaissance architecture is integrated with the rapid development of the early capitalist city states of northern Italy.

Figure 62 The Italian Renaissance as the birth of architecture, Filarete's Sforzinda: invented city, the architect as innovative creator

The second epochal style was the Baroque.[9] It coincides with the era of political absolutism ruling over the economically integrated mercantilist state. The architectural order of the ideal city of the Renaissance stopped at the city walls. Beyond the city walls was still the mostly amorphous, wild, medieval hinterland. The Baroque style projected the architectural order of the city beyond the confines of the city, staking the claim for territorial control by the absolute sovereign, symbolizing the integration of the land into a single, unified state territory. This process had its early precursors during the late Renaissance. Architecture is geometry – geo- 'earth', -metri 'measurement' – the founding technique of man's appropriation of space. Following Mark Cousins,[10] the history of mankind, in relation to space, might be described as a successive internalization, in real as well as in conceptual terms, the successive integration of the surroundings into the interior of the city. Athens still had an edge-condition, whereby it met the unknown and uncontrolled 'other'. Greek cosmology still asked questions concerning the end of the world. The whole Middle Ages existed within Aristotelian cosmology. The city remained a closed circle. Departure from it implied adventure. All maps stopped somewhere surrendering to the white terra incognita. Architecture's formal systems first started tentatively to conquer the surrounding landscape during the Renaissance. The Italian villa emerged as the *castello* could shed its fortifications and the control over the hinterland was asserted by way of extending architecture's geometry and placing the landscape under its spell. This finds its pendant in the representation of space through perspective construction which, according to Alberti, starts with the gridded horizontal plane, thus domesticating everything in advance. Everything that might happen to occupy space is safely positioned. The medieval realms are transcended. City, landscape and villa are unified in the *integrazione scenica*. Venice's reclamation of the Veneto in the 16th century was the politico-economic agenda setting the task for the Palladian villa. The villa transposes the urban architectural order into the hinterland, formally seizing upon the colonizing grid imposed under the *centuriatio* system that divided the land relentlessly into squares of 625 metres.[11] The villa was placed at major crossing points within this system formally enhancing the

9 The Renaissance style transitioned to the Baroque style via Mannerism.

10 The author followed some of Mark Cousins' lectures at the Architectural Association School of Architecture during the mid to late 1990s.

11 Clemens Steenbergen and Wouter Reh, *Architecture and Landscape*, Prestel Verlag (Munich), 1996. A brilliant study attentive to the various formal strategies by which the ever-resistant geo-morphology is forced under architecture's rule.

intersecting axes. Palladio recommends raising the axial streets against the fields and lining them with a regular rhythm of trees, while the *piano nobile* was again raised above the intersection. This was the first precise articulation of a comprehensive modular and hierarchical order.

These processes that began tentatively during the late Renaissance intensified decisively during the Baroque era which found its historical peak in the service of 17th-century French absolutism, as the land was built into a state. Only with the advent of the Baroque style, during the era of absolutism (integrating economies on a national scale) did the architectural order stretch all the way to the horizon, brought under the controlling gaze of monumental, panoramic perspectives. The France of Louis XIV was the paradigmatic case where the Baroque's capacity to integrate large territories and to unify large building complexes was put to work most effectively. Further, roads – measured by milestones – and canals were cut through the landscape. State boundaries were precisely defined and maps surveyed the state territory. A unified currency was imposed. At the same time, large administrative complexes had to be built, much larger than anything hitherto required or known. The Palace of Versailles is the paradigmatic monument that shows off the power of Baroque architecture in line with the power of the absolutist sovereign and his administration. Another example is Baroque Rome with the monumental complex of the papal basilica of Saint Peter. The Baroque style was rolled out across Europe representing and reasserting the power of the Catholic Church.

Formally the main advance of Baroque architecture over the architecture of the Renaissance is the degree to which it is able visually to integrate the ramifying parts of a large building or complex of buildings into a unified whole. The Baroque style is able to make the functional integration of large building complexes perceptually palpable. The typical features of the Baroque style – the use of convex and concave curvature, enhanced depth and plasticity, as well as details like double columns and split gables – all contribute to this unifying capacity. Curvature unifies, deep relief and plasticity enhances conspicuity from distant views imposed by the size of the ensembles, split gables are a part of the game of breaking the symmetry of the parts of a facade in order to emphasize its overall unity. This effect of making the parts of a composition asymmetrical, turning them into radicals that demand a resolution in the overall symmetry of the global complex, is the most powerful unifying device here. Robert Venturi noted this effect and termed it 'inflection'.[12]

12 Robert Venturi, *Complexity and Contradiction in Architecture*, Museum of Modern Art (New York), 1966.

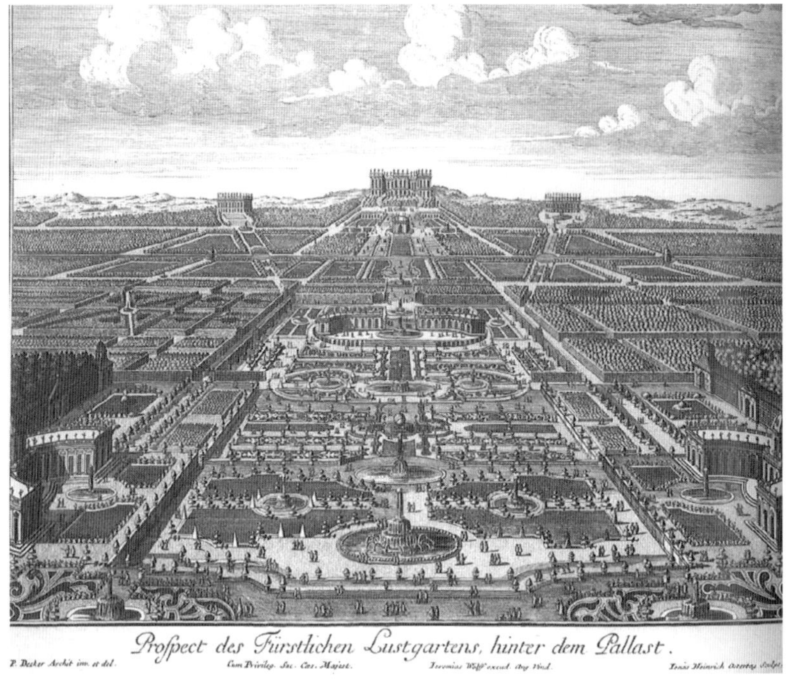

Figure 63 Baroque projection of absolutist power, from Paulus Decker, *Princely Architect, or Architectura Civilis*, 1711

In contrast, all parts of a Renaissance composition rest symmetrically within themselves. They are self-sufficient and do not call for resolution within a larger whole, ie, they are not inflected towards the centre of the composition. Renaissance compositions are thus additive whereas Baroque compositions are integrative. The same effect whereby local asymmetry enhances global symmetry can be observed in the famous inkblots that Hermann Rorschach used in his psychological experiments.[13] The strongly unifying impact of such symmetries built on asymmetry increases their impressiveness, thus commanding heightened attention.

The next epochal style that needs to be accounted for is Neo-Classicism leading to Historicism. This style is aligned with Classical bourgeois capitalism and the nation states of the 19th century, most paradigmatically with Napoleon's post-revolutionary France, an era marked by a challenging variety of societal demands both in terms of the

13 See Figure 42: Inkblot #1, from Hermann Rorschach, *Psychodiagnostik*, H Hubert (Berlin/Leipzig), 1921.

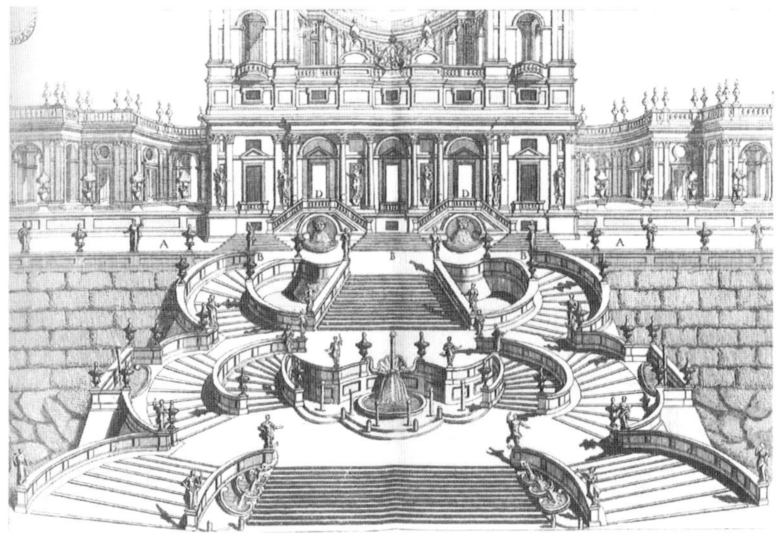

Figure 64 Baroque, local asymmetry enhances global symmetry: Bernardo Antonio Vittone, palace with stairs, 1760

variety of building types and in terms of the individual variations that had to be accommodated in each design project. Neo-Classicism is a bourgeois style in its decisive differentiation against the Baroque style of the Ancien Régime and against the subsidiary Rococo style that was associated with aristocratic frivolity. The austere simplicity of Neo-Classicism expressed bourgeois virtues and was associated with the civic values of republican Rome. Neo-Classicism was also the first stage of the more general phenomenon of Historicism, ie, tapping into the large reservoir of prior historical styles to build up a rich repertoire of stylistic expression to cope with the increasingly extensive task domain of architecture. The diversity of function-types that had to be accommodated had grown significantly. During the era of absolutism, architecture was still confined to palaces and churches. Now there was a new set of public institutions to be designed. Typical alignments emerged between certain function-types and specific historical styles. Law courts, banks and central government buildings were biased towards the Neo-Grec style. Churches and town halls were biased towards the Neo-Gothic style. Private villas and townhouses were biased towards the Neo-Renaissance style. Thus a loose system emerged that had a larger capacity to articulate the institutional variety of society. At the same time a new, versatile method of composing diverse plan configurations was devised and propagated. This was the achievement of JNL Durand. In

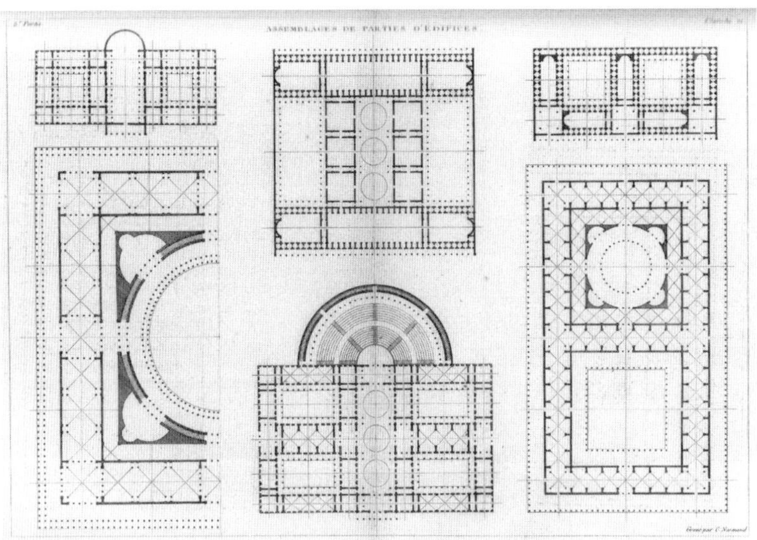

Figure 65 Neo-Classicism, combinatorial process coping with typological diversification. JNL Durand, *Précis des leçons d'architecture, 1802-5*

terms of plan organization, Durand's system of architectural composition implies a massive expansion of the repertoire of architecture. Durand talks about the 'near-infinite variety of classes of buildings', each in turn 'susceptible of an infinity of modifications' because 'the particular requirements of any one building might be varied by places, times, persons, sites, costs, and so on'.[14]

The next great transition was from Historicism to Modernism. Compared with all prior styles, Modernism is distinguished by a marked increase in its compositional versatility made possible by its formal openness. This openness is achieved on the basis of the radical abstraction afforded by the concept of space in contrast to the mimetic boundedness of all prior architecture. It is this new level of abstraction – afforded by the idea of architectural design as the configuration of space – that gives Modern architecture its much - increased innovative prowess and that allows it to take on the massively increased scope of its task domain.[15] However, this relative level of innovative openness and

14 Jean-Nicolas-Louis Durand, *Précis des leçons d'architecture données à l'École royale polytechnique* (Paris), 1802–5, English translation by David Britt, published by The Getty Research Institute (Los Angeles), 2000, p 140.

15 For a more detailed interpretation of the concept of space in this vein see Volume 1, chapter 5.4.1 *The Emergence of Architectural Space* and chapter 5.4.2 *The Hegemony of Architectural Space.*

versatility of Modernism – when compared with all prior architecture – is at the same time subject to very specific formal constraints and compositional principles that become clear when compared with the later stylistic development beyond Modernism. The Modernist repertoire had unleashed itself from the Classical impositions of symmetry, proportion and completeness. However, it remained tied to orthogonality. Further, it is committed to hierarchical organization on the basis of the principles of ***separation, specialization*** and ***repetition***. These formal constraints and compositional principles are well adapted to the industrial era of Fordist mass production which is at the same time the era of social democracy where the masses become the client of architecture, and architecture/design for the first time claims universal competency and responsibility for the totality of the built environment and the world of artefacts.

The term 'Fordism' denotes a general category of socio-economic history initiated by the Ford Motor Company as the first paradigmatic case for a system of industrial mass production that was able to produce complex consumer goods on a scale and at a price that made them universally accessible. Fordism gave workers access to the results of their productive efforts as the new scale and methods of production turned luxury goods like the motor car into affordable commodities for every worker. The system could thus produce its own market in a self-amplifying economic expansion. The material basis of modern mass society was established. As a production system Fordism is premised on Taylorism, ie, the scientific decomposition of the work process into a system of measurable operations lined up along a continuous assembly line. This required the transference of production knowledge from the worker into the mechanism of the assembly line. At each point a single, repetitive task is required. All these tasks are easy to learn and in their simplicity similar to each other, thus leading to the homogenization of labour. Fordism understood as a socio-economic category, rather than a merely technological paradigm, presupposes the systematic integration of the reproduction of labour into a new and totalizing reproduction cycle. The advance of Fordism was a qualitative shift in the ability of industry to render workers' 'basic needs' (processing food, clothing, housing, transport etc) the object of comprehensive commodification, achieving an unprecedented general standard of living. The totalizing logic of Fordism became instrumental to the underlying rationality of Modern architecture and urbanism. In Europe, this regime of Fordist urbanization became possible after the working class (through the mediation of social democracy) gained a degree of power sharing after the First World War, establishing the socio-economic basis for Modern architecture: the social welfare state, guaranteeing a general consumption standard via institutionalized collective bargaining and public welfare provision. The state was increasingly engaged in regulating the economy and was nationalizing many sectors. This also affected architecture directly via massive public investment in the built environment: new towns, social housing, schools, hospitals, recreational facilities etc.

Modern architecture reinvented the discipline by identifying in the mundane (mass housing, mass-produced domestic furnishings, factories) worthy and urgent tasks for architecture.[16] The social democratic institutions of the welfare state became the mechanisms through which modern urbanism was advanced. In line with the principles of Fordism, the task posed was the development of an optimally efficient standard of modern living, the house for the 'Existenzminimum', as the universal receptacle for a series of universal mass consumer goods: living room, dining room, (Frankfurt-) kitchen, bathroom, washing machine and later the refrigerator, television and automobile. Modern architectural composition was assimilated to the principles of Fordist organization: separation, specialization and repetition. This logic is evident in the organization of separate functions into specialized and separately optimized volumes. The Dessau Bauhaus (Figure 67) is paradigmatic in this respect. Here residential, administrative and workshop functions are separately articulated, allocating to each function a different volume with distinct proportions, spatial depth, floor-to-floor height and facade pattern, separately optimized for each respective function (instead of forcing all functions into a single, formally prefigured shape as was the case with Classical architecture). Within each separate part dominates the order of repetition. There is no sense of completeness in the overall composition. The exact same principles can be observed in the design for the Moscow Lenin Library by the Vesnin brothers (Figure 66). Each volume has different proportions. The internal order of each area is repetitive. The different volumes of the complex are kept apart and are connected only by small passages. Further additions are always possible. A more complex composition comprising more functionally specialized buildings, and articulated series of buildings, is exhibited in Nicolai Kusmin's design for a residential complex for Soviet miners. The similarity of this composition to the design of machines or factory complexes is obvious. The same organizational patterns apply to the bureaucratic, social organization of the industrial corporations of this era:

16 These developments also implied a revolution in the leadership of the architectural profession. The Historicist architects educated in the academies were replaced by self-educated architects like Corb and Mies.

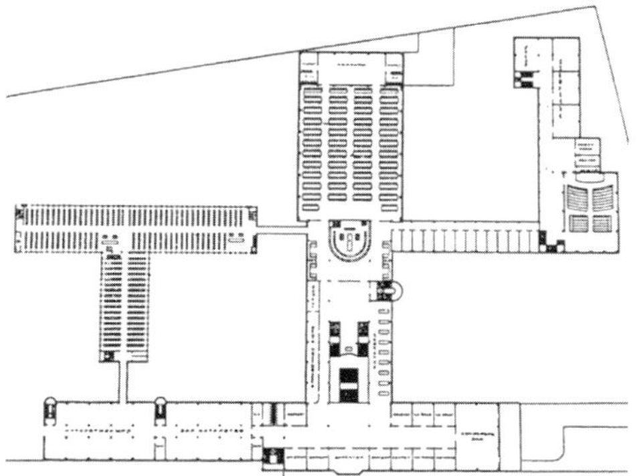

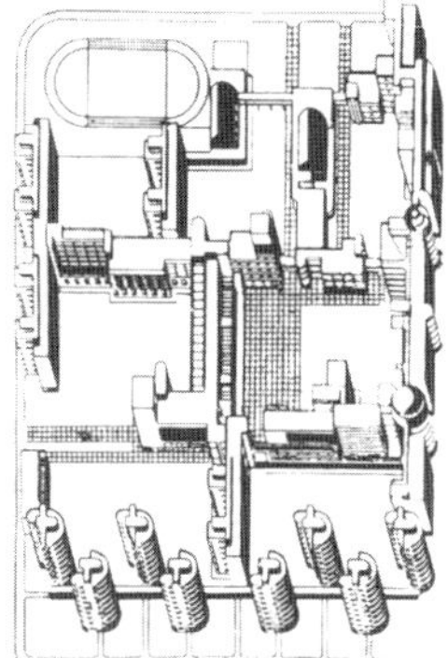

Figure 66 Modernist organization: separation – specialization – repetition, Vesnin brothers' Lenin Library; Nicolai Kusmin's miners' complex

separation, specialization and repetition. Again, the same principles are at work in the canonical conception of the Modernist city. Le Corbusier's Ville Radieuse (1933) is a comprehensive and rigorous application of this logic of separation (zoning), specialization (distinct functionalist articulation of each zone) and repetition (seriality/homogeneity within each zone). Another example is W Kalmykow's 1930 design of an Industrial City for the Soviet Union (Figure 68). Fordism and its architectural complement – Modernist urbanism – did indeed find its most logical expression in the Soviet Union.[17] The whole Western world was eventually subsumed under this pattern of social organization. Everywhere the same pattern of social organization dominated: bureaucracies that established rigid, functional hierarchies separating out different job-descriptions, each with its own domain of competency, repetitive task and position within the chain (tree) of instruction/reporting. The Modernist institutional building is the projection of this organizational pattern into space. The Modernist pattern of urbanization is the spatial projection of the total social machine of functionally differentiated, Fordist mass society.

In the late 1960s, the Fordist system of repetitive mass production, corporate concentration, collective bargaining, universal consumption standard and bureaucratic state-regulation was challenged on all fronts.[18]

17 One might indeed argue that socialism was the most appropriate political form for this stage of economic development.

18 Its fundamental premise – the stability and predictability of its socio-economic environment – was fractured. The first serious break in the post-war boom occurred with the recession of 1966/67. The political struggles of 1968, the oil crisis in 1973, the breakdown of the international exchange-rate system, and a deepening of the recession in 1974 followed.

Figure 67 Modernist articulation: separation – specialization – repetition, W Gropius, Bauhaus 1926

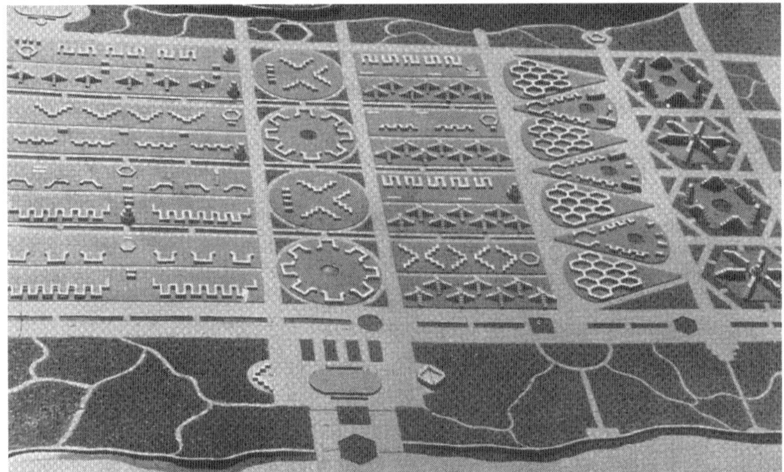

Figure 68 Modernist City, separation – specialization – repetition, W Kalmykow, Industrial City, about 1930

By the end of the 1970s, it was clear that world society was facing a structural (systemic) crisis that called for new political and economic strategies.[19] Modernist architecture faced its own, related crisis. The solutions offered by Modernism that had successfully dominated the development of the built environment for 50 years seemed bankrupt. Modernism with its sprawling, zoned urbanism, with its satellite sleeping cities and corporate administrative complexes on suburban green-field sites, was no longer viable. The Modernist solutions were abandoned. The massive housing estate Pruitt-Igoe in the US city of St Louis was

19 See UNIDO (United Nations Industrial Development Organization), *Structural Change in Industry* (Vienna), 1979, and OECD (Organisation for Economic Co-operation and Development), *Positive Adjustment Policies: Managing Structural Change* (Paris), 1983.

demolished in 1974, only 20 years after its construction. No new answers were as yet available within the autopoiesis of architecture. The most vital societal processes moved into the historical centres seeking out a new density of communication. The social and technological conditions of Fordism had been undermined by its own material successes. With the growing complexity of the division of labour and the proliferation of white-collar labour, salary stratification increased. Affluence beyond the saturation of the most basic needs meant that markets began to diversify, allowing for status- and identity-consumption and leading to an acceleration of aesthetically motivated product cycles. These developments placed a reward on innovation and flexibility rather than cost reductions achieved through mass-market economies of scale. The house, as the main site of consumption, was itself drawn into the logic of differential incomes and identities. Problems arose in terms of an increasing economic volatility. As products and markets differentiated, economies of scale were recuperated through international expansion.

The resultant international economic interdependency had the effect of eroding the economic competence of the nation state, ie its ability to regulate the economy and smooth out disturbances in the business cycle. As markets globalized, the less economically feasible it became to protect national producers and the less feasible became Keynesian macro-economic regulation. The increasing internationalization of mobile capital implied that the erosion of the welfare state would become inevitable. The Fordist regime was premised on long-term stability that makes it feasible to concentrate and build up economies of scale via colossal (but inherently rigid) production bureaucracies. On the positive side, new computer-based production technologies made possible greater product diversity (small runs) without the enormous cost of handicraft production that had previously limited deviations from the standard. The crucial material factor was the micro-electronic revolution that offered greater productivity through desired economies of scope, rather than scale. Flexible specialization became a technological possibility, and the subsequent fluidity of production demanded the dissolution of static Fordist labour and management arrangements.[20] The result of these new

20 All these interlocking technological, economic, social and political phenomena have been analyzed under the label of Post-Fordism. See Ash Amin, *Post-Fordism – A Reader,* Blackwell (Oxford/Cambridge, MA), 1994; Robin Murray, 'Fordism and Postfordism', in S Hall & M Jacques (Eds), *New Times: Changing Face of Politics in the 1990s*, Lawrence & Wishart (London), 1989; W Ruigrok & R van Tulder, *The Logic of International Restructuring*, Routledge (London/New York), 1995; Paul Hirst & Jonathan Zeitlin, 'Flexible Specialization versus Post-Fordism', *Economy and Society*, Vol 20, No 1, February 1991. There are two further books that discuss Post-Fordism in the context of urbanism: David Harvey, *The Condition of*

constraints and opportunities was a comprehensive restructuring from the Fordist mass society to a much more diverse and dynamic Post-Fordist network society.[21] Nationalized industries are being privatized. The large, integrated corporations are breaking up into loosely coupled networks via outsourcing. The intensity of communications is increasing exponentially, everywhere: within firms, between firms, between firms and consumers as well as between firms and their potential workers. Everybody's life is becoming more communication intensive: continuous learning, career shifts, multiple careers, multiple projects with many, ever-changing participants etc.[22] The urban texture, as well as all buildings and spaces within it, is required to facilitate an increased diversity of communicative situations, as well as the increased communicative density, complexity and dynamism of social life. Postmodernism and Deconstructivism started to respond, haphazardly trying to capture and cater for the salient new features of social life in the emerging era of Post-Fordism.

The key issues that contemporary avant-garde architecture and urbanism must address can thus be summarized in the slogan: organization and articulation of the increased complexity of ***Post-Fordist network society***. The philosophical re-orientation of architecture in this

Postmodernity, Basil Blackwell (Oxford/Cambridge, MA), 1989; Edward W Soja, *Postmodern Geographies*, Verso (London/New York), 1989. Concerning the introduction of the concept into architectural discourse see Patrik Schumacher, 'Productive Patterns', in: *architect's bulletin, Operativity*, Vol 135–136, and Vol 137–138, Slovenia; abbreviated German version: 'Produktive Ordnungen', in: *ARCH+* 136, *Your Office Is Where You Are* (Berlin), 1997.

21 Post-Fordism as an analytical category is of distinctively Marxist provenance. The underlying notion of 'Fordism', originally put forward by Antonio Gramsci, characterizes the epoch of corporate and state capitalism since the First World War (and coming into its own fully after the Second World War). This notion was systematically developed by the French Regulation School of (Marxist) economic analysis, initiated with Michel Aglietta's *A Theory of Capitalist Regulation*. Aglietta attempts to reconceptualize and systematize Marxist conceptions of the stages of capitalist development (free market-, monopoly-, state-capitalism) by organizing their progression around the following dimensions: *the techno-industrial paradigm* (production process), *the regime of accumulation* (circulation/growth cycle of capital) and *the mode of regulation* (political institutional framework). Each particular stage of capitalist development is defined by the systemic cohesion of those three dimensions. Following Louis Althusser, Aglietta asserts that those dimensions are engaged in a dialectic that grants each a status of semi-autonomy, although in the long run the development of the forces of production supposedly remains 'determination in the last instance'. A structural crisis arises if one or more of those dimensions breaks out of this synchronized ensemble. An extended period of crisis and intensified class-struggle creates revolutionary potentials for a solution beyond capitalism, or a new regime might crystallize and allow the stabilization of a new stage of development within capitalism. See Michel Aglietta, *A Theory of Capitalist Regulation – The US Experience*, Verso (London), 1979.

22 Patrik Schumacher, 'Arbeit, Spiel und Anarchie', in: Herbert Lachmayer & Eleonora Luis (Eds), *Work & Culture – Büro.Inszenierung von Arbeit*, Ritterverlag (Klagenfurt), 1998.

direction was effected during the 1980s by the reception of Post-Structuralism and especially since the early 1990s by the reception of Deleuze and Guattari's *A Thousand Plateaus*. Since then the consequences of this re-orientation have been worked through. The task was to develop an architectural and urban repertoire geared up to create complex, urban fields that allow for the near simultaneous participation in multiple events, and thus for the quick orientation and fast connection of many diverse spaces. This challenge has been pressing on architecture's autopoiesis for over 30 years. Postmodernism and Deconstructivism made some attempts. These styles, however, could not be generalized to take over the mainstream. It seemed as if Postmodernism was taking over during the 1980s but the mainstream soon reverted back to a pragmatic kind of Modernism (as well as to a more rarefied Modernism in the guise of Minimalism). Deconstructivism never took off in the real world. However, the key formal advances of Deconstructivism and its general lust for complexity were taken up in the next wave of the architectural avant-garde that formed in the early 1990s under the label of Folding. During this period the utilization of animation software took off and strongly shaped the direction of the design research. The exploration of computationally based design processes intersected with the aesthetic and programmatic exploration of the complex geometries that were becoming available through these processes. The new processes and forms are addressing the demand for an increased level of articulated complexity by means of a rich panoply of parametric design techniques. However, we are confronted with a new style rather than just with a new set of techniques. The techniques in question – the employment of animation, simulation and form-finding tools, as well as parametric modelling and scripting – have inspired a new collective movement with radically new ambitions and values. This has led to many new systematically connected design problems that are being worked on competitively within a global network of design researchers.[23] Within this collective design research, the new heuristic principles of Parametricism have matured to the point where they can now be explicitly stated with the confidence that a whole generation of young designers recognizes that they have become a priori premises of their work. Parametricism can also point to a whole series of successful, high-profile built projects, on all scales and across many programme types. There are also some large-scale urban planning projects that make the possibility of a Parametricist

23 ZHA and AADRL together form just one node within this fast growing network.

urbanism plausible. Parametricism can therefore be posited here as a serious contender to become the epochal style of the current era.

Including Parametricism, the history of architecture's autopoiesis has produced five epochal styles during its nearly 600 years of self-determined evolution: Renaissance (15th and 16th centuries), Baroque (17th and 18th centuries), Neo-Classicism/Historicism (19th century), Modernism (20th century), Parametricism (21st century). The Gothic style prepared the way by transitioning from tradition-bound building to the advent of architecture. The table below summarizes the alignment of these epochal styles with the stages of societal (socio-economic) evolution.

Epochal Tradition/Epochal Style	*Societal Environment/Socio-economic Epoch*
tradition-bound building	
Medieval Vernacular	feudalism
Romanesque	feudalism
transition	
Gothic	feudalism + rising cities
architectural history: succession of active styles	
Renaissance	early capitalism, city states
Baroque	mercantilism, absolutism
Neo-Classicism/Historicism	bourgeois capitalism, nation states
Modernism	Fordism, (socialist) welfare state
Parametricism	Post-Fordist network society, global

Epochal Alignment of Styles

11.1.2 A UNIFIED STYLE FOR THE 21ST CENTURY

Can there still be a unified style in the 21st century? Yes there can. In 2008, the author first communicated that a new, profound style has been maturing within the avant-garde segment of architecture during the last 10 years. It seemed urgent that the style acquired a name in order to recognize itself and in order to be recognized in the world at large. Therefore 'Parametricism' was enunciated during the 11th Venice Architecture Biennale.[24] The term has since been circulating and gathering momentum – largely via critical challenges[25] – within the architectural discourse. So far, this event has remained largely confined

24 The 'Parametricist Manifesto' was displayed on site and published in the Biennale catalogue.

25 That a progressive discourse thrives on criticism rather than statements of approval is to be expected.

within architecture. However, one might suspect that the news will spread quickly once it has been picked up somewhere in the mass media. Outside architectural circles, 'style' is virtually the only category through which architecture is observed and recognized. A named style needs to be put forward in order to stake the claim to act in the name of architecture. What complicates matters is that the concept of style(s) has long been losing traction within the architectural discourse.[26] Therefore the announcement of Parametricism involves two simultaneous discursive moves: the presentation of a new vital architectural movement and the reassertion of the concept of style(s) as valid and productive category of discursive orientation and self-description.

The concept of style(s) deserves to be defended. To let this concept wither away would only impoverish the discourse within architecture. This would also imply the renunciation of a powerful asset for communicating architecture to society. However, the resuscitation of this drained and battered concept requires conceptual reconstruction in terms that are intellectually credible today. What stands in the way of such a reconstruction is the tendency to regard style as merely a matter of appearance as well as the related tendency to confuse styles with superficial, short-lived fashions. Although aesthetic appearance matters enormously in architecture and design, neither architecture as a whole nor its styles can be reduced to matters of mere appearance. Nor must the phenomenon of styles be assimilated to the phenomenon of fashion. The concept of style(s) must therefore be sharply distinguished and cleansed of all these trivializing and distracting connotations. It denotes the unity of the difference between the architectural periods of Gothic, Renaissance, Baroque, Neo-Classicism, Historicism and Modernism. The historical self-consciousness of architecture demands the revitalization of the concept of style(s) as a profound historical phenomenon that can be projected into the future. The theory of architectural autopoiesis proposes that architectural styles are best understood as ***design research programmes*** conceived in analogy to the way paradigms frame scientific research programmes.[27] A new style in architecture/design is akin to a new paradigm in science: it redefines the fundamental categories,

26 For instance, in his 1967 introduction to *Space, Time and Architecture* Sigfried Giedion suggested the elimination of the concept from architectural discourse: 'There is a word we should refrain from using to describe contemporary architecture – "style". The moment we fence architecture within a notion "style", we open the door to a formalistic approach.' Sigfried Giedion, *Space, Time, and Architecture*, 5th edition, Harvard University Press (Cambridge, MA), 1967, p xxxiii.

27 The author has elaborated this concept in the following article: Patrik Schumacher, 'Style as Research Programme', in: *DRL TEN – A Design Research Compendium*, AA Publications (London), 2008. This analogy does not imply that architecture is a science. Quite the contrary,

purposes and methods of a coherent collective endeavour. Innovation in architecture proceeds within the framework of styles or via the progression of styles so understood. This implies the alternation between periods of cumulative advancement within a style and revolutionary periods of transition between styles. Styles represent long, sustained cycles of innovation, gathering design research efforts into a collective movement so that individual efforts are mutually relevant, spurring and enhancing.

From the inside, within architecture, the identification of Parametricism demarcates and further galvanizes a maturing avant-garde movement and thus might serve to accelerate its progress and hegemony as a collective research and development effort that is ready to go mainstream. At least this is the author's hope and motivation. As a piece of retrospective description and interpretation, the announcement of Parametricism seems justified given 10 years of consistent, cumulative design research. Prospectively the announcement of the style should further consolidate the achievements attained and prepare the transition from avant-garde to mainstream hegemony. The author believes that Parametricism finally offers a credible, sustainable answer to the drawn out crisis of Modernism that resulted in 30 years of stylistic searching. Parametricism is the great new style after Modernism.[28] Postmodernism and Deconstructivism were mere transitional episodes, similar to Art Nouveau and Expressionism as transitions from Historicism to Modernism. The distinction of *epochal styles* from *transitional styles* is important. In a period of transition there might emerge a rapid succession of styles, or even a plurality of simultaneous, competing styles. The crisis and demise of Modernism led to a deep and protracted transitional period, but this is no reason to believe that this pluralism cannot be overcome by the hegemony of a new unified style. The potential for such a unification is indeed what we are witnessing.

Besides epochal styles and transitional styles we can identify *subsidiary styles* that emerge under the umbrella of epochal styles. These subsidiary styles represent either parallel variations or historical sequences that enrich and progress the respective epochal style. Within Historicism we can distinguish Neo-Grec, Neo-Gothic, Neo-Renaissance, Neo-Baroque and Eclecticism. Within Modernism we can distinguish

the author insists upon the demarcation of architecture and the design disciplines against both science and art.

28 The author has elaborated this thesis in the following article: Patrik Schumacher, 'Parametricism: A New Global Style for Architecture and Urban Design', in: Neil Leach, Helen Castle (Eds), *Digital Cities*, Architectural Design, Vol 79, No 4, July/August 2009.

Functionalism, Rationalism, Organicism, Brutalism, Metabolism and High-Tech. All these subsidiary styles adhere fully to the basic design principles of Modernism: *separation, specialization and repetition*, ie, separation between specialized subsystems and repetition within each subsystem. Postmodernism and Deconstructivism reject the order of separation and repetition by positing historical diversity and then diversity via collage and superposition (without establishing a new order). Parametricism is able to recuperate and enhance the Deconstructivist capacity to absorb diversity within a complex order. The Modernist order of separation and repetition is being supplanted by the Parametricist order of continuous differentiation within systems and intensive correlation across systems. Within the broad new paradigm many subsidiary styles might be expected to enrich and progress the coming epoch of Parametricism.

The experience of Modernism's crisis and its architectural aftermath – together with the failure to distinguish epochal styles from transitional and subsidiary styles – has led many critics to believe that our civilization (and this means today global civilization) can no longer be expected to forge a unified style. Did the profound developmental role of styles in the history of architecture as evidenced in the sequence Gothic–Renaissance–Baroque–Historicism–Modernism come to an end? Did history come to an end? Or did it fragment into criss-crossing and contradictory trajectories? If so, are we to celebrate this fragmentation of efforts under the slogan of pluralism?

Architecture today is world architecture. Every architectural project is immediately exposed and assessed in comparison to all other projects. Global convergences are possible. This does not spell homogenization and monotony. It merely implies a consistency of principles, ambitions and values to build upon so that different efforts add up, are relevant to each other, compete constructively with each other, to establish the conditions for cumulative progress rather than pursuing contradictory efforts that misconstrue and deny each other, going round in circles by continuously battling over fundamentals. This is the idea of a unified style, initially as a unified avant-garde design research programme, and eventually as a unified system of principles, ambitions and values that constitute global best practice. The parametric design paradigm is fast penetrating all corners of the discipline. Its claim for hegemony is universal. Systematic, adaptive variation, *continuous* differentiation and multi-system correlation concerns *all* architectural design tasks across all functional domains and across all scales, from urbanism to the level of tectonic detail.

11.1.3 THE MATURITY OF PARAMETRICISM

Over and above aesthetic recognizability it is this widespread, long-term consistency of shared design ambitions and problems that is the defining criterion that justifies the enunciation of a style in the most profound sense of an epochal phenomenon.

Parametricism is a mature style. That the parametric paradigm is becoming pervasive in avant-garde architecture and design has been evident for quite some time. There has been talk about versioning, iteration and mass customization etc for quite a while within the architectural avant-garde discourse. The fundamental desire that has come to the fore in this tendency had already been formulated at the beginning of the 1990s with the key slogan of 'continuous differentiation'.[29] Since then there has been both a widespread, even hegemonic dissemination of this tendency as well as a cumulative build up of virtuosity, resolution and refinement within it. This development was facilitated by the attendant development of parametric design tools and scripting languages that allow the precise formulation and execution of intricate correlations between elements and subsystems. The shared concepts, computational techniques, formal repertoires and tectonic logics that characterize this work are crystallizing into a solid new paradigm for architecture.

Parametricism emerges from the creative exploitation of parametric design systems in view of articulating increasingly complex social processes and institutions. The parametric design tools by themselves cannot account for this profound shift in style from Modernism to Parametricism. This is evidenced by the fact that Late Modernist architects are employing parametric tools in ways which result in the maintenance of a Modernist aesthetic, ie, using parametric modelling inconspicuously to absorb complexity. The Parametricist sensibility pushes in the opposite direction and aims for a maximal emphasis on conspicuous differentiation and the visual amplification of differentiating logics. Aesthetically it is the elegance[30] of ordered complexity and the sense of seamless fluidity akin to natural systems that constitute the hallmark of Parametricism. Both elegance and seamlessness are premised on differentiation and complexity rather than simplicity and repetition.

The new style claims relevance at all scales from architecture and interior design to large-scale urban design. The larger the scale of the

29 The credit for coining this key slogan goes to Greg Lynn and Jeff Kipnis.

30 For a pertinent concept of elegance that is related to the visual resolution of complexity see: Patrik Schumacher, 'Arguing for Elegance', in: H Castle, A Rahim & H Jamelle (Eds), *Elegance*, Architectural Design, January/February 2007, Vol 77, No 1, Wiley Academy (London).

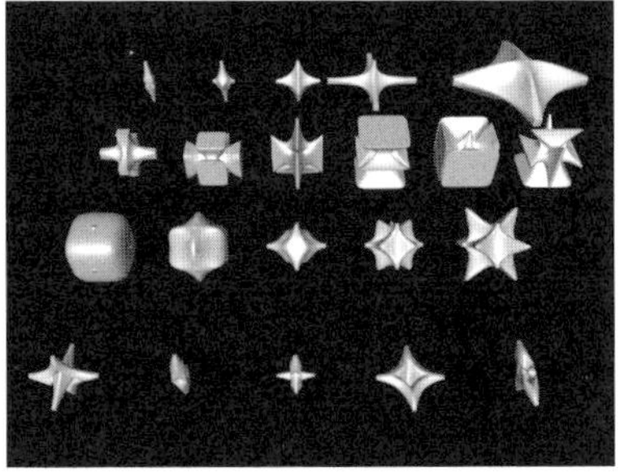
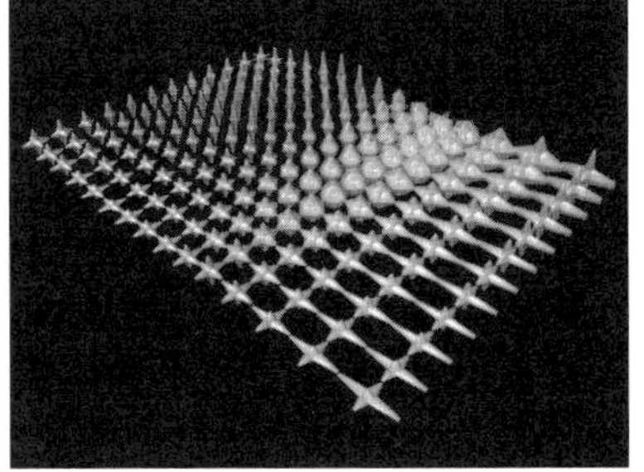

Figure 69 From pure difference to continuous differentiation, Masterclass Hadid, University of Applied Arts, Vienna

project, the more pronounced is Parametricism's superior capacity to organize and articulate an unprecedented level of programmatic complexity. The urbanist potential of Parametricism has been explored in a three-year research agenda at the AADRL – *Parametric Urbanism* – and was demonstrated by a series of competition-winning urban masterplans by Zaha Hadid Architects.

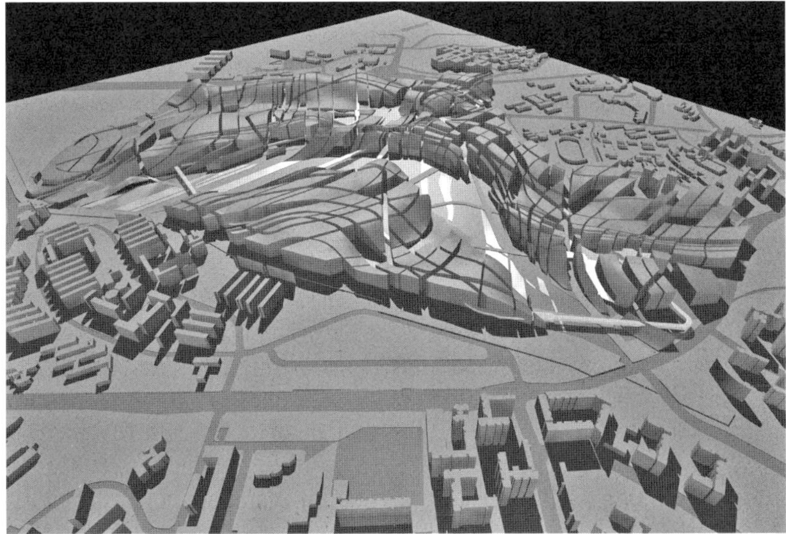

Figure 70 Continuous differentiation: One-North Masterplan, Network – Fabric – Buildings, Singapore, Zaha Hadid Architects 2001–3

11.1.4 POLARIZED CONFRONTATION: PARAMETRICISM VERSUS MINIMALISM

As alluded to above, many theorists presume that the demise of Modernism ushered in an era of stylistic pluralism. Accordingly, the search for a new, unified style is seen as an anachronism. Any style today – so it seems – can only be one among many other simultaneously operating styles, thus adding one more voice to the prevailing cacophony of many voices. The idea of a pluralism of styles is just one symptom of the more general trivialization and denigration of the concept of style. The author repudiates the complacent acceptance (and even celebration) of the apparent pluralism of styles. A unified style has many advantages over a condition of stylistic fragmentation. Parametricism is therefore posed to aim for hegemony and combats all other styles. Within an urban field or masterplan designed according to the principles of Parametricism, the admixture of a Postmodernist, Deconstructivist or Minimalist design can only disrupt the Parametricist continuity and intensity of relations. The reverse does not hold because there is no equivalent degree of continuity in Postmodernist, Deconstructivist or Minimalist urbanism. In fact, Parametricism can take up vernacular, Classical, Modernist, Postmodernist, Deconstructivist and Minimalist urban conditions and forge a new network of affiliations and continuities between any given number of urban fragments and conditions.

What are the current styles that must be combated by Parametricism? Is there really still the kind of stylistic pluralism posited by Charles Jencks? In fact, Postmodernism has disappeared. The same goes for Deconstructivism. (The contributions/advances of both have been incorporated within Parametricism.) The mainstream has in fact returned to a form of pragmatic Modernism with a slightly enriched palette: a kind of Modernist eclecticism mixing and matching elements from all of Modernism's subsidiary styles. The inability of Postmodernism and Deconstructivism to formulate a new viable paradigm led to the return of Modernism, in the guise of two variants: Minimalism as the principled, pronounced re-enactment and even radicalization of Modernism on the one hand, and the unprincipled, pragmatic, diffuse variant one might call Pragmatic Modernism, on the other. Minimalism is as ideological and intransigent as Parametricism (although it does so without explicit theory). Perhaps the best example is David Chipperfield's impressive oeuvre. Minimalism operates with taboos and dogmas that are as sharply defined as those of Parametricism. In contrast, Pragmatic Modernism is introduced here nearly as a residual category. It contains everything else that goes on today, including all mainstream work. This does not imply that the term 'Pragmatic Modernism' is to be taken as in any way

Figure 71 Parametricism is going mainstream: Zaha Hadid Architects, Business Complex, Cairo

derogatory. We also include here the brilliant work of OMA and its spin-offs. However, the primary confrontation in the struggle for stylistic hegemony is the confrontation between Parametricism and Minimalism. Minimalism is nothing but a sophisticated neo-Modernism. The confrontation between Parametricism and Minimalism is thus the confrontation between a progressive, untested hypothesis and a regressive, falsified hypothesis. Modernism had flourished for 50 years but cannot flourish any longer. It experienced a shattering crisis and proved unsustainable as universal style for our contemporary era.

Parametricism is ready to go mainstream. There is sufficient evidence to support this thesis. For instance, the latest built works from Zaha Hadid Architects are much more than experimental manifesto projects; they are succeeding as high-performance projects in the real world. The Innsbruck train stations are a good example. No other style could have achieved this coincidence of adaptive variation to the very different site conditions with such a high degree of genotypical coherence across those phenotypical variants. The project demonstrates the principle of correlated subsystems. In each station, two subsystems are at play: the platforms and staircases form one system executed in concrete and following a geometry restricted to developable surfaces; the roofs – executed in steel and glass – form the second system that is

Figure 72 Parametricism delivers high-performance architecture, Zaha Hadid Architects, Nordkettenbahn, Innsbruck

geometrically based on nurb surfaces. Despite the characteristic (ontological) difference that is thus established between these subsystems, they are made to resonate with each other creating an organic unity between them. Instead of introducing further discrete elements like columns, the roof surfaces adapt their shape to meet the platforms directly. Instead of adding gutters as additional elements, this function is accommodated by slicing/peeling the glass surface. These inconspicuous gutter folds are integrated in the tessellation pattern of the roof. Each of the four stations displays its own variation on these themes. These design strategies use the principles of Parametricism to articulate complex affiliations while absorbing visual complexity. The result produces the effect of elegance based on the confident resolution of a complex task, rather than the Minimalist elegance based on a reduction and simplification that suppresses rather than articulates complex relations.

Simplicity in design can only be a relative value, relative to the complexity of the task. Relative simplicity produces true elegance. An elegant solution is as simple as possible without obliterating essential aspects of the functional organization. Simplicity goes hand in hand with order, and indeed with complex order. The simplicity we mean should not be opposed to complexity. If we had to choose between simplicity and complexity we would choose complexity. But this is a false dichotomy. ***Relative simplicity*** articulates complexity with a precise economy of means. Differences that make a difference must be expressed – as simply as possible. Simplicity must thus be tied to the agenda of articulation: reducing visual complexity for the sake of visual clarification of the functional organization. The value of relative simplicity is compatible with Parametricism. At ZHA this often translates into dynamic curvilinearity as the means to differentiate space without polluting the visual scene with corners or other breaks of continuity. Simplicity also implies an abstracting attitude to detailing: do not allow tectonic detail to distract from the global organization of the space. Details are either suppressed or utilized as means of articulation. The simplicity we pursue allows minimalism in detail but rejects minimalism in the overall composition. The overriding headline here remains: reduction of unnecessary visual complexity for the sake of orientation *within complex organizations*. The superiority of Parametricism to Minimalism is most pronounced in the domain of urbanism and urban design. The larger the scale and the more diverse and complex the programme, the more evident become the superiority of Parametricism and the inadequacy of Minimalism. Parametricism and Minimalism converge at the small scale. However, even at the very small scale the design strategies of Parametricism remain valid, although Minimalism can survive here too. In interior and furniture design Parametricism remains superior to Minimalism. In product and fashion design the same holds true. Contemporary high-tech sports wear might serve here as example: a contemporary running shoe, cycling suit or skiing under-shirt. The fabric of these items is differentiated and correlated with the local, body-hugging geometric shapes and functions these items of clothing take on.

11.1.5 STYLES AS DESIGN RESEARCH PROGRAMMES

As elaborated in detail in section 3.7, avant-garde styles might be interpreted and evaluated in analogy to new scientific paradigms or *research programmes*, affording a new conceptual framework, and formulating new aims, methods and values for design research. Thus with a new avant-garde style, a new direction for concerted research work is established.[31] My thesis is therefore: *styles are design research programmes.*[32]

31 This interpretation of styles is valid only with respect to the avant-garde phase of any style. Mainstream styles are routine programmes that operationalise architecture's double code of utility and beauty.

32 See section 3.7 *Styles as Research Programmes*. It is important to distinguish between research programmes in the literal sense of institutional research plans and the meta-scientific

Innovation in architecture proceeds via the progression of styles so understood. This implies the alternation between periods of cumulative advancement within a style and revolutionary periods of transition between styles. Styles represent cycles of innovation, gathering the design research efforts into a collective endeavour. Stable self-identity is here as much a necessary precondition of evolution as it is in the case of organic life. To hold on to the new principles in the face of difficulties is crucial for the chance of eventual success. Only on the basis of widespread and long-term stable ambitions and problematics can there be a chance to make substantial progress. This is incompatible with an understanding of styles as transient fashions. Basic principles and methodologies need to be preserved and defended with tenacity in the face of initial difficulties and setbacks. This tenacity – abundantly evident within the AADRL, ZHA, as well as in the wider contemporary avant-garde – might at times appear as dogmatic obstinacy. For instance, the obstinate insistence on solving everything with a folding single surface, project upon project, only slowly wrenching the plausible from the implausible. This kind of pursuit might seem both implausible and over - ambitious in its singlemindedness and in its claim of universality. However, this is the way substantial advances are eventually achieved. One might observe how sustained advances are achieved in the sciences. The overambitious singlemindedness of Parametricism might seem less irrational if it is compared to the initially implausible Newtonian insistence on explaining everything from planets to bullets to atoms in terms of the same principles. The 18th- and 19th-century quest for a Newtonian explanation of the totality of the physical world paid off in a long, fruitful scientific project. Many eventual success stories in science did proceed stubbornly in the face of initial implausibility, ongoing failure and continuous refutation. 'Newton's theory of gravitation, Einstein's relativity theory, quantum mechanics, Marxism, Freudianism, are all research programmes, each with a characteristic hard core stubbornly defended, ... each with its elaborate problem-solving machinery. Each of them, at any stage of its development, has unsolved problems and undigested anomalies. All theories, in this sense, are born refuted and die refuted.'[33] The same can be said of styles: initial refutation is inevitable. Each avant-garde style has its hard core of principles that are stubbornly defended on the basis

conception of research programmes that has been introduced into the philosophy of science: whole new research traditions that are directed by a new fundamental theoretical framework. It is this latter concept that is utilized here for the reinterpretation of the concept of style. See Imre Lakatos, *The Methodology of Scientific Research Programmes*, Cambridge University Press (Cambridge), 1978.

33 Ibid, p 5.

of an initially implausible overreach. This makes sense to the extent that avant-garde architecture produces manifestos: paradigmatic expositions of a new style's unique potential, not buildings that are balanced to function in all respects. There can be neither verification nor final refutation of an avant-grade style merely on the basis of its built results.[34] Verification comes eventually in the form of mainstream proliferation.

Rigour and tenacity are necessary virtues for any burgeoning style. The consistency of the style as a collective design research programme depends upon the unfailing adherence to its strictures and impositions. (The good news is that a whole generation of young architects is already unfailingly adhering to the strictures and impositions (taboos and dogmas) of Parametricism – whether this is always explicitly reflected or not.) Any unprincipled vacillation or compromise in this respect – falling back upon old, suspended solutions – compromises the status of the design as rigorous avant-garde design research hypothesis. The principles have to be upheld tenaciously – even in the face of initial difficulties and failures – for the sake of giving radical innovation a chance. Without this tenacity and without the attendant methodological tolerance of failures a culture gets stuck in local maxima.[35]

Rigorous adherence to the principles across all design tasks is a necessary condition to test Parametricism's claim of universal competency. However, beside this methodological argument there is an important substantial reason to insist on absolute consistency. The performative advantage of Parametricism over all prior styles is premised on this consistency of adherence to its principles. This is so because Parametricism's ability to set up continuities and correspondences across many diverse and distant elements relies on its principles' holding uninterrupted sway. Only this way can perceptual orientation and navigability be maximized in the face of everybody's requirement to participate in increasingly diverse and complex life-processes. Parametricism allows for the design of information-rich environments. When all elements are part of differentiated subsystems, and these differentiations are lawful (algorithmic) and thus retrievable, as well as correlated with many other differentiations, then the various differentiated subsystems become each other's representations. In such a dense network of associations that radiate deep through the urban fabric, many system-to-system (locale-to-locale) inferences as well as

34 The final reckoning takes place later, in the arena of the mainstream adoption which only indirectly feeds back into the central, discursive arena of the discipline.

35 The discipline has differentiated into avant-garde and mainstream in order to escape from local maxima via high-risk test projects. The avant-garde segment functions as a zone where high-risk strategies are rewarded and a certain level of dysfunctionality is tolerated.

local-to-global inferences become possible. The pervasiveness of Parametricist interdependencies does not at all imply monotony or homogeneity. It also does not imply that large parts of the city must be designed by a single design team or even that there must be a masterplan that integrates individual efforts. It only implies that the continuities that have been forged should not be disrupted by the intervention of non-Parametricist designers. Parametricist continuation is always possible in myriad, qualitatively diverse ways, but it is never random. Satisfying Parametricist continuation is admittedly a difficult, elaborate process that demands a high level of talent (or acquired sensibility) and technical expertise. However, fortunately the community of designers that is gearing up for the task is growing by the day. Parametricist urbanism is delivering a variegated, complex order while older styles can only either suppress contemporary social complexity or descend into visual chaos.

11.2 The Parametricist Research Programme

THESIS 58

The eventual success of grand, unifying schemes in science relies on the underlying coherence of reality. The rationality of a style's claim to universality lies in the advantage a coherent built environment offers to society. Modernism did achieve universality during the course of the 20th century. Parametricism aims for an equivalent achievement in the 21st century.

11.2.1 CONCEPTUAL DEFINITION OF PARAMETRICISM

As conceptual definition of Parametricism one might offer the following formula: Parametricism implies that all architectural elements and complexes are parametrically malleable. This implies a fundamental ontological shift within the basic, constituent elements of architecture. Instead of the Classical and Modern reliance on ideal (hermetic, rigid) geometrical figures – cubes, cylinders, pyramids and (semi-)spheres – the new primitives of Parametricism are animate (dynamic, adaptive, interactive) geometrical entities – splines, nurbs and subdivs – as fundamental geometrical building blocks for dynamical systems like 'hair', 'cloth', 'blobs' and 'metaballs' etc that react to 'attractors' and that can be made to resonate with each other via scripts.

In principle every property of every element or complex is subject to parametric variation. The key technique for handling this variability is the scripting of functions that establish associations between the properties of the various elements. However, although the new style is to a large extent dependent upon these new design techniques, the style cannot be

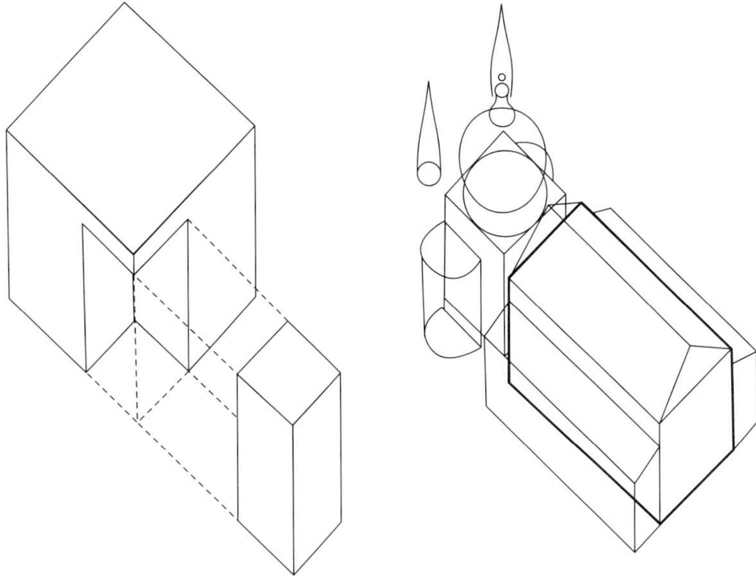

Figure 73 Classical/Modernist ontology, F Ching

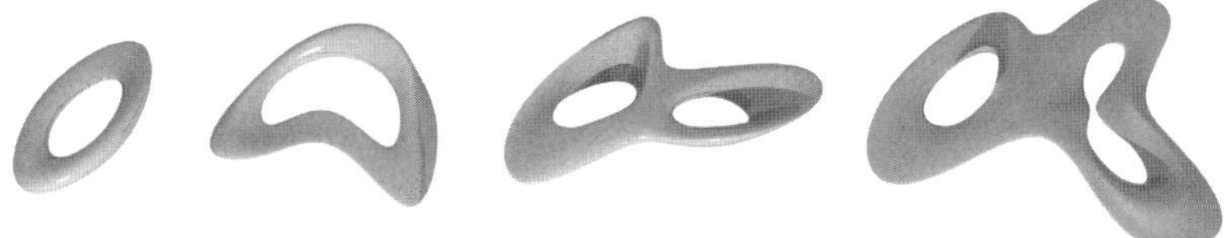

Figure 74 Parametricist ontology

reduced to the mere introduction of new tools and techniques. What characterizes the new style are new ambitions and new values – both in terms of form and in terms of function – that are to be pursued with the aid of the new tools and techniques. Parametricism pursues the very general aim: to organize and articulate the increasing diversity and complexity of social institutions and life-processes within the most advanced arenas of Post-Fordist network society. For this task, Parametricism aims to establish a complex variegated spatial order. It uses scripting lawfully to differentiate and correlate all elements and subsystems of a design. The goal is to ***intensify the internal interdependencies*** within an architectural design as well as the ***external affiliations and continuities*** within complex, urban contexts. Parametricism

Figure 75 Zaha Hadid Architects, Galaxy, Beijing, 2009

offers a new, complex order via the principles of differentiation and correlation. This general verbal and motivational definition of Parametricism can and must be complemented by an operational definition. It is necessary to operationalize the intuitive values of a style in order to make its hypotheses testable, to make its dissemination systematic, to be exposed to constructive criticism, including self-critique.

11.2.2 OPERATIONAL DEFINITION OF PARAMETRICISM: THE DEFINING HEURISTICS OF PARAMETRICISM

The operational definition of a style must formulate general instructions that guide the creative process in line with the general ambitions and expected qualities of the style. A style is not only concerned with the elaboration and evaluation of architectural form. Each style offers a specific way of understanding and handling functions. Accordingly, the operational definition of Parametricism comprises both a ***formal heuristics***: establishing rules and principles that guide the elaboration and evaluation of the design's formal development and resolution: and a ***functional heuristics***: establishing rules and principles that guide the elaboration and evaluation of the design's functional performance. For each of these two dimensions the operational definition formulates the heuristics of the design process in terms of *taboos* (negative heuristics) and *dogmas* (positive heuristics) specifying what to avoid and what to pursue.

Parametricism - as avant-garde style- is a design research programme. A research programme can be defined via its methodological rules: some tell us what paths of research to avoid (negative heuristics), and others what paths to pursue (positive heuristics). The ***negative heuristics*** prevent the relapse into old patterns that are not fully consistent with the new research programme, and the ***positive heuristics*** offers guiding principles and preferred techniques that allow the work to fast-forward in a determinate direction.

In line with architecture's lead-distinction of form vs function, there are two sets of heuristic principles that define an architectural style:

1. ***Functional heuristics***: principles that guide the interpretation of the brief and the functional elaboration of the design. These principles operationalize the code of utility.
2. ***Formal heuristics:*** principles that delimit the formal repertoire and guide the formal elaboration of the design. These principles operationalize the code of beauty.

Each of these two sets of principles comprises both a positive and a negative heuristics, ie, the design is guided by dogmas and taboos with respect to both formal and functional aspects. The defining heuristics of Parametricism – both formal and functional – are fully reflected in the taboos and dogmas of contemporary avant-garde design culture. Parametricism can thus be operationally defined by the following system of heuristic principles:

1.1 **Negative functional heuristics (functional taboos):**

1.1.1 avoid rigid functional stereotypes,
ie, avoid thinking in terms of fixed essences. Avoid the reduction of the brief to generic or essentializing functional designations. Functions can no longer be represented by simple schedules of accommodation.

1.1.2 avoid segregative functional zoning,
ie, avoid the Modernist principle of specialization in combination with urban separation. Do not insist on pure, either/or definitions for function zones. Do not insist on monofunctional territories.

1.2 **Positive functional heuristics (functional dogmas):**

1.2.1 all functions are parametric activity/event scenarios,
ie, think in terms of gradient fields of activity. Formulate the substantial functional expectations in terms of the anticipated life-process that is to be accommodated, fostered and sustained by the project in question. This formulation will

proceed via the description of social activities that are expected to unfold within the respectively designed spaces. These descriptions describe viable social scenarios – calibrated via multiple event parameters – that correlate actor to actor, actor to artefact, and artefact to artefact interactions. The description is thus elaborated as a parametric definition of variably determinable action-artefact networks. Allow the domains of activity to interpenetrate and gradually transform into each other. Allow for the simultaneity of multiple audiences or user groups. Also: function, rather than being only considered in relation to a predetermined purpose, might be understood as capacity or affordance that opens itself up for an evolutionary formation of new purposes.

1.2.2 all activities communicate with each other, ie, all territories and spaces are designed and oriented with a view towards maximizing the perceptual relatedness and easy accessibility of their respectively accommodated events/activities within an integrated ensemble of events/activities.

2.1 **Negative formal heuristics (formal taboos):**

2.1.1 avoid rigid forms, ie, avoid rigid geometric primitives like squares, triangles and circles, or cubes, pyramids or spheres because these forms lack malleability, they lack adaptive capacity and thus the ability to enter into articulated relations. These forms cannot react to each other's presence in any nuanced way. They remain blind, inert, uninflected.

2.1.2 avoid simple repetition, ie, avoid Modernist seriality and monotony because this implies a lack of variety or diversity of spatial offerings.

2.1.3 avoid collage of unrelated elements, ie, avoid the mere juxtaposition of isolated, unrelated elements, subsystems or territories because this implies a lack of order.

2.2 **Positive formal heuristics (formal dogmas):**

2.2.1 all forms must be soft, ie, consider all forms to be parametrically malleable. Local deformations might give information about the form's content or context. This implies the definition of rules of deformation.

2.2.2 all systems must be differentiated, ie, iterate and vary elements systematically, according to rules, to build up (sub)systems. Differentiate gradually (at variant rates) or according to rule-based thresholds. Parametric variation might thus be intelligent, ie, it responds to an inbuilt, performance-based constraint.

2.2.3 all systems must be correlated, ie, build up ordered complexity by correlating subsystems, by defining interdependencies. The differentiation of any posited subsystem (inclusive of the given context) might become the input data-set for a correlated differentiation in any further subsystem. One system's parametric differentiation is transcoded into the next system's differentiation.[36] Thus all subsystems become mappings or mathematical representations of each other. The ambition of articulation suggests that these resonances should be perceptually palpable. Mathematical representation should become visual representation. In terms of the design process, the demand for correlation implies that any design action needs to be followed by a corresponding re-action.[37]

The theory of architectural autopoiesis is emphasizing that a progressive style – understood as a genuine design research programme – must try to innovate both form and function, *and* their relation. It is indeed crucial to first distinguish and then relate form and function. There must be both an explicit formal discourse leading to a fruitful formal heuristics, and an explicit functional discourse leading to a viable functional heuristics. But only if both dimensions are addressed *together* can real, sustained progress be secured. Only if Parametricism can *coherently* propose fruitful and viable heuristics on both planes of engagement can the claim be made that Parametricism constitutes the most promising candidate for contemporary high-performance architecture.The requirement to advance both a formal and a functional heuristics raises the stakes considerably compared with a one-sided effort from either side. Not only must each set of principles be internally consistent, but the formal approach has to be consistent with the functional approach which in turn has to be viable with respect to the demands of society. Is there a good fit between the formal and the functional heuristics of Parametricism? The formulation of the principles

36 Note that correlation presupposes differentiation.

37 This heuristic principle is very open. Any inherently malleable system might be posited. Any further systems might added, even if such additional systems possess a radically different ontology, as long as a systematic correlation can be defined that allows the two systems to mutually adapt and resonate with each other. The more radical the ontological difference between the correlated systems, the more challenging and interesting will be the invention and crafting of correlations between these subsystems.

above is trying to make the compatibility, and indeed the good fit, between the two sets of heuristic principles discernible.

11.2.3 GENEALOGY OF THE PARAMETRICIST HEURISTICS

The Parametricist understanding and way of handling functions has evolved in parallel rather than hand in hand with the Parametricist principles of form generation. The functional heuristics of Parametricism evolved primarily within the OMA-inspired Dutch avant-garde of the last 15 to 20 years. The formal heuristics of Parametricism evolved primarily within the Eisenman-inspired American avant-garde of the last 15 to 20 years. Although these two genealogical strands were running in parallel – often with mutual misgivings – there were also definite points of cross-fertilization. The two strands overlapped at the Architectural Association School of Architecture (AA) in London in the second half of the 1990s. Jeff Kipnis had been teaching at the AA during the first half of the 1990s. His unit promoted the formalism of Folding that lies at the origin of the formal values of Parametricism. Starting in the mid-1990s, the AA Design Research Lab,[38] the AA diploma unit of Zaera-Polo/Moussavi, as well as Ben van Berkel's unit, tried to combine the formalism of Folding with the methods of conceiving functions by means of variable data-sets rather than by functional stereotypes. The inspiration for the parametric Folding formalism came from Eisenman, Lynn and Kipnis, while the inspiration for the data-driven, parametric functionalism came from Rem Koolhaas (OMA) and Winy Maas (MVRDV). During the mid-1990s, Winy Maas had radicalized OMA's method of diagramming under the programmatic banner of 'datascapes'. Maas interpreted urban landscapes with their urban morphologies and distribution of densities as the expression of forces and pressures that could be registered through underlying data-sets in the form of population parameters, consumer preferences, economic indicators, regulatory constraints, as well as technological and environmental parameters. This initially analytical concept was turned into a design engine whereby the respectively assumed parameters became the input data for simple, form-generating functions, not unlike three-dimensional bar-charts. The approach emphasized the functional input parameters without much reflection or discussion about the respective formal a priori that is inevitably involved when a data-scaping machine is constructed.

38 The Design Research Lab was founded in 1996 at the Architectural Association School of Architecture when the author, together with Brett Steele, took over and remodelled the postgraduate design unit of Jeff Kipnis and Bahram Shirdel.

The formal a priori determines the form the spatialization of the data takes. Depending on the formal repertoire at the designer's command, there is great creative freedom here, just like the choice one has among the various modes of graphic information display in a program like Excel. However, sole focus on the data per se often prevents the well-considered, deliberate choice of the formalism of spatialization. Instead a conventional formalism is treated as the natural expression of the data per se. The formal a priori of the whole operation remains implicit, hidden from critique, and shielded from the competition of possible alternative formalisms. This 'Radical Functionalism' had the false self-conception that its method would allow functions to come through unfettered by formal prejudice. This lack of reflection upon the inevitable formal premises of all function-led design is the blind spot of both the historical version of Radical Functionalism and of its updated reincarnation under the banner of Datascapes.

The AA Design Research Lab (AADRL) took up Maas' notion and method of Datascapes,[39] but without its blind spot. A formal agenda was explicitly stated. From the very start, the AADRL was firmly committed to the formal repertoire of Folding (which constitutes the true precursor to the formal heuristics of Parametricism). At the same time, it was clear that the polemic Formalism of Eisenman, Kipnis and Lynn was not a viable stance. It signified the need for an initial protective shield for the formal research against being overburdened too early by functional demands. In 1996 the founders of the DRL felt that after about five years of experimental work and three years after the manifesto-style promotion of this work under the banner of 'Folding',[40] it was high time to test and demonstrate the performative capacity, and indeed the potential performative superiority, of the formal repertoire of Folding. There was the anticipation that if such a demonstration was not delivered soon, the new style would be discredited, and all too easily dismissed as wilful, fanciful indulgence. Rather than taking up a typical avant-garde project task like a villa or contemporary art centre, the first design task posed was to design an airport. This was to test the formal repertoire of Folding in a task environment where functional requirements were foregrounded and the pursuit of form for the sake of form was out of the question. On the basis of the same motivation the next three years were dedicated to demonstrating the superior capacity of Folding with respect to the spatial organization of corporate headquarters in line with the most advanced

39 Winy Maas was invited to teach a workshop in 1997.

40 In 1993 a programmatic issue of *AD* was published: Greg Lynn (ed), *Folding in Architecture, Architectural Design* (*AD*), Academy Editions, Vol 63, no 3–4, March/April 1993.

ideas in management and organization theory. It was important to go beyond the requirements of quantitatively focused, physical ordering of the kind posed by airports and train stations and instead involve the requirements of both physical and perceptual ordering in the context of complex patterns of social communication. The claim was made for a high-performance architecture that can indeed succeed within the most advanced and most competitive domain of contemporary society. This claim still stands, with enhanced confidence, with respect to Parametricism.[41]

The evolution of Parametricism demonstrates the importance of first distinguishing and then explicitly relating form and function. The agenda of the AADRL involved the conscious confrontation and then the integration of the functionally innovative Datascape approach with the formally innovative approach of Folding. The two one-sided discourses were brought together to form the basis of a new style that integrates a sophisticated formal discourse with a sophisticated functional discourse, both based on advanced computational techniques.

However, in the current state of the architectural avant-garde it sometimes seems as if there are still two strands that stand apart from each other. The launch of the label 'Parametricism' on the occasion of the Venice Architecture Biennale in 2008[42] brought together young

41 The first significant, realized Parametricist project was perhaps FOA's Yokohama ferry terminal (1995–2002), closely followed by ZHA's Phaeno Science Musem in Wolfsburg (1998–2005) and by ZHA's MAXXI museum in Rome (1998–2010). As mature statements of Parametricism one might count the following projects by Zaha Hadid Architects: the four stations plus bridge designed for the Hungerburg Bahn in Innsbruck (2004–7), the Zaragoza Bridge Pavilion for the Zaragoza World Expo 2008 (2005–8), the Chanel Mobile Art Pavilion that was travelling from Hong Kong, via Tokyo to New York (2006–8), as well as the Guangzhou Opera House (2002–10). The Central Building for Leipzig's new BMW plant (2002–6) is significant as an example of high-performance architecture within a contemporary business environment.

42 See Patrik Schumacher, *Parametricism as Style – Parametricist Manifesto*, London 2008, presented and discussed at the Dark Side Club, 11th Architecture Biennale, Venice 2008. The Dark Side Club is a critical salon initiated and organized by Robert White to coincide with the Architecture Biennale. Three successive events were conceived as a critical salon to debate some of the themes Aaron Betsky had set for the 2008 Biennale. The first session – curated and introduced by Patrik Schumacher was titled: *Parametricism as New Style*. The following eight architectural studios were presenting: MAD, f-u-r, UFO, Plasma Studio, Minimaforms, Aranda/Lasch, AltN Research+Design, MOH. Jeff Kipnis acted as moderator. See also: Patrik Schumacher, 'Experimentation within a Long Wave of Innovation', published in: *Out There – Architecture Beyond Building*, Volume 3: *Experimental Architecture*, Catalogue of the 11th Architecture Biennale, Venice 2008, also: Zaha Hadid and Patrik Schumacher, 'Parametricist Manifesto', published in: *Out There – Architecture Beyond Building*, Vol 5, *Experimental Architecture*, Catalogue of the 11th Architecture Biennale, Venice, 2008.

protagonists who seem to stand rather closer to the formalist American strand than to the functionalist Dutch strand. The primary interest is still in complex geometry, algorithmic design processes and advanced fabrication processes rather than in the social performativity of this new repertoire. To this extent the agendas of Parametricism appear once more overly biased towards the formal side of the discourse. The underlying reason for the re-emergence of the formalist bias is that a whole new wave of digitally supported formal possibilities has entered the scene via the practice of scripting and parametric modelling alongside (and instead of) simple 3D modelling. The rapid ascendance of scripting and parametric modelling since 2005 played a similar role to the advent of 3D modelling and animation software a decade earlier. The experimental appropriation of the new tools and their attendant concepts, once more, had to take precedence. The initial emphasis on the formal side of a style is thus to be expected, just like a new theoretical approach in science often gears up its conceptual apparatus and its mathematical techniques before going deep into the thicket of empirical reality. Stretching exercises and shadow boxing are recommended before entering the real arena. However, dry runs and rehearsals lose their meaning if the real engagement is not firmly placed on the agenda of future ambitions. The exposure of the new formal possibilities to functional challenges is to follow suit now. Formal research is in danger of losing its credibility and might come to be seen as indulgence the longer the engagement with serious functional concerns is delayed. However, the introduction of serious functional challenges within a design research programme does not imply that the formal research is complete, or even temporarily to be arrested. The formal research continues hand in hand with the exploration of more and more functional domains where the new style might exercise its design prowess.

11.2.4 ANALOGIES: EMULATING NATURAL SYSTEMS

Parametricism instructs its adherents always to differentiate and correlate. Differentiation here implies rule-based differentiation and thus produces a series of interdependent differences rather than pure difference. The further instruction is to correlate various differentiated series. Thus every design move that follows the Parametricist heuristic implies a relative increase in the design's complexity.

This build up of a complex organization is cumulative and implies that an initially arbitrary beginning leads to a more and more self-constraining organization where each further additional element or design intervention must be ever more carefully elaborated to satisfy and continue the complex web of rules and interdependencies already established. The overall organization remains open – it never achieves completion or perfection like, for example, a Palladian villa – but the probability that an arbitrary move or mutation disrupts rather than enhances the design increases with every further move. To find a satisfying solution to a design problem posed late in the design becomes increasingly difficult the more the design has advanced. (A sense of necessity is therefore the subjective corollary of this situation from the designer's perspective.) Successful Parametricist designs share this feature with highly evolved organisms. Modernist, Postmodernist and Deconstructivist designs do not experience this increasing tightening of the remaining space of possibilities and the attendant increase in the difficulty of elaborating satisfying solutions for further design requirements or details. A late design move is nearly as easy and unconstrained as an early move. Anything goes.

The Parametricist build up of organized complexity often proceeds hierarchically, whereby interdependent sets of items (systems) are set into correlations (functions, mappings) with other such integrated sets of items or systems. Such systems are often functional units or subsystems.

One might think of the subsystems of a tower, such as envelope, structural skeleton, system of spatial divisions, circulation system etc. Each of these systems is itself comprised of interrelated parts. According to the design research programme of Parametricism one would expect each of these systems to be internally diffentiated rather than repetitive (as one could assume in Modernism), ie, the skeleton's elements and their pattern of connections should be differentiated along the vertical axis of the tower in accordance with load and moment/stability parameters. The skeleton's particular pattern and trajectory of differentiation can now become the input data-set for driving (aspects of) the facade's internal differentiation while other aspects/properties might be differentiated in accordance with environmental parameters.

To the extent to which these system differentiations are articulated and become legible, their organization contributes to the establishment of ***architectural order***. For instance, the visible differentiation of the skeleton offers clues (facilitating positional local to global inferences) as to whether one is relatively high or low within the building, or the visible differentiation of the facade's shading devices along the tower's circumference might offer clues (facilitating positional local to global inferences) as to one's orientation. Again, to the extent to which the correlation between these two subsystems of the tower is legible, ie, to the extent to which the skeleton's differentiation shines through the facade or is even further accentuated and revealed by the facade, organization is elevated to become order. In this case the subsystems involved in the scripted correlations become indeed ***representations***[43] of each other.

Above we emphasized that a Parametricist design transforms an arbitrary beginning into a highly elaborate, complex order that assumes the semblance of necessity for the designer. To the extent to which this ever more tightened network of organizing correlations is articulated and thus visible, an awe-inspiring elegance is the subjective corollary from the observer's perspective.

The example of correlated subsystems is only one of many organizational patterns through which interdependencies can be established. This particular pattern of correlated subsystems is analogous to the way organisms, in particular higher organisms like vertebrates, are organized, in terms of radically distinct but morphologically and functionally highly correlated subsystems (skin, skeleton, muscular system, nervous system, blood circulation, etc). There is, however, an important difference between the organization of an animal organism and a Parametricist design. An organism is autonomous, self-enclosed and complete, while a Parametricist design project remains incomplete, open to extension and further elaboration. Parts can be added or subtracted as long as the network of correlations is being re-established/adjusted.

In what follows, various types of natural phenomena are briefly considered as source domains for the analogical transference leading to different organizational patterns and forms of architectural order that are equally pertinent for the tasks and ambitions of contemporary architecture:

- inorganic systems
- swarms
- superorganisms
- organisms
- symbioses
- ecologies

These distinctions are not absolute, not even in biology itself, and far less so once we consider them as source domains for analogical transference or inspirational models for architectural concepts. One might, for instance, understand an organism as an ecology of cells. However, there are important distinctive aspects that make it meaningful to work with this classification of six analogical domains rather than using only a single

43 The German word for mathematical function 'Abbildung' literally translates as 'representation'.

analogy like organism or ecology. Each category of natural system leads the design concept in a different direction and the classification provides a useful intellectual tool for the expansion of the universe of Parametricist possibilities as well as for comparative orientation within this universe.

Inorganic systems

Inorganic natural systems that have been used as models or inspiration in architecture are usually single systems made up from a rather homogeneous material or mass of particles, for example, elastic membranes, fabrics, hair simulations, fluid dynamic systems etc. There are plenty of computational simulations available that can emulate the self-organizing, morphogenetic behaviour of such material systems for use in architectural designs. Fluid dynamic systems are interesting to the extent to which the field is continuously differentiated by waves, eddies and turbulences. It becomes more interesting if a second system, for example, obstacles, is introduced that engenders typical reactions in the fluid. In the terms of architectural ordering, the fluid responds and thus announces, represents and amplifies the presence of the obstacle in the field. It is also rather commonplace to move from single dynamic systems with fixed obstacles to systems with two or more interacting fluids. These fluids might be distinguished merely by their trajectories and quantities. However, they might also be distinguished by different parameters (for example, viscosity) that result in differences of qualitative behaviour. The fascinating property of fluids that is utilized in Parametricist architectural and urban designs is its capacity to absorb and mediate many different edge conditions and obstacles without ever losing its formal coherence and gradient transitioning between zones of different character. Simulated fluids have been used as basic data substrate that fills and structures a site (in a context sensitive manner) as a basis for driving the parametric differentiation of building genotypes that are to populate the site.

Swarms

Swarms (swarms, flocks, herds etc) are composed of loosely coupled organisms. The fact that the components of swarms are very complex animal organisms does not imply that the swarm formation itself is very complex. The specific internal structure of the components does not enter into the order/formation of the swarm which is defined by rather simple behavioural rules that sustain the integrity and coordinated movement of the swarm. As a result, swarms behave in a similar way to fluids. So in terms of analogical transference into architecture, results might be similar. The difference is that swarms – computationally modelled via multi-agent systems rather than via particle systems – offer more scope for the definition of the swarm members' behavioural rules and thus more scope for the configurational behaviour of the swarm. Usually, swarms – moving within largely homogeneous media like water or air – are organized around simple, direct feedback rules set up between the proximate members of the swarm. This scenario might be enriched by the introduction of a differentiated ground surface and stigmergic mechanisms. Here the analogy is using the self-organization of foraging patterns of ant swarms.

Swarm members in natural swarms (school of fish, flock of birds etc) are usually identical replicas, all from undifferentiated species. This constraint can be suspended in the analogical transference into the design world of Parametricism. When we think of swarms of buildings we might allow for significant variation within the swarm. These variations might correlate with the building's position within the swarm. We might even construct swarms with rather different species as members, each species with a different behavioural profile, yet still coordinated into a unified swarm. We might also think of the interaction of multiple swarms, each internally differentiated etc. All these variants might be modelled by multi-agent systems.

Superorganisms

Superorganisms are collective organisms, ie, clusters of organisms that are tied together much more tightly than swarms, flocks or herds. The main point of difference between swarms and superorganisms is the fact that the individual organisms comprising the superorganism are functionally (sometimes also morphologically) differentiated and thus become dependent upon each other with little or no chance of an individual metabolism/survival. Examples are social insect colonies as well as coral colonies. In both cases, the inert physical structures (termite mounds, coral reefs etc) that emerge from the collective life-process become an integral part of the superorganism. What is of interest here for the sake of architectural analogies is the superorganism's hierarchical, modular organization. Subsets of individual organisms (modules) form subsystems of the superorganism. However, unlike the subsystems of an organism proper, on the one hand these subsystems can grow without bounds and on the other they are able to survive the loss of many individual modules. The superorganism is super-redundant and thus super-robust and flexible. These qualities – an open-ended growth-potential and robustness/flexibility combined with a functionally differentiated organization – make the superorganism a pertinent model for urbanism.

Organisms

The primary point of distinction between the organization of an organism in comparison with the three types of natural systems explored so far is its bounded, self-enclosed nature. The organism's enclosure is the precondition for the intensive build up of internal complexity via rule-based differentiation and correlation. The density and diversity of internal interdependencies afford a relative autonomy/independence from the surrounding environment, although this is only a relative rather than an absolute autonomy. Dependency upon the surrounding environment is not fully suspended. However, the organism's interfacing with the environment is highly selective and specific, in accordance with the specialized subsystems that mediate the exchanges with the environment (for example, sensing nervous system, breathing system, ingestive/digestive system, skeleton and muscular system etc). This combination of compact enclosure with complex internal organization and specialized, selective interface capacities makes the organism a good model for compact, complex buildings like towers. Internal functional differentiation leads here to the following interdependent and interpenetrating subsystems: environmental envelope, structural skeleton, occupiable surfaces, internal divisions, circulation/navigation system.

Symbioses

The interesting aspect of symbioses – in comparison with unitary organisms – is the fact that here two complex entities of radically different constitution, for instance, two organisms of different species, or one organism plus many organisms of another species, or one organism plus a superorganism, engage in a set of very tight interdependencies. What is very interesting here for the development of architectural analogies is the possibility of positing two initially wholly independent and radically dissimilar systems, perhaps each discharging radically different functions for different user groups, and yet developing synergies via the establishment of intricate, non-trivial correlations. These correlations must be non-trivial as they map across an ontological abyss. Mixed-use developments might be an occasion for the employment of this organizational strategy.

Ecologies

Ecologies might be defined as an all-encompassing symbiosis of all life-forms within a realm. They might involve all of the natural systems distinguished above. The concept of ecology internalizes all relations. The distinction of system vs environment dissolves. The Concept of a living system that confronts all the other natural systems as its external, constraining environment that demands adaptation is suspended. In this radical sense, planet earth is an ecology. As a source for architectural analogy, the concept of ecology suggests a totalizing approach to the design of built environments. The 19th-century artistic concept of 'Gesamtkunstwerk' (total work of art) hinted at such a possibility. However, the 21st-century concept of ecology implies different strategies of synthesis, allowing for radical ontological heterogeneity and looking for inspiration in self-organizing processes. Also, totalization does not imply closure. It is a continuous, open process.

11.2.5 AGENDAS ADVANCING PARAMETRICISM

The analogical transference and inspiration drawn from natural systems into architecture are supported by the importation of computational processes that were originally developed as tools for (scientific) simulation. The current stage of advancement within Parametricism is as much to the continuous advancement of those computational capabilities (and the attendant computational design techniques) as it is due to the designer's realization of the unique formal and organizational opportunities that are afforded by these capabilities. Parametricism can only progress via the continuous advancement and appropriation of sophisticated computational techniques. Finally, computationally advanced design techniques like scripting (in MEL script or RhinoScript) and parametric modelling (with tools like GC or DP) are becoming a pervasive reality. The incorporation of dynamic simulation techniques and agent-based systems as generative/morphogenetic approaches to design is also becoming more widespread, at least within the avant-garde segment of the discipline. Today it is impossible to compete within the contemporary avant-garde scene without mastering and advancing these techniques. However, the mastering and advancement of techniques should go hand in hand with the formulation of further, related ambitions and agendas.

The following seven agendas are proposed here to inject new aspects into the parametric paradigm and to push the development of Parametricism further:

1. *Parametric Inter-articulation of Subsystems*

   The ambition is to move from single system differentiation – for example, a swarm of facade components – to the scripted association of multiple subsystems including envelope, structure, occupiable surfaces, internal subdivisions and navigation system. The

Figure 76 Accentuation: Maori facial tattoos

differentiation in any posited system is to be correlated with differentiations in the other systems. The result is a dense network of associations/dependencies within each system as well as between systems.[44]

2. *Parametric Accentuation*
The ambition is to enhance the legibility of a complex form through intricate correlations that favour deviation amplification rather than compensatory or ameliorating adaptations. For instance, when generative components populate a surface with a subtle curvature modulation, the component correlation should amplify and thus accentuate the initial differentiation. This might include the deliberate setting of accentuating thresholds or singularities. Thus a far richer

44 Parametricism involves the conceptual shift from part-to-whole relationships to component-system relationships, system-to-system relationships and system-subsystem relationships. Parametricism prefers open systems that always remain incomplete. As the density of associations increases, components might be associated into multiple systems. The correlation of an initially independent system implies the formation of a new encompassing system etc.

Figure 77 Accentuation: network correlates with surface

articulation can be achieved and more orienting information can be made conspicuous and perceptually palpable.

3. *Parametric Figuration*[45]

   Complex configurations that are latent with multiple readings can be constructed as a parametric model. The parametric model might be set up so that the variables are figuration-sensitive. Small parametric variations trigger strongly felt reconfigurations ('Gestalt-catastrophes'), ie, the quantitative modifications of these parameters trigger qualitative shifts in the perceived order of the configuration. This notion of parametric figuration implies an expansion in the types of parameters considered within parametric design. Beyond the usual

45 We might also use the term 'Parametric Phenomenology' here. The term 'Parametric Figuration' featured in studios the author taught (with Zaha Hadid) at Yale and at the University of Applied Arts, Vienna. It also featured in the author's studio at the AADRL.

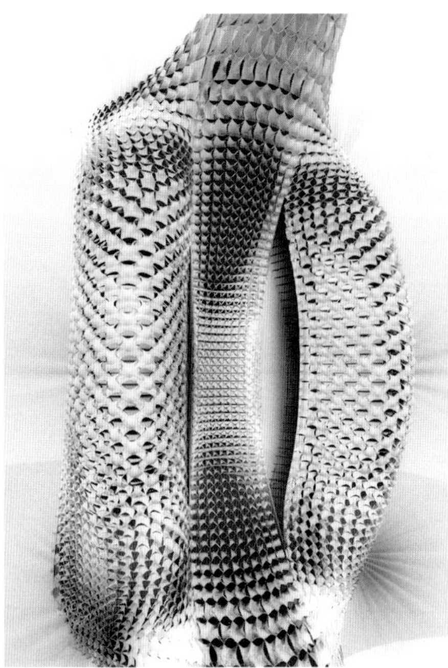

Figure 78 Accentuation: enhancing plasticity

geometric object parameters, ambient parameters (variable lighting conditions) and observer parameters (variable 'camera' positions and view angles) have to considered and integrated into the parametric system. The specific agenda of parametric figuration – with its ambitions for figural latency and parametrically controlled, perceptual re-figuration – is considered here as a special case of the broad agenda of the phenomenological project.

4. *Parametric Semiology*
   The theory of architectural autopoiesis has established the importance of the semantic dimension of architecture. Architectural ensembles of sufficient size and programmatic richness might therefore be taken as an occasion to design a coherent system of signification that, on the one hand, provides for the formal/positional coding of all prevalent distinctions of function-types, social-types and location-types[46] and, on the other, provides a functional, social or locational interpretation for all conspicuous formal/positional distinctions. The establishment of meaning (coding/interpreting) can only be achieved by means of establishing systematic correlations between the domain of the

46 See Chapter 6.9.1 *The Scope of Architecture's Signified.*

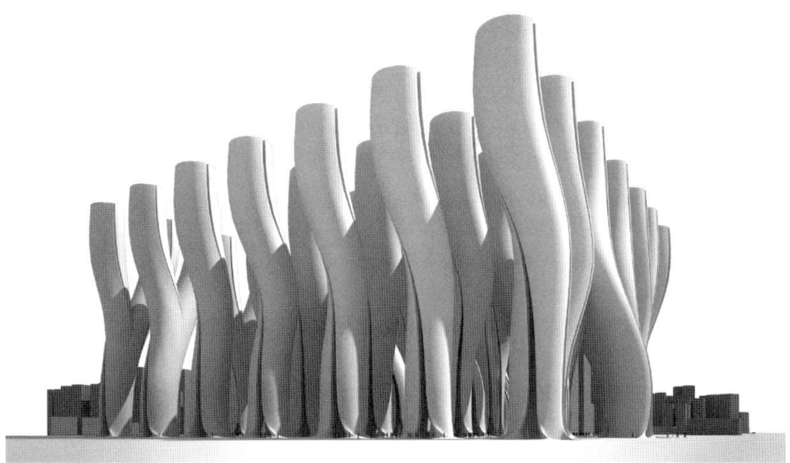

Figure 79 Parametric figuration: cluster of towers, Masterclass Hadid, Vienna, 2006

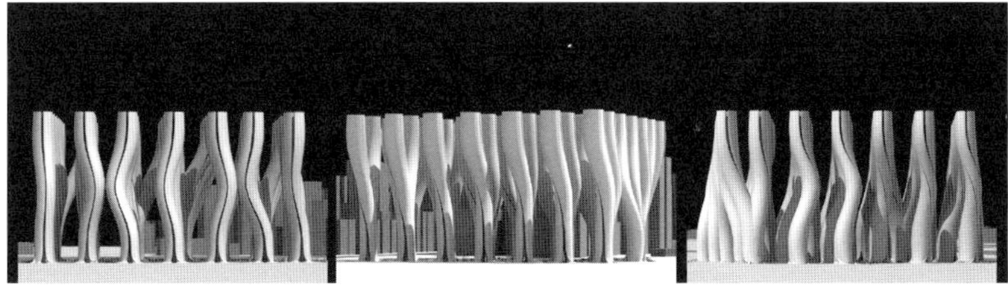

Figure 80 Parametric figuration: cluster of towers, apparent figure from different observer positions

signified (function-type, social-type, location-type) and the domain of the signifier (position, shape, materiality). The parametric paradigm is thus well prepared to take the semiological project to a new level. The designed semiological system (system of signification) should be conceived as a parametric system, ie, the various distinctions and their correlations are subject to parametric variation. The programme domain, the domain of the signified, is best understood in terms of interaction patterns or communicative activities. These patterns of communicative interaction can be modelled via programmed agents that respond to the coded environmental clues. This implies that – for the first time in the history of architecture – the meaning of the architectural language can enter the digital model (design medium) and thus becomes the object of cumulative design elaboration. The system of signification works if the agents consistently respond to the relevant positional and morphological clues so that behaviours to be expected can be read off the articulated environmental configuration.

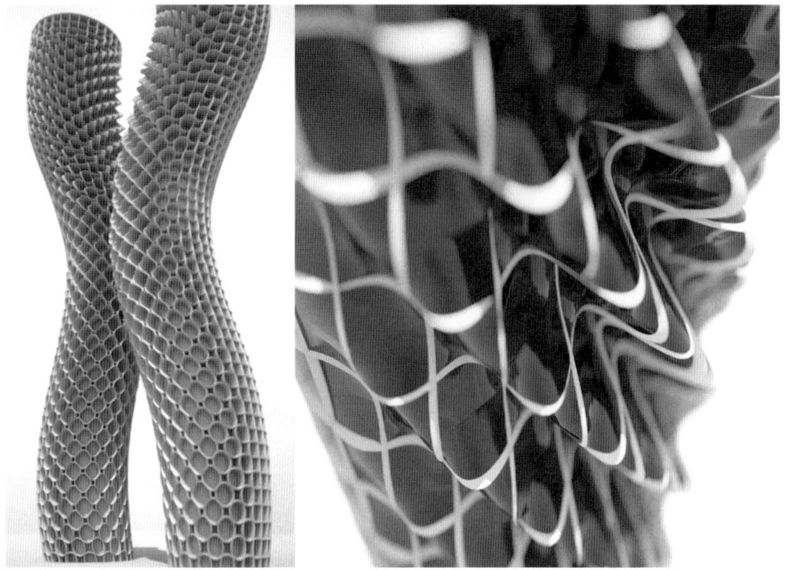

Figure 81 Parametric figuration, facade

The meaning of architecture, the prospective life-processes it frames and sustains, can be modelled and assessed within the design process, thus becoming a direct object of creative speculation.

5. *Parametric Responsiveness*[47]
   We propose that urban and architectural (interior) environments can be designed with an inbuilt kinetic capacity that allows those environments to reconfigure and adapt themselves in response to the prevalent patterns of occupation and use. The real-time registration of use-patterns produces the parameters that drive the (real-time) kinetic adaptation process. Cumulative registration of use patterns might result in semi-permanent morphological transformations. The built environment thus acquires responsive agency at different time scales.
6. *Parametric Ecology*
   The agenda of parametric ecology suggests turning the ecological challenge architecture faces into an opportunity to push Parametricism forward. The fundamental working hypothesis here is that rule-based, morphological adaptations to environmental parameters – sun exposure, temperature, wind pressure, rainfall etc – could allow for the reduction/elimination of energy-intensive

47 Parametric Responsiveness was at the heart of our three-year design research agenda 'Responsive Environments' at the AADRL in London, 2001–4.

Figure 82 Regional and local environmental adaptations – Toledo Museum Competition, Zaha Hadid Architects, 2010

mechanized systems. The morphological and material intelligence of the built environment has generally been degraded since the introduction of AC systems. Working with passive systems on the basis of parametric differentiation allows architecture to recuperate this lost adaptive intelligence. There is a lot to learn from a scientifically informed analysis of the vernacular building traditions of the world. However, the new tools and techniques of parametric design, as well as the abundance of available environmental data, allow contemporary architecture to go beyond what was possible for vernacular traditions. Within each individual project this approach would differentiate the building fabric according to its immediate environmental orientation and context, thus enhancing the legibility and navigability of the designed spatial complex. In global terms, this agenda leads to the regional-climatic differentiation of the global style of Parametricism.

7. *Parametric Urbanism*[48] *– Deep Relationality*

   The assumption is that the urban massing describes a swarm formation of many buildings. These buildings form a continuously changing field, whereby lawful continuities cohere this manifold of buildings. Parametric Urbanism implies that the systematic modulation of the buildings' morphologies produces powerful urban effects and facilitates field orientation. We might refer to this ambition to integrate the building morphology – all the way to the detailed tectonic articulation and the interior organization – as the ambition of *deep relationality*. Parametric Urbanism might involve parametric accentuation, parametric figuration and parametric responsiveness as registers to fulfil its ambition of deep relationality.

48 'Parametric Urbanism' is the title of our recently completed design research cycle at the AADRL, 2005–8.

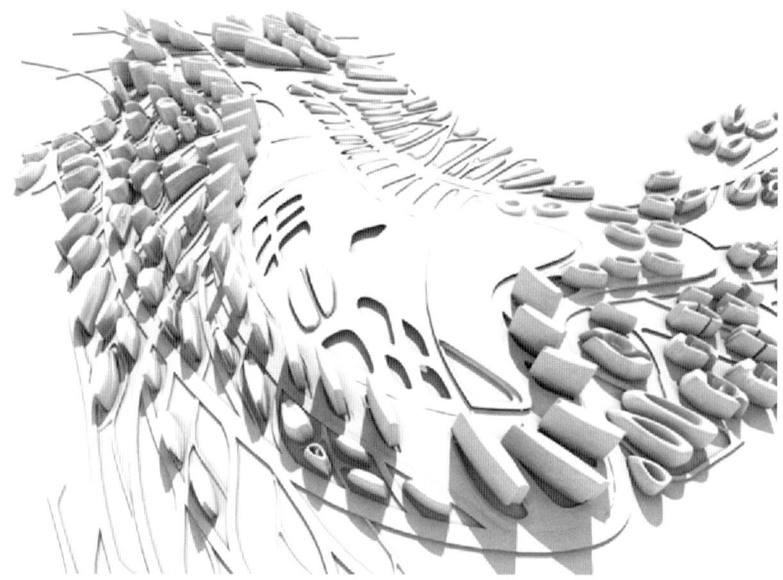

Figure 83 Parametric Urbanism, Zaha Hadid Architects, Appur Masterplan competition, 2008, mutually accentuating systems: topography, massing, path network

11.2.6 THE AGENDA OF ECOLOGICAL SUSTAINABILITY

Our technologically - based world civilization has expanded its power of wealth creation to the point where it becomes its own barrier. We are finally compelled to recognize the finitude of our planet. Our world has shrunk to this single, fragile, shared 'spaceship planet earth'. Every new enterprise must now involve an additional reflective loop about its potential ecological consequences.

Cities are a crucial conduit of our global consumption of energy, air and water. Buildings consume energy and pollute during their life cycle as well as during their fabrication and construction. The ecological sustainability of our civilization depends on our ability to find more intelligent and light-footed ways to harness and utilize the finite resources of our natural environment. This necessity imposes a new constraint upon the design of our built environment, not only in terms of new technology and innovative engineering solutions, but also in terms of the architectural order and stylistic expression of the built environment. However, the imperative of energy saving must *not* imply that the shutters are coming down. The task is to create cities that are sustainably adapted to the natural environment *without* arresting the progressive, developmental thrust of our civilization.

Cultural advancement has to continue. This is not only an end in itself but the *sine qua non* of our continued survival on spaceship earth. Continuous technological innovation is a necessary precondition for our ability to ascertain our ongoing ecological sustainability. Therefore the tightening of ecological constraints that impose themselves on the design of cities must not constrain the vitality and productivity of the life-processes they accommodate. Cities must continue to provide the living conditions that are favourable to innovative work. Thus before we can fully address the question of how to optimize our cities in terms of environmental engineering, we must answer the question of which urban patterns and architectural morphologies are most likely to vitalize and advance the productive life and communication processes upon which everything else depends.

This latter question involves architecture's enduring core competency and societal function, namely to order and frame societal communication via the innovative/adaptive design of the built environment. All social communication requires institutions. All institutions require architectural frames.

The prevalent institutions and communication patterns of society have undergone momentous changes during the last 30 years. Social communication has been dynamized, differentiated and intensified. The static organizing principles of Fordist mass society – separation, specialization and mass repetition – have been replaced by the dynamic principles of self-organization of the emerging Post-Fordist network society: variation, flexible specialization and networking. Accordingly, Modernist urbanism (zoning) and Modernist architecture (serial monotony) experienced a fatal crisis.

The inherent limitations of the linear models of expansion that characterized Fordism had become apparent in terms of the ecological, the socio-economic, as well as the urban crises of the 1970s. The pertinent theoretical answer developed in the form of complexity theory analyzing and simulating self-regulating systems ranging from simple, homeostatic feedback mechanisms via organisms to evolving ecosystems. The same theoretical resources and computational techniques that allow meteorologists to reconstruct and predict the global weather system and scientists to speculate about the earth's evolving climate are available to contemporary urbanists and architects in their effort to meet the challenges posed by the ongoing Post-Fordist socio-economic restructuring. The task is to project the growth and transformation of cities as a rule-based, largely self-regulating morphogenetic process. However, this emergent morphogenesis of the city is 'designed' via computational processes (for example, genetic algorithms) involving both generative processes as well as inbuilt selection criteria. This method of urban design is compatible (congenial) with a free market development dynamic.

The emerging network society implies that the intensity of communication increases exponentially. Even while the use of the Internet and mobile devices increases, the demand for face to face communication – mediated by architectural and urban spaces – increases too. That is why the solution to the global ecological crisis cannot involve the shutting down of urban porosity and urban flow. Post-Fordism requires variegated, complex and densely integrated patterns of spatial ordering that are inherently multivalent and adaptive. In retrospect, Postmodernism (1980s) and Deconstructivism (1990s) might be understood as the first groping steps in this direction. Their partial insights and discoveries have been preserved and expanded by Parametricism. Parametricism confronts both the remaining vestiges of Modernism's monotony, and the cacophony of the urban chaos that has sprung up in the wake of Modernism's demise, with a complex, variegated order inspired by the self-organizing processes of nature. Key design processes are variation and correlation. The designer invents and formulates correlations or rules akin to the laws of nature. Thus everything is potentially made to network and resonate with everything else. This should result in an overall intensification of relations that gives the urban field a performative density, informational richness and cognitive coherence that make for good legibility, easy navigation and thus quick, effective participation in a complex social arena where everybody's ability to scan an ever-increasing simultaneity of events and to move through a rapid succession of communicative encounters constitutes the quintessential cultural skill.

The ecological challenge referred to above is among the defining moments of our epoch. Its impact on contemporary architecture and urbanism is second only to the challenge posed by the dynamic and complexity of Post-Fordist network society. Indeed, the general paradigm of 'ecosystems' applies to both, and is embraced as founding paradigm of Parametricism. The same design concepts, techniques and tools of Parametricism that allow contemporary architects to ramp up the communicative complexity of the built environment are also conducive to the agenda of optimizing architectural forms with respect to ecological performance criteria. Morphological output variables can be programmed to respond to environmental input parameters. For instance, a data-set like a sun exposure map that maps the radiation intensities that a facade is exposed to during a given time period can become the data-input for the adaptive modulation of a sun-shading system. As the system of

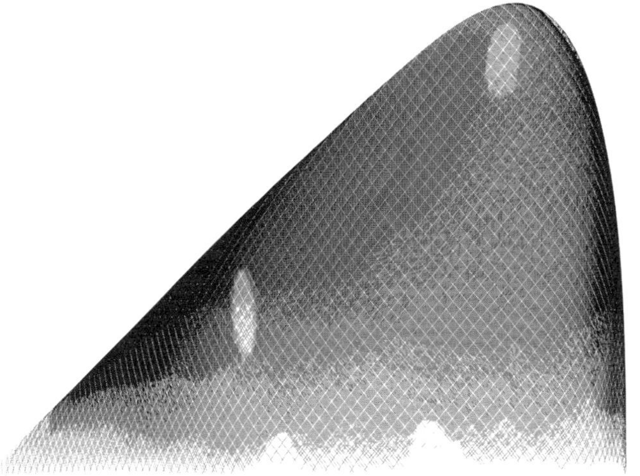

Figure 84 Environmental parameters: sunlight exposure map

Figure 85 Scripted transcoding: sunlight exposure to louvre pattern

shading elements wraps around the facade, the spacing, shape and orientation of the individual elements gradually transform and adapt to the specific exposure conditions of their respective location on the facade. The result is a gradient, continuously changing facade pattern that optimizes sun-protection relative to light intake for each point on the facade. At the same time, this adaptive modulation gives the building a differentiated appearance that also makes the orientation of the building in the environment legible and thus facilitates the comprehension and navigation of the urban environment. The differentiated articulation of the facade contains and transmits information about its position rather than remaining indifferent and blind. The same principle of conspicuous, adaptive variation and correlation is being applied to the activity and event parameters of the urban life-process. The disorientating generic neutrality and monotony of Modernism give way to the ecologically adaptive eloquence of Parametricism. The cities of the future can only be sustainable if they become truly parametric. Parametricism is well prepared to take on the ecological challenge.

11.3 Parametricist vs Modernist Urbanism

THESIS 59

The work of Frei Otto is the only true precursor of Parametricism.

In its urban application, Parametricism offers a convincing alternative to both Modernist monotony and Postmodernist laissez-faire. The former produces order without complexity and the latter produces complexity without order. Both result in disorientation. Parametricist urbanism offers orientation within a complex order. Modernist monotony obliterates the social complexity of Post-Fordist network society. Postmodernist laissez-faire urbanism allows the richness of societal life-processes to be accommodated, albeit without being able to order and articulate this rich complexity. Parametricism can indeed deliver something that produces a decisive advantage. Laissez-faire urbanism proceeds via arbitrary juxtapositions that lack all aesthetic rhyme and reason. This process always results in visual chaos, even if the pragmatic logics of urban life are accommodated within this chaos. The contemporary choice of typologies, construction options and styles is simply too large to expect pragmatic logics to become legible. The result is a cacophony of pure difference.

Parametricism affords the build up of a complex visual and semiological order that facilitates orientation by making the complex order of the urban life-processes legible. Parametricism is able to coordinate pragmatic concerns and articulate them with all their rich differentiations and relevant associations. The danger of overriding real life richness is minimized because variety and adaptiveness are written into the very genetic make up of Parametricism.

11.3.1 SIMPLE ORDER, DISORDER, COMPLEX ORDER

Le Corbusier's first great theoretical statement on urbanism starts with a eulogy on the straight line and the right angle as means by which man conquers and goes beyond nature. The first two paragraphs of the book famously contrast man's way with the pack-donkey's way: 'Man walks in a straight line because he has a goal and knows where he is going; he has made up his mind to reach some particular place and he goes straight to it. The pack-donkey meanders along, meditates a little in his scatter-brained and distracted fashion, he zig-zags in order to avoid larger stones, or to ease the climb, or to gain a little shade; he takes the line of least resistance.'[49] Le Corbusier admires the urban order of the Romans and rejects our sentimental attachment to the picturesque irregularity of the medieval cities: 'The curve is ruinous, difficult and dangerous; it is a paralyzing thing.'[50]

Le Corbusier insists that: 'the house, the street, the town ... should be ordered; ... if they are not ordered, they oppose themselves to us.'[51] Le Corbusier's limitation is not his insistence upon order but his limited concept of order in terms of Classical geometry. Complexity theory (or chaos theory) in general, and the research of Frei Otto[52] in particular, have since taught us to recognize, measure and simulate the complex patterns of order that emerge from processes of self-organization. Phenomena like the 'donkey's path' and the urban patterns resulting from unplanned settlement processes can now be analyzed and appreciated in terms of their underlying logic and rationality, ie, in terms of their hidden regularity and related performative power that result from the consistent constraining pressures that have been underlying their process of formation.

Le Corbusier realized that although 'nature presents itself to us as a chaos ... the spirit which animates nature is a spirit of order'.[53] However, his understanding of nature's order was limited by the science of his day. He lacked the concepts and computational tools that can now reveal the complex order of those apparently chaotic patterns by means of simulating their lawful 'material computation'. Parametricist sensibility gives more credit to the 'pack-donkey's path' as a form of adaptive material computation than to the simplicity of clear geometries that can be imposed in one sweeping move.

49 Le Corbusier, *The City of Tomorrow and its Planning*, Dover Publications (New York), 1987, translated from French original *Urbanisme,* Editions Crès & Cie (Paris), 1925, p 5.

50 Ibid, p 8.

51 Ibid, p 15.

52 The work of Frei Otto might be considered as the sole true precursor of Parametricism.

53 Le Corbusier, *The City of Tomorrow and its Planning*, p 18.

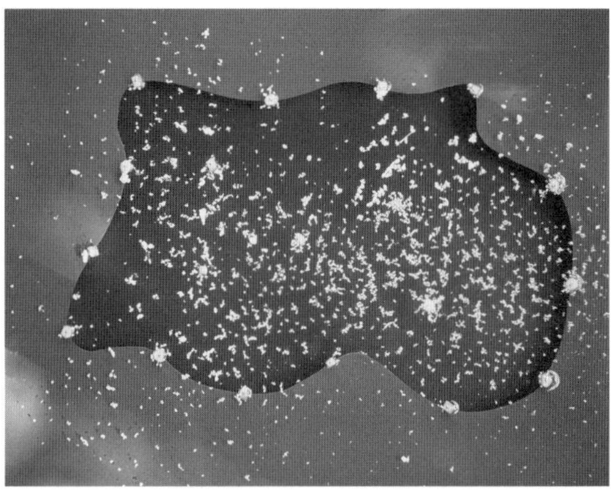

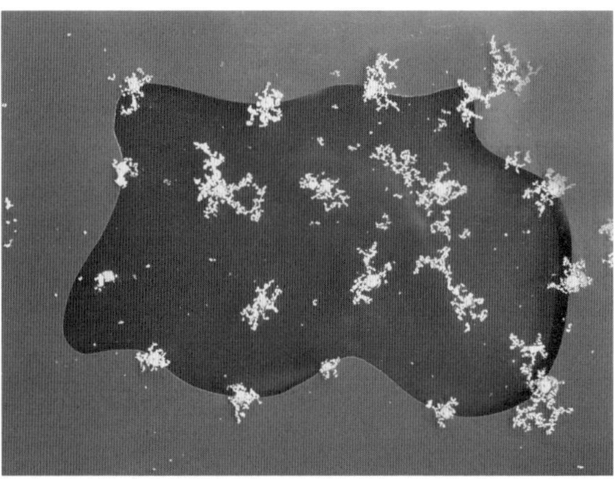

Figure 86 Occupation with simultaneous distancing and attracting forces, Frei Otto, Stuttgart, 1992

Frei Otto's pioneering work on natural structures included work on settlement patterns. His starting point is the distinction and interplay of *occupying* and *connecting* as the two fundamental processes that are involved in all processes of urbanization.[54] His mapping of existing patterns and their geometric analyses was paralleled by physical experiments that were conceived as analogues modelling crucial features of the settlement process. In terms of occupation, he distinguished distancing and attractive occupations. For distancing occupation he used

54 Frei Otto, *Occupying and Connecting – Thoughts on Territories and Spheres of Influence with Particular Reference to Human Settlement*, Edition Axel Menges (Stuttgart/London), 2009.

magnets floating in water and for attractive occupation he used floating polystyrene chips. A more complex model integrates both distancing and attractive occupation whereby the polystyrene chips cluster around the floating magnetic needles that maintain distance among themselves.[55] The result closely resembles the typical settlement patterns found in real urban landscapes.[56]

With respect to processes of connection, Frei Otto empirically distinguishes three scalar levels of path networks – each with its own typical configuration: settlement path networks, territory path networks and long-distance path networks. All start as forking systems that eventually close into continuous networks. On the plane of abstract theory, Frei Otto distinguishes three fundamental types of configuration: direct path networks, minimal path networks and minimizing (optimizing) detour networks. Again he conceives material analogues that are able to self-organize into relatively optimized solutions. For the material computation of minimal path networks, Frei Otto devised the soap bubble skin apparatus where a glass plate is held over a water surface and the minimal path system forms itself from needles.[57] For the more widespread and more interesting optimized detour networks, researchers around him devised the famous wool-thread models[58] that are able to compute a network solution between given points that optimizes the relationship of total network length and the average detour factor imposed by the network. For each set of points and for each adopted sur-length over the theoretical direct paths, an optimizing solution is produced. Although no unique optimal solution exists and each computation is different, characteristic patterns emerge in different regions of the parametric space.

What is so powerful about Frei Otto's material models of self-organizing form-finding is that they bring a large multitude of components – mass particles or path channels – into a simultaneous organizing force-field. Any variation of the parametric profile of any of the elements – size/attractive force of particle or end-points and sur-length of path thread – is being responded to by all other elements within the

55 Ibid, p 45.

56 Within the AADRL research agenda of 'Parametric Urbanism' we also always started with material analogues that were then transposed into the domain of digitally simulated self-organization.

57 Frei Otto, *Occupying and Connecting* – p 64.

58 Institute for Lightweight Structures, SFB 230, *Natural Structures – Principles, Strategies, and Models in Architecture and Nature,* Proceedings of the 2nd International Symposium of the Sonderforschungsbereich 230 (Stuttgart), 1991, p 139.

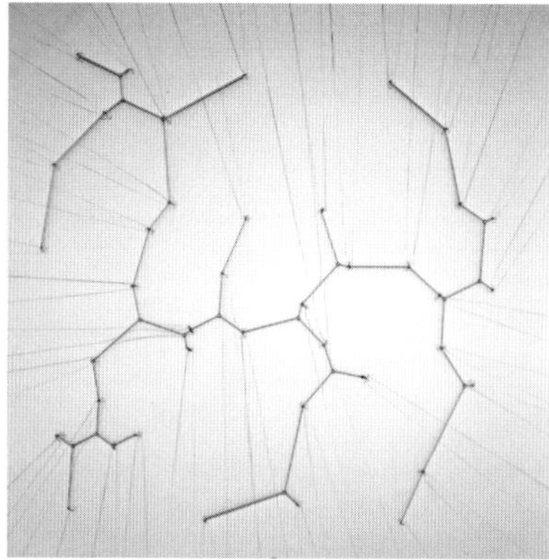

Figure 87 Apparatus for computing minimal path systems, Frei Otto, Stuttgart, 1988

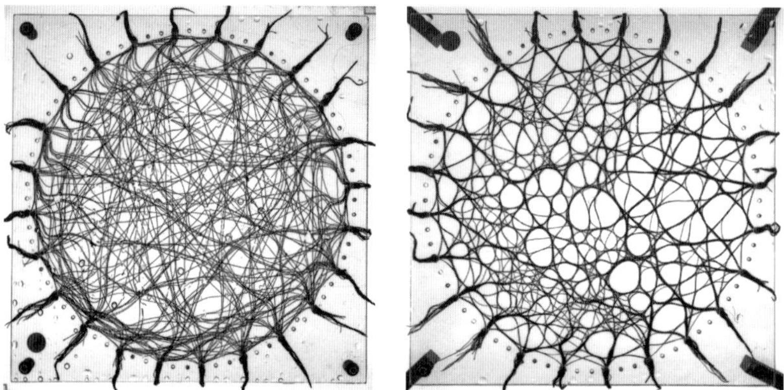

Figure 88 Wool thread model to compute optimized detour path networks, Marek Kolodziejczyk, Stuttgart, 1991

system. What is even more remarkable is that such nuanced quantitative adaptations often cross thresholds into new emergent qualities.

If such an associative sensitivity holds sway within a system we can talk about ***relational fields***. Such relational fields might comprise mutually correlated sub-layers (subsystems), for instance the correlation of patterns of occupation with patterns of connection. The growth-process of unplanned settlement patterns does indeed continuously oscillate between moments when points of occupation spawn paths and paths in turn attract/encourage occupation. The continuous differentiation of the path network – linear stretches, forks, crossing points – correlates with the continuous differentiation of the occupying fabric in terms of its density, programmatic type and morphology. The organizing and articulating capacity of such relational fields is striking in comparison with the pure grid of the modern American city. This modern grid is undifferentiated and therefore non-adaptive. Its 'freedom' to receive any urban fabric and architectural morphology whatsoever is now limiting: it leads to indifference and arbitrary juxtapositions that soon result in impenetrable visual chaos.

Modernism was founded on the concept of universal space. Parametricism differentiates fields. Space is empty. Fields are full, as if filled with a fluid medium. We might think of liquids in motion, structured by radiating waves, laminal flows and spiralling eddies. Swarms have also served as paradigmatic analogues for the field concept. We would like to think of swarms of buildings that drift across the landscape. There are no Platonic, discrete figures or zones with sharp outlines. Within fields, only the global and regional field qualities matter: biases, drifts, gradients, and perhaps conspicuous singularities like radiating centres. Deformation no longer spells the breakdown of order but the *lawful* inscription of information. Orientation in a complex, lawfully differentiated field affords navigation along vectors of transformation. The contemporary condition of arriving in a metropolis for the first time, without prior hotel arrangements, without a map, might instigate this kind of field navigation. Imagine there are no more landmarks to rely on, no axes to follow and no more boundaries to cross.

Parametricist urbanism aims to construct new field logics that operate via the mutually accentuating correlation of multiple urban systems: fabric modulation, street systems, system of open spaces etc. The agenda of deep relationality implies that the fabric modulation also extends to the tectonic articulation of the building mass. For instance, both massing and fenestration might – each in its own way – be driven by sunlight orientation. In this case there is a mutual enhancement of the visual orienting effect so that local perceptions (of the facade) can give clues about the relative position within the global system of the urban massing. Another example: the location and articulation of building entrances might be correlated with the urban navigation system. (This is what ZHA imposed within the urban guidelines for the Singapore masterplan.) This correlation might even extend to the internal circulation patterns of the buildings. This concept of deep relationality might also operate in reverse so that, for example, the internal organization of a major institutional building might lead to multiple entrances that in turn trigger adaptations (additional streets or pedestrian paths) within the urban navigation system. What is important in this respect is that such laws of correlation are adhered to across sufficiently large stretches. However, this does not imply a rigid determinism. Nearly anything can be correlated and there are always many ways to correlate.

11.3.2 IMPLEMENTING PARAMETRICIST URBANISM

The real world implementation of the urban strategies of Parametricism is still in its infancy. However, the fact that ZHA was able to win a series of international masterplanning competitions with schemes that embody the key features of Parametricism constitutes a promising beginning. The projects that have been won include the 200 hectare One-North Masterplan for a mixed-use urban business park (including residential space) for 150,000 people in Singapore, Soho City in Beijing comprising 2.5 million square metres of residential and retail programme, the mixed-use masterplan for Bilbao including the river island and both opposing embankments, and the Kartal-Pendik Masterplan,[59] a mixed-use urban field of 55 hectares with 6 million square metres of gross buildable area comprising all programmatic components of a city including the full panoply of public programmes.

The project is located on the Asian side of Istanbul and is supposed to constitute a new sub-centre that should re-orient this side of Istanbul and thus release the pressure that a growing population places on the historic centre. The site is being reclaimed from industrial estates and stretches from a dedicated highway off-ramp next to a great quarry all the way to the coastline. It is flanked on both sides by the dense, low-rise, small grain fabric of the suburban towns of Kartal and Pendik respectively. Zaha Hadid Architects were encouraged to consider the site as a blank sheet. However, the Parametricist taboo of unmediated juxtapositions implied that the adjacent context – in particular the incoming lines of circulation – had to be taken into account as input for the generation of a new urban geometry. ZHA used Maya's hair dynamic tool to achieve a parametrically tuned bundling of the many incoming paths into larger roads enclosing larger sites. The bundling action produced a path system that exhibits the basic properties of Frei Otto's minimizing detour network between the two sides. This net was strongly biased in the lateral east–west direction. The north–south direction was then imposed via a primary artery with a series of subsidiary roads running in parallel. The result is a hybrid system between the minimizing detour network and a

59 Zaha Hadid Architects, design team: Zaha Hadid, Patrik Schumacher, Saffet Bekiroglu, Daewa Kang, Daniel Widrig, Bozana Komljenovic, Sevil Yazici, Vigneswaran Ramaraju, Brian Dale, Jordan Darnell, Elif Erdine, Melike Altinisik, Ceyhun Baskin, Inanc Eray, Fluvio Wirz, Gonzalo Carbajo, Susanne Lettau, Amit Gupta, Marie-Perrine Placais, Jimena Araiza.

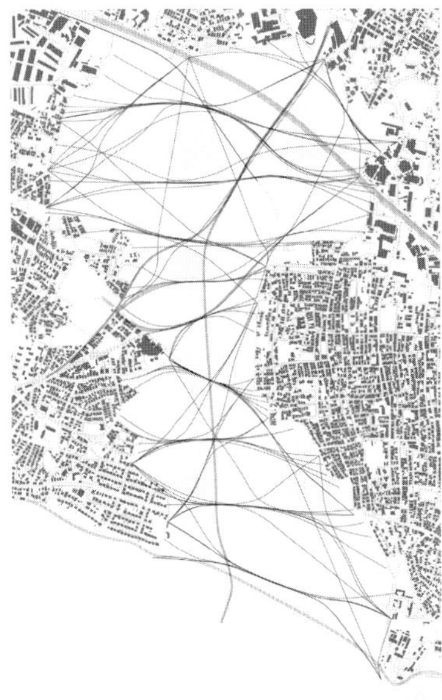

Figure 89 ZHA, Istanbul, path network – digital wool-thread model

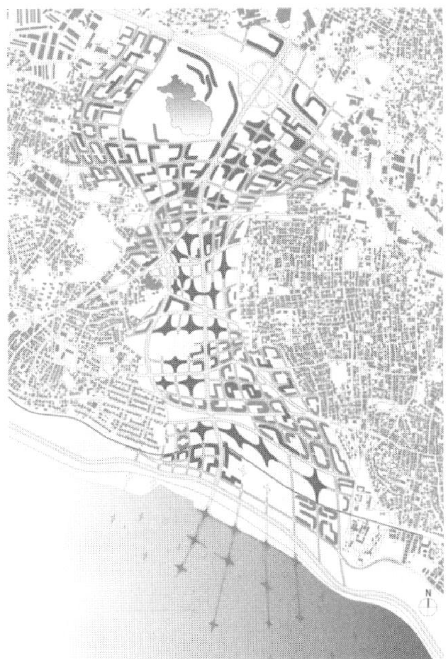

Figure 90 ZHA, Istanbul Masterplan, final urban layout of streets and urban fabric

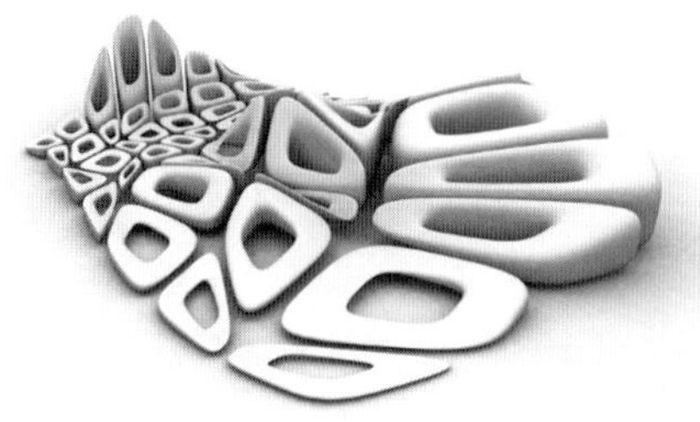

Figure 91 Fabric studies 1: block variations

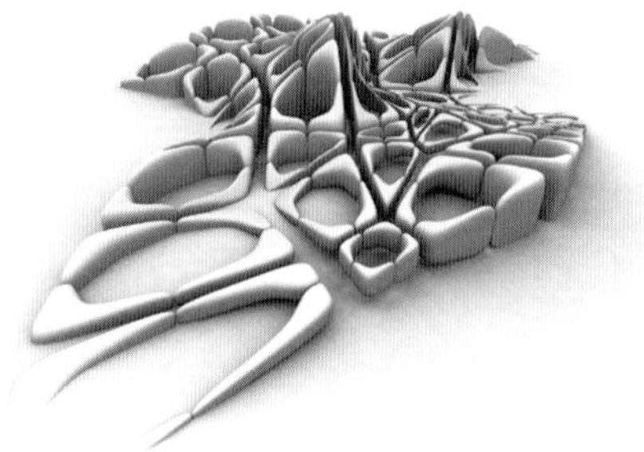

Figure 92 Fabric studies 2: split block variations

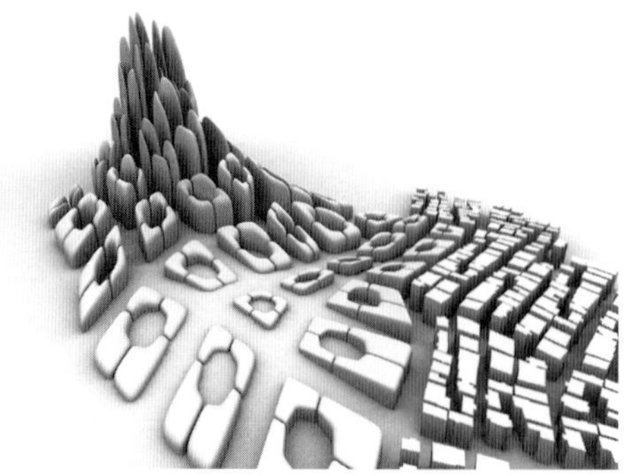

Figure 93 Fabric studies 3: point buildings variation

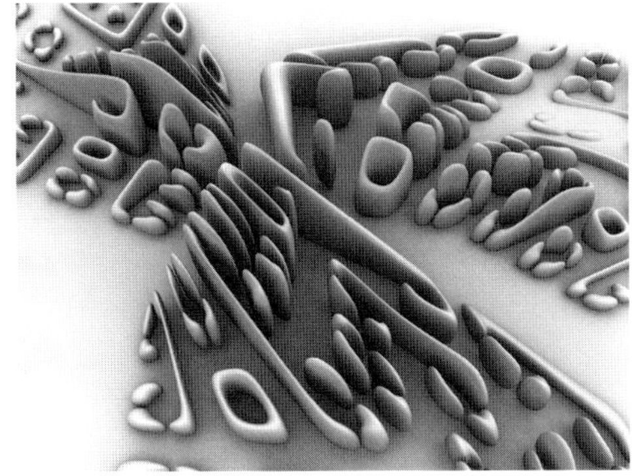

Figure 94 Fabric studies 4: calligraphy blocks

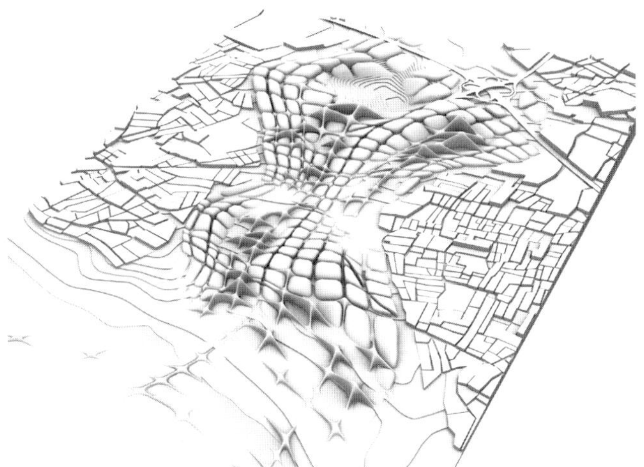

Figure 95 Istanbul, global Maya model

deformed grid that affords a useful range of parcels – differentiated in terms of shape and size.

In parallel, we studied potential fabric typologies. We decided to work with two primary types: towers and perimeter blocks, each conceived as generative components or genotypes that allow for a wide range of phenotypical variation. The towers were conceived as cross towers, initially placed literally over the crossing points of the network. Some cross towers are replacing those crossing points to create larger sites. Further cross towers are placed on a secondary pedestrian network that is directly offset from the primary street network. The towers thus

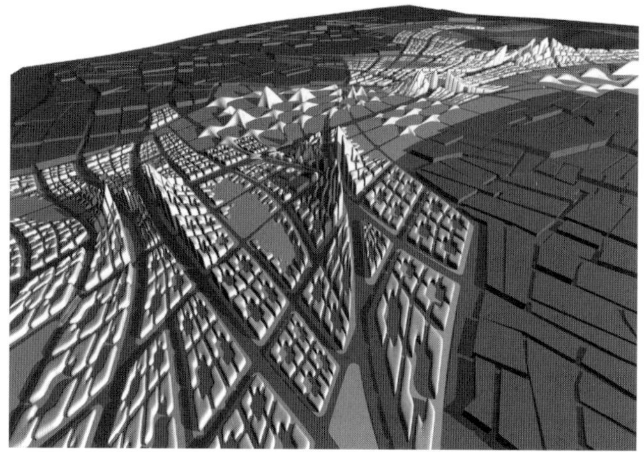

Figure 96 Istanbul, global Rhino model

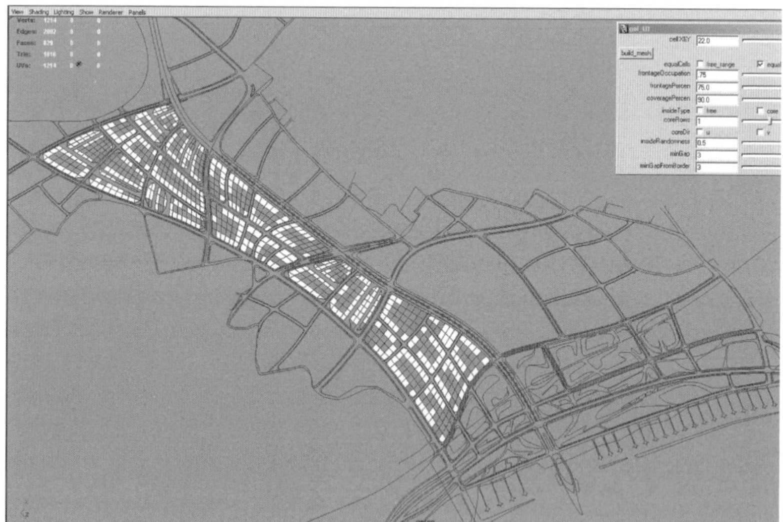

Figure 97 Scripting calligraphy block patterns 2D

accentuate the path network. The perimeter block type inversely correlates height with parcel area. Courtyards morph into internal atria as sites get smaller and the blocks get taller. The next move was to split the perimeter blocks along the lines of the secondary path network. This move, together with the height differentiation, allows the block type, at certain instances, to be assimilated to the cross-tower type. Accordingly,

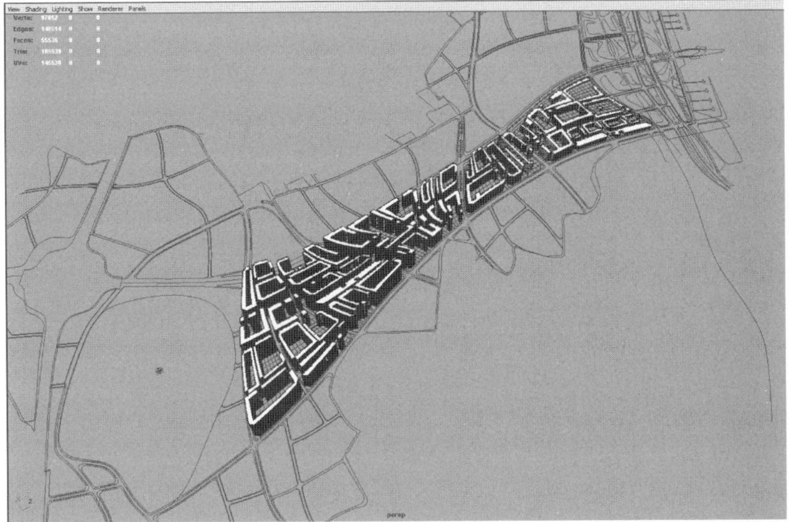

Figure 98 Scripting calligraphy block patterns 3D

Figure 99 New Parametricist city-scape, Kartal-Pendik Masterplan, Istanbul, Zaha Hadid Architects, 2007

'pseudo-towers' are formed at some crossing points by pulling up the four corners of the four blocks that meet at such a corner. Thus an overall sense of continuity is achieved in spite of starting with two rather distinct urban typologies.

In terms of the global height regulation – beyond the local dependency of height upon parcel size – the scheme correlates the conspicuous build

Figure 100 Calligraphy blocks – tectonic detail

up of regional height within the urban field with the regional spaciousness (width) of the field. Thus the rhythm of urban peaks maps and indicates the rhythm of the widening and narrowing of the urban field. The result is an elegant, coherently differentiated city-scape that facilitates navigation through its lawful constitution and through the architectural accentuation of both global and local field properties.

This much might be possible to institute with the imposition of strict planning guidelines using strict building lines and height regulation. Strong political support and private buy-in are required to make it happen. All constituencies need to be convinced that the restrictions placed upon all sites really deliver a worthwhile collective value that cannot be achieved otherwise. Here the collective value is the unique character and coherent order of the urban field. All players benefit from this if adherence can be enforced. Ordered complexity here replaces both the monotony of Fordist, planned developments and the disorienting visual chaos that marks virtually all contemporary laissez-faire city expansions.

This new density of highly differentiated, urban regulation can deliver a coherent urban vision. However, to go yet further, in terms of the concept of deep relationality the architect's involvement needs to extend from urbanism to architecture. Only architectural design affords the opportunity to further intensify the elaboration of accentuating correlations via the systematic modulation of tectonic features. For instance, in terms of the calligraphy blocks – a third perimeter block variation that has been designed to open up the interior of the parcels and

Figure 101 Cross towers – close up

to cross parcels – the architectural design proposes a continuous facade differentiation that leads from the streetside to the courtyard on the basis of an initial distinction of two facade articulations: inside versus outside. Another moment of deep articulation is the coordination of the parcel's landscape design with the design of the public spaces. Furthermore, the design proposes the correlation of the secondary path system with the cross-tower axes and with the building's internal navigation systems.

Doubts might be felt when confronted with the possibility of designing an urban field of up to 6 million square metres with a single design team. Is this a worthwhile and realistic ambition or are ZHA overreaching here? The complex order and deep relationality we seek does not rely on a single hand. Multiple authors can contribute and continue the project, as long as their creativity is guided by the heuristics of Parametricism. Parametricism can indeed deliver something that produces a decisive surplus value when compared with the alternative of arbitrary juxtapositions. Current urban development patterns lack aesthetic coherence, even when the pragmatic logics of a vital urban life-process are secured via the rationality of market forces. The contemporary choice of typologies, construction options and styles is simply too large to expect pragmatic logics to become legible. The result is visual chaos, a

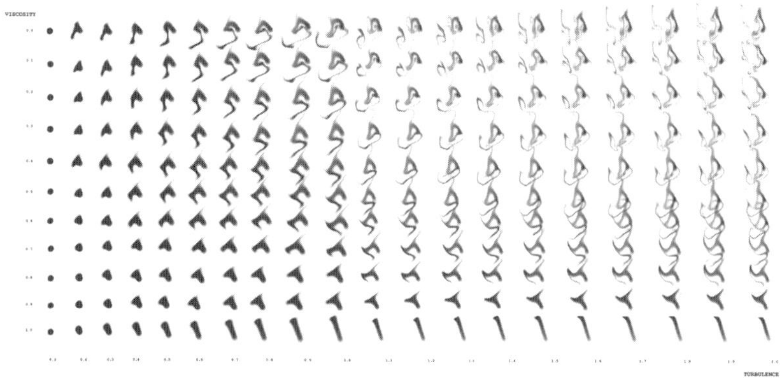

Figure 102 Fluid dynamic – parametric variations, Parametric Urbanism, AADRL, 2008

cacophony of pure difference. Parametricism is able to further coordinate pragmatic concerns and articulate them with all their rich differentiations and relevant associations. The danger of overriding real-life richness is minimized because variety and adaptiveness are written into the heuristics of Parametricism.

The inherent advantages of Parametricism become most salient at the urban scale. The competition-winning urban schemes of Zaha Hadid Architects indicate that Parametricism has the chance to be recognized as a rational approach that can deliver large-scale, high-performance projects. This initial, societal success of Parametricist urbanism is important as context for the more radical design research that has been conducted under the title of 'Parametric Urbanism',[60] at the AA Design Research Lab (AADRL). Parametric Urbanism takes the tools of parametric design into the domain of urbanism. The power of parametric design systems is usually exploited to cope with the rapid succession of design changes, ie, for the ability to produce variations of a single building, or for generating versions of building components for a complex building geometry that does not allow for the repetition of elements. Parametric Urbanism suggests that these techniques of versioning can be applied to an array of buildings, so that a new version does not replace an older version but comes to join and extend the field of simultaneous versions in the build up of a complex urban field. Whole buildings are treated as generative components that populate an urban site according to a rule of differentiation that is correlated with chosen aspects of the site's initial differentiation. Thus the build up of multiple urban layers is

60 This research agenda was pursued for three years, from 2006 to 2009.

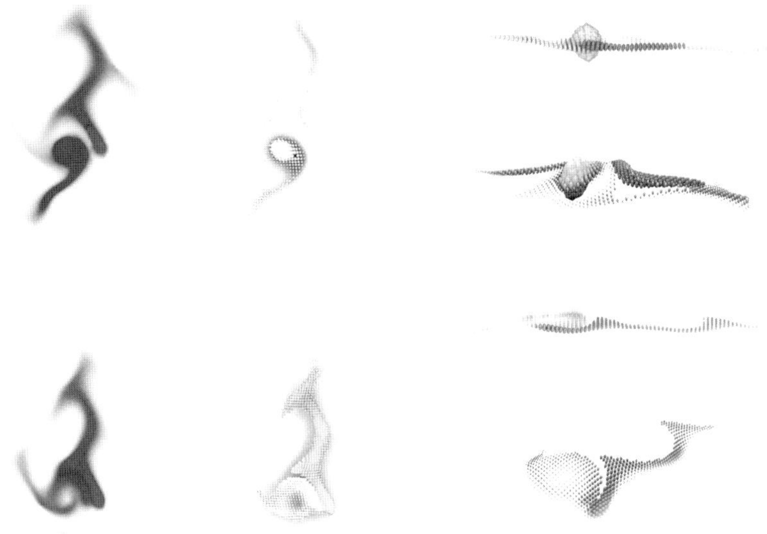

Figure 103 Interaction of two fluids, Parametric Urbanism, AADRL, 2008

being initiated, each with its own logic of differentiation as well as with its own way of resonating with the other layers.

The project presented here was using Maya fluid as a tool for the initial generation of a basic urban geometry. The tool simulates the dynamic of fluids and makes a fluid's typical characteristics subject to parametric control. The particle flow is sensitive to contextual features like boundaries and obstacles. Two fluids flowing into each other form complex patterns of nesting and intermixing. The project proposed to 'represent' the different programmatic layers of the urban brief via different fluids. These different fluids were initially colour-coded and released into the site at strategic locations. The hypothetical site was the development site of China's Shanghai Expo 2010.

The fluids negotiate each other as well as the site boundaries. The emergent patterns are regulated by the laws of quasi-nature that can be parametrically manipulated. The designer thus gains a certain (loose) control over the emergent configuration. He/she might freeze the process at any time and choose from the successive patterns that emerge as stages of the dynamic process. Iterative series working is called for. The resultant patterns appeal (more or less) due to their coherence, their degree of legible mixity and due to their responsiveness with respect to contextual constraints. An 'elegant' pattern is chosen. The next step is

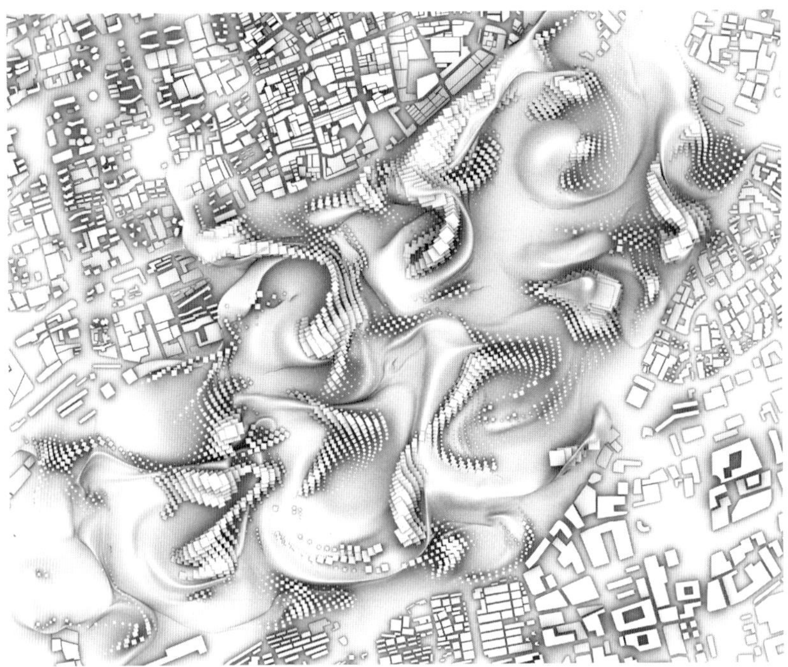

Figure 104 Fluid deployed – simple geometric translation, Parametric Urbanism, AADRL, 2008

the three-dimensional, morphological interpretation of the pattern (which is nothing but a certain vector distribution). The geometric translation of the rather generic data-sets produced by the fluids might take any imaginable form. The field of particles or vectors might be analyzed in terms of local particle directions, densities and velocities, thus producing a data-set for further computational operations. These three variables provide the input parameters for the definition of a scripted, geometric transcoding. The most diverse transcoding scripts are imaginable. This radical openness with respect to translation turns these dynamical systems into Deleuzian design diagrams. To be more precise, the design medium (design world, modelling space) provided by Maya fluids becomes here a medium for ***parametric-extraordinary diagrams***.[61] In the terms of Nelson Goodman's conceptual apparatus for the analysis of the 'languages of art',[62] adopted by the theory of architectural autopoiesis for

61 See Volume 1, chapter 4.2.2 *The Diagram.*

62 Nelson Goodman, *Languages of Art*, Hackett Publishing Company (Indianapolis/Cambridge), 1976.

the characterization of architecture's modelling spaces,[63] the sketching space of Maya fluids is at least as ***non-notational***, ***ambiguous, dense*** and ***replete*** as a compositional hand sketch. These characteristics are not due to the inherent aspects of Maya fluids. Rather, they are connected with the Deleuzian character of a design process that has not yet settled on a fixed routine of translation. The fluids are ambiguous because the transcoding possibilities are unconstrained. Understood as a symbol system, the fluid model is replete because there are many potential measures that might be taken as relevant inputs for the next step. The system is dense because the thresholds at which a difference is measured and registered as a difference can be set arbitrarily fine. However, the possibility of writing a transcoding script implies that the designer has the opportunity to turn this modelling space into a strict notational system. It seems, that once the transcoding idea has been decided on and implemented as a script, the system transforms into a notation eliminating ambiguity. Now the 'meaning' of each run of the model is predetermined. However, the lack of control over the precise behaviour of the fluid and the potential difficulty (depending on the specific script) to anticipate all the possible geometric results of the transcodings make this process rather different from the usual use of a notational system. The system remains – to a certain extent – generative.

The strategic choice is made to transcode different fluids rather differently. Figure 104 shows the interaction of two differently transcoded fluids. One of the two fluids is transcoded into a smooth topography. The second fluid, in stark contrast, is transcoded into a field of voxels. Despite the ontological difference between the two systems, their systematic interaction ensures a sense of overall coherence. However, these translations demonstrate a principle rather than constituting a design. They produce a diagram that merely demonstrates the idea of correlating different systems. Even at this level of abstraction the interim result can be criticized: both translations make insufficient use of the information provided by the vector field. The topography only reads one of the three variables – translating it into height values. The voxel field seems to register two variables – via voxel density and voxel size. Neither of the two transcodings seems to be registering/translating all three variables. Directionalities do not come through. This abstract/formal critique has been superseded in the next, much more demanding step of defining meaningful architectural genotypes that can translate the underlying data-set into meaningful urban fields. One

63 See section 7.7 *Modelling Spaces.*

Figure 105 Fluid 1 transcoded into courtyard morphology

difficulty here is to preserve (or perhaps even enhance) the elegance and sense of animate interaction that was the appeal of the initial fluids.

The programmatic layers to be accommodated were stipulated as residential accommodation (two typologies), public/cultural facilities and landscape/park areas. Figures 105 and 106 show two very different residential typologies. Both transcodings display the fluidity of the original diagrams. This shared character assimilates the two systems to each other despite their radical differences. The juxtaposition of these two images demonstrates the power of this design process to produce unity within difference (as well as difference within unity). The modelling space of the Maya fluids displays its strong formative power that is able to maintain an anticipated global order and character while leaving the detailed morphology wide open.

A third and a fourth morphological system were developed, also as transcodings of the same type of underlying data-set. Thus a system of four types of fluids, each type pouring into the field from several emitter locations, was set up. Each of the four fluid types was interpreted in radically distinct ways: a residential tower system, a residential courtyard system, a public podium system and a topographical landscape system. The shared, underlying fluid system ensures that these four systems are

Figure 106 Fluid 2 transcoded into tower morphology

Figure 107 Fluid integration of three urban morphologies, Parametric Urbanism, AADRL, London, 2008. Authors: Ludovico Lombardi, Du Yu, Victoria Goldstein, Xingzhu Hu; tutor: Patrik Schumacher

able to participate in a single, coherent, multi-layer urban field, despite their morphological distinctness.

It should be clear that a result like that shown in Figure 107 cannot be the outcome of a single, quick computational process. Such a result requires an intense design process that moves through even more trial and error loops than any ordinary (Modernist or Postmodernist) design process. The difference is that the trial and error process here focuses on the development of the scripted systems rather than working directly on a singular scheme. Once the systems operate and collaborate satisfactorily across a certain range of input data-sets and across certain ranges of parameter inputs, 'the result' is much more than a singular scheme. Even if only one of the instances of the system is considered, it should be clear that the combination of variability, intricacy and coherence – both organizationally and phenomenologically – could not have been achieved without harnessing the power of the new computational processes. The complex order and elegance shown here depend on these new design tools and processes. Parametricism can only progress together with its tools and methods, explored and honed in design research projects that take up more and more of the challenges posed to architecture, on all scales.

11.4 Elegance

THESIS 60

Elegance is the aesthetic expression of complex order.

'Elegance' is here promoted as the general watchword of Parametricism's aesthetics, ie, 'elegance' is the name of the kind of beauty that can be accomplished by adhering to the formal heuristics of Parametricism. 'Elegance' suggests sophistication and refinement. It is an unquestioned value of immediate appeal and in no need of argument. The immediate appeal of 'elegance' should be an asset in Parametricism's push into the mainstream. The mainstream appeal of elegance runs counter to any raw/radical avant-gardism. The promotion of the concept indicates that Parametricism has matured to the point that refinement and mastery are becoming the order of the day.

Elegance articulates complexity. This concept of elegance is opposed to the elegance of Minimalism. Minimalist elegance thrives on simplicity. It eliminates complexity. In contrast, the elegance that is promoted here thrives on complexity. It coordinates variety. It achieves a visual reduction of an underlying complexity that is thereby sublated rather than eliminated.

Attributed to a person, elegance suggests the effortless display of sophistication. We also talk about an elegant solution to a complex problem. In fact only if the problem is complex and difficult does the solution deserve the attribute 'elegant'. While simplistic solutions are pseudo-solutions, the elegant solution is marked by an economy of means by which it conquers complexity and resolves (unnecessary) complications. It is this kind of connotation that we would like to

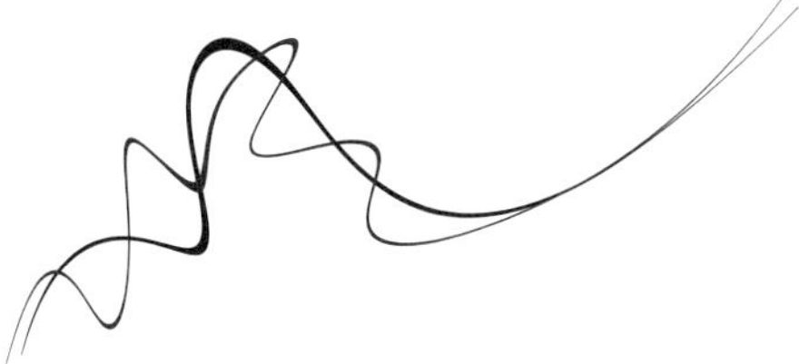

Figure 108 Curved lines running along with each other

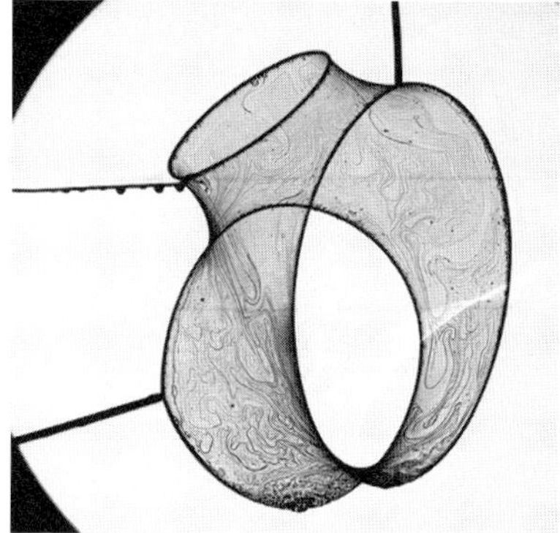

Figure 109 Soap film – minimal surface, Frei Otto, 1988

Figure 110 Competition Kunsthaus Graz, Zaha Hadid Architects, 1999

Figure 111 Abu Dhabi Performing Arts Centre, Zaha Hadid Architects, 2007

harness. An elegant building or urban design should therefore be able to manage considerable complexity without descending into disorder.

Robert Venturi's notion of the 'difficult whole' is concerned with the compositional integration of diversity. 'It is the difficult unity through inclusion rather than the easy unity through exclusion.'[64] One of the specific techniques he has identified is the technique he has termed 'inflection'. 'By inflecting towards something outside themselves, the parts contain their own linkage.'[65] He identified this technique and its integrative effect in Baroque architecture, in comparison with the more additive structure of Renaissance compositions where each subsystem rests complete within itself. In contrast, Baroque inflection achieves the integration of parts (subsystems) by means of imposing an overarching curvature which leaves the part asymmetrical/incomplete requiring the other complementary parts to continue and complete the curvature.

64 Robert Venturi, *Complexity and Contradiction in Architecture*, 2nd edition, Museum of Modern Art (New York), 1977, p 88.

65 Ibid, p 89.

The concept of inflection can be generalized, so that we can propose: elegance requires that the layers and subsystems of a complex composition are mutually inflected. Every new element or new layer that enters the complex will both inflect the overall composition and will in turn be inflected. Elegance can never result from a merely additive complication.[66]

Current digital modelling tools are able to facilitate integrative effects: lofting, spline-networks, soft-bodies, force-fields etc. Intensive coherence (Kipnis), pliancy, multiple affiliations, intricacy (Lynn) etc are the concepts coined to describe the compositional ambitions that emerged early in the wake of the new modelling tools. In fact it has become increasingly easy to achieve abstract sketch-designs (surfaces) that satisfy these terms and thereby achieve a measure of elegance as defined here. However, surface compositions are only the first sketchy step in the design of an elegant architecture. Seamless surface models do not translate directly into a built reality. Buildings cannot be single surfaces or single systems. The obvious task that Folding posed for itself was to go beyond pure surfaces and to elaborate structural systems that are compatible with the ambition for continuous differentiation. One of the most convincing contributions was Jesse Reiser's notion of a 'space-frame' exemplified in his competition entry for Manhattan's West Side in 1999. In the work of Reiser + Umemoto, the space-frame becomes a space-filling medium that could receive continuous deformations that inform the system by allowing disturbances (squeezes, clearances, inserted objects) to radiate through the space-frame. These more complex models displayed more ordered complexity. The next step was the focus on the envelope: how to tessellate or panelize continuously changing double-curved surfaces and, further, how to integrate (rather than merely impose) openings. With each step the maintenance of elegance became more difficult but if the difficulty was mastered a new, higher order of elegance was attained. Naturally, on the way to the elaboration of fully functional, fully detailed designs, whereby ever more systems or layers need to be integrated, the principle of inflection (organic inter-articulation) becomes ever more difficult to achieve. Also, the visual field is in danger of being overcrowded, compromising legibility and orientation.

It is at this moment of mounting difficulty – in the face of bringing the new paradigm into large-scale realization – that elegance must become

66 For instance, Tschumi's Parc de la Villette, in contrast, still operates with layers that remain indifferent to each other. The introduction of inflection marks the shift from Deconstructivism to Folding as the immediate precursor of Parametricism.

an explicit priority. Every new layer of function or detailing requires a new, increasing ingenuity to be incorporated with seeming effortlessness. With a view to execution, further demands of geometric precision (for example, high order surface continuity) become paramount concerns. Contemporary car design affords a challenging benchmark both in terms of the tight inflective nesting of multiple functional features and in terms of surface continuity. The obvious progress of car design in the last few years is equally reliant upon digital design and manufacturing. (For instance, observe the way the headlights of the latest Mercedes sports cars are massaged into the subtle surface of the chassis.)

The notion of elegance promoted here still gives a certain relevance to Alberti's criterion of beauty: you can neither add, nor subtract without destroying the harmony achieved. Except, in the case of contemporary elegance, the overall composition lacks the sense of perfect closure that is implied in Alberti's conception. Alberti focused on key ordering principles, like symmetry and proportion. These principles were seen as integrating the various parts into a whole by means of setting those parts into definite relations of relative position and proportion in analogy to the human figure. Perhaps the best example of this ideal is the Palladian villa. In contrast, contemporary projects remain incomplete compositions, more akin to the Deleuzian notion of assemblage than to the Classical conception of the organism. Our current idea of organic integration does not rely on fixed ideal types. Neither does it presuppose any proportional system. Nor does it privilege symmetry. Instead the parts or subsystems mutually inflect and adapt to each other achieving integration by various modes of spatial interlocking, soft transitions at the boundaries between parts, morphological affiliation, scripted correlations etc.

The principle of elegance postulates: *do not add or subtract without elaborate inflections, mediations or correlations.* While the Classical concept of preordained perfection has thus been abandoned, there still remains a strong sense of increasing tightness and stringency, approaching even a sense of internal necessity, as the network of compositional relations is elaborated and tightened. Every designer knows this from his/her own design experience. The more the compositional cross-referencing, inflection and integration within the design have been advanced, the harder it becomes to add or subtract elements. This kind of design trajectory – although wide open at the beginning – beyond a certain point becomes heavily self-constraining. One might be inclined to talk about the increasing ***self-determination*** of a composition: an emergent (rather than preordained) 'perfection'.

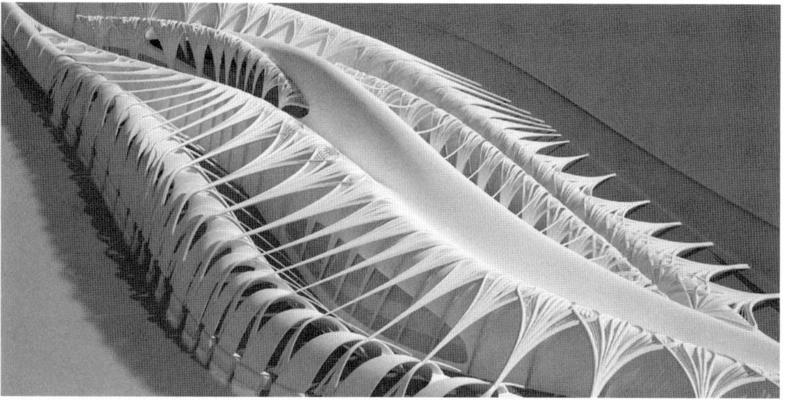

Figure 112 Parametric differentiation of Gothic system, proto-design, AADRL, 2010

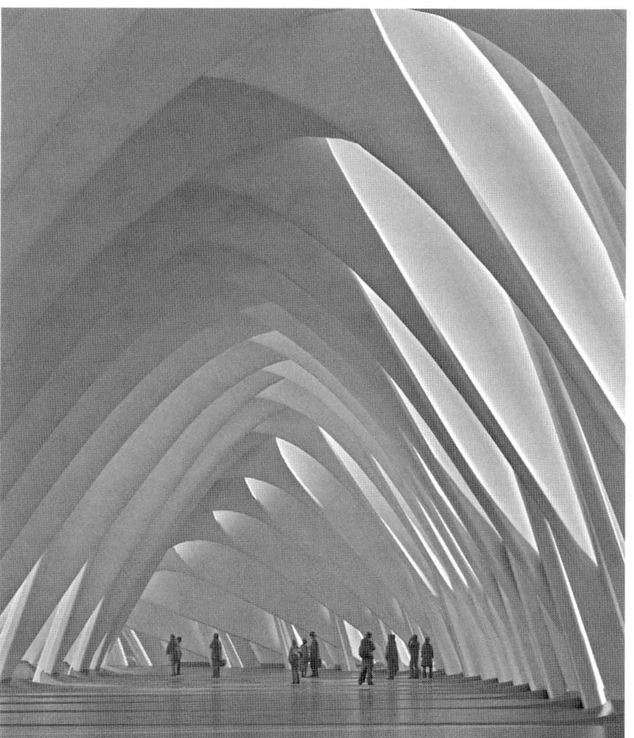

Figure 113 Parametric Gothic, interior; authors: Gerry Cruz, Spyridon Kaprinis, Natalie Popik, Maria Tsironi; tutor: Patrick Schumacher

Figure 114 Correlating fabric differentiation with topographic differentiation, Bilbao Masterplan, Zaha Hadid Architects, 2004

Niklas Luhmann has emphasized this phenomenon – which he has termed the 'self-programming'[67] of the individual art work – that might be observed within all artistic work that is concerned with the elaboration of complex artefacts, whether they be elaborate paintings, musical compositions or literary works. Luhmann takes account of 'the necessity that manifests itself in the artwork'. He elaborates: 'In this sense, creating a work of art ... generates the freedom to make decisions on the basis of which one can continue one's work. The freedoms and necessities one encounters are entirely ... consequences of decisions made within the work. The necessity of certain consequences one experiences in one's work ... is not imposed ... but results from the fact that one began, and how. This entails the risk of running into insoluble problems ...'.[68]

Every designer knows how a design-trajectory can lead to a dead end, can fail to 'work', or remain unresolved. The elegance implied here – elegance on top of complexity – is a tall order, and cannot be secured in advance. Although the formal heuristic of Parametricism provides procedural guidelines, and although we can come up with many concrete recipes – for example, the employment of global distortions to cohere a field of fragments etc – the elegant result cannot be guaranteed as the complexity of the problem increases. With increasing complexity the maintenance of elegance becomes increasingly demanding. Complexity and elegance stand in a relation of precarious mutual amplification: a

67 Niklas Luhmann, *Art as a Social System*, Stanford University Press (Stanford, CA), 2000, p 204.
68 Ibid, pp 203–4.

relation of ever more improbable mutual enhancement, ie, mutual amplification with increasing probability of collapse.

Why should we strive for this increasingly difficult elegance? Does this elegance serve a purpose beyond itself?

The overriding headline here is: ***orientation within complex scenes.*** Contemporary architectural briefs are marked by a demand for ever more complex and simultaneous programmatic provisions to be organized within ever more complex urban contexts. Elegance allows for an increased programmatic complexity to coincide with a relative reduction of visual complication by means of integrating multiple elements into a coherent and continuous formal and spatial system. The general challenge is to find modes of composition that can articulate complex arrangements and relationships without losing legibility and the capacity to orient users. Elegance as defined here signifies this capacity to articulate complex life-processes in a way that can maintain overall comprehension, legibility and continuous orientation within the composition.

The ability to navigate dense and complex urban environments is an important aspect of our overall productivity today. Post-Fordist network society demands that we keep continuously connected and informed. We cannot afford to beaver away in isolation. In order to remain relevant and productive we need to network and coordinate our efforts with what everybody else is doing. Everything must communicate with everything else. In terms of urban environments this implies that we should be able to see and participate in as many events as possible, always exposed to further choices to select the next move. This is facilitated best, if the visual field presents a rich, ordered scene of manifold offerings that also provides anticipations of what lies behind the currently visible layer. The speed and confidence with which one cam make new experiences and connections is decisive. Parametricism enables the design of environments that facilitate such a hyper-connectivity.

An elegant, legible scene should deliver what it promises, ie, an efficient, physical organization of the vital life-processes must be assumed. Its elegant articulation is a further boon to its efficiency. Aesthetic values and performance values engage in mutual amplification. Finally, if we consider real urban scenes rather than rendered designs, the smooth functioning of the framed life-processes is an indispensable ingredient of the scene's ultimate elegance. The demanded 'correlation of the subsystems' ultimately includes the layer of the anticipated or observed communicating users. That is why many current avant-garde design research projects – and in future all state-of-the-art mainstream projects – incorporate user simulations within their design models.[69]

Architecture's societal function is the innovative ordering of social communication via spatial frames, on an ever more complex, more productive level. Opportunities for innovation lie primarily in the domain of enhanced phenomenological and semiological articulation. All three aspects of architecture's task – the organizational, the phenomenological and the semiological project – enhance architecture's functionality. The latter two rely also on aesthetic appeal to fulfil their function.[70] Beauty conquers everything, as the promise of a higher level of vitality. It can be sustained only if it delivers on its promise. The elegance that expresses complex order can – in principle – deliver vital, productive spaces of interaction within Post-Fordist network society. For the foreseeable future the physiognomy of these spaces might therefore be best determined by the heuristics of Parametricism.

How can we anticipate what might lie beyond Parametricism? What lies beyond Parametricism cannot yet be foreseen. It depends on the further evolution of world society. World society is an evolving, open, indeterminate project, with many degrees of freedom. In order to try to anticipate what might lie beyond Parametricism we would have to speculate about latent utopias within world society rather than only speculating about architecture's possible responses to society's manifest demands or emergent tendencies. It might be the art system's societal function to confront us with speculative anticipations of different, possible futures (although this is perhaps too big a job for any system). Art – *not* architecture/design – was set free from all immediate, tangible tasks. Only the art system opens a clearing, an unconstrained platform for freewheeling, experimental, 'irresponsible' communications. All other function systems observe these latter-day court jesters, to find inspiration

69 The author has made this an a priori imposition for all of his AADRL design projects.

70 Aesthetic appeal can be distinguished from perceptual palpability and legibility. It is the first point of access for the users of architecture that operates via their emotions, perceptions and cognitions. Organization operates via the physical distancing and channelling of bodies. Here aesthetic values are *not* coming into play. However, the design process is still guided by aesthetic values – the formal heuristics of the style employed – *even* with respect to the organizational project. All interim design stages, including organizational diagrams, are subject to the quest for formal resolution. Otherwise the design process would have to admit random decisions because forms can never be derived on the basis of functional criteria and arguments alone. Completion on the basis of formal/aesthetic principles is advantageous in comparison with random choices. One very basic advantage is the avoidance of indecision. More importantly, general aspects of organizational functionality might be condensed into aesthetic values that allow the designer to do the right thing without too much analytical effort.

or warning. The art system's platforms of unconstrained experimentation can be used, on occasion, by the other function systems, not least by avant-garde architecture and design. But unlike artists, designers have to return from these excursions to make tangible contributions that have a chance to work in the near future, if not in the immediate here and now. This puts a definite brake on the forward fancy of architects. Architectural innovation cannot substitute itself for the trajectory of overall society. It must stay close to the ground. The science, politics and economics that architecture must recognize are the real science, real politics and real economics of today. The avant-garde must not be confused with science fiction or utopian speculation. The science, politics and economics that *avant-garde* architecture must relate to are those real tendencies on the ground that state-of-the-art scientific, political and economic discourses identify as most promising. The architectural avant-garde must not attempt to substitute itself for these discourses. It does so only at peril of escaping from the autopoiesis of architecture. The revolution, when it comes, will surprise us all, including artists and the most radical of radicals. Revolutionary periods – inherently – arrive unannounced. The theory of architectural autopoiesis thus suggests that – until then – cumulative design research within the broad framework of Parametricism is the most sensible 'order of the day' for the architectural avant-garde.

12. Epilogue – The Design of a Theory

The Autopoiesis of Architecture is the result of a comprehensive sense-making effort by a practising architect. It is the theoretical rationalization of the architect/author's ongoing practical investments and commitments. As such it has succeeded. The architect/author's practice is staying on course. This is no coincidence as this course was forged and refined in parallel with its theoretical reflection. The architect/author practises what he preaches because he set out to theorize/preach what he practises, ie, the architect/author's theory was informed by his practice and his practice was a theory-led practice all along. The result of this architect's theoretical reflections presents itself in the form of a comprehensive theoretical edifice that – although based on an elaborate discourse analysis of the discipline – takes on a normative shape and intervenes within the contemporary debate about the future direction of architecture.

Is there such a debate? Before such a debate can commence we need to answer a fundamental question concerning our discursive culture: should we – the participants/protagonists of architecture – commit/submit ourselves to a collective debate arguing about *the* broad direction in which architecture should progress?[1] Or are we saying: anything goes, let every individual architect do as he/she pleases (without demanding a coherent account of the rationality of the practice pursued)?[2] The very existence as well as the whole edifice of *The Autopoiesis of Architecture* are premised on the understanding that the latter stance is not an option. The author of the theory of architectural autopoiesis must therefore take a position against indifference and the live-and-let-live tolerance that suffocates debate. The unity of architecture requires *comprehensive* debate. The unity of a hegemonic style requires *conclusive* debate. Coherent practice requires that debates are concluded to become premises for decisive action. The underlying sensibility and thrust of the arguments about Parametricism as new global, epochal style are based on the desire to enhance the power of collective discourse over all individual

1 The well-founded argument about the direction in which architecture should progress requires the prior clarification of architecture's societal function.

2 Which of the two attitudes is in need of a comprehensive theory?

endeavours. This implies a shift in discursive sensibility, a reduction of anything goes tolerance and an insistence on forging a coherent, collective movement forward. However, the appropriate level of discursive tolerance is itself a historical variable. The theory of architectural autopoiesis recognizes the value of discursive tolerance at certain historical junctures. During periods of crisis – requiring a radical rethinking of the discipline – discursive tolerance must be very high. A freewheeling brainstorming is required to break intellectual deadlock. During a period when the established wisdom of the discipline is bankrupt, all heresies are welcome. After a series of new approaches have emerged and gained support they might be pursued in parallel in a competitive battle of ideas. Selection follows mutation. Now the name of the game is to find the most productive way forward. The debate sharpens. Mutual critique takes over from mutual inspiration. Finally, the best outcome is for one of the competing tendencies to win hegemony. Moving forward in one coherent direction allows for cumulative design research and a new, coherent mainstream practice. This is more effective than fragmenting into several criss-crossing trajectories where different projects might end up obstructing each other.

Cumulative design research and a new, coherent mainstream practice require that fundamental premises have been settled (and need not be revisited every Monday morning). There will be less interest in heresies and less patience with those who keep going back to fundamentals.

If the character of the discipline's discursive culture is a historical variable, where do we stand in this respect today? In 2011 the discursive culture of architecture needs to sharpen decisively in order to accelerate the collective discursive formation of a strong, maturing, unified style. Parametricism is pushing forward with cumulative research and needs to develop the confidence and intransigence it takes decisively to reshape mainstream practice.

During the 1970s, after 50 years of cumulative research, development and implementation under the auspices of Modernism, the discipline entered a deep crisis. The situation demanded a decisive shift in discursive culture and called forth a different cut of protagonists, with different abilities and sensibilities. Radical questions and experiments were the order of the day. In the previous era the discipline had assimilated itself closer and closer to science. Now it turned towards artistic practice as a conducive domain with which to affiliate. Radical philosophical reflection and free experimentation were indeed necessary to find ways forward in a situation where all accumulated competencies, as well as the principles they were built upon, were bankrupt. New paths had to be charted. It is the conviction of the author, and the two Volumes of *The Autopoiesis of Architecture* attest to this, that this period of deep reflection and experimentation has resulted in the emergence of a new, viable paradigm the basis of which is a new, shared design research practice. This new avant-garde practice is inaugurating a new era of disciplined, cumulative research. However, the fact that the ethos of freewheeling play, hostile to all demands for rigour, still lingers, perhaps even as dominant ethos, is holding the discipline back. The shift from revolutionary to cumulative research/practice requires, once more, a decisive shift of discursive culture, a new ethos and indeed a change in the cast of characters that are thriving within the discipline. A live-and-let-live attitude in this respect is not an option. It is precisely the infinite tolerance and acceptance of every idiosyncratic self-expression, a corollary of architecture's assimilation to art, that needs to be broken at the current historical juncture. The historical justification for this freewheeling discursive culture has vanished. A new culture and ethos need to win hegemony, and take responsibility for architecture's role within society. It is the author's conviction that a more frank and sharp discursive culture would facilitate the ongoing convergence of intellectual and creative efforts that is under way under the banner of Parametricism.

The theory of architectural autopoiesis is a comprehensive, unified theory of architecture. Within it, Parametricism is theorized as architecture's best bet today. Despite the confident display of both the style and the wider theoretical edifice, the author is conscious of their contingency. Both are theoretical constructs that either live or die within the ongoing autopoiesis of architecture. They live by being taken up, connected to, built upon and modified in the ongoing discourse and practice. *The Autopoiesis of Architecture* presents itself as a ***post-metaphysical*** theoretical edifice that sets itself contingent as a designed construct that asks to be judged not primarily by its rather abstract premises but on the basis of its comprehensiveness, internal coherence and mnemotechnic elegance as aspects of its capacity to make sense of what goes on in architecture. It should also be judged by the plausibility and coherence of the practical conclusions it suggests.

Within a ***constructivist*** epistemological framework – as it has been adopted here – it is understood that reality and knowledge are constructed rather than being discovered. Reality and knowledge are constructed within autopoietic systems of communication. Autopoietic systems of communication are self-organizing historical machines that are evolving without being under the control of any preconceived goal. They are beyond the control of any deliberate, controlling agency. This must be remembered despite the fact that goal-setting self-descriptions might circulate within this autopoiesis. The overall trajectory always exceeds any such aspirations. The individual communications that occur within these historical machines are individually attributed to individual persons, or organizations, although it should be understood to what extent the respective communication was framed and prestructured by the specific language and schemata provided by the specific social communication system within which the individual communication is embedded. These attributions of individual responsibility/authorship are themselves following a general schema – the schema of individual attribution – and are in this sense constructed. Theories – to the extent that they are contained within a single book – are individual communications, at least initially. As such they can and must be attributed to its author, without however forgetting the above reminder concerning the inevitable prestructuredness of all communications. On the basis of the constructivist epistemology adopted here we must therefore be aware of and reflect the fact that theories are constructions in two senses. They are constructions in the sense that they are preformed by the social construction that is the discourse they are embedded in, and they are constructions as they are constructed by the individual author, who has selected the themes, sharpened the definition of the terms employed, set up the contrasts with theoretical predecessors and opponents, selected and fitted the evidence, constructed the arguments, drawn the conclusions, organized and articulated the final presentation etc. All these aspects of the development of the theory involve (hopefully conscious rather than unconscious) theoretical decisions that are in many ways analogues to design decisions. In this second sense, therefore, a theory is a designed construction. The more conscious, explicit and reflected this design of the theory is, the more mature, sophisticated and effective should be the result.

This notion of designing a theory is unusual. It seems to infringe upon the supposed objectivity of the theory. Therefore the concept of design is usually only admitted with respect to the final presentation of the work. However, the concept of design offers a pertinent conceptualization for aspects of the theoretical work from its very inception. The build up of the theoretical edifice requires many design decisions, as indicated above. This statement is more than a loose metaphor.

The theory of architectural autopoiesis adopts a distinct theoretical edifice: Niklas Luhmann's social systems theory. This edifice is here adopted and adapted to serve as global theoretical framework for the analysis of architecture. Within this general framework, a distinct and detailed analysis of architecture as a self-referentially closed system of communications is being elaborated. This analysis is based on the author's own insider observations, readings, as well as his own communication and design practice. The analysis is guided by the rich theoretical apparatus provided by Luhmann's social systems theory. From the perspective of architectural theory, this apparatus has the status of a meta-theory that guides the design of the theory of architectural autopoiesis. The concrete analysis of architecture as autopoietic system of communications results in a rational reconstruction rather than a mere description of the discipline. The theory establishes a system of categories and theses that are bound to be read as normative. More than that, the theory of architectural autopoiesis also takes an explicit position within contemporary architecture. It evaluates prevalent architectural tendencies with respect to their contribution to architecture's actual and potential performance within contemporary world society. The criterion here is a tendency's adaptive pertinence with respect to fulfilling architecture's societal function within Post-Fordist network society.

This epilogue is trying to reflect the elaboration of the theory of architectural autopoiesis as a process of theory design. It therefore confronts the elaborated theory with theoretical choices that have *not* been pursued but might have been. This might – in a final turn of circumspection – throw further light on what *has* been done here.

12.1 Theoretical Foundation: Communication Theory vs Historical Materialism?

The first point of confrontation concerns the most fundamental base categories adopted here. About 12 years ago the author – after many years of intellectual investment in Historical Materialism – decided to leave Marxism behind to ground the elaboration of his intended unified theory of architecture in Luhmann's social systems theory. The shift turned out to be very productive. A lot of new insights were facilitated without losing sight of the insights that had accumulated while thinking about architecture within the Marxist framework. The fact that Luhmann's system could take over and recuperate most of these accumulated insights suggests that the two systems might be philosophically compatible. A creative synthesis between the two systems might be possible.[3] But this is not the task of an architectural theoretician, and thus no option for the author. The detailed theoretical elaboration of a single, unified theory for architecture had to involve the decision to abandon Marx's system and terminology, and with it many of the author's prior theoretical formulas. Luhmann's system offered so many new,

3 In the section *Parametricism as Epochal Style* (section 11.1), the theory of architectural autopoiesis effects the integration of Marxist categories of historical periodization without compromising the integrity of the Luhmannian theoretical edifice.

detailed conceptual resources that the choice, once posed, seemed inevitable. Here and now, however, with (the initial draft of) the unified theory of architecture fully formulated, there arises the opportunity to confront the work, once more, with Marx's most profound intuition.

Niklas Luhmann's fundamental base category is the category of communication. Everything social is understood as communication. This move provides an enormously powerful theoretical abstraction/reduction. What does this abstraction abstract from? In Luhmann's terms, it abstracts from human beings as psychic and organic systems. In Marxist terms, it seems to abstract from the fundamental material conditions of social reproduction. From a Marxist perspective, Luhmann's approach seems to be a form of idealism. This is not accurate. Although not elaborated within the theory, the theory is fully compatible with a materialist philosophy. The origins of Luhmann's theory include cybernetics, artificial intelligence, complexity theory etc. These paradigms indicate that communications are material processes. Within sociology it is not only scientifically respectable, but indeed necessary, to abstract from many of the immediate material conditions of communication. The question here can only be: is it sensible to abstract from all material conditions of communication? For instance, we might ask: how can Foucault's insights into the material aspects of discursive formations be integrated? By expanding the concept of communication to include physical artefacts such as clinics as premises for acts like health checks. The theory of architectural autopoiesis is precisely the locus where some of these Foucauldian insights are being integrated within Luhmann's edifice.

There *is* indeed a compelling plausibility in abstracting from the materiality of our existence. Within our contemporary life all problems are problems of communication. Everybody's relationship with the material world is mediated by social communication. This also applies to our most basic, material needs as organisms. If we are wounded or sick, we need to find and communicate with medical staff within the medical system. To find shelter from the elements we need to communicate in order to gain access to buildings. If we are hungry we need to communicate: within the family, within the economy etc. If we want to move across space and overcome distance our problems are social problems, ie, the problems associated with travel: the price of travel, congestion, security controls etc. All material problems are always mediated by social systems. The difficulty to overcome is always a difficulty of communication, a social constraint: no health insurance, no right of access, no friends, no money, no ticket, no passport. It seems reality already abstracts from the materiality of our life situations. In this sense

Luhmann's theoretical abstraction – adopted within the theory of architectural autopoiesis – seems pertinent. It is an abstraction performed by the the real social life process itself.

But what is driving the evolution of social systems? According to Luhmann, the most general problem formula for social systems is 'coping with complexity'. Increasing (self-generated) societal complexity is being coped with via system differentiation and the build up of internal complexity. However, this formula remains overly abstract. What is the *advantage* of building up complexity? Marx's answer is that the advantage must be – in the last analysis – the social system's productivity, ie, its capacity to advance material (re)production. Marx's base category and axiom of productivity provides the immediate plausibility that Luhmann's problem formula is lacking. It directly relates to the material conditions of social life. The concept of productivity is posited here as the ***ultimate evolutionary attractor*** and therefore deserves to be the ultimate criterion of all societal evaluations. This concept of productivity cannot be narrowly defined in terms of the production of material plenty. Two further factors have to be incorporated in an updated concept of productivity: working conditions and ecological sustainability.

According to Marx's Historical Materialism, historical stages must be distinguished in terms of *modes of production* (rather than in terms of modes of societal differentiation). 'A certain mode of production, or industrial stage, is always combined with a certain mode of co-operation, or social stage, and this mode of co-operation is itself a productive force.'[4] That means that the productivity of a society is not only a matter of society's economy, although the issue surfaces in the economy. There is no implication that the economy 'determines' the structure of the other function systems or of society as a whole, even if we assume 'productivity' to be the ultimate endgame and 'coping with complexity' as its most immediate proxy. The achievement of productivity gains is a matter of the successful coevolution[5] of all interdependent, autopoietic function systems. The economy itself has no monopoly over the category of productivity. Also, the economy's code of profitability measures productivity only obliquely. Profitability leaves out key externalities that would have to be incorporated into a substantial notion of productivity

4 Karl Marx & Friedrich Engels, 'The German Ideology', in: L Easton & K Guddat (Eds), *Writings of the Young Marx on Philosophy and Society*, Doubleday (New York), 1967, p 421.

5 For Marx, as for Luhmann, the historical process is a process that should be compared to the evolution rather than to the deterministic processes of physics. Both Marx and Luhmann favour functional explanations over causal explanations.

that can serve as fundamental base category for both the analysis of history and for giving orientation into the future.[6]

Although this cannot be worked through here, it should be possible to align Luhmann's social systems theory with (an updated) Historical Materialism. The author's intuition is that the updated base category of productivity can be slipped in underneath the theory of social systems. The extensions of Luhmann's and Marx's historical periodization coincide sufficiently. (The stage of capitalism coincides with the epoch of functionally differentiated society.) The category of productivity could be given the status of a meta-theoretical base category without giving the economic system an absolute priority over the other great function systems of society. On the other hand, it has to be recognized that not all the services of the different function systems are of equal urgency in the short run. It should be possible for social systems theory to give up the symmetry between function systems in order to incorporate the Marxian insight concerning the relative importance of the economy – for instance, in comparison to the art system – for the (ultimately material) reproduction of society. A general ranking of the function systems in terms of importance or urgency is not possible. Since all function systems make necessary provisions for society's reproduction so that it can continue on its accomplished level of complexity/productivity, the most urgent service will be the service that has been somehow lacking or compromised. Legal order becomes most urgent in a situation where legal order has been compromised. Mass media services become most urgent where the mass media are being suppressed. Life, dependent upon material plenty, and a worthwhile, contemporary life, dependent on the enjoyment of material plenty in freedom, security and charity, requires that all autopoietic function systems continue to provide and progress. However, if the ultimate endgame is the (free, secure and charitable) *enjoyment of material plenty* and a society's attained *standard of living* its ultimate criterion of competitive evaluation, then it seems that the economy might be marked out somehow as being most immediately related to this ultimate criterion. This does not imply its higher importance or higher urgency under all circumstances. (All function systems are ultimately equally necessary to maintain and further upgrade total societal reproduction on the attained level of productivity.) It does, however, suggest the possibility of a certain theoretical ordering of the relationships between the various autopoietic function systems, an

6 The most immediate externalities that are often excluded from the economic concept of productivity – if operationalized in terms of profitability – are working conditions and ecological sustainability. The Marxist critique of capitalism reflects this fact.

ordering that highlights the contribution every function system makes to the functioning of the economy.

This might take the form of ordering all function systems according to Marx's base vs superstructure distinction. The consequences of such a theoretical decision are not immediately clear. Would the autopoiesis of architecture belong to the base or to the superstructure? Or does the mainstream belong to the base and the avant-garde to the superstructure? Its discourse analysis and rational reconstruction as autopoietic function system could remain more or less as presented within the two volumes of *The Autopoiesis of Architecture*. Perhaps its services to the economy in general and its ability to accommodate and frame the high productivity communications within advanced business organizations would have received even more attention.[7] References to Post-Fordism and Post-Fordist network society as the latest/current stage of capitalist, functionally differentiated society would sit more easily within a materialist social systems theory so theorized.

Productivity is the base criterion for the total societal process. As long as there were different competing societies, productivity was the fundamental, long-term selection criterion of the historical process, ie, its evolutionary attractor. Within a single world society there is no longer any sense in which one society is selected over another, but within each subsystem ways forward are competing with each other. Within each subsystem, the pursued aims can be achieved more or less time efficiently. This can be recognized by a generalized concept of productivity as the unity of the difference of political productivity, legal productivity, scientific productivity, economic productivity, architectural productivity etc. Each subsystem's services impact the economy as the primary site for the advancement of material life. To the extent to which these specialized productivities can be somehow summed up[8] we might speak of overall societal productivity. The specific productivity of each function system indirectly contributes to economic productivity, architectural productivity etc. The economy is the only subsystem of society where productivity can be measured because it is the only communication system in which the specialized medium of communication is fundamentally quantitative. Economic productivity thus makes overall societal productivity indirectly measurable. Economic

7 The theory of architectural autopoiesis indeed emphasizes the function-type of work environments as one of the key arenas where architecture's adaptive pertinence must be tested and upgraded.

8 There can be no more than a qualitative comparison of two or more societies along a series of incommensurable dimensions. A plausible quantitative arithmetic that would allow us to add up special productivities is not to be expected.

productivity depends on the productivity of all other autopoietic function systems. It might thus serve as an indicator for overall societal productivity. These hints must suffice here to give a sense of the author's intention to seek out lines of theorizing along which the premises of Marxism can be integrated into social systems theory.

12.2 The Theory of Architectural Autopoiesis as Unified Theory of Architecture

The theory of architectural autopoiesis proceeds by means of a comprehensive discourse analysis. This analysis is being conducted by an active participant ordering his observations, experiences and readings by means of the distinct conceptual grid adopted. On this analytical basis, a comprehensive theoretical edifice is being *constructed* that claims to explicate the totality of all things architectural. The claim to constitute a theoretical edifice relies on the elaborate effort to integrate all key concepts into a close-knit network of interlocking definitions and mutually supportive propositions (theses). The result is a unified theory of architecture that integrates various partial theories – a theory of architecture's societal function, a theory of the avant-garde, the demarcation of the discipline, aesthetic theory, media theory, a theory of the design process etc – into a coherent theoretical edifice. This theoretical edifice aims rationally to reconstruct the actual system of architectural communications. The systematic nature of the theoretical edifice is thus meant to reflect and enhance the inner coherence of architecture as integral *system* of communications.

The most fundamental premise of the theory of architectural autopoiesis is the thesis that architecture is one of the great, autopoietic function systems that – according to Luhmann's social systems theory – together constitute the primary social structure of contemporary world society. Luhmann's social systems theory projects a functionalist paradigm. Instead of merely trying to pin down isolated cause-effect relations between observed phenomena and aiming for causal explanations, the functionalist research paradigm tries to explicate observed communication structures in terms of their integration and functional contribution to an encompassing system which in turn collaborates and functions within an even larger system, and ultimately within evolving world society. The theory adopts a problem focused perspective. The aim of this problem focused, functionalist research agenda is not so much the precise reproduction of isolated effects as the identification of the systemic problems or challenges certain communication structures respond to – always considered within the double-context of the overall architectural system *and* the overarching system of society. On this basis functional equivalents and thus potential alternative routes of system viability can be projected. Thus the theoretical framework in general and the fundamental premise in particular, ie, the premise that architecture is one of the great function systems of world society, steer the analysis towards the functional explication of all identified structural features of architecture's autopoiesis. The typical question is always: which challenge is being responded to here? Which problem is being solved by the communication structure in question? And then: which consequent new problems and challenges are now posed? This kind of questioning leads to the explication of architecture's specific communication structures in terms of their contribution to architecture's overall societal performance. This explication then serves as a basis for critical evaluations and confident programmatic proclamations with respect to the direction contemporary architecture should take.

Within the overarching theoretical edifice – Luhmann's functionalist social systems theory – all prevalent features of architecture's autopoiesis are theoretically reinterpreted and integrated. This leads to a series of specific theoretical components:

- a theory of architectural theory
- a theory of the architectural avant-garde
- a theory of the discipline's (self-)demarcation
- a theory of the discipline's historical emergence
- a theory of form and function as architecture's lead-distinction
- a theory of utility and beauty as architecture's double code
- a theory of aesthetic values
- a theory of architectural styles
- a theory of architecture's medium of communication
- a theory of architecture's societal function
- a theory of architecture's organizational, phenomenological and semiological tasks
- a theory of the design process
- a theory concerning architecture's relationship to politics
- a theory concerning a new epochal style: Parametricism

Many of these theoretical components might convince on account of their individual plausibility or individual resonance with experience. This might perhaps be the case with the theory of the avant-garde as evolutionary accelerator. The theory of styles as research programmes might also convince on account of its own merit. Other theoretical components might – if taken in isolation – remain largely counterintuitive. For example, the insistence that architecture commences with the

Renaissance or the insistence that architecture is sharply demarcated against art, both seem to violate widely cherished presumptions. However, as soon as it is understood that architecture requires architectural theory and a compelling medium to fulfil its societal function of innovation, the thesis that architecture commences in the Renaissance gains traction: architecture as autopoietic system emerges together with the invention of perspective (allowing for comprehensive design speculation on paper) and the first architectural treatises (disseminated via the new medium of print). In a similar way the promotion of Parametricism as new epochal style gains traction on the basis of media theory, the theory of the avant-garde and the theory of styles. To take these subtheories one by one, each on its own plausibility or implausibility, misses the point. The various theories listed above have to be understood in their relation as interlocking and collaborating components of a coherent edifice. In each other's immediate company, the subtheories are mutually illuminating. Through their collaboration, all subtheories gain credibility. They become compelling to the extent to which they participate in the reconstruction of architecture's global rationality.

The key to a full appreciation of the theory of architectural autopoiesis is to engage with its ambition to construct an integral and comprehensive theoretical edifice that is supposed to reflect the systemic totality of architecture. That such a totality exists as a single, self-referentially enclosed and internally coherent system of communications is the point of departure of the whole theoretical endeavour. The cross-referenced and correlated components of the theory correspond to the collaborating subsystems, institutions and communication structures of architecture understood as integral communication system.

The theoretical re-presentation of the various communication structures should serve as their reinvigorating recuperation. Most of these communication structures had been identified and named before. Reflexive descriptions are a feature of all modern function systems. The naming of emerging communication structures serves their further promotion. For example, during the 19th century, the identification of ***styles*** as structures through which architectural history progresses led to the active search for a new style that would advance architecture to the next level meeting the challenges of the industrial age. The explicit positing of the need for a modern style as necessary ingredient of architecture's development played its productive part in the eventual emergence of Modernism as successful style of the age. The retrospective identification of the heroic promoters of Modernism as historical ***avant-garde*** strengthened the resolve of the 1970s' neo-avant-garde to pursue its radical agendas against the ongoing hegemony of mainstream

Modernism. These examples show how the reflexive identification of communication structures can enhance these structures. However, any explicit exposure implies exposure to criticism. Within the polemical discursive culture of modern society any reflexive identification is likely to trigger a backlash. This is not necessarily counterproductive. All theoretical convergences are achieved via controversy. The more controversies have been worked through and overcome, the more robust is the tendency that survived and absorbed those controversies. The same applies to the progress of Parametricism.

12.3 Notes on the Architecture of the Theory

Beyond the important emphasis on the theoretical freedom (design freedom) and on the resultant contingency of the choices made, the statement that theories are designed constructions is stating the potential for an analogy between theory design and architectural design that can be fruitfully elaborated by probing the applicability of concepts like design world, organization, articulation, elegance etc.

The analogy between architecture and systematic thinking is not new. It has often been applied to philosophical systems by way of referring to the architecture of the system. Thus phrases like 'the theoretical edifice' or 'the architecture of the theory' are rather well established. 'The architecture of the theory' is understood to refer to the extent to which a theoretical construct is an integrated, ordered whole with features like hierarchy, symmetry and a sense of completeness. This traditional version of the analogy did not emphasize the aspect of design as contingent decision making, because this concept of design freedom and contingent decision making was not prevalent within Classical architecture. The analogy was originally trying to convey a sense of natural and necessary order. Classical architecture imposed a narrow repertoire of schemata, and each schema came with prescriptions for its appropriate institutional application. Similar rigidities operated in the domain of philosophy. That is why the analogy made sense. The old analogy was already elaborated to some extent: there was the idea of *grounding* a philosophical system, and the idea of *building* onto *solid foundations*.[9] There was further the utilization of the distinction between *structure* and *ornament*, the notion of a *pyramid of concepts* and the analogy between *pillars* and arguments as *supports*.

9 This long-standing utilization of architectural metaphors and ordering tropes has been investigated by Mark Wigley through the writings of Jacques Derrida. See Mark Wigley, *The Architecture of Deconstruction – Derrida's Haunt*, MIT Press (Cambridge, MA), 1993.

In the meantime the underlying idea of an essential, or necessary, natural order disappeared both in architecture and in philosophy. In both domains the deployed ordering patterns became more complex and varied, so that if we look back at both older architectures and older philosophical systems we are struck by the seemingly obsessive insistence upon certain formal devices like symmetry, repetition and clean orders of subsumption. We perceive these patterns with suspicion, as implausible formalist straitjackets that must do violence to the content. However, we might expect a later generation that has further expanded the repertoire of recognized conceptual ordering devices to look back at our theoretical productions with a similar sense of pity for the naivety with which we place confidence in the formal devices we deploy. However, this reflection, although a heuristically healthy invitation to look further for ordering options, does not allow us to jump out of our straitjacket altogether. Thus we might as well start to see the positive achievements and enabling characteristics of our current theory design world or panoply of conceptual ordering devices. Once we have gone through the loop of epistemological reflection on the revealing-concealing dependence on ordering tropes, we keep this loop as latent option in readiness, with permanent alert. But we also have to move forward with our specific theoretical ambitions, and then the deployment of architecture as the discipline of spatial organization and articulation becomes a potentially fertile source domain of analogical transference for any theory building, including the theory of architecture.

One of the primary services that theoretical architectures render resides in their mnemotechnic economy and navigability. On this count, the degree to which the network of concepts and theorems can be overlooked by means of mental maps becomes a criterion that is independent of the number and final utility of all the theses and conclusions that might be drawn from the theory in question. This implies that the build up of conceptual complexity should proceed with an acute alertness towards the legibility of the conceptual architecture as well as towards the economy of conceptual means. The concern with a legible theoretical architecture cannot be divorced from the more 'superficial' aspects of how the text is segmented into chapters, because this more outward organization of the text should be instrumentalized as an opportunity to make the structure of the theory conspicuous.

The most conspicuous outward structuring feature of *The Autopoiesis of Architecture* is the fact that it is split into two volumes, a white volume and a grey volume, each with its own subtitle. The white volume presents the result of the discourse analysis as theoretical framework, and the grey volume – although it continues to elaborate the framework – utilizes this framework to formulate agendas for architecture's future adaptive progress. This very strong articulation of the treatise into two volumes is being deliberately countered by imposing a continuous chapter numbering. Volume 1 ends with part 5 and Volume 2 starts with part 6. The same principle has been applied to the Theses. They form a continuous set: Volume 1 contains theses 1–24 and Volume 2 contains theses 25–60. The use of a three-level hierarchy – parts, sections and chapters – is another 'architectural' organizing device utilized here. The table of contents gives a synoptic overview. However, there is an additional reminder of the content hierarchy carried forward in the margin, so that within each chapter the reader is offered a convenient reminder of both the section title and the title of the part within which the chapter is framed. The use of chapter titles, in general, is a common quasi-architectural device. They bind the chapter's content into a common theme. The three-level hierarchy of titles establishes an order of subsumption in terms of levels of abstraction and generality. This helps to build up a mental map of the overall theoretical edifice and allows more detail to be absorbed and ordered. It is a primary mnemotechnical device. Three-level hierarchies are rather rare these days. The great system builders like Kant and Hegel used up to five levels in their content hierarchies.[10]

Another device used within *The Autopoiesis of Architecture* is the extraction of numbered theses. Theses are aligned with sections rather than parts or chapters because 11 theses seemed too small and 250 too large a number. The point of the theses is not only to supply another level of summary condensation for mnemotechnical convenience. Rather than rehearsing the conceptual system via key definitions and axioms, the theses are trying to extract substantial, potentially controversial statements that make a difference. The theses pull together the claims that give the theory of architectural autopoiesis its sharp edge and distinctiveness. Because their selection was not based on their respective systematic position and importance, they are just numbered in sequence producing a final list that is independent of the treatise's logical order of subsumption (content hierarchy).

A further, truly spatial ordering device is the extensive use of tables and matrices. This device is utilized here to conspicuously order the concepts and statements of the theory. Most important and most prominent is *Appendix 1* of Volume 1: *Comparative Matrix of Societal*

10 For instance, Immanuel Kant's *Kritik der reinen Vernunft* has five levels: Abteilung (part), Buch (book), Hauptstück (main segment), Abschnitt (section) and within these sections he lists several chapters.

Function Systems. It is a 10 x 10 matrix offering 100 content slots. The fact that the matrix is square and produces this round number of cells is not emphasized. There is certainly no numerology implied here. Neither is there any suggestion of a natural order with symmetry and completeness intended, as it is in Kant's table of judgements.[11] Quite the opposite is intended here, namely an indication of the fundamental artificiality and therefore arbitrariness and contingency of any conceptual system. On the horizontal axis of the matrix are plotted the key analytical categories by which the discourse analysis of architecture and its rational reconstruction are structured. Here the sequence from right to left mirrors (to a certain extent) a possible logical sequence by which the categories might be related to each other, building upon one another. That this sequence works rather well has been demonstrated in the concluding remarks of Volume 1 where this list of categories is utilized to formulate a condensed summary of the theory of architectural autopoiesis. Along the vertical axis of the matrix are listed the other autopoietic function systems that have all along been compared and related to the autopoiesis of architecture. The demonstration that their analyses can be brought under a single set of categories was Luhmann's great achievement and the starting point for the theoretical project presented in *The Autopoiesis of Architecture*.[12]

Another matrix offers yet another global summary view of the theory of architectural autopoiesis – this time in the context of a comparison with three great classic texts that had offered influential theoretical self-descriptions during earlier epochs. This matrix is attached here as Appendix 3: *The Autopoiesis of Architecture in the Context of Three Classic Texts*.

The theory of architectural autopoiesis is the only recent theory of architecture that presents itself as a comprehensive theoretical edifice. In terms of its comprehensive scope, systematicity and integration into an encompassing theory of society, the theory of architectural autopoiesis is indeed an altogether unique effort. Most of its conceptual organization was prefigured by Niklas Luhmann's grand edifice. Beyond the basic analytic grid Luhmann offered, his thinking in distinctions rather than isolated concepts and his preference for binary distinctions was adopted. The pervasiveness of the functional mode of explanation has already been referred to in the introduction to Volume 1.[13]

11 See Figure 54, chapter 8.6.2 *From Spatial Order to Conceptual Order*.

12 Luhmann, however, never published such a matrix, neither did he ever analyze architecture in these terms.

13 See Volume 1, section 0.3 *Functional vs Causal Explanations*.

What are the primary characteristics of a systematic work? Despite the ability to produce summary condensations and synoptic matrices of the kind referred to above, it is the recursive build up of the theory, ie, the continuous reutilization of the already established concepts throughout the further elaboration of the theory. This also implies that the different aspects and topics of the theory are theorized with the same set of concepts, respecting the same set of axioms. Thus the different aspects and topics become integrated subtheories of an encompassing unified theory. This implies two heuristic principles for the development of such a theoretical edifice: first, this implies the continuous effort to bring in, employ and thus enrich concepts/distinctions already defined earlier in the theory. Since a full theory is a network of interdependent distinctions rather than a linear sequence, it also implies the anticipation and preliminary employment of concepts/distinctions only fully elaborated later. Second, it implies the continuous confrontation of the different claims the theory makes. The theorems (claims) that are elaborated in one part are to be confronted and tested for compatibility with respect to all the other theorems derived or claims made in the other parts of the overall theory. The hallmark and great advantage of a theoretical edifice over and above, for example, a collection of essays is this level of explicit, worked through coherence. This also entails the ability to achieve an overall reduction in distinctions, terms and statements, made possible by their re-use in many contexts. Compared with essay collections, a systematic treatise thus achieves a relative reduction of conceptual complexity combined with a relative increase in its theoretical sensitivity and richness. This increase of sensitivity and richness is due to the fact that the overall apparatus serves as a probing checklist in each theoretical subdomain, thus making the theoretician more perceptive and allowing him/her to mine more insights and connections than otherwise, without accumulating contradictions. This process of confronting the different parts of the theory with each other, as well as the parallel process of confronting the theory with the ongoing experiences made in professional practice, or with the accumulating record of the history of architecture's autopoiesis, is far from complete. This must be an ongoing process of confrontation, modification, further systematization and refinement.

12.4 The Theory as the Result of Contingent Theory Design Decisions

This section of the book tries to trace how some of the key theoretical questions were decided: which options came into consideration at each juncture, and which arguments helped to determine the decision taken in each case. The author's experience with the design of the theory of architectural autopoiesis suggests that at the beginning theory-design decisions are as contingent or arbitrary as the initial design decisions in the case of architectural design. On what basis was it decided to design/construct[14] a general theory of architecture as autopoietic system of communications? Even with this first premise being settled, many different routes remain open. Just as is the case with the design of a large, complex building, the initial series of moves is largely arbitrary. There is usually a surplus of possibilities. Although initially rather arbitrary and unconstrained, the decisions made have consequences, they constrain all further moves. However, all the consequences of an early move can rarely be anticipated at the beginning. Therefore, backtracking and the revisiting of earlier decisions is to be expected. This applies to theory design as much as it applies to architectural design. (The experience of multiple starts induced the comparison with architectural design in the first place.) The very fact that certain key decisions had been reversed when difficulties arose in the elaboration of the edifice meant that theoretical propositions are not decided one by one on their individual merit but on the basis of their fit within an evolving theoretical edifice.

For example, there were two reversals with respect to the status of buildings as architectural communications. The theory of architectural autopoiesis, as it is being presented here, theorizes designed buildings as a special type of architectural communication: the final framing communications that the societal function system of architecture delivers to society. In the same way, all designed artefacts are to be regarded as framing communications that variously service all the different social systems within society. However, at an earlier stage in its development, the design of the theory assumed that buildings should be excluded from the definition of architecture. At that stage buildings were not included in the panoply of types of communications that make up the autopoiesis of architecture. They had instead been located within the relevant environment of architecture, as a primary domain of architecture's observations. Why did the author resist or hesitate to consider buildings as one more type of architectural communication? In order to understand this it might be useful to quote here a prior version of the manuscript,

14 Unlike the case of architecture proper, in the case of theory, design and construction are not separated, they coincide. This might serve as one more point of evidence to keep the metaphorical use of 'architecture' and 'design' separate from their literal use. Theory design questions in general are not architectural questions. They are not a part of architecture's societal function.

more precisely, a prior version of the epilogue.[15] Ironically, the author's first intuition had been to include buildings within the domain of communications. Then, this decision was temporarily reversed. At this interim stage, the following reflection was placed into the epilogue:

> Nothing compels us to exclude buildings here, and someone else might try to proceed with the design and construction of a general theory of architecture as autopoietic system of communications where all or some buildings are interpreted as architectural communications. The author is confident about this because he tried this and got quite far with it. In fact, although this is a rather fundamental decision that should have taken place at the beginning, the theoretical decision to exclude the buildings themselves from participating within the autopoiesis of architecture came rather late in the build up of the theory. The theory had started assuming that at least avant-garde buildings, as manifesto buildings, ought to be included among the communications that constitute the autopoiesis of architecture. The final decision[16] not to do so, is not due to the fact that we need to keep communication and object of communication apart. After all, most communications within society are communications about communications. There is nothing inherently wrong in considering buildings as communications within the discipline of architecture. Robin Evans' reminder that architects draw but do not build was a first indication to question the status of buildings as communications next to verbal communications, drawings, books and exhibitions. But this reminder was not in itself decisive, because – after all – some architects let draw rather than draw themselves just as they let build rather than building themselves. And the group of those who do not draw – or at least who no longer draw – includes the leading figures of the field that head large design studios and thus no longer have time to draw themselves. And both drawings and buildings are attributed to these figures in much the same way. The fact that buildings are heavy, physical objects rather than ephemeral events like most communications is also no decisive point. Architectural books, magazines and drawings are also physical objects. All communication proceeds via one or another material substrate, and this also includes the spoken word. Perhaps what excludes buildings is the fact that they are fixed to a specific location. However, this also cannot be decisive as this feature is shared by architectural exhibitions. The complexity (and thus potential ambiguity) of buildings is again shared with exhibitions as well as with books. The reason why buildings are excluded is twofold: on the one hand,

15 The idea of writing an epilogue dealing with the development of the theory as a theory design process with deliberate and therefore contingent theory design decisions had developed early on. The various attempts at designing/constructing the theory led to the reflective realization that theorizing is analogous to designing and that it would be useful to reveal this by documenting some of the design options and the considerations that led to certain theory design decisions.

16 In fact, this 'final decision' turned out to be only an interim decision.

published photographs of designed buildings can sufficiently substitute for the theoretical absence of the buildings themselves. This way the idea of architecture as autopoietic system of communications can be plausible without including the completed buildings. On the other hand, the completed buildings pose the following problem: they function within social systems other than the autopoiesis of architecture. For instance, school-buildings function within the education system, in particular for the particular social systems – the school – they accommodate. Buildings thus exist in architecture's environment. They are the object of architectural communications rather than being themselves architectural communications.[17]

Although such a theoretical arrangement could have been pursued further, the author was dissatisfied with this. The very broad concept of communication should also encompass buildings. Further, if buildings are the final services of architecture to society they should be communications because the services of all the other function systems Luhmann describes consist of communications: the collectively binding decisions that politics delivers to order and regulate the economy, the court decisions and legal arguments through which the legal system structures all social acts, the continuous updates of our shared world view which the system of the mass media delivers to us on a daily basis, all these are communications delivered to virtually all social systems of society. In the same way, the designed spaces that architecture delivers into society, to nearly all social systems, might be theorized as communications. This set up seemed indeed more coherent. Further, the author/architect's prior realization of the importance of articulation in architecture soon led to a re-evaluation of semiology and the semiological project in architecture. This aspect too implied that buildings/spaces should be theorized as communications, as framing communications that operate as permanently broadcast premises for the social interactions that are to unfold within their ambit. The difficulty that the completed spaces/buildings belong to the social systems they accommodate was overcome with the formula of the double-connectivity and double meaning of buildings as communications. They are special in that they connect both within architecture – they are visited and discussed as exemplars, as manifestos manifesting certain themes and styles – and are accommodated within their respective social system. In the first context they are attributed to the designer/architect, and in the second context they are attributed to the accommodated social system, ie, the client organization that commissioned and/or occupies the building. This

17 Quoted from unpublished, prior manuscript of *The Autopoiesis of Architecture*.

seemed to be a more satisfying arrangement and on this basis the further elaborations of the theoretical edifice proceeded.

Another story of theoretical recalibration can be told with respect to the distinction of avant-garde vs mainstream. It was obvious to the author – working for Zaha Hadid and teaching at the AA in London – that there is an avant-garde, ie, a special subsystem (sub-culture) within architectural discourse and design practice that is focused on pushing the boundaries of established practice, even if the term 'avant-garde' is only reluctantly applied by the protagonists of this subsystem. During the same period of theory design development, when buildings were excluded from the system of architectural communications, the autopoiesis of architecture was theorized as being restricted to the avant-garde. Since the avant-garde rarely builds, this made the exclusion of buildings less problematic. However, in principle the two theory decisions are independent. The main reason to consider restricting the autopoiesis of architecture to avant-garde architecture was that it seemed coherent with the emphasis on innovation and theory. Also, the avant-garde discourse seemed to be a distinct discourse. The distinction of avant-garde vs mainstream was treated as a theoretically sharpened, updated version of the distinction of architecture vs mere building. The distinction between science and its textbook dissemination seemed to offer an analogue. Only original, new science is science. In analogy one might say only original, new architecture is architecture.

Soon many drawbacks to this approach transpired. That it would constitute a very controversial thesis was *not* a deterrent. However, there were many genuine difficulties in attempting to construct a comprehensive theory on the premise that only avant-garde architecture is architecture. First of all, the avant-garde is a relatively recent phenomenon. The consequence would be that the autopoiesis of architecture started only in the 1920s. This consequence would have impoverished the theory too much. (The formula of architecture's refoundation during the 1920s is the way the theoretical edifice finally presented here registers the grain of truth that was contained in the otherwise implausible statement that architecture came into being during the 1920s.) Second, despite that fact that the distinction of architecture vs building offered a certain hook or connection back to aspects of the ongoing discourse, the formula 'architecture = avant-garde architecture' clearly drew the demarcation line too narrowly. Could the concept of architecture still be applied to Foster + Partners? To exclude this firm seemed difficult. To classify it as an avant-garde firm seemed equally implausible. An all too narrow definition of architecture also conflicts with the fundamental premise that architecture is one of the great function systems of society claiming exclusive and universal competency/ responsibility for an important societal requirement. Just as everybody participates in the economy, just as everybody's actions are under the continuous purview of the legal system, just as everybody has the right to vote, follow the debates of the political system and is subject to the collectively binding decisions that are made there, just as everybody updates his/her world view via the global mass media, so everybody is continuously communicating within the frames provided by architecture and design. At this point it is also important to stress that the communications within self-referentially enclosed function systems are not restricted to expert communications only. Although the expert discourses dominate the evolution of the function systems, in terms of their communication structures, non-expert communications utilize those communication structures in certain everyday contexts that belong to the respective function system's domain of competency. For instance, lay-people might engage in political discussions, or people might wonder about the legality of certain actions that concern them. In these situations their communications are guided by the respective codes of these function systems, ie, by the code conservative vs progressive in their political debates, and by the code legal vs illegal in their debates concerning the law. In the same way, the laity has occasion to communicate according to architecture/design's double code of utility and beauty. While the final destiny of architecture/design's services to society is their utilization in all social interactions[18] as their spatial/artefactual frames, the laity might have occasion to reflect and communicate about the appropriateness of these frames. On such occasions, the users of architecture/design communicate in terms of the function system of architecture/design. For instance, when friends go shopping together they have occasion to compare and discuss the elegance and functionality of certain dresses, or a client who has just moved into his/her new house might guide his/her friends to see and judge the elegance and functionality of the house and its various spaces. Depending on the sophistication of the respective clients of design and architecture, their reflections and communications might be informed by concepts and turns of arguments that had originated in the expert discourse of architecture/design but had since been disseminated by architectural/design critics operating via the mass media.

The more complex and nuanced the framing requirements of society are, the more sophistication is required, not only from the expert

18 Interactions are communications where the participating parties communicate within each other's presence.

discourse but also from the clients and consumers. Expert fashion designers design but the selection and combination of the designed items for the different communicative occasions is usually left to the consumer. In the same way, the spaces designed by architects are often furnished by the users themselves. In doing so the users try to inform themselves about the prevailing ideas and sensibilities emanating from the expert discourses. The pervasiveness of mediating fashion magazines and home decoration magazines testifies to the fact that the laity feels the need for expert guidance. Corporate clients usually engage professional architects and interior designers. The risk of blundering is here too high. However, the fact remains that the utilization of design cannot be fully controlled by the experts. This implies that for architecture/design to fulfil its societal function (parts of) its evolving expert discourse must be disseminated into society at large. The general societal utilization of the concepts of utility and beauty should be influenced by the latest expert discourses. Delays are inevitable here. The everyday applicability of concepts like beauty, elegance, style, and of even more specific concepts like Modern Functionalism, Minimalism, Eclecticism etc, testifies to the fact that architecture/design as a system of communications is not restricted to expert communications, just as the legal system, understood as a system of communications, is not restricted to expert communications. The ability to distinguish the basic relevancy criteria (codes) of society's great function systems is a communicative competency that is expected from any adult member of world society. A more sophisticated understanding of the contemporary state of the art within those different domains might be expected at least from the educated strata. All this implies that the restriction of the autopoiesis of architecture to the avant-garde would be highly problematic, or indeed untenable. The avant-garde discourse is an exclusive expert discourse. The mainstream discourse comprises both the mainstream expert discourse as well as the use of architecture's codes (as well as mainstream architectural ideas) by the lay users of architecture/design.

These reflections won the argument against narrowing architecture to its avant-garde segment. However, the distinction between avant-garde and mainstream was not discarded. It was incorporated within the theory and had to be functionally explained. Its function/advantage was identified as providing a mechanism of accelerated evolution.

Another question that arose was the question of how to relate the distinction of avant-garde vs mainstream with the Kuhnian distinction of revolutionary vs cumulative (design) research. The initial hypothesis was that the two distinctions might be aligned. This would imply that the avant-garde was a temporary phenomenon that only appears during revolutionary periods of paradigm shift, and should disappear during periods of work under a stable paradigm. This seemed to concur with the history of the first half of the 20th century. However, it seemed to be at odds with the history of the second half of the 20th century, and it was at odds with the author's desire to maintain his own avant-garde research affiliation while pushing the style of Parametricism into the mainstream. The question arose of how a continuous existence of an avant-garde segment can be theorized. The assumption in the final version of the theory is that the avant-garde is the permanent research segment of the discipline, engaging in revolutionary research during periods of paradigm shift and engaging in cumulative design research during periods in which new hegemonic style has been established. The assumption is that cumulative design research continues even if the new, hegemonic avant-garde style – Parametricism being the currently most promising candidate – has conquered mainstream professional practice. The assumption here is that the societal environment of Post-Fordist network society, in contrast to Fordist mass society, demands permanent innovation and thus justifies the continuous existence of an avant-garde segment.

How did this relate to the theory of styles as programmes of architecture? Initially it was considered to discard the nearly defunct concept of style(s) and to introduce Kuhn's much more popular and cool concept of paradigm in its stead. Then, however, the decision was made to retain and reconstruct the concept of style(s). The expected increase in controversy was welcome rather than a deterrent. The main advantage that settled the decision was that the concept delivers profound continuities with the history of architecture's autopoiesis. A second advantage is the concept's presence and potency outside the confines of the discipline, in society at large, mediated by the broader mass media discourses. The role of the avant-garde is to research, experiment and innovate within a style, or to develop a new style. In fact, the most original avant-garde research is concerned with the development of a new style. This idea can be reconciled with the thesis of the continuity of the avant-garde by introducing the distinction between epochal, transitional and subsidiary styles. During revolutionary periods, the avant-garde is engaged in the experimental production of new candidates for epochal styles. Some of those attempts converge to establish transitional styles. Such a transitional style might even make it into the mainstream. The example here is Postmodernism. Some of its protagonists such as Michael Graves moved with their style from the avant-garde into the mainstream segment of the discipline. However, despite Postmodernism's success, avant-garde research moved on to produce

Deconstructivism which, however, never made it into the mainstream on the scale that the concept of mainstream practice requires. Deconstructivism spurned Folding which in turn led to Parametricism. The sequence Postmodernism, Deconstructivism and Folding describes a continuous sequence of transitional avant-garde styles.

Parametricism is the only recent movement that has gained sufficient maturity and pervasiveness to be acknowledged as hegemonic avant-garde style with a credible claim of being posited as the next epochal style of architecture. Avant-garde research under the auspices of Parametricism has been cumulative for at least a whole decade. As this style starts to conquer mainstream practice, avant-garde research continues. It will also continue to produce new styles, albeit these will be either subsidiary styles within the overarching research programme of Parametricism or irrelevant heresies. (Epochal styles cannot be produced every Monday morning.) How does the author theorize his own work with Zaha Hadid Architects? ZHA might be described as a firm that moves into the mainstream to the extent to which Parametricism is able to conquer the mainstream and its principles (heuristics) can be established as 'state of the art' or 'best practice' within the autopoiesis of architecture. The second arena of the author's practice – the AADRL – will remain a vehicle of cumulative avant-garde design research, potentially contributing to the development of new subsidiary styles. This applies also to the dedicated research unit that has been set up within ZHA. The bulk of the author's work will (hopefully) fulfil architecture's societal function as part of a mainstream best practice. The ambition to go mainstream is built into the very concept of the avant-garde as the subsystem where spearheaded innovations are advanced that deserve to be followed and generalized.

The concrete ambition to push parametricism into the mainstream is one of the author's most urgent ambitions, an ambition that animates the book throughout. However, 'The Autopoeisis of Architecture', cannot be reduced to such a motivation. It points beyond any finite set of conclusions.

Concluding Remarks

In conclusion one might ask: does the theory of architectural autopoiesis – as it has been elaborated so far – really offer orientation and guidance with respect to the assessment of current trends, and with respect to viable ways forward? There are quite a number of claims and critical assessments that can and have been drawn out of this theoretical edifice. This was possible partly because these assessments have been incorporated in it and have guided and constrained the design/construction of the theory. To the extent to which this is the case, the main advantage of the systematic theory is the mnemotechnically relevant ability to systematize, condense, package and order these prior intuitions and assessments. Another part of the assessments and theses were discoveries that were made through the theory, and thus were drawn out as fresh conclusions or theorems that emerged from the re-descriptions and systematic connections between the initial opinions that were input like a priori axioms. The reference to 'axioms' and theoretical 'conclusions' should not imply that a theoretical edifice like the theory of architectural autopoiesis really operates analogously to a strict mathematical apparatus that – on the basis of an initial set of definitions and axioms – allows for the endless, rigorous extraction of conclusive theorems. Even in the case of mathematics, the derivation of interesting theorems is not a mechanical process. Rather it involves confronting the edifice with interesting questions. Even in the case of mathematical systems a final answer cannot always be derived. All other theoretical structures are far less complete and far less rigorous. Whether assessments and theses have been incorporated from the beginning or whether they emerged through the elaboration of the theory implies something about the degree of its heuristic fertility. However, once a significant range of theses and practically relevant assessments has been gathered, their origin matters perhaps less than the theory's ability to gather, cohere and present them in a convincing and concise way. A lot hinges here on the consistency of the conceptual/terminological apparatus.

What are the theory's most relevant claims and recommendations that make a difference in terms of guiding architecture's future practice? The attempt to list them here would inevitably produce a sense of disappointment. (Is this all? After all this effort?) The most urgent, general conclusion is perhaps simply: join Parametricism's drive to conquer the mainstream of world architecture! The importance of investing in architecture's semiological project is certainly one of the most pertinent conclusions of the theory of architectural autopoiesis.[1] The best place to (quickly) find further distinctive, suggestive and potentially productive claims is the list of 60 theses. However, we should also reflect on the fact that a general theory is an apparatus with an only loosely defined purpose, and in this sense such a theory is perhaps comparable to a computer, ie, it is a general purpose machine, a tool with an attached invitation to be put to many creative uses. The theory of architectural autopoiesis is a general, unified theory of architecture for architecture. As such it has been designed/constructed with a view towards the open-ended derivation/discovery of future insights and practice-relevant suggestions. To remain fruitful, the theoretical edifice must be probed and confronted with new experiences and questions. New, suggestive theorems might be drawn out from it, or read into it,[2] in ways that are at this moment unforeseeable.

1 The theory also offers concrete guidance concerning the best way to introduce and advance the semiological project. In fact, on this basis, the author started to experiment with the design of project specific semiological systems as soon as he arrived at a theoretical understanding of its importance and feasibility.

2 This distinction cannot always be maintained or settled with certainty.

Appendix 3
The Autopoiesis of Architecture in the Context of Three Classic Texts

treatise problematic	*De re aedificatoria*	*Précis des leçons d'architecture*	*Vers une architecture*	*The Autopoiesis of Architecture*
1. societal function	– architecture brings/holds the community together – architecture and urbanism manifest the political constitution and the social divisions that order society	– demands unitary purpose – not delightful sensation – not mimesis – purpose is public and private utility, ie, happiness and protection for individuals and society	– architecture is society's most important tool, allows society to create its own universe – architecture or revolution: a new architecture is required to satisfy the rising masses, to save society's social peace	– societal function as evolutionary attractor of system differentiation – single, unique, exclusive, universal societal function: framing communicative interaction
2. avant-gardism	– history/progress of architecture as process of perfection	– no historical self-location	– heightened historical sense. Machine age as new epoch – architecture must progress, adapt to new social, economic and technological conditions	– historical context: Post-Fordist network society as latest form of functionally differentiated society – the avant-garde as mechanism of evolutionary acceleration
3. demarcation	– inaugural demarcation of architecture against the building trades – builders are mere tools for theory-based architectural design	– alignment with science – separation from arts like painting and sculpture: utility instead of pleasure, fitness and economy instead of imitation	– alignment with art – demarcation against engineering and science	– sharp demarcation against art, engineering and science – inside-outside dialectic as *differentia specifica* within the design disciplines

4. form-function relation	– treats functional and formal concerns as equally indispensable – oscillates between giving utility priority and giving beauty priority	– hierarchy of form determinants: utility/construction, tradition, easy apprehension – systematic classification of function-types	– functionalism: solutions which spring from a problem that has been clearly stated (a house is a machine for living in) – form poses an additional task, the task of perfection, moving our emotions	– form vs function as lead-distinction, re-entry of system vs environment – forms are framing communications, functions are framed communications
5. programme of utility	– differentiation of building types relates to societal subsystems and social classes – key distinctions: public vs private, and leading strata vs commoners – achieving social control – focus on life-processes	– utility: fitness and economy – fitness comprises solidity, salubrity and commodity – economy leads to simplicity and regularity	– establishment of standards for function-types – mass production – functional separation and specialization	– functional heuristics: negative: avoid stereotypes, avoid segregative zoning positive: all functions are parametric activity/event scenarios, all activities and events communicate with each other
6. programme of beauty	– beauty as *concinnitas* via symmetry and proportions – universally recognized – general principle of nature – wholeness of organism – variety as aesthetic value	– beauty: grandeur, character and variety – beauty results from the rigorous pursuit of utility: fitness and economy – direct pursuit of beauty results in its opposite	– utility is a necessary but insufficient precondition of beauty – primary geometric forms – avoid ambiguity – avoid ornament – importance of proportions	– formal heuristics: negative: no rigid figures, no repetition, no collage positive: parametric malleability, gradient differentiation, intensive correlation

(*Continued*)

treatise problematic	*De re aedificatoria*	*Précis des leçons d'architecture*	*Vers une architecture*	*The Autopoiesis of Architecture*
7. programme of originality	– original innovations based on experience and prior achievements – avoid arbitrary novelty – avoid slavish dependency	– no acknowledgement of novelty/originality (Enlightenment rationality as absolute, timeless)	– new needs require new solutions: a period of analysis and experiment – rejection of all fixed preconceptions – beauty too requires originality	– originality is finally recognized as indispensable code of architecture, albeit only within architecture's avant-garde segment – original innovation demands more than novelty: shared style
8. style formation	Renaissance active style	Neo-Classicism active style	Modernism active-reflective style	Parametricism active-reflective style
9. repertoire expansion	– recuperating the repertoire of Roman architecture in terms both of organization and articulation – increasing precision of design anticipation	– expansion of repertoire of plan organization to cater for (new) variety of classes of buildings (function-types) – each susceptible to many individual modifications	– no explicit recognition of the need for repertoire expansion – instead insistence on pure geometric forms – objective expansion through radical abstraction and rejection of symmetry	– promoting the expansion of the repertoire for both organization and articulation – explicit proposals for new Parametricist agendas: correlation, accentuation, figuration, deep relationality etc

10. process guidance	– rational design sequence: location, site, compartition, roof, walls, openings – sequence of concerns: first utility and then beauty	– hierarchical composition: whole, parts, elements – successive division starts from global geometric forms – grid, rules of alignment – plans first, then elevations, then sections – combinatorial richness	– selection of standard solution precedes artistic refinement – design from the inside to the outside (exterior is the result of interior) – plan as generator	– theoretical process reflection – design process as problem solving, as search in a state space with well-defined generating/testing operators – parametric systems enhance generative power, constraining power and analytical power
11. design medium	– new medium: perspective making the absent present – mathematics for systems of proportions – scale models to fully anticipate and resolve all aspects of the project ahead of construction	– purification of the medium: economical, abstract line drawings, diagrams – functional differentiation of drawing types: orthographic projections to define shape and arrangement, perspective to test visual effect	– new design media: abstract diagram and axonometric projection – warning against succumbing to the 'illusions of the plan'	– the medium opens and delimits a universe of possibilities – the medium of the model is a specialized success medium like money, power and truth – scripting replaces modelling – it better combines design progress with reversibility
12. self-reflection	– practice must be based on coherent theory/method – theory/method via study of nature, past achievements, experiments, search for principles	– architectural theory is important to society – it is a deductive system based on architecture's general purpose and principles derived from it	– no self-reflection – assertive, proselytizing manifesto-style	– the theory of autopoiesis reflects itself as super-theory – as contemporary self-description of architecture aligned with the epochal style of Parametricism

Comparative matrix: *The Autopoiesis of Architecture* in the context of three classic texts

Appendix 4 Theses 25–60

THESIS 25 (section 6.1 Functions)
While functional typology remains indispensable as initial orienting framework, functional reasoning in architecture has to upgrade towards a conceptualization of function in terms of action-artefact networks.

THESIS 26 (section 6.2 Order via Organization and Articulation)
Architectural order is symbiotic with social order and its effective realization requires organization and articulation as crucial registers of the design effort.

THESIS 27 (section 6.3 Organization)
Proficiency in establishing compelling new form-function relationships requires a system of abstract mediating concepts that can guide the correlation of spatial with social patterns.

THESIS 28 (section 6.4 Supplementing Architecture with a Science of Configuration)
The task of organization today requires a more explicit and more elaborate repertoire of organizational patterns and more explicit, precise criteria for their evaluation than what can be reasonably expected from the tacit knowledge and accumulated wisdom of an experienced architect.

THESIS 29 (section 6.5 Articulation)
The degree to which the effective functioning of architecture must (and can) rely upon articulation rather than mere physical organization is a barometer of societal progress.

THESIS 30 (section 6.6 The Phenomenological vs the Semiological Dimension of Architecture)
Phenomenology and semiology address different dimensions of the task of architectural articulation that are equally indispensable for the built environment's functionality: the perception of spatial order and the comprehension of social order.

THESIS 31 (section 6.7 The Phenomenological Dimension of Architectural Articulation)
Within the avant-garde stage of a style, articulation strategies must emphasize the phenomenological dimension as independent, pre-semantic arena of articulation that gives scope to creative appropriation beyond fixed meanings.

THESIS 32 (section 6.8 The Semiological Dimension of Architectural Articulation)
The semiological dimension makes a significant contribution to the architecturally inspired process of social structuration that occurs all the time, at all scales.

THESIS 33 (section 6.9 Prolegomenon to Architecture's Semiological Project)
Contemporary architecture must push the expressive power of its architectural language far beyond the simple correlations between forms and designations that have usually been considered under the heading of 'meaning in architecture'.

THESIS 34 (section 6.10 The Semiological Project and the General Project of Architectural Order)
The semiological dimension of architecture engages most directly with architecture's unique societal function. It is the leading dimension of architecture's task. It is the expertise in this dimension that is most required to succeed in the provision of effective communicative spatial frames.

THESIS 35 (section 7.1 Contemporary Context and Aim of Design Process Theory)
Design process theories (with rationalizing methodological ambitions) make sense only during the cumulative periods of disciplinary advancement, under the auspices of a hegemonic style. The time has come for a new theoretical investment in design process theory with the aim of advancing contemporary design methodology under the auspices of Parametricism.

THESIS 36 (section 7.2 Towards a Contemporary Design Process Reflection and Design Methodology)
At a certain stage within a maturing avant-garde style, prevalent processes have to evolve into self-critical methods. This requires the rational reconstruction of the prevalent processes rather than the invention of new processes, or the imposition of abstract ideals of rationality.

THESIS 37 (section 7.3 The Design Process as Problem-Solving Process)

Within a design process theory that intends to probe and enhance the rationality of design, the design process must be theorized as problem-solving process. Problem solving – especially at the level of such a complex endeavour like designing the built environment – can only be adequately theorized as accomplishment of an autopoietic communication system, geared up with its whole panoply of communication structures.

THESIS 38 (section 7.4 Differentiating Classical, Modern and Contemporary Processes)

Design via scripted rules is replacing design via the direct manipulation of individual forms. Scripts can uniquely enhance both the design process's generative power and its analytical power. The ability to combine the explorative potential for surprise discoveries with the guaranteed adherence to key criteria is the unique advantage of the new computational techniques. Through these techniques the design process simultaneously gains breadth and depth.

THESIS 39 (section 7.5 Problem Definition and Problem Structure)

The architectural design process is self-determined. There are only very few, very general constraints that are accepted in advance. The design process then proceeds by continuous self-stimulation on the basis of its own intermediate states. This self-determination is a correlate of the autonomy of architecture as autopoietic subsystem of society.

THESIS 40 (section 7.6 Rationality: Retrospective and Prospective)

The rationality of the specific characteristics, affordances and limitations of the various, radically different problem spaces a project typically moves through can be broadly aligned with the three fundamental dimensions of architecture's task: the organizational, the phenomenological and the semiological dimension.

THESIS 41 (section 7.7. Modelling Spaces)

A historically well-adapted style is a necessary precondition of any credible design process rationality.

THESIS 42 (section 8.1 World Architecture within World Society)
Contemporary architecture exists as a single, unified world architecture.

THESIS 43 (section 8.2 Autonomy vs Authority)
The autonomy of architecture implies its discursive authority but lacks the power to impose its authority. Within a polycontextual societal environment, architecture needs to sustain its autonomy precisely to be able to respond to all the disparate challenges of the different societal subsystems. However, its proposed solutions are no longer backed up by power.

THESIS 44 (section 8.3 Architecture's Conception of Society)
Architecture must periodically adapt and upgrade its internal representation of society. To do this it must draw on external theoretical resources.

THESIS 45 (section 8.4 Architecture in Relation to Other Societal Subsystems)
Architecture coevolves with all the other major autopoietic subsystems of society in relations of mutual facilitation and irritation.

THESIS 46 (section 8.5 Architecture as Profession and Professional Career)
Architecture no longer tolerates that the bearer of architectural reputation has any outside ambitions.

THESIS 47 (section 8.6 The Built Environment as Primordial Condition of Society)
Architectural figures offer the archetypical paradigm of any concept or order. The emergence and stabilization of any social order require that the spatial traces of social interactions ossify into a sedimented social memory that acts both as an organizing framework and as system of signification.

THESIS 48 (section 9.1 Is Political Architecture Possible?)
The notion of a political architecture has transformed from a tautology to an oxymoron.

THESIS 49 (section 9.2 Theorizing the Relationship between Architecture and Politics)
To respond to hegemonic political trends is a vital capacity of architecture. It has no capacity to resolve political controversy. Political debate within

architecture overburdens the discipline. The autopoiesis of architecture consumes itself in the attempt to substitute itself for the political system.

THESIS 50 (section 9.3 Architecture Adapts to Political Development)

Architecture responds to resolved and thus depoliticized politics. To bind architectural positions to an ongoing political polemic is counterproductive. The intransigence of political positions operating in the medium of power leads to communicative dysfunction within the architectural discourse.

THESIS 51 (section 9.4 The Limitations of Critical Practice in Architecture)

The vitality of architecture depends on its ability to register and address the political agendas empowered within the political system. Those forms of theoretical politics that are merely be desired or hoped for cannot become productive within architecture.

THESIS 52 (section 10.1 Theoretical Underpinnings)

Architecture, as a self-reflective system of communications, is trying to steer itself via theoretical self-descriptions that attempt to theorize and define architecture's role within society. The complexity and sophistication of the contemporary societal environment demand increasingly complex and sophisticated architectural self-explications. Convincing autological self-inclusion is now one of the indispensable conditions that any serious candidate for architectural self-description must fulfil.

THESIS 53 (section 10.2 The Necessity of Reflection: Architectural Theory as Reflection Theory)

Like all other great function systems, architecture tries to unify and orient itself via self-descriptions that reflect/define its raison *d'être* and identify/define its tasks within its societal environment. Although necessary, these self-descriptions, like all descriptions, are fallible and risky self-simplifications. The fact that these descriptions might become influential, and thus might indeed seem to shape the reality of what they describe, does not vitiate the prior fact that the reality of architecture's autopoiesis always already exceeds its simplified descriptions.

THESIS 54 (section 10.3 Classic Treatises)

All classics of architectural theory are self-descriptions. Only this theory type explicitly addresses and interprets the general, underlying, permanent problematic of architecture. The continued relevance of the classics of architectural theory is based on this stability of their underlying problematic

even when the more particular historical problems/solutions that have been formulated within these theories are no longer applicable.

THESIS 55 (section 10.4 Architectural Historiography)

Architectural historiography is always committed historiography. It is an integral part of architecture's self-description. It is a reflection theory rather than a science. Its organizing principle and coherence can only be derived from a principle that identifies a particular historical problematic and task for contemporary architecture.

THESIS 56 (10.5 Architectural Criticism)

Architectural criticism provides the interface (structural coupling) between architecture and the mass media. The results of architecture's internal evaluation processes are supplied with a new set of reasons satisfying the values and criteria of mass media communication. Therefore architectural criticism can neither share in nor convey architectural intelligence. Instead it can productively irritate this intelligence.

THESIS 57 (section 11.1. Parametricism as Epochal Style)

Avant-garde architecture and urbanism engage in an ongoing cycle of innovative adaptation – retooling the discipline in order to elaborate its capacity to adapt the architectural/urban environment to the demands of the socio-economic era of Post-Fordism.

THESIS 58 (section 11.2 The Parametricist Research Programme)

The eventual success of grand, unifying schemes in science relies on the underlying coherence of reality. The rationality of a style's claim to universality lies in the advantage of a coherent built environment. Modernism did achieve universality during the course of the 20th century. Parametricism aims for an equivalent achievement in the 21st century.

THESIS 59 (section 11.3 Parametricist vs Modernist Urbanism)

The work of Frei Otto is the only true precursor of Parametricism.

THESIS 60 (section 11.4 Elegance)

Elegance is the aesthetic expression of complex order.

References

ABC Group, 'ABC Demands the Dictatorship of the Machine', in: Ulrich Conrads (Ed), *Programs and Manifestoes on 20th-Century Architecture*, MIT Press (Cambridge, MA), 1971; original: 'ABC fordert die Diktatur der Maschine', in: *ABC – Beiträge zum Bauen* 4, 1928

Aglietta, Michel, *A Theory of Capitalist Regulation – The US Experience*, Verso (London), 2001 (1979)

Akin, Ömer, *Psychology of Architectural Design*, Pion (London), 1986

Akin, Ömer, "Exploration of the Design Process" in: *Design Methods & Theories*, 1979, vol. 13

Alberti, Leon Battista, *On the Art of Building in Ten Books*, translated by Joseph Rykwert, Neil Leach & Robert Tavernor, MIT Press (Cambridge, MA), 1988

Alberti, Leon Battista, *Opere volgari*, C Grayson (Ed), Laterza (Bari), 1960–73

Alexander, Christopher, 'A City is not a Tree', in: *Zone 1/2*, *The Contemporary City*, ed Jonathan Crary, published by Urzone (New York), 1987, p 130; first published in: *Architectural Forum*, Vol 122, Nos 1 & 2, 1965

Alexander, Christopher, *Notes on the Synthesis of Form*, Harvard University Press (Cambridge, MA), 1964

Alexander, Christopher, *A Pattern Language*, Oxford University Press (New York), 1977

Amin, Ash, *Post-Fordism – A Reader*, Blackwell Publishing (Oxford), 1994

Austin, John L, *How to Do Things with Words*, Clarendon Press (Oxford), 1962

Baecker, Dirk, *Die nächste Stadt: Ein Pflichtenheft,* unpublished manuscript, 2009/2010, www.dirkbaecker.com

Baecker, Dirk, *Studien zur nächsten Gesellschaft*, Suhrkamp (Frankfurt am Main), 2007

Banham, Reyner, *Theory and Design in the First Machine Age*, The Architectural Press (London), 1960

Barthes, Roland, *The Semiotic Challenge,* Basil Blackwell (Oxford), 1988, French original: *Líaventure sémiologique*, Éditions du Seuil (Paris), 1985

Becker, Mirco, 'The Generative and the Synthetic', in: *Modulor*, February 2010

Behne, Adolf, *The Modern Functional Building*, Getty Research Institute (Santa Monica, CA), 1996

Benevolo, Leonardo, *The History of the City*, MIT Press (Cambridge, MA), 1980

Benjamin, Walter, 'The Work of Art in the Age of Mechanical Reproduction', in: Walter Benjamin, *Illuminations: Essays and Reflections*, Schocken Books (New York), 1968

Bentham, Jeremy, *An Introduction to the Principles of Morals and Legislation*, Dover Publications (New York), 2009, originally published in 1781

Berkel, Ben van & Bos, Caroline (UN Studio), 'Deep Plan', in: *AA files 38*, Architectural Association School of Architecture (London), 1999

Berkel, Ben van & Bos, Caroline, 'Diagrams – Interactive Instruments in Operation', in: *Any* magazine 23, *Diagram Work* (New Jersey), 1998

Best, Steven & Kellner, Douglas, *Postmodern Theory: Critical Interrogations*, MacMillan and Guildford Press (London/New York), 1991

Blondel, Jacques-François, *Course of Architecture*, 1771, excerpt in: Harry Francis Mallgrave (Ed), *Architectural Theory*, Blackwell Publishing (Oxford), 2006

Boffrand, Germain, *Book of Architecture Containing the General Principles of the Art*, Ashgate Publishing (Aldershot), 2003, French original *Livre d'architecture*, 1745, excerpt in: Harry Francis Mallgrave (Ed), *Architectural Theory*, Blackwell Publishing (Oxford), 2006

Bourdieu, Pierre, *The Logic of Practice*, Polity Press (Cambridge), 1990

Broadbent, Geoffrey, 'Meaning into Architecture', in: Charles Jencks & George Baird (Eds), *Meaning in Architecture*, George Braziller (New York), 1970

Carnap, Rudolf, *The Logical Syntax of Language*, Kegan Paul, Trench Trubner & Co Ltd (London), 1937

Castells, Manuel, *The Rise of the Network Society: The Information Age: Economy, Society, and Culture*, Vol 1, 2nd edition, Wiley-Blackwell (London), 2009

Chan-Magomedow, Selim O, *Pioniere der Sowjetischen Architektur*, Löcker Verlag (Vienna/Berlin), 1983

Ching, Francis DK, *Architecture – Form, Space and Order*, 2nd edition, John Wiley & Sons (New York), 1996

Chomsky, Noam, *On Language*, New Press (New York), 2007

Chomsky, Noam, *Syntactic Structures*, Mouton de Gruyter (Berlin/New York), 2002, 1st edition published in 1957

Coates, Paul, *Programming Architecture*, Routledge (London), 2010

Conrads, Ulrich (Ed), *Programs and Manifestoes on 20th-Century Architecture*, MIT Press (Cambridge, MA), 1971

Cross, Nigel (Ed), *Developments in Design Methodology*, John Wiley & Sons (Chichester), 1984

Cross, Nigel, 'Natural Intelligence in Design', in: *Design Studies*, Vol 20, No 1, January 1999, reprinted in: Nigel Cross, *Designerly Ways of Knowing*, Birkhäuser (Basel), 2007

Cunningham, David, 'Architecture as Critical Knowledge', in: Jane Rendell et al (Eds), *Critical Architecture*, Routledge (London), 2007

Cuvier, Georges, *The Animal Kingdom – Arranged in Conformity with its Organization*, G & C & H Carvill (New York), 1832

Darke, Jane, 'The Primary Generator and the Design Process', in: *Design Studies 1*, 1979, reprinted in: Nigel Cross (Ed), *Developments in Design Methodology*, John Wiley & Sons (Chichester), 1984

Daskalakis, G, Waldheim, C & Young, J (Eds), *Stalking Detroit*, Actar (Barcelona), 2001

Deco, G, Pollatos, O, Zihl, J, 'The Time Course of Selective Visual Attention: Theory and Experiments', in: *Vision Research* 42, (2002), 2925–2945

Deleuze, Gilles & Guattari, Félix, *A Thousand Plateaus*, The Athlone Press (Minneapolis), 1987, French original: *Mille Plateaux*, Les Editions de Minuit (Paris), 1980

Durand, Jean-Nicolas-Louis, *Précis des leçons d'architecture données à l'École royale polytechnique* (Paris), 1802–5, English translation by David Britt, published by The Getty Research Institute (Los Angeles, CA), 2000

Eastman, Charles M., *Explorations of the Cognitive Processes of Design*, Department of Computer Science, Carnegie-Mellon University, Pittsburgh 1968, ARPA Report, Defense Documentation Report No. AD 671158

Eco, Umberto, 'The Influence of Roman Jakobson on the Development of Semiotics', in: Martin Krampen et al (Eds), *Classics of Semiotics*, Plenum Press (New York), 1987
Eisenman, Peter, 'Post-Functionalism', in: *Oppositions* 6, Fall 1976, reprinted in: K Michael Hays, *Oppositions Reader*, Princeton Architectural Press (New York), 1998
El Lissitzky (Lazar Markovich Lissitzky), *Russia: An Architecture for World Revolution*, MIT Press (Cambridge, MA), 1984
Evans, Robin, 'Figures, Doors and Passages', in: *Translations from Drawing to Building and Other Essays*, AA Documents 2, Architectural Association (London), 1997
Feldtkeller, Christoph, *Der architektonische Raum: eine Fiktion. Annäherung an eine funktionale Betrachtung*, Bauwelt Fundamente 83, Vieweg (Braunschweig), 1989
Forty, Adrian, *Words and Buildings – A Vocabulary of Modern Architecture*, Thames & Hudson (London), 2000
Foucault, Michel, *The Archaeology of Knowledge*, Routledge (London), 1989, French: *L'Archéologie du Savoir*, Éditions Gallimard (Paris), 1969
Gabo, Naum & Pevsner, Antoine, 'Basic Principles of Constructivism', in: Ulrich Conrads (Ed), *Programs and Manifestoes on 20th-Century Architecture*, MIT Press (Cambridge, MA), 1971
Gandelsonas, Mario, 'From Structure to Subject: The Formation of an Architectural Language', in: *Oppositions 17*, Summer 1979
Gerber, David Jason, *The Parametric Affect – Computation, Innovation and Models for Design Exploration in Contemporary Architectural Practice*, Harvard Design School, Department of Architecture, Design and Technology Report Series, 2009
Giedion, Sigfried, *Space, Time and Architecture – The Growth of a New Tradition*, 5th edition, Harvard University Press (Cambridge, MA), 1967
Goel, Vinod, *Sketches of Thought*, MIT Press (Cambridge, MA), 1995
Goffman, Erving, *The Presentation of Self in Everyday Life*, Anchor Books (New York), 1959, Penguin Books (London), 1990
Goodman, Nelson, *Languages of Art – An Approach to a Theory of Symbols*, Hackett Publishing Company (Indianapolis/Cambridge), 1976
Goodman, Nelson, *Ways of Worldmaking*, Hackett Publishing Company (Indianapolis/Cambridge), 1978
Gould, Stephen J & Vrba, Elizabeth S, 'Exaptation: A Missing Term in the Science of Form', in: *Paleobiology* 8(1), 1982
Grafton, Anthony, *Leon Battista Alberti – Master Builder of the Italian Renaissance*, Penguin Books (London), 2002
Hadid, Zaha & Schumacher, Patrik (Eds), *Latent Utopias – Experiments within Contemporary Architecture*, Springer Verlag (Vienna/New York), 2002
Hadid, Zaha & Schumacher, Patrik, 'Parametricist Manifesto', published in: *Out There – Architecture beyond Building*, Vol 5: Experimental Architecture, Catalogue of the 11th Architecture Biennale (Venice), 2008
Harvey, David, *The Condition of Postmodernity: An Enquiry into the Origins of Cultural Change*, Blackwell Publishers (Cambridge, MA/Oxford), 1990
Hays, Michael K (Ed), *Oppositions Reader*, Princeton Architectural Press (New York), 1998
Heidegger, Martin, 'On the Essence of Truth', in: Martin Heidegger, *Being and Truth*, Indiana University Press (Bloomington), 2010
Hilberseimer, Ludwig, *Groszstadtarchitektur*, Julius Hoffman Verlag (Stuttgart), 1927

Hillier, Bill, *Space is the Machine – A Configurational Theory of Architecture*, Cambridge University Press (Cambridge), 1996

Hillier, Bill & Hanson, Julienne, *The Social Logic of Space*, Cambridge University Press (Cambridge), 1984

Hirst, Paul & Zeitlin, Jonathan, *Flexible Specialization versus Post-Fordism*, Routledge (London), 1991

Hübsch, Heinrich, *In What Style Should We Build?*, German original from 1828: *In welchem Style sollen wir bauen?*, excerpt in: Harry Francis Mallgrave (Ed), *Architectural Theory*, Blackwell Publishing (Oxford), 2006

Huet, Bernard, 'Les trois fortunes de Durand', in: Werner Szambien, *Jean-Nicolas-Louis Durand 1760–1834: De l'imitation à la norme*, Picard (Paris), 1984

Institute for Lightweight Structures, SFB 230, *Natural Structures – Principles, Strategies, and Models in Architecture and Nature*, Proceedings of the 2nd International Symposium of the Sonderforschungsbereich 230 (Stuttgart), 1991

Jencks, Charles & Baird, George (Eds), *Meaning in Architecture*, George Braziller (New York), 1970

Jencks, Charles, 'Semiology and Architecture', in: Charles Jencks & George Baird (Eds), *Meaning in Architecture*, George Braziller (New York), 1970

Jencks, Charles, *The Language of Post-Modern Architecture*, 5th edition, Rizzoli (New York), 1987 (1st edition 1977)

Kant, Immanuel, *Critique of Pure Reason*, Cambridge University Press (Cambridge), 1998, original German: *Kritik der reinen Vernunft* (Riga), first published in 1781

Kepes, György, *Language of Vision*, Dover Publications (New York), 1995, originally published by Paul Theobald (Chicago), 1944

King, Ross, *Brunelleschi's Dome: How a Renaissance Genius Reinvented Architecture*, Vintage Random House (London), 2008

Kling, RE, *A Paradigm for Reasoning by Analogy*, Proceedings of the 2nd International Joint Conference on Artificial Intelligence, British Computer Society (London), 1971

Koffka, Kurt, 'Perception: An Introduction to the Gestalt-Theorie', in: *Psychological Bulletin*, 19, 531–85, 1922

Köhler, Wolfgang, 'Gestalt Psychology Today', in: *American Psychologist*, 14, 1959

Koolhaas, Rem, *Delirious New York: A Retroactive Manifesto for Manhattan*, Oxford University Press (New York), 1978

Krampen, M et al (Eds), *Classics of Semiotics*, Plenum Press (New York), 1987

Kuhn, Thomas S, *The Structure of Scientific Revolutions*, University of Chicago Press (Chicago), 1970

Lakatos, Imre, *The Methodology of Scientific Research Programmes*, Cambridge University Press (Cambridge), 1978

Latour, Bruno, 'A Cautious Prometheus? A Few Steps Toward a Philosophy of Design (with special attention to Peter Sloterdijk)', keynote lecture for the Networks of Design meeting of the Design History Society (Falmouth, Cornwall), 3 September 2008

Latour, Bruno, *Reassembling the Social: An Introduction to Actor-Network-Theory*, Oxford University Press (Oxford), 2005

Latour, Bruno, *Von der Realpolitik zur Dingpolitik*, Merve Verlag (Berlin), 2005

Laugier, Marc-Antoine, *An Essay on Architecture*, Hennessey & Ingalls (Los Angeles), 1977, original French: *Essai sur l'architecture*, 1753

Le Corbusier, *The City of Tomorrow and its Planning*, Dover Publications (New York), 1987, translated from French original *Urbanisme*, Crès & Cie (Paris), 1925
Le Corbusier, *Towards a New Architecture*, Dover Publications (New York), 1986, unaltered republication of English translation of 13th French edition, published by John Rodker (London), 1931, French original: *Vers une architecture,* Editions Crès (Paris), 1923
Legendre, George, 'Excerpt: New Things', in: *GSD 08 Platform*, Harvard University Graduate School of Design, Actar (Barcelona), 2008
Lettvin, JY, Maturana, HR, McCulloch, WS, & Pitts, WH, 'What the Frog's Eye tells the Frog's Brain', in: William C Corning, & Martin Balaban (Eds), *The Mind: Biological Approaches to its Functions*, John Wiley & Sons (New York), 1968
Lévi-Strauss, Claude, *Structural Anthropology*, Basic Books (New York), 1963
Leymore, Varda Langholz, *Hidden Myths: Structure and Symbolism in Advertising*, Basic Books (New York), 1975
Lootsma, Bart, 'Ausblick auf eine reflexive Architektur', in: *Arch+* 143, October 1998
Lootsma, Bart, 'Reality Bytes', in: *Daidalos* 69/70, December 1998/January 1999
Luhmann, Niklas, *Art as a Social System*, Stanford University Press (Stanford, CA), 2000
Luhmann, Niklas, 'Der Politische Code', in: *Soziologische Aufklärung 3*, 4th edition, VS Verlag für Sozialwissenschaften (Wiesbaden), 2005
Luhmann, Niklas, *Die Gesellschaft der Gesellschaft*, Suhrkamp Verlag (Frankfurt am Main), 1998
Luhmann, Niklas, *Die Politik der Gesellschaft*, Suhrkamp Verlag (Frankfurt am Main), 2000
Luhmann, Niklas, *Die Wirtschaft der Gesellschaft*, 2nd edition, Suhrkamp Verlag (Frankfurt am Main), 1996
Luhmann, Niklas, *Die Wissenschaft der Gesellschaft*, Suhrkamp Verlag (Frankfurt am Main), 1992
Luhmann, Niklas, *Gesellschaftsstruktur und Semantik – Studien zur Wissenssoziologie der modernen Gesellschaft*, Suhrkamp Verlag (Frankfurt am Main), 4 vols, 1995
Luhmann, Niklas, *Social Systems*, Stanford University Press (Stanford, CA), 1995
Luhmann, Niklas, 'The Modernity of Science', in: *New German Critique*, Winter 1994, Issue 61, Telos Press (New York)
Luhmann, Niklas, *The Reality of the Mass Media*, Stanford University Press (Stanford, CA), 2000
Luhmann, Niklas, *Theories of Distinction*, Stanford University Press (Stanford, CA), 2002
Luhmann, Niklas, *Zweckbegriff und Systemrationalität Über die Funktion von Zwecken in Sozialen Systemen*, Suhrkamp Verlag (Frankfurt am Main), 1973
Lynn, Greg (Ed), *Folding in Architecture*, Architectural Design Profile No 102, 1993
Lyotard, Jean-François, *The Postmodern Condition: A Report on Knowledge*, University of Minnesota Press (Minneapolis), 1984, original French by Les Éditions de Minuit (Paris), 1979
Maas, W, van Rijs, J, & Koek, R (Eds), *MVRDV FARMAX*, 010 Uitgeverij (Rotterdam), 1998
Mach, Ernst, *The Analysis of Sensations and the Relation of the Physical to the Psychical*, Open Court Publishing Company (Chicago/London), 1914. German original: *Die Analyse der Empfindungen und das Verhältnis des Physischen zum Psychischen*, Verlag Gustav Fischer (Jena), 1886

Mallgrave, Harry Francis (Ed), *Architectural Theory*, Blackwell Publishing (Oxford), 2006
March, JG & Olsen, JP, *Ambiguity and Choice in Organizations*, Universitetsforlaget (Bergen), 1976
March, Lionel & Steadman, Philip, *The Geometry of Environment – An Introduction to Spatial Organization in Design*, RIBA Publications (London), 1971
Martin, Reinhold, 'Critical of What? Toward a Utopian Realism', in: William S Saunders (Ed), *The New Architectural Pragmatism*, University of Minnesota Press (Minneapolis/London), 2007
Martin, Reinhold, 'Moment of Truth', in: *Log*, vol 7, Winter/Spring 2006, Anyone Corporation
Marx, Karl & Engels, Friedrich, 'The German Ideology', in: L Easton & K Guddat (Eds), *Writings of the Young Marx on Philosophy and Society*, Doubleday Anchor (New York), 1967
Maturana, Humberto R & Varela, Francisco J, *Autopoiesis and Cognition – The Realization of the Living*, Reidel Publishing Company (Dordrecht), 1980
Meyer, Hannes, 'bauen', in: *Bauhaus* Year 2, No 4, Bauhaus (Dessau), 1928
Meyer, Hannes, *Der Architekt im Klassenkampf*, in: *Der Rote Aufbau* #5 (Berlin), 1932
Mitchell, William J, *The Logic of Architecture – Design, Computation and Cognition*, MIT Press (Cambridge, MA), 1990
Montesquieu, Charles de Secondat, Baron de, *The Spirit of the Laws*, Cambridge University Press (Cambridge), 1989, original French: *L'esprit des lois*, originally published anonymously in 1748
Murray, Robin, 'Fordism and Postfordism', in: Stuart Hall & Martin Jacques (Eds), *New Times: Changing Face of Politics in the 1990s*, Lawrence & Wishart (London), 1989
Muthesius, Hermann, *Style-Architecture and Building-Art: Transformations of Architecture in the Nineteenth Century and its Present Condition*, University of Chicago Press (Chicago), 1994, original German: *Stilarchitektur und Baukunst: Wandlungen der Architektur im XIX Jahrhundert und ihr heutiger Standpunkt*, Schimmelpfeng (Mülheim-Ruhr), 1902
Naumann, Friedrich, 'Die Kunst im Zeitalter der Maschine', in: Kunstwart 17, July 1904
Neander, Karen, 'Functions as Selected Effects: The Conceptual Analyst's Defense', in: *Philosophy of Science*, Vol 58, No 2, June 1991
Newell, Allen, Heuristic Programming: 'Ill-Structured Problems', in: JA Aronofsky (Ed), *Progress in Operations Research*, Vol 3, John Wiley (New York), 1970
Newell, Allen & Simon, Herbert A, *Human Problem Solving*, Prentice-Hall International (London), 1972
Norberg-Schulz, Christian, *Architecture: Presence, Language, Place*, Skira Editore (Milan), 2000
OECD (Organisation of Economic Co-operation and Development), *Positive Adjustment Policies: Managing Structural Change*, OECD (Paris), 1983
Otto, Frei, *Occupying and Connecting – Thoughts on Territories and Spheres of Influence with Particular Reference to Human Settlement*, Edition Axel Menges (Stuttgart/London), 2009
Otto, Frei & Rasch, Bodo, *Finding Form – Towards an Architecture of the Minimal*, Edition Axel Menges (Stuttgart), 1995
Parsons, Talcott, *Essays in Sociological Theory*, The Free Press (New York), 1954
Pawson, John, *Minimum*, Phaidon (London), 2006

Peirce, Charles S, *Prolegomena to an Apology for Pragmaticism* (1906), in: Charles S Peirce, *Philosophy of Mathematics – Selected Writings*, Indiana University Press (Bloomington/Indianapolis), 2010
Perrault, Claude, *Ordonnance des cinq espèces de colonnes selon la méthode des anciens*, original French 1683; *Ordonnance for the Five Kinds of Columns after the Method of the Ancients,* Getty Publications (Santa Monica, CA), 1993
Pfammatter, Ulrich, *The Making of the Modern Architect and Engineer: The Origins and Development of a Scientific and Industrially Oriented Education*, Birkhäuser (Basel), 2000
Picon, Antoine, 'From "Poetry of Art" to Method: The Theory of Jean-Nicolas-Louis Durand', in: Jean-Nicolas-Louis Durand, *Précis des leçons d'architecture données à l'École royale polytechnique* (Paris), 1802–5, The Getty Research Institute (Los Angeles), 2000
Preziosi, Donald, *Architecture, Language, and Meaning – The Origins of the Built World and its Semiotic Organization*, Mouton Publishers (The Hague/Paris/New York), 1979
Preziosi, Donald, *The Semiotics of the Built Environment – An Introduction to Architectonic Analysis*, Indiana University Press (Bloomington), 1979
Rahim, Ali, *Catalytic Formations – Architecture and Digital Design*, Taylor & Francis (London/New York), 2006
Rajchman, John, 'The Virtual House', in: *Any* magazine, September 1997
Reitman, Walter R, *Cognition and Thought – An Information Processing Approach*, John Wiley & Sons, Inc (New York/London/Sydney), 1965
Rittel, Horst WJ & Webber, Melvin M, 'Dilemmas in a General Theory of Planning', in: *Policy Sciences 4*, 1973
Rorschach, Hermann, *Psychodiagnostik*, H Huber (Berlin/Leipzig), 1921
Rothbard, Murray N, *Man, Economy, and State – A Treatise on Economic Principles*, Scholar's Edition, 2nd edition, Ludwig von Mises Institute (Auburn, AL), 2009
Rowe, Colin & Koetter, Fred, *Collage City*, MIT Press (Cambridge, MA), 1978
Rowe, Colin & Slutzky, Robert, 'Transparency: Literal and Phenomenal', in: *Perspecta 8* (Yale Architectural Journal), Yale University, 1963
Ruigrok, W & Tulder, R van, *The Logic of International Restructuring*, Routledge (London/New York), 1995
Russell, Bertrand, *Our Knowledge of the External World*, Routledge Classics (London/New York), 2009, first published by Open Court Publishing Company (Chicago), 1914
Russell, Bertrand, 'The Philosophy of Logical Atomism', first published in: *The Monist 1918/1919,* also in: Bertrand Russell, *Logic and Knowledge – Essays 1901–1950*, Capricorn Books (New York), 1951
Russell, Bertrand, *The Problems of Philosophy*, Home University Library, 1912, Oxford University Press paperback (Oxford/New York), 1959
Sapers, Carl, 'Losing and Regaining Ground: A Jeremiad on the Future of the Profession', in: William Saunders (Ed), *Reflections on Architectural Practices in the Nineties*, Princeton Architectural Press (New York), 1996
Saunders, William S (Ed), *Reflections on Architectural Practices in the Nineties*, Princeton Architectural Press (New York), 1996
Saunders, William S (Ed), *The New Architectural Pragmatism*, University of Minnesota Press (Minneapolis/London), 2007

Saussure, Ferdinand de, *Course in General Linguistics*, 4th edition, Duckworth (London), 1995, original French: *Cours de linguistique générale*, Payot (Paris), 1916

Schinkel, Karl Friedrich, *Das Architektonische Lehrbuch*, Deutscher Kunstverlag (Munich/Berlin), 2001

Schumacher, Patrik, 'Arbeit, Spiel und Anarchie', in: Herbert Lachmayer & Eleonora Luis (Eds), *Work & Culture – Büro.Inszenierung von Arbeit*, Ritterverlag (Klagenfurt), 1998

Schumacher, Patrik, 'Arguing for Elegance', in: H Castle, A Rahim & H Jamelle (Eds), *Elegance*, Architectural Design, January/February 2007, Vol 77, No 1, Wiley – Academy (London)

Schumacher, Patrik, 'Business – Research – Architecture', in: *Daidalos* 69/70, December 1998/January 1999

Schumacher, Patrik, 'Experimentation within a Long Wave of Innovation', published in: *Out There – Architecture Beyond Building*, Volume 3: *Experimental Architecture*, Catalogue of the 11th Architecture Biennale (Venice), 2008

Schumacher, Patrik, 'Parametricism: A New Global Style for Architecture and Urban Design', in: Neil Leach, Helen Castle (Eds), *Digital Cities*, Architectural Design Vol 79, No 4, July/August 2009

Schumacher, Patrik, 'Produktive Ordnungen', in: *ARCH+* 136, *Your Office Is Where You Are*, April 1997 (Berlin)

Schumacher, Patrik, 'Productive Patterns – Restructuring Architecture', Part 1, in: *architect's bulletin, Operativity*, Vols 135–136, June 1997, & 'Productive Patterns – Restructuring Architecture', Part 2, in: *architect's bulletin*, Vols 137–138, November 1997, Slovenia

Schumacher, Patrik, 'Research Agenda: Spatializing the Complexities of Contemporary Business', in: Brett Steele (Ed), *Corporate Fields – New Office Environments by the AADRL*, AA Publications (London), 2005

Schumacher, Patrik, 'Responsive Environments – From Drawing to Scripting', in: Katja Grillner, Per Glembrandt, Sven-Olov Wallenstein (Eds), *01 AKAD – Experimental Research in Architecture and Design – Beginnings*, Royal Institute of Technology (Stockholm), 2005

Schumacher, Patrik, 'Style as Research Programme', in: *DRL TEN – A Design Research Compendium*, AA Publications (London), 2008

Schumacher, Patrik & Rogner, Christian, 'After Ford', published in: Georgia Daskalakis, Charles Waldheim, Jason Young (Eds), *Stalking Detroit*, Actar (Barcelona), 2001

Searle, John, *Speech Acts*, Cambridge University Press (Cambridge), 1969

Semper, Gottfried, *Style in the Technical and Tectonic Arts, or Practical Aesthetics*, Getty Publications (Los Angeles), 2004, original German: *Der Stil in den technischen und tektonischen Künsten oder Praktische Aesthetik: Ein Handbuch für Techniker, Künstler und Kunstfreunde*, Vol 1, Verlag für Kunst und Wissenschaft (Frankfurt am Main), 1860, Vol 2, Bruckmann Verlag (Munich), 1863

Semper, Gottfied, *Wissenschaft, Industrie und Kunst*, Neue Bauhausbücher, Florian Kupferberg Verlag (Mainz), 1966

Silverman, David & Torode, Brian, *Postmodern Theory: Critical Interrogations, Critical Architecture, The Material World: Some Theories of Language and its Limits*, Routledge & Kegan Paul (London), 1980

Simon, Herbert A, *Administrative Behavior – A Study of Decision-Making Processes in Administrative Organizations*, The Free Press (New York), 1945

Simon, Herbert A, *Models of Bounded Rationality*, MIT Press (Cambridge, MA), 1997
Simon, Herbert, 'The Structure of Ill-Structured Problems', in: *Artificial Intelligence 4* (1973), reprinted in: Nigel Cross (Ed), *Developments in Design Methodology*, John Wiley & Sons (New York/Chichester), 1984
Smith, Adam, *An Inquiry into the Nature and Causes of the Wealth of Nations*, University of Chicago Press (Chicago), 1976, originally published 1776
Smith Capon, David, *The Vitruvian Fallacy – A History of the Categories in Architecture and Philosophy*, John Wiley & Sons (Chichester), 1999
Soane, John, *The Royal Academy Lectures*, Cambridge University Press (Cambridge), 2000
Soja, Edward W, *Postmodern Geographies*, Verso (London/New York), 1989
Spencer-Brown, George, *Laws of Form*, Allen & Unwin (London), 1969
Steele, Brett (Ed), *Corporate Fields – New Office Environments by the AADRL*, AA Publications (London), 2005
Steenbergen, Clemens & Reh, Wouter, *Architecture and Landscape*, Prestel Verlag (Munich), 1996
Stiny, George, *Shape: Talking about Seeing and Doing*, MIT Press (Cambridge, MA), 2006
Sudjic, Deyan, *The Edifice Complex: How the Rich and Powerful Shape the World*, Penguin Books (New York), 2005
Summerson, John, *The Classical Language of Architecture*, MIT Press (Cambridge, MA), 1963
Tafuri, Manfredo, *Architecture and Utopia: Design and Capitalist Development*, MIT Press (Cambridge, MA), 1976
Tafuri, Manfredo, *Theories and History of Architecture*, Harper & Row Publishers (New York), 1976
Tinniswood, Adrian, *Visions of Power: Ambition and Architecture from Ancient Rome to Modern Paris*, Mitchell Beazley (London), 1998
Trotsky, Leon, 'The Social Roots and the Social Function of Literature' (1923), in: Leon Trotsky, *Art and Revolution: Writings on Literature, Politics and Culture*, Pathfinder (Atlanta), 1992
UNIDO (United Nations Industrial Development Organization), *Structural Change in Industry* (Vienna), 1979
Van Berkel, Ben & Bos, Caroline, *'Deep Plan', in:* AA files 38, Architectural Association School of Architecture (London), 1999
van Dijk, Jan, *The Network Society: Social Aspects of New Media*, Sage Publications (London), 2006
van Toorn, R, Arets, W, & Zaera-Polo, A, *Hunch – the Berlage Institute Report* No 6/7, N/A Publishers (Amsterdam), 2003
van Toorn, Roemer, 'Dirty Details', in: Zaha Hadid & Patrik Schumacher (Eds), *Latent Utopias*, Springer Verlag (Vienna/New York), 2002
van Toorn, Roemer, *Hunch 5*, Berlage Institute, N/A Publishers (Amsterdam), 2002
Venturi, Robert, *Complexity and Contradiction in Architecture*, Museum of Modern Art (New York), 1966
Viollet-le-Duc, EE, *Lectures on Architecture*, 2 vols (1863, 1872), trans B Bucknall (1877, 1881), Dover Publications (New York), 1987
Vitruvius, *The Ten Books on Architecture*, Dover Publications (New York), 1960
Weaver, Warren, 'Science and Complexity', in: *American Scientist*, 36: 536 (1948)

Weber, Max, *Economy and Society*, The Free Press (New York), 1947, German original: *Wirtschaft und Gesellschaft*, Mohr (Tübingen), 1922

Wertheimer, Max, *Gestalt Theory*, German original: 'Über Gestalttheorie' (an address before the Kant Society, Berlin, 7 December 1924), Erlangen, 1925, translation published in W Ellis, *Source Book of Gestalt Psychology*, Harcourt, Brace & Co (New York), 1938

Wertheimer, Max, *Laws of Organization in Perceptual Forms*, first published in 1923, German: 'Untersuchungen zur Lehre von der Gestalt II', in: *Psychologische Forschung*, 4, 301–50. Translation published in W Ellis, *A Source Book of Gestalt Psychology* (pp 71–88), Harcourt, Brace & Co (New York), Routledge & Kegan Paul (London), 1938

Whitehead, Hugh, Foreword in: Robert Woodbury, *Elements of Parametric Design*, Routledge (London/New York), 2010

Wigley, Mark, *Architectural Weaponry*, Interview, bldgblog.blogspot.com/2007/04/architectural-weaponry

Wigley, Mark, *The Architecture of Deconstruction – Derrida's Haunt*, MIT Press (Cambridge, MA), 1993

Wigley, Mark, 'The Future of the Architect', Dean's Statement, Website of GSAPP, Columbia University

Wingler, Hans M, *Das Bauhaus 1919–1933 Weimar Dessau Berlin und die Nachfolge in Chicago seit 1937*, 3rd edition, Verlag Gebr Rasch & Co (Wiesbaden), 1975

Wittgenstein, Ludwig, *Philosophical Investigations*, Blackwell Publishers (Oxford), 1953

Woodbury, Robert, *Elements of Parametric Design*, Routledge (London/New York), 2010

Work Council for Art, 'Under the Wing of a Great Architecture', in: Ulrich Conrads (Ed), *Programs and Manifestoes on 20th-Century Architecture*, MIT Press (Cambridge, MA), 1971

Wright, Georg Henrik von, *Explanation and Understanding*, Cornell University Press (Ithaca/London), 1971

Yates, Frances A, *The Art of Memory*, Routledge & Kegan Paul (London), 1966

Zaera-Polo, Alejandro, 'The Politics of the Envelope – A Political Critique of Materialism', in: *Volume* #17, Archis 2008

Zevi, Bruno, *The Modern Language of Architecture*, University of Washington Press (Seattle), 1978, Italian original *Il linguaggio moderno dell'architettura*, Einaudi (Turin), 1973

Index

AADRL (AA Design Research Lab) 227, 401, 647, 652, 661, 662, 694, 734
Aalto, Alvar 315, 384
ABC Group 460, 462–66, 467, 507
absorption of uncertainty 418–19
abstract art 224, 588
action 11, 12
action system 240
action type 11
action-artefact networks 34–37, 39, 40, 71, 83, 113, 140, 311, 358, 658, 742
adaptation 14–15, 45, 68, 221, 341, 381, 385, 406, 439, 454, 459, 622
adaptive pertinence 387
aesthetic values 434, 533, 534, 548, 556–59, 576, 577, 585, 596, 720, 739
agendas 46
Akin, Ömer 266, 286
Alberti, Leon Battista 3, 9, 44, 45, 47–50, 150, 203–4, 251, 413, 436, 484, 497, 510, 511–42, 543, 583, 605, 607, 704
Alexander, Christopher 31, 82–83, 92, 106, 107, 109–13, 261, 294, 337, 488
analog vs digital 370
analogy 9, 47, 105, 111, 170, 176–81, 190, 206, 213–14, 219, 229
analytical power 311, 316, 604, 744
arbitrariness 57, 61, 62, 85, 113, 210–15, 217
arbitrariness, absolute 212
arbitrariness, relative 210, 212, 214
archetypes 24–25, 29
Archigram 453
architect's project 357, 361, 362, 372
Architectural Association (AA) 227, 350, 401, 409, 660, 730
architectural excess 247, 249
architectural language 170, 174, 175, 178, 194, 198, 200, 203–6, 209, 211, 219, 222, 224, 225, 226, 228, 232, 235–36, 239, 244–46, 247, 673
architectural morphology 136, 189, 685
architectural order 17, 31, 42, 44, 45, 46, 50, 52–56, 58, 61, 70, 71, 87, 133, 143, 167, 178, 197, 238, 246, 621, 664, 676, 742
architectural surplus 247
architecture 1–4
architecture vs building 730
Aristotle 89–90, 515
Arnhem Central project 341–46, 350, 353
arrangement 49
art 381, 410, 412, 413, 446, 505, 506, 507, 546, 549, 550, 573, 574–75, 595, 708
art history 611–12
Art Nouveau 529, 644
art system 400, 612, 708, 709, 717
artefacts 5, 6, 7, 9, 10, 17–20, 30, 32, 34, 35, 54, 80, 83, 171, 173, 174, 176, 205, 220, 255, 275, 364–65, 402, 423, 425, 428, 454, 514, 595, 598, 658, 706, 715
articulation 2, 7, 19–22, 27, 28, 42, 43, 44, 46, 47, 50, 53–56, 58, 60, 61, 63, 71, 87, 124, 125, 132–47, 163, 167, 175, 188, 218, 219, 221, 227, 228, 229, 234, 246–50, 359, 372, 376, 378, 399, 401, 402, 458, 459, 465, 476, 505, 507, 509, 524–25, 535, 537, 559, 594, 600, 651, 722, 742, 743
articulation, morphological 53, 55, 56, 61, 233, 400, 614
articulation, phenomenological 7, 46, 146–47, 205, 234, 238, 598
articulation, semiological 7, 46, 205, 229, 238, 242, 359, 424, 425, 598
articulation, tectonic 537, 557, 675
assemblage 424, 437, 557, 704
atmosphere 19, 21, 43, 44, 51, 141, 175, 231, 477
atmospheric priming 136
authority 385, 386, 411, 536
authorship 413–14
autological 488, 566, 591, 592, 593

autological self-inclusion 4, 484–87, 509, 606
autonomization 594, 608, 625
autonomy 39, 385, 387, 414, 446, 745
autopoeisis 42, 268, 281, 282, 383, 387, 399, 420, 421, 448, 449, 490, 497, 498, 625, 712
autopoeisis of architecture 1–8, 10, 11, 17, 20, 21, 22, 24, 33, 34, 36, 37, 40, 43, 44, 46–47, 49, 53, 58, 61, 71, 72, 74–75, 80, 81, 83, 85, 87, 113, 131, 132, 142, 144, 145, 149, 168–73, 176, 180, 186, 199, 204, 206, 221, 238, 239, 243, 244, 245, 251, 253, 257, 263, 264, 266–69, 273, 276, 283, 323, 333, 334, 357, 358, 361, 365, 371, 381, 385, 386, 387, 389–92, 394, 396–98, 400, 407, 408, 409, 411, 412, 414, 416, 417, 420, 421, 424, 434, 439, 441, 443, 446–52, 454, 457, 467, 469, 471, 472, 474, 476, 478, 479, 480, 483, 484, 486, 488, 495–98, 500, 501, 504–7, 509, 510, 519, 521, 524, 525, 536, 553, 573, 576, 577, 578, 590, 592–97, 599, 600, 603, 605, 606, 608, 611–16, 623, 626, 628, 639, 659, 672, 696–97, 709, 711–16, 719–22, 724, 725, 727, 728, 732–36, 741, 746
avant-garde 1, 3, 15, 23, 42, 46, 69, 71, 74, 75, 92, 111, 112, 140, 145, 214, 226, 237, 246, 253, 256, 257, 311, 312, 315, 318, 328, 329, 338, 342, 343, 361, 378, 382–83, 386–89, 393, 397, 398, 401–2, 406–7, 410, 412, 422, 441, 449, 465, 471, 477, 495, 496, 505, 508, 509, 511, 568, 594, 597, 598, 605, 608, 610, 611, 613, 615, 617, 618, 622, 623, 641, 644, 645, 646, 651, 652–53, 657, 661, 669, 700, 709, 720, 721, 730, 732, 733–34, 738, 743, 747
avant-garde vs mainstream 730, 732
Aviler, Augustin-Charles d' 48

Baecker, Dirk 56, 626
Baird, George 169
Banham, Reyner 169, 572–73
Baroque 55, 139, 150, 163, 388, 403, 440, 529, 560, 630–32, 633, 642, 643, 645, 702
Barthes, Roland 167–68, 169
Bateson, Gregory 175
Baudrillard, Jean 169
Bauhaus 202, 314, 409, 466, 468, 568, 636
beautiful vs ugly 434, 435, 436, 557, 596
beauty 41, 42, 49, 269, 434, 435, 436, 485, 507, 525, 527, 528, 530, 531, 533, 535, 539, 542, 576, 577, 586, 708, 720, 732, 739, 740
beauty, code of 44, 48, 375, 378, 403, 437, 449, 477, 505, 508, 509, 511, 517, 519, 527–35, 537–38, 555–60, 576, 580–84, 596, 611, 623, 657, 739
Beck, Ulrich 443, 444
Behne, Adolph 460, 569
Behrens, Peter 413
Bentham, Jeremy 500
Berkel, Ben van 341, 342–43, 344, 345, 351, 660
Blondel, Jacques-François 48, 510, 543, 544, 545
Boffrand, Germain 51
Bos, Caroline 341, 342–43, 344, 345, 351
boundary 31, 73, 74, 75, 78, 87, 97, 125, 141, 185, 187, 188, 322, 327, 349, 429, 455
Braque, Georges 153
brief 253, 264, 279, 293, 335, 351
Broadbent, Geoffrey 169
Brutalism 588, 645
bubble diagrams 90, 187
built environment 1, 3, 6, 56, 62, 79, 112, 125, 137, 138, 139, 143, 146, 150, 153, 167, 170, 171, 172, 176, 177, 179, 180, 183, 186, 187, 188, 193–96, 198, 199, 201, 215, 219, 220, 222, 225, 229, 237, 245, 263, 275, 359, 381, 386, 387, 399–400, 422–38, 514, 525, 537, 580, 584, 597, 598, 627, 628, 635, 638, 676, 677, 742, 747

CAD 270, 273, 275, 285, 286, 291, 298, 335, 375, 377, 605
capacities 10–18, 20, 24, 25, 37, 46, 93, 94, 110–11, 133, 136, 145, 147, 170, 211, 227, 232, 266, 362, 474
capacities, functional 26, 28, 83, 84
Caravaggio 150
career 410–13
Carnap, Rudolph 210
causal explanation 261
centre-periphery differentiation 414–18, 624
character 50–51, 54
Chipperfield, David 648
Chomsky, Noam 207–8, 223, 224, 235, 274, 329
CIAM 394, 460–61
circularity 332
classic treatise 509–606, 738–41, 746–47
Classical architecture 21, 45, 48, 51, 55, 57, 178–79, 181, 198, 201, 217, 314, 315, 317, 431, 436, 440, 501, 555, 603, 617, 635, 636, 654, 704, 722
Classical orders 21, 48, 533, 534, 559
client's project 357, 361
closure, law of 158, 160
code 49–50, 168, 171, 172, 198, 215, 233, 234, 235, 237, 448–49, 454
cognition 54, 137, 146, 281
collage 59–60
Colquhoun, Alan 169
Columbia University 409
communication 2, 7, 10, 11, 13, 19, 32–35, 37–45, 47, 52, 54, 72, 77, 83, 136, 137, 138, 141, 143, 171–89, 194, 195, 196, 198, 201, 203–6, 208, 209, 221, 227, 236, 239, 240, 241, 250, 257, 263, 266, 268, 282, 331, 350, 359, 379, 386, 398, 399, 400, 406, 408, 409, 422, 425, 427, 428, 489, 504, 551, 595, 610
communication, political 446, 448–52, 454–58, 472, 473, 474
communication, social 5, 12, 16, 17, 32, 34, 43, 54, 56, 77, 110, 136, 167, 176, 180, 241, 254, 263, 266, 267, 268, 275, 276, 281, 315, 333, 379, 380, 400, 424, 448, 454, 456, 471, 477, 482, 490, 492, 514, 523, 662, 677, 715
communication structure 268, 276, 281
communication structure, categorical 510
communication structure, permanent 7, 47, 245, 519, 627
communication structure, variable 246, 627
communicative operation 257, 448, 449, 489
compartition 47–48, 49, 50, 54, 70, 537
complexity 5, 29, 31, 54, 56, 58, 61, 63, 64, 66, 67, 68, 72, 87, 92, 107, 109, 139, 142, 225, 226, 231, 247, 249, 252, 254–58, 275, 289, 291, 317, 337, 341, 356, 360, 375, 422, 434, 495, 599, 646, 651, 692
complexity, determined 64
complexity, social 16, 134, 181, 200, 246, 283, 403, 432, 535, 600
complexity, societal 423, 614, 716
complexity theory 393, 395, 397, 428, 677, 681
composition 30, 48, 50, 51, 54–57, 69, 70, 159, 163, 164, 181, 199, 209, 273, 330, 376, 465, 475, 487, 529, 530, 533, 543, 561, 564, 582, 632, 634, 651, 707
comprehensive theory 75, 85, 113, 132, 194, 397
concepts of order 55
conceptual schemata 426
conditioning 208, 209, 434
configuration 16, 27, 33, 35, 41, 42, 48, 54, 57, 61–63, 65–68, 79, 80, 82–88, 93, 112–16, 123–26, 128, 130, 131, 147, 159, 162, 165–66, 223, 335, 347, 673
configuration, heterogenous 80, 82
configuration, homogeneous 80, 81, 82
configuration, logical 95, 96
configuration, ordered 437
configuration, random 437
configuration, spatial 16, 38, 40, 58, 61, 64, 93, 95, 96, 99, 112, 114, 116, 119, 125, 126, 128, 133, 136, 137, 158, 242, 396
configuration predictability 58
connection 31, 43, 47, 75, 76, 78, 79, 93, 125, 429

connectivity 2, 121, 130, 132, 182, 455, 503
connotation 168, 188, 203, 205
connotation vs denotation 186, 204
Constant 453
constraining power 316, 318, 604
Constructivism 453, 460, 465
Constructivist epistemology 428
continuation, law of 158, 160
continuously differentiated field 74, 78, 187–88
contractor's project 357, 361, 371, 372
Coop Himmelb(l)au 384, 413
core competency 2, 139
correlation 6, 8, 9, 42, 55, 65–71, 79, 124, 131, 132–33, 138, 143, 144, 148, 180, 209, 211, 212, 219, 220, 224, 226, 233, 237, 250, 255, 276, 280, 331, 437, 597–98, 602, 621–22, 649, 656, 670, 672–73
crisis of Modernism 169, 252, 253, 394–96
critical architecture 458, 470, 471, 473, 475
Critical Regionalism 385
criticism 615–16, 656, 747
Cross, Nigel 297
Cubism 150–51, 153, 385
Cubism, Analytical 150
cultural evolution 14, 423
cumulative advance 15
cumulative vs revolutionary research 733
Cuvier, Georges 8

data-structure 273, 599
datascape 343, 344, 661
decision tree 292, 345, 346, 429
decomposition 30–32, 67, 106, 110, 121, 122, 146, 152, 153, 154, 159, 160, 164, 188, 201, 238, 261, 294, 304–9, 311, 330, 337, 345, 360, 376, 390, 602, 603, 635
Deconstruction 395, 397, 428, 678
Deconstructivism 57, 69, 91–92, 140, 199, 243, 396, 432, 507, 613, 617, 619, 640, 641, 644, 645, 648, 664, 678, 734
deep relationality 740
degree of conventionality 217
degree of informational integration 287
DEGW 39–40, 41
Deleuze, Gilles 74, 393, 641, 697, 704
Deleuzian diagram 349, 350, 696
demarcation 36, 39, 136, 146, 183, 185, 196, 235, 330, 417, 427, 488, 494–95, 505, 509, 511, 516, 517, 551, 573–75, 594–95, 627, 644, 720, 738
denotation 168, 203, 204, 205, 362–63, 376, 377
dependency 57, 82, 85, 144, 210, 218, 304, 305, 308, 386, 390, 391, 395
Derrida, Jacques 169, 173, 428
design decision 52, 167, 257, 258, 263, 275, 276, 277, 289, 378
design disciplines 5, 17, 112
design medium 33, 34, 38, 43, 142, 187, 194, 250, 275, 292, 362, 422, 505, 508, 509, 511, 538–39, 564–65, 600, 604–6, 741
design methodology 254, 257–62, 318, 319, 743
design methods movement 252, 266, 302, 318, 507
design process 2, 20, 36, 37, 40, 41, 52, 68, 142, 223, 251–378, 435, 437, 492, 493, 505, 507–8, 509, 511, 527, 535, 560, 589–91, 599–600, 602, 603, 674, 720, 744
design process guidance 509, 511, 537–38, 561–64, 589–91, 599–604, 618, 741
design process theory 251–57, 263, 266, 271, 275, 283, 599, 600, 743, 744
design progress predictability 58
design research 13, 46, 145, 165, 227–28, 237, 253, 356, 392, 401–2, 573, 590, 598, 623, 644, 709, 711
design research programme 52, 140, 244, 414, 590, 618, 623, 643, 645, 651–54
design studio 420–22
design tools 349, 373, 646
design world 348–49, 356, 696, 722
differentiation 24, 30, 31, 45, 61, 64, 65, 68, 70, 75, 77, 78, 80, 92, 96, 98, 114, 115, 123, 127, 139, 193, 203, 213, 246, 366, 368, 381, 415, 422, 436, 446, 500, 626, 645, 646, 656, 663, 670

differentiation, adaptive 22
differentiation, functional 23–24, 203, 381, 472, 479, 557, 565, 624, 625, 626
differentiation, morphological (morphing) 26, 78, 134
differentiation, societal 472, 479, 551, 610, 624
differentiation, system 597
digital models 220, 285, 286, 330, 331, 335, 357, 360, 362, 452, 492, 703
discipline 1, 3, 4, 6, 20, 22, 25, 39, 40, 41, 46, 72, 87, 139, 142, 167, 170, 176, 252, 268, 270, 334, 349, 378, 386, 390, 393, 397, 400, 402, 407, 415, 417, 426, 438, 440, 442, 448, 451, 470, 476, 484, 503, 505, 508, 511, 516, 519, 535, 536, 542, 543, 551, 567, 594, 606, 607, 608, 710, 711
discourse 9, 12, 16, 22, 24, 29, 33, 34, 36, 40, 41, 42, 46, 204, 226, 243, 253, 254, 275, 343, 383, 387, 389, 392, 406–7, 408, 411, 413, 418, 439, 451, 458, 459, 467, 470, 477, 510, 583, 616
discourse analysis 1
discursive formation 428
distinction 44, 86, 87, 427, 439, 491
distribution 48–51, 54, 126, 127
  occupational 21
  spatial 19, 44, 45, 49
division 49, 73, 74, 75, 77, 78, 79, 428
dogma 656, 657–59
dogmatism 378
double code 44, 508, 517, 519, 527, 537, 623, 720
double contingency 241
drawing 33, 43, 94–95, 142, 187, 194, 218, 269, 298, 330, 331, 349–50, 357, 360, 361, 362, 371, 372, 377, 452, 492, 502, 509, 510, 538–39, 565, 628
Durand, Jean-Nicolas-Louis 3, 223, 252, 484, 487, 500–501, 511, 543–67, 576, 633–34

Eastman, Charles M 266
Eclecticism 529, 644, 732
Eco, Umberto 169, 182
ecological sustainability 676–80, 716
ecology 41, 447, 665, 668–69
economic conditions 404, 406
economics 278, 498, 709
economy 379, 380, 381, 398, 400–403, 410, 415, 416, 420, 445, 454, 455, 460, 472, 498, 499, 547, 548, 549, 551, 553–56, 625, 716, 731
education 39, 202, 381, 386, 400, 407–10, 414, 415–16, 420, 445, 446, 499, 500, 502, 548–49
Eisenman, Peter 92, 145, 223–24, 225, 329, 338, 483, 506, 507, 660, 661
El Lissitzky 465
elegance 70, 436, 535, 646, 700–709, 722, 732, 747
elemental operation 257
elementary information process (eips) 270, 271, 273, 274, 277, 285, 317
emergence 3
enclosure 73, 74, 75, 77, 79, 80, 86, 97, 98, 164, 195, 377, 627
engineering 11, 18, 21, 22, 36, 42, 49, 139, 140, 195, 234, 241, 252, 297, 321, 323, 336, 352, 404, 412, 413, 417, 418, 505, 507, 517, 548, 554, 567, 573–74, 580, 595, 738
engineer's project 357, 361, 371
environment 3, 5, 13, 24, 26, 27, 28, 32, 33, 37, 38, 70, 134, 137, 143, 171, 199, 219, 221, 225, 227, 229, 231, 233, 239, 246, 247, 270, 272, 274, 279, 280, 281, 296, 355, 365, 380, 385, 386, 390, 400, 401, 405, 415, 417, 459, 477, 485, 490, 491, 503, 594, 608, 609, 612, 676, 746
epochal style 1, 4, 484, 503, 507, 510, 584, 593, 598, 614, 622, 623, 627–42, 644, 710, 733, 734
Evans, Robin 728
evolution 14, 15, 139, 147, 192, 209, 261, 353, 386, 387, 407, 409, 428, 505, 543, 610, 618, 625, 627, 628
evolution, cultural 423, 435, 437
evolution, language 213, 215
evolution, social 6, 214
evolution, societal 275, 389, 496
evolution, socio-cultural 3, 189, 422–23
exaption 14, 15

exemplars 729
exemplification 362, 363–64, 376, 377
exhibition design 433–34
explanation vs understanding 240
expression 27, 50–51, 54, 180, 208, 243, 362, 364, 376, 377
Expressionism 503, 644
expressive power 99, 206, 232, 236, 238
external reference 404

fashion 203, 204, 643
Felderer, Brigitte 164
Feldtkeller, Christoph 9
field 24, 26, 41, 42, 64, 68, 75–76, 78, 79, 80, 93, 99, 121–22, 188, 617
figural after-effects 151
figure 36, 57, 278, 339, 341, 346, 347, 350, 351, 422, 426, 428, 530, 654, 745
figure-ground 155, 157, 158, 159
Finsterlin, Hermann 503
Folding 641, 660, 661, 662, 734
Fordism 389, 394, 405, 580, 584, 625, 626, 635, 636, 637, 639, 640, 677, 692, 733
form vs function 6, 10, 44, 185, 517, 519, 525, 595, 657
form-function relations 21, 26, 28, 70, 139, 390, 451, 502, 508, 509, 511, 517–19, 551–53, 575–77, 739
form-to-function inferences 133
form-to-programme 15, 314, 338
formal heuristics 244, 618, 658–59, 660
formal a priori 31
formal repertoire 12, 34, 54, 255, 315, 338
formalism 94, 96, 98, 338, 429–30, 431, 660, 661
formally resolved vs formally unresolved 449
Forty, Adrian 9
Foster + Partners 730
Foster, Norman 384, 411, 615
Foucault, Michel 169, 428, 472, 715
Fourier, Charles 440–41
frame 5, 8, 18, 183, 184, 229, 240, 241, 380, 381, 423, 448, 457, 731
frame vs interaction 5
framing 5, 6, 16, 17, 19, 30, 32, 34, 43, 58, 72, 172, 173, 185, 188, 241, 379, 380, 381, 456, 458, 485
framing communications 10, 11, 33
Frampton, Kenneth 169
Friedman, Yona 453
fully articulated 248
fully interpreted 247, 248
fully systematized 248
function, latent 12, 16, 18, 19
function, manifest 12, 13, 16, 18, 19
function systems 3, 47, 391–92, 398, 399, 401, 404, 407, 410–11, 414–15, 419, 420, 423, 439, 445, 447, 448, 456, 464, 471, 477, 479, 482, 489, 496, 500, 501, 510, 512, 551, 610–11, 627, 708–9
function-type 6, 9, 17, 22–24, 26, 29, 32, 125, 201–6, 227, 228, 229, 231, 233–36, 245, 250, 553, 584, 633, 672, 673
functional equivalence 20
functional heuristics 34, 560, 596, 618, 656–60
functional vs disfunctional 449
Functionalism 253, 460, 575, 645
Futurism, Futurists 572, 594

Gabo, Naum 460
Gandelsonas, Mario 198, 201, 222–23
Gehry, Frank 411, 469, 615
generate-and-test method 265, 299, 300, 301, 303, 304, 311, 312, 601
generative power 311, 316, 318, 604, 744
Gestalt 2, 153, 154, 155, 157, 166, 230, 231, 360, 376, 671
Gestalt psychology 145, 153, 154
Gestalt-grouping principles 144, 157–60, 163, 166
Gestalt-perception 63, 153–65, 239
Giddens, Anthony 443
Giedion, Siegfried 145, 478–79, 506, 511, 569, 607, 612
Ginzburg, Moisei 569
Glass, Ruth 110
globalization 199, 383, 639
goal state 264, 284, 285, 288, 290, 291, 296, 297, 324, 335, 341, 600
Goel, Vinod 309–10, 362, 364, 371–74, 377
Goffman, Erving 424

Goodman, Nelson 362–65, 367–74, 376, 696
Gothic style 55, 217, 436, 440, 537, 628, 642, 643, 645
Grafton, Anthony 538
grammar 178, 181, 190, 198, 199, 200, 208, 209, 211, 218, 219, 222, 223, 225, 226, 228, 230, 231, 232, 235, 245
graph theory 32, 88, 93, 94, 95, 98, 99, 106, 292, 350, 600
Graves, Michael 92, 145
Gropius, Walter 384, 464, 467, 568
Guarini, Guarino 510
Guattari, Felix 74, 393, 641

Hadid, Zaha 412, 615, 730
hard functioning 141
Hegel, Georg Wilhelm Friedrich 623, 724
hegemony 253, 254, 256, 446, 471, 644, 645, 648, 649, 710, 712, 743
Heidegger, Martin 428
Herzog & DeMeuron 384
heuristic method 311, 312
heuristic search method 265, 303, 602
heuristics 2, 15, 34, 69, 72, 86, 88, 99, 130, 225, 244, 245, 267, 276, 283, 318, 326, 338, 375, 378, 436–37, 596, 622, 641, 656, 693, 706, 708, 734
High-Tech 588, 645
Hillier, Bill 24, 42, 62, 99, 112, 113–14, 116–17, 119, 121, 124–28, 130, 132, 204, 483
Historical Materialism 428, 466, 716, 717
Historicism 436, 632, 633, 634, 642–45
historiography, architectural 606–14, 747
historiography, scientific 611
Hitchcock, Henry-Russell 198, 569
Hübsch, Heinrich 586
Huet, Bernard 547–48
hypostatization 20
hypothesis 322, 612, 613, 618, 649, 656

icon 168, 216, 218, 219, 372
iconic 144
iconic sign 216–19
ideology 339, 340, 413
idiom 178
ill-structured problem 319, 323–32, 333
immersion 136, 231
impartation 175, 205, 219, 220, 221, 232, 239, 263
Impressionism 150
improbability 16, 38–39, 162, 304
in absentia 197
in praesentia 179, 197
incommensurability 67, 302, 349
index 137, 216, 217, 219, 222
indexical 144, 219, 220, 222
indexical sign 144, 216–19, 222
information 65, 175, 189, 201–2, 205–6, 227, 229–32, 236, 237, 239, 263, 268, 270, 286–91, 297, 321, 327–32, 375, 418, 434
information processing 52, 194, 263, 268, 269, 332–36, 362, 415, 599
information rich 133, 206, 331–34
information-processing system (IPS) 266, 267, 270–72, 273–76, 278–81, 286, 287, 289, 293, 295, 299, 306, 313, 324, 326, 328, 332, 334, 353
information-processing theory of cognition 264, 265–66
informative theory 260, 261, 262
initial state 264, 284, 285, 288–89, 290, 307, 313, 341, 600
innovation 2, 6, 16, 36–37, 41, 55, 74, 75, 142, 144, 214, 253, 255, 256, 380, 386, 388, 389, 399, 411, 414, 422, 432, 447, 483, 495, 536, 546, 547, 555, 585, 594, 595, 597, 605, 617, 628, 644, 652, 708, 709
inorganic system 665, 666
input vs output 270, 271
inside vs outside 74
institution 12, 16, 35, 37, 52, 72, 209, 242, 409, 410, 416, 432, 721
institution, political 456, 457, 458
institution, public 633
institution, social 6, 7, 15, 16, 25, 31, 34, 35, 52, 71, 135, 137, 138, 141, 195, 203, 204, 215, 249, 399, 425, 432, 433, 474, 476, 530, 614, 655
integration 29, 40, 42, 76, 77, 78, 79, 96, 114, 115, 119, 121–24, 128, 130, 131, 383, 397, 704
integration, articulatory 22

integration, functional 9, 10
integration, global 19, 127, 130, 131, 132
integration, local 19, 123, 127, 130, 131, 132
integration, system 30, 31, 36
integration, three-dimensional 75
intelligibility 53, 58, 127, 128, 130, 131–34, 378
intensive coherence 703
intermediate state 264, 265, 279, 284, 285, 286, 288, 289–90, 292, 297, 313, 314, 315, 318, 324, 600, 603
internal reference 15, 33, 185
International Style 384, 385, 464, 507
irritation 358, 359, 390, 402, 405, 406, 407, 443, 445, 446, 447, 449, 451, 454, 455, 459, 471, 476, 594, 616, 745, 747

j-graphs (justified graphs) 116, 117, 119
Jakobson, Roman 169
Jencks, Charles 169, 178, 199, 648
Johnson, Philip 198, 569

Kant, Immanuel 280, 281, 431, 499–500, 724
Kartal-Pendik Masterplan 686
Kepes, György 145
Kipnis, Jeffrey 483, 506, 507, 660, 661, 703
Klenze, Leo von 433, 543
Koffka, Kurt 151, 153, 154–55, 157–58
Köhler, Wolfgang 153, 154
Königsberg Bridges problem 93–94
Koolhaas, Rem 27, 411–12, 413, 458–59, 478, 481, 482, 506, 615, 660
Krier, Leon 503
Kristeva, Julia 169
Kuhn, Thomas 573, 732

Lachmayer, Herbert 164
Lakatos, Imre 294
language 56, 73, 170, 172, 174–83, 188–95, 197, 198, 200, 201, 203, 204, 206–15, 218, 219, 221–29, 231, 232, 233, 236, 237, 244, 245, 246, 274, 362, 369, 372, 382, 395, 428, 432, 490, 673, 743
language games 192
Late Modernism 646
latency 12, 163, 166
latent utopias 708
Latour, Bruno 444
Laugier, Marc-Antoine 413, 510–11, 543–44, 545, 607
law 415, 416, 445, 499
Le Corbusier 3, 86–87, 145, 151–52, 163–64, 315, 384, 445–46, 466, 467, 484, 497, 506, 511, 568–606, 637, 681
lead-distinction 2, 6, 7, 10, 44, 454, 505, 517, 519, 525, 595, 657, 720
legal system 379, 381, 382, 383, 398, 400, 401, 413, 416, 420, 453, 455, 499, 500, 731
legibility 56, 134, 136, 137, 138–39, 220, 222, 227, 675, 723
Leonardo da Vinci 150, 413
Lévi-Strauss, Claude 169, 180
linguistic value 190
Lloyd's headquarters, London 294
local to global inferences 131, 132
location-type 205, 206, 227, 228, 231, 233, 236, 359, 672, 673
long-term memory (LTM) 270, 273, 306, 328, 329, 330, 333, 334, 335, 353
Loos, Adolf 507
loose coupling 182
Luhmann, Niklas 3, 10, 170, 173, 175, 176, 181, 182, 239, 240, 281, 381, 382, 387–88, 394, 397, 398, 411, 415, 416, 418–19, 428, 446, 449, 452, 454, 455, 457, 479, 489, 490, 491, 493, 494, 497, 499, 593, 609, 610–11, 623–27, 706, 713–16, 719, 720, 725, 729
Lynn, Greg 483, 660, 661, 703
Lyotard, Jean-François 169

Maas, Winy 507, 660
McLuhan, Marshall 173
macro-political 465, 471, 474
macro-politics 472, 475, 4712
mainstream 75, 144, 253–57, 312, 315, 328, 386–89, 392–93, 394, 407, 409, 410, 458, 469–70, 471, 493, 495, 505, 506, 573, 594, 597, 598, 619, 641, 644, 648, 649, 653, 700,

708, 711, 718, 721–22, 730, 732, 733, 734, 736
manifesto project 441, 649
manner 51, 83, 209, 272, 278
March, James 339–40, 418, 419
March, Lionel 112
Martin, Reinhold 469–70
Marx, Karl 381, 428, 462, 623, 624, 625, 714, 715, 716, 717, 718
Marxism 392, 463, 465, 466, 468, 623, 624, 652, 714, 715
mass media 381, 391, 400, 401, 410, 412, 413, 420, 446, 452, 615, 616, 731, 747
Maturana, Humberto 280, 281, 282
May, Ernst 441, 465
meaning 268, 455, 672–73
medial substrate 195, 211, 215
Melnikov, Konstantin 315
metabolism 379, 380
Metabolism 453, 588–89, 645
method vs process 258–62
methodological tolerance 653
Meyer, Hannes 343, 465–66, 467, 468, 507
Michelangelo 413
Michelozzo di Bartolomeo 44
micro-political 474–78, 480, 481, 482
micro-politics 472, 473, 474
Mies van der Rohe, Ludwig 315, 464–68, 507, 568
Minimalism 199, 246, 403, 447, 641, 648–51, 700, 732
Mitchell, William J 266
modal qualifications 236
modality 236
mode of attention 229–30, 231
mode of distraction 229, 230, 231
modelling spaces 361–78, 600, 696, 697
models 38, 43, 53, 214, 218, 265, 269–70, 272, 274, 282, 285, 298, 317, 318–19, 332–36, 352, 361, 377, 485, 536, 538–39, 605
Modern Functionalism 223, 314, 315, 384, 385, 403, 568, 732
Modernism, Modernists 4, 57, 59, 69, 74, 82, 86, 121, 169, 186, 198–99, 201, 202, 203, 245, 252, 253, 310, 315, 317, 384, 385, 389, 393, 395, 403, 431, 436, 454, 459–60, 464–67, 479, 484, 498, 501, 506, 507, 511, 529, 543, 546, 547, 564, 568, 569, 577, 579, 580, 584, 588, 589, 591, 592, 593, 595, 598, 602, 603, 607, 617, 619, 634, 635, 637, 638, 641–46, 648, 649, 654, 657, 658, 664, 677, 678, 680, 685, 699, 711, 721, 740, 747
modernization theory 395, 396
modes of differentiation 381
Moholy-Nagy, László 145
Montesquieu, Baron de 500
Moos, Stanislaus von 201
morphogenesis 677–78
morphology 16, 20, 22, 25, 44, 45, 52, 54, 124, 136, 184, 189, 220, 353, 361, 424, 435, 475, 665, 673, 674, 675, 677, 678, 685, 696, 698
Morris, William 587
Moussavi, Farshid 660
multi-modal 171, 194
multiple affiliation 92
Muthesius, Hermann 511, 568, 587
MVRDV 343

Naumann, Friedrich 506, 568
navigation 54, 58, 132, 136, 137, 147, 205, 231, 678, 685
negative heuristics 528, 582, 656, 657
Neo-Baroque 644
Neo-Classicism 4, 403, 484, 487, 511, 529, 555, 560, 561, 593, 607, 632, 633, 642, 643, 740
Neo-Gothic 529, 633, 644
Neo-Grec style 644, 733
Neo-Historicism 246, 619
Neo-Renaissance 633, 644
network theory 2, 88, 93–106, 350, 360
Newell, Allen 264–65, 266, 267, 269, 271, 272, 273, 274, 276, 277, 278, 279, 280, 282, 285, 286, 291, 293, 294, 303, 310, 325, 333
Nicholson, Simon 111
Niemeyer, Oscar 384
Nolli, Giambattista 157
Norberg-Schulz, Christian 145, 169, 487–88
norm 260, 261, 431

normal vs revolutionary politics 445-8
normative theory 260–61, 262
notational system 362, 364, 365, 366, 368, 369, 372, 373, 374, 375
novelty 337, 356, 449, 536, 740
novelty, code of 449, 560, 597

object permanence 147
observation 28, 147, 281, 295, 391, 439
OCEAN 420, 422
oeuvre 414
Olsen, Johann 339–40
OMA 384, 413, 481, 483, 649, 660
One-North Masterplan 478, 686
ontology 10, 79, 88, 93, 98, 149, 352, 353, 605, 650, 654, 697
operational definition 61, 131, 437, 527, 618, 656
order 17, 45, 48, 53, 55, 57, 58, 70, 73, 87, 426, 427, 428, 431, 436, 437, 438
order, architectural *see* architectural order
order, conceptual 432
order, creative destruction of 432
order, social 31, 42, 52, 53, 56, 61, 71, 73, 137, 163, 167, 203, 400, 422, 423
order, spatial 73, 139, 141, 142, 165, 431
order vs chaos 437
Organicism 645
organism 8, 9, 13, 14, 47, 69, 147, 274, 275, 280, 281, 434, 528, 610, 665, 666, 668, 704, 715, 739
organization 2, 7, 19, 20, 29, 42, 43, 44, 46, 47, 48, 50, 53–58, 61–74, 80–88, 113, 133–36, 195, 227, 238, 419, 420, 424, 458, 459, 476, 505, 523, 524–25, 554, 594, 600, 663, 664, 722, 742
organization, articulate 134, 138–39
organization, functional 8, 137, 650
organization, inarticulate 138
organization, physical 134, 135, 138, 141, 143
organization, spatial 50, 53, 56, 57, 60–63, 71, 72–77, 79, 87, 90, 93, 98, 111, 133, 135, 137, 139, 141, 143, 146, 167, 183, 188, 205, 228, 229, 233, 238, 246, 341, 359, 375, 378, 379, 402, 522, 591, 661, 723
organization vs articulation 49, 134–36
organizational dimension 357, 358, 744
organizational project 46, 242, 269, 358, 359, 360, 361, 720
orientation 3, 42, 43, 54, 70, 71, 74, 122, 131, 132, 136, 137, 139, 146, 147, 167, 231, 234, 249, 253, 446, 472, 508, 643, 651, 675, 685, 707
orientation, avant-gardist 508, 511, 516, 547, 571–73, 594
original vs conventional 449
originality 41, 42, 507
originality, code of 505, 509, 511, 535–36, 560, 584–86, 596–98, 740
ornament, ornamentation 48, 54, 55, 124, 219, 234, 384, 423, 519, 525–26, 527, 529, 535, 539, 542, 560, 565
Otto, Frei 87, 619, 621, 681, 682–83, 747
outside-to-inside inferences 133
Owen, Robert 440–41

Palladio, Andrea 510, 631
paradigmatic relations 179, 196, 197
parametric accentuation 670–71
parametric ecology 674–75
parametric figuration 165–67, 671–72, 675
parametric inter-articulation 669–70
parametric modelling 40, 250, 336, 603, 641, 646, 663, 671
parametric responsiveness 674, 675
parametric semiology 672–74
parametric urbanism 26, 675, 686–700
Parametricism 1, 4, 47, 58, 69, 70, 71, 92, 228, 244, 246, 253–56, 283, 310, 315, 317, 318, 336, 338, 385, 389, 394, 403, 418, 433–34, 436–37, 447, 484, 593, 596, 597, 598, 600, 602, 603, 605–6, 608, 613, 614, 617–712, 720, 721, 722, 733, 734, 740, 741, 743, 747
parametrics 29
Parc de la Villette, Paris 68, 92
Parsons, Talcott 411
part-to-whole 19
particle 666, 667, 683, 695, 696
partitioning 97
Peirce, Charles Sanders 168, 177, 189, 216, 365
penetration 76

perception 43, 47, 54, 63, 111, 132, 134, 136, 142–55, 157, 158, 159, 163, 166, 171, 187, 191, 193, 217, 239, 241, 280
performance values 534
permeability 27, 73, 76, 116, 126
Perrault, Claude 413, 543
perturbation 387
Pevsner, Antoine 460
phenomenal transparency 111, 163–65
phenomenological dimension 134, 141, 142–46, 250, 357, 358, 743, 744
phenomenological project 46, 238, 239, 242, 269, 356, 358–61, 372, 672, 720
phenomenology 46, 149, 167, 228, 238, 501, 742
philosophy 427, 428, 431, 432, 465, 542
Piaget, Jean 147
Piano, Renzo 384
Picasso, Pablo 153
Picon, Antoine 543, 553
planning space 295–98, 335, 601
Plato 427, 515
playfulness 340
political agenda 447, 448, 449, 457–60, 467, 471, 472, 479
political agitation 452, 462
political architecture 440, 441, 442, 445, 446, 447, 482, 745
political controversy 468, 745
political power 387, 442, 452, 473, 474, 513
political system 379, 381, 382, 391, 400, 401, 405, 416, 439, 440, 442, 448, 450, 451, 452, 455, 456, 457, 459, 460, 461, 468, 470, 480, 499, 500, 521, 566, 611, 746
politics 3, 323, 410, 415, 416, 439–83, 709, 720, 746
politics, code of 449
politics, normal 445–48
politics, revolutionary 445–48
polycontextural (polycontextual) 3, 385, 397, 404, 745
positive heuristics 656, 657
positivism 500
Post-Fordism 58, 199, 283, 389, 391, 392, 394, 402, 421, 580, 594, 625, 626, 627, 640, 655, 677, 678, 680, 708, 714, 718, 733, 738
post-metaphysical 606
Post-Structuralism 169, 393, 395, 396, 397, 486, 501, 641
Postmodernism 57, 59, 69, 140, 199, 203, 222, 243, 245, 396, 613, 617, 619, 640, 644, 645, 648, 664, 678, 680, 699, 733, 734
power 17, 28, 37, 43, 47, 77, 98, 99, 141, 162, 179, 180, 200, 206, 219, 223, 232, 236, 237, 238, 249, 250, 261, 297, 311, 312, 316, 317–18, 384, 385, 387, 388, 433, 446, 451, 452, 453, 458, 459, 467, 472, 473, 474, 521, 604, 746
pragmatics 516
predictability 58, 86, 87, 220, 455
Preziosi, Donald 171, 172, 186–87
primitive 93, 98, 264, 271, 272, 277, 312, 352, 599
Prix, Wolf 413
problem definition 318–23
problem solving 263–310, 312, 333, 341, 460, 485, 599, 600, 601
problem space 264, 279–88, 291–301, 303, 306, 307, 308, 310, 313, 314, 317, 324, 325, 327, 333–37, 348, 353, 356–59, 600, 601
problem state 264, 285–90, 298–307, 313, 316, 324, 327, 330, 601, 602
problem structure 318–36, 744
problem-types vs solution-types 24–29
process 258, 493
product design 11, 146, 203
profession 320, 410–11, 414, 416, 417–18, 487, 606
programme 27, 93, 272–77, 439, 599–600
programme types 22, 23, 641
progressive vs conservative 447
project 24, 26, 32, 33, 34, 38, 39, 41, 46, 52, 68, 71, 80, 81, 165, 168, 170, 174, 199, 200, 219, 222–29, 231, 233, 236, 238, 239, 241–44, 246, 248, 250, 599
propositional calculus 236
proximity, law of 158, 159

psychology of perception 151, 153, 154, 163, 193, 239
public competitions 477–83

quantifiers 236

Radical Constructivism 394
Radical Functionalism 294, 465, 501, 507, 595, 661
Rahim, Ali 256
random, randomness 40, 57, 61–62, 65, 66, 69, 84, 85, 86, 113
rational in retrospect 341–55
Rationalism 385, 460, 645
rationality 2, 20, 21, 45, 50, 162, 212–13, 243, 252, 253, 255–58, 260, 262, 268–69, 278, 292, 294, 295, 300, 310, 316, 317, 323, 324, 331, 332, 333, 337, 339–42, 344–45, 348, 349, 353, 354, 355, 359, 361, 378, 411, 413, 414, 419, 435, 524, 540, 560, 564, 599, 601, 602, 613, 681, 743, 744, 747
rationality, bounded 278, 355
rationality, design 2, 3, 255, 301, 302, 338, 341, 355
rationality, prospective 355–58
re-entry 337
recursive network 174, 263
recursivity 63, 65, 489, 491–92, 495
redundancy 198, 215, 232, 243, 368, 374, 503, 536
reflection 2, 3, 148, 149, 153, 169, 181, 215, 227, 251, 254, 255, 258, 281, 286, 391, 426, 441, 486, 491, 493–95, 507, 508
reflection theory 1–2, 402, 486, 496–509, 610, 747
reflectivity 491, 493–96
reflexivity 491, 492–93, 495
registers of morphological articulation 233
registers of spatial organization 233
regularity 63, 80, 86–87, 137, 143, 179, 198, 212, 219, 220
Reiser & Umemoto 703
Reiser, Jesse 703
Reitman, Walter 267, 269, 319, 323, 328, 329, 330
relational field 684
Rembrandt 150
Renaissance 4, 7, 44, 45, 55, 139, 163, 198, 403, 430, 431, 436, 440, 479, 484, 501, 510, 511, 529, 537, 593, 594, 627–32, 642, 643, 645, 702, 740
repertoire expansion 509, 511, 537, 561, 598–99, 740
repetition 57–60, 432, 635
repleteness 369–70, 376
representation 27, 28, 36, 37, 56, 70, 89, 93, 95, 98, 115, 131, 140, 150, 258, 281, 348, 349, 357, 362, 665
reproduction 12–13, 38, 353, 386, 387, 401, 407, 434, 717
reputation 411–13, 414, 615, 745
requisite variety 246–50
research programme 253, 447, 505
response versatility 58
retroactive manifesto387
revolution 23, 37, 439, 446, 461, 570, 709
revolution vs reform 464
revolutionary period 439, 441, 733
RIBA Outline Plan of Works 295
Rietveld, Gerrit 315, 568
risk 37, 407
Rittel, Horst 319–23, 325
Rococo 560
Rogers, Richard 294
Rorschach, Hermann 632
Rorschach test 162, 632
Rossi, Aldo 24
Rothbard, Murray 498
Rousseau, Jean-Jacques 566
routine utilization 12–13
Rowe, Colin 92, 111, 145, 157, 163
Rubin, Edgar 151, 155
Russell, Bertrand 148–49, 153
Russian Constructivism 385

Saarinen, Eero 216
Sapers, Carl 417–18
Saussure, Ferdinand de 168, 169, 170, 177, 178–79, 182, 189–94, 196–97, 210–15, 216, 218, 229, 240, 428
Scharoun, Hans 588
Schinkel, Karl Friedrich 48–49, 413, 543
Schmidt, Hans 465–66

science 2, 9, 42, 149, 189, 226, 252, 294, 320, 322, 323, 381, 382, 386, 387–88, 398, 399, 404, 410, 418, 428, 431, 445, 446, 499, 549, 550, 573, 611, 628, 709, 730, 738
science of configuration 88–134
scripting, script 67, 285–86, 311, 313, 316, 317, 318, 336, 604, 617, 641, 663, 744
search graph 292, 294, 600
second order observation 295
segmentation 19, 23, 92, 96, 97, 192, 415, 624
selection 353
self-criticism 257, 343, 656, 743
self-description 1, 3, 4, 203, 243, 393, 484–90, 496–506, 508–12, 514, 527, 537, 545, 561, 566, 577, 592, 593, 594, 598, 606, 610, 613, 623, 712, 746
self-determination 318, 328, 335, 405, 704, 744
self-organization 61, 87, 214
self-reference 185, 263, 489–96
self-reference, basal 489, 490, 491, 492, 495
self-reference vs world-reference 490
self-reflectiveness 509, 511, 539–42, 566–68, 591–92, 606, 741
self-regulation 389, 390, 399
semantic density 369
semantic disjointness 365, 367–68, 374
semantic finite differentiation 365, 368
semantic unambiguity 365, 367
semantics 496
semiological code 134, 135, 145
semiological differentiation 45
semiological dimension 46, 125, 134, 140, 141, 142–45, 169, 172, 173, 238, 239, 357, 358, 364, 424, 458, 743, 744
semiological potential 214, 249
semiological project 2, 46, 200, 219, 222–29, 231, 233, 238, 239, 241–44, 246, 250, 269, 356, 358, 359, 360, 361, 372, 612, 613, 720, 736
semiological unit 187
semiological virtuality 214, 249
semiology 2, 140, 166–71, 177, 181, 182, 183, 189, 206, 218, 219, 222, 224, 228, 238, 742
semiosis 144, 145, 168, 176, 183, 187, 199, 200, 204, 209, 212, 214, 215–22, 225, 238, 245, 246, 358, 361
semiosis, architectural 179, 187, 188, 219
semiosis, linguistic 179
semiosis, natural 199
semiotic power 179
Semper, Gottfried 177–78, 506, 511, 586, 587, 607
sense-data 148, 149, 150, 153
service 39, 42, 43, 241, 399, 400, 415, 416, 418, 456
service provisions 453–59, 521
SERVO 420, 422
set theory 88–92, 96, 106
short-term memory (STM) 270, 273, 330, 331
sign 143–44, 168, 180–83, 185, 189, 190, 192, 197, 200, 201, 205, 206, 207, 209, 210, 212, 215, 221, 230, 232, 233, 235
sign, iconic 216–19
sign, indexical 144, 216–19, 222
sign, symbolic 144, 216–19
sign systems 171, 172, 185, 189, 195, 196, 201, 212, 225, 229, 232
sign-radical 206–9, 211–12, 218, 219, 222, 230, 231, 234, 235, 237
signified 168, 182, 185, 189, 192–93, 194, 196, 200–203, 205, 206, 210, 211, 212, 216–19, 227, 228, 231, 233, 250, 365
signifier 2–6, 168, 182, 185, 186, 189, 192, 196, 199, 205, 210, 212, 216–19, 231, 233, 236, 250, 365
signifier vs signified 185, 211
similarity, law of 158, 159
Simon, Herbert 264–69, 271–74, 276–80, 282, 285, 286, 291, 293–96, 303, 310, 323–30, 332–33, 353, 355, 418, 419
simultaneity 658, 678
situation 48
Slutzky, Robert 92, 111

Smith, Adam 499, 500
Soane, Sir John 49, 50
social interaction 5, 6, 17, 22, 56, 71, 136, 143, 183–86, 188, 198, 201, 202, 203, 211, 222, 226, 228, 229, 231, 233, 234, 239, 241, 250
social order 31, 42, 52, 53, 56, 61, 71, 73, 137, 163, 167, 203, 400, 422, 423, 514, 742, 745
social power 473, 474, 475, 477, 478
social systems 5, 6, 10, 13, 19, 23, 30, 33, 34, 56, 110, 139, 141, 153, 172, 174, 175, 177, 181, 190, 209, 214, 220, 221, 227, 247, 267, 268, 281, 319, 379, 386, 399, 400, 412, 420, 426, 448, 455–56, 489, 490–91, 493, 494, 714, 715, 716, 719, 729
social systems theory 10, 170, 240, 394, 397, 398, 428, 446, 626, 717, 718, 720
social-type 204, 205, 206, 227, 228, 229, 231, 233, 234, 250, 672, 673
societal function 1, 3, 5, 6, 47, 136, 166, 172, 238, 240, 241, 242, 357, 359, 371, 380, 381, 388, 390, 393, 396, 397, 411, 447, 448, 455, 456, 459, 474, 482, 484, 497, 499, 503–6, 508, 510, 511, 513, 514, 519, 542, 544, 545, 546, 548, 569, 571, 575, 592, 593, 594, 597, 606, 612, 614, 677, 708, 714, 719, 720, 721, 727, 732, 734, 738, 743
society 1, 3, 5, 6, 16, 23, 43, 56, 58, 60, 78, 79, 109–10, 135, 176, 199, 203, 209, 214, 323, 328, 379–438, 445, 470, 472, 512–15, 605, 624, 662, 712, 738, 745
sociology 12, 23, 227, 239, 424, 426, 611, 715
soft function 141
soft functioning 141
Soho City, Beijing 686
solution-types 24, 25, 29
space 5, 7, 12, 18, 20, 21, 27–30, 32, 34, 39, 40, 43–44, 49, 51, 55, 73, 74, 75, 77–80, 95, 98, 110, 114, 119, 121, 122, 125, 126, 128, 130, 136, 140, 141, 153, 163, 171–76, 193, 197, 201, 228, 230, 241, 247, 249, 279, 353, 458, 473, 589, 617, 630, 634, 651
space syntax 41–42, 99, 112–31, 204, 250
Space Syntax Laboratory 38, 40, 41, 112
space-making 186
spatial order 73, 139, 141, 142, 165, 423, 433, 513, 655, 742
Speaks, Michael 469
Spuybroek, Lars 483
Stam, Mart 465, 466
state space 284, 286, 333, 600
state space schema 284, 341, 600
state transformation 264, 284, 285, 286, 290–91, 292, 600
Steadman, Philip 9, 112, 483
stratification 23, 203, 204, 381, 479, 624, 625
structural coupling 355, 454, 479, 480, 481, 616, 747
Structuralism 169, 275, 588–89
style 586–87, 721, 740
style, active 596
style, active-reflective 598
style, epochal 1, 4, 484, 503, 507, 510, 584, 593, 598, 614, 622, 623, 627–42, 644, 710, 733, 734
style, hegemonic 710
style, implied 511, 536–37, 560
style, passive 628
style, subsidiary 644–65
style, transitional 644, 645
style, unified 644
sub-systematized 247, 248
subsidiary function 9, 10, 17, 18, 19, 20
subsidiary style 598
substantial function 9, 17, 18, 19, 20, 21, 22, 23, 24, 25, 26, 34, 37, 39, 44, 52
substantial vs subsidiary function 9, 578
substantially articulated 248
subsystem 3, 19, 30, 31, 32, 35, 69, 70, 79, 80, 106, 139, 174, 274, 282–83, 305, 306, 308, 310, 311, 318, 328, 330, 336, 337, 344, 358, 381, 382, 385, 390, 392, 398, 416, 445, 475, 477, 500, 594, 597–98, 600, 602, 608, 617, 621, 622, 623, 625, 649–50, 659, 664–65, 668, 669, 718, 721, 730, 734, 744, 745

Summerson, John 178
super-position 92
super-theory 486, 592
superorganism 665, 667, 668
Superstudio 37, 453
swarm 665, 666–67, 675, 685
syllogism 89–90, 429
symbioses 665, 668
symbol 217, 219, 265, 272, 362, 599
symbol structure 270, 272–75, 285, 291, 296, 599
symbol system 265, 268, 270, 272, 275, 277, 285, 288, 291, 336, 348, 349, 354, 362–65, 368, 369, 371, 372, 374, 376–77, 599
symbol token 271, 599
symbol type 271
symbolic sign 144, 216–19
symbolically generalized media 43
symbolism 185–86, 201
symbolism, self-referential 186, 201
symmetry, law of 158, 161–64
syntactic density 369
syntactic disjointness 365–66
syntactic finite differentiation 365, 366–67
syntagmatic relations 179, 196, 197
syntagmatic vs paradigmatic 196–200
syntax 208, 209, 223, 224, 225, 227, 235, 247
system vs environment 668
system-of-signification 2, 125, 170, 171, 174, 177, 182, 189, 198, 204, 211, 215, 219, 222, 233, 235, 240, 241, 242, 244, 245, 359, 361, 365
system-reference 10, 30, 449, 493–94

taboo 656, 657, 658, 686
Tafuri, Manfredo 607–8
Tange, Kenzo 109, 384
task environment 12, 270, 271, 277–84, 287, 293, 600
taste 539
Taut, Bruno 569
technique 256
tectonics 7, 19–22, 45, 55, 218, 233, 234, 645, 651
tenacity 323
territorial demarcation 235
territorial unit 18, 19, 30, 32, 74, 75, 77–78, 79, 183, 185–88, 204, 205, 206, 233, 242
territorialization 74–79, 86, 183, 187
territory 16, 17, 19, 30, 73–79, 141, 146, 147, 153, 163, 164, 165, 172, 183–88, 201–206, 211, 219, 227, 230, 231, 233–36, 250, 360, 361, 473
theme 164, 404, 492, 508, 574, 622, 650, 713, 729
theory 497
theory, analytic 258
theory, descriptive 2
theory, informative 260, 261, 262
theory, normative 2, 260
time 38
total articulation 248
totalization 669
transitional style 598
tree vs semi-lattice 106–7, 113–14
Trotsky, Leon 466
truth 42, 427
truth, code of 42, 611
Tschumi, Bernard 68, 92
Twynstra Gudde 39, 41
typology 7, 22–26, 28, 29, 37, 82, 113–14, 186, 202, 216, 689, 691, 698, 742

UIA (International Union of Architects) 415
Ultra-Historicism 503
UN Studio 341, 342, 343, 347, 351
unambiguity 365, 367, 371
uncertainty absorption 289–90, 418–19
under-articulated 248
under-interpreted 248
understanding 7, 8, 20, 32, 34, 37, 143, 145, 171, 175, 196, 205, 207, 208, 212, 231, 239, 240, 251, 263, 276, 358
unified style 1, 642–45, 648
unified theory 1, 251
unit of interaction 153, 280
United Architects 469
universality 566, 652, 654, 747
universe of possibilities 72, 287, 604

urbanism 29, 41, 80, 91, 93, 99, 112, 180, 202, 204, 233, 381, 395, 401, 514, 579, 598, 599, 622, 637, 638, 640, 645, 648, 667, 677, 680, 685, 692, 694, 738, 747
useful vs useless 520
utility 9, 41, 42, 50, 269, 485, 507, 518, 528, 541, 546, 555–56, 557, 559, 577, 580, 583, 720, 732, 739
utility, code of 44, 48, 403, 449, 452, 476, 477, 505, 508, 509, 511, 517, 519, 520–27, 537–38, 553–55, 576, 577–80, 596, 611, 623, 739
utility vs beauty 49–50
utilization effect 12

van Eyck, Aldo 169
Van Toorn, Roemer 442, 443, 445, 481–82, 483
variation 215
Venn diagrams 89–90, 96, 97, 107, 360, 374, 376, 377, 429
Venturi, Robert 216, 223, 225, 631, 702
Viollet le Duc, E.E. 8–9
Vitruvius 7, 487, 502, 511–12, 541, 543, 544, 545

Wagner, Martin 466
Wagner, Otto 568
Webber, Melvin 325
Wertheimer, Max 153, 155, 158, 160
Whitehead, Hugh 356
wicked problem 319–23, 325
Wigley, Mark 475, 478, 481, 483
Wittgenstein, Ludwig 192, 208, 214, 428
Wittwer, Hans 465
Work Council for Art 460, 461–62
world architecture 200, 255, 381, 382–85, 447, 621, 645, 736, 745
world society 3, 378–85, 394, 580, 719
world-reference 10, 23, 39, 185, 490

Zaera-Polo, Alejandro 26–28, 444, 445, 473, 475, 481, 660
Zaha Hadid Architects (ZHA) 26, 384, 478, 483, 647, 649, 651, 652, 685, 686, 693, 694, 734
Zevi, Bruno 178